Arctic Ocean

80N

ARCTIC CIRCLE

60N

NORWAY

SWEDEN FINLAND

RUSSIA

● Sungir

DENMARK

Spy ● Neander Valley

NETH. ● Heidelberg (Mauer)

FRANCE ● Mladeč, Předmostí, Dolní Věstonice

Krapina ● Oase

Arago ●

Ceprano ● Petralona

Tighenif ●

Amud ●

Skhūl/Tabun Jebel Qafzeh ● Shanidar

KAZAKHSTAN

UZBEKISTAN

Teshik Tash ●

Dmanisi ●

GEORGIA

AZERBAIJAN

TURKMENISTAN

KYRGYZSTAN

TAJIKISTAN

AFGHANISTAN

PAKISTAN

NEPAL BHUTAN

MONGOLIA

NORTH KOREA

SOUTH KOREA

JAPAN

40N

Jinniushan ●

Zhoukoudian ●

Ordos ● Lantian ● Dali ●

CHINA Hexian ●

Liujiang ● Maba ●

TAIWAN

HONG KONG MACAU

Pacific Ocean

TROPIC OF CANCER

20N

NORTHERN MARIANA ISLANDS (U.S.)

REPUBLIC OF THE MARSHALL ISLANDS

NIGER CHAD SUDAN

Toros-Menalla ●

ETHIOPIA

Hadar ●

Bodo ● ● Middle Awash (Aramis, Bouri, Herto, Dikika)

Omo ●

UGANDA ● East and West Turkana

Tugen Hills ● ● Kanapoi

KENYA

● Olduvai/Laetoli

TANZANIA

Kabwe ● ZAMBIA

Taung ● ● Sterkfontein/Swartkrans/Drimolen

Florisbad ● SWAZILAND

SOUTH AFRICA ● Border Cave

Klasies River Mouth ●

INDIA

MYANMAR (BURMA)

THAILAND

VIETNAM

LAOS

CAMBODIA

PHILIPPINES

BRUNEI

MALAYSIA ● Niah Cave

Borneo

SINGAPORE

Sumatra

INDONESIA

Sangiran ● ● Trinil ● Ngandong

● Flores

PAPUA NEW GUINEA

FEDERATED STATES OF MICRONESIA

EQUATOR 0

SOLOMON ISLANDS

TUVALU

VANUATU

FIJI

NEW CALEDONIA (Fr.)

20S

Indian Ocean

SRI LANKA

MALDIVES

SEYCHELLES

COMOROS IS.

MADAGASCAR

MAURITIUS

AUSTRALIA

TROPIC OF CAPRICORN

Lake Mungo ●

Kow Swamp ●

NEW ZEALAND

40S

1. SLOVENIA
2. CROATIA
3. BOSNIA AND HERZEGOVINA
4. ALBANIA
5. MACEDONIA
6. SERBIA AND MONTENEGRO

60S

ANTARCTICA

ANTARCTIC CIRCLE

80S

20E 40E 60E 80E 100E 120E 140E 160E 180

Essentials
of Physical
Anthropology

Essentials of Physical Anthropology

SEVENTH EDITION

Robert Jurmain
Professor Emeritus, San Jose State University

Lynn Kilgore
University of Colorado, Boulder

Wenda Trevathan
New Mexico State University

WADSWORTH
CENGAGE Learning

Australia • Brazil • Japan • Korea • Mexico • Singapore • Spain • United Kingdom • United States

Essentials of Physical Anthropology, Seventh Edition
Robert Jurmain, Lynn Kilgore, and Wenda Trevanthan

Anthropology Editor: Lin Marshall Gaylord

Development Editor: Renee Deljon

Editorial Assistant: Paige Leeds

Technology Project Manager: Alexandria Brady

Marketing Manager: Meghan Pease

Marketing Assistant: Mary Anne Payumo

Marketing Communications Manager: Tami Strang

Creative Director: Rob Hugel

Art Director: Caryl Gorska

Print Buyer: Karen Hunt

Permissions Editor: Scott Bragg

Production Service: Patti Zeman / Hespenheide Design

Text and Cover Designer: Yvo Riezebos

Copy Editor: Janet Greenblatt

Cover Image: Lordkipanidze / National Museum
     of Georgia

Compositor: Hespenheide Design

For product information and technology assistance, contact us at
Cengage Learning Customer & Sales Support, 1-800-354-9706.

For permission to use material from this text or product, submit all requests online at **cengage.com/permissions**. Further permissions questions can be e-mailed to **permissionrequest@cengage.com**

Library of Congress Control Number: 2007942784

Student Edition:
ISBN-13: 978-0-495-50939-4
ISBN-10: 0-495-50939-6

Loose-leaf Edition:
ISBN-13: 978-0-495-51011-6
ISBN-10: 0-495-51011-4

Wadsworth
10 Davis Drive
Belmont, CA 94002-3098
USA

Cengage Learning is a leading provider of customized learning solutions with office locations around the globe, including Singapore, the United Kingdom, Australia, Mexico, Brazil, and Japan. Locate your local office at **international.cengage.com/region**.

Cengage Learning products are represented in Canada by Nelson Education, Ltd.

For your course and learning solutions, visit **academic .cengage.com**.

Purchase any of our products at your local college store or at our preferred online store **www.ichapters.com**.

Printed in Canada
1 2 3 4 5 6 7 12 11 10 09 08

Brief Contents

Contents

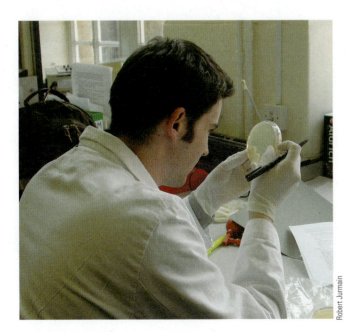

Robert Jurmain

CHAPTER 4

Heredity and Evolution **56**

CHAPTER 5

Macroevolution: Processes of Vertebrate and Mammalian Evolution **77**

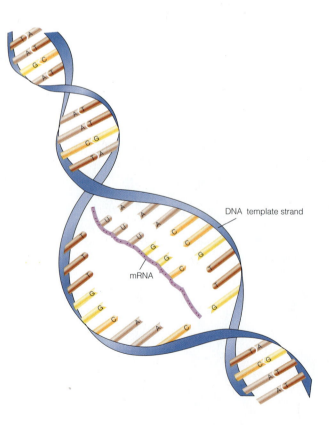

DNA template strand

mRNA

Ellen Ingmanson

© Russell Ciochon

CHAPTER 9

The First Dispersal of the Genus *Homo*: *Homo erectus* and Contemporaries

CHAPTER 10

Premodern Humans

CHAPTER **11**

The Origin and Dispersal of Modern Humans

CHAPTER **12**

Human Variation and Adaptation

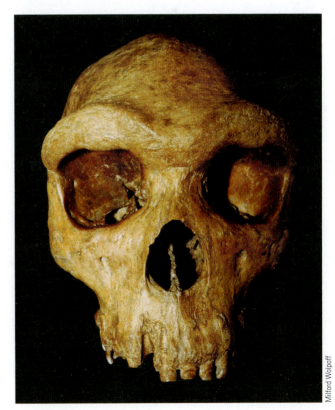

Milford Wolpoff

Lynn Kilgore

Preface

Welcome to all students and instructors using *Essentials of Physical Anthropology,* Seventh Edition. Not everyone reads a book preface, but we're glad you are reading it, because here we have our best opportunity to explain what's in this book and why we've written it.

First off, this book is about the biology of humans as understood from an evolutionary point of view. What we are and how we came to be this way is the underlying *biological* story of this text. In fact, physical anthropology is frequently also called *biological anthropology.*

Few readers should be surprised to learn they are reading a book concerning biological topics. After all, at most colleges, introductory courses in physical/biological anthropology are incorporated into general education programs as a biology (or "life science") requirement.

All three authors of this text are physical anthropologists as well as teachers, and we have all taught introductory physical anthropology as a general education course. So, this book is a product of our experience, and our goal is to provide a constructive educational aid to students from nonscience backgrounds. Moreover, most students are probably not anthropology majors or biology majors, and we've written and organized this textbook to provide as much help to as many students as possible.

For those with a nonscience background, scientific topics can sometimes prove difficult, as various theories, technical data, specialized terminology, and discoveries are discussed. We recognize that these challenges will be demanding for both teachers and students. But the effort is worth it, and we mean this in more ways than simply satisfying a graduation requirement. The topics we discuss are important. Being anthropologists, we also think that the material is interesting, and it's our hope that you will too. Because we live in a remarkably fast changing world, it is all the more crucial that we all have adequate knowledge of how biology affects the human species.

As educated and engaged citizens in a twenty-first century democracy, it's your responsibility to be well informed. More than likely, advances in molecular biological studies have already had a direct influence on someone you know. In your lifetime they are certain to have far greater impact. Think about the changes that molecular science has brought about in our ability to diagnose and treat a variety of diseases. So, too, will it vastly enhance our understanding of the specific evolutionary changes that have occurred during the history of life on earth. Indeed, what we are and how we came to be this way is a story that, in large part, is contained within our genes. The keys to unlock these ancient mysteries are now within reach, and dramatic new discoveries are just around the corner. There is no question that this knowledge will have profound social, medical, economic, and even philosophical impacts. The real question is: Will you be ready?

What's New in the Seventh Edition?

This revised version of *Essentials of Physical Anthropology* contains a great amount of updated information derived from further advances in molecular biology, primate behavioral studies, and many new discoveries of fossil hominids. Moreover, we have endeavored throughout to make this edition more readable and more accessible to as wide an audience as possible.

Several chapters have been reorganized and streamlined; there are new versions of all maps, and many of the diagrams have been redrawn. Dozens of new photos have been added, enhancing the pedagogy as well as improving the visual appeal of the book. We've also added a new feature at the end of each chapter called "Why It Matters." We've tried in these short discussions to address some of the "So what?" questions asked by many students, illustrating how our knowledge about a particular subject of the chapter has improved our lives or otherwise made a difference in the world we live in. We expect that you'll be able to think of other examples of why this information is relevant.

When the previous edition was written, the molecular sequencing of chimpanzee DNA (the species' genome) was not quite complete. We predicted that once completed and published, this information would have immediate impact and contribute tremendously to understanding what it is to be human.

In the three years since that edition, biologists have identified many specific regions in human DNA that differ from regions in the DNA of chimpanzees. Some of these differences are currently being investigated to provide better understanding of genetic influences on human language and other complex brain functions. Several other DNA regions are providing insight into underlying causes of major human diseases, including diabetes and coronary artery disorders. And while recognizing all this research is new and still preliminary, we discuss the findings and possible implications.

Moreover, there have been astounding breakthroughs in studies of ancient DNA— derived from minuscule fragments preserved in partially fossilized hominid bones dating as far back as 50,000 years ago. We cover these new discoveries in Chapters 10 and 11. In late 2006, two teams of researchers announced they had sequenced large sections of Neandertal DNA from the vast portion found in the nucleus of cells (that is, "nuclear DNA"). It's interesting too that scientific assessment of just how different we are from Neandertals is made much more accurate by comparison with the newly available genomic information from chimpanzees. Indeed, exciting new work has helped identify specific Neandertal genes that may tell us about the aptitude of Neandertals for language and other genes that provide evidence about their skin color!

Primatologists continue to report new examples of tool use in nonhuman primates, including the recent observation that female chimpanzees in one population sometimes use sharpened sticks to kill prey (covered in Chapter 7). Unfortunately, nonhuman primates continue to decline in numbers, and in Chapter 6 we provide new information from central Africa of just how seriously threatened is the continued existence of mountain gorillas there and elsewhere.

Many new fossil finds are discussed in Chapters 8 through 11, including a remarkably well-preserved infant skeleton from Ethiopia of an early hominid who died more than 3 million years ago. We also discuss new finds of other early African hominids, including early members of our genus, *Homo*.

New discoveries from southeastern Europe (in the Republic of Georgia) have recently provided significant insight into what the earliest hominids outside Africa looked like. Other recent discoveries, as well as crucial new dating of previously known fossils, updated in this edition, also enhance our understanding of later phases of hominid evolution. As discussed in Chapter 12, we now have a clearer time frame for the appearance of the earliest modern humans in Africa, China, and Indonesia.

Then, too, there are the "little people" from an island in Indonesia, whom the press refers to as "hobbits." These extremely unusual hominids were discussed in the previous edition, but since then, anthropologists have intensely debated what sort of hominid these fossils represent. The debate continues and is discussed in some detail in Chapter 11; as you'll see, the latest and most detailed studies provide more conclusive evidence than was previously available.

In-Chapter Learning Aids

- Chapter outlines at the beginning of each chapter list all major topics covered.
- Focus Questions appear at the beginning of each chapter and highlight the central topic of that chapter.
- A running glossary in the margins provides definitions of terms immediately adjacent to the text when the term is first introduced. A full glossary is provided at the back of the book.
- Quick Review boxes, found throughout the book, summarize complex or controversial material in a visually understandable fashion.
- Figures, including numerous photographs, line drawings, and maps, most in full color, are carefully selected to clarify and support discussion in the text.
- Summary "What's Important" figures are placed at the end of each of the fossil hominid chapters (Chapters 8 through 11) and are designed to offer crucial pedagogical support to students and make it easier for them to identify and organize the most important information in the chapter.
- A "Why It Matters" feature at the end of each chapter provides examples of contemporary applications of information relating to the chapter material and asks students to think about the relevance of this knowledge.
- Critical Thinking Questions at the end of each chapter reinforce key concepts and encourage students to think critically about what they have read.
- Full bibliographical citations throughout the book provide sources from which the materials are drawn. This type of documentation guides students to published source materials and illustrates for students the proper use of references. All cited sources are listed in the comprehensive bibliography at the back of the book.
- A "Click!" guide at the beginning of each chapter directs students to the appropriate media covering materials pertinent to that chapter. One or more of the three supplemental multimedia products will be listed:
  - Online Virtual Laboratories for Physical Anthropology CD-ROM, Fourth Edition
  - Basic Genetics for Anthropology CD-ROM 2.0: Principles and Applications
  - Hominid Fossils CD-ROM: An Interactive Atlas.

Acknowledgments

Over the years many friends and colleagues have assisted us with our books. For this edition we are especially grateful to the reviewers, focus group participants, and survey respondents who so carefully commented on the text and made so many helpful suggestions:

William Belcher, University of Hawaii–West Oahu; Rene Bobe, University of Georgia; Evangeline Catungal, Oakton Community College; Isabelle Champlin, University of Pittsburgh at Bradford; Janet Culbert, Sierra College; Maia Greenwell Cunningham, Citrus College; Marie Danforth, University of Southern Mississippi; Mark Dobbs, Ohlone College; David H. Dye, University of Memphis; Toni Edge, Los Angeles Valley College and Los Angeles Pierce College; Alejandra A. Estrin, University of Milwaukee; Gloria Everson, Lyon College; Josef Gamper, Monterey Peninsula College; Sharon Gursky, Texas A&M University; Tori Heflin, University of San Diego; Amelia Hubbard, Ohio State University; Marianne Jacobs, Green River Community College; Richard Jones, Lee University; Jennifer L. Kalfsbeek, Saint Paul College; Robert F. Manlove, Contra Costa College; Debra L. Martin, University of Nevada, Las Vegas; Jim Mielke, University of Kansas; Derek Milne, Pasadena City College; Jennifer Molina-Stidger, Sierra College; M. J. Mosher, Western Washington University; Elizabeth Pain, Palomar Community College; Melissa Remis, Purdue University; Patricia Richards, University of Wisconsin–Milwaukee; Ruth M. Riles, Bakersfield College; Stephen Schlecht, Ohio State University; Sue Short, College of Visual Arts in St. Paul, Minnesota; Jennifer Spence, Ohio State University; Lewis H. Tarrant, Shoreline Community College; Carolyn Tasa, Erie Community College; Laura Turner, University of Indianapolis; Giuseppe Vercellotti, Ohio State University; Rachel J. Watkins, American University; Daniel Wescott, University of Missouri; Lisa Westwood, Butte College; William Wheeler, University of Massachusetts–Amherst; Mary Williams Walker, Los Angeles Southwest College; RoxiAnn Wolfe, Linfield College.

We also wish to thank the following at Wadsworth: Lin Marshall, Anthropology Editor; Renee Deljon, Senior Development Editor; Paige Leeds, Editorial Assistant; and the former staff members at Wadsworth who have moved on to other professional pursuits, especially Eve Howard, Sherry Symington, Dave Lionetti, and Jessica Jang. Moreover, for their unflagging expertise and patience, we are grateful to our copy editor, Janet Greenblatt, together with our production team at Hespenheide Design, especially principal Gary Hespenheide, production coordinator Patti Zeman, and proofreader Bridget Neumayr.

To the many friends and colleagues who have generously provided photographs we are greatly appreciative: Zeresenay Alemsegel, Brenda Benefit, C.K. Brain, Günter Bräuer, Michel Brunet, Peter Brown , Desmond Clark, Ron Clarke, Raymond Dart, Henri de Lumley, Jean deRousseau, Denis Etler, Diane France, Robert Franciscus, David Frayer, Kathleen Galvin, Philip Gingerich, David Haring, Almut Hoffman, Ellen Ingmanson, Fred Jacobs, Peter Jones, John Kappelman, Richard Kay, William Kimbel, Leslie Knapp, Arlene Kruse, Richard Leakey, Carol Lofton, David Lordkipanidze, Giorgio Manzi, Margaret Maples, Lorna Moore, John Oates, Bonnie Pedersen, Lorna Pierce, David Pilbeam, William Pratt, Judith Regensteiner, Sastrohamijoyo Sartono, Jeffrey Schwartz, Eugenie Scott, Rose Sevick, Elwyn Simons, Meredith Small, Fred Smith, Thierry Smith, Judy Suchey, Li Tianyuan, Phillip Tobias, Erik Trinkaus, Alan Walker, Carol Ward, Dietrich Wegner, Randy White, Milford Wolpoff, and Xinzhi Wu.

February, 2008
Robert Jurmain
Lynn Kilgore
Wenda Trevathan

Supplements

Essentials of Physical Anthropology, **Seventh Edition,** is accompanied by a wide array of supplements prepared to create the best learning experience inside as well as outside the classroom for both the instructor and the student. All the supplements for the seventh edition have been thoroughly revised and updated, and several are new to this edition. The Wadsworth anthropology team invites you to take full advantage of the teaching and learning tools available to you.

Supplements for the Instructor

Instructor's Edition
This comprehensive resource contains a visual guide that illustrates and provides a walk-through of the book's features.

Instructor's Manual with Test Bank
Written by M. Leonor Monreal of Fullerton College, this comprehensive manual includes chapter outlines, learning objectives, key terms and concepts, suggested student activities, lecture suggestions and enrichment topics, as well as 40–60 test questions per chapter. A sample syllabus integrating material from the Wadsworth Anthropology Resource Center is also included.

NEW! Power Lecture With PowerPoint, JoinIn And Examview CD-ROM for Anthropology 2009
This easy-to-use, one-stop digital library and presentation tool includes the following book-specific resources as well as direct links to many of Wadsworth's highly valued electronic resources for anthropology:
- Ready-to-use **Microsoft® PowerPoint®** lecture slides with photos and graphics from the text, making it easy for you to assemble, edit, publish, and present custom lectures for your course.
- Video-based polling and quiz questions that can be used with the easy-to-use JoinIn™ on TurningPoint personal response system, which enables instant classroom assessment and learning.
- ExamView® testing software, which provides all the test items from the text's printed *test bank* in electronic format, enabling you to create customized tests of up to 250 items that can be delivered in print or online.
- The text's *instructor's resource manual* in electronic format.

Supplements for the Student

Premium Companion Website for *Essentials of Physical Anthropology,* Seventh Edition
academic.cengage.com/login
This protected site offers a wealth of resources, such as interactive exercises, video exercises, map exercises, and quizzing. It includes Robert Jurmain's "The Latest Dirt" on new fossil finds, with maps and information on the newest discoveries; map exercise: Primates and their geographic regions; interactive exercise: Identifying the bones of humans and chimps; video example: South Africa: Bones of 3,000-year-old ape man found.

Student Companion Website for *Essentials of Physical Anthropology,* Seventh Edition
academic.cengage.com/anthropology/Jurmain
This site provides students with basic learning resources including tutorial quizzes, a final exam, learning objectives, web links, flash cards, and more!

Study Guide for *Essentials of Physical Anthropology,* Seventh Edition
Written by Daniel D. White, this comprehensive student study guide includes chapter outlines, key terms, Internet activities, and practice tests (answers provided) with a variety of question types—ideal for test prep!

NEW! Telecourse Study Guide

Print study guide for the Physical Anthropology Telecourse *Physical Anthropology: The Evolving Human* provides study aids, quizzing and exercises correlated with *Essentials of Physical Anthropology*, Seventh Edition.

NEW! Classic Readings in Physical Anthropology

Edited by Mary K. Sandford, this reader presents primary articles with introductions and questions for discussion, helping students to better understand the nature of scientific inquiry. Students will read highly accessible classic and contemporary articles on key topics, including the science of physical anthropology, evolution and heredity, primates, human evolution, and modern human variation.

Anthropology Resource Center

This hands-on online center offers a wealth of information and useful tools for both instructors and students in all four fields of anthropology: cultural anthropology, physical anthropology, archaeology, and linguistics. It includes interactive maps, learning modules, video exercises, a Case Study Forum with abstracts and critical thinking questions, and breaking news in anthropology.

Virtual Laboratories for Physical Anthropology, Online Version 4.0
academic.cengage.com/anthropology

Through the use of video segments, interactive exercises, quizzes, 3-D animations, sound and digital images, students can actively participate in 12 labs on their own terms—at home, in the library—at any time! Recent fossil discoveries are included, as well as exercises in behavior and archaeology and critical thinking and problem-solving activities. When you order Virtual Laboratories on the web-based CengageNOW platform, a powerful course management component allows you to reorder the labs, move content within the labs, utilize the pre-lab and post-lab tests for each lab, and track how much time students spend on each lab. Virtual Laboratories includes web links, outstanding fossil images, exercises, a notebook feature, and a post-lab self-quiz. This supplement is also available on CD-ROM (with a portion of the features and functionality of the online version).

Basic Genetics for Anthropology CD-ROM: Principles and Applications, Version 2.0

This student CD-ROM expands on basic biological concepts covered in the book, focusing on biological inheritance (such as genes and DNA sequencing) and its applications to modern human populations. Interactive animations and simulations bring these important concepts to life so that students can fully understand the essential biological principles underlying human evolution. Also available are quizzes and interactive flash cards

for further study. (An updated version of this CD-ROM will be available in spring 2008.)

Hominid Fossils CD-ROM: An Interactive Atlas

This CD-based interactive atlas includes over 75 key fossils that are important for a clear understanding of human evolution. The QuickTime Virtual Reality (QTVR) "object" movie format for each fossil will enable students to have a near-authentic experience working with these important finds by allowing them to rotate the fossil 360°. Unlike some VR media, QTVR objects are made using actual photographs of the real objects and thus better preserve details of color and texture. The fossils used are high-quality research casts and real fossils.

The organization of the atlas is nonlinear, with three levels and multiple paths, enabling students to start with a particular fossil and work their way "up" to see how the fossil fits into the map of human evolution in terms of geography, time, and evolution. The CD-ROM offers students an inviting, authentic learning environment, one that also contains a dynamic quizzing feature that will allow students to test their knowledge of fossil and species identification as well as provide more detailed information about the fossil record.

Wadsworth Anthropology's Module Series

This series includes:

- **Human-Environment Interactions: New Directions in Human Ecology** This module by Kathy Galvin, of Colorado State University, begins with a brief discussion of the history and core concepts of the field of human ecology, the study of how humans interact with the natural environment, before looking in depth at how the environment influences cultural practices (environmental determinism) as well as how aspects of culture, in turn, affect the environment. Human behavioral ecology is presented within the context of natural selection, examining how ecological factors influence the development of cultural and behavioral traits and how people subsist in different environments. The module concludes with a discussion of resilience and global change as a result of human-environment interactions. This module in chapter-like print format can be packaged for free with the text.

- **Evolution of the Brain Module: Neuroanatomy, Development, and Paleontology** The human species is the only species that has ever created a symphony, written a poem, developed a mathematical equation, or studied its own origins. The biological structure that has enabled humans to perform these feats of intelligence is the human brain. This module, created by Daniel D. White, explores the basics of neuroanatomy, brain development, lateralization, and sexual dimorphism and provides the fossil evidence for hominid brain evolution. This module in chapter-like print format can be packaged for free with the text.

Forensics Anthropology Module
The forensic application of physical anthropology is exploding in popularity. Written by Diane France, this module explores the myths and realities of the search for human remains in crime scenes, what can be expected from a forensic anthropology expert in the courtroom, some of the special challenges in responding to mass fatalities, and the issues a student should consider if pursuing a career in forensic anthropology. This module in chapter-like print format can be packaged for free with the text.

Molecular Anthropology Module
This module by Leslie Knapp, of Cambridge University, explores how molecular genetic methods are used to understand the organization and expression of genetic information in humans and nonhuman primates. Students will learn about the common laboratory methods used to study genetic variation and evolution in molecular anthropology. Examples are drawn from up-to-date research on human evolutionary origins and comparative primate genomics to demonstrate that scientific research is an ongoing process with theories frequently being questioned and reevaluated. Mitochondrial DNA and the human-chimp biological connection are also examined in this fascinating and timely module. This module in chapter-like print format can be packaged for free with the text.

These resources are available to qualified adopters, and ordering options for student supplements are flexible. Please consult your local Cengage sales representative for more information, or to evaluate examination copies of any of these resources or receive product demonstrations. You may also contact the Wadsworth Academic Resource Center at 800-423-0563 or visit us at **academic.cengage. com.** Additional information is also available at **academic. cengage.com/anthropology/jurmain.**

CHAPTER 1

Introduction to Physical Anthropology

© Russell Ciochon

Craig King

David Haring

FOCUS QUESTIONS

What do physical anthropologists do?

Why is physical anthropology a scientific discipline, and what is its importance to the general public?

▶ Click!

Go to the following media resources for interactive activities, more information, and study materials on topics covered in this chapter:

■ Anthropology Resource Center
■ Student Companion Website for *Essentials of Physical Anthropology,* Seventh Edition
■ Online Virtual Laboratories for Physical Anthropology CD-ROM, Fourth Edition
■ Basic Genetics for Anthropology CD-ROM 2.0: Principles and Applications
■ Hominid Fossils CD-ROM: An Interactive Atlas

Introduction

One day, perhaps during the rainy season some 3.7 million years ago, two or three animals walked across a grassland **savanna** in what is now northern Tanzania, in East Africa. These individuals were early members of the taxonomic family **Hominidae,** the family that also includes ourselves, modern *Homo sapiens.* Fortunately for us, a record of their passage on that long-forgotten day remains in the form of fossilized footprints, preserved in hardened volcanic deposits.

As chance would have it, shortly after heels and toes were pressed into the damp soil, a nearby volcano erupted. The ensuing ashfall blanketed everything on the ground, including the hominid footprints. In time, the ash layer hardened into a deposit that preserved them for almost 4 million years (Fig. 1-1).

These now famous prints indicate that two **hominids,** one smaller than the other and perhaps walking side by side, left parallel sets of tracks. But because the larger animal's prints are blurred, possibly by those of a third, it's unclear how many individuals actually made that journey so long ago. But what is clear is that the prints were made by an animal that habitually walked **bipedally** (on two feet), and that fact tells us that those ancient travelers were hominids.

FIGURE 1-1

Early hominid footprints at Laetoli, Tanzania. The tracks to the left were made by one individual, while those to the right appear to have been formed by two individuals, the second stepping in the tracks of the first.

Peter Jones

In addition to the footprints, scientists working at this site (called Laetoli) and at other locations have discovered many fossilized parts of skeletons of an animal we call *Australopithecus afarensis*. After analyzing these remains, we know that these hominids were anatomically similar to ourselves, although their brains were only about one-third the size of ours. And even though they may have used stones and sticks as simple tools, there's no evidence to suggest that they actually *made* stone tools. In fact, these early hominids were very much at the mercy of nature's whims. They certainly couldn't outrun most predators, and since their canine teeth were fairly small, they were pretty much defenseless.

Chimpanzees often serve as living models for our early ancestors, and there are several good reasons for this, as you will learn later. But the earliest hominids probably occupied a somewhat different habitat than chimpanzees and they probably had more to fear from predators. So, however much we may be tempted to compare early forms to living ones, we need to remind ourselves that there is no living animal that perfectly represents them. Just like every other living thing, extinct **species** were also unique.

We've asked hundreds of questions about the Laetoli hominids, but we'll never be able to answer them all. They walked down a path into what became their future, and their immediate journey ended long ago. So it remains for us to learn as much as we can about them and their species; and as we continue to do so, their greater journey continues.

On July 20, 1969, a television audience numbering in the hundreds of millions watched as two human beings stepped out of a spacecraft onto the surface of the moon. The significance of that first moonwalk can't be overstated, because it represents humankind's presumed mastery over the natural forces that govern our presence on earth. For the first time ever, people had actually walked upon the surface of a celestial body that, as far as we know, has never given birth to biological life.

As the astronauts gathered geological specimens and frolicked in near weightlessness, they left traces of their fleeting presence in the form of footprints in the lunar dust (Fig. 1-2). On the surface of the moon, where no rain falls and no wind blows, the footprints remain undisturbed to this day. They survive as mute testimony to a brief visit by a medium-sized, big-brained creature who presumed to challenge the very forces that created it.

You may be wondering why anyone would care about early hominid footprints and how they can possibly be relevant to your life. You may also wonder why a physical anthropology textbook would begin by discussing two such seemingly unrelated events as early hominids walking across a savanna and a moonwalk. The fact is, these two events aren't unrelated at all.

Physical, or biological, anthropology is a scientific discipline concerned with the biological and behavioral characteristics of human beings; our ancestors; and our closest relatives, the nonhuman **primates** (apes, monkeys, and prosimians). This kind of research helps us explain what it means to be human. This is an ambitious goal and it probably isn't fully attainable, but it's certainly worth pursuing. We're the only species to ponder our own existence and wonder how we fit into the spectrum of life on earth. Most people view humanity as separate from the rest of the animal kingdom. But at the same time, some are curious about the similarities we share with other species. Maybe, as a child, you looked at your dog and tried to figure out how her front legs might correspond to your arms. Perhaps, during a visit to the zoo, you noticed the similarities between a chimpanzee's hands or facial expressions and your own. Did you think that maybe they also shared your thoughts and feelings? If the answer to this question is yes, then you've indeed been curious about humankind's place in nature.

We humans, who can barely comprehend a century, can't begin to grasp the enormity of nearly 4 million years. But we still want to know more about those creatures who walked across the savanna that day. We want to know how an

© Bettmann/Corbis

FIGURE 1-2

Human footprint left on the lunar surface during the *Apollo* mission.

savanna (also spelled savannah) A large flat grassland with scattered trees and shrubs. Savannas are found in many regions of the world with dry and warm to hot climates.

Hominidae The taxonomic family to which humans belong; also includes other, now extinct, bipedal relatives.

hominids Colloquial term for members of the family Hominidae, which includes all bipedal hominoids back to the divergence from African great apes.

bipedally On two feet; walking habitually on two legs.

species A group of organisms that can interbreed to produce fertile offspring. Members of one species are reproductively isolated from members of all other species (that is, they can't mate with them to produce fertile offspring).

primates Members of the order of mammals Primates (pronounced "pry-may´-tees"), which includes prosimians, monkeys, apes, and humans.

evolution A change in the genetic structure of a population. The term is also frequently used to refer to the appearance of a new species.

adaptation An anatomical, physiological, or behavioral response of organisms or populations to the environment. Adaptations result from evolutionary change (specifically, as a result of natural selection).

macroevolution Large-scale changes that occur in populations only after many generations, such as the appearance of a new species, or speciation.

microevolution Small genetic changes that occur within a species. A human example is the variation seen in the different ABO blood types.

culture Behavioral aspects of human adaptation, including technology, traditions, language, religion, marriage patterns, and social roles. Culture is a set of learned behaviors transmitted from one generation to the next through learning and not by biological or genetic mechanisms.

worldview General cultural orientation or perspective shared by members of a society.

behavior Anything organisms do that involves action in response to internal or external stimuli; the response of an individual, group, or species to its environment. Such responses may or may not be deliberate, and they aren't necessarily the result of conscious decision making (as in one-celled organisms or insects).

predisposition The capacity or inclination to do something. An organism's capacity for behavioral or anatomical modification is related to the presence of preexisting traits.

insignificant but clever bipedal primate like *Australopithecus afarensis* (or, more likely, a close relative) gave rise to a species that would eventually walk on the surface of the moon, some 230,000 miles from earth.

How did *Homo sapiens,* a result of the same evolutionary forces that produced all other life on this planet, gain the power to control the flow of rivers and alter the very climate in which we live? As tropical animals, how were we able to leave the tropics and eventually occupy most of the earth's land surfaces? How did we adjust to different environmental conditions as we spread throughout the world? How could our species, which numbered fewer than 1 billion until the mid-nineteenth century, come to number more almost 7 billion worldwide today and, as we now do, add another billion people every 11 years?

These are some of the many questions that physical anthropologists try to answer through the study of human **evolution,** variation, and **adaptation.** These issues, and many others, are the topics covered in this textbook, because physical anthropology is, in part, human biology seen from an evolutionary perspective.

As biological organisms, humans are subjected to the same evolutionary forces as all other species are. On hearing the term *evolution,* most people think of the appearance of new species. Certainly, new species formation is one important consequence of evolution; but it isn't the only one, because evolution is an ongoing biological process with more than one outcome. Simply stated, evolution is a change in the genetic makeup of a population from one generation to the next, and it can be defined and studied at two levels. Sometimes, genetic changes over time in populations do result in the appearance of a new species, or *speciation,* especially when those populations are isolated. Change at this level is called **macroevolution.** At the other level, there are genetic alterations *within* populations; and while this type of change may not lead to speciation, it often causes populations of a species to differ from one another regarding the frequency of certain traits. Evolution at this level is referred to as **microevolution.** Evolution at both these levels will be addressed in this book.

But biological anthropologists don't just study physiological and biological systems. When these topics are considered within the broader context of human evolution, another factor must be considered, and that factor is **culture.** Culture is an extremely important concept, not only as it relates to modern human beings but also because of its critical role in human evolution. Quite simply, and in a very broad sense, culture is the strategy by which humans adapt to the natural environment. In fact, culture is the environment in which we live. Culture includes technologies ranging from stone tools to computers; subsistence patterns, from hunting and gathering to global agribusiness; housing types, from thatched huts to skyscrapers; and clothing, from animal skins to high-tech synthetic fibers (Fig. 1-3). Technology, religion, values, social organization, language, kinship, marriage rules, gender roles, inheritance of property, and so on, are all aspects of culture. And each culture shapes people's perceptions of the external environment, or **worldview,** in particular ways that distinguish that culture from all others.

One basic point to remember is that culture isn't genetically passed from one generation to the next. Culture is *learned,* and the process of learning one's culture begins at birth. All humans are products of the culture they're raised in, and since most of human **behavior** is learned, it follows that most behaviors, perceptions, and reactions are shaped by culture. But even though culture isn't genetically determined, the human **predisposition** to assimilate culture and function within it is profoundly influenced by biological factors. Most nonhuman animals, including birds and especially primates, rely to varying degrees on learned behavior. This is especially true of the great apes (orangutans, chimpanzees, gorillas, and bonobos), which, as you will learn later, exhibit numerous aspects of culture.

The predisposition for culture is perhaps the most critical component of human evolutionary history, and it was inherited from early hominid or prehomi-

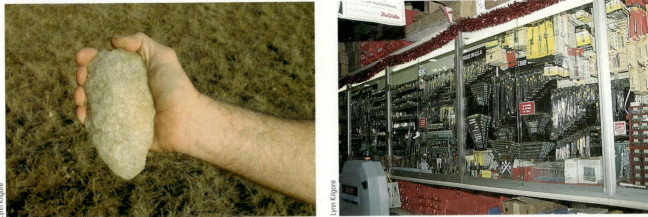

(a)   (b)

(c)   (d)

nid ancestors. In fact, the common ancestor we share with chimpanzees may have had this predisposition. But during the course of human evolution, the role of culture became increasingly important. Over time, culture came to influence biology; and in turn, aspects of biology influenced cultural practices. For this reason, humans are said to be the result of interactions between biology and culture, or **biocultural evolution.**

Many major anatomical and behavioral changes (larger brains, reorganization of brain structures, smaller teeth, bipedalism, and the development of language) all came about through biocultural interactions during the course of human evolution. Biocultural interactions are still critically important, and they even continue to influence changes in disease patterns. For example, global warming is increasing the range of mosquitoes that carry malaria and West Nile virus. Another example is Africa, where rapid culture change (driven by several centuries of contact with Western cultures and technological change) has facilitated the spread and perhaps even the evolution of HIV, the virus that causes AIDS.

So how does biological anthropology differ from human biology? In many ways it doesn't, because human biologists also study human physiology, genetics, and adaptation. But human biology, as a discipline, doesn't include studies of nonhuman primates or human evolution. So when biological research also includes these topics as well as how cultural factors have shaped our species, it's placed within the discipline of anthropology.

FIGURE 1-3

(a) An early stone tool from East Africa. This artifact represents one of the oldest types of stone tools found anywhere. (b) Assortment of implements available today in a modern hardware store. (c) A Samburu woman building a simple, traditional dwelling of stems, plant fibers, and mud. (d) These Hong Kong skyscrapers are typical of cities in industrialized countries today.

biocultural evolution The mutual, interactive evolution of human biology and culture; the concept that biology makes culture possible and that developing culture further influences the direction of biological evolution; a basic concept in understanding the unique components of human evolution.

What Is Anthropology?

Stated ambitiously but simply, **anthropology** is the study of humankind. The word *anthropology* is derived from the Greek words *anthropos*, meaning "human," and *logos*, meaning "word" or "study of." The goals of anthropology are shared by other disciplines within the social, behavioral, and biological sciences. The main difference between anthropology and these related fields is that anthropology integrates the findings of many disciplines, including sociology, economics, history, psychology, and biology.

In the United States and in some Canadian universities, anthropology comprises three main subfields: cultural, or social, anthropology; archaeology; and physical, or biological, anthropology. Additionally, some universities include linguistic anthropology as a fourth area. Each of these subdisciplines, in turn, is divided into several specialized areas of interest. Following is a brief discussion of the main subdisciplines of anthropology.

Cultural Anthropology

Cultural anthropology is the study of all aspects of human behavior. The beginnings of cultural anthropology are found in the nineteenth century, when Europeans became increasingly aware of what they termed "primitive" societies in Africa and Asia. Also, in the New World, there was considerable interest in the vanishing cultures of Native Americans.

The interest in traditional societies led early anthropologists to study and record lifeways that unfortunately are now all but extinct. These studies produced many descriptive **ethnographies** that covered a range of topics, including religion, ritual, myth, use of symbols, taboos, subsistence strategies, dietary preferences, technology, medical practices, gender roles, and child-rearing practices. Ethnographic accounts, in turn, formed the basis for comparative studies of numerous cultures. By examining the similarities and differences between cultures, anthropologists have been able to formulate many theories about fundamental aspects of human behavior.

The focus of cultural anthropology shifted over the course of the twentieth century. For example, in recent decades, ethnographic techniques have been used to study diverse subcultures and their interactions with one another in contemporary metropolitan areas (urban anthropology). Another relevant area for cultural anthropologists today is the resettlement of refugees in many parts of the world.

Medical anthropology is the subfield of cultural anthropology that explores the relationship between various cultural attributes and health and disease. One area of interest is how different groups view disease processes and how these views affect treatment or the willingness to accept treatment. When a medical anthropologist focuses on the social dimensions of disease, physicians and physical anthropologists may also collaborate. In fact, many medical anthropologists have received much of their training in physical anthropology.

Many cultural anthropology subfields (for example, medical anthropology) have practical applications and are pursued by anthropologists working outside the university setting. This approach is called **applied anthropology,** and all anthropological disciplines have wide practical applications. Indeed, the various fields of anthropology, as practiced in the United States, overlap considerably, which, after all, was the reason for combining them under the umbrella of anthropology in the first place.

Archaeology

Archaeology is the study of earlier cultures and lifeways by anthropologists who specialize in the scientific recovery, analysis, and interpretation of the material remains of past societies. Although archaeology often deals with cultures that existed before the invention of writing (the period commonly known as *prehistory*), historic

anthropology The field of inquiry that studies human culture and evolutionary aspects of human biology; includes cultural anthropology, archaeology, linguistics, and physical, or biological, anthropology.

ethnographies Detailed descriptive studies of human societies. In cultural anthropology, an ethnography is traditionally the study of a non-Western society.

applied anthropology The practical application of anthropological and archaeological theories and techniques. For example, many biological anthropologists work in the public health sector.

archaeologists examine the evidence of later, more complex societies that produced written records.

Although archaeologists are concerned with culture, they don't study living people. Instead, they study the **artifacts** left behind by earlier societies and people. Obviously, no one has ever excavated such aspects of culture as religious belief, spoken language, or a political system. However, the surviving evidence of human occupation (buildings, foundations, tools, and so on) can tell us many things about these and many other important characteristics of the society that created them.

Today, the main goal of archaeology is to answer specific questions about human behavior. Sites are no longer excavated just because they exist or for the artifacts they may contain. Patterns of behavior are reflected in the dispersal of human settlements across a landscape and in the distribution of cultural remains within them. Through the identification of these patterns, archaeologists can identify the commonalities shared by many or all populations as well as those features that differ between groups.

In the United States, the greatest expansion in archaeology since the 1960s has been in the area of *cultural resource management (CRM)*. This applied approach arose from environmental legislation requiring archaeological evaluation and sometimes excavation of sites that may be threatened by development. (Canada and many European countries have similar legislation.) Many contract archaeologists (so called because their services are contracted out to developers or contractors) are affiliated with private consulting firms, state or federal agencies, or educational institutions. In fact, an estimated 40 percent of all archaeologists in the United States now fill such positions.

Linguistic Anthropology

Linguistic anthropology is the study of human speech and language, including the origins of language in general. By examining similarities between contemporary languages, linguists have been able to trace historical ties between languages and groups of languages, thus facilitating the identification of language families and perhaps past relationships between human populations. Linguistic anthropologists are also interested in the relationship between language and culture. For example, they may want to know how language reflects the way members of a society perceive phenomena and how the use of language shapes perceptions in different cultures.

Because the spontaneous acquisition and use of language is a uniquely human characteristic, it's an important topic for linguistic anthropologists, who, along with specialists in other fields, study the process of language acquisition in infants. Since insights into the process may well have implications for the development of language skills in human evolution, as well as in growing children, it's also an important subject to physical anthropologists.

Physical Anthropology

As we've already said, *physical anthropology* is the study of human biology within the framework of evolution and with an emphasis on the interaction between biology and culture. This subdiscipline is also referred to as *biological anthropology,* and you'll see the terms used interchangeably. *Physical anthropology* is the original term, and it reflects the initial interests of anthropologists in describing human physical variation. The American Association of Physical Anthropologists, its journal, as well as many college courses and numerous publications, retain this term. The designation *biological anthropology* reflects the shift in emphasis to more biologically oriented topics, such as genetics, evolutionary biology, nutrition, physiological adaptation, and growth and development. This shift occurred largely because of advances in the field of genetics since the late 1950s. Although we've continued to use the traditional term in the title of this textbook, you'll find that all the major topics pertain to biological issues.

artifacts Objects or materials made or modified for use by modern humans and their ancestors. The earliest artifacts tend to be tools made of stone or, occasionally, bone.

FIGURE 1-4
Paleoanthropologists excavating at an early hominid site in South Africa.

paleoanthropology The interdisciplinary approach to the study of earlier hominids, their chronology, physical structure, archaeological remains, habitats, etc.

anthropometry Measurement of human body parts. When osteologists measure skeletal elements, the term *osteometry* is often used.

FIGURE 1-5
This anthropology student is measuring the length of a human cranium with spreading calipers.

The origins of physical anthropology can be found in two principal areas of interest among nineteenth-century European and American scholars. First, many scientists (at the time called *natural historians*) were becoming increasingly curious about the origins of modern species. In other words, they were beginning to doubt the literal interpretation of the biblical account of creation at a time when scientific explanations emphasizing natural processes, rather than supernatural phenomena were becoming more popular. Eventually, these sparks of interest in biological change over time were fueled into flames by the publication of Charles Darwin's *On the Origin of Species* in 1859.

Today, **paleoanthropology,** or the study of human evolution, particularly as revealed in the fossil record, is a major subfield of physical anthropology (Fig. 1-4). Thousands of specimens of human ancestors (mostly fragmentary) are now kept in research collections. Taken together, these fossils span about 7 million years of human prehistory; and although incomplete, they provide us with significantly more knowledge than was available just 15 years ago. It's the ultimate goal of paleoanthropological research to identify the various early hominid species, establish a chronological sequence of relationships among them, and gain insights into their adaptation and behavior. Only then will we have a clear picture of how and when humankind came into being.

Human variation was the other major area of interest for early anthropologists. They were especially concerned with observable physical differences, skin color being the most obvious. Enormous effort was aimed at describing and explaining the biological differences between various human populations. Although some attempts were misguided and downright racist, they gave birth to literally thousands of body measurements that are sometimes still used to compare people. Physical anthropologists also use many of the techniques of **anthropometry** to study skeletal remains from archaeological sites (Fig. 1-5). Moreover, anthropometric techniques have had considerable application in the design of everything from wheelchairs to office furniture. (Undoubtedly, they've also been used to determine the absolute minimum amount of leg room a person must have in order to complete a 3-hour flight on a commercial airliner and remain sane.)

Today, anthropologists are concerned with human variation because of its possible *adaptive significance* and because they want to identify the genetic and other evolutionary factors that have produced variation. In other words, some traits that typify certain populations evolved as biological adaptations, or adjustments, to local environmental conditions such as sunlight, altitude or, infectious disease. Other traits may simply be the results of geographical isolation or the descent of populations from small founding groups. Examining biological variation between populations of any species provides valuable information as to the mechanisms of genetic change in groups over time, and this is really what the evolutionary process is all about.

Modern population studies also examine other important aspects of human variation, including how various groups respond physiologically to different kinds of environmentally induced stress (Fig. 1-6). Environmental stressors can include high altitude and/or temperature extremes, and human individuals and populations differ in some of the ways they respond to these conditions.

Many biological anthropologists conduct nutritional studies, investigating the relationships between various dietary components, cultural practices, physiology, and certain aspects of health and disease (Fig. 1-7). Investigations of human fertility, growth, and development also are closely related to the topic of nutrition; they're fundamental to studies of adaptation in modern human populations and they can also provide insights into hominid evolution.

It would be impossible to study evolutionary processes without knowledge of how traits are inherited. For this reason and others, **genetics** is a crucial field for physical anthropologists. Modern physical anthropology wouldn't exist as an evolutionary science if it weren't for advances in the understanding of genetic mechanisms.

In this exciting time of rapid advances in genetic research, *molecular anthropologists* use cutting-edge technologies to investigate evolutionary relationships between human populations and between humans and nonhuman primates. To do this, they examine similarities and differences in **DNA** sequences between individuals, populations, and species. What's more, by extracting DNA from fossils, they've contributed to our understanding of relationships between extinct and living species. As genetic technologies continue to be developed, molecular anthropologists will play a key role in explaining human evolution, adaptation, and our biological relationships with other species (Fig. 1-8).

Primatology, the study of nonhuman primates, has become increasingly important since the late 1950s (Fig. 1-9). Behavioral studies, especially those conducted on groups in natural environments, have implications for many scientific disciplines. Because nonhuman primates are our closest living relatives, identifying the underlying factors related to social behavior, communication, infant care, reproductive

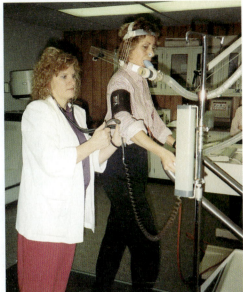

Judith Regensteiner

FIGURE 1-6
Researcher using a treadmill test to assess a subject's heart rate, blood pressure, and oxygen consumption.

genetics The study of gene structure and action and the patterns of inheritance of traits from parent to offspring. Genetic mechanisms are the foundation for evolutionary change.

DNA (deoxyribonucleic acid) The double-stranded molecule that contains the genetic code, a set of instructions for producing bodily structures and functions. DNA is a main component of chromosomes.

primatology The study of the biology and behavior of nonhuman primates (prosimians, monkeys, and apes).

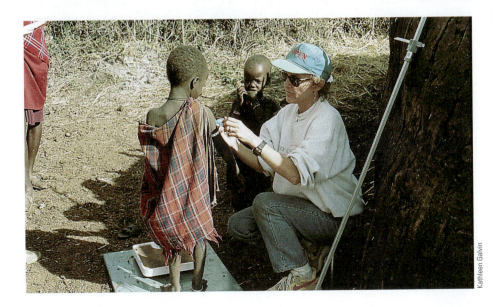

Kathleen Galvin

FIGURE 1-7
Dr. Kathleen Galvin measures upper arm circumference in a young Maasai boy in Tanzania. Data derived from various body measurements, including height and weight, were used in a health and nutrition study of groups of Maasai cattle herders.

FIGURE 1-8
Cloning and sequencing methods are frequently used to identify genes in humans and nonhuman primates. This graduate student identifies a genetically modified bacterial clone.

FIGURE 1-9
Yahaya Alamasi, a member of the field staff at Gombe National Park, Tanzania. Alamasi is recording behaviors in free-ranging chimpanzees.

osteology The study of skeletal material. Human osteology focuses on the interpretation of skeletal remains from archaeological sites, skeletal anatomy, bone physiology, and growth and development. Some of the same techniques are used in paleoanthropology to study early hominids.

behavior, and so on, helps us to better understand the natural forces that have shaped so many aspects of modern human behavior.

But sadly, an even more important reason to study nonhuman primates is that most species are now threatened or seriously endangered. Indeed, as you will learn, some are very close to extinction. Only through research will scientists be able to recommend policies that can better ensure the survival of many nonhuman primates and thousands of other species as well.

Primate paleontology, the study of the primate fossil record, has implications not only for nonhuman primates but also for hominids. Virtually every year, fossil-bearing beds in North America, Africa, Asia, and Europe yield important new discoveries. By studying fossil primates and comparing them with anatomically similar living species, primate paleontologists can learn a great deal about such things as diet or locomotion in earlier forms. They can also make assumptions about social behavior in some extinct primates and try to clarify what we know about evolutionary relationships between extinct and living species, including ourselves.

Osteology, the study of the skeleton, is central to physical anthropology. In fact, it's so important that when many people think of biological anthropology, the first thing that comes to mind is bones (although they often ask about dinosaurs). The emphasis on osteology is partly due to the fact that a thorough knowledge of skeletal structure and function is critical to the interpretation of fossil material.

Bone biology and physiology are of major importance to many other aspects of physical anthropology. Many osteologists specialize in studies that emphasize various measurements of skeletal elements. This type of research is essential, for example, to determine stature and growth patterns in archaeological populations.

One subdiscipline of osteology, called **paleopathology,** is the study of disease and trauma in skeletons from archaeological sites. Paleopathology is a prominent subfield that investigates the prevalence of trauma, certain infectious diseases (such as syphilis and tuberculosis), nutritional deficiencies, and many other conditions that can leave evidence in bone (Fig. 1-10). This research tells us a great deal about the lives of individuals and populations from the past. Paleopathology also yields information regarding the history of certain disease processes, and for this reason it's of interest to scientists in biomedical fields.

Forensic anthropology is directly related to osteology and paleopathology, and many people have become interested in it because of forensic shows on television. Technically, this approach is the application of anthropological (usually osteological and sometimes archaeological) techniques to legal issues (Fig. 1-11a). Forensic

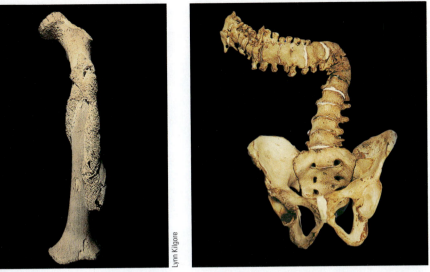

Lynn Kilgore

(a)   (b)

Lynn Kilgore

FIGURE 1-10

(a) A partially healed fracture of the femur (thigh bone) from a child's skeleton (estimated age at death is 6 years). Cause of death was probably an infection resulting from this injury. (b) Very severe congenital scoliosis in an adult male from Nubia. The curves are due to several developmental defects that affect individual vertebrae. (this is not the most common form of scoliosis).

paleopathology The branch of osteology that studies the evidence of disease and injury in human skeletal (or, occasionally, mummified) remains from archaeological sites.

forensic anthropology An applied anthropological approach dealing with legal matters. Forensic anthropologists work with coroners, police, and others in identifying and analyzing human remains.

anthropologists help identify skeletal remains in mass disasters or other situations where a human body has been found.

Forensic anthropologists have been involved in numerous cases having important legal, historical, and human consequences. They were instrumental in identifying the skeletons of most of the Russian imperial family, executed in 1918; and many participated in the overwhelming task of trying to identify the remains of victims of the September 11, 2001, terrorist attacks in the United States (Fig. 1-11b).

Anatomical studies are another area of interest for physical anthropologists. In living organisms, bones and teeth are intimately linked to the muscles and other tissues that surround and act on them. Consequently, a thorough knowledge of soft tissue anatomy is essential to the understanding of biomechanical relationships involved in movement. Knowledge of such relationships is fundamental to the interpretation of the structure and function of limbs and other structures in extinct animals now represented only by fossilized remains. For these reasons and others, many physical anthropologists specialize in anatomical studies. In fact, several physical anthropologists hold professorships in anatomy departments at universities and medical schools (Fig. 1-12).

As we mentioned in our discussion of medical anthropology, applied approaches in biological anthropology are numerous. While *applied anthropology* is the practical application of anthropological theories and methods outside the academic setting, applied and academic anthropology aren't mutually exclusive approaches. Applied anthropology relies on the research and theories of academic anthropologists and at

FIGURE 1-11

(a) Physical anthropologists Lorna Pierce (left) and Judy Suchey (center) working as forensic consultants. The dog has just located a concealed human cranium during a training session. (b) Forensic anthropologists at the location on Staten Island where all materials from the World Trade Center were taken for investigation after September 11, 2001. The scientists are wearing HAZMAT (hazardous materials) suits for protection.

Lorna Pierce/Judy Suchey

(a)   (b)

D. France

FIGURE 1-12

Dr. Linda Levitch teaching a human anatomy class at the University of North Carolina School of Medicine.

Linda Levitch

theory A broad statement of scientific relationships or underlying principles that has been substantially verified through the testing of hypotheses.

continuum A set of relationships in which all components fall along a single integrated spectrum. All life reflects a single biological continuum.

science A body of knowledge gained through observation and experimentation; from the Latin *scientia,* meaning "knowledge."

empirical Relying on experiment or observation; from the Latin *empiricus,* meaning "experienced."

hypotheses (*sing.,* hypothesis) A provisional explanation of a phenomenon. Hypotheses require verification or falsification through testing.

scientific method An approach to research whereby a question is asked, a hypothesis (or provisional explanation) is stated, and that hypothesis is tested by collecting and analyzing data.

the same time has much to contribute to **theory** and techniques. Within biological anthropology, forensic anthropologists are a good example of the applied approach. But the practical application of the techniques of physical anthropology isn't new. During World War II, for example, physical anthropologists were extensively involved in designing gun turrets and airplane cockpits. Since then, many physical anthropologists have pursued careers in genetic and biomedical research, public health, evolutionary medicine, medical anthropology, and conservation of nonhuman primates, and many have positions in museums and zoos. In fact, a background in physical anthropology is excellent preparation for almost any career in the medical and biological fields.

From this brief overview, you can see that physical anthropology is the subdiscipline of anthropology that focuses on many varied aspects of the biological and behavioral nature of human beings. Humans are a product of the same forces that produced all life on earth. As such, we're a contemporary component of a vast biological **continuum** at one point in time; and in this regard, we aren't particularly unique. Stating that humans are part of a continuum doesn't imply that we're at the peak of development on that continuum. Depending on the criteria used, humans can be seen to exist at one end of the spectrum or the other or perhaps somewhere in between, but we don't necessarily occupy a position of inherent superiority over other species.

However, human beings are truly unique in one way, and that is intellect. After all, humans are the only species, born of earth, to stir the lunar dust. We're the only species to develop language and complex culture as a means of buffering nature's challenges. And we're the only species capable of writing and reading textbooks that attempt to explain what it means to be human.

Physical Anthropology and the Scientific Method

Science is a process of explaining natural phenomena through observation and experimentation. That is, it involves an **empirical** approach, developing explanations or **hypotheses,** and then devising a research design or series of experiments to test those hypotheses. Because biological anthropologists are scientists, they adhere to the principles of the **scientific method,** whereby they identify a research question and then gather information to answer it.

Once a question has been asked, the first step usually is to explore the existing literature (books and journals) to determine what other people have done to resolve the issue. Based on this preliminary research and other observations, one or even several provisional explanations (hypotheses) are then proposed. The next step is to develop a research design or methodology aimed at testing the hypothesis. These methods involve collecting information, or **data,** that can then be studied and analyzed. Data can be analyzed in many ways, most of them involving various statistical tests. During the data collection and analysis phase, it's important for scientists to use a highly controlled approach so they can precisely describe their techniques and results. This precision is critical because it enables others to repeat the experiments and allows scientists to make comparisons between their research and the work of others.

For example, when scientists collect data on tooth size in hominid fossils, they specify which teeth are being measured, how they're measured, and the results of the measurements, expressed numerically or **quantitatively.** Then, by analyzing the data, the investigators try to draw conclusions about the meaning and significance of their measurements. This body of information then becomes the basis of future studies, perhaps by other researchers, who can compare their own results with those already obtained.

Hypothesis testing is the very core of the scientific method, and although it may seem contradictory at first, it's based on the potential to *falsify* the hypothesis. Falsification doesn't mean that the entire hypothesis is untrue, but it does indicate that there may be exceptions to it or that the hypothesis may need to be refined and subjected to further testing.

Eventually, if a hypothesis stands up to repeated testing, it may become part of a theory or perhaps a theory itself. There's a popular misconception that a theory is mere conjecture, or a "hunch". But in science, theories are proposed explanations of relationships between natural phenomena. Theories usually concern a broader, more universal view than hypotheses, which have a narrower focus and deal with more specific relationships between phenomena. But like hypotheses, theories aren't facts. *They're tested explanations of facts.* For example, it's a fact that when you drop an object, it falls to the ground. The explanation for this fact is the theory of gravity. But, like hypotheses, theories can be altered over time with further experimentation and by using newly developed technologies in testing. **Scientific testing** of hypotheses may take several years (or longer) and may involve researchers who weren't involved with the original work. What's more, new methods may permit different kinds of testing that weren't previously possible, and this is a strength of scientific research.

There's one more important fact about hypotheses and theories: *Any proposition that's stated as absolute and/or doesn't allow the possibility of falsification is not a scientific hypothesis and should never be considered as such.* A crucial aspect of scientific statements is that there must be a way to evaluate their validity. Statements such as "Heaven exists" may well be true (that is, they may describe some actual state), but there's no rational, empirical means, based on experience or experiment, of testing them. Therefore, acceptance of such a view is based on faith rather than on scientific verification. Contrary to what many people think, the purpose of scientific research is not to establish absolute truths; rather, it's to generate ever more accurate and consistent explanations of phenomena in our universe, based on observation and testing. At its very heart, scientific methodology is an exercise in rational thought and critical thinking.

The development of critical thinking skills is an important and lasting benefit of a college education. Such skills enable people to evaluate, compare, analyze, critique, and synthesize information so they won't accept everything they hear at face value. Perhaps the most glaring need for critical thinking is in how we evaluate advertising claims. For example, people spend billions of dollars every year on "natural" dietary supplements based on marketing claims that in fact may not have been tested. So when a salesperson tells you that, for example, echinacea helps prevent colds, you should ask if that statement has been scientifically tested, how it was

data (*sing.,* datum) Facts from which conclusions can be drawn; scientific information.

quantitatively Pertaining to measurements of quantity and including such properties as size, number, and capacity. When data are quantified, they're expressed numerically and can be tested statistically.

scientific testing The precise repetition of an experiment or expansion of observed data to provide verification; the procedure by which hypotheses and theories are verified, modified, or discarded.

QUICK REVIEW   The Scientific Method

THE OBSERVABLE UNIVERSE

Data collection → Human perceptions and human rational thought

Search for patterns

Further testing → Hypothesis generated

Verification → Hypothesis strengthened and more generalized
Further testing

Further testing → Development of theory

OR

Falsification

Hypothesis modified or rejected

---

tested, when, and by whom. Similarly, when politicians make claims in 30-second sound bytes, check those claims before you accept them as truth. Be skeptical. And if you do check the validity of advertising and political statements, you'll find that frequently they're either misleading or just plain wrong.

The Anthropological Perspective

Perhaps the most important benefit you'll receive from this textbook, and this course, is a wider appreciation of the human experience. To understand human beings and how our species came to be, we need to broaden our viewpoint, both through time and space. All branches of anthropology fundamentally seek to do this in what we call the *anthropological perspective*.

Physical anthropologists, for example, are interested in how humans differ from, and are similar to, other animals, especially nonhuman primates. For example, unlike other primates, we're bipedal. But what are the major anatomical components of bipedal locomotion, and how do they differ from, say, those in a quadrupedal ape? To answer these questions, anthropologists have for years studied human locomotion and compared the anatomy of our spine, pelvis, legs, and feet with that of various nonhuman primates. Through this type of broadened perspective, we can begin to grasp the diversity of the human experience within the context of biological and behavioral continuity with other species. In this way, we may better understand the limits and potentials of humankind. Furthermore, by extending our knowledge to include cultures other than our own, we may hope to avoid the **ethnocentric** pitfalls that are inherent to a more limited view of humanity.

This **relativistic** view of culture is perhaps more important now than ever before, because in our increasingly interdependent global community, it allows us to understand other people's concerns and to view our own culture from a broader perspective. Likewise, by examining our species as part of a wide spectrum of life,

ethnocentric Viewing other cultures from the inherently biased perspective of one's own culture. Ethnocentrism often results in other cultures being seen as inferior to one's own.

relativistic Pertaining to relativism; viewing entities as they relate to something else. Cultural relativism is the view that cultures have merits within their own historical and environmental contexts and that they shouldn't be judged through comparison with one's own culture.

we realize that we can't judge other species using human criteria. Each species is unique, with needs and a behavioral repertoire not exactly like that of any other. By recognizing that we share many similarities (both biological and behavioral) with other animals, perhaps we may come to recognize that they have a place in nature just as surely as we ourselves do.

In addition to broadening perspectives over space (that is, encompassing many cultures and ecological circumstances as well as nonhuman species), an anthropological perspective also extends our horizons through time. For example, in Chapter 13, we'll discuss human nutrition. The vast majority of the foods people eat today (coming from domesticated plants and animals) were unavailable until 10,000 years ago. But human physiological mechanisms for chewing and digesting foods were already well established long before that date. In fact, these adaptive complexes go back millions of years. Besides the obviously different diets prior to the development of agriculture (approximately 10,000 years ago), earlier hominids might well have differed from humans today in average body size, **metabolism,** and activity patterns. How, then, does the basic evolutionary "equipment" (that is, physiology) inherited from our forebears accommodate our modern diets? Clearly, the way to understand such processes isn't just to look at contemporary human responses. We also need to put them in the perspective of evolutionary development through time.

We hope that reading the following pages will help you develop an increased understanding not only of the similarities we share with other biological organisms but also of the processes that have shaped the traits that make us unique. We live in what may well be the most crucial time for our planet in the past 65 million years. We are members of the one species that, through the very agency of culture, has wrought such devastating changes in ecological systems that we must now alter our technologies or face potentially unspeakable consequences. In such a time, it's vital that we attempt to gain the best possible understanding of what it means to be human. We believe that the study of physical anthropology is one endeavor that aids in this attempt, and indeed, that is the goal of this text.

Summary

In this chapter, we've introduced you to the field of physical, or biological, anthropology, placing it within the overall context of anthropological studies. As a major academic discipline within the social sciences, anthropology also includes cultural anthropology, archaeology, and linguistic anthropology as major subfields.

Physical anthropology is the study of many aspects of human biology, including genetics, genetic variation, adaptations to environmental factors, nutrition, and anatomy. These topics are discussed within an evolutionary framework because all human characteristics are either directly or indirectly the results of biological evolution, which in turn is driven by genetic change. Hence, biological anthropologists also study our closest relatives, the nonhuman primates, primate evolution, and the genetic and fossil evidence for human evolution.

Because biological anthropology is a scientific discipline, we also discussed the role of the scientific method in research. We presented the importance of objectivity, observation, data collection, and analysis; and we described the formation and testing of hypotheses to explain natural phenomena. We also emphasized that this approach is an empirical one that doesn't rely on supernatural explanations.

Because evolution is the core of physical anthropology, in the next chapter we present a brief historical overview of changes in Western scientific thought that led to the discovery of the basic principles of biological evolution. As you're probably aware, evolution is a highly controversial subject (much more so in the United States than elsewhere). In the next chapter, we'll address some of the reasons for this controversy and discuss the evidence for evolution as the single thread uniting all the biological sciences.

metabolism The chemical processes within cells that break down nutrients and release energy for the body to use. When nutrients are broken down into their component parts, such as amino acids, energy is released and made available for use by the cell.

WHY IT MATTERS

Today, the trend in advanced education is toward greater and greater specialization, with the result that very few people or professions have the broad overview necessary to implement policy and make effective changes that could lead to improved standards of living, a safer geopolitical world, and better planetary health. This is acutely felt in medicine, where specialists focusing on one part of the body sometimes ignore other parts, often to the detriment of overall health (especially mental and emotional) of the patient. Anthropology is one of the few disciplines that encourages a broad view of the human condition.

An example is seen in AIDS prevention research. The wealth of knowledge that biologists and medical researchers have provided on the characteristics and behavior of HIV (the virus that causes AIDS) is useless for preventing its transmission unless we also have an understanding of human behavior at both the individual and the sociocultural levels. Behavioral scientists, including anthropologists, are prepared to examine the range of social, religious, economic, political, and historical contexts surrounding sexuality to devise AIDS prevention strategies that will vary from population to population and even from subculture to subculture. Whether or not you choose a career in anthropology, the perspectives that you gain from studying this discipline will enable you to participate in research and policy decisions on future challenges to human and planetary health and well-being.

Critical Thinking Questions

1 Given that you've only just been introduced to the field of physical anthropology, why do you think subjects such as anatomy, genetics, nonhuman primate behavior, and human evolution are integrated into a discussion of what it means to be human?

2 Is it important to you, personally, to know about human evolution? Why or why not?

3 Do you see a connection between hominid footprints that are almost 4 million years old and human footprints left on the moon in 1969? If so, do you think this relationship is important? What does the fact that there are human footprints on the moon say about human adaptation? (You may wish to refer to both biological and cultural adaptation.)

CHAPTER 2

The Development of Evolutionary Theory

ORIGIN OF SPECIES

DARWIN

LONDON
JOHN MURRAY

Introduction

Has anyone ever asked you, "If humans evolved from monkeys, then why do we still have monkeys?" Or maybe you've heard this: "If evolution happens, then why don't we ever see new species?" These are the kinds of questions asked by people who don't understand evolutionary processes and who usually don't believe they exist. Given the overwhelming genetic evidence for biological evolution today, the fact that anyone would ask such questions is a reflection of the poor quality of biological education. Evolution is one of the most fundamental of biological processes, and it's also one of the most misunderstood. This is partly because, at least in the United States, the topic is commonly avoided in primary and secondary schools, so students aren't exposed to it. Also, at colleges and universities, evolution is covered only in classes that directly relate to it. Indeed, if you're not an anthropology or biology major and you're taking a class in biological anthropology mainly to fill a science requirement, you'll probably never study evolution again.

By the end of this course, you'll know the answers to the two questions in the previous paragraph. Briefly, no one who studies evolution would ever say that humans evolved from monkeys, because they didn't. They didn't evolve from chimpanzees either. The earliest human ancestors evolved from a species that lived some 5 to 8 million years ago (mya). That ancestral species was the *last common ancestor* we share with chimpanzees, and it was one of a group of animals that separated from monkey-like ancestors some 20 mya. Monkeys are still around because, as primate lineages diverged from one another, each one went its separate way. Some lineages eventually became extinct, but a few gave rise to apes and humans while others evolved into monkeys. Therefore, each living species that we see today is the product of processes that go back millions of years. Because evolution takes time, and lots of it, we rarely witness the appearance of new species except in microorganisms such as bacteria and viruses. But we do see *microevolutionary* changes in many species.

The subject of evolution is controversial, especially in the United States, because some religious views hold that evolutionary statements run counter to biblical teachings. In fact, as you're probably aware, there is strong opposition to the teaching of evolution in public schools.

People who deny that evolution happens often comment that "evolution is only a theory," implying that evolution is mere supposition. You'll remember from Chapter 1 that scientific theories aren't just suppositions or guesses, although that's how the word *theory* is commonly used in everyday conversation. Actually, when dealing with scientific issues, referring to a concept as "theory" supports it. As we discussed in Chapter 1, theories have been tested and subjected to verification through accumulated evidence—and they haven't been disproved, sometimes even after decades of experimentation. It's true; evolution *is* a theory, one that's being supported by a mounting body of genetic evidence that, quite literally, expands daily.

It's a theory that explains how biological change occurs in species over time, and it's stood the test of time. Today, evolutionary theory stands as the most fundamental unifying force in biological science.

Because physical anthropology is concerned with all aspects of how humans came to be and how we adapt physiologically to the external environment, the details of the evolutionary process are crucial to the field. Given the central importance of evolution to biological anthropology, it's beneficial to know how the mechanics of the process came to be discovered. Also, if we want to understand and make critical assessments of the controversy still surrounding the issue today, we need to explore the social and political events that influenced the discovery of evolutionary principles.

A Brief History of Evolutionary Thought

The discovery of evolutionary principles first took place in western Europe and was made possible by advances in scientific thinking that date back to the sixteenth century. Having said this, we must recognize that Western science borrowed many of its ideas from other cultures, especially the Arabs, Indians, and Chinese. In fact, intellectuals in these cultures and in ancient Greece had developed notions of biological evolution (Teresi, 2002), but they never formulated them into a cohesive theory.

Charles Darwin was the first person to explain the basic mechanisms of the evolutionary process. But while he was developing his theory of **natural selection,** a Scottish naturalist named Alfred Russel Wallace independently reached the same conclusion. The fact that natural selection, the single most important force of evolutionary change, should be proposed at more or less the same time by two British men in the mid-nineteenth century may seem like a strange coincidence. But if Darwin and Wallace hadn't made their simultaneous discoveries, someone else soon would have, and that someone would probably have been British or French. That's because the groundwork had already been laid in Britain and France, and many scientists there were prepared to accept explanations of biological change that would have been unacceptable even 25 years before.

Like other human endeavors, scientific knowledge is usually gained through a series of small steps rather than giant leaps. And just as technological change is based on past achievements, scientific knowledge builds on previously developed theories. For this reason, it's informative to examine the development of ideas that led Darwin and Wallace to independently develop the theory of evolution by natural selection.

Throughout the Middle Ages, one predominant feature of the European worldview was that all aspects of nature, including all forms of life and their relationships to one another, never changed. This view was partly shaped by a feudal society that was itself a hierarchical, rigid class system that hadn't changed much for centuries. But the most important influence was an extremely powerful religious system wherein the teachings of Christianity were taken literally. Consequently, it was generally accepted that all life on earth had been created by God exactly as it existed in the present, and this belief (that life-forms couldn't change) came to be known as **fixity of species.** To question the assumptions of fixity, especially publicly, was seen as a challenge to God's perfection and could be considered heresy, a crime punishable by a nasty and potentially fiery death.

The plan of the entire universe was seen as God's design. In what's called the "argument from design," anatomical structures were planned to meet the purpose for which they were required. Wings, arms, and eyes all fit the functions they performed; and they, along with the rest of nature, were a deliberate plan of the Grand Designer. Also, pretty much everybody believed that the Grand Designer had completed his works fairly recently. An Irish archbishop named James Ussher (1581–1656) analyzed the "begat" chapter of Genesis and determined that the earth was created the morning of October 23, 4004 B.C. While Ussher wasn't the

natural selection The most critical mechanism of evolutionary change, first articulated by Charles Darwin; refers to genetic change or changes in the frequencies of certain traits in populations due to differential reproductive success between individuals.

fixity of species The notion that species, once created, can never change; an idea diametrically opposed to theories of biological evolution.

first person to suggest a recent origin of the earth, he was the first to propose a precise date for it.

The prevailing notion of the earth's brief existence, together with fixity of species, was a huge obstacle to the development of evolutionary theory. Evolution takes time; and the idea of immense geological time, which today we take for granted, simply didn't exist. In fact, until the concepts of fixity and time were fundamentally altered, it was impossible to conceive of evolution by means of natural selection.

The Scientific Revolution

So, what transformed centuries-old beliefs in a rigid, static universe to a view of worlds in continuous motion? How did the earth's brief history become an immense expanse of incomprehensible time? How did the scientific method as we know it today develop? These are important questions, but it would be equally appropriate to ask why it took so long for Europe to break from the constraints of traditional belief systems. After all, Arab and Indian scholars had developed concepts of planetary motion, for example, centuries earlier.

For Europeans, the discovery of the New World and circumnavigation of the globe in the fifteenth century overturned some very basic ideas about the planet. For one thing, the earth could no longer be thought of as flat. Also, as Europeans began to explore the New World, their awareness of biological diversity was greatly expanded as they became aware of plants and animals they'd never seen before.

There were other attacks on traditional beliefs. In 1514, a Polish mathematician named Copernicus challenged a notion proposed more than 1,500 years earlier by the fourth-century B.C. Greek philosopher Aristotle. Aristotle had taught that the sun and planets existed in a series of concentric spheres that revolved around the earth (Fig. 2-1). This system of planetary spheres was, in turn, surrounded by the stars, and this meant that the earth was the center of the universe. In fact, in India, scholars had figured out that the earth orbited the sun long before Copernicus came to this conclusion; but Copernicus is generally credited with removing the earth as the center of all things by proposing a sun-centered system.

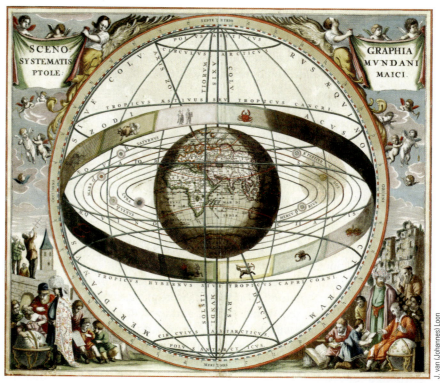

FIGURE 2-1

This beautifully illustrated seventeenth-century map shows the earth at the center of the solar system. Around it are seven concentric circles depicting the orbits of the moon, sun, and the five planets that were known at the time. (Note also the signs of the zodiac.)

J. van (Johannes) Loon

Copernicus' theory was openly discussed in intellectual circles, but it didn't attract much attention from the Catholic Church. Nevertheless, it did contradict a major premise of church doctrine. By the 1300s, the church had accepted Aristotle's teachings as dogma because it reinforced the notion that the earth, and the humans on it, was the central focus of God's creation and must therefore have a central position in the universe.

However, in the early 1600s, an Italian mathematician named Galileo Galilei restated Copernicus' views in print, and he used logic and mathematics to support his claim. To his misfortune, Galileo eventually was confronted by the Catholic Church regarding his publications and spent the last nine years of his life under house arrest. Nevertheless, in intellectual circles, the solar system had changed; the sun was now at its center and, instead of being static or fixed, it was in motion.

Throughout the sixteenth and seventeenth centuries, European scholars developed methods and theories that revolutionized scientific thought. The seventeenth century, in particular, saw the discovery of the principles of physics, motion, and gravity. Other achievements included the discovery of the true function of the heart and circulatory system as well as the development of numerous scientific instruments, including the telescope (perfected by Galileo), barometer, and microscope. These advances permitted investigations of natural phenomena and opened up entire new worlds for discoveries that had never before been imagined. But even with these advances, the idea that living forms could change over time simply didn't occur to people.

Precursors to the Theory of Evolution

Before early naturalists could begin to understand the many forms of organic life, they needed to list and describe them. And as research progressed, scholars were increasingly impressed with the amount of biological diversity they saw.

The concept of species, as we think of it today, wasn't proposed until the seventeenth century, when John Ray, a minister educated at Cambridge University, developed the concept. He recognized that groups of plants and animals could be differentiated from other groups by their ability to mate with one another and produce offspring. He placed such groups of **reproductively isolated** organisms into a single category, which he called the species (*pl.,* species). Thus, by the late 1600s, the biological criterion of reproduction was used to define species, much as it is today (Young, 1992).

Ray also recognized that species frequently shared similarities with other species, and he grouped these together in a second level of classification he called the genus (*pl.,* genera). He was the first person to use the labels *genus* and *species* in this way, and they're the terms we still use.

Carolus Linnaeus (1707–1778) was a Swedish naturalist who developed a method of classifying plants and animals. In his famous work, *Systema Naturae* (Systems of Nature), first published in 1735, he standardized Ray's use of genus and species terminology and established the system of **binomial nomenclature.** He also added two more categories: class and order. Linnaeus' four-level system became the basis for **taxonomy,** the system of classification we continue to use.

Linnaeus also put humans in his classification of animals, placing them in the genus *Homo* and species *sapiens*. Including humans was controversial because it went against contemporary thought that humans, made in God's image, should be considered unique and separate from the rest of the animal kingdom.

For all his progressive tendencies, Linnaeus still believed in fixity of species, although in later years, faced with mounting evidence to the contrary, he came to question it. Indeed, fixity was being challenged on many fronts, especially in France, where voices were being raised in favor of a universe based on change and, more to the point, in favor of a biological relationship between similar species based on descent from a common ancestor.

reproductively isolated Pertaining to groups of organisms that, mainly because of genetic differences, are prevented from mating and producing offspring with members of other groups.

binomial nomenclature (*binomial,* meaning "two names") In taxonomy, the convention established by Carolus Linnaeus whereby genus and species names are used to refer to species. For example, *Homo sapiens* refers to human beings.

taxonomy The branch of science concerned with the rules of classifying organisms on the basis of evolutionary relationships.

A French naturalist, Georges-Louis Leclerc de Buffon (1707–1788), recognized the dynamic relationship between the external environment and living forms. In his *Natural History,* first published in 1749, he emphasized that species could change. Buffon believed that when groups of organisms migrated to new areas, they gradually altered as a result of adapting to a somewhat different environment. Although Buffon rejected the idea that one species could give rise to another, his recognition of the external environment as an agent of change in species was extremely important.

Erasmus Darwin (1731–1802) is best known as Charles Darwin's grandfather. But he was also a physician, inventor, philosopher, naturalist, and leading member of an important intellectual community in England. Erasmus Darwin was also a famous poet, and in his most famous work, he expressed his views that life had originated in the seas and that all species had descended from a common ancestor. Thus, he introduced many of the ideas that his grandson would propose 56 years later. These concepts include vast expanses of time for life to evolve, competition for resources, and the importance of the environment in evolutionary processes. From letters and other sources, we know that Charles Darwin read his grandfather's writings, but we don't know how much he was influenced by them.

Even though Buffon and Erasmus Darwin believed that species could change, neither tried to explain how this could happen. The first person to do this was a French naturalist named Jean-Baptiste Lamarck (1744–1829). Lamarck (Fig. 2-2) suggested a dynamic relationship between species and the environment such that if the external environment changed, an animal's activity patterns would also change to accommodate the new circumstances. This would result in the decreased or increased use of certain body parts; consequently, those body parts would be modified. According to Lamarck, those parts that weren't used would disappear over time. However, the parts that continued to be used, in somewhat different ways, would undergo physical changes in response to bodily "needs." If a particular part of the body felt a certain need to change, "fluids and vital forces"* would be directed to that point, and the structure would be modified. And because the alteration would make the animal better suited to its habitat, the new trait would be passed on to offspring.

Lamarck's theory is known as the *inheritance of acquired characteristics,* or the *use-disuse* theory, and the giraffe is often used as a hypothetical example. Having stripped all the leaves from the lower branches of a tree (environmental change), the giraffe tries to reach leaves on upper branches. As "vital forces" move to tissues of the neck, it becomes slightly longer, and the giraffe can reach higher. The longer neck is then passed on to offspring, with the eventual result that all giraffes have longer necks than their predecessors had (Fig. 2-3). So, according to this theory, *a trait acquired by an animal during its lifetime can be passed on to offspring.* Today we know that this explanation is incorrect, because only those traits that are influenced by genetic information contained within sex cells (eggs and sperm) can be inherited (see Chapter 3).

Because Lamarck's explanation of species change isn't genetically correct, it's often criticized and dismissed. But actually, Lamarck deserves a lot of credit for emphasizing the importance of interactions between organisms and the external environment in the evolutionary process. What's more, he coined the term *biology* to refer to studies of living organisms.

Lamarck's most vehement opponent was a French vertebrate paleontologist named Georges Cuvier (1769–1832). Cuvier (Fig. 2-4) introduced the concept of extinction to explain the disappearance of animals represented by fossils. Although he was a brilliant anatomist, Cuvier never grasped the dynamic concept of nature, and he insisted on the fixity of species. So, rather than assuming that similarities

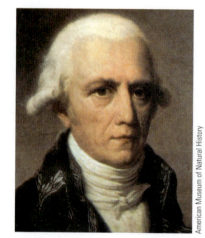

American Museum of Natural History

FIGURE 2-2

Lamarck believed that species change was influenced by environmental change. He is best known for his theory of the inheritance of acquired characteristics.

---

* Although today the notion of "vital forces" sounds odd, during Lamarck's time most scientists believed such substances existed and that they were the foundation of life itself.

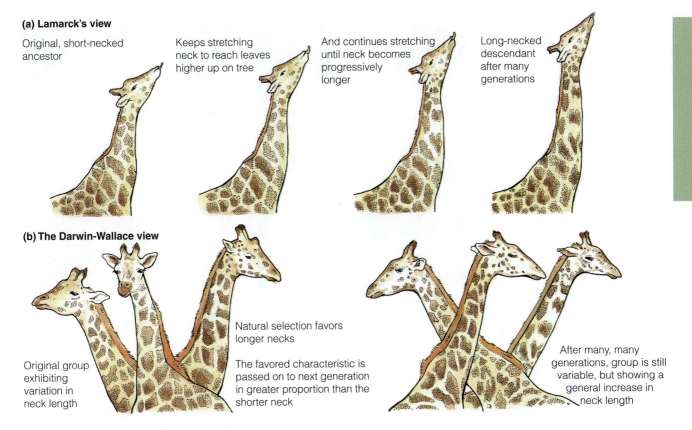

(a) Lamarck's view

Original, short-necked ancestor

Keeps stretching neck to reach leaves higher up on tree

And continues stretching until neck becomes progressively longer

Long-necked descendant after many generations

(b) The Darwin-Wallace view

Original group exhibiting variation in neck length

Natural selection favors longer necks

The favored characteristic is passed on to next generation in greater proportion than the shorter neck

After many, many generations, group is still variable, but showing a general increase in neck length

FIGURE 2-3

Contrasting ideas about the mechanism of evolution. (a) Lamarck's theory holds that acquired characteristics can be passed to subsequent generations. Short-necked giraffes stretched their necks to reach higher into trees for food, and, according to Lamarck, this acquired trait was passed on to offspring, who were born with longer necks. (b) The Darwin-Wallace theory of natural selection states that among giraffes there is variation in neck length. If having a longer neck provides an advantage for feeding, the trait will be passed on to a greater number of offspring, leading to an overall increase in the length of giraffe necks over many generations.

catastrophism The view that the earth's geological landscape is the result of violent cataclysmic events. Cuvier promoted this view, especially in opposition to Lamarck.

between fossil forms and living species indicated evolutionary relationships, Cuvier proposed a variation of a doctrine known as **catastrophism**.

Catastrophism was the belief that the earth's geological features are the results of sudden, worldwide cataclysmic events. Cuvier's version of catastrophism suggested that a series of regional disasters had destroyed most or all of the local plant and animal life in many places. These areas were then restocked with new, similar forms that migrated in from unaffected regions. But he needed to be consistent with emerging fossil evidence that indicated that organisms had become more complex over time. So Cuvier proposed that after each disaster, the incoming migrants had a more modern appearance because they were the results of more recent creation events. (The last of these creations occurred after the Noah flood, described in Genesis.) In this way, Cuvier's explanation of increased complexity over time avoided any notion of evolution while still being able to account for the evidence for change that was preserved in the fossil record.

In 1798, an English economist named Thomas Malthus (1766–1834) wrote *An Essay on the Principle of Population* (Fig. 2-5). In his essay, Malthus pointed out that, in nature, population size increases exponentially but food supplies remain relatively stable. Thus, the tendency for populations to increase in size is always checked by the limited availability of food and water and this results in competition for resources.

Mathieu-Ignace van Brée

FIGURE 2-4

Cuvier explained the fossil record as the result of a succession of catastrophes followed by new creation events.

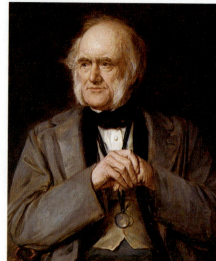

FIGURE 2-5

Thomas Malthus' *Essay on the Principle of Population* led both Darwin and Wallace to the principle of natural selection.

FIGURE 2-6

Portrait of Charles Lyell.

Actually, Malthus wasn't concerned with species change. Instead he was arguing for limits to human population growth. However, his essay inspired both Charles Darwin and Alfred Russel Wallace because both men recognized that competition between individuals is a key factor in natural selection.

Charles Lyell (1797–1875) is considered the founder of modern geology (Fig. 2-6). He was a lawyer, a geologist, and, for many years, Charles Darwin's friend and mentor. Before meeting Darwin in 1836, Lyell had earned acceptance in Europe's most prestigious scientific circles, thanks to his highly praised *Principles of Geology,* first published during the years 1830–1833.

In this immensely important work, Lyell argued that the geological processes observed in the present are the same ones that occurred in the past. This theory, called **uniformitarianism,** didn't originate entirely with Lyell, having been proposed by James Hutton in the late 1700s. Even so, it was Lyell who demonstrated that forces such as wind, water erosion, local flooding, frost, decomposition of vegetable matter, volcanoes, earthquakes, and glacial movements had all contributed in the past to produce the geological landscape that we see today. What's more, the fact that these processes could still be seen in operation indicated that geological change was continuing to happen and that the forces that drove such change were consistent, or *uniform,* over time. In other words, various aspects of the earth's surface (for example, climate, plants, animals, and land surfaces) are variable through time, but the *underlying processes* that influence them are constant. Additionally, Lyell emphasized the obvious: namely, that for such slow-acting forces to produce momentous change, the earth must be far older than anyone had previously suspected.

By providing an immense time scale and thereby altering perceptions of earth's history from a few thousand to many millions of years, Lyell changed the framework within which scientists viewed the geological past. So the concept of "deep time" (Gould, 1987) remains one of Lyell's most significant contributions to the discovery of evolutionary principles. The immensity of geological time permitted the necessary time depth for the inherently slow process of evolutionary change.

As you can see, the roots of evolutionary theory are deeply imbedded in the late eighteenth and early nineteenth centuries. During that time, many lesser-known people also contributed greatly to this intellectual movement. One such individual was Mary Anning (1799–1847), who lived in the town of Lyme Regis on the south coast of England (Fig. 2-7).

uniformitarianism The theory that the earth's features are the result of long-term processes that continue to operate in the present as they did in the past. Elaborated on by Lyell, this theory opposed catastrophism and contributed strongly to the concept of immense geological time.

Anning's father died when she was 11 years old, leaving his family destitute. But fortunately, he had taught Mary to recognize marine fossils embedded in the cliffs near the town, and she began to collect and sell these fossils to support her family. She was able to do this because of a growing public interest in collecting fossils, many of which were believed to be the remains of creatures killed in the Noah flood.

After Anning's discovery of the first *Pleiosaurus* fossil (an ocean-dwelling reptile), some of the most famous scientists in England repeatedly visited her home. Over the years, Anning supplied researchers and museums with hundreds of fossils and she became known as one of the world's leading "fossilists." By sharing her extensive knowledge of fossil species with many of the leading scientists of the day, she contributed to their understanding of the evolution of marine life during a period of over 200 million years. But because she was a woman and of lowly social position, she wasn't acknowledged in the numerous scientific publications she facilitated. In recent years, however, she has achieved the recognition she deserves; her portrait hangs prominently in the British Museum (Natural History) in London, near one of her famous *Pleiosaurus* fossils.

The Discovery of Natural Selection

Charles Darwin Having already been introduced to Erasmus Darwin, you shouldn't be surprised that his grandson Charles grew up in an educated family with ties to intellectual circles. Charles Darwin (1809–1882) was one of six children of Dr. Robert and Susanna Darwin (Fig. 2-8). Being the grandson not only of Erasmus Darwin but also of the wealthy Josiah Wedgwood (of Wedgwood china fame), Charles grew up enjoying the comfortable lifestyle of the landed gentry in rural England. As a boy, he had a keen interest in nature and spent his days fishing and collecting shells, birds' eggs, and rocks. However, this interest in natural history didn't dispel the generally held view of family and friends that he was in no way remarkable. In fact, his performance at school was no more than ordinary.

After his mother's death when he was 8 years old, Darwin was raised by his father and older sisters. Because he showed little interest in anything except hunting, shooting, and perhaps science, his father sent him to Edinburgh University to study medicine. It was there that Darwin first became acquainted with the evolutionary theories of Lamarck and others. During that time (the 1820s), notions of evolution were becoming feared in England and elsewhere. Anything identifiable with postrevolutionary France (the French Revolution, which overthrew the monarchy, began in 1789) was viewed with suspicion by the established order in England, and Lamarck, partly because he was French, was especially vilified by British scientists.

It was also a time of growing political unrest in Britain. The Reform Movement, aimed at undoing the many inequalities of the traditional class system, was in full swing, and like most social movements, it had a radical faction. Because many of the radicals were atheists and socialists who also supported Lamarck's ideas, many people came to associate evolution with atheism and political subversion. Such was the growing fear of evolutionary ideas that many believed that if these ideas were generally accepted, "the Church would crash, the moral fabric of society would be torn apart, and civilized man would return to savagery" (Desmond and Moore, 1991, p. 34). It's unfortunate that some of the most outspoken early proponents of **transmutation** were so vehemently anti-Christian, because their rhetoric helped establish the entrenched suspicion and misunderstanding of evolutionary theory that persists today.

While at Edinburgh, Darwin studied with professors who were outspoken supporters of Lamarck. So, even though he hated medicine and left Edinburgh after two years, his experience there was a formative period in his intellectual development. Although Darwin was fairly indifferent to religion, he next went to Cambridge, to study theology. It was during his Cambridge years that he seriously cultivated his interests in natural science and immersed himself in botany and geology. For this reason, after his graduation in 1831, at the age of 22, he was invited to join a scientific expedition that would circle the globe. And so it was that Darwin set sail aboard

FIGURE 2-7
Portrait of Mary Anning.

transmutation The change of one species to another. The term *evolution* did not assume its current meaning until the late nineteenth century.

FIGURE 2-8
Charles Darwin, photographed five years before the publication of *Origin of Species*.

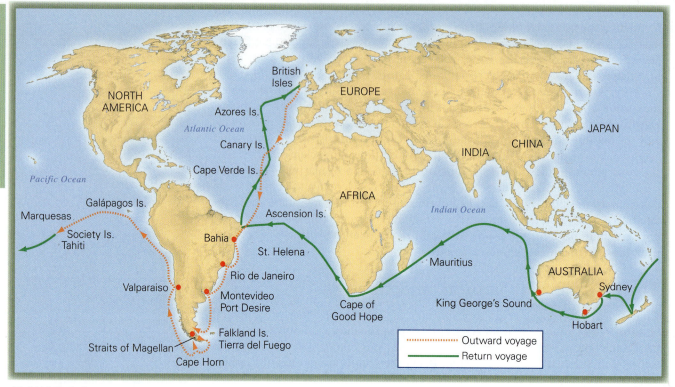

FIGURE 2-9
The route of HMS *Beagle.*

HMS *Beagle* on December 17, 1831. The famous voyage of the *Beagle* would take almost five years and would forever change not only the course of Darwin's life but also the history of biological science (Fig. 2-9).

When Darwin first stepped onto the deck of the *Beagle,* he believed in fixity of species. But during the voyage, he privately began to have doubts. While exploring the geology of foreign lands, he came across the fossilized remains of ancient giant animals that, except for size, looked very much like species that still lived in the same vicinity, and he began to wonder if the fossils represented ancestors of the living forms. During the famous stopover at the Galápagos Islands, off the coast of Ecuador (see Fig. 2-9), Darwin noticed that the vegetation and animals (especially birds) shared many similarities with those on the mainland of South America but they weren't identical to them. What's more, the birds of one island were somewhat different from those on another. Darwin collected 13 varieties of Galápagos finches, and it was clear that they represented a closely affiliated group; but some of their physical traits were different, particularly the shape and size of their beaks (Fig. 2-10). He also collected finches from the mainland, and these appeared to represent only one group.

The insight that Darwin gained from the finches is legendary. He recognized that the various Galápagos finches had all descended from a common mainland ancestor and had been modified over time in response to different island habitats and dietary preferences. But actually, it wasn't until *after* he returned to England

FIGURE 2-10
Beak variation in Darwin's
Galápagos finches.

(a) Ground finch
Main food: seeds
Beak: heavy

(b) Tree finch
Main food: leaves, buds,
blossoms, fruits
Beak: thick, short

(c) Tree finch (called
woodpecker finch)
Main food: insects
Beak: stout, straight

(d) Ground finch (known
as warbler finch)
Main food: insects
Beak: slender

that he recognized the significance of the variation in beak structure. In fact, during the voyage, he had paid little attention to the finches. It was only later that he considered the factors that could lead to the modification of one species into many (Gould, 1985; Desmond and Moore, 1991).

Darwin arrived back in England in October of 1836 and was immediately accepted into the most prestigious scientific circles. He married his cousin, Emma Wedgwood, and moved to the village of Down, near London, where he spent the rest of his life writing on topics ranging from fossils to orchids. But the question of species change was his overriding passion.

At Down, Darwin began to develop his views on what he called *natural selection.* This concept was borrowed from animal breeders, who choose, or "select," as breeding stock those animals that have certain traits they want to emphasize in offspring. Animals with undesirable traits are "selected against," or prevented from breeding. (A dramatic example of the effects of selective breeding can be seen in the various domestic dog breeds shown in Fig. 2-11.) Darwin applied his knowledge of domesticated species to naturally occurring ones—recognizing that in undomesticated organisms, the selective agent was nature, not humans.

By the late 1830s, Darwin had realized that biological variation within a species (that is, differences among individuals) was crucial. He also recognized that sexual reproduction increased variation, although he didn't know why. Then, in 1838, he read Malthus' essay; and there he found the answer to the question of how new species came to be. He accepted from Malthus the idea that animal populations increase at a faster rate than resources do. He also recognized that population size is continuously checked by limited supplies of food and water. He also accepted the observation that in nature there is a constant "struggle for existence." The idea that in each generation more offspring are born than will survive to adulthood, coupled with the notions of competition for resources and biological diversity, was all Darwin needed to develop his theory of natural selection. He wrote: "It at once struck me that under these circumstances favourable variations would tend to be preserved, and unfavourable ones to be destroyed. The result of this would be the formation of a new

FIGURE 2-11

All domestic dog breeds share a common ancestor, the wolf. The extreme variation exhibited by dog breeds today has been achieved in a relatively short time through artificial selection. In this situation, humans allow only certain dogs to breed to emphasize specific characteristics. (We should note that not all traits desired by human breeders are advantageous to the dogs themselves.)

species" (F. Darwin, 1950, pp. 53–54). Basically, this quotation summarizes the entire theory of natural selection.

By 1844, Darwin had written a short summary of his views on natural selection, but he didn't think he had enough data to support his hypothesis, so he continued his research without publishing. He had other reasons for hesitating to publish what he knew would be a highly controversial work. For one thing, he was deeply troubled that his wife, Emma, believed that his ideas ran counter to her strong religious convictions (Keynes, 2002). Also, as a member of the established order, he knew that many of his friends and associates were concerned with threats to the status quo, and evolutionary theory was seen as a very serious threat. So he waited.

Alfred Russel Wallace's (1823–1913) background couldn't have been more unlike Darwin's. Born into a family of modest means, Wallace (Fig. 2-12) went to work when he was just 14, and with little formal education, he moved from one job to the next. But he became interested in collecting plants and animals and joined expeditions to the Amazon and Southeast Asia, where he acquired firsthand knowledge of many natural phenomena.

In 1855, Wallace published an article suggesting that species were descended from other species and that the appearance of new species was influenced by environmental factors (Trinkaus and Shipman, 1992). At that point, Lyell and others urged Darwin to publish his theories, but much to their consternation, he continued to hesitate. Then, in 1858, Wallace sent Darwin another paper in which he described evolution as a process driven by competition and natural selection. When he read Wallace's paper, Darwin was finally stirred to action by the fear that Wallace might actually get credit for a theory (natural selection) that he himself had developed. He quickly wrote a paper presenting his ideas, and both men's papers were read before the Linnean Society of London. However, neither author was present. Wallace was out of the country, and Darwin was mourning the recent death of his young son.

The papers received little notice at the time. But in December 1859, when Darwin completed and published his greatest work, *On the Origin of Species,** the storm broke; and it still hasn't abated. Although public opinion was negative, there was much scholarly praise for the book, and scientific opinion gradually came to Darwin's support. The riddle of species was now explained: Species were mutable (changeable), not fixed; and they evolved from other species through the mechanism of natural selection.

FIGURE 2-12
Alfred Russel Wallace independently discovered the key to the evolutionary process.

© National Portrait Gallery, London

Natural Selection

Darwin had realized early on that selection was the key to evolution, and with the help of Malthus' ideas, he saw *how* selection in nature could be explained. In the struggle for existence, those *individuals* with favorable variations would survive and reproduce, but those with unfavorable variations wouldn't. For Darwin, the explanation of evolution was simple. These are the basic processes, as he understood them:

1. All species are capable of producing offspring at a faster rate than food supplies increase.

2. There is biological variation within all species.

3. Because in each generation more offspring are produced than can survive, and owing to limited resources, there is competition among individuals. (*Note:* This statement doesn't mean that there is constant fierce fighting.)

4. Individuals who possess favorable variations or traits (for example, speed, resistance to disease, protective coloration) have an advantage over those who don't

---

* The full title is *On the Origin of Species by Means of Natural Selection, or the Preservation of Favoured Races in the Struggle for Life.*

have them. In other words, favorable traits increase the likelihood of survival and reproduction.

5. The environmental context determines whether or not a trait is beneficial. What is favorable in one setting may be a liability in another. Consequently, the traits that become most advantageous are the results of a natural process.

6. Traits are inherited and passed on to the next generation. Because individuals who have favorable traits contribute more offspring to the next generation than those who don't, over time, those favorable traits become more common in the population; less favorable ones aren't passed on as frequently, so they become less common. Individuals who produce more offspring in comparison to others are said to have greater **reproductive success** or fitness.

7. Over long periods of geological time, successful variations accumulate in a population, so that eventually, later generations may be distinct from ancestral ones. Thus, in time, a new species may appear.

8. Geographical isolation also contributes to the formation of new species. As populations of a species become geographically isolated from one another for whatever reason (for example, natural barriers such as rivers, oceans, or mountain ranges), they begin to adapt to different environments. Over time, as populations continue to respond to different **selective pressures** (that is, different ecological circumstances), they may become distinct species. The 13 species of Galápagos finches are presumably all descended from a common ancestor on the South American mainland, and they provide an excellent example of how geographical isolation can lead to speciation.

Before Darwin, individual members of species weren't considered important, so they weren't studied. But as we've seen, Darwin recognized the uniqueness of individuals and realized that variation among them could explain how selection occurs. Nature selects (or chooses) variations that increase the likelihood of survival; and unfavorable variations are weeded out. Darwin realized that *natural selection operates on individuals,* either favorably or unfavorably, but *it's the population that evolves.* It's important to emphasize that the unit of natural selection is the individual; the unit of evolution is the population. This is because individuals don't change genetically, but over time, populations do.

Natural Selection in Action

One of the most frequently cited examples of natural selection is change in the coloration of "peppered" moths around Manchester, England. In recent years, the moth story has come under some criticism; but the premise remains valid, so we use it to illustrate how natural selection works.

Before the nineteenth century, the most common variety of the peppered moth in England was a mottled gray color. During the day, as the moths rested on lichen-covered tree trunks, their coloration provided camouflage (Fig. 2-13). There was also a dark gray variety of the same species, but since the dark moths weren't well

reproductive success The number of offspring an individual produces and rears to reproductive age; an individual's genetic contribution to the next generation.

selective pressures Forces in the environment that influence reproductive success in individuals.

Michael Tweedie/Photo Researchers

(a)

Breck P. Kent/Animals Animals

(b)

FIGURE 2-13
Variation in the peppered moth. (a) The dark form is more visible on the light, lichen-covered tree. (b) On trees darkened by pollution, the lighter form is more visible.

camouflaged, they were more frequently eaten by birds and so they were less common. In this example, the birds are the *selective agent,* and they apply *selective pressures* on the moths. Therefore, the dark moths produced fewer offspring than gray camouflaged moths. Yet, by the end of the nineteenth century, the dark form had almost completely replaced the gray one. Why?

The traditionally cited answer is air pollution. Near towns and cities during the industrial revolution, coal dust from factories and fireplaces settled on trees, turning them dark gray and killing the lichen. With this environmental change, the lighter moths became more conspicuous and more vulnerable to birds. Since fewer of them were living long enough to reproduce, their contribution to the next generation decreased; as a result, the darker moths became more common.

In recent years, the role of lichen has been questioned, partly because the same color shift in moths had also occurred in North America, where lichen wasn't generally present on trees. Also, there's evidence that birds can see ultraviolet (UV) light, and in the UV spectrum, moths and lichen wouldn't look alike. So, a resemblance to lichen may not have actually helped protect the lighter moths (Weiss, 2003). Nevertheless, the color shift did occur in both regions during periods of increased air pollution. As clean air acts in both Britain and the United States have reduced the amount of air pollution (at least from coal), the light gray moth has become more common again. Even though the explanation for the observed changes in moth color is probably more complex than originally believed and may involve factors in addition to bird predation, this color change is still a good example of microevolution in a contemporary population.

The medium ground finch of the Galápagos Islands is another example of natural selection in action. In 1977, drought killed many of the plants that produced the smaller, softer seeds favored by these birds. This forced a population of finches on one of the islands to feed on larger, harder seeds. Even before 1977, some of these birds had smaller, less robust beaks than others (that is, there was variation); and during the drought, because they were less able to process the larger seeds, more of these smaller-beaked birds died than did birds with larger beaks. As you might expect, many birds died and the population was greatly reduced. But average beak thickness in the group increased because survivorship was higher in the larger-beaked birds, and these birds subsequently produced more offspring; in other words, they had greater reproductive success. But during heavy rains in 1982–1983, smaller seeds became more plentiful again, and the pattern in beak size reversed itself, demonstrating again how reproductive success is related to environmental conditions (Grant, 1975, 1986; Ridley, 1993).

The best illustration of natural selection, however, and certainly one with potentially grave consequences for humans, is the recent increase in resistant strains of disease-causing microorganisms. When antibiotics were first introduced in the 1940s, they were hailed as the cure of bacterial disease. But that optimistic view didn't take into account that bacteria, like other organisms, possess genetic variability. Consequently, while an antibiotic will kill most bacteria in an infected person, any bacterium with an inherited resistance to that particular therapy will survive. The surviving bacteria then reproduce and pass their drug resistance to future generations. Eventually, the bacterial population is mostly composed of organisms that don't respond to treatment. Moreover, because bacteria reproduce (usually through cell division) every few hours, the majority won't be susceptible to antibiotics. This is why antibiotic-resistant strains of many bacterial diseases are appearing, and many types of infection no longer respond to treatment. Tuberculosis, for example, was once thought to be well controlled, but there's been a resurgence of this serious disease in recent years because some strains of the bacterium that causes it are resistant to most of the antibiotics used to treat it.

These three examples (moths, finches, and bacteria) provide the following insights into the fundamentals of evolutionary change produced by natural selection:

1. *A trait must be inherited if natural selection is to act on it.* A characteristic that isn't hereditary (such as a temporary change in hair color produced by the

hairdresser) won't be passed on to offspring. In finches, for example, beak size is a hereditary trait.

2. *Natural selection can't occur without population variation in inherited characteristics.* If, for example, all the peppered moths had initially been the lighter gray color (you'll recall that there were always some dark forms) and the trees had become darker, survival and reproductive rates could have been so reduced that the population might have become extinct. The point is, *selection can work only when variation exists.*

3. *Fitness is a relative measure that changes as the environment changes.* **Fitness** is simply *differential reproductive success.* In the initial stage, the lighter moths were more fit simply because they produced more offspring. But when the environment changed, the dark gray moths became more fit. Then an additional change reversed the pattern back to what it had been. Likewise, the majority of Galápagos medium ground finches will have larger or smaller beaks, depending on external conditions. So it should be obvious that statements regarding the "most fit" don't mean anything without reference to specific environments.

4. *Natural selection can act only on traits that affect reproduction.* If a characteristic isn't expressed until later in life, after organisms have reproduced, then natural selection can't influence it. This is because the trait's inherited components have already been passed on to offspring. Many forms of cancer and cardiovascular disease are influenced by hereditary factors, but because these diseases usually affect people after they've had children, natural selection can't act against them. Conversely, if a condition usually kills or severely compromises the individual before he or she reproduces, natural selection can act against it because the trait won't be passed on.

So far, our examples have shown how different death rates influence natural selection (for example, moths or finches that die early leave fewer offspring). But mortality isn't the complete picture. Another important aspect of natural selection is **fertility,** because an animal that gives birth to more young passes its genes on at a faster rate than one that bears fewer offspring. But fertility isn't the entire story either, because the crucial element is the number of young raised successfully to the point

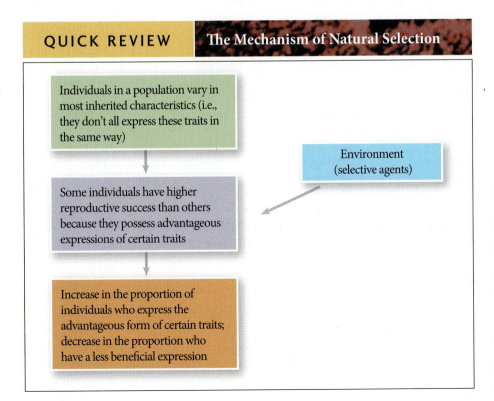

QUICK REVIEW **The Mechanism of Natural Selection**

Individuals in a population vary in most inherited characteristics (i.e., they don't all express these traits in the same way)

Environment (selective agents)

Some individuals have higher reproductive success than others because they possess advantageous expressions of certain traits

Increase in the proportion of individuals who express the advantageous form of certain traits; decrease in the proportion who have a less beneficial expression

fitness Pertaining to natural selection, a measure of *relative* reproductive success of individuals. Fitness can be measured by an individual's genetic contribution to the next generation compared to that of other individuals. The terms *genetic fitness, reproductive fitness,* and *differential reproductive success* are also used.

fertility The ability to conceive and produce healthy offspring.

where they themselves reproduce. We call this *differential net reproductive success.* The way this mechanism works can be demonstrated through another example.

In swifts (small birds that resemble swallows), data show that producing more offspring doesn't necessarily guarantee that more young will be successfully raised. The number of eggs hatched in a breeding season is a measure of fertility. The number of birds that mature and are eventually able to leave the nest is a measure of net reproductive success, or successfully raised offspring. The following table shows the correlation between the number of eggs hatched (fertility) and the number of young that leave the nest (reproductive success), averaged over four breeding seasons (Lack, 1966):

Number of eggs hatched (fertility)	2 eggs	3 eggs	4 eggs
Average number of young raised (reproductive success)	1.92	2.54	1.76
Sample size (number of nests)	72	20	16

As you can see, the optimum number of eggs is three, because that number yields the highest reproductive success. Raising two offspring is less beneficial to the parents, since the end result isn't as successful as with three eggs. Trying to raise more than three is actually detrimental, since the parents may not be able to provide enough nourishment for any of the offspring. Offspring that die before reaching reproductive age are, in evolutionary terms, the same as never being born. Actually, death of an offspring can be a minus to the parents, because before it dies, it drains parental resources. It may even inhibit their ability to raise other offspring, thus reducing their reproductive success even further. Selection favors those genetic traits that yield the maximum net reproductive success. If the number of eggs laid is a genetic trait in birds (and it seems to be), natural selection in swifts should act to favor the laying of three eggs as opposed to two or four.

Constraints on Nineteenth-Century Evolutionary Theory

Darwin argued for the concept of evolution in general and the role of natural selection in particular. But he didn't understand the exact mechanisms of evolutionary change. As we have seen, natural selection acts on *variation* within species, but no one in the nineteenth century knew the actual source of this variation. No one understood how parents pass traits to offspring either. Almost without exception, nineteenth-century scholars believed that inheritance was a *blending* process in which parental characteristics were combined to produce intermediate expressions in offspring.

With blending theory the established premise, we can see why the true nature of genes was unimaginable; and with no alternative explanations, Darwin accepted it. As it turns out, a contemporary of Darwin's had actually worked out the rules of heredity. However, the work of this Augustinian monk named Gregor Mendel (whom you'll meet in Chapter 4) wasn't recognized until the beginning of the twentieth century. The first three decades of the twentieth century saw the merger of natural selection theory and Mendel's discoveries. This was a crucial development because until then, scientists thought these concepts were unrelated. Then, in 1953, the structure of DNA was discovered. This landmark achievement has been followed by even more amazing advances in the field of genetics, including the sequencing of the human **genome.** Today, we are finally on the threshold of revealing the remaining secrets of the evolutionary process—if only Darwin could know!

Opposition to Evolution Today

Almost 150 years after the publication of *Origin of Species,* the debate over evolution is far from over, especially in the United States, where opposition is mostly based in religious beliefs. For the majority of biological scientists today, evolution is indisput-

genome The entire genetic makeup of an individual or species.

able. The genetic evidence for it is solid and accumulating daily. Moreover, most Christians don't believe that biblical depictions should be taken literally. Yet, surveys consistently indicate that about half of all Americans don't believe that evolution occurs. There are a number of reasons for this.

The mechanisms of evolution are complex and don't lend themselves to simple explanations. Understanding them requires some familiarity with genetics and biology, a familiarity that most people (not just Americans) don't have. What's more, many people want definitive, clear-cut answers to complex questions. But as you learned in Chapter 1, science doesn't always provide definitive answers to questions; it doesn't establish absolute truths; and it doesn't *prove* facts. Another thing to consider is that regardless of their culture, most people are raised in belief systems that don't emphasize **biological continuity** between species or offer scientific explanations for natural phenomena.

The relationship between science and religion has never been easy (remember Galileo), even though both systems serve, in their own ways, to explain natural phenomena. Scientific explanations are based in data analysis, hypothesis testing, and interpretation. Religion is a system of faith-based beliefs that, like science, often attempts to explain natural phenomena. One difference between science and religion is that religious beliefs and explanations aren't amenable to scientific testing. Religion and science concern different aspects of the human experience, and they aren't inherently mutually exclusive approaches. That is, belief in God doesn't exclude belief in biological evolution; and acknowledgment of evolutionary processes doesn't preclude the existence of God. In fact, most people who accept evolution as fact also believe in God. What's more, evolutionary theories aren't opposed by all religions or by most forms of Christianity. Some years ago, the Vatican hosted an international conference on human evolution; and in 1996, Pope John Paul II issued a statement that "fresh knowledge leads to recognition of the theory of evolution as more than just a hypothesis." Today, the official position of the Catholic Church is that evolutionary processes do occur, but that the human soul is of divine creation and not subject to evolutionary processes. Likewise, mainstream Protestants don't generally see a conflict. But, those who believe in an absolutely literal interpretation of the Bible (called *fundamentalists*) accept no compromise.

The teaching of evolution in public schools has unfortunately become an important political issue, especially in the United States. Unfortunately, most people aren't very well informed about the nature of this controversy or its history. Because this is such an important topic, we conclude this chapter with a short discussion of the controversy, its historical context, and the significance of the constitutional guarantee of separation of church and state.

Reacting to rapid cultural change after World War I, conservative Christians in the United States sought a revival of what they considered "traditional values." In their view, one way to do this was to prevent any mention of Darwinism in public schools. One result of this effort was a law passed in 1925 that banned the teaching of any theory (particularly evolution) that doesn't support the biblical version of the creation of humankind. To test the validity of the law, the American Civil Liberties Union persuaded a high school teacher named John Scopes to agree to be arrested and tried for teaching evolution. The subsequent trial, called the Scopes Monkey Trial, was a 1920s equivalent of current celebrity trials, and in the end, Scopes was convicted and fined $100, though the conviction was later overturned. Although most states didn't actually forbid the teaching of evolution, Arkansas, Tennessee, and a few others continued to prohibit any mention of it until 1968, when the U.S. Supreme Court struck down the ban against teaching evolution in public schools. (One of the authors of this textbook remembers when her junior high school science teacher was fired for mentioning evolution in Little Rock, Arkansas.)

As coverage of evolution in textbooks increased by the mid-1960s, **Christian fundamentalists** renewed their campaign to eliminate evolution from public school curricula or to introduce antievolutionary material into public school classes. Out of this effort, the *creation science* movement was born. The premise of creation science

biological continuity Refers to a biological continuum. When expressions of a phenomenon continuously grade into one another so that there are no discrete categories, they exist on a continuum. Color is one such phenomenon, and life-forms are another.

Christian fundamentalists Adherents to a movement in American Protestantism that began in the early twentieth century. This group holds that the teachings of the Bible are infallible and are to be taken literally.

is that the biblical account of the earth's origins and the Noah flood can be supported by scientific evidence.

Creationists have insisted that what they used to call "creation science" and now call "intelligent design" (ID) is based in science and they claim that there's scientific evidence to support creationist views. They've argued that in the interest of fairness, a balanced view should be offered: If evolution is taught as science, then creationism should also be taught as science. Sounds fair, doesn't it? But creation science, or ID, isn't science at all for the simple reason that creationists insist that their view is absolute and infallible. Therefore, creationism isn't a hypothesis that can be tested, nor is it amenable to falsification; and because hypothesis testing is the basis of all science, creationism, by its very nature, cannot be considered science.

Since the 1970s, creationists have promoted laws that mandate the teaching of creationism in public schools. In 1981, the Arkansas state legislature passed one such law that was subsequently overturned in 1982. In his ruling against the state, the judge justifiably argued that "a theory that is by its own terms dogmatic, absolutist and never subject to revision is not a scientific theory." And he added: "Since creation is not science, the conclusion is inescapable that the only real effect of [this law] is the advancement of religion."

In Dover, Pennsylvania, ID proponents suffered a setback in 2004 when voters ousted all eight of the nine-member Dover Area School Board who were up for reelection. This school board, composed entirely of ID supporters, had established a policy requiring high school teachers to discuss ID as an alternative to evolution. Then, in late 2005, U.S. District Judge John Jones struck down the policy because it violated the First Amendment to the Constitution. In his written opinion, Judge Jones stated: "ID is not science and cannot be adjudged a valid, accepted scientific theory. . . . [It] is grounded in theology, not science. . . . It has no place in a science curriculum." State and federal courts consistently overrule such laws because they violate the "establishment clause" of the First Amendment of the U.S. Constitution, which states that "Congress shall make no law respecting an establishment of religion, or prohibiting the free exercise thereof." This statement guarantees the separation of church and state. Therefore, the use of public institutions (including schools), paid for by public funds (tax revenues), to promote any particular religion is unconstitutional. Of course, this doesn't mean that students and teachers can't have private religious discussions or pray in public places; but it does mean that public places can't be used for organized religious events.

The establishment clause was initially proposed to ensure that the government could neither promote nor restrict any particular religious view, as it did in England at the time the U.S. Constitution was written. Nevertheless, creationists continue to encourage teachers to claim "academic freedom" to teach creationism. By the mid-1980s, creationists dropped the terms *creationism* and *creation science* in favor of the less religious-sounding term *intelligent design theory*. The term *intelligent design* is based on the notion that most biological functions and anatomical traits are too complex to be explained by a theory that doesn't include the presence of a creator or designer. To avoid objections based on the guarantee of separation of church and state, proponents of ID claim that they don't emphasize any particular religion. But this argument doesn't address the essential point that teaching *any* religious views in a way that promotes them in publicly funded schools is a violation of the U.S. Constitution.

But even after numerous defeats in state, district, and federal courts, the attacks on evolution continue. In the first six weeks of 2006 alone, 12 antievolution bills were introduced in nine states. That's more than in any year in the history of the United States (Gross, 2006). Clearly, antievolution sentiment remains strong among many politicians. The president of the United States (as of this writing) has publicly supported teaching intelligent design in public schools; and in 1999, one very powerful U.S. congressman went so far as to state that the teaching of evolution is a factor behind violence in America today! Now, that's a stretch!

Summary

Our current understanding of evolutionary processes is directly traceable to developments in intellectual thought in western Europe, with significant influences from the East, over the past 400 years. Many people contributed to this shift in perspective, and we've named only a few. Linnaeus placed humans in the same taxonomic scheme as all other animals. With remarkable insight, Lamarck and Buffon both recognized that species could change in response to environmental circumstances; Lamarck also attempted to explain *how* the changes occurred. He proposed the idea of the *inheritance of acquired characteristics,* which was later discredited. Lyell, in his theory of geological uniformitarianism, provided the necessary expanse of time for evolution to occur, and Malthus discussed how population size is kept in check by the availability of resources.

Darwin and Wallace, influenced by their predecessors, independently recognized that because of competition for resources, individuals with favorable characteristics would tend to survive and pass those beneficial traits on to offspring. Those lacking such traits would produce fewer offspring, if they survived to reproductive age at all. That is, they would have lower reproductive success and reduced fitness. Therefore, over time, advantageous characteristics accumulate in a population (because selection has favored them) while disadvantageous ones are eliminated (selected against). This, in a nutshell, is the theory of evolution by means of natural selection.

Despite mounting evidence in support of evolutionary theory for almost 150 years, there is still very strong public sentiment against it, especially in the United States. The opposition has been fueled mostly by fundamentalist Christian groups attempting to either ban the teaching of evolution in public schools or introduce religious-based views into public school curricula in the name of "fair and balanced treatment." These attempts have repeatedly been struck down in state and federal courts because they violate the First Amendment to the U.S. Constitution.

WHY IT MATTERS

As you've just seen, one of the greatest controversies regarding education in the United States and other parts of the world is the teaching of evolution. While some political leaders advocate "equal time" for intelligent design, they also express concern over the threat of avian flu (H5N1), for fear that the virus that now affects birds will change (that is, evolve) into a form that can infect humans. But many of these leaders don't recognize the link between developing vaccines or other medical tools to fight an emerging disease and the teaching of evolution in the public schools. (While creationists accept that microorganisms change, they don't believe that these changes are evolutionary ones.)

Actually, there are several ways an evolutionary view can contribute to understanding contemporary health challenges. One of these is the recognition that the inevitable outcome of more and more aggressive interventions to fight disease-causing pathogens will be pathogens that have evolved to resist therapies such as antibiotics. (This is because the antibiotics and other treatments we develop actually weed out vulnerable pathogens but leave less vulnerable ones to reproduce.)

For example, we've seen the appearance of resistant strains of *Staphylococcus* bacteria, tuberculosis, and *E. coli.* The virus that causes AIDS (HIV) and the organism that causes malaria mutate so quickly that all attempts to develop a vaccine against them have failed so far. For the most part, the antibiotic-pathogen arms race has led to the development of increasingly lethal strains of disease. However, the evolutionary process doesn't have to lead in that direction. In fact, one suggestion for defeating disease-causing organisms like HIV is to turn the evolutionary process around so that it produces less virulent strains. Ewald (1994, 1999) has called this procedure "domesticating" pathogens and cites as an example diphtheria, which has apparently evolved into milder strains because of vaccination. The primary argument is that medical interventions that can respond to the processes of disease emergence and evolution are much more likely to be successful in the long run than those that target specific disease variants and their manifestations.

Consider, for example, the influenza viruses that appear every autumn. Medical researchers work hard to predict which of several strains will pose the most serious threat. Then they try to develop a vaccine that targets that specific strain. If their prediction is wrong, an influenza epidemic may emerge. If future physicians and biomedical researchers don't understand evolutionary processes, then there is little hope that they can do anything to forestall the potential medical crises that lie ahead as the pace of change in pathogens exceeds that of the antibiotics designed to defeat them.

Critical Thinking Questions

1 After having read this chapter, how would you answer the question, "If humans evolved from monkeys, why do we still have monkeys?"

2 Given what you've read about the scientific method in Chapter 1, how would you explain the differences between science and religion as methods of explaining natural phenomena? Do you personally see a conflict between evolutionary and religious explanations of how species came to be?

3 Can you think of a few examples of artificial and natural selection that weren't discussed in this chapter? For your examples, what traits have been selected for? In the case of natural selection, what was the selective agent?

CHAPTER 3

The Biological Basis of Life

ORIGIN
OF
SPECIES
·
DARWIN

LONDON
JOHN MURRAY

What is the biological basis of life? Does it vary from species to species?

How do human beings fit into a biological continuum?

genetics The study of gene structure and action, and the patterns of inheritance of traits from parent to offspring. Genetic mechanisms are the foundation for evolutionary change.

nucleic acids Organic acids made up of nucleotides. DNA and RNA are nucleic acids.

organelles Structures contained within cells. There are many kinds of organelles, and each type has a different function.

Introduction

Envision yourself after a rotten day, watching the news on TV. The first story, following an endless string of commercials, is about genetically modified foods, a newly cloned species, or the controversy over stem cell research. What do you do? Change the channel? Leave the room? Go to sleep? Or do you follow the story? And if you do follow it, do you understand it? Do you think it's important or relevant to you personally? Well, the fact is, you live in an age when genetic discoveries and genetically based technologies are advancing daily, and they're going to profoundly affect your life.

At some point, you or someone you love will probably need lifesaving medical treatment, perhaps for cancer, and this treatment will be based on genetic research. Like it or not, you already eat genetically modified foods. You may take advantage of developing reproductive technologies, and sadly, you may soon see the development of biological weapons based on genetically altered bacteria and viruses. But fortunately, you'll also live to see many of the secrets of evolution revealed through genetic research. So even if you haven't been particularly interested in genetic issues (or maybe you've been intimidated by them), you should be aware that they affect your life every day.

As you already know, this book is about human evolution and adaptation, both of which are intimately linked to life processes that involve cells, the duplication and decoding of genetic information, and the transmission of this information between generations. So, to present human evolution and adaptation in the broad sense, we need to examine the basic principles of **genetics**. Genetics is the study of how genes work and how traits are transmitted from one generation to the next. Even though many physical anthropologists don't actually specialize in this field, it's genetics that ultimately links the various subdisciplines of biological anthropology.

The Cell

To discuss genetic and evolutionary principles, it's necessary to understand basic cell functions. Cells are the fundamental units of life in all living organisms. In some forms, such as bacteria, the entire organism consists of only a single cell (Fig. 3-1). However, more complex *multicellular* forms, such as plants, insects, birds, and mammals, are composed of billions of cells. As a matter of fact, an adult human is made up of perhaps as many as 1,000 billion (1,000,000,000,000) cells, all functioning in complex ways that ultimately promote the survival of the individual.

Life on earth began at least 3.7 billion years ago in the form of single-celled organisms, represented today by bacteria and blue-green algae. Structurally more complex cells, called eukaryotic cells, appeared approximately 1.2 billion years ago, and since they're the kind of cell that multi-cellular organisms are made of, they will be the focus of this chapter. Despite the numerous differences between various life-forms and the cells that constitute them, it's important to understand that the cells of all living organisms share many similarities as a result of their common evolutionary past.

In general, a eukaryotic cell is a three-dimensional structure composed of carbohydrates, lipids (fats), **nucleic acids,** and proteins. It also contains several kinds of substructures called **organelles,** one of which is the **nucleus** (*pl.,* nuclei), a discrete unit surrounded by a thin membrane called the *nuclear membrane* (Fig. 3-2). Inside the nucleus are two kinds of nucleic acids, **molecules** that contain the genetic information that controls the cell's functions. These two nucleic acids are **DNA (deoxyribonucleic acid)** and **RNA (ribonucleic acid)** (In single-celled organisms, genetic information isn't contained within a nucleus.) The nucleus is surrounded by a gel-like substance called the **cytoplasm,** which contains numerous other types of organelles involved in various activities, such as breaking down nutrients and converting them to other substances, storing and releasing energy, eliminating waste, and manufacturing **proteins** through a process called **protein synthesis.**

Two of these organelles, **mitochondria** (*sing.,* mitochondrion) and **ribosomes,** require further mention. Mitochondria (see Fig. 3-2) are responsible for producing energy within the cell, and they can be loosely thought of as the cell's engines. Mitochondria are oval structures enclosed within a folded membrane, and they contain their own distinct DNA, called **mitochondrial DNA (mtDNA),** which directs mitochondrial activities. Mitochondrial DNA has the same molecular structure and

Dr. Michael S. Donnenberg

FIGURE 3-1

Each one of these oval-shaped structures is a single-celled bacterium.

nucleus A structure (organelle) found in all eukaryotic cells. The nucleus contains chromosomes (nuclear DNA).

molecules Structures made up of two or more atoms. Molecules can combine with other molecules to form more complex structures.

DNA (deoxyribonucleic acid) The double-stranded molecule that contains the genetic code, a set of instructions for producing bodily structures and functions. DNA is a main component of chromosomes.

ribonucleic acid (RNA) A single-stranded molecule similar in structure to DNA. Three forms of RNA are essential to protein synthesis: messenger RNA (mRNA), transfer RNA (tRNA), and ribosomal RNA (rRNA).

cytoplasm The portion of the cell contained within the cell membrane, excluding the nucleus. The cytoplasm consists of a semifluid material and contains numerous structures involved with cell function.

proteins Three-dimensional molecules that serve a wide variety of functions through their ability to bind to other molecules.

protein synthesis The assembly of chains of amino acids into functional protein molecules. The process is directed by DNA.

mitochondria (*sing.,* mitochondrion) Structures contained within the cytoplasm of eukaryotic cells that convert energy, derived from nutrients, to a form that's used by the cell.

ribosomes Structures composed of a form of RNA called ribosomal RNA (rRNA) and protein. Ribosomes are found in the cell's cytoplasm and are essential to the manufacture of proteins.

mitochondrial DNA (mtDNA) DNA found in the mitochondria. mtDNA is inherited only from the mother.

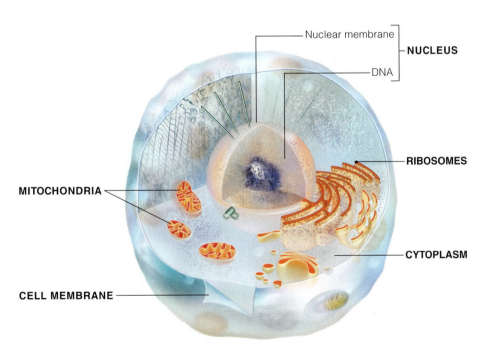

FIGURE 3-2

Structure of a generalized eukaryotic cell, illustrating the cell's three-dimensional nature. Various organelles are shown, but for simplicity only those we discuss are labeled.

function as nuclear DNA (that is, DNA found in the nucleus), but it's organized somewhat differently. In recent years, mtDNA has attracted a lot of attention because of the numerous traits it influences and because it can be used to study certain evolutionary processes. For these reasons, we'll discuss mitochondrial inheritance in more detail in Chapters 4 and 11. Ribosomes are roughly spherical and are partly composed of RNA. They're important because they're essential to protein synthesis (see p. 42).

There are basically two types of cells: **somatic cells** and **gametes.** Somatic cells are the cellular components of body tissues, such as muscle, bone, skin, nerve, heart, and brain. Gametes, or sex cells, are specifically involved in reproduction and aren't important as structural components of the body. There are two types of gametes: egg cells, produced in female ovaries, and sperm cells, which develop in male testes. The sole function of a sex cell is to unite with a gamete from another individual to form a **zygote,** which has the potential of developing into a new individual. In this way, gametes transmit genetic information from parent to offspring.

DNA Structure

Because it directs all cellular functions, DNA is the very basis of life. The exact physical and chemical properties of DNA were unknown until 1953 when, at the University of Cambridge in England, an American researcher named James Watson and three British scientists, Francis Crick, Maurice Wilkins, and Rosalind Franklin, developed a structural and functional model (Fig. 3-3) of DNA (Watson and Crick, 1953a, 1953b). It's impossible to overstate the importance of this achievement because it completely revolutionized the fields of biology and medicine and forever altered our understanding of biological and evolutionary mechanisms.

The DNA molecule is composed of two chains of even smaller molecules called **nucleotides.** A nucleotide, in turn, is made up of three components: a sugar molecule (deoxyribose), a phosphate unit, and one of four nitrogenous bases (Fig. 3-4). In DNA, nucleotides are stacked on top of one another to form a chain that is bonded along its bases to another nucleotide chain. Together the two chains twist to form a spiral, or helical, shape. The DNA molecule, then, is double-stranded and is described

somatic cells All the cells in the body except gametes (eggs and sperm).

gametes Reproductive cells (eggs and sperm in animals), developed from precursor cells in ovaries and testes.

zygote A cell formed by the union of an egg cell and a sperm cell. It contains the full complement of chromosomes (in humans, 46) and has the potential to develop into an entire organism.

nucleotides Basic units of the DNA molecule, composed of a sugar, a phosphate, and one of four DNA bases.

FIGURE 3-3

James Watson (left) and Francis Crick in 1953 with their model of the structure of the DNA molecule.

A. Barrington Brown / Photo Researchers, Inc.

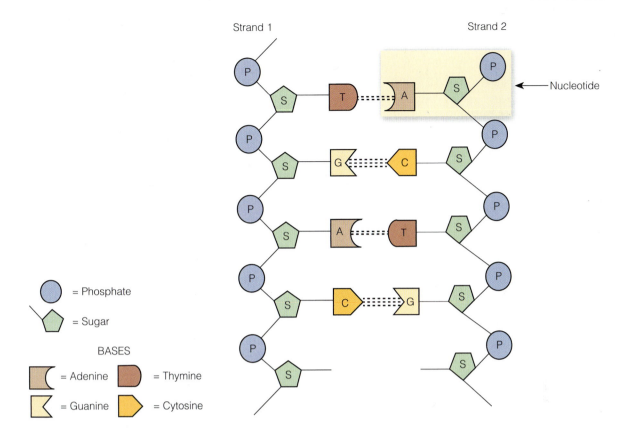

Strand 1   Strand 2

Nucleotide

= Phosphate

= Sugar

BASES

= Adenine   = Thymine

= Guanine   = Cytosine

FIGURE 3-4

Part of a DNA molecule. The illustration shows the two DNA strands with the sugar and phosphate backbone and the bases extending toward the center.

as forming a *double helix* that resembles a twisted ladder. If we follow the twisted ladder analogy, the sugars and phosphates represent the two sides, while the bases and the bonds that join them form the rungs (Fig. 3-5).

The four bases are the key to how DNA works. These bases are *adenine, guanine, thymine,* and *cytosine,* and they're usually referred to by their initial letters: A, G, T, and C. In forming the double helix, one type of base can pair, or bond, with only one other type. Therefore, *base pairs* can form *only* between adenine and thymine and between guanine and cytosine (see Figs. 3-4 and 3-5). This specificity is essential to the DNA molecule's ability to **replicate** or make an exact copy of itself.

DNA Replication

Cells multiply by dividing, making exact copies of themselves. This, in turn, enables organisms to grow and injured tissues to heal. There are two kinds of cell division. In the simpler form, cells divide in a way that ensures that each new cell receives a full set of genetic material. This is important, because a cell can't function properly without the appropriate amount of DNA. But before a cell can divide, its DNA must replicate.

Replication begins when **enzymes** break the bonds between bases throughout the DNA molecule, leaving the two previously joined strands of nucleotides with their bases exposed (see Fig. 3-5). These exposed bases then attract unattached DNA nucleotides (made by the DNA), which are present in the cell nucleus. Since each base can pair with only one other, the attraction between bases occurs in a **complementary** way. What this means is that the two previously joined parental nucleotide chains serve as models, or templates, for forming new strands of nucleotides. As each new strand is formed, its bases are joined to the bases of an original strand. When the process is complete, there are two double-stranded DNA molecules exactly like the original one, and each newly formed molecule consists of one original nucleotide chain joined to a newly formed chain (see Fig. 3-5).

replicate To duplicate. The DNA molecule is able to make copies of itself.

enzymes Specialized proteins that initiate and direct chemical reactions in the body.

complementary In genetics, referring to the fact that DNA bases form base pairs in a precise manner. For example, adenine can bond only to thymine. These two bases are said to be complementary because one requires the other to form a complete DNA base pair.

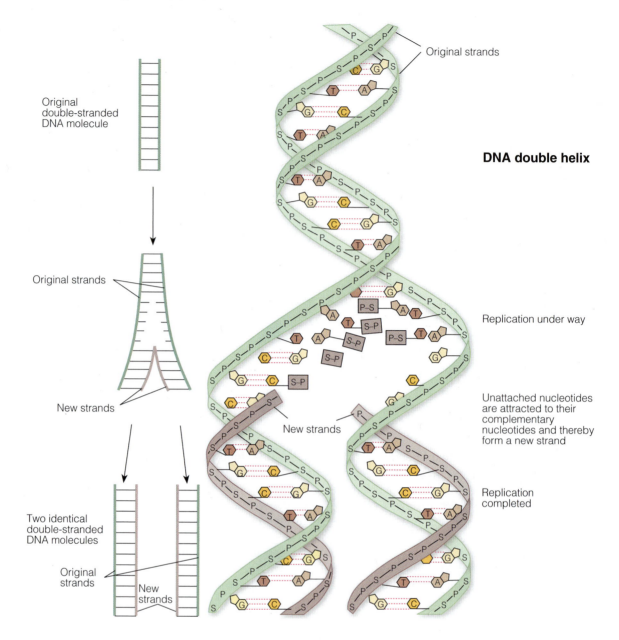

Original double-stranded DNA molecule

Original strands

New strands

Two identical double-stranded DNA molecules

Original strands

New strands

Original strands

DNA double helix

Replication under way

Unattached nucleotides are attracted to their complementary nucleotides and thereby form a new strand

New strands

Replication completed

FIGURE 3-5
DNA replication. During DNA replication, the two strands of the DNA molecule are separated, and each strand serves as a template for the formation of a new strand. When replication is complete, there are two DNA molecules. Each molecule consists of one new and one original DNA strand.

hemoglobin A protein molecule found in red blood cells. Hemoglobin binds to oxygen, an ability that allows the blood to carry oxygen throughout the body.

Protein Synthesis

One of the most important activities of DNA is to direct protein synthesis within the cell. Proteins are complex, three-dimensional molecules that function through their ability to bind to other molecules (Fig. 3-6). For example, the protein **hemoglobin,** found in red blood cells, is able to bind to oxygen, which it carries to cells throughout the body.

Proteins function in countless ways. Some, like collagen, are structural components of tissues. Collagen is the most common protein in the body and is a major component of all connective tissues. Enzymes are also proteins, and they regulate chemical reactions. For instance, a digestive enzyme called *lactase* breaks down *lactose,* or milk sugar, into two simpler sugars. Another class of proteins includes many types of **hormones.** Hormones are produced by specialized cells and then released into the bloodstream to circulate to other areas of the body, where they produce specific effects in tissues and organs. Insulin, for example, is a hormone produced by cells in the pancreas, and it causes cells in the liver to absorb energy-producing glucose (sugar) from the blood. (Enzymes and hormones are discussed in more detail in Chapter 13.) Lastly, many kinds of proteins can enter a cell's nucleus and attach directly to its DNA. This is very important because when these proteins bind to the DNA, they can regulate its activity. From this brief description, you can see that proteins make us what we are. So, protein synthesis has to occur accurately, because if it doesn't, physiological development and cellular activities can be disrupted or even prevented.

Proteins are made up of chains of smaller molecules called **amino acids.** In all, there are 20 amino acids, 8 of which must be obtained from foods (see Chapter 13). The remaining 12 are produced in cells. These 20 amino acids are combined in different amounts and sequences to produce at least 90,000 different proteins. What makes proteins different from one another is the number and sequence of their amino acids.

In part, DNA is a recipe for making a protein, since it's the sequence of DNA bases that ultimately determines the order of amino acids in a protein molecule. In the DNA instructions, a *triplet,* or group of three bases, refers to a particular amino acid. For example, if a triplet consists of the base sequence cytosine, guanine, and adenine (CGA), it specifies the amino acid arganine (Table 3-1). Therefore, a small

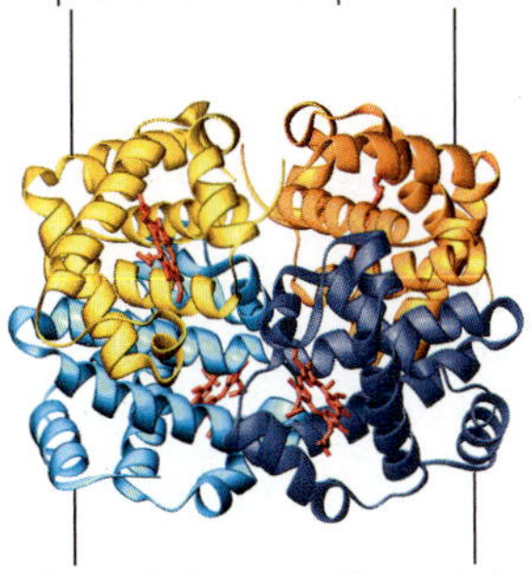

Alpha chain   Alpha chain

Beta chain   Beta chain

FIGURE 3-6
Diagrammatic representation of a hemoglobin molecule. Hemoglobin molecules are composed of four chains of amino acids (two "alpha" chains and two "beta" chains). The red structures are the portions that bind to oxygen.

hormones Substances (usually proteins) that are produced by specialized cells and travel to other parts of the body, where they influence chemical reactions and regulate various cellular functions.

amino acids Small molecules that are the components of proteins.

TABLE 3.1	The Genetic Code		
Amino Acid Symbol	**Amino Acid**	**mRNA Codon**	**DNA Triplet**
Ala	Alanine	GCU, GCC, GCA, GCG	CGA, CGG, CGT, CGC
Arg	Arginine	CGU, CGC, CGA, CGG, AGA, AGG	GCA, GCG, GCT, GCC, TCT, TCC
Asn	Asparagine	AAU, AAC	TTA, TTG
Asp	Aspartic acid	GAU, GAC	CTA, CTG
Cys	Cysteine	UGU, UGC	ACA, ACG
Gln	Glutamine	CAA, CAG	GTT, GTC
Glu	Glutamic acid	GAA, GAG	CTT, CTC
Gly	Glycine	GGU, GGC, GGA, GGG	CCA, CCG, CCT, CCC
His	Histidine	CAU, CAC	GTA, GTG
Ile	Isoleucine	AUU, AUC, AUA	TAA, TAG, TAT
Leu	Leucine	UUA, UUG, CUU, CUC, CUA, CUG	AAT, AAC, GAA, GAG, GAT, GAC
Lys	Lysine	AAA, AAG	TTT, TTC
Met	Methionine	AUG	TAC
Phe	Phenylalanine	UUU, UUC	AAA, AAG
Pro	Proline	CCU, CCC, CCA, CCG	GGA, GGG, GGT, GGC
Ser	Serine	UCU, UCC, UCA, UCG, AGU, AGC	AGA, AGG, AGT, AGC, TCA, TCG
Thr	Threonine	ACU, ACC, ACA, ACG	TGA, TGG, TGT, TGC
Trp	Tryptophan	UGG	ACC
Tyr	Tyrosine	UAU, UAC	ATA, ATG
Val	Valine	GUU, GUC, GUA, GUG	CAA, CAG, CAT, CAC
Terminating triplets		UAA, UAG, UGA	ATT, ATC, ACT

portion of a DNA recipe might look like this (except there would be no spaces between the triplets): AGA CGA ACA ACC TAC TTT TTC CTT AAG GTC.

Protein synthesis actually takes place outside the cell nucleus, in the cytoplasm at one of the organelles we mentioned earlier, the ribosomes. But the DNA molecule can't leave the cell's nucleus. So the first step in protein synthesis is to copy the DNA message into a form of RNA called **messenger RNA (mRNA),** which can pass through the nuclear membrane into the cytoplasm. RNA is similar to DNA, but it's different in some important ways:

1. It's single-stranded. (This is true for the forms we discuss here, but it's not true for all.)
2. It contains a different type of sugar.
3. It contains the base uracil as a substitute for the DNA base thymine. (Uracil binds to adenine in the same way thymine does.)

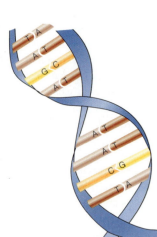
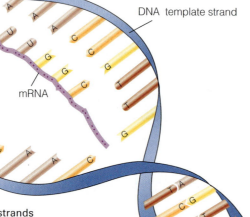

DNA template strand

mRNA

The mRNA molecule forms on the DNA template in pretty much the same way that new DNA molecules are assembled. As in DNA replication, the two DNA strands separate, but only partially, and one of these strands attracts free-floating RNA nucleotides (also produced in the cell), which are joined together on the DNA template. The formation of mRNA is called *transcription* because, in fact, the DNA code is being copied, or transcribed (Fig. 3-7). Once the appropriate segment has been copied, the mRNA strand peels away from the DNA model, and a portion of it travels through the nuclear membrane to the ribosome. Meanwhile, the bonds between the DNA bases are reestablished, and the DNA molecule is once more intact.

As the mRNA strand arrives at the ribosome, its message is translated. (This stage of the process is called *translation* because at this point, the genetic instructions are decoded.) Just as each DNA triplet specifies one amino acid, so do mRNA triplets, which are called **codons.** Therefore, the mRNA strand is "read" in codons, or groups of three mRNA bases at a time (see Table 3-1). Subsequently, another form of RNA molecule, called **transfer RNA (tRNA),** brings the amino acid specified by the codon being read to the ribosome. The ribosome then joins that amino acid to another one in the order dictated by the sequence of mRNA codons (or, ultimately, DNA triplets). In this way, amino acids are linked together to form a molecule that will eventually be a protein or part of a protein. But it's important to mention that if a DNA base or a sequence of bases is changed through **mutation,** some proteins may not be made or they may be defective. In this case, cells won't function properly, if at all.

What Is a Gene?

For decades, biologists have defined a **gene** as the entire sequence of DNA bases responsible for the synthesis of a protein or, in some cases, part of a protein. Or, put another way, a gene is a segment of DNA that specifies the sequence of amino acids in a particular protein. This definition, based on the concept of a one gene–one protein relationship, has been a core principle in biology for almost 50 years, but it's been qualified partly in recognition of the fact that DNA also codes for RNA and other DNA nucleotides. (Incidentally, this situation is a good example of what we discussed in Chapter 1—that hypotheses and theories can, and do, change over time as we acquire additional knowledge.) A more inclusive definition simply states that a gene

FIGURE 3-7

Transcription. The two DNA strands have partly separated. Free messenger RNA (mRNA) nucleotides have been drawn to the template strand, and a strand of mRNA is being made. Note that the mRNA strand will exactly complement the DNA template strand, except that uracil (U) replaces thymine (T).

messenger RNA (mRNA)
A form of RNA that's assembled on a sequence of DNA bases. It carries the DNA code to the ribosome during protein synthesis.

codons Triplets of messenger RNA bases that code for specific amino acids during protein synthesis.

transfer RNA (tRNA) The type of RNA that binds to amino acids and transports them to the ribosome during protein synthesis.

is "a complete chromosomal segment responsible for making a functional product" (Snyder and Gerstein, 2003).

It's important to understand that gene action is incredibly complex and still only partly understood. For example, only some of the DNA segments in a gene, called *exons,* are actually translated into amino acids; most of the DNA in a gene isn't expressed during protein synthesis. In fact, some segments, called *introns,* are initially transcribed (that is, mRNA copies are manufactured) but subsequently deleted (Fig. 3-8). But even though introns aren't instrumental in protein synthesis, they're still part of the DNA molecule and may have other functions. So it's the combination of introns and exons, interspersed along a strand of DNA, that makes up the unit we call a gene.

Regulatory Genes

Some genes act solely to control the expression of other genes. Basically, these **regulatory genes** make proteins that switch other DNA segments (genes) on or off. Thus, their functions are critical for individual organisms, and they also play an important role in evolution. In fact, as information about regulatory genes accumulates, we should be able to answer many of the questions we still have about the evolution of species.

Homeobox genes, or *Hox* **genes,** are extremely important regulatory genes. *Hox* genes direct early segmentation of embryonic tissues, including those that give rise to the spine and thoracic muscles. They also interact with other genes to determine the identity and characteristics of developing body segments and structures, but not their actual development. For example, homeobox genes determine where,

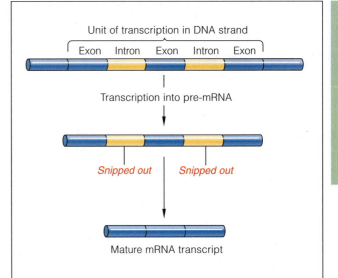

FIGURE 3-8

Diagram of a DNA sequence being transcribed. The introns are deleted from the pre-mRNA before it leaves the cell nucleus. The remaining mature mRNA contains only exons.

QUICK REVIEW   Coding and Noncoding DNA

CODING DNA	"NONCODING" DNA
Codes for sequences of amino acids (i.e., functional proteins) or RNA molecules	Not involved in protein synthesis—functions not fully understood, but is involved in gene regulation
Comprises approximately 2% of human nuclear DNA	Comprises about 98% of human nuclear DNA
Includes exons within functional genes	Includes introns within functional genes and multiple repeated segments elsewhere on chromosomes (e.g., microsatellites)

Introns spliced out during RNA processing

mutation A change in DNA. The term can refer to changes in DNA bases as well as to changes in chromosome number or structure.

gene A sequence of DNA bases that specifies the order of amino acids in an entire protein, a portion of a protein, or any functional product. A gene may be made up of hundreds or thousands of DNA bases organized into coding and noncoding segments.

regulatory genes Genes that code for the production of proteins that can bind to DNA and modify the action of genes. Many are active only during certain stages of development.

homeobox genes (*Hox* genes) An evolutionarily ancient family of regulatory genes that directs the development of the overall body plan and the segmentation of body tissues.

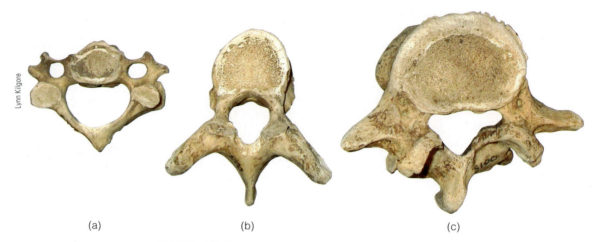

(a)   (b)   (c)

FIGURE 3-9

The differences in these three vertebrae, from different regions of the spine, are caused by the action of *Hox* genes during embryonic development. The cervical (neck) vertebrae (a) have characteristics that differentiate them from the thoracic vertebrae (b) that are attached to the ribs, and also from the lumbar vertebrae (c) of the lower back. *Hox* genes determine the overall pattern not only of each type of vertebra but also of each individual vertebra.

in a developing embryo, limb buds will appear. They also establish the number and overall pattern of the different types of vertebrae, the bones that make up the spine (Fig. 3-9).

Homeobox genes are highly conserved, meaning they've been maintained pretty much throughout evolutionary history. They're present in all invertebrates (such as worms and insects) and vertebrates, and they don't vary greatly from species to species. This type of conservation means not only that these genes are vitally important, but also that they evolved from genes that were present in some of the earliest forms of life. Moreover, changes in the behavior of homeobox genes are responsible for various physical differences between closely related species.

There's one final point to be made about genes and DNA: The genetic code is universal, and at least on earth, DNA is the genetic material in all forms of life. The DNA of all organisms, from bacteria to oak trees to human beings, is composed of the same molecules using the same kinds of instructions. Consequently, the DNA triplet CGA, for example, specifies the amino acid alanine, regardless of species. These similarities imply biological relationships among, and an ultimate common ancestry for, all forms of life. What makes oak trees distinct from humans isn't differences in the DNA material itself, but differences in how that material is arranged.

Cell Division

Throughout much of a cell's life, its DNA (all 6 feet of it!) directs cellular functions and exists as an uncoiled, granular substance. However, at various times in the life of most types of cells, normal activities cease and the cell divides. Cell division produces new cells, and at the beginning of this process, the DNA becomes tightly coiled and is visible under a microscope as a set of discrete structures called **chromosomes** (Fig. 3-10).

Every species has a specific number of chromosomes in somatic cells (Table 3-2). Humans, have 46, while chimpanzees and gorillas have 48. This difference doesn't mean that humans have less DNA than chimpanzees and gorillas do. It just means that the DNA is packaged differently.

chromosomes Discrete structures composed of DNA and protein found only in the nuclei of cells. Chromosomes are visible under magnification only during certain phases of cell division.

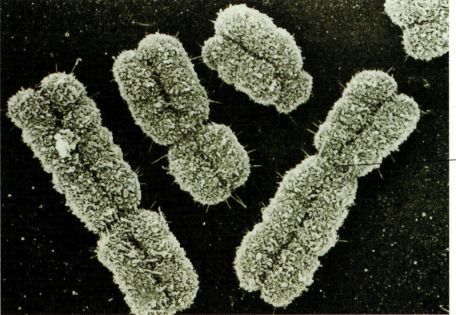

— Centromere

FIGURE 3–10

Scanning electron micrograph of human chromosomes during cell division. Note that these chromosomes are composed of two strands, or two DNA molecules.

Chromosomes

A chromosome is composed of a DNA molecule and proteins (Fig. 3-11). During normal cell function, if chromosomes were visible, they would look like single-stranded structures. However, during the early stages of cell division, they're made up of two strands, or two DNA molecules, joined together at a constricted area called the **centromere.** The reason there are two strands is simple: The DNA molecules have *replicated* and one strand is an exact copy of the other.

TABLE 3.2	Standard Chromosomal Complement in Various Organisms	
Organism	**Chromosome Number in Somatic Cells**	**Chromosome Number in Gametes**
Human (*Homo sapiens*)	46	23
Chimpanzee (*Pan troglodytes*)	48	24
Gorilla (*Gorilla gorilla*)	48	24
Dog (*Canis familiaris*)	78	39
Chicken (*Gallus domesticus*)	78	39
Frog (*Rana pipiens*)	26	13
Housefly (*Musca domestica*)	12	6
Onion (*Allium cepa*)	16	8
Corn (*Zea mays*)	20	10
Tobacco (*Nicotiana tabacum*)	48	24

Source: Cummings, 2000, p. 16.

centromere The constricted portion of a chromosome. After replication, the two strands of a double-stranded chromosome are joined at the centromere.

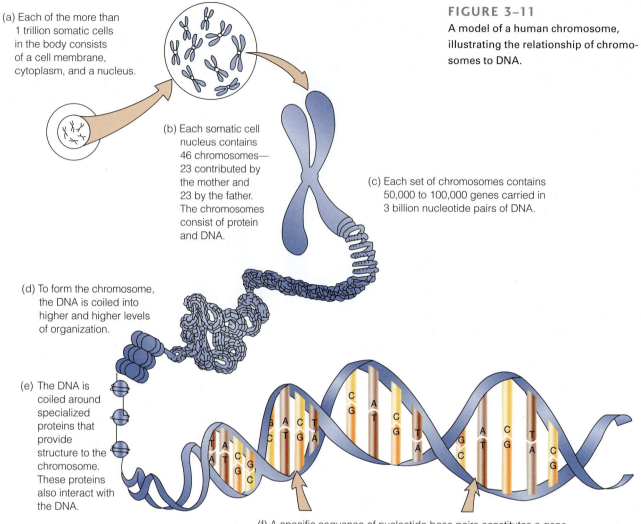

(a) Each of the more than 1 trillion somatic cells in the body consists of a cell membrane, cytoplasm, and a nucleus.

FIGURE 3–11

A model of a human chromosome, illustrating the relationship of chromosomes to DNA.

(b) Each somatic cell nucleus contains 46 chromosomes— 23 contributed by the mother and 23 by the father. The chromosomes consist of protein and DNA.

(c) Each set of chromosomes contains 50,000 to 100,000 genes carried in 3 billion nucleotide pairs of DNA.

(d) To form the chromosome, the DNA is coiled into higher and higher levels of organization.

(e) The DNA is coiled around specialized proteins that provide structure to the chromosome. These proteins also interact with the DNA.

(f) A specific sequence of nucleotide base pairs constitutes a gene.

There are two basic types of chromosomes: **autosomes** and **sex chromosomes.** Autosomes carry genetic information that governs all physical characteristics except primary sex determination. The two sex chromosomes are the X and Y chromosomes; in mammals, the Y chromosome is directly involved in determining maleness. Although the X chromosome is called a "sex chromosome," it acts more like an autosome because it's not involved in primary sex determination, and it influences several other traits. Among mammals, all genetically normal females have two X chromosomes (XX), and they're female only because they don't have a Y chromosome. (In other words, female is the default setting.) All genetically normal males have one X and one Y chromosome (XY). In other classes of animals, such as birds, reptiles, or insects, primary sex determination is governed by various other chromosomal mechanisms and factors.

Chromosomes occur in pairs, so all normal human somatic cells have 22 pairs of autosomes and 1 pair of sex chromosomes. Offspring inherit one member of each pair from the father, and the other member is inherited from the mother. Members of chromosomal pairs are alike in size and position of the centromere, and they carry genetic information governing the same traits. But this doesn't mean that partner chromosomes are genetically identical; it just means they influence the same traits.

Abnormal numbers of autosomes, with few exceptions, are fatal—usually soon after conception. Although abnormal numbers of sex chromosomes aren't usually fatal, they may cause sterility and can have other consequences as well. So, to function normally, human cells must have both members of each chromosomal pair, or a total of 46 chromosomes.

autosomes All chromosomes except the sex chromosomes.

sex chromosomes In mammals, the X and Y chromosomes.

Mitosis

Cell division in somatic cells is called **mitosis.** In the early stages of mitosis, a human somatic cell has 46 double-stranded chromosomes, and as the cell begins to divide, these chromosomes line up along its center and split apart so that the two strands separate (Fig. 3-12). Once the two strands are apart, they pull away from each other and move to opposite ends of the dividing cell. At this point, each strand is now a distinct chromosome, *composed of one DNA molecule.* Following the separation of chromosome strands, the cell membrane pinches in and seals, so that there are two new cells, each with a full complement of DNA, or 46 chromosomes.

Mitosis is referred to as "simple cell division" because a somatic cell divides one time to produce two daughter cells that are genetically identical to each other and to the original cell. In mitosis, the original cell possesses 46 chromosomes, and each new daughter cell inherits an exact copy of all 46. This precision is made possible by the DNA molecule's ability to replicate. Therefore, DNA replication is what ensures that the amount of genetic material remains constant from one generation of cells to the next.

mitosis Simple cell division; the process by which somatic cells divide to produce two identical daughter cells.

FIGURE 3-12

A diagrammatic representation of mitosis. Above four of the illustrations are photomicrographs of the actual events depicted in the drawings.

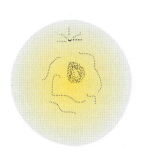

(a) The cell is involved in metabolic activities. DNA replication occurs, but chromosomes are not visible.

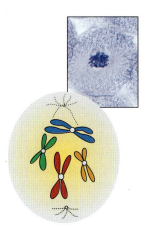

(b) The nuclear membrane disappears, and double-stranded chromosomes are visible.

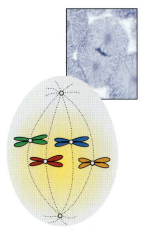

(c) The chromosomes align themselves at the center of the cell.

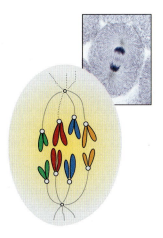

(d) The chromosomes split at the centromere, and the strands separate and move to opposite ends of the dividing cell.

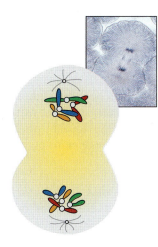

(e) The cell membrane pinches in as the cell continues to divide. The chromosomes begin to uncoil (not shown here).

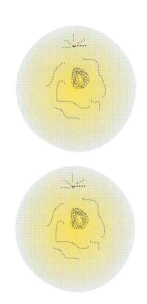

(f) After mitosis is complete, there are two identical daughter cells. The nuclear membrane is present, and chromosomes are no longer visible.

Meiosis

While mitosis produces new cells, **meiosis** can lead to the development of an entire new organism because it produces reproductive cells. Although meiosis is similar to mitosis, it's a more complicated process. In meiosis, there are two divisions instead of one. Also, meiosis produces four daughter cells, not two, and each of these four cells contains only half the original number of chromosomes.

During meiosis, specialized cells in male testes and female ovaries divide and eventually develop into sperm and egg cells. Initially, these cells contain the full complement of chromosomes (46 in humans), but after the first division (called "reduction division"), the number of chromosomes in the two daughter cells is 23, or half the original number (Fig. 3-13). This reduction of chromosome number is crucial because the resulting gamete, with its 23 chromosomes, may eventually unite with another gamete that also has 23 chromosomes. The product of this union is a *zygote,* or fertilized egg, in which the original number of chromosomes (46) has been restored. In other words, a zygote inherits the exact amount of DNA it needs (half from each parent) to develop and function normally. But if it weren't for *reduction division* in meiosis, it wouldn't be possible to maintain the correct number of chromosomes from one generation to the next.

During the first division, partner chromosomes come together to form pairs of double-stranded chromosomes that line up along the cell's center. Pairing of partner chromosomes is essential, because while they're together, members of pairs exchange genetic information in a process called **recombination.** Pairing is also important because it ensures that each new daughter cell receives only one member of each pair.

As the cell begins to divide, the chromosomes themselves remain intact (that is, double-stranded), but *members of pairs* pull apart and move to opposite ends of the cell. After the first division, there are two new daughter cells, but they aren't identical to each other or to the parental cell. They're different because each cell contains only one member of each chromosome pair (that is, only 23 chromosomes), each of which still has two strands. Also, because of recombination, each chromosome now contains some combinations of genes it didn't have before.

The second meiotic division happens pretty much the same way as in mitosis. (For a comparison of mitosis and meiosis, see Fig. 3-14.) In the two newly formed cells, the 23 double-stranded chromosomes line up at the cell's center, and as in mitosis, the strands of each chromosome separate and move apart. Once this second division is completed, there are four daughter cells, each with 23 single-stranded chromosomes, or 23 DNA molecules.

The Evolutionary Significance of Meiosis Meiosis occurs in all sexually reproducing organisms, and it's an extremely important evolutionary innovation because it increases genetic variation in populations. As you've already learned, genetic variation is essential if species are to adapt to changing selective pressures. Members of sexually reproducing species aren't genetically identical **clones** of other individuals because they inherit a combination of genes from two parents. Furthermore, recombination between partner chromosomes increases the genetic uniqueness of each individual by producing new arrangements of genetic information. And these rearrangements potentially provide additional material for natural selection to act upon.

Problems with Meiosis In order for fetal development to occur normally, the meiotic process needs to be exact. If chromosomes or chromosome strands don't separate during either of the two divisions, serious problems can develop. This failure to separate is called *nondisjunction.* The result of nondisjunction is that one of the daughter cells receives two copies of the affected chromosome, while the other daughter cell receives none. If such an affected gamete unites with a normal gamete containing 23 chromosomes, the resulting zygote will have either 45 or 47 chromosomes. If there are

---

meiosis Cell division in specialized cells in ovaries and testes. Meiosis involves two divisions and results in four daughter cells, each containing only half the original number of chromosomes. These cells can develop into gametes.

recombination Sometimes called crossing over; the exchange of genetic material between partner chromosomes during meiosis.

clones Organisms that are genetically identical to another organism. The term may also be used in referring to genetically identical DNA segments, molecules, and cells.

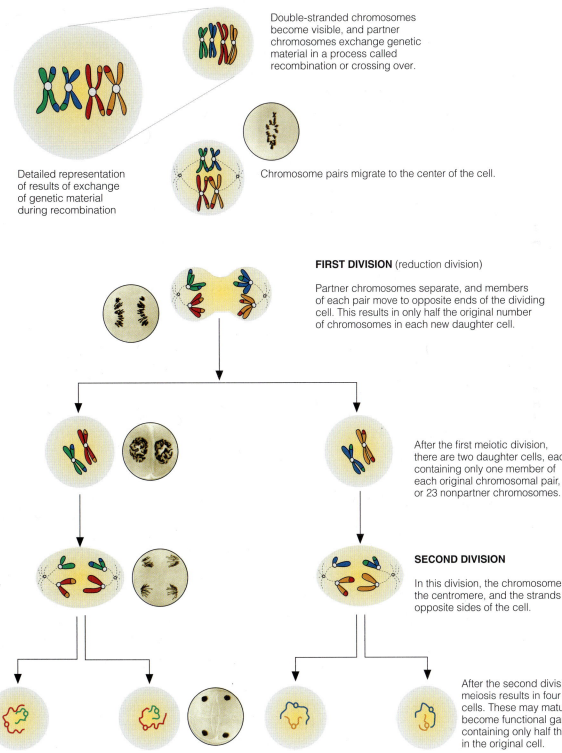

FIGURE 3-13
A diagrammatic representation of meiosis. The five brownish circles are photomicrographs of the stages being illustrated.

Chromosomes are not visible as DNA replication occurs in a cell preparing to divide.

Double-stranded chromosomes become visible, and partner chromosomes exchange genetic material in a process called recombination or crossing over.

Detailed representation of results of exchange of genetic material during recombination

Chromosome pairs migrate to the center of the cell.

FIRST DIVISION (reduction division)

Partner chromosomes separate, and members of each pair move to opposite ends of the dividing cell. This results in only half the original number of chromosomes in each new daughter cell.

After the first meiotic division, there are two daughter cells, each containing only one member of each original chromosomal pair, or 23 nonpartner chromosomes.

SECOND DIVISION

In this division, the chromosomes split at the centromere, and the strands move to opposite sides of the cell.

After the second division, meiosis results in four daughter cells. These may mature to become functional gametes, containing only half the DNA in the original cell.

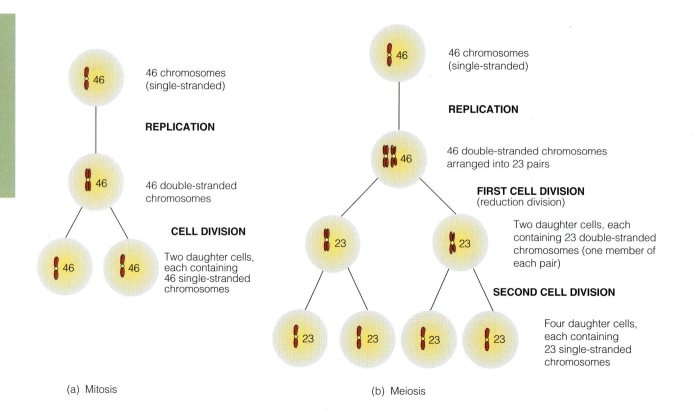

(a) Mitosis

(b) Meiosis

FIGURE 3-14

Mitosis and meiosis compared. (a) In mitosis, one division produces two daughter cells, each of which contains 46 chromosomes. (b) Meiosis is characterized by two divisions. After the first, there are two cells, each containing only 23 chromosomes (one member of each original chromosome pair). Each daughter cell divides again, so that the final result is four cells, each with only half the original number of chromosomes.

47, then there will be three copies of one chromosome instead of two and the term for this situation is *trisomy*.

You can appreciate the potential effects of an abnormal number of chromosomes if you remember that, through mitosis, the zygote ultimately gives rise to all the cells in the developing body. Consequently, every one of these cells will inherit the abnormal chromosome number. And, since most abnormal numbers of autosomes are lethal, the embryo is usually spontaneously aborted, frequently before the pregnancy is even recognized.

Trisomy 21 (formerly called Down syndrome) is the only example of an abnormal number of autosomes that's compatible with life beyond the first few years after birth. Trisomy 21 is caused by the presence of three copies of chromosome 21, it occurs in approximately 1 out of every 1,000 live births, and is associated with a number of developmental and health problems. These problems include congenital heart defects (seen in about 40 percent of affected newborns), increased susceptibility to respiratory infections, and leukemia. However, the most widely recognized effect is mental impairment, which is variably expressed and ranges from mild to severe.

Nondisjunction also occurs in sex chromosomes. For example a man may have two X chromosomes and one Y chromosome, or one X chromosome and two Y chromosomes. Likewise a woman may have only one X chromosome or she may have more than two. Although abnormal numbers of sex chromosomes don't always result in spontaneous abortion or death, they can cause sterility and other problems. Clearly, normal development depends on the presence of the correct number of chromosomes.

New Frontiers

polymerase chain reaction (PCR) A method of producing thousands of copies of a DNA segment using the enzyme DNA polymerase.

Since the discovery of DNA structure and function in the 1950s, the field of genetics has revolutionized biological science and reshaped our understanding of inheritance, genetic disease, and evolutionary processes. For example, a technique developed in 1986, called **polymerase chain reaction (PCR),** enables scientists to make thousands of copies of small samples of DNA that can then be analyzed. In the past,

DNA samples such as those from crime scenes or from fossils were too small to be studied. But PCR has made it possible to examine nucleotide sequences in, for example, Neandertal fossils and Egyptian mummies. As you can imagine, PCR has limitless potential for many disciplines, including forensic science, medicine, and paleoanthropology.

Another application of PCR allows scientists to identify *DNA fingerprints,* so called because they appear as patterns of repeated DNA sequences that are unique to each individual. For example, one person might have a segment of six bases such as ATTCTA repeated 3 times; another might have the same sequence repeated 10 times (Fig. 3-15).

DNA fingerprinting is perhaps the most powerful tool available for human identification. Scientists have used it to identify scores of unidentified remains, including members of the Russian royal family murdered in 1918 and victims of the September 11, 2001, terrorist attacks. It also provided the DNA evidence in the O. J. Simpson murder trial. Moreover, the technique has been used to exonerate many innocent people wrongly convicted for crimes—in some cases decades after they were imprisoned.

Over the last two decades, scientists have used the techniques of **recombinant DNA technology** to transfer genes from the cells of one species into those of another. The most common method has been to insert human genes that direct the production of various proteins into bacterial cells. The altered bacteria can then produce human gene products such as insulin. Until the early 1980s, diabetic patients relied on insulin derived from nonhuman animals. However, this insulin wasn't plentiful, and some patients developed allergies to it. But since 1982, abundant supplies of human insulin, produced by bacteria, have been available; and bacteria-derived insulin doesn't cause allergic reactions.

In recent years, genetic manipulation has become increasingly controversial owing to questions related to product safety, environmental concerns, animal welfare, and concern over the experimental use of human embryos. For example, the insertion of bacterial DNA into certain crops has made them toxic to leaf-eating insects, thus reducing the need for pesticides. Cattle and pigs are commonly treated with antibiotics and genetically engineered growth hormone to increase growth rates. (There's no current evidence that humans are susceptible to the insect-repelling bacterial DNA or harmed by consuming meat and dairy products from animals treated with growth hormone. But there are concerns over the unknown effects of long-term exposure.

No matter how contentious these new techniques may be, nothing has generated as much controversy as cloning. The controversy escalated in 1997 with the birth of Dolly, a clone of a female sheep (Wilmut et al., 1997). Actually, cloning isn't as new as you might think. Anyone who has ever taken a cutting from a plant and rooted it to grow a new one has produced a clone. Currently, the list of cloned mammals includes mice, rats, rabbits, cats, sheep, cattle, horses, a mule, and a dog (Woods et al., 2003).

How successful cloning will be hasn't been determined yet. Dolly, who had developed health problems, was euthanized in February 2003 at the age of 6 years (Giles and Knight, 2003). Long-term studies have yet to show whether cloned animals live out their normal life span, but some evidence from mice suggests that they don't.

As exciting as these innovations are, probably the single most important advance in genetics has been the progress made by the **Human Genome Project.** The goal of this international effort, begun in 1990, was to sequence the entire human genome which consists of some 3 billion bases comprising approximately 25,000 genes. In 2003, the project was completed; now, all human chromosomes have been provisionally mapped. The next step is to sort out which DNA segments operate as functional genes and which don't. It will also be several years before scientists identify the functions of many of the proteins produced by these genes. It's one thing to know a gene's chemical makeup but quite another to know what it does. Still, the magnitude

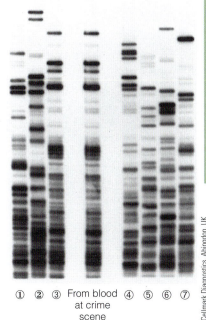

① ② ③ From blood at crime scene ④ ⑤ ⑥ ⑦

Cellmark Diagnostics, Abingdon, UK

FIGURE 3-15

Eight DNA fingerprints, one of which is from a blood sample left at an actual crime scene. The other seven are from suspects. By comparing the banding patterns, it is easy to identify the guilty person.

recombinant DNA technology
A process in which genes from the cell of one species are transferred to somatic cells or gametes of another species.

Human Genome Project An international effort aimed at sequencing and mapping the entire human genome, completed in 2003.

and importance of the achievement can't be overstated; it will ultimately transform biomedical and pharmaceutical research, changing forever the way many human diseases are diagnosed and treated.

The potential for anthropological applications is also enormous. While scientists were sequencing human genes, the genomes of other organisms were also being studied. As of now the genomes of hundreds of species have been sequenced. In December 2002, the mouse genome had been completely sequenced (Waterston et al., 2002). The sequence of the chimpanzee genome was announced in 2005 (The Chimpanzee and Analysis Consortium, 2005), and in 2007 the genome of the rhesus macaque was published (The Rhesus Macaque Genome Sequencing and Analysis Consortium, 2007). Two different groups are also currently working to reveal the Neandertal genome (Noonan et al., 2006; Green et al, 2006). The availability of these genomes will allow comparisons between human DNA and the DNA of Neandertals and nonhuman primates. This research, called *comparative genomics,* has enormous implications not only for biomedical research but also for studies of evolutionary relationships among species, including ourselves.

Eventually, comparative genome analysis should provide a thorough assessment of genetic similarities and differences, and thus the evolutionary relationships, between humans and other primates. What's more, we can already look at human variation in an entirely different light than we could even 10 years ago (see Chapter 12). Among other things, genetic comparisons between human groups can inform us about population movements in the past and what selective pressures may have been exerted on different populations to produce some of the variability we see. We may even be able to speculate to some extent on patterns of infectious disease in the past. The possibilities are extraordinary, and it wouldn't be exaggerating to say that this is the most exciting time in the history of evolutionary biology since Darwin published *On the Origin of Species.*

Summary

The topics covered in this chapter relate to discoveries made after Darwin and Wallace described the fundamentals of natural selection. But all the issues presented here are basic to an understanding of biological evolution, adaptation, and human variation.

Cells are the fundamental units of life, and in multicellular organisms, there are basically two types. Somatic cells make up body tissues, while gametes (eggs and sperm) are reproductive cells that transmit genetic information from parents to offspring.

Genetic information is contained in the DNA molecule, found in the nuclei of cells. The DNA molecule is capable of replication, or making copies of itself. Replication makes it possible for daughter cells to receive a full complement of DNA (contained in chromosomes).

DNA also controls protein synthesis by directing the cell to arrange amino acids in the proper sequence for each particular type of protein. Also involved in the process of protein synthesis is another, similar molecule called RNA.

There are many genes that regulate the function of other genes. One class of regulatory genes, the homeobox genes, direct the development of the body plan. Other regulatory genes turn genes on and off.

There are also many segments of DNA that don't code for protein production, and much of their function is unknown. Some of these noncoding sequences, called introns, are contained within genes, and these are initially transcribed into mRNA but are then deleted before the mRNA leaves the cell nucleus.

Cells multiply by dividing, and during cell division, DNA is visible under a microscope in the form of chromosomes. In humans, there are 46 chromosomes (23 pairs). If the full complement isn't precisely distributed to succeeding generations of cells, there may be serious consequences.

Somatic cells divide during growth or tissue repair or to replace old, or dead cells. Somatic cell division is called mitosis. A cell divides one time to produce two daughter cells, each possessing a full and identical set of chromosomes. Sex cells are produced when specialized cells in the ovaries and testes divide during meiosis. Unlike mitosis, meiosis is characterized by two divisions that produce four non-identical daughter cells, each containing only half the amount of DNA (23 chromosomes) that's carried by the original cell.

WHY IT MATTERS

You may be wondering why it's important to compare human genes with those of other species. Actually, there are countless reasons for this kind of research. The latest developments in assessing the complete genetic sequences of chimpanzees and humans have confirmed the many similarities in genes that code for proteins, but they also show many previously unanticipated differences in sequences that *don't* code for proteins. Also, research has shown how tiny differences in protein-coding sequences may explain why humans are susceptible to diseases like cholera, malaria, and influenza while chimpanzees apparently are not. For example, the human form of a molecule called sialic acid differs from the chimpanzee molecule by a single oxygen atom (Varki, 2000). The chimpanzee version of the sialic acid gene is the one found in other mammals, so it's been suggested that the human sialic acid gene probably evolved after the chimpanzee and human lines split (see Chapter 8).

Sialic acid serves as a binding site for microorganisms that cause diseases such as cholera, malaria, and some forms of influenza (Muchmore, Diaz, and Varki, 1998), and the discovery of this genetic difference may lead to treatments for these diseases. It's also an important reminder that even one genetic difference between humans and chimpanzees can have an extensive and as yet unforeseen impact. Without full knowledge of the gene sequences of humans, chimpanzees, and other animals, we wouldn't be aware of these tiny differences that may have huge impacts on individual health, growth, and development.

Critical Thinking Questions

1   We only briefly touched on the topic of recombinant DNA technologies. From what we said and from things you've heard elsewhere, what is your view on this important topic? Are you generally in favor of most of the goals of recombinant DNA research? What are your objections?

2   Before reading this chapter, were you aware that the DNA in your body is structurally the same as in all other organisms? Do you see this fact as having potential to clarify some of the many questions we still have regarding biological evolution? Why?

3   Do you think proteins are exactly the same in all species? If not, how do you think they would differ in terms of their composition, and why might these differences be important to physical anthropologists?

CHAPTER 4

Heredity and Evolution

ORIGIN OF SPECIES

DARWIN

LONDON
JOHN MURRAY

Introduction

Have you ever had a cat with five, six, or even seven toes? Even if you haven't, you may have seen one, because it's fairly common in cats. Maybe you've known someone with an extra finger or toe, because it's not unheard of in people. Anne Boleyn, mother of England's Queen Elizabeth I and the first of Henry VIII's wives to lose her head, apparently had an extra little finger. (Of course, this had nothing to do with her early demise—that's another story.)

Having extra digits (fingers and toes) is called *polydactyly,* and it's fairly certain that one of Anne Boleyn's parents was also polydactylous. It's also likely that any polydactylous cat has a parent with extra toes. But how do we know this? Actually, it's fairly simple. We know this because polydactyly is a Mendelian characteristic, meaning that it's one of many characteristics that's inherited according to one of the principles discovered almost 150 years ago by a monk named Gregor Mendel (Fig. 4-1).

For at least 10,000 years, people have raised domesticated plants and animals. However, it wasn't until the twentieth century that scientists understood *how* selective breeding could increase the frequency of desirable traits in domestic plants and animals. From the time ancient Greek philosophers considered the question of how traits were inherited until well into the nineteenth century, one predominant belief was that characteristics of offspring resulted from the *blending* of parental traits. Blending supposedly occurred because of certain particles found in every part of the body. These particles contained miniature versions of the body part (limbs, organs, etc.) they came from, and they traveled through the blood to the reproductive organs and ultimately blended with particles of another individual during reproduction. There were variations on this theme, and numerous scholars, including Charles Darwin, adhered to some aspects of the theory.

The Genetic Principles Discovered by Mendel

It wasn't until Gregor Mendel (1822–1884) considered the question of heredity that it began to be resolved. Mendel was living in an abbey in what is now the Czech Republic. At the time he began his research, he had already studied botany, physics, and mathematics at the University of Vienna, and he had also performed various

Raychel Ciemma and Precision Graphics

FIGURE 4-1
Portrait of Gregor Mendel.

Click!

Go to the following media resources for interactive activities, more information, and study materials on topics covered in this chapter:

- Anthropology Resource Center
- Student Companion Website for *Essentials of Physical Anthropology,* Seventh Edition
- Online Virtual Laboratories for Physical Anthropology CD-ROM, Fourth Edition
- Basic Genetics for Anthropology CD-ROM 2.0: Principles and Applications

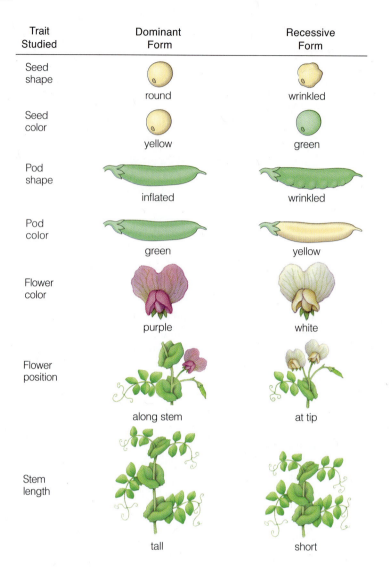

Trait Studied	Dominant Form	Recessive Form
Seed shape	round	wrinkled
Seed color	yellow	green
Pod shape	inflated	wrinkled
Pod color	green	yellow
Flower color	purple	white
Flower position	along stem	at tip
Stem length	tall	short

FIGURE 4-2
The traits Mendel studied in peas.

experiments in the monastery gardens. These experiments led him to investigate the ways that physical traits, such as color or height, could be expressed in plant **hybrids.**

Mendel worked with garden peas, concentrating on seven different traits, each of which could be expressed two ways (Fig. 4-2). We want to emphasize that we discuss Mendel's pea experiments only to illustrate the basic rules of inheritance. The principles Mendel discovered apply to all biological organisms, including humans.

Segregation

Mendel called the plants he used in the first cross the P (parental) generation, and in the first stage of the experiment, he crossed tall plants with short ones. But the hybrid offspring of the P generation (called the F_1 generation) weren't intermediate in height, as blending theories of inheritance would have predicted. Instead, they were all tall (Fig. 4-3).

Next, Mendel allowed the F_1 plants to self-fertilize and produce a second generation (the F_2 generation). But this time, only approximately ¾ of the offspring were tall, and the remaining ¼ were short. One expression of the trait (in this case, plant height) had completely disappeared in the F_1 generation and then reappeared in the F_2 generation. Moreover, the expression that was present in all the F_1 plants was more common in the F_2 plants, occurring in a ratio of approximately 3:1. (For every three tall plants there was one short plant.)

hybrids Offspring of parents who differ from one another with regard to certain traits or certain aspects of genetic makeup; heterozygotes.

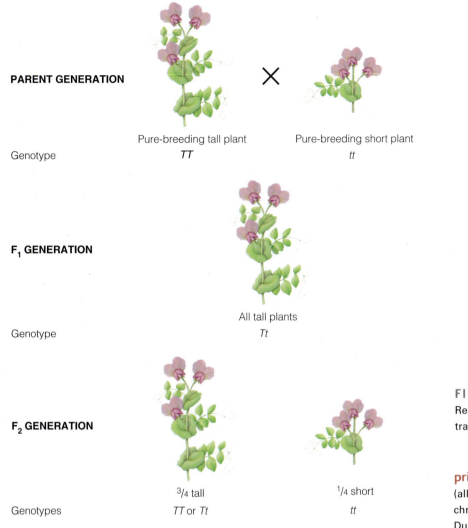

PARENT GENERATION

Genotype

Pure-breeding tall plant
TT

Pure-breeding short plant
tt

F₁ GENERATION

Genotype

All tall plants
Tt

F₂ GENERATION

Genotypes

³/₄ tall
TT or *Tt*

¹/₄ short
tt

FIGURE 4–3
Results of crosses when only one trait at a time is considered.

These results suggested that different expressions of a trait were controlled by discrete *units* (we would call them genes), which occurred in pairs, and that offspring inherited one unit from each parent. Mendel realized that the members of a pair of units that controlled a trait somehow separated into different sex cells and were again united with another member during fertilization of the egg. This is Mendel's *first principle of inheritance*, known as the **principle of segregation.**

Today we know that meiosis explains Mendel's principle of segregation. You will remember that during meiosis, paired chromosomes, and the genes they carry, separate from each other and are distributed to different gametes. However, in the zygote, the full complement of chromosomes is restored, and both members of each chromosome pair are present in the offspring.

Dominance and Recessivenes

Mendel also realized that the expression that was absent in the F₁ plants hadn't actually disappeared at all. It had remained present, but somehow was masked and couldn't be expressed. Mendel described the trait that seemed to be lost as "**recessive**," and he called the expressed trait "**dominant.**" Thus, the important principles of *dominance* and *recessiveness* were developed, and today they're still important concepts in the field of genetics.

As you already know, one definition of a gene is a segment of DNA that directs the production of a specific protein, part of a protein, or any functional product.

principle of segregation Genes (alleles) occur in pairs (because chromosomes occur in pairs). During gamete production, the members of each gene pair separate, so that each gamete contains one member of each pair. During fertilization, the full number of chromosomes is restored, and members of gene or allele pairs are reunited.

recessive Describing a trait that isn't expressed in heterozygotes; also refers to the allele that governs the trait. For a recessive allele to be expressed, there must be two copies of it (i.e., the individual must be homozygous).

dominant Describing a trait governed by an allele that can be expressed in the presence of another, different allele (i.e., in heterozygotes). Dominant alleles prevent the expression of recessive alleles in heterozygotes. (This is the definition of *complete* dominance.)

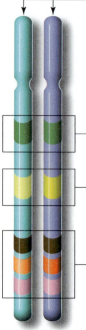

Members of a pair of chromosomes, one from a male parent and its partner from a female parent

Gene locus. The location for a specific gene on a specific type of chromosome

Pair of alleles. Although they influence the same characteristic, their DNA varies slightly, so they produce somewhat different expressions of the same trait.

Three pairs of alleles (at three loci on this pair of homologous chromosomes). Note that at two loci the alleles are identical (homozygous), and at one locus they are different (heterozygous).

FIGURE 4–4

As this diagram illustrates, alleles are located at the same locus on paired chromosomes, but they aren't always identical. For the sake of simplicity, they are shown here on single-stranded chromosomes.

locus (*pl.*, loci) (lo´-kus, lo-sigh´) The position on a chromosome where a given gene occurs. The term is sometimes used interchangeably with *gene,* but this usage is technically incorrect.

alleles Alternate forms of a gene. Alleles occur at the same locus on partner chromosomes and thus govern the same trait. However, because they are slightly different, their action may result in different expressions of that trait. The term is sometimes used synonymously with *gene.*

homozygous Having the same allele at the same locus on both members of a chromosome pair.

heterozygous Having different alleles at the same locus on members of a chromosome pair.

Furthermore, the location of a gene on a chromosome is its **locus** (*pl.,* loci). At many genetic loci, however, there are more than one possible form of the gene, and these variations of genes at specific loci are called **alleles** (Fig. 4-4). Put simply, alleles are different versions of a gene, each of which can direct the cell to produce a slightly modified form of the same protein and, ultimately, a different expression of the trait.

As it turns out, plant height in garden peas is controlled by two different alleles at the same genetic locus. (We'll call it the *height locus.*) The allele that specifies tall is dominant to the allele for short. (It's worth mentioning that height isn't controlled this way in all plants.) In Mendel's experiments, all the parent (P) plants had two copies of the same allele, either dominant or recessive, depending on whether they were tall or short. When two copies of the same allele are present, the individual is said to be **homozygous.** Thus, all the tall P plants were homozygous for the dominant allele, and all the short P plants were homozygous for the recessive allele. (This explains why tall plants crossed with tall plants produced only tall offspring, and short plants crossed with short plants produced all short offspring. All the plants in the P generation lacked genetic variation at the height locus. However, all the F_1 plants (hybrids) inherited one allele from each parent plant (one tall allele and one short allele). Therefore, they all inherited two different alleles at the height locus. Individuals that have two different alleles at a locus are **heterozygous.**

Figure 4-3 illustrates the crosses that Mendel initially performed. (Letters that represent alleles or genes are conventionally italicized.) Uppercase letters refer to dominant alleles (or dominant traits), and lowercase letters refer to recessive alleles (or recessive traits). Therefore,

T = the allele for tallness
t = the allele for shortness

The same symbols are combined to describe an individual's actual genetic makeup, or **genotype.** The term *genotype* can be used to refer to an organism's entire genetic makeup or to the alleles at a specific genetic locus. Thus, the genotypes of the plants in Mendel's experiments were

TT = homozygous tall plants
Tt = heterozygous tall plants
tt = homozygous short plants

Figure 4-5 is a *Punnett square.* It demonstrates the different ways alleles can be combined when the F_1 plants are self-fertilized to produce an F_2 generation. Therefore, the figure shows all the *genotypes* that are possible in the F_2 generation, and statistically speaking, it demonstrates that we would expect ¼ of the F_2 plants to be homozygous dominant (TT), ½ to be heterozygous (Tt), and the remaining ¼ to be homozygous recessive (tt).

The Punnett square also shows the proportions of F_2 **phenotypes,** the observed physical manifestations of genes, illustrating why Mendel saw approximately three tall plants for every short plant in the F_2 generation. You can see that ¼ of the F_2 plants are tall because they have the TT genotype. Furthermore, an additional ½, which are heterozygous (Tt), are also tall because T is dominant to t and so it's expressed in the phenotype. The remaining ¼ are homozygous recessive (tt), and they're short because no dominant allele is present. It's important to note that the *only* way a recessive allele can be expressed is if it occurs with another recessive allele, that is, if the individual is homozygous recessive at the particular locus in question.

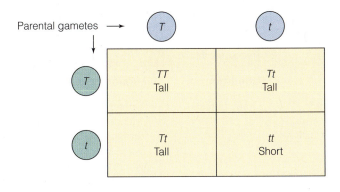

Parental gametes →

	T	t
T	TT Tall	Tt Tall
t	Tt Tall	tt Short

FIGURE 4-5
Punnett square representing possible genotypes and phenotypes and their proportions in the F_2 generation. The circles across the top and at the left of the Punnett square represent the gametes of the F_1 parents. The four squares illustrate that ¼ of the F_2 plants can be expected to be homozygous tall (*TT*); another ½ also can be expected to be tall but will be heterozygous (*Tt*); and the remaining ¼ can be expected to be short (*tt*). Thus, ¾ can be expected to be tall and ¼ to be short."

Independent Assortment

Mendel also demonstrated that different characteristics aren't necessarily inherited together by showing that plant height and seed color are independent of each other. That is, any tall pea plant had a 50-50 chance of producing either yellow or green peas. This relationship, called the **principle of independent assortment,** indicates that the units (genes) that code for different traits (in this example, plant height and seed color) assort independently of each other during gamete formation. Today we know that this happens because the genes that control plant height and seed color are located on different, nonpartner chromosomes, and during meiosis, the chromosomes travel to newly forming cells independently of one another in a process called **random assortment.**

But if Mendel had used just *any* two traits, his results would have been different at least some of the time. Genes on the same chromosome aren't independent of each other, and they usually stay together during meiosis. While Mendel didn't know about chromosomes, he was certainly aware that all characteristics weren't independent of one another in the F_2 generation. Therefore, he reported only on those traits that did in fact illustrate independent assortment, which is what he was interested in.

In 1866, Mendel's results were published, but the methodology and statistical nature of the research were beyond the thinking of the time, and their significance was overlooked and unappreciated. However, by the end of the nineteenth century, several investigators had made important contributions to the understanding of chromosomes and cell division. These discoveries paved the way for the acceptance of Mendel's work in 1900, when three different groups of scientists came across his paper. Regrettably, Mendel had died 16 years earlier and never saw his work vindicated.

Mendelian Inheritance in Humans

Mendelian traits, also called *discrete traits,* are controlled by alleles at only one genetic locus (or, in some cases, two or more very closely linked loci). The most comprehensive listing of Mendelian traits in humans is V. A. McKusick's (1998) *Mendelian Inheritance in Man,* first published in 1965 and now in its twelfth edition. This volume, as well as its continuously updated Internet version, *Online Mendelian Inheritance in Man* (www.ncbi.nlm.nih.gov/omim/), currently lists more than 18,000 human characteristics known or believed to be inherited according to Mendelian principles.

Although there are some Mendelian characteristics that have readily visible phenotypic expressions, most don't. The majority of Mendelian traits are biochemical in nature, and many genetic disorders (some of which do produce visible abnormalities) result from harmful alleles inherited in Mendelian fashion (Table 4-1). So if it seems like textbooks overly emphasize genetic disease in discussions of Mendelian traits, it's because many of the known Mendelian characteristics are the results of harmful alleles.

genotype The genetic makeup of an individual. Genotype can refer to an organism's entire genetic makeup or to the alleles at a particular locus.

phenotypes The observable or detectable physical characteristics of an organism; the detectable expressions of genotypes.

principle of independent assortment The distribution of one pair of alleles into gametes does not influence the distribution of another pair. The genes controlling different traits are inherited independently of one another.

random assortment The chance distribution of chromosomes to daughter cells during meiosis; along with recombination, a source of variation resulting from meiosis.

Mendelian traits Characteristics that are influenced by alleles at only one genetic locus. Examples include many blood types, such as ABO. Many genetic disorders, including sickle-cell anemia and Tay-Sachs disease, are also Mendelian traits.

TABLE 4.1	Some Mendelian Traits in Humans		
Dominant Traits		**Recessive Traits**	
Condition	**Manifestations**	**Condition**	**Manifestations**
Achondroplasia	Dwarfism due to growth defects involving the long bones of the arms and legs; trunk and head size usually normal.	Cystic fibrosis	Among the most common genetic (Mendelian) disorders among European Americans; abnormal secretions of the exocrine glands, with pronounced involvement of the pancreas; most patients develop obstructive lung disease. Until the recent development of new treatments, only about half of all patients survived to early adulthood.
Brachydactyly	Shortened fingers and toes.		
Familial hyper-cholesterolemia	Elevated cholesterol levels and cholesterol plaque deposition; a leading cause of heart disease, with death frequently occurring by middle age.		
Neurofibromatosis	Symptoms range from the appearance of abnormal skin pigmentation to large tumors resulting in severe deformities; can, in extreme cases, lead to paralysis, blindness, and death.	Tay-Sachs disease	Most common among Ashkenazi Jews; degeneration of the nervous system beginning at about 6 months of age; lethal by age 2 or 3 years.
		Phenylketonuria (PKU)	Inability to metabolize the amino acid phenylalanine; results in mental retardation if left untreated during childhood; treatment involves strict dietary management and some supplementation.
Marfan syndrome	The eyes and cardiovascular and skeletal systems are affected; symptoms include greater than average height, long arms and legs, eye problems, and enlargement of the aorta; death due to rupture of the aorta is common. Abraham Lincoln may have had Marfan syndrome.		
		Albinism	Inability to produce normal amounts of the pigment melanin; results in very fair, untannable skin, light blond hair, and light eyes; may also be associated with vision problems. (There is more than one form of albinism.)
Huntington disease	Progressive degeneration of the nervous system accompanied by dementia and seizures; age of onset variable but commonly between 30 and 40 years.		
		Sickle-cell anemia	Abnormal form of hemoglobin (HbS) that results in collapsed red blood cells, blockage of capillaries, reduced blood flow to organs, and, without treatment, death.
Camptodactyly	Malformation of the hands whereby the fingers, usually the little finger, is permanently contracted.		
Hypodontia of upper lateral incisors	Upper lateral incisors are absent or only partially formed (peg-shaped). Pegged incisors are a partial expression of the allele.	Thalassemia	A group of disorders characterized by reduced or absent alpha or beta chains in the hemoglobin molecule; results in severe anemia and, in some forms, death.
Cleft chin	Dimple or depression in the middle of the chin; less prominent in females than in males.	Absence of permanent dentition	Failure of the permanent dentition to erupt. The primary dentition is not affected.
PTC tasting	The ability to taste the bitter substance phenylthiocarbamide (PTC). Tasting thresholds vary, suggesting that alleles at another locus may also exert an influence.		

Blood groups, such as the ABO system, provide some of the best examples of Mendelian traits in humans. The ABO system is governed by three alleles, *A, B,* and *O,* found at the ABO locus on the ninth chromosome.* These alleles determine a person's ABO blood type by coding for the production of molecules called **antigens**

antigens Large molecules found on the surface of cells. Several different loci govern various antigens on red and white blood cells.

* Human chromosomes are numbered in order of size of the autosomes (1 through 22) plus X and Y.

TABLE 4.2	ABO Genotypes and Associated Phenotypes	
Genotype	**Antigens on Red Blood Cells**	**ABO Blood Type (Phenotype)**
AA, AO	A	A
BB, BO	B	B
AB	A and B	AB
OO	None	O

on the surface of red blood cells. If only antigen A is present, the blood type (phenotype) is A; if only B is present, the blood type is B; if both are present, the blood type is AB; and when neither is present, the blood type is O (Table 4-2).

Dominance and recessiveness are clearly illustrated by the ABO system. The *O* allele is recessive to both *A* and *B;* therefore, if a person has type O blood, he or she must be have two copies of the *O* allele. However, since both *A* and *B* are dominant to *O,* an individual with blood type A can actually have one of two genotypes: *AA* or *AO.* The same is true of type B, which results from the genotypes *BB* and *BO* (see Table 4-2). However, type AB presents a slightly different situation and is an example of **codominance.**

Codominance is seen when a person has two different alleles (that is, they're heterozygous); but instead of one allele having the ability to mask the expression of the other, the products of *both* are present in the phenotype. Therefore, when both *A* and *B* alleles are present, both A and B antigens can be detected on the surface of red blood cells.

A number of genetic disorders are caused by dominant alleles (see Table 4-1). This means that if a person inherits only one copy of a harmful dominant allele, the condition it causes will be present, regardless of the presence of a different, recessive allele on the partner chromosome.

Recessive conditions are commonly associated with the lack of a substance, usually an enzyme (see Table 4-1). For a person actually to have a recessive disorder, he or she must have *two* copies of the recessive allele that causes it. Heterozygotes who have only one copy of a harmful recessive allele are unaffected. Such individuals are frequently called *carriers* because, even though they don't actually have the recessive condition, they can still pass the allele that causes it to their children. (Remember, half their gametes will carry the recessive allele.) If their mate is also a carrier, then it's possible for them to have a child who will be homozygous for the allele, and that child will be affected. In fact, in a mating between two carriers, the risk of having an affected child is 25 percent (refer back to Fig. 4-5).

Misconceptions about Dominance and Recessiveness

Most people have the impression that dominance and recessiveness are all-or-nothing situations. This misconception especially pertains to recessive alleles, and the general view is that when these alleles occur in heterozygotes (carriers), they have no effect on the phenotype; that is, they are completely inactivated by the presence of another (dominant) allele. Certainly, this is how it appeared to Gregor Mendel.

However, various biochemical techniques available today show that many recessive alleles *do* influence the phenotype, although these effects aren't usually detectable through simple observation. In fact, many recessive alleles only reduce the amount of whatever gene product they influence but don't eliminate it entirely. Clearly, our perception of recessive alleles greatly depends on whether we examine them at the directly observable phenotypic level or the biochemical level.

codominance The expression of two alleles in heterozygotes. In this situation, neither allele is dominant or recessive; thus, both influence the phenotype.

There are also a number of misconceptions about dominant alleles. The majority of people see dominant alleles as somehow "stronger" or "better," and there is always the mistaken notion that dominant alleles are more common in populations because natural selection favors them. This idea undoubtedly stems from the label "dominant" and the connotations that the term carries. But in genetic usage, this view of dominance is misleading. Just think about it. If dominant alleles were always more common, then a majority of people would be affected by such conditions as achondroplasia and Marfan syndrome (see Table 4-1). But clearly, this isn't the case.

Previously held views of dominance and recessiveness were guided by available technologies; as genetic technologies continue to change, new theories emerge, and our perceptions will be further altered. (This another example of how new techniques and continued hypothesis testing can lead to a revision of hypotheses and theories.) In fact, although dominance and recessiveness will remain important factors in genetics, it's clear that the ways in which these concepts will be taught will be adapted to accommodate new discoveries.

Polygenic Inheritance

Mendelian traits are also referred to as *discrete*, or *discontinuous*, because their phenotypic expressions don't overlap; instead, they fall into clearly defined categories (Fig. 4-6a). For example, Mendel's pea plants were either short or tall, but none was intermediate in height. In the ABO system, the four phenotypes are completely distinct from one another; that is, there is no intermediate form between type A and type B. In other words, Mendelian traits don't show *continuous* variation.

However, many traits do have a wide range of phenotypic expressions that form a graded series. These are called **polygenic,** or *continuous,* traits (Fig. 4-6b and c). While Mendelian traits are governed by only one genetic locus, polygenic characteristics are influenced by alleles at two or more loci, and each locus makes a contribution to the phenotype. One of the most frequently cited examples of polygenic inheritance in humans is skin color; and the single most important factor influencing skin color is the amount of melanin, a pigment that is produced by cells in the skin.

Melanin production is influenced by several different loci, some of which have been identified (Lamason et al, 2005). The traditional view has been that each locus has at least two codominant alleles. Given that there are several loci and alleles involved, there are numerous ways in which these alleles can combine to influence skin color. If a person inherits 11 alleles coding for maximum pigmentation and only 1 for reduced melanin production, his or her skin will be very dark. Someone who inherits a higher proportion of reduced pigmentation alleles will have lighter skin. This is because in this system, as in some other polygenic systems, there is an *additive effect*. This means that each allele that codes for melanin production makes a contribution to increased amounts of melanin (although for some characteristics the contributions of the alleles aren't all equal). Likewise, each allele coding for reduced melanin production contributes to lighter skin. Therefore, the effect of multiple alleles at several loci, each making a contribution to individual phenotypes, is to produce continuous variation from very dark to very fair skin within the species. (Skin color is also discussed in Chapter 12.)

The additive effects of several alleles at different genes are still believed to play a critical role in human skin color. But a recent study by Lamason, et al (2005) showed that one single highly conserved gene with two alleles makes a significant (and perhaps disproportionate) contribution to the amount of melanin cells produce (see page 283 for further discussion). In addition, at least four other pigmentation genes have been identified and this is important because, until recently, none had been found. Thus, it appears that many long-standing questions about variation in human skin color may be answered in the foreseeable future.

polygenic Referring to traits that are influenced by genes at two or more loci. Examples of such traits are stature, skin color, and eye color. Many polygenic traits are also influenced by environmental factors.

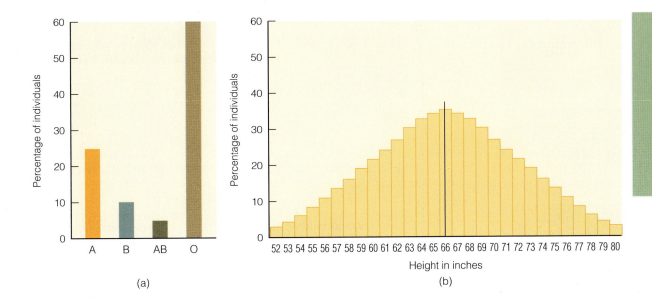

(a)   (b)

FIGURE 4-6

(a) This bar chart shows the discontinuous distribution of a Mendelian trait (ABO blood type) in a hypothetical population. Expression of the trait is described in terms of frequencies. (b) This histogram represents the continuous expression of a polygenic trait (height) in a large group of people. Notice that the percentage of extremely short or tall individuals is low; most people are closer to the mean, or average, height, represented by the vertical line at the center of the distribution. (c) A group of male students arranged according to height. The most common height is 70 inches (5'10"), which is the mean, or average, for this group.

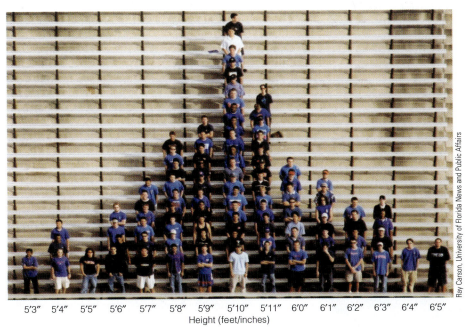

(c)

Ray Carson, University of Florida News and Public Affairs

Polygenic traits actually account for most of the readily observable phenotypic variation seen in humans, and they have traditionally served as a basis for racial classification (see Chapter 12). In addition to skin color, polygenic inheritance in humans is seen in hair color, height, stature, shape of the face, fingerprint pattern, and eye color (Fig. 4-7). Because they exhibit continuous variation, most polygenic traits can be measured on a scale composed of equal increments. For example, height (stature) is measured in feet and inches (or meters and centimeters). If one were to measure height in a large number of individuals, the distribution of measurements would continue uninterrupted from the shortest extreme to the tallest. That's what is meant by the term *continuous traits*.

Because polygenic traits can be measured, physical anthropologists treat them statistically. Although statistical analysis can be complicated, the use of simple summary statistics, such as the *mean* (average) or *standard deviation* (a measure of variation within a group), permits basic descriptions of, and comparisons between, populations. For example, one might be interested in average height in two different

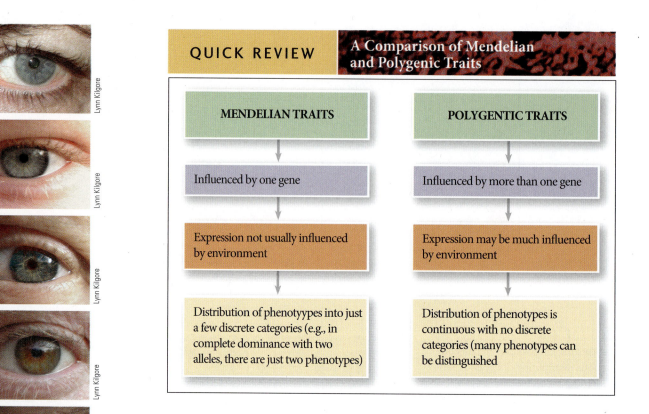

QUICK REVIEW A Comparison of Mendelian and Polygenic Traits

MENDELIAN TRAITS	POLYGENTIC TRAITS
Influenced by one gene	Influenced by more than one gene
Expression not usually influenced by environment	Expression may be much influenced by environment
Distribution of phenotyypes into just a few discrete categories (e.g., in complete dominance with two alleles, there are just two phenotypes)	Distribution of phenotypes is continuous with no discrete categories (many phenotypes can be distinguished

FIGURE 4-7
Examples of the continuous variation seen in human eye color.

populations and whether or not differences between the two are significant, and if so, why. (Incidentally, *all* physical traits measured and statistically treated in fossils are polygenic in nature.)

These particular statistical descriptions aren't possible with Mendelian traits simply because those traits can't be measured in the same way. But Mendelian characteristics can be described in terms of frequency within populations, and then we can compare groups for differences in prevalence. (For example, one population may have a high frequency of blood type A, while in another group, type A may be almost completely absent.) Also, Mendelian traits can be analyzed for mode of inheritance (dominant or recessive). Finally, for many Mendelian traits, the approximate or exact positions of genetic loci are known, and this makes it possible to examine the mechanisms and patterns of inheritance at these loci. This type of study isn't yet possible for polygenic traits because they're influenced by several genes and they can't yet be traced to specific loci.

Genetic and Environmental Factors

By now, you may have the impression that phenotypes are completely the expressions of genotypes, but that's not true. (Here the terms *genotype* and *phenotype* are used in a broader sense to refer to an individual's *entire* genetic makeup and *all* observable or detectable characteristics.) The genotype sets limits and potentials for development, but it also interacts with the environment, and many (but not all) aspects of the phenotype are influenced by this genetic-environmental interaction. Adult stature is a trait that's influenced by both genes and the environment. Even though maximum height is genetically determined, nutrition (an environmental factor) during childhood is also crucial. However, for many characteristics, it's not possible to identify the *specific* environmental components that influence the phenotype.

Mendelian traits are less likely to be influenced by environmental factors. For example, ABO blood type is determined at fertilization and remains fixed throughout the individual's lifetime, regardless of diet, exposure to ultraviolet radiation, temperature, and so on.

Mendelian and polygenic inheritance show different patterns of phenotypic variation. In the former, variation occurs in discrete categories, while in the latter, it's continuous. However, it's important to understand that even for polygenic characteristics, Mendelian principles still apply at individual loci. In other words, if a trait is influenced by six loci, each one of those loci may have two or more alleles, with some perhaps being dominant to others. It's the combined action of the alleles at all six loci, interacting with the environment, that produces the phenotype.

Mitochondrial Inheritance

Another component of inheritance involves the organelles called *mitochondria* (see p. 38). All cells contain several hundred of these oval-shaped structures that convert energy (derived from the breakdown of nutrients) to a form that can be used by the cell.

Each mitochondrion contains several copies of a ring-shaped DNA molecule, or chromosome. While *mitochondrial DNA (mtDNA)* is distinct from chromosomal DNA, its molecular structure and functions are the same. The entire molecule has been sequenced and is known to contain around 40 genes that direct the conversion of energy within the cell.

Mitochondrial DNA is subject to mutations just like nuclear DNA, and some mutations cause certain genetic disorders that result from impaired energy conversion. Importantly, animals of both sexes inherit all their mtDNA, and thus all mitochondrial traits, from their mothers. This is so because mitochondria are found only in a cell's cytoplasm, and while egg cells retain their cytoplasm, sperm cells lose theirs just prior to fertilization. Because mtDNA is inherited from only one parent, meiosis and recombination don't occur. This means that all the variation in mtDNA among individuals is caused by mutation, which makes mtDNA extremely useful for studying genetic change over time. So far, geneticists have used mutation rates in mtDNA to investigate evolutionary relationships between species; to trace ancestral relationships within the human lineage; and to study genetic variability among individuals and/or populations. While these techniques are still being refined, it's clear that we have a lot to learn from mtDNA.

Modern Evolutionary Theory

By the beginning of the twentieth century, the foundations for evolutionary theory had already been developed. Darwin and Wallace had described natural selection 40 years earlier, and the rediscovery of Mendelian genetics in 1900 contributed the other major component—a mechanism for inheritance. We might expect that these two basic contributions would have been combined into a consistent theory of evolution, but they weren't. For the first 30 years of the twentieth century, some scientists argued that mutation was the main factor in evolution, while others emphasized natural selection. What they really needed was a merger of the two views rather than an either-or situation; but this didn't happen until the mid-1930s.

The Modern Synthesis

Biologists working on mathematical models of evolutionary change in the late 1920s and early 1930s realized that mutation and natural selection weren't opposing processes and that both actually contributed to biological evolution. The two major foundations of the biological sciences had thus been brought together in what is called the Modern Synthesis. From such a "modern" (that is, the middle of the twentieth century onward) perspective, we define evolution as a two-stage process. These two stages are:

1. The production and redistribution of **variation** (inherited differences among organisms)
2. *Natural selection* acting on this variation, whereby inherited differences, or variation, among individuals differentially affect their ability to successfully reproduce.

A Current Definition of Evolution

As we discussed in Chapter 2, Darwin saw evolution as the gradual unfolding of new varieties of life from previous forms over long periods of time. Indeed, this is one result of the evolutionary process. But these long-term effects can come about only through the accumulation of many small genetic changes occurring over the generations. Today, we're able to demonstrate how evolution works by looking at some of the small genetic changes that occur between generations. From such a modern genetic perspective, we define evolution as *a change in* **allele frequency** *from one generation to the next.*

Allele frequencies are indicators of the genetic makeup of an interbreeding group of individuals, or **population.** To show how allele frequencies change, we use a simplified example of an inherited characteristic, again the ABO blood groups (see p. 62). (*Note:* There are several blood type systems, such as the Rh system, that are controlled by different genes than the ones that influence the ABO blood types.

Let's assume that the students in your anthropology class represent a population, an interbreeding group of individuals, and that we've determined the ABO blood type of each member. (To be considered a population, individuals must choose mates more often from *within* the group than from outside it. Obviously, your class won't meet this requirement, but we'll overlook this point.) The proportions of the *A, B,* and *O* alleles are the allele frequencies for this trait. If 50 percent of all the ABO alleles in your class are *A*, 40 percent are *B*, and 10 percent are *O*, then the frequencies of these alleles are *A* = .50, *B* = .40, and *O* = .10.

Since the frequencies for these alleles represent proportions of a total, it's obvious that allele frequencies can refer only to groups of individuals, or populations. Individuals don't have allele frequencies; they have either *A, B,* or *O* in any combination of two. Also, from conception onward, a person's genetic composition is fixed. If you start out with blood type A, you'll always have type A. Therefore, only a population can evolve over time; individuals can't.

Assume that 25 years from now, we calculate the frequencies of the ABO alleles for the children of our classroom population and find the following: *A* = .30, *B* = .40, and *O* = .30. We can see that the relative proportions have changed: *A* has decreased, *O* has increased, and *B* has remained the same. This wouldn't be a big deal, but in a biological sense, minor changes such as this constitute evolution. Over the short span of just a few generations, changes in the frequencies of inherited traits may be very small; but if they continue to happen, and particularly if they go in one direction as a result of natural selection, they can produce new adaptation and even new species.

Whether we are talking about the short-term effects (as in our classroom population) from one generation to the next, which is sometimes called **microevolution,** or the long-term effects through time, called speciation or **macroevolution,** the basic evolutionary mechanisms are similar. But how do allele frequencies change? Or, to put it another way, what causes evolution? As we've already said, evolution is a two-stage process. Genetic variation must first be produced by mutation, and then it can be acted on by natural selection.

---

variation (genetic) Inherited differences among individuals; the basis of all evolutionary change.

allele frequency In a population, the percentage of all the alleles at a locus accounted for by one specific allele.

population Within a species, a community of individuals where mates are usually found.

microevolution Small genetic changes that occur within a species. A human example is the variation seen in the different ABO blood types.

macroevolution Large-scale changes that occur in populations after many generations, such as the appearance of a new species (speciation).

Factors That Produce and Redistribute Variation

Mutation

You've already learned that a change in DNA is a type of mutation. A gene may exist in one of several alternative forms, which we've defined as alleles (*A, B,* or *O,* for example). If one allele changes to another, that is, if the gene itself is altered, a mutation has occurred. In fact, alleles are the results of mutation. Even the substitution of one single DNA base for another, called a *point mutation,* can cause the allele to change. But point mutations have to occur in sex cells if they're going to be important to the evolutionary process. This is because evolution is a change in allele frequencies *between* generations. If a mutation doesn't occur in a gamete, the individual will have it but won't pass it on to offspring. If, however, a genetic change occurs in the sperm or egg of one of the students in our classroom (*A* mutates to *B,* for instance), the offspring's blood type will be different from that of the parent, causing a minute shift in the allele frequencies of the next generation.

Actually, except in microorganisms, it would be rare to see evolution occurring by mutation alone. Mutation rates for any given trait are usually low, so we wouldn't really expect to see a mutation at the ABO locus in so small a population as your class. In larger populations, mutations might be observed in, say, 1 individual out of 10,000, but by themselves they would have little impact on allele frequencies. However, when mutation is combined with natural selection, evolutionary changes not only can occur, but they can occur more rapidly.

It's important to remember that mutation is the basic creative force in evolution, since it's the *only* way to produce *new* genes (that is, variation). Its role in the production of variation is key to the first stage of the evolutionary process.

Gene Flow

Gene flow is the exchange of genes between populations. The term *migration* is also sometimes used; but strictly speaking, migration means movement of people, whereas gene flow refers to the exchange of *genes* between groups, and this can only happen if the migrants interbreed. Also, even if individuals move temporarily and have offspring in the new population (thus leaving a genetic contribution), they don't necessarily remain in the population. For example, the children of U.S. soldiers and Vietnamese women represent gene flow, even though the fathers returned to their native population.

Human population movements (particularly in the last 500 years) have reached enormous proportions, and very few breeding isolates remain. However, significant population movements also took place in the past. Migration between populations has been a consistent feature of hominid evolution since the first dispersal of our genus, and gene flow between populations (even though sometimes limited) helps explain why, in the last million years, speciation has been rare.

An interesting example of how gene flow influences microevolutionary changes in modern human populations is seen in African Americans. African Americans in the United States are largely of West African descent, but there has also been considerable genetic admixture with European Americans. By measuring allele frequencies for specific genetic loci, we can estimate the amount of migration of European alleles into the African American gene pool. Data from northern and western U.S. cities (including New York, Detroit, and Oakland) have shown the migration rate (that is, the proportion of *non-*African genes in the African American gene pool) at 20 to 25 percent (Cummings, 2000). However, more restricted data from the southern United States (Charleston and rural Georgia) have suggested a lower degree of gene flow (4 to 11 percent).

gene flow Exchange of genes between populations.

Genetic Drift and Founder Effect

Genetic drift is the random factor in evolution, and it's a function of population size. *Drift occurs solely because the population is small,* and in small populations, alleles with low frequencies may, just by chance, not be passed on to offspring. If this happens, these alleles may completely disappear from the population.

A particular kind of genetic drift called **founder effect** is seen in many modern human and nonhuman populations. Founder effect can occur when a small band of "founders" leaves its parent group to live in a different area. Over time, a new population is established, and as long as mates are chosen only from within this population, all of its members will be descended from just a few individuals. Therefore, all the genes in the expanding group will have come from the original colonists. In such a case, an allele that was rare in the founders' parent population but was carried by even one of the founders can become common among the founders' descendants (Fig. 4-8).

Colonization isn't the only way founder effect can happen. Small founding groups may be a few survivors of a larger group that's been decimated by disaster (famine, war,

Time

A small population with considerable genetic variability. Note that the dark green and light blue alleles are less common than the other alleles.

After just a few generations, the population is approximately the same size, but genetic variation has been reduced. Both the dark green and blue alleles have been lost. Also, the red allele is less common and the frequency of the light green allele has increased.

Population size

(a)

Original population with considerable genetic variation

A small group leaves to colonize a new area, or a bottleneck occurs, so that population size decreases and genetic variation is reduced.

Population size is restored, but the dark green and purple alleles have been lost. The frequencies of the red and yellow alleles have also changed.

Population size

(b)

FIGURE 4-8

Small populations are subject to genetic drift where rare alleles can be lost because, just by chance, they weren't passed to offspring. Also, although more common alleles may not be lost, their frequencies may change for the same reason. (a) This diagram represents six alleles (different-colored dots) that occur at one genetic locus in a small population. You can see that in a fairly short period of time (three or four generations), rare alleles can be lost and genetic diversity consequently reduced. (b) This diagram illustrates founder effect, a form of genetic drift where diversity is lost because a large population is drastically reduced in size and consequently passes through a genetic "bottleneck." Founder effect also happens when a small group leaves the larger group and "founds" a new population elsewhere. (In this case, the group of founders is represented by the bottleneck.) Those individuals that survive (or the founders) and the alleles they carry represent only a sample of the variation that was present in the original population. And future generations, all descended from the survivors (founders), will therefore have less variability.

genetic drift Evolutionary changes—that is, changes in allele frequencies—produced by random factors. Genetic drift is a result of small population size.

founder effect A type of genetic drift in which allele frequencies are altered in small populations that are taken from, or are remnants of, larger populations.

or disease, for example). The small group of survivors becomes a founder population, possessing only a sample of all the alleles that were present in the original group.

As you can see, some alleles may be completely removed from a population's **gene pool** while others may become the only allele at a locus that previously had two or more. Whatever the cause, the outcome is a reduction of genetic diversity, and the allele frequencies of succeeding generations may be substantially different from those of the original, larger population. The loss of genetic diversity in this type of situation is called a *genetic bottleneck,* and the effects can be very detrimental to a species.

There are many known examples (both human and nonhuman) of species or populations that have passed through genetic bottlenecks. (In fact, many species are currently going through genetic bottlenecks.) Genetically, cheetahs (Fig. 4-9) are an extremely uniform species, and biologists believe that at some point in the past, these magnificent cats suffered a catastrophic decline in numbers. For reasons we don't know but that are related to the species-wide loss of numerous alleles, male cheetahs produce a high percentage of defective sperm compared to other cat species. Decreased reproductive potential, greatly reduced genetic diversity, and other factors (including human hunting) have combined to jeopardize the continued existence of this species. Other examples include California elephant seals, sea otters, and condors. Indeed, our own species is genetically uniform, compared to chimpanzees, and it appears that all modern human populations are the descendants of a few small groups (see Chapter 11).

Many examples of founder effect in human populations have been documented in small, usually isolated populations (such as island groups or small agricultural villages in New Guinea or South America). Even larger populations that are descended from fairly small groups of founders can show the effects of genetic drift many generations later. For example, French Canadians in Quebec, who currently number close to 6 million, are all descended from about 8,500 founders who left France during the sixteenth and seventeenth centuries. Because the genes carried by the initial founders represented only a sample of the gene pool from which they were derived, a number of alleles now occur in different frequencies from those of the current population of France. These differences include an increased presence of several harmful alleles, including those that cause some of the diseases listed in Table 4-1, such as cystic fibrosis, a variety of Tay-Sachs, thalassemia, and PKU (Scriver, 2001).

In small groups, drift plays an evolutionary role because fairly sudden fluctuations in allele frequency occur solely because of population size. Throughout much of human evolution (at least the last 4–5 million years), hominids probably lived in small groups, and drift would have had a significant impact. But even though genetic drift has caused evolutionary change in certain circumstances, its effects have been irregular. That's because drift isn't directional; that is, it doesn't consistently increase or decrease the frequency of a given allele. But by altering allele frequencies in small populations, drift can provide significantly greater opportunities for natural selection, the only truly directional force in evolution.

As we've seen, both gene flow and genetic drift can produce some evolutionary changes by themselves. However, these changes are usually *microevolutionary* ones; that is, they produce changes within species over the short term. To have the kind of evolutionary changes that ultimately result in entire new groups (for example, the diversification of the first primates or the appearance of the hominids), natural selection is necessary. But natural selection can't operate independently of the other evolutionary factors: mutation, gene flow, and genetic drift.

Recombination

In sexually reproducing species, both parents contribute genes to offspring, and the genetic information is reshuffled (or recombined) in every generation (see Chapter 3). By itself, recombination doesn't change allele frequencies (cause evolution). However, it does produce different combinations of genes that natural selection may be able to act on. In fact, the reshuffling of chromosomes during meiosis can produce literally trillions of gene combinations, making every human being genetically unique.

Lynn Kilgore

FIGURE 4-9
Cheetahs, like many other species, have passed through a genetic bottleneck. Consequently, as a species they have little genetic variation.

gene pool The total complement of genes shared by the reproductive members of a population.

Natural Selection Is Directional and Acts on Variation

The evolutionary factors just discussed: mutation, gene flow, genetic drift, and recombination, interact to produce variation and to distribute genes within and between populations. But there is no long-term *direction* to any of these factors. So how do populations adapt and evolve? The answer is natural selection, which causes **directional change** in allele frequencies. This means that natural selection can increase or decrease the frequency of certain alleles over time in ways that are beneficial in specific environmental settings. Remember that in the moth example on page 29, the increase in frequency of dark or light moths depended on environmental change. Such a functional shift in allele frequencies is what we mean by *adaptation*. If there are long-term environmental changes in a consistent direction, then allele frequencies should also shift gradually each generation.

In Chapter 2, we discussed the general principles underlying natural selection and gave some nonhuman examples. In humans, the best-documented example of natural selection involves *hemoglobin S*, an abnormal form of hemoglobin that results from a point mutation in the gene that produces part of the hemoglobin molecule (refer back to Fig. 3-6, p. 43, and to p. 278). Most people are homozygous for the Hb^A allele (Hb^A/Hb^A), and they produce normal hemoglobin. But people who inherit the Hb^S allele from both parents (Hb^S/Hb^S) produce no normal hemoglobin, and they have a very serious condition called **sickle-cell anemia.** People who have one copy of each allele (that is, they're heterozygotes with the Hb^A/Hb^S genotype) have a condition called *sickle-cell trait,* and although some of their hemoglobin is abnormal, enough of it is normal to enable them to function normally under most circumstances.

Sickle-cell anemia has numerous manifestations, but basically, the abnormal hemoglobin S reduces the ability of red blood cells to transport oxygen throughout the body. When people with sickle-cell anemia increase their body's demand for oxygen (for example, while exercising or traveling to high altitude), their red blood cells collapse and form a shape similar to a sickle (Fig. 4-10). Consequently, these cells can't carry adequate amounts of oxygen. What's more, they also clump together and block small capillaries, restricting blood flow and depriving vital organs of oxygen. Even with treatment, life expectancy in the United States today is less than 45 years for patients with sickle-cell anemia. Worldwide, sickle-cell anemia causes an estimated 100,000 deaths each year, and in the United States, approximately 40,000 to 50,000 individuals, mostly of African descent, suffer from this condition.

The Hb^S mutation occurs occasionally, and at pretty much the same rate in all human populations. In some populations, however, especially in western and central Africa, the Hb^S allele is more common than elsewhere, with frequencies as high as 20 percent. The Hb^S allele is also fairly common in parts of Greece and India (Fig. 4-11). Given the devastating effects of hemoglobin S in homozygotes, you may wonder why it's so common in some populations. It seems like natural selection would act to eliminate it, but it doesn't. The explanation for this situation can be summed up in one word: malaria.

Malaria is an infectious disease that currently kills an estimated 1 to 3 million people a year worldwide. It's caused by a single-celled parasitic organism that's transmitted to humans by mosquitoes. Very briefly, after an infected mosquito bite, these parasites invade red blood cells, where they obtain the oxygen they need to reproduce. The consequences of this infection include fever, chills, headache, nausea, vomiting, and, frequently, death. In parts of western and central Africa, where malaria is always present, the burden of the disease is borne by children, with as many as 50 to 75 percent of 2- to 9-year-olds being afflicted.

In the mid-twentieth century, the geographical correlation between malaria and the distribution of the sickle-cell allele (Hb^S) was the only evidence of a biological relationship between the two (Figs. 4-11 and 4-12). But now we know that people with sickle-cell trait have greater resistance to malaria than people who have only

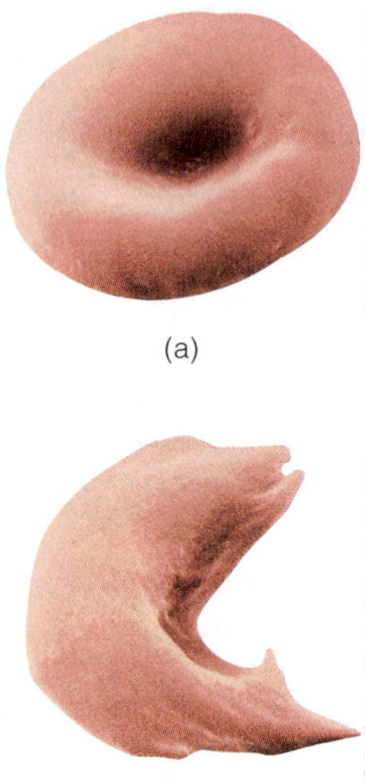

(a)

(b)

FIGURE 4-10

(a) Scanning electron micrograph of a normal, fully oxygenated red blood cell. (b) Scanning electron micrograph of a collapsed, sickle-shaped red blood cell that contains Hb^S.

directional change In a genetic sense, the nonrandom change in allele frequencies caused by natural selection. The change is directional because the frequencies of alleles consistently increase or decrease (they change in one direction), depending on environmental circumstances and the selective pressures involved.

sickle-cell anemia A severe inherited hemoglobin disorder in which red blood cells collapse when deprived of oxygen. It results from inheriting two copies of a mutant allele. This mutation is caused by a single base substitution in the DNA.

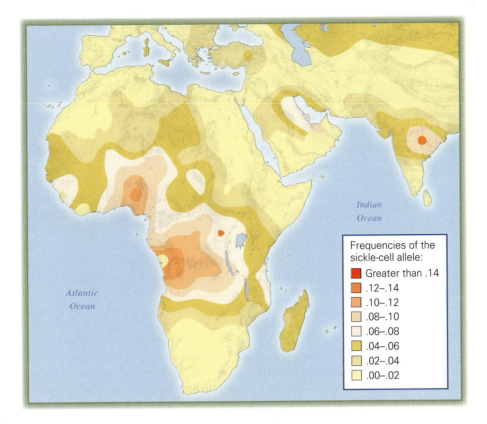

FIGURE 4-11
The distribution of the sickle-cell allele in the Old World.

normal hemoglobin. This is because people with sickle-cell trait have some red blood cells that contain hemoglobin S, and these cells don't provide a suitable environment for the malarial parasite. In other words, having some hemoglobin S is beneficial because it affords some protection from malaria. So, in malarial areas, malaria acts as a selective agent that favors the heterozygous phenotype, since individuals with sickle-cell trait have higher reproductive success than those with normal hemoglobin, who may die of malaria. But selection for heterozygotes means that the Hb^S allele will be maintained in the population. Thus, there will always be some people with sickle-cell anemia, and they, of course, have the lowest reproductive success, since without treatment, most die before reaching adulthood.

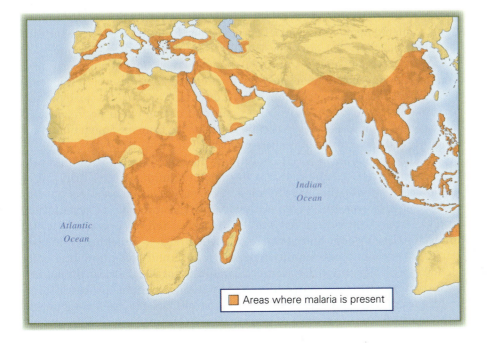

FIGURE 4-12
The distribution of malaria in the Old World.

Review of Genetics and Evolutionary Factors

In this chapter, we discussed how genetic information is passed from individuals in one generation to those in the next. We also reviewed evolutionary theory, emphasizing the crucial role of natural selection. The different levels (molecular, cellular, individual, and populational) are different components of the evolutionary process, and they're related to each other in a way that can eventually produce evolutionary change. A step-by-step example will make this clear.

We begin with a population in which almost everyone has the same type of hemoglobin, hemoglobin A. Therefore, there's almost no variation regarding this trait, and without some source of new variation, evolution isn't possible. But a few individuals in each generation carry a spontaneous mutation that changes just one DNA base in the Hb^A gene. Furthermore, this single base substitution (which actually creates a new allele) in the DNA sequence slightly alters the protein product (the hemoglobin molecule) and ultimately the phenotype of the individual. But for the mutated allele to be passed on to succeeding offspring, it must be present in the gametes. Moreover, for a mutation to have any evolutionary potential, it must be transmitted to offspring.

Once a mutation has occurred, it will be contained within a chromosome, which, along with other chromosomes, will be passed to offspring. We can see the results of this process by looking at phenotypes (traits) in individuals, and the mode of inheritance is described simply by Mendel's principle of segregation. If a person has a mutation in only one member of a pair of alleles, which in turn occur on paired chromosomes, there is a 50 percent chance that the mutation will be passed on to each offspring produced.

But what does all this have to do with *evolution?* To repeat an earlier definition, evolution is a change in allele frequency in a *population* from one generation to the next. The key point here is that we are considering populations, and it's the populations that may change over time.

We know whether allele frequencies have changed in a population where sickle-cell hemoglobin is found by determining the percentage of individuals with the sickling allele (Hb^S) versus those with the normal allele (Hb^A). If the relative proportions of these alleles change with time, evolution has occurred. But it's also important to know why. There are several possible explanations. First, the only way the new Hb^S allele could have arisen is by mutation, and we've shown how this can happen in a single individual. But this isn't an evolutionary change, since in a relatively large population, the alteration of one individual's genes won't change the allele frequencies of the entire population. Somehow, this new allele must *spread* in the population.

One way this can happen is in a small population, where mutations in one or just a few individuals and their offspring may indeed alter the overall frequency quite quickly. This would be genetic drift. As discussed, drift acts in small populations, where random factors may cause significant changes in allele frequencies. Consequently, some alleles may be completely removed from the population, while others may end up being the only allele at a particular locus.

In the course of human evolution, drift has probably played a significant role, and it's important to remember that at this microevolutionary level, drift and/or gene flow can (and will) produce evolutionary change, even in the absence of natural selection. However, *directional* evolutionary trends can only be sustained by natural selection. The way this has worked in the past and still operates today (as with sickle-cell) is through differential reproduction. That is, individuals who carry a particular allele or combination of alleles produce more offspring than other individuals with different alleles. Hence, the frequency of a new allele in the population increases slowly from generation to generation. When this process is compounded over hundreds of generations for numerous loci, the result is significant evolutionary change. The levels of organization in the evolutionary process are summarized in Table 4-3.

TABLE 4.3	Levels of Organization in the Evolutionary Process		
Evolutionary Factor	**Level**	**Evolutionary Process**	**Technique of Study**
Mutation	DNA	Storage of genetic information; ability to replicate; influences phenotype by production of proteins	Biochemistry, electron microscope, recombinant DNA
Mutation	Chromosomes	A vehicle for packaging and transmitting genetic material (DNA)	Light or electron microscope
Recombination (sex cells only)	Cell	The basic unit of life that contains the chromosomes and divides for growth and for production of sex cells	Light or electron microscope
Natural selection	Organism	The unit, composed of cells, that reproduces and which we observe for phenotypic traits	Visual study, biochemistry
Drift, gene flow	Population	A group of interbreeding organisms; changes in allele frequencies between generations; it's the population that evolves	Statistical analysis

Summary

We've seen how Gregor Mendel discovered the principles of segregation, independent assortment, and dominance and recessiveness by doing experiments with pea plants. Although the field of genetics progressed dramatically during the twentieth century, the concepts first put forth by Gregor Mendel remain the basis of our current knowledge of how traits are inherited.

Basic Mendelian principles are applied to the study of the various modes of inheritance we are familiar with today. The most important factor in all the Mendelian modes of inheritance is the role of segregation of chromosomes, and the alleles they carry, during meiosis.

Building on fundamental nineteenth-century contributions by Charles Darwin and the rediscovery of Mendel's work in 1900, advances in genetics throughout the twentieth century contributed to contemporary evolutionary thought. In particular, the combination of natural selection with Mendel's principles of inheritance and experimental evidence concerning the nature of mutation have all been synthesized into a modern understanding of evolutionary change, appropriately termed the Modern Synthesis. In this, the contemporary theory of evolution, evolutionary change is seen as a two-stage process. The first stage is the production and redistribution of variation. The second stage is the process whereby natural selection acts on the accumulated genetic variation.

Mutation is crucial to all evolutionary change because it's the only source of completely new genetic material (that is, new alleles, which increase variation). In addition, the factors of recombination, genetic drift, and gene flow redistribute variation within individuals (recombination), within populations (genetic drift), and between populations (gene flow).

Natural selection is the central determining factor that influences the long-term direction of evolutionary change. How natural selection works can best be explained as differential net reproductive success, or how successful individuals are, compared to others, in leaving offspring to succeeding generations. The detailed history of the evolutionary spread of the sickle-cell allele provides the best-documented example of natural selection among recent human populations. It must be remembered that evolution is an integrated process, and this chapter concluded with a discussion of how the various evolutionary factors can be integrated into a single comprehensive view of evolutionary change.

WHY IT MATTERS

As you learned on page 62, many human disorders are caused by mutations in genes (alleles) at one locus. This has practical implications for many of us who may eventually have to make important life decisions due to a family history of genetic disease. Obviously, the more we know about Mendelian disorders, the better prepared we are to make such decisions.

Huntington disease is a neurological disorder that affects approximately 1 out of every 100,000 people. It's caused by a dominant mutation on chromosome 4. Since the disease is a dominant trait, you will eventually have it if you inherit only one copy of the mutant allele. Also, a person who has the allele has a 50-50 chance of passing it on to each child he or she has.

In Huntington disease, brain cells are destroyed. Symptoms include erratic behavior, confusion, uncontrollable movement, loss of cognitive abilities, and eventually death. There is no cure and tragically, the symptoms of most forms of Huntington disease don't appear until a person is between the ages of 35 and 45. By this time most people who want children have already had them and may have unknowingly passed the mutant allele on to their offspring.

There is a test for Huntington disease, and people who have a parent with symptoms can learn whether or not they themselves have inherited the disease. Certainly, anyone who has such a parent should be tested before they, in turn, have children. But just suppose that one of your parents has been diagnosed with Huntington disease and you've already decided not to have children. What would you do? Would you be tested? Because you know about Mendelian traits, you know that you have a 50 percent chance of having the allele for Huntington. If you have the test, you will either be greatly relieved by the results or you'll have to deal with the knowledge that inevitably you'll develop a severe neurological disease that ultimately will kill you. It's just this kind of scenario that makes it important for people to be at least minimally informed about how traits are inherited. After all, every one of us has inherited many detrimental genes.

Critical Thinking Questions

1. If two people with blood type A, both with the *AO* genotype, have children, what *proportion* of these children would be expected to have blood type O? Why? Can these two parents have a child with AB blood? Why or why not?

2. After having read this chapter, do you understand evolutionary processes more completely? What questions do you still have?

3. Sickle-cell anemia is frequently described as affecting only Africans or people of African descent; it is construed as a "racial" disease that doesn't affect other populations. How would you explain to someone that this view is incorrect?

4. Give some examples of how selection, gene flow, genetic drift, and mutation have acted on populations or species in the past. Try to think of at least one human and one nonhuman example. Why do you think genetic drift might be important today to endangered species?

CHAPTER 5

Macroevolution: Processes of Vertebrate and Mammalian Evolution

ORIGIN
OF
SPECIES
DARWIN

LONDON
JOHN MURRAY

© Russell L. Ciochon,

*In what ways do humans
fit into a biological
continuum (as
vertebrates and
mammals)?*

Introduction

Many people think of paleontology as pretty boring and only interesting to overly serious academics. But have you ever been to a natural history museum—or perhaps to one of the larger, more elaborate toy stores? If so, you may have seen a full-size mock-up of *Tyrannosaurus rex,* one that might even have moved its head and arms and screamed threateningly. These displays are usually encircled by flocks of noisy children who seem anything but bored.

The study of the history of life on earth is full of mystery and adventure. The bits and pieces of fossils are the remains of once living, breathing animals (some of them extremely large and dangerous). Searching for these fossils in remote corners of the globe is not a task for the faint of heart. Piecing together the tiny clues and ultimately reconstructing what *Tyrannosaurus rex* (or, for that matter, a small, 50-million-year-old primate) looked like and how it might have behaved is really much like detective work. Sure, it can be serious; but it's also a lot of fun.

In this chapter, we review the evolution of vertebrates and, more specifically, mammals. It's important to understand these more general aspects of evolutionary history so that we can place our species in its proper biological context. *Homo sapiens* is only one of millions of species that have evolved. More than that, humans have been around for just an instant in the vast expanse of time that life has existed, and we want to know where we fit in this long and complex story of life on earth. To discover where humans belong in this continuum of evolving life on earth, we also discuss some contemporary issues relating to evolutionary theory. In particular, we emphasize concepts relating to large-scale evolutionary processes, that is, *macroevolution* (in contrast to the microevolutionary focus of Chapters 3 and 4). The fundamental perspectives reviewed here concern geological history, principles of classification, and modes of evolutionary change. These perspectives will serve as a basis for topics covered throughout much of the remainder of this book.

The Human Place in the Organic World

There are millions of species living today; if we were to include microorganisms, the total would likely exceed tens of millions. And if we added in the multitudes of species that are now extinct, the total would be staggering—perhaps *hundreds* of millions!

How do we deal scientifically with all this diversity? As humans, biologists approach complexity by simplifying it. One way to do this is to develop a system of **classification** that organizes diversity into categories and, at the same time, indicates evolutionary relationships.

Multicellular organisms that move about and ingest food (but don't photosynthesize, as do plants) are called animals (Fig. 5-1). Within the Kingdom Animalia,

classification In biology, the ordering of organisms into categories, such as orders, families, and genera, to show evolutionary relationships.

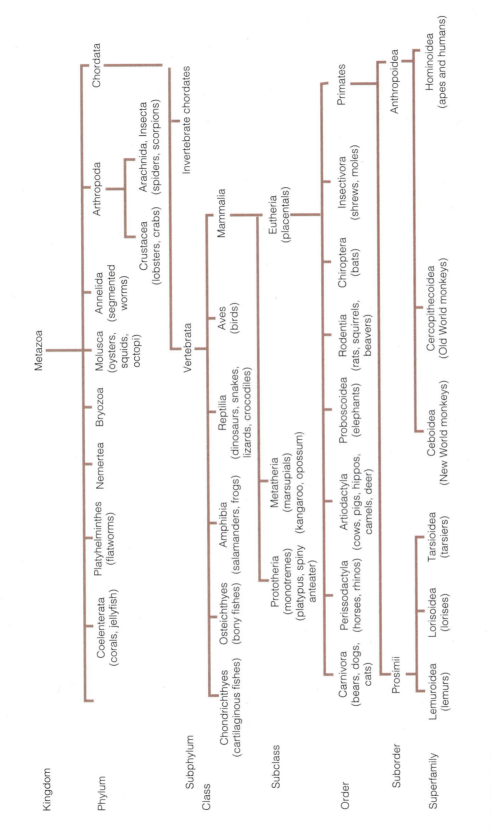

FIGURE 5-1

In this classification chart, modified from Linnaeus, all animals are placed in certain categories based on structural similarities. Not all members of categories are shown; for example, there are up to 20 orders of placental mammals (8 are depicted). Chapter 6 presents a more comprehensive classification of the primate order.

there are more than 20 major groups called *phyla* (*sing.,* phylum). One of these phyla is **Chordata,** containing animals with a nerve cord, gill slits (at some stage of development), and a supporting cord along the back. In turn, most (but not all) chordates are **vertebrates**—so called because they have a vertebral column. Vertebrates also have a developed brain and paired sensory structures for sight, smell, and balance.

The vertebrates themselves are subdivided into six classes: cartilaginous fishes, bony fishes, amphibians, reptiles, birds, and mammals. We'll discuss mammalian classification later in this chapter.

By putting organisms into increasingly narrow groupings, this hierarchical arrangement organizes diversity into categories. It also makes statements about evolutionary and genetic relationships between species and groups of species. Further dividing mammals into orders makes the statement that, for example, all carnivores (Carnivora) are more closely related to each other than they are to any species placed in another order. Consequently, bears, dogs, and cats are more closely related to each other than they are to cattle, pigs, or deer (Artiodactyla). At each succeeding level (suborder, superfamily, family, subfamily, genus, and species), finer distinctions are made between categories until, at the species level, only those animals that can potentially interbreed and produce viable offspring are included.

Principles of Classification

Before we go any further, we need to discuss the basis of animal classification. The field that specializes in establishing the rules of classification is called *taxonomy.* Organisms are classified first, and most traditionally, according to their physical similarities. Such was the basis of the first systematic classification devised by Linnaeus in the eighteenth century (see Chapter 2).

Today, basic physical similarities are still considered a good starting point. But for similarities to be useful, they *must* reflect evolutionary descent. For example, the bones of the forelimb of all air-breathing vertebrates initially adapted to land (terrestrial) enviroments are so similar in number and form (Fig. 5-2) that the obvious

Chordata The phylum of the animal kingdom that includes vertebrates.

vertebrates Animals with segmented, bony spinal columns; includes fishes, amphibians, reptiles, birds, and mammals.

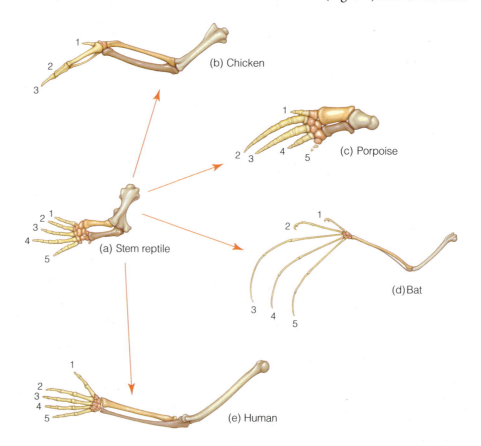

FIGURE 5-2

Homologies. Similarities in the forelimb bones of these animals can be most easily explained by descent from a common ancestor.

explanation for the striking resemblance is that all four kinds of these "four-footed" (tetrapod) vertebrates ultimately derived their forelimb structure from a common ancestor. What's more, recent discoveries of remarkably well-preserved fossils from Canada have provided exciting new evidence of how the transition from aquatic to land living took place and what the earliest land vertebrates looked like (Daeschler et al., 2006; Shubin et al., 2006).

How could such seemingly major evolutionary modifications in structure occur? They quite likely began with only relatively minor genetic changes. For example, recent research shows that forelimb development in all vertebrates is directed by just a few regulatory genes, called *Hox* genes (see p. 45; Shubin et al., 1997; Riddle and Tabin, 1999). A few mutations in certain *Hox* genes in early vertebrates led to the basic limb plan seen in all subsequent vertebrates. With further additional, small mutations in these genes, or in the genes they regulate, the varied structures that make up the wing of a chicken, the flipper of a porpoise, or the upper limb of a human developed. You should recognize that *basic* genetic regulatory mechanisms are highly conserved in animals; that is, they've been maintained relatively unchanged for hundreds of millions of years. Like a musical score with a basic theme, small variations on the pattern can produce the different "tunes" that define one organism from another. This is the essential genetic foundation for most macroevolutionary change. Large anatomical modifications, therefore, don't always require major genetic rearrangements.

Structures that are shared by species on the basis of descent from a common ancestor are called **homologies.** Homologies, alone, are reliable indicators of evolutionary relationship, but we have to be careful not to draw hasty conclusions from superficial similarities. For example, both birds and butterflies have wings, but they shouldn't be grouped together on the basis of this single characteristic; butterflies (as insects) differ dramatically from birds in several other, even more fundamental ways. (For example, birds have an internal skeleton, central nervous system, and four limbs; insects don't.)

Here's what's happened in evolutionary history: From quite distant ancestors, both butterflies and birds have developed wings *independently*. So their (superficial) similarities are a product of separate evolutionary responses to roughly similar functional demands. Such similarities, based on independent functional adaptation and not on shared evolutionary descent, are called **analogies.** The process that leads to the development of analogies (also called analogous structures) such as wings in birds and butterflies is termed **homoplasy.** In the case of butterflies and birds, the homoplasy has occurred in evolutionary lines that share only very remote ancestry. Here, homoplasy has produced analogous structures separately from any homology. In some cases, however, homoplasy can occur in lineages that are more closely related (and share considerable homology as well). Homoplasy in closely related lineages is evident among the primates (for example, New and Old World monkeys show considerable homoplasy, and so do the great apes; see Chapter 6).

Constructing Classifications and Interpreting Evolutionary Relationships

Evolutionary biologists typically use two major approaches, or "schools," when interpreting evolutionary relationships with the goal of producing classifications. The first approach, called **evolutionary systematics,** is the more traditional. The second approach, called **cladistics,** has emerged primarily in the last two decades. While aspects of both approaches are still used by most evolutionary biologists, in recent years cladistic methodologies have predominated among anthropologists. Indeed, one noted primate evolutionist commented that "virtually all current studies of primate phylogeny involve the methods and terminology" of cladistics (Fleagle, 1999, p. 1).

Before we begin drawing distinctions between these two approaches, it's first helpful to note features shared by both evolutionary systematics and cladistics. First,

homologies Similarities between organisms based on descent from a common ancestor.

analogies Similarities between organisms based strictly on common function, with no assumed common evolutionary descent.

homoplasy (*homo,* meaning "same," and *plasy,* meaning "growth") The separate evolutionary development of similar characteristics in different groups of organisms.

evolutionary systematics A traditional approach to classification (and evolutionary interpretation) in which presumed ancestors and descendants are traced in time by analysis of homologous characters.

cladistics An approach to classification that attempts to make rigorous evolutionary interpretations based solely on analysis of certain types of homologous characters (those considered to be derived characters).

both schools are interested in tracing evolutionary relationships and in constructing classifications that reflect these relationships. Second, both schools recognize that organisms must be compared using specific features (called *characters*) and that some of these characters are more informative than others. And third (deriving directly from the previous two points), both approaches focus exclusively on homologies.

But these approaches also have some significant differences—in how characters are chosen, which groups are compared, and how the results are interpreted and eventually incorporated into evolutionary schemes and classifications. The primary difference is that cladistics more explicitly and more rigorously defines the kinds of homologies that yield the most useful information. For example, at a very basic level, all life (except for some viruses) shares DNA as the molecule underlying all organic processes. However, beyond inferring that all life most likely derives from a single origin (a most intriguing point), the mere presence of DNA tells us nothing further regarding more specific relationships among different kinds of life-forms. To draw further conclusions, we need to look at particular characters that certain groups share as the result of more recent ancestry.

This perspective emphasizes an important point: Some homologous characters are much more informative than others. We saw earlier that all terrestrial vertebrates share homologies in the number and basic arrangement of bones in the forelimb. Even though these similarities are broadly useful in showing that these large evolutionary groups (amphibians, reptiles, birds, and mammals) are all related through a distant ancestor, they don't provide information we can use to distinguish one group from another (a reptile from a mammal, for example). These kinds of characters (also called traits) that are shared through such remote ancestry are said to be **ancestral** or primitive. We prefer the term *ancestral* because it doesn't reflect negatively on the evolutionary value of the character in question. In biological anthropology, the term *primitive* or *ancestral* simply means that a character seen in two organisms is inherited in both of them from a distant ancestor.

In most cases, analyzing ancestral characters doesn't supply enough information to make accurate evolutionary interpretations of relationships between different groups. In fact, misinterpretation of ancestral characters can easily lead to quite inaccurate evolutionary conclusions. Cladistics focuses on traits that distinguish particular evolutionary lineages; such traits are far more informative than ancestral traits. Lineages that share a common ancestor are called a **clade,** giving the name *cladistics* to the field that seeks to identify and interpret these groups. The characters of interest are said to be **derived,** or **modified.** Thus, while the general ancestral bony pattern of the forelimb in land vertebrates doesn't allow us to distinguish among them, the further modification of this pattern in certain groups (as hooves, flippers, or wings, for instance) does.

A simplified example might help clarify the basic principles used in cladistic analysis. Figure 5-3a shows a hypothetical "lineage" of passenger vehicles. All of the "descendant" vehicles share a common ancestor, the prototype passenger vehicle. The first major division (I) differentiates passenger cars from trucks. The second split (that is, diversification) is between luxury cars and sports cars (you could, of course, imagine many other subcategories). Modified (derived) traits that distinguish trucks from cars might include type of frame, suspension, wheel size, and, in some forms, an open cargo bed. Derived characters that might distinguish sports cars from luxury cars could include engine size and type, wheel base size, and a decorative racing stripe.

Now let's assume that you're presented with an "unknown" vehicle (meaning one as yet unclassified). How do you decide what kind of vehicle it is? You might note such features as four wheels, a steering wheel, and a seat for the driver, but these are *ancestral* characters (found in the common ancestor) of all passenger vehicles. If, however, you note that the vehicle lacks a cargo bed and raised suspension (so it's not a truck) but has a racing stripe, you might conclude that it's a car, and more than that, a sports car (since it has a derived feature presumably of *only* that group).

ancestral (primitive) Referring to characters inherited by a group of organisms from a remote ancestor and thus not diagnostic of groups (lineages) that diverged after the character first appeared.

clade A group of organisms sharing a common ancestor. The group includes the common ancestor and all descendants.

derived (modified) Referring to characters that are modified from the ancestral condition and thus are diagnostic of particular evolutionary lineages.

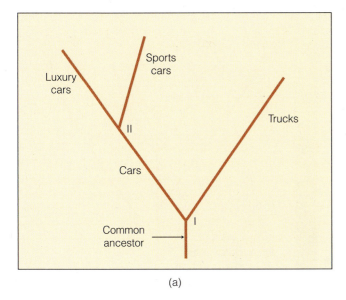

(a)

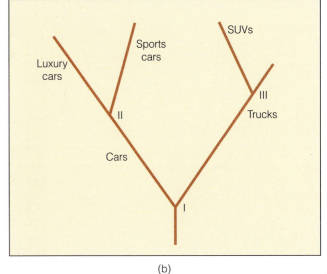

(b)

From a common ancestor of all passenger vehicles, the first major divergence is that between cars and trucks (I). A later divergence also occurs between luxury cars and sports cars (II). Derived features of each grouping ("lineage") appear only after its divergence from other groups (e.g., cargo beds are found only in trucks, cushioned suspension only in cars; likewise, only sports cars have a decorative racing stripe).

In this "tree," SUVs diverge from trucks, but like sports cars, they have a decorative racing stripe. This feature is a homoplasy and does not make SUVs sports cars. The message is that classifications based on just one characteristic that can appear independently in different groups can lead to an incorrect conclusion. *Note:* In (a), two clades are defined (I and II), while in (b), three clades (I, II, and III) are recognized.

FIGURE 5-3
Evolutionary "trees" showing development of passenger vehicles.

All this seems fairly obvious, and you've probably noticed that this simple type of decision making characterizes much of human mental organization. Still, we frequently deal with complications that aren't so obvious. What if you're presented with a sports utility vehicle (SUV) with a racing stripe (Fig. 5-3b)? SUVs are basically trucks, but the presence of the racing stripe could be seen as a homoplasy with sports cars. The lesson here is that we need to be careful, look at several traits, decide which are ancestral and which are derived, and finally try to recognize the complexity (and confusion) introduced by homoplasy.

Our example of passenger vehicles is useful up to a point. Because it concerns human inventions, the groupings possess characters that humans can add and delete in almost any combination. Naturally occurring organic systems are more limited in this respect. Any species can possess only those characters that have been inherited from its ancestor or that have been subsequently modified (derived) from those shared with the ancestor. So any modification in *any* species is constrained by that species' evolutionary legacy—that is, what the species starts out with.

Another example, one drawn from paleontological (fossil) evidence of actual organisms, can help clarify these points. Most people know something about dinosaur evolution, and some of you may know about the recent controversies surrounding this topic. There are several intriguing issues concerning the evolutionary history of dinosaurs, and recent fossil discoveries have shed considerable light on them. We'll mention some of these issues later in the chapter, but here we consider one of the more fascinating: the relationship of dinosaurs to birds.

Traditionally, it was thought that birds were a quite distinct group from reptiles and not especially closely related to any of them (including extinct forms, such as the dinosaurs; Fig. 5-4a). Still, the early origins of birds were clouded in mystery and have been much debated for more than a century. In fact, the first fossil evidence of a very primitive bird (now known to be about 150 million years old) was discovered in 1861, just two years following Darwin's publication of *Origin of Species.* Despite some initial and quite remarkably accurate interpretations by Thomas Huxley

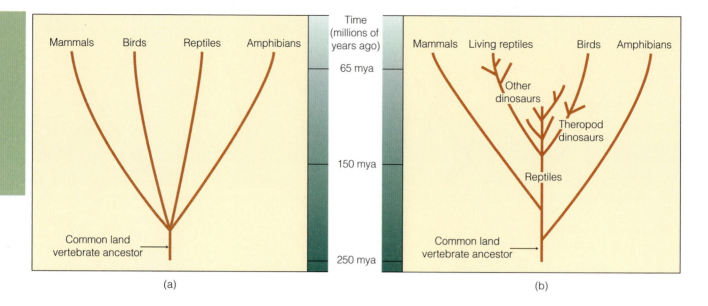

FIGURE 5-4

Evolutionary relationships of birds and dinosaurs. (a) Traditional view, showing no close relationship. (b) Revised view, showing common ancestry of birds and dinosaurs.

theropods Small- to medium-sized ground-living dinosaurs, dated to approximately 150 mya and thought to be related to birds.

shared derived Relating to specific character traits shared in common between two life-forms and considered the most useful for making evolutionary interpretations.

phylogenetic tree A chart showing evolutionary relationships as determined by evolutionary systematics. It contains a time component and implies ancestor-descendant relationships.

cladogram A chart showing evolutionary relationships as determined by cladistic analysis. It's based solely on interpretation of shared derived characters. It contains no time component and does not imply ancestor-descendant relationships.

linking these early birds to dinosaurs, most experts concluded that there was no close relationship. This view persisted through most of the twentieth century, but events of the last two decades have swung the consensus back to the hypothesis that birds *are* closely related to some dinosaurs. Two developments in particular have influenced this change of opinion: the remarkable discoveries in the 1990s from China, Madagascar, and elsewhere and the application of cladistic methods to the interpretation of these and other fossils.

Recent finds from Madagascar of chicken-sized, primitive birds dated to 70–65 million years ago (mya) show an elongated second toe (similar, in fact, to that in the dinosaur *Velociraptor,* made infamous in the film *Jurassic Park*). Indeed, these primitive birds from Madagascar show many other similarities to *Velociraptor* and its close cousins, which together comprise a group of small- to medium-sized ground-living, carnivorous dinosaurs called **theropods.** Even more extraordinary finds have been unearthed recently in China, where the traces of what were once *feathers* have been found embossed in fossilized sediments! For many researchers, these new finds have finally solved the mystery of bird origins (Fig. 5-4b), leading thems to conclude that this evidence "shows that birds are not only *descended* from dinosaurs, they *are* dinosaurs (and reptiles)—just as humans are mammals, even though people are as different from other mammals as birds are from other reptiles" (Padian and Chiappe, 1998, p. 43).

There are some doubters who remain concerned that the presence of feathers in dinosaurs (145–125 mya) might simply be a homoplasy (that is, these creatures developed the trait independently from its appearance in birds). Certainly, the possibility of homoplasy must always be considered, as it can add considerably to the complexity of what seems like a straightforward evolutionary interpretation. Indeed, strict cladistic analysis assumes that homoplasy is not a common occurrence; if it were, perhaps no evolutionary interpretation could be very straightforward! In the case of the proposed relationship between some (theropod) dinosaurs and birds, the presence of feathers looks like an excellent example of a **shared derived** characteristic, which therefore *does* link the forms. What's more, cladistic analysis emphasizes that several characteristics should be examined, since homoplasy might muddle an interpretation based on just one or two shared traits. In the bird/dinosaur case, several other characteristics further suggest their evolutionary relationship.

One last point needs to be mentioned. Traditional evolutionary systematics illustrates the hypothesized evolutionary relationships using a *phylogeny,* more properly called a **phylogenetic tree.** Strict cladistic analysis, however, shows relationships in a **cladogram** (Fig. 5-5). If you examine the charts in Figures 5-4 and 5-5, you'll see some obvious differences. A phylogenetic tree incorporates the dimension

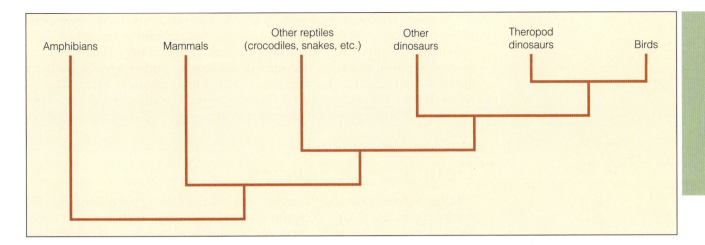

Amphibians   Mammals   Other reptiles (crocodiles, snakes, etc.)   Other dinosaurs   Theropod dinosaurs   Birds

of time, shown approximately in Figure 5-4 (you can find many other examples in this and upcoming chapters). A cladogram doesn't indicate time; all forms (fossil and modern) are shown along one dimension. Phylogenetic trees usually attempt to make some hypotheses regarding ancestor-descendant relationships (for example, theropods are ancestral to modern birds). Cladistic analysis (through cladograms) makes no attempt whatsoever to discern ancestor-descendant relationships. In fact, strict cladists are quite skeptical that the evidence really permits such specific evolutionary hypotheses to be scientifically confirmed (since there are many more extinct species than living ones).

FIGURE 5-5

This cladogram shows relationships of birds, dinosaurs, and other terrestrial vertebrates. Notice that there's no time scale, and both living and fossil forms are shown along the same dimension—that is, ancestor-descendant relationships aren't indicated.

QUICK REVIEW   **Comparing Two Approaches to Interpretations of Evolutionary Relationships**

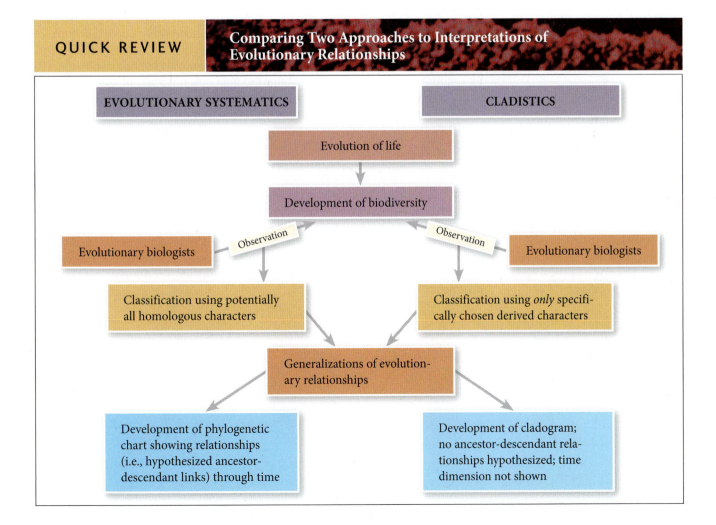

EVOLUTIONARY SYSTEMATICS   CLADISTICS

Evolution of life

Development of biodiversity

Evolutionary biologists —Observation→   ←Observation— Evolutionary biologists

Classification using potentially all homologous characters   Classification using *only* specifically chosen derived characters

Generalizations of evolutionary relationships

Development of phylogenetic chart showing relationships (i.e., hypothesized ancestor-descendant links) through time   Development of cladogram; no ancestor-descendant relationships hypothesized; time dimension not shown

In practice, most physical anthropologists (and other evolutionary biologists) utilize cladistic analysis to identify and assess the utility of traits and to make testable hypotheses regarding the relationships between groups of organisms. They also frequently extend this basic cladistic methodology to further hypothesize likely ancestor-descendant relationships shown relative to a time scale (that is, in a phylogenetic tree). In this way, aspects of both traditional evolutionary systematics and cladistic analysis are combined to produce a more complete picture of evolutionary history.

Definition of Species

Whether biologists are doing a cladistic or more traditional phylogenetic analysis, they're comparing groups of organisms—that is, different species, genera (*sing., genus*), families, orders, and so forth. Fundamental to all these levels of classification is the most basic, the species. It's appropriate, then, to ask, how do biologists define species? We addressed this issue briefly in Chapter 1, where we used the most common definition, one that emphasizes interbreeding and reproductive isolation. While it's not the only definition of species (others are discussed shortly), this view, called the **biological species concept** (Mayr, 1970), is the one preferred by most zoologists.

To understand what species are, you might consider how they come about in the first place—what Darwin called the "origin of species." This most fundamental of macroevolutionary processes is called **speciation.** According to the biological species concept, the way new species are first produced involves some form of isolation. Picture a single species (baboons, for example) composed of several populations distributed over a wide geographical area. Gene exchange between populations (gene flow) will be limited if a geographical barrier, such as an ocean or mountain range, effectively separates these populations. This extremely important form of isolating mechanism is called *geographical isolation.*

If one baboon population (A) is separated from another baboon population (B) by a mountain range, individual baboons of population A will not mate with individuals from B (Fig. 5-6). As time passes (perhaps hundreds or thousands of generations), genetic differences will accumulate in both populations. If population size is small, we can assume that genetic drift will also cause allele frequencies to change in both populations. And since drift is *random,* we wouldn't expect the effects to be the same. Consequently, the two populations will begin to diverge genetically.

As long as gene exchange is limited, the populations can only become more genetically different over time. What's more, further difference can be expected if the baboon groups are occupying slightly different habitats. These additional genetic differences would be incorporated through the process of natural selection. Certain individuals in population A would be more reproductively fit in their own environment, but they would show less reproductive success in the environment occupied by population B. So allele frequencies will shift further, resulting in even greater divergence between the two groups.

biological species concept A depiction of species as groups of individuals capable of fertile interbreeding but reproductively isolated from other such groups.

speciation The process by which a new species evolves from an earlier species. Speciation is the most basic process in macroevolution.

FIGURE 5-6
This speciation model illustrates branching evolution, pushed along through the influence of increasing reproductive isolation.

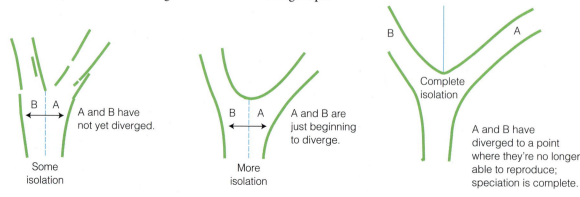

B A   A and B have not yet diverged.
Some isolation

B A   A and B are just beginning to diverge.
More isolation

B   A
Complete isolation
A and B have diverged to a point where they're no longer able to reproduce; speciation is complete.

With the cumulative effects of genetic drift and natural selection acting over many generations, the result will be two populations that—even if they were to come back into geographical contact—could no longer interbreed. More than just geographical isolation might now apply. There may, for instance, be behavioral differences that interfere with courtship—what we call *behavioral isolation*. Using our *biological* definition of species, we would now recognize two distinct species where initially only one existed.

Another related process that can contribute to the further differentiation of populations into incipient species concerns mate recognition. This is sometimes called the **recognition species concept,** though the crucial process, again, concerns reproduction (that is, who's mating with whom; Ridley, 1993).

Assume in our baboon example that some isolation has already occurred and that phenotypic (and genotypic) differences are beginning to be established between two populations. In this situation, coloration patterns of faces or the size, location, coloration, or even smell of the female genital swelling might vary from group to group. If so, then a female from population A might not recognize a male from population B as an appropriate mate (and vice versa, of course). Natural selection would quickly favor such discrimination if hybrids were less reproductively successful than within-population crosses. Indeed, once such "selective breeding" became established, speciation would be accelerated considerably.

Another definition of species focuses primarily on natural selection and emphasizes that speciation is the result of influences of varied habitats. In this view, called the **ecological species concept,** a species is defined as a group of organisms exploiting a single niche. Also called an **ecological niche,** this is the physical as well as biological position of an organism within the biological world (that is, within the full ecosystem). For each population, the ecological niche will vary slightly, and different phenotypes will be slightly more advantageous in each. For example, one population might be more arboreal and another more terrestrial; but there would not be an intermediate population equally successful on the ground and in the trees.

In recent years, the ecological species concept has attracted support from several evolutionary biologists, especially among physical anthropologists. While the biological species concept emphasizes gene flow and reproductive isolation, the ecological species concept stresses the role of natural selection. Clearly, our approach in this text has been to focus on the evolutionary contribution of natural selection; thus, the ecological species concept has much to offer here. Nevertheless, our understanding of species need not entail an either-or choice between the biological species concept and the ecological species concept. Some population isolation could indeed *begin* the process of speciation, and at this stage, the influence of genetic drift could be crucial. The process might then be reinforced by natural selection through habitat differentiation as well as mate recognition.

A final approach that biologists use to define species is primarily a practical one. How can species be defined when neither reproductive isolation nor ecological separation can be clearly tested? This type of difficulty plagues the interpretation of fossil organisms but sometimes crops up in discussions of contemporary species as well. For example, Colin Groves, of the Australian National University, has recently advocated splitting many populations of primates into separate species (Groves, 2001b). He utilizes a definition of species called the **phylogenetic species concept,** based on an identifiable pattern of ancestry (that is, who is *clearly* related to whom).

For living species, characteristics that define a phylogenetic species could be phenotypic or more directly genotypic (identifying shared patterns in the karyotype or in specific DNA sequences). For extinct groups, with a few notable exceptions (from which ancient DNA has been extracted), the *only* evidence available comes from phenotypic characters that can be identified in fossil forms (see p. 89 for further discussion).

recognition species concept A depiction of species in which the key aspect is the ability of individuals to identify members of their own species for purposes of mating (and to avoid mating with members of other species). In theory, this type of selective mating is a component of a species concept emphasizing mating and is therefore compatible with the biological species concept.

ecological species concept The concept that a species is a group of organisms exploiting a single niche. This view emphasizes the role of natural selection in separating species from one another.

ecological niche The position of a species within its physical and biological environment. A species' ecological niche is defined by such components as diet, terrain, vegetation, type of predators, relationships with other species, and activity patterns, and each niche is unique to a given species. Together, ecological niches make up an ecosystem.

phylogenetic species concept Splitting many populations into separate species based on an identifiable parental pattern of ancestry.

Interpreting Species and Other Groups in the Fossil Record

Throughout much of this text, we'll be using various taxonomic terms for fossil primates (including fossil hominids). You'll be introduced to such terms as *Ardipithecus, Australopithecus,* and *Homo.* Of course, *Homo* is still a living primate. But it's especially complex to make these types of designations from remains of animals that are long dead (and only partially preserved as skeletal remains). In these contexts, what do such names mean in evolutionary terms?

Our goal when applying species, genus, or other taxonomic labels to groups of organisms is to make meaningful biological statements about the variation that's represented. When looking at populations of living or long-extinct animals, we certainly are going to see variation; this happens in *any* sexually reproducing organism due to recombination (see Chapter 3). As a result of recombination, each individual organism is a unique combination of genetic material, and the uniqueness is usually reflected to some extent in the phenotype.

Besides such *individual variation,* we see other kinds of systematic variation in all biological populations. *Age changes* alter overall body size, as well as shape, in many mammals. One pertinent example for fossil human and ape studies is the change in number, size, and shape of teeth from deciduous (also known as baby or milk) teeth (only 20 teeth are present) to the permanent dentition (32 are present). It would be an obvious error to differentiate fossil forms based solely on such age-dependent criteria. If one individual were represented just by milk teeth and another (seemingly very different) individual were represented just by adult teeth, they easily could be different-aged individuals from the *same* population. Variation due to sex also plays an important role in influencing differences among individuals observed in biological populations. Differences in physical characteristics between males and females of the same species, called **sexual dimorphism,** can result in marked variation in body size and proportions in adults of the same species (in Chapter 6, we'll discuss this important topic in more detail).

Recognition of Fossil Species Keeping in mind all the types of variation present within interbreeding groups of organisms, the minimum biological category we'd like to define in fossil primate samples is the *species*. As already defined (according to the biological species concept), a species is a group of interbreeding or potentially interbreeding organisms that is reproductively isolated from other such groups. In modern organisms, this concept is theoretically testable by observations of reproductive behavior. In animals long extinct, such observations are obviously impossible. Our only way, then, of getting a handle on the variation we see in fossil groups is to refer to living animals.

When studying a fossil group, we may observe obvious variation, such as some individuals being larger and with bigger teeth than others. The question then becomes: What is the biological significance of this variation? Two possibilities come to mind. Either the variation is accounted for by individual, age, and sex differences seen *within* every biological species (that is, it is **intraspecific**), or the variation represents differences *between* reproductively isolated groups (that is, it is **interspecific**).How do we decide which answer is correct? To do this, we have to look at contemporary species.

If the amount of morphological variation we observe in fossil samples is comparable to that seen today *within species of closely related forms,* then we shouldn't "split" our sample into more than one species. We must, however, be careful in choosing modern analogues, because rates of morphological evolution vary among different groups of mammals. So, for example, when studying extinct fossil primates, we need to compare them with well-known modern primates. Even so, studies of living groups have shown that defining exactly where species boundaries begin and end is often difficult. In dealing with extinct species, the uncertainties are even greater. In addition to the overlapping patterns of variation *spatially* (over space),

sexual dimorphism Differences in physical characteristics between males and females of the same species. For example, humans are slightly sexually dimorphic for body size, with males being taller, on average, than females of the same population.

intraspecific Within species; refers to variation seen within the same species.

interspecific Between species; refers to variation beyond that seen within the same species to include additional aspects seen between two different species.

variation also occurs *temporally* (through time). In other words, even more variation will be seen in **paleospecies,** since individuals may be separated by thousands or even millions of years. Applying strict Linnaean taxonomy to such a situation presents an unavoidable dilemma. Standard Linnaean classification, designed to take account of variation present at any given time, describes a static situation. But when we deal with paleospecies, the time frame is expanded and the situation can be dynamic (that is, later forms might be different from earlier forms). In such a dynamic situation, taxonomic decisions (where to draw species boundaries) are ultimately going to be somewhat arbitrary.

Because the task of interpreting paleospecies is so difficult, paleoanthropologists have sought various solutions. Most researchers today define species using clusters of derived traits (identified cladistically). But owing to the ambiguity of how many derived characters are required to identify a fully distinct species (as opposed to a subspecies), the frequent mixing of characters into novel combinations, and the always difficult problem of homoplasy, there continues to be disagreement. A good deal of the dispute is driven by philosophical orientation. Exactly how much diversity should one *expect* among fossil primates, especially among fossil hominids?

Some researchers, called "splitters," claim that speciation occurred frequently during hominid evolution, and they often identify numerous fossil hominid species in a sample being studied. As the nickname suggests, these scientists are inclined to split groups into many species. Others, called "lumpers," assume that speciation was less common and see much variation as being intraspecific. These scientists lump groups together, so that fewer hominid species are identified, named, and eventually plugged into evolutionary schemes. As you'll see in the following chapters, debates of this sort pervade paleoanthropology, perhaps more than in any other branch of evolutionary biology.

Recognition of Fossil Genera The next and broader level of taxonomic classification, the **genus** (*pl.,* genera), presents another problem. To have more than one genus, we obviously must have at least two species (reproductively isolated groups), and the species of one genus must differ in a basic way from the species of another genus. A genus is therefore defined as a group of species composed of members more closely related to each other than they are to species from any other genus.

Grouping species into genera can be quite subjective and is often much debated by biologists. One possible test for contemporary animals is to check for results of hybridization between individuals of different species—rare in nature, but quite common in captivity. If members of two normally separate species interbreed and produce live (though not necessarily fertile) offspring, the two parental species probably are not too different genetically and should therefore be grouped in the same genus. A well-known example of such a cross is horses with donkeys (*Equus caballus* × *Equus asinus*), which normally produces live but sterile offspring (mules).

As previously mentioned, we can't perform breeding experiments with extinct animals, which is why another definition of genus becomes highly relevant. Species that are members of the same genus share the same broad adaptive zone. An adaptive zone represents a general ecological lifestyle more basic than the narrower ecological niches characteristic of individual species. This ecological definition of genus can be an immense aid in interpreting fossil primates. Teeth are the most frequently preserved parts, and they often can provide excellent general ecological inferences. Cladistic analysis also helps scientists to make judgments about evolutionary relationships. That is, members of the same genus should all share derived characters not seen in members of other genera.

As a final comment, we should stress that classification by genus is not always a straightforward decision. For instance, in emphasizing the very close genetic similarities between humans (*Homo sapiens*) and chimpanzees (*Pan troglodytes*), some current researchers (Wildman et al., 2003) place both in the same genus (*Homo sapiens, Homo troglodytes*). This philosophy has even been argued by some to advocate extension of basic human rights to great apes. Such thinking underscores the point that when it gets this close to home, it's often difficult to remain objective!

paleospecies Species defined from fossil evidence, often covering a long time span.

genus (*pl.,* genera) A group of closely related species.

Vertebrate Evolutionary History: A Brief Summary

Besides the staggering array of living and extinct life-forms, biologists must also contend with the vast amount of time that life has been evolving on earth. Again, scientists have devised simplified schemes—but in this case to organize *time*, not biological diversity.

To this end, geologists have formulated the **geological time scale** (Fig. 5-7), in which very large time spans are organized into eras that include one or more periods. Periods, in turn, can be broken down into epochs. For the time span encompassing vertebrate evolution, there are three eras: the Paleozoic, the Mesozoic, and the Cenozoic. The first vertebrates are present in the fossil record dating to early in the Paleozoic at 500 mya, and their origins probably go back considerably further. It's the vertebrates' capacity to form bone that accounts for their more complete fossil record *after* 500 mya.

During the Paleozoic, several varieties of fishes (including the ancestors of modern sharks and bony fishes), amphibians, and reptiles appeared. At the end of the Paleozoic, close to 250 mya, several varieties of mammal-like reptiles were also diversifying. It's generally thought that some of these forms ultimately gave rise to the mammals.

geological time scale The organization of earth history into eras, periods, and epochs; commonly used by geologists and paleoanthropologists.

ERA	PERIOD	(Began mya)	EPOCH	(Began mya)
CENOZOIC	Quaternary	1.8	Holocene	0.01
			Pleistocene	1.8
			Pliocene	5
			Miocene	23
			Oligocene	33
			Eocene	55
	Tertiary	65	Paleocene	65
MESOZOIC	Cretaceous	136		
	Jurassic	190		
	Triassic	225		
PALEOZOIC	Permian	280		
	Carboniferous	345		
	Devonian	395		
	Silurian	430		
	Ordovician	500		
	Cambrian	570		
PRE-CAMBRIAN				

FIGURE 5-7
Geological time scale.

The evolutionary history of vertebrates and other organisms during the Paleozoic and Mesozoic was profoundly influenced by geographical events. We know that the positions of the earth's continents have dramatically shifted during the last several hundred million years. This process, called **continental drift,** is explained by the geological theory of *plate tectonics,* which states that the earth's crust is a series of gigantic moving and colliding plates. Such massive geological movements can induce volcanic activity (as, for example, all around the Pacific rim), mountain building (for example, the Himalayas), and earthquakes. Living on the juncture of the Pacific and North American plates, residents of the Pacific coast of the United States are acutely aware of some of these consequences, as illustrated by the explosive volcanic eruption of Mt. St. Helens and the frequent earthquakes in Alaska and California.

While reconstructing the earth's physical history, geologists have established the prior, much altered, positions of major continental landmasses. During the late Paleozoic, the continents came together to form a single colossal landmass called *Pangea.* (In reality, the continents had been drifting on plates, coming together and separating, long before the end of the Paleozoic around 225 mya.) During the early Mesozoic, the southern continents (South America, Africa, Antarctica, Australia, and India) began to split off from Pangea, forming a large southern continent called *Gondwanaland* (Fig. 5-8a). Similarly, the northern continents (North America, Greenland, Europe, and Asia) were consolidated into a northern landmass called *Laurasia.* During the Mesozoic, Gondwanaland and Laurasia continued to drift apart and to break up into smaller segments. By the end of the Mesozoic (about 65 mya), the continents were beginning to assume their current positions (Fig. 5-8b).

The evolutionary ramifications of this long-term continental drift were profound. Groups of land animals became effectively isolated from each other by oceans, significantly influencing the distribution of reptiles and mammals. These continental movements continued in the Cenozoic and indeed are still happening, although without such dramatic results.

During most of the Mesozoic, reptiles were the dominant land vertebrates, and they exhibited a broad expansion into a variety of *ecological niches,* which included aerial and marine habitats. The most famous of these highly successful Mesozoic reptiles were the dinosaurs, which themselves evolved into a wide array of sizes and species and adapted to a variety of lifestyles. Dinosaur paleontology, never a boring field, has advanced several startling notions in recent years: that many dinosaurs were "warm-blooded" (see p. 93); that some varieties were quite social and probably also engaged in considerable parental care; that many forms became extinct because

continental drift The movement of continents on sliding plates of the earth's surface. As a result, the positions of large landmasses have shifted drastically during the earth's history.

FIGURE 5-8

Continental drift. (a) Positions of the continents during the Mesozoic (ca. 125 mya). Pangea is breaking up into a northern landmass (Laurasia) and a southern landmass (Gondwanaland). (b) Positions of the continents at the beginning of the Cenozoic (ca. 65 mya).

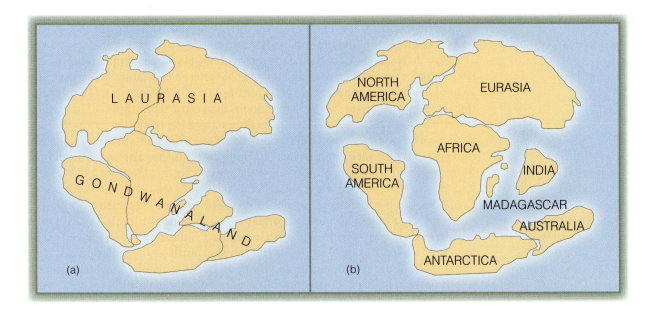

(a)   (b)

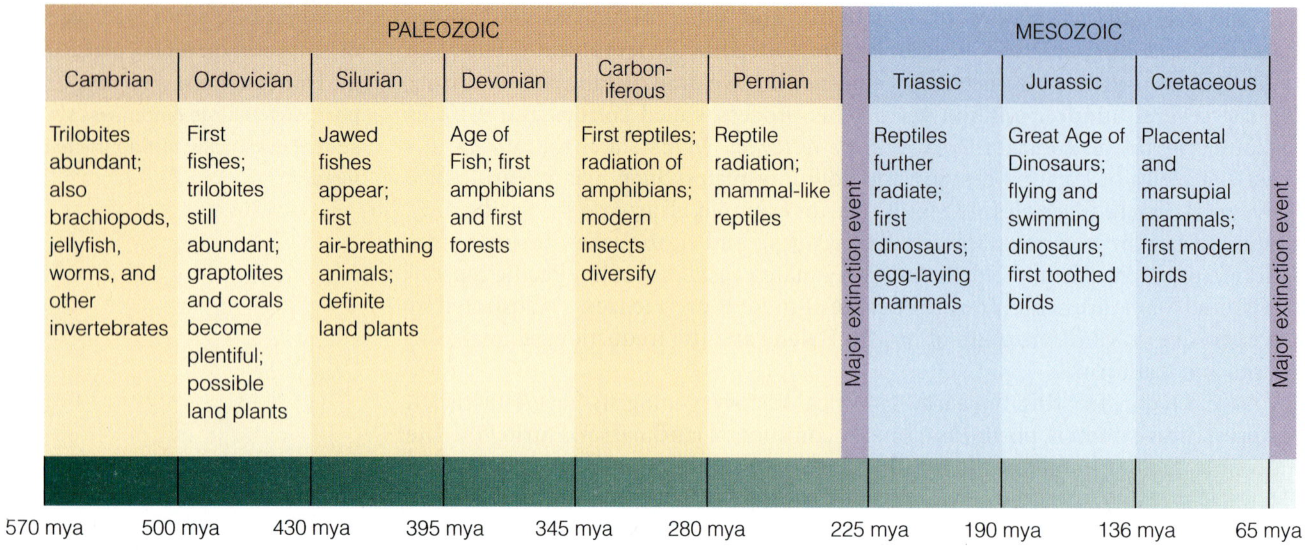
PALEOZOIC
MESOZOIC
Cambrian
Ordovician
Silurian
Devonian
Carbon-iferous
Permian
Triassic
Jurassic
Cretaceous
Trilobites abundant; also brachiopods, jellyfish, worms, and other invertebrates
First fishes; trilobites still abundant; graptolites and corals become plentiful; possible land plants
Jawed fishes appear; first air-breathing animals; definite land plants
Age of Fish; first amphibians and first forests
First reptiles; radiation of amphibians; modern insects diversify
Reptile radiation; mammal-like reptiles
Major extinction event
Reptiles further radiate; first dinosaurs; egg-laying mammals
Great Age of Dinosaurs; flying and swimming dinosaurs; first toothed birds
Placental and marsupial mammals; first modern birds
Major extinction event
570 mya
500 mya
430 mya
395 mya
345 mya
280 mya
225 mya
190 mya
136 mya
65 mya

FIGURE 5-9
This time line depicts major events in early vertebrate evolution.

of major climatic changes to the earth's atmosphere from collisions with comets or asteroids; and finally, that not all dinosaurs became entirely extinct and have many descendants still living today (that is, all modern birds). (See Fig. 5-9 for a summary of major events in early vertebrate evolutionary history.)

The Cenozoic is divided into two periods, the Tertiary (about 63 million years duration) and the Quaternary, from about 1.8 mya up to and including the present (see Fig. 5-7). Paleontologists often refer to the next, more precise level of subdivision within the Cenozoic as the **epochs.** There are seven epochs within the Cenozoic: the Paleocene, Eocene, Oligocene, Miocene, Pliocene, Pleistocene, and Holocene, the last often referred to as the Recent epoch.

Mammalian Evolution

We can learn about mammalian evolution from fossils as well as from studying the DNA of living species (Bininda-Emonds et al., 2007). Studies using both of these approaches suggest that all the living groups of mammals (that is, all the orders; see p. 79) had diverged by 75 mya. Later, only after several million years following the beginning of the Cenozoic, did the various current mammalian subgroups (that is, the particular families) begin to diversify.

Today, there are over 4,000 species of mammals, and we could call the Cenozoic the Age of Mammals. It is during this era that, along with birds, mammals replaced reptiles as the dominant land-living vertebrates.

How do we account for the relatively rapid success of the mammals during the late Mesozoic and early Cenozoic? Several characteristics relating to learning and general flexibility of behavior are of prime importance. To process more information, mammals were selected for larger brains than those typically found in reptiles. In particular, the cerebrum became generally enlarged, especially the outer covering, the neocortex, which controls higher brain functions (Fig. 5-10). In some mammals, the cerebrum expanded so much that it came to comprise most of the brain volume; the number of surface convolutions also increased, creating more surface area and thus providing space for even more nerve cells (neurons). As we'll soon see in Chapter 6, this is a trend even further emphasized among the primates.

For such a large and complex organ as the mammalian brain to develop, a longer, more intense period of growth is required. Slower development can occur internally (*in utero*) as well as after birth. Internal fertilization and internal development aren't unique to mammals, but the latter is a major innovation among terrestrial vertebrates. Other forms (birds, most fishes, and reptiles) incubate their

epochs Categories of the geological time scale; subdivisions of periods. In the Cenozoic, epochs include the Paleocene, Eocene, Oligocene, Miocene, and Pliocene (from the Tertiary) and the Pleistocene and Holocene (from the Quaternary).

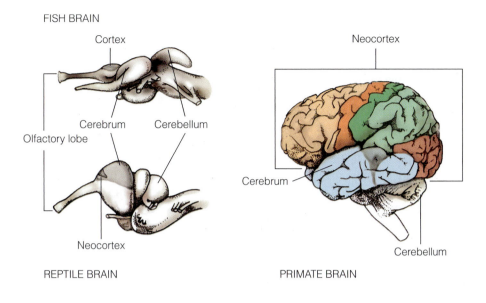

FISH BRAIN

Cortex

Cerebrum Cerebellum

Olfactory lobe

Neocortex

REPTILE BRAIN

Neocortex

Cerebrum

Cerebellum

PRIMATE BRAIN

FIGURE 5-10
Lateral view of the brain in fishes, reptiles, and primates. You can see the increased size of the cerebral cortex, also called the neocortex, of the primate brain. The cerebral cortex integrates sensory information and selects responses.

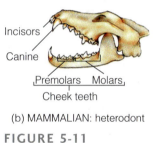

(a) REPTILIAN (alligator): homodont

Incisors

Canine

Premolars Molars
Cheek teeth

(b) MAMMALIAN: heterodont

FIGURE 5-11
Reptilian and mammalian teeth.

placental A type (subclass) of mammal. During the Cenozoic, placentals became the most widespread and numerous mammals and today are represented by upward of 20 orders, including the primates.

heterodont Having different kinds of teeth; characteristic of mammals, whose teeth consist of incisors, canines, premolars, and molars.

endothermic (*endo,* meaning "within" or "internal") Able to maintain internal body temperature by producing energy through metabolic processes within cells; characteristic of mammals, birds, and perhaps some dinosaurs.

young externally by laying eggs, while mammals, with very few exceptions, give birth to live young. Even among mammals, however, there's considerable variation among the major groups in how mature the young are at birth. As you'll see, it is in mammals like us—the **placental** forms—that *in utero* development goes farthest.

Another distinctive feature of mammals is seen in the dentition. While living reptiles consistently have similarly shaped teeth (called a *homodont* dentition), mammals have differently shaped teeth (Fig. 5-11). This varied pattern, termed a **heterodont** dentition, is reflected in the ancestral (primitive) mammalian array of dental elements, which includes 3 incisors, 1 canine, 4 premolars, and 3 molars in each quarter of the mouth. Since the upper and lower jaws are usually the same and are symmetrical for both sides, the "dental formula" is conventionally illustrated by dental quarter (see p. 105 for a more complete discussion of dental patterns as they apply to primates). So with 11 teeth in each quarter of the mouth, the ancestral mammalian dental complement includes a total of 44 teeth. Such a heterodont arrangement allows mammals to process a wide variety of foods. Incisors can be used for cutting, canines for grasping and piercing, and premolars and molars for crushing and grinding.

A final point regarding teeth relates to their disproportionate representation in the fossil record. As the hardest, most durable portion of a vertebrate skeleton, teeth have the greatest likelihood of becoming fossilized (that is, mineralized, since teeth are predominantly mineral to begin with). As a result, the vast majority of available fossil data (particularly early on) for most vertebrates, including primates, consists of teeth.

Another major adaptive complex that distinguishes contemporary mammals from reptiles is the maintenance of a constant internal body temperature. Known colloquially (and incorrectly) as warm-bloodedness, this crucial physiological adaptation is also seen in contemporary birds (and may have characterized many dinosaurs as well). In fact, many contemporary reptiles are able to approximate a constant internal body temperature through behavioral means (especially by regulating activity and exposing the body to the sun). In this sense, reptiles (along with birds and mammals) could be said to be *homeothermic.* So a more useful distinction is to see how the energy to maintain body temperature is produced. In reptiles, it's obtained directly from exposure to the sun; reptiles are thus said to be *ectothermic.* In mammals and birds, however, the energy is generated *internally* through metabolic activity (by processing food or by muscle action); for this reason, mammals and birds are referred to as **endothermic.**

FIGURE 5-12
A wallaby with an infant in the pouch (marsupials).

The Emergence of Major Mammalian Groups

There are three major subgroups of living mammals: the egg-laying mammals, or monotremes; the pouched mammals, or marsupials (Fig. 5-12); and the placental mammals. The monotremes (of which the platypus and wallaby are two examples) are extremely primitive and are considered more distinct from marsupials or placentals than these two subgroups are from each other.

The most notable difference between marsupials and placentals concerns fetal development. In marsupials, the young are born extremely immature and must complete development in an external pouch. But placental mammals develop over a longer period of time *in utero,* made possible by the evolutionary development of a specialized tissue (the placenta) that provides for fetal nourishment.

With a longer gestation period, the central nervous system develops more completely in the placental fetus. What's more, after birth, the "bond of milk" between mother and young allows more time for complex neural structures to form. We should also emphasize that from a *biosocial* perspective, this dependency period not only allows for adequate physiological development but also provides for a wider range of learning stimuli. That is, a vast amount of information is channeled to the young mammalian brain through observation of the mother's behavior and through play with age-mates. It's not enough to have evolved a brain capable of learning. Collateral evolution of mammalian social systems has ensured that young mammal brains are provided with ample learning opportunities and are thus put to good use.

Processes of Macroevolution

As we noted earlier, evolution operates at both microevolutionary and macroevolutionary levels. We discussed evolution primarily from a microevolutionary perspective in Chapters 3 and 4; in this chapter, our focus is on macroevolution. Macroevolutionary mechanisms operate more on the whole species than on individuals or populations, and they take much longer than microevolutionary processes to have a noticeable impact.

Adaptive Radiation

As we mentioned in Chapter 2, the potential capacity of a group of organisms to multiply is practically unlimited, but its ability to increase its numbers is regulated largely by the availability of resources (food, water, shelter, and space). As population size increases, access to resources decreases, and the environment will ultimately prove inadequate. Depleted resources induce some members of a population to seek an environment in which competition is reduced and the opportunities for survival and reproductive success are increased. This evolutionary tendency to exploit unoccupied habitats may eventually produce an abundance of diverse species.

This story has been played out countless times during the history of life, and some groups have expanded extremely rapidly. This evolutionary process, known as **adaptive radiation,** can be seen in the divergence of the stem reptiles into the profusion of different forms of the late Paleozoic and especially those of the Mesozoic. It's a process that takes place when a life-form rapidly takes advantage, so to speak, of the many newly available ecological niches.

The principle of evolution illustrated by adaptive radiation is fairly simple, but important. It may be stated this way: A species, or group of species, will diverge into as many variations as two factors allow. These factors are (1) its adaptive potential and (2) the adaptive opportunities of the available niches.

In the case of reptiles, there was little divergence in the very early stages of evolution, when the ancestral form was little more than one among a variety of amphibian water dwellers. Later, a more efficient egg (one that could incubate out of water) developed in reptiles; this new egg, with a hard, watertight shell, had great adaptive

adaptive radiation The relatively rapid expansion and diversification of life-forms into new ecological niches.

potential, but initially there were few zones to invade. When reptiles became fully terrestrial, however, a wide array of ecological niches became accessible to them. Once freed from their attachment to water, reptiles were able to exploit landmasses with no serious competition from any other animal. They moved into the many different ecological niches on land (and to some extent in the air and sea), and as they adapted to these areas, they diversified into a large number of species. This spectacular radiation burst forth with such evolutionary speed that it may well be termed an adaptive explosion.

Of course, the rapid expansion of placental mammals during the late Mesozoic and throughout the Cenozoic is another excellent example of adaptive radiation.

Generalized and Specialized Characteristics

Another aspect of evolution closely related to adaptive radiation involves the transition from *generalized* characteristics to *specialized* characteristics. These two terms refer to the adaptive potential of a particular trait. A trait that's adapted for many functions is said to be generalized, while one that's limited to a narrow set of functions is said to be specialized.

For example, a generalized mammalian limb has five fairly flexible digits, adapted for many possible functions (grasping, weight support, and digging). In this respect, human hands are still quite generalized. On the other hand (or foot), there have been many structural modifications in our feet to make them suited for the specialized function of stable weight support in an upright posture.

The terms *generalized* and *specialized* are also sometimes used when speaking of the adaptive potential of whole organisms. Consider, for example, the aye-aye of Madagascar, an unusual primate species. The aye-aye is a highly specialized animal, structurally adapted to a narrow, rodent/woodpecker-like econiche—digging holes with prominent incisors and removing insect larvae with an elongated bony finger.

It's important to note that only a generalized ancestor can provide the flexible evolutionary basis for rapid diversification. Only a generalized species with potential for adaptation to varied ecological niches can lead to all the later diversification and specialization of forms into particular ecological niches.

An issue that we've already raised also bears on this discussion: the relationship of ancestral and derived characters. It's not always the case, but ancestral characters *usually* tend to be more generalized. And specialized characteristics are nearly always derived ones as well.

Modes of Evolutionary Change

Until fairly recently, evolutionary biologists generally agreed that microevolutionary mechanisms could be translated directly into the larger-scale macroevolutionary changes, especially the most central of all macroevolutionary processes, speciation. In the past three decades, this view has been seriously challenged. Many scientists now believe that macroevolution can't be explained solely in terms of accumulated microevolutionary changes. Consequently, these researchers are convinced that macroevolution is only partly understandable through microevolutionary models.

Gradualism versus Punctuated Equilibrium The traditional view of evolution has emphasized that change accumulates gradually in evolving lineages, an idea called *phyletic gradualism.* Accordingly, the complete fossil record of an evolving group (if it could be recovered) would display a series of forms with finely graded transitional differences between each ancestor and its descendant; that is, many "missing links" would be present. The fact that such transitional forms are only rarely found is attributed to the incompleteness of the fossil record, or, as Darwin called it, "a history of the world, imperfectly kept, and written in changing dialect."

For more than a century, this perspective dominated evolutionary biology. But in the last 30 years, some biologists have called it into question. The evolutionary mechanisms operating on species over the long run aren't always gradual. In some cases, species persist, basically unchanged, for thousands of generations. Then, rather suddenly (at least in geological terms), a "spurt" of speciation occurs. This uneven, nongradual process of long stasis and quick spurts has been termed **punctuated equilibrium** (Gould and Eldredge, 1977). What the advocates of punctuated equilibrium are disputing are the tempo (rate) and mode (manner) of evolutionary change as commonly understood since Darwin's time. Rather than a slow, steady tempo, this alternate view postulates long periods of no change (that is, equilibrium) punctuated (interrupted) only occasionally by sudden bursts. From this observation, many researchers concluded that the mode of evolution, too, must be different from that suggested by classical Darwinists. Rather than gradual accumulation of small changes in a single lineage, advocates of punctuated equilibrium believe that an additional evolutionary mechanism is required to push the process along. In fact, they postulate *speciation* as the major influence in bringing about rapid evolutionary change.

How well does the paleontological record agree with the predictions of punctuated equilibrium? Considerable fossil data do, in fact, show long periods of stasis punctuated by occasional quite rapid changes (taking from about 10,000 to 50,000 years). The best supporting evidence for punctuated equilibrium has come from marine invertebrate fossils. Intermediate forms are rare, not so much because the fossil record is poor but because the speciation events and longevity of these transitional species were so short that we shouldn't expect to find them very often.

And while some of the fossil evidence of other animals, including primates (Gingerich, 1985; Brown and Rose, 1987; Rose, 1991), doesn't fit the expectations of punctuated equilibrium, it would be misleading to assume that evolutionary change in these groups must thus be taking place at a completely gradual tempo. Moreover, recent molecular evidence suggests that both gradual change and rapid punctuated change occurred in the evolution of both plants and animals (Pagel et al., 2006). In all lineages, the pace assuredly speeds up and slows down due to factors that influence the size and relative isolation of populations. Environmental changes that influence the pace and direction of natural selection must also be considered. So in general accordance with the Modern Synthesis and as indicated by molecular evidence, microevolution and macroevolution don't need to be "decoupled," or considered separately, as some evolutionary biologists have suggested.

Summary

In this chapter, we've surveyed the basics of vertebrate and mammalian evolution, emphasizing a macroevolutionary perspective. Given the huge amount of organic diversity displayed, as well as the vast amount of time involved, two major organizing perspectives prove indispensable: (1) schemes of formal classification to organize organic diversity and (2) the geological time scale to organize geological time. We reviewed the principles of classification in some detail, contrasting two differing approaches: evolutionary systematics and cladistics. Because primates are vertebrates and, more specifically, mammals, we briefly reviewed these broader organic groups, emphasizing major evolutionary trends.

Theoretical perspectives relating to contemporary understanding of macroevolutionary processes (especially the concepts of species and speciation) are crucial to any interpretation of long-term aspects of evolutionary history, be it vertebrate, mammalian, or primate.

Since genus and species designation is the common form of reference for both living and extinct organisms (and we use it frequently throughout the text), we discussed its biological significance in depth. From a more general theoretical perspective, evolutionary biologists have postulated two different modes of evolutionary change: gradualism and punctuated equilibrium. Currently, even though the available fossil record does not conform entirely to the predictions of punctuated equilibrium, we should not conclude that evolutionary tempo was necessarily strictly gradual (which it certainly was not).

punctuated equilibrium The concept that evolutionary change proceeds through long periods of stasis punctuated by rapid periods of change.

Question: Why is it important to know something about the early evolutionary history of vertebrates, mammals, and primates? Isn't it enough to just know how humans evolved?

Answer: One of the taxonomic characteristics that helps us distinguish between mammals is placental type. There are four different types of placenta in mammals, but only two of these are found in primates. One, the epitheliochorial placenta of lemurs and lorises, has six membranes between the maternal and fetal circulatory systems, three of maternal origin and three of fetal origin. The hemochorial placenta of monkeys, apes, and humans has only three membranes, all of fetal origin. In an evolutionary sense, the epitheliochorial placenta allows greater variability between generations in that large genetic differences between the mother and fetus are not as readily detected, meaning that the fetus is less likely to be rejected. Greater variability means greater flexibility in responding to environmental change and more rapid divergence of lines. The adaptive radiation of lemurs on Madagascar probably wouldn't have occurred if these primates had hemochorial placentas, because very little genetic change would have been tolerated between generations.

On the other hand, the hemochorial placenta is very efficient at delivering oxygen to the fetus, which is important for a species like ours, in which a developing brain is an important component of gestation. Species like ours, with hemochorial placentas, may experience more early fetal loss, but the trade-off is greater brain growth, clearly a positive feature of human evolution. Another downside of the hemochorial placenta is that many substances readily cross from the maternal system to the fetal system. For example, the drug thalidomide apparently has little effect on the fetuses of lorises and lemurs (with their epitheliochorial placentas), but has well-known tragic effects on primates with hemochorial placentas. In the 1950s, when thalidomide was given to women early in pregnancy as a "wonder drug" to prevent morning sickness, the result was the birth of infants with severe developmental and physical abnormalities. Apparently, the drug readily crosses the hemochorial placenta and interferes with normal development; but since it did not have any negative effect on animals with epitheliochorial placentas, it was deemed safe for human use during pregnancy. Fetal alcohol syndrome similarly results from high levels of alcohol consumption during pregnancy.

Critical Thinking Questions

1 What are the two goals of classification? What happens when meeting both goals simultaneously becomes difficult or even impossible?

2 Remains of a fossil mammal have been found on your campus. If you adopt a cladistic approach, how would you determine (a) that it's a mammal rather than some other kind of vertebrate (discuss specific characters), (b) what kind of mammal it is (again, discuss specific characters), and (c) how it *might* be related to one or more living mammals (again, discuss specific characters)?

3 For the same fossil find (and your interpretation) in question 2, draw an interpretive figure using cladistic analysis (that is, draw a cladogram). Next, using more traditional evolutionary systematics, construct a phylogeny. Lastly, explain the differences between the cladogram and the phylogeny (be sure to emphasize the fundamental ways the two schemes differ).

4 Humans are fairly generalized mammals. What do we mean by this, and what specific features (characters) would you select to illustrate this statement?

CHAPTER 6

An Overview of the Primates

Lynn Kilgore

What are the major characteristics of primates?

Why are humans considered primates?

Why are so many nonhuman primates becoming endangered today? Do you think anything can be done to save them, and if so, what?

Introduction

Chimpanzees aren't monkeys. Neither are gorillas and orangutans. They're apes, and even though most people think they're basically the same, they aren't. Yet, how many times have you seen a greeting card or advertisement with a picture of a chimpanzee and a phrase that goes something like, "Don't monkey around" or "No more monkey business"? Or maybe you've seen people at zoos teasing and making fun of captive primates. While these things might seem trivial, they aren't, because they show how little most people know about their closest relatives. This is extremely unfortunate, because by better understanding these relatives, not only can we know more about ourselves; we can also try to preserve the many primate species that are now critically endangered.

One way to better understand any organism is to compare its anatomy and behavior with the anatomy and behavior of other, closely related species. This comparative approach helps explain how and why physiological and behavioral systems evolved as adaptive responses to various selective pressures throughout the course of evolution. This statement applies to human beings just as it does to any other species. So if we want to identify the components that have shaped the evolution of our species, a good starting point is to compare ourselves with our closest living relatives, the approximately 230 species of nonhuman primates (**prosimians**, monkeys, and apes). (Groves, 2001b, suggests that there may be as many as 350 primate species.)

This chapter describes the physical characteristics that define the order Primates; gives a brief overview of the major groups of living primates; and introduces some methods of comparing living primates through genetic data. (For a comparison of human and nonhuman skeletons, see Appendix A.) But before we go any further, we again want to call attention to a few common misunderstandings about evolutionary processes.

Evolution isn't a goal-directed process. Therefore, the fact that prosimians evolved before **anthropoids** doesn't mean that prosimians "progressed," or "advanced," to become anthropoids. Living primate species aren't in any way "superior" to their predecessors or to one another. Consequently, in discussions of major groupings of contemporary nonhuman primates, there is no implied superiority or inferiority of any of these groups. Each lineage or species has come to possess unique qualities that make it better suited to a particular habitat and lifestyle. Given that all living organisms are "successful" results of the evolutionary process, it's best to completely avoid using such loaded terms as *superior* and *inferior*. Finally, you shouldn't make the mistake of thinking that contemporary primates (including humans) necessarily represent the final stage or apex of a lineage. Actually, the only species that represent final evolutionary stages of particular lineages are the ones that become extinct.

Click!

Go to the following media resources for interactive activities, more information, and study materials on topics covered in this chapter:

- Anthropology Resource Center
- Student Companion Website for *Essentials of Physical Anthropology,* Seventh Edition
- Online Virtual Laboratories for Physical Anthropology CD-ROM, Fourth Edition

prosimians Members of a suborder of Primates, the suborder Prosimii (pronounced "pro-sim´-ee-eye"). Traditionally, the suborder includes lemurs, lorises, and tarsiers.

anthropoids Members of a suborder of Primates, the suborder Anthropoidea (pronounced "ann-throw-poid´-ee-uh"). Traditionally, the suborder includes monkeys, apes, and humans.

Primate Characteristics

All primates share many characteristics with other mammals (see Chapter 5). Some of these basic mammalian traits are body hair; a relatively long gestation period followed by live birth; mammary glands (thus the term *mammal*); different types of teeth (incisors, canines, premolars, and molars); the ability to maintain a constant internal body temperature through physiological means, or *endothermy*; increased brain size; and a considerable capacity for learning and behavioral flexibility. Therefore, to differentiate primates, as a group, from other mammals, we need to describe those characteristics that, taken together, set primates apart from other mammalian groups.

Identifying single traits that define the primate order isn't easy because compared to many mammals, primates have remained quite *generalized*. That is, primates have retained many ancestral, or primitive, mammalian traits that some other mammals have lost over time. In response to particular selective pressures, many mammalian groups have become increasingly **specialized,** or derived. For example, through the course of evolution, horses and cattle have undergone a reduction of the number of digits (fingers and toes) from the ancestral pattern of five to one and two, respectively. Moreover, these species have developed hard, protective coverings over their feet in the form of hooves (Fig. 6-1a). This limb structure is adaptive in prey species, whose survival depends on speed and stability, but it restricts them to only one type of locomotion. Moreover, limb function is limited entirely to support and movement, while the ability to manipulate objects is completely lost.

Primates can't be defined by one or even a few traits they share in common because they *aren't* so specialized. Therefore, anthropologists have drawn attention to a group of characteristics that, taken together, more or less typify the entire primate order. But these are a set of *general* tendencies that aren't equally expressed in all primates. In addition, while some of these traits are unique to primates, many others are retained primitive mammalian characteristics shared with other mammals. So the following list is meant to give an overall structural and behavioral picture of the primates in general, and it emphasizes the characteristics that tend to set primates apart from other mammals. Concentrating on certain ancestral mammalian traits along with more specific derived ones has been the traditional approach of **primatologists,** and it's still used today. In their limbs and locomotion, teeth and diet, senses, brain, and behaviors, primates reflect a common evolutionary history with adaptations to similar environmental challenges, mostly as highly social, arboreal animals.

A. *Limbs and locomotion*
   1. *A tendency toward erect posture (especially in the upper body).* Present to some degree in almost all primates, this tendency is variously associated with sitting, leaping, standing, and, occasionally, bipedal walking.
   2. *A flexible, generalized limb structure, which allows most primates to practice a number of locomotor behaviors.* Primates have retained some bones (for example, the clavicle, or collarbone) and certain abilities, (like rotation of the forearm) that have been lost in some more specialized mammals. Various aspects of hip and shoulder anatomy also provide primates with a wide range of limb movement and function (walking on four, or sometimes, two limbs, climbing, hanging, etc.). Thus, by maintaining a generalized locomotor anatomy, primates aren't restricted to one form of movement, such as quadrupedalism. Primate limbs are also used for many activities besides locomotion.
   3. *Hands and feet with a high degree of **prehensility** (grasping ability).* All primates use their hands, and frequently their feet, to grasp and manipulate objects (Fig. 6-1b through e). This is variably expressed and is enhanced by a number of characteristics, including:

specialized Evolved for a particular function; usually refers to a specific trait (e.g., incisor teeth), but may also refer to the entire way of life of an organism.

primatologists Scientists who study the evolution, anatomy, and behavior of nonhuman primates. Those who study behavior in non-captive animals are usually trained as physical anthropologists.

prehensility Grasping, as by the hands and feet of primates.

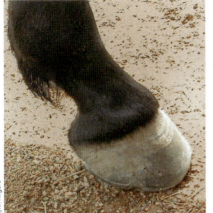
(a)

(b)

(c)

(d)

(e)

FIGURE 6-1

(a) A horse's front foot, homologous with a human hand, has undergone reduction from 5 digits to one. (b) While raccoons are capable of considerable manual dexterity and can readily pick up small objects with one hand, they have no opposable thumb.
(c) Many monkeys are able to grasp objects with an opposable thumb, while others have very reduced thumbs. (d) Humans are capable of a "precision grip."
(e) Chimpanzees, with their reduced thumbs, are also capable of a precision grip, but they frequently use a modified form.

a. *Retention of five digits on hands and feet.* This characteristic varies somewhat throughout the order, with some species showing reduction or absence of the thumb or second digit (first finger).

b. *An opposable thumb and, in most species, a divergent and partially opposable big toe.* Most primates are capable of moving the thumb so that it comes in contact (in some fashion) with the second digit or the palm of the hand (see Fig. 6-1c through e).

c. *Nails instead of claws.* This characteristic is seen in all primates except some New World monkeys. All prosimians also possess a claw on one digit.

d. *Tactile pads enriched with sensory nerve fibers at the ends of digits.* This enhances the sense of touch.

B. *Diet and teeth*
  1. *Lack of dietary specialization.* This is typical of most primates, who tend to eat a wide assortment of food items. In general, primates are **omnivorous.**
  2. *A generalized dentition* The teeth aren't specialized for processing only one type of food, a pattern related to the lack of dietary specialization.

C. *The senses and the brain.* Primates, especially **diurnal** ones, rely heavily on the visual sense and less on the sense of smell. This emphasis is reflected in evolutionary changes in the skull, eyes, and brain.
  1. *Color vision.* This is a characteristic of all diurnal primates. **Nocturnal** primates don't have color vision.

omnivorous Having a diet consisting of many kinds of foods, such as plant materials (seeds, fruits, leaves), meat, and insects.

diurnal Active during the day.

nocturnal Active during the night.

stereoscopic vision The condition whereby visual images are, to varying degrees, superimposed on one another. This provides for depth perception, or the perception of the external environment in three dimensions. Stereoscopic vision is partly a function of structures in the brain.

binocular vision Vision characterized by overlapping visual fields provided for by forward-facing eyes. Binocular vision is essential to depth perception.

hemispheres Two halves of the cerebrum that are connected by a dense mass of fibers. (The cerebrum is the large rounded outer portion of the brain.)

2. *Depth perception.* **Stereoscopic vision,** or the ability to perceive objects in three dimensions, is made possible through a variety of mechanisms, including:

   a. *Eyes positioned toward the front of the face (not to the sides).* This provides for overlapping visual fields, or **binocular vision** (Fig. 6-2).

   b. *Visual information from each eye transmitted to visual centers in both hemispheres of the brain.* In nonprimate mammals, most optic nerve fibers cross to the opposite hemisphere through a structure at the base of the brain. In primates, about 40 percent of the fibers remain on the same side, so that each hemisphere receives information from both eyes (see Fig. 6-2).

   c. *Visual information organized into three-dimensional images by specialized structures in the brain itself.* The capacity for stereoscopic vision depends on overlapping visual fields and on each hemisphere of the brain receiving visual information from both eyes.

3. *Decreased reliance on the sense of smell (olfaction).* This trend is expressed in an overall reduction in the size of olfactory structures in the brain. Corresponding reduction of the entire olfactory apparatus has also resulted in decreased size of the snout. In some species, such as baboons, the large muzzle isn't related to olfaction, but to the presence of large teeth, especially the canines (Fig. 6-3).

4. *Expansion and increased complexity of the brain.* This is a general trend among placental mammals, but it's especially true of primates (Fig. 6-4). In

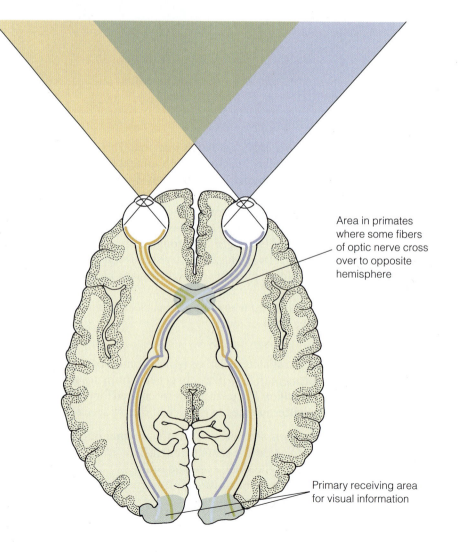

FIGURE 6-2

Simplified diagram showing overlapping visual fields that permit binocular vision in primates with eyes positioned at the front of the face. (The green shaded area represents the area of overlap.) Stereoscopic vision (three-dimensional vision) is provided in part by binocular vision and in part by the transmission of visual stimuli from each eye to *both* hemispheres of the brain. (In nonprimate mammals, most, if not all, visual information crosses over to the hemisphere opposite the eye in which it was initially received.)

Area in primates where some fibers of optic nerve cross over to opposite hemisphere

Primary receiving area for visual information

(a)

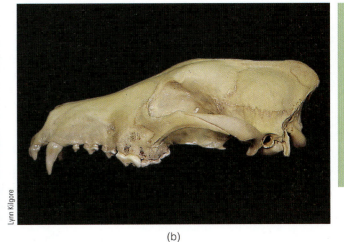
(b)

primates, this expansion is most evident in the visual and association areas of the **neocortex** (portions of the brain where information from different **sensory modalities** is integrated).

D. *Maturation, learning, and behavior*
1. *A more efficient means of fetal nourishment, longer periods of gestation, reduced numbers of offspring (with single births the norm), delayed maturation, and longer life span.*
2. *A greater dependence on flexible, learned behavior.* This trend is correlated with delayed maturation and longer periods of infant and childhood dependency on at least one parent. As a result of both these trends, parental investment in each offspring is increased, so that although fewer offspring are born, they receive more intense rearing.
3. *The tendency to live in social groups and the permanent association of adult males with the group.* Except for some nocturnal species, primates tend to associate with other individuals. The permanent association of adult males with the group is uncommon in most mammals but widespread in primates.
4. *The tendency toward diurnal activity patterns.* This is seen in most primates; only one monkey species and some prosimians are nocturnal.

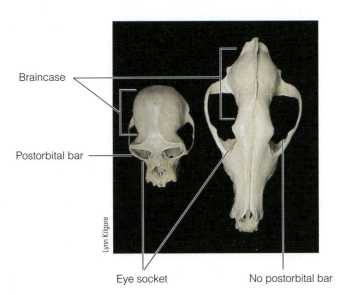

Braincase

Postorbital bar

Eye socket

No postorbital bar

FIGURE 6-3

The skull of a male baboon (a) compared with that of a red wolf (b). Note the forward-facing eyes positioned above the snout in the baboon, compared with the lateral position of the eyes at the sides of the wolf's face. Also, the baboon's large muzzle doesn't reflect a heavy reliance on the sense of smell. Rather, it supports the roots of the large canine teeth, which curve back through the bone for as much as 1½ inches.

neocortex The more recently evolved portions of the brain's cortex that are involved with higher mental functions and composed of areas that integrate incoming information from different sensory modalities.

sensory modalities Different forms of sensation (e.g., touch, pain, pressure, heat, cold, vision, taste, hearing, and smell).

FIGURE 6-4

The skull of a gibbon (left) compared with that of a red wolf (right). Note that the absolute size of the braincase in the gibbon is slightly larger than that of the wolf, even though the wolf (at about 80 to 100 pounds) is six times the size of the gibbon (about 15 pounds).

Primate Adaptations

In this section, we'll consider how primate anatomical traits evolved as adaptations to environmental circumstances. It's important to remember that when you see the phrase "environmental circumstances," it refers to several interrelated variables, including climate, diet, habitat (such as woodland, grassland, forest), and predation.

Evolutionary Factors

Traditionally, the suite of characteristics shared by primates has been explained as the result of adaptation to **arboreal** living. While other placental mammals were adapting to various ground-dwelling lifestyles and even marine environments, the primates found their **adaptive niche** in the trees. Some other mammals were also adapting to arboreal living, but while many of them nested in trees, they continued to come to the ground to find food. But throughout the course of evolution, primates increasingly found food (leaves, seeds, fruits, nuts, insects, birds' eggs, and small mammals) in the branches themselves. Over time, this dietary shift enhanced a general trend toward increased *omnivory;* and this trend in turn led to the retention of the generalized dentition we see in primates today.

This adaptive process is also reflected in how heavily primates rely on vision. In a complex, three-dimensional environment with uncertain footholds, acute color vision with depth perception is, to say the least, extremely beneficial. Grasping hands and feet also reflect an adaptation to living in the trees. Obviously, grasping hands aren't essential to climbing, as many animals (such as cats, squirrels, and raccoons) demonstrate quite effectively. But all the same, the primates adopted a technique of grasping branches with prehensile hands and feet (and tails in some species), and grasping abilities were further enhanced with the appearance of flattened nails instead of claws.

Cartmill (1972,1992) proposed an alternative to the traditional *arboreal hypothesis,* called the *visual predation hypothesis.* Cartmill pointed out that while some animals (squirrels, for example) don't have forward-facing eyes, visual predators like cats and owls do, and this fact may suggest an additional factor that could have shaped primate evolution.

Actually, forward-facing eyes (which facilitate binocular vision), grasping hands and feet, and the presence of nails instead of claws may not have come about as adaptive advantages in a purely arboreal setting. But they may have been the hallmarks of an arboreal visual predator. So it's possible that early primates may first have adapted to shrubby forest undergrowth and the lowest tiers of the forest canopy, where they hunted insects and other small prey primarily through stealth. In fact, many smaller primates today occupy just such an econiche.

In a third scenario, Sussman (1991) suggested that the basic primate traits developed along with another major evolutionary occurrence: the appearance of flowering plants around 140 million years ago. Flowering plants provide numerous resources, including nectar, seeds, and fruits, and their appearance coincided with the emergence of ancestral forms of major groups of insects, birds and mammals. Sussman argued that visual predation isn't common among modern primates. Therefore, forward-facing eyes, grasping hands and feet, omnivory, and color vision may have come about in response to the demand for fine visual and tactile discrimination, which would benefit an animal that feeds on small food items (berries and seeds) among branches and stems (Dominy and Lucas, 2001).

These hypotheses aren't mutually exclusive. The complex of primate characteristics might well have begun in nonarboreal settings and certainly may have been stimulated by the new econiches provided by evolving flowering plants. But at some point, the primates did take to the trees, and that's where the majority of them still live today.

arboreal Tree-living; adapted to life in the trees.

adaptive niche The entire way of life of an organism: where it lives, what it eats, how it gets food, how it avoids predators, etc.

Geographical Distribution and Habitats

With just a couple of exceptions, primates are found in tropical or semitropical areas of the New and Old Worlds. In the New World, these areas include southern Mexico, Central America, and parts of South America. Old World primates are found in Africa, India, Southeast Asia (including numerous islands), and Japan (Fig. 6-6 on pages 106–107).

While the majority of primates are mostly arboreal and live in forest or woodland habitats, some Old World monkeys (for example, baboons) have adapted to life on the ground in places where trees are sparsely distributed. Moreover, the African apes (gorillas, chimpanzees, and bonobos) spend a considerable amount of time on the ground in forested and wooded habitats. Nevertheless, no nonhuman primate is adapted to a fully terrestrial lifestyle, so they all spend some time in the trees.

Diet and Teeth

Omnivory is one example of the overall lack of specialization in primates. Although the majority of primate species tend to emphasize some food items over others, most eat a combination of fruits, nuts, seeds, leaves, other plant materials, and insects. Many also get animal protein from birds and amphibians, and some occasionally kill and eat small mammals, including other primates. Others, such as African colobus monkeys and the leaf-eating monkeys (langurs) of India and Southeast Asia, have become more specialized and mostly feed on leaves. Such a wide array of choices is highly adaptive, even in fairly predictable environments.

Like the majority of other mammals, most primates have four kinds of teeth: incisors and canines for biting and cutting, and premolars and molars for chewing. Biologists use what's called a *dental formula* to describe the number of each type of tooth a species has in each quadrant of the mouth (Fig. 6-5). For example, all Old World *anthropoids* (monkeys, apes, and humans) have two incisors, one canine, two premolars, and three molars on each side of the **midline** in both the upper and lower jaws, for a total of 32 teeth. This is represented as a dental formula of:

$$\frac{2.1.2.3 \text{ (upper)}}{2.1.2.3 \text{ (lower)}}$$

The dental formula for a generalized placental mammal is 3.1.4.3. (three incisors, one canine, four premolars, and three molars). But primates have fewer than this because of the evolutionary trend toward a reduced number of teeth in many mammal groups. But, the number of each type of tooth varies among primate lineages. For example, in most New World monkeys, the dental formula is 2.1.3.3. (two incisors, one canine, three premolars, and three molars). In contrast, humans, apes, and all Old World monkeys have a dental formula of 2.1.2.3; that is, they have one less premolar than most New World monkeys.

The lack of dietary specialization in primates is reflected in the lack of specialization in the size and shape of the teeth, because tooth form is directly related to diet. For example, carnivores typically have premolars and molars with high pointed **cusps** adapted for tearing meat; but herbivores, such as cattle and horses, have molars with broad, flat surfaces suited to chewing tough grasses and other plant materials. Most primates have premolars and molars with low, rounded cusps, and this kind of molar **morphology** allows them to process most types of foods. So throughout their

midline An anatomical term referring to a hypothetical line that divides the body into right and left halves.

cusps The elevated portions (bumps) on the chewing surfaces of premolar and molar teeth.

morphology The form (shape, size) of anatomical structures; can also refer to the entire organism.

FIGURE 6-5

The human maxilla (a) illustrates a dental formula of $\frac{2.1.2.3}{2.1.2.3}$ characteristic of all Old World monkeys, apes, and humans. The *Cebus* maxilla (b) shows the $\frac{2.1.3.3}{2.1.3.3}$ dental formula that is typical of most New World monkeys.

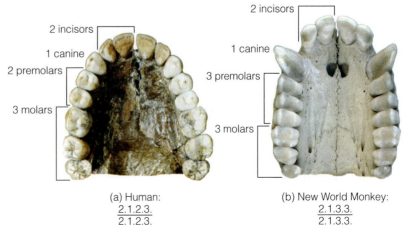

2 incisors
1 canine
2 premolars
3 molars

(a) Human:
$$\frac{2.1.2.3.}{2.1.2.3.}$$

2 incisors
1 canine
3 premolars
3 molars

(b) New World Monkey:
$$\frac{2.1.3.3.}{2.1.3.3.}$$

FIGURE 6-6
Geographical distribution of living nonhuman primates. Much original habitat is now very fragmented.

Spider monkeys and muriquis (Central and South America)

Howler species (Central and South America)

Prince Bernhard's titi (Brazil, Amazon rain forest)

Uakari (Brazil, near Jurua River)

Squirrel monkeys (South America)

White-faced capuchins (South America)

Muriqui (southeastern Brazil)

Marmosets and tamarins (South America)

Macaque species
(North Africa, India,
Southeast Asia,
China, and Japan)

Baboon species
(throughout sub-Saharan
Africa)

Gibbons and siamangs
(Southeast Asia,
islands, and China)

Cercopithecus
species (throughout
sub-Saharan Africa)

Tarsier species
(Southeast
Asia, islands,
and China)

Loris species
(Africa, India, and
Southeast Asia)

Mountain and lowland
gorillas (western and
central Africa)

Langur species
(colobines) (India,
southern Asia, and
south China)

Orangutans
(Borneo and Sumatra)

Lemurs
(Madagascar)

Chimpanzees and
bonobos
(across central Africa)

Colobus species
(throughout sub-Saharan
Africa)

Galagos (bush babies)
(throughout sub-Saharan
Africa)

evolutionary history, the primates have developed a dentition adapted to a varied diet, and the capacity to exploit many foods has contributed to their overall success during the last 50 million years.

Locomotion

quadrupedal Using all four limbs to support the body during locomotion; the basic mammalian (and primate) form of locomotion.

macaques (muh-kaks´) A group of Old World monkeys comprising several species, including rhesus monkeys. Most macaque species live in India, other parts of Asia, and nearby islands.

Almost all primates are, at least to some degree, **quadrupedal,** meaning they use all four limbs to support the body during locomotion. However, most primates use more than one form of locomotion, and they're able to do this because of their generalized anatomy.

Although the majority of quadrupedal primates are arboreal, terrestrial quadrupedalism is fairly common and is typical of some lemurs, baboons, and **macaques.** The limbs of terrestrial quadrupeds are approximately the same length (Fig. 6-7a), but in arboreal quadrupeds, forelimbs are somewhat shorter (Fig. 6-7b).

Vertical clinging and leaping, another form of locomotion, is characteristic of many prosimians. As the term implies, vertical clingers and leapers support themselves vertically by grasping onto tree trunks with their knees and ankles tightly flexed (Fig. 6-7c). Forceful extension of their long hind limbs allows them to spring powerfully forward or backward.

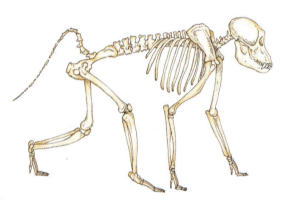

(a) Skeleton of a terrestrial quadruped (savanna baboon).

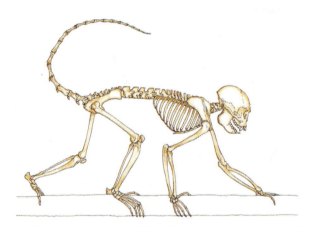

(b) Skeleton of an arboreal New World monkey (bearded saki).

FIGURE 6–7

Differences in skeletal anatomy and limb proportions reflect differences in locomotor patterns. (Redrawn from original art by Stephen Nash in John G. Fleagle, *Primate Adaptation and Evolution,* 2nd ed., 1999. Reprinted by permission of publisher and Stephen Nash.)

(c) Skeleton of a vertical clinger and leaper (indri).

(d) Skeleton of a brachiator (gibbon).

Brachiation, or arm swinging, is another type of primate locomotion where the body is alternatively supported under either forelimb (Fig. 6-7d). Because of anatomical modifications at the shoulder joint, apes and humans are capable of true brachiation. However, only the small gibbons and siamangs of Southeast Asia brachiate almost exclusively.

Species that brachiate tend to have arms that are longer than legs, a short stable lumbar spine, long curved fingers, and reduced thumbs. Because these are traits seen in all the apes, it's believed that although none of the great apes (orangutans, gorillas, bonobos, and chimpanzees) habitually brachiate today, they may have inherited these characteristics from brachiating or perhaps climbing ancestors.

Some New World monkeys (for example, muriquis and spider monkeys) are called *semibrachiators,* as they practice a combination of leaping with some arm swinging. Also, some New World species enhance arm swinging and other suspensory behaviors by using a *prehensile tail,* which in effect serves as a grasping fifth hand. It's important to mention that no Old World monkeys have prehensile tails.

Lastly, all the apes (to varying degrees) have arms that are longer than legs, and some (gorillas, bonobos, and chimpanzees) practice a special form of quadrupedalism called knuckle walking. Because their arms are so long relative to their legs, instead of walking with the palms of their hands flat on the ground like some monkeys do, they support the weight of their upper body on the back surfaces of their bent fingers (Fig. 6-8).

FIGURE 6-8
Chimpanzee knuckle walking. Note how the weight of the upper body is supported on the knuckles and not on the palm of the hand.

Primate Classification

The living primates are commonly categorized into their respective subgroups as shown in Figure 6-9. This taxonomy is based on the system originally established by Linnaeus. (Remember that the primate order, which includes a diverse array of approximately 230 species, belongs to a larger group, the class Mammalia.)

As you learned in Chapter 5, in any taxonomic system, animals are organized into increasingly specific categories. For example, the order Primates includes *all* primates. But at the next level down, the *suborder,* primates have conventionally been divided into two large categories, Prosimii (all the prosimians: lemurs, lorises, and, customarily, the tarsiers) and Anthropoidea (all the monkeys, apes, and humans). Therefore, as you can see, the suborder distinction is more specific than the order.

At the suborder level, the prosimians are distinct as a group from all the other primates, and this classification makes the biological and evolutionary statement that all the prosimian species are more closely related to each other than they are to any of the anthropoids. Likewise, all anthropoid species are more closely related to one another than they are to the prosimians.

The taxonomy shown in Figure 6-9 is the traditional one, and it's based on physical similarities between species and lineages. However, this approach isn't foolproof. For instance, two primate species that resemble each other anatomically (for example, some New and Old World monkeys) may not be closely related at all. By looking only at physical characteristics, it's possible to overlook the unknown effects of separate evolutionary history (see our discussion of homoplasy on p. 81). But genetic evidence overcomes this problem and shows that Old and New World monkeys are evolutionarily quite distinct and may have evolved from a common ancestor as long ago as 35 million years.

Primate classification is currently in a state of transition, mainly because of genetic evidence that has emerged over the past few years. Beginning in the 1970s, scientists began to apply a few different genetic techniques to help identify biological and phylogenetic relationships between species. One of these methods was to compare the amino acid sequences of particular proteins in different species. If the proteins were very similar, then the species were closely related, and they probably inherited their genetic blueprint from a common ancestor. For example, there's only one difference between chimpanzees and humans in the 146 amino acids that make up the hemoglobin beta chain.

brachiation A form of locomotion in which the body is suspended beneath the hands and support is alternated from one forelimb to the other; arm swinging.

FIGURE 6-9

Primate taxonomic classification. This abbreviated taxonomy illustrates how primates are grouped into increasingly specific categories. Only the more general categories are shown, except for the great apes and humans.

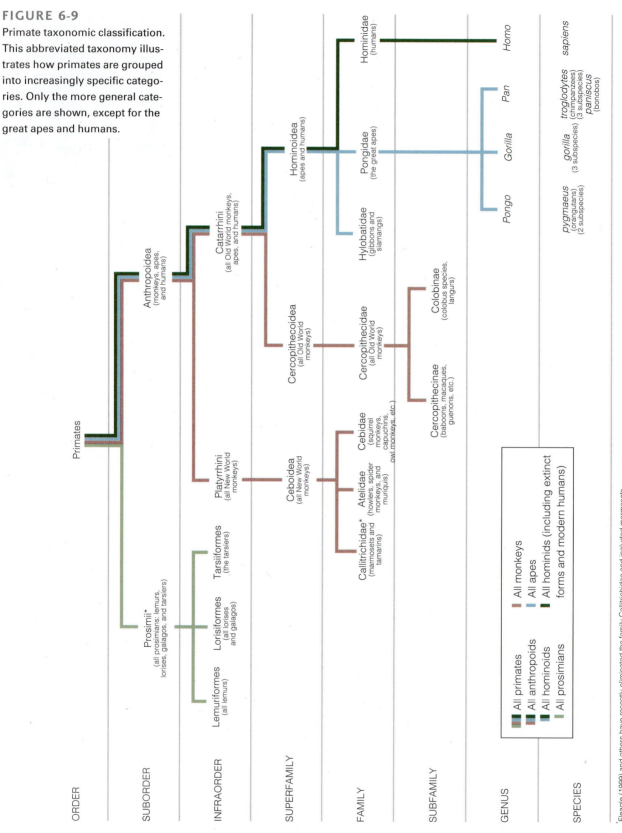

Legend:

— All monkeys
— All apes
— All hominids (including extinct forms and modern humans)

— All primates
— All anthropoids
— All hominoids
— All prosimians

*Fleagle (1999) and others have recently eliminated the family Callitrichidae and included marmosets and tamarins in the family Cebidae.

As useful as these techniques were, they're still only *indirect* methods of comparing DNA sequences between species. But now, the techniques of DNA sequencing used in the Human Genome Project make it possible to make direct between-species comparisons of DNA sequences. This approach is called *comparative genomics.*

A complete draft sequence of the chimpanzee genome was completed in 2005 (The Chimpanzee Sequencing and Analysis Consortium, 2005), and it represents a major advance in human comparative genomics. But even prior to this, molecular anthropologists had already compared the sequences of several chimpanzee and human genes. For example, Wildman et al. (2003) compared nearly 100 human genes with their chimpanzee, gorilla, and orangutan counterparts and determined that humans are most closely related to chimpanzees and that their "functional elements," or **coding DNA sequences,** are between 98.4 and 99.4 percent identical. These results are consistent with the findings of several other previous studies that suggested a genetic difference between chimpanzees and ourselves of approximately 1.2 percent (Chen et al., 2001). Other studies have substantiated these figures, but they've also revealed more variation in **noncoding DNA segments** and portions that have been inserted, deleted, or duplicated. So when the *entire* genome is considered, reported differences between chimpanzees and humans range from 2.7 percent (Cheng et al., 2005) to 6.4 percent (Demuth, et al., 2006,). Still, these aren't substantial differences, and as of now, the genetic evidence suggests that humans and chimpanzees last shared a common ancestor with gorillas around 6–8 mya and that the chimpanzee and human lineages diverged between 4 and 6 mya (Chen, et al., 2001). However, a recent new fossil discovery has perhaps pushed the date of divergence between the gorilla lineage and chimpanzees and humans back to at least 10 mya (Suwa et al., 2007).

The genetic similarities together with relatively recent divergence from a common ancestor have caused many primatologists to consider changing how they classify the hominoids (Goodman et al., 1998; Wildman et al., 2003). Although there's no formal acceptance of suggested changes, most biological anthropologists support placing all the great apes in the family Hominidae along with humans. However, many anthropologists still use the term *hominid* to refer to humans and their bipedal ancestors. (We'll return to this important topic in Chapter 8.)

Another area where changes have been suggested concerns tarsiers (see p. 114). Tarsiers are highly specialized animals that display several unique physical characteristics. Because they possess a number of prosimian traits, tarsiers have traditionally been classified as prosimians (with lemurs and lorises). But they also have certain anthropoid features, and they're more similar to the anthropoids biochemically (Dene et al., 1976).

Primatologists who maintain that tarsiers are more closely related to anthropoids have supported a reclassification. Instead of simply moving tarsiers into the suborder Anthropoidea, one scheme (Fig. 6-10) places lemurs and lorises in a different suborder, Strepsirhini, instead of Prosimii, while tarsiers are included with monkeys, apes, and humans in another suborder, Haplorhini (Szaley and Delson, 1979). In this classification, the traditionally named suborders Prosimii and Anthropoidea are replaced by Strepsirhini and Haplorhini, respectively. This designation hasn't been universally accepted. In fact, a cross-species comparison of almost 10,000 DNA base pairs in 64 species showed that tarsiers are more closely

coding DNA sequences DNA sequences that code for the production of a detectable protein product.

noncoding DNA sequences sequences that do not code for identifiable proteins but in many cases influence the actions of coding sequences.

FIGURE 6-10

Revised partial classification of the primates. In this system, the names Prosimii and Anthropoidea would be replaced by Strepsirhini and Haplorhini, respectively. Tarsiers would be included in the same suborder as monkeys, apes, and humans to reflect a closer relationship with these species than with lemurs and lorises. (Compare with Fig. 6-9.)

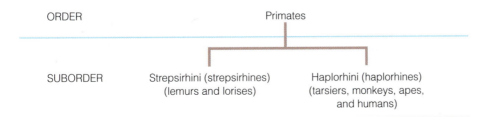

ORDER — Primates

SUBORDER — Strepsirhini (strepsirhines) (lemurs and lorises) — Haplorhini (haplorhines) (tarsiers, monkeys, apes, and humans)

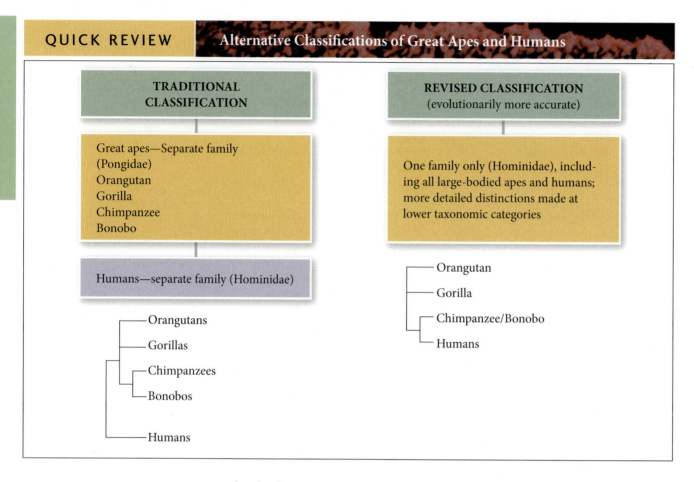

QUICK REVIEW — Alternative Classifications of Great Apes and Humans

TRADITIONAL CLASSIFICATION

Great apes—Separate family (Pongidae)
Orangutan
Gorilla
Chimpanzee
Bonobo

Humans—separate family (Hominidae)

Orangutans
Gorillas
Chimpanzees
Bonobos
Humans

REVISED CLASSIFICATION (evolutionarily more accurate)

One family only (Hominidae), including all large-bodied apes and humans; more detailed distinctions made at lower taxonomic categories

Orangutan
Gorilla
Chimpanzee/Bonobo
Humans

related to lemurs (Murphy et al., 2001). Nevertheless, the terminology is now common, especially in technical publications. So if you see the term *strepsirhine,* you know that the author is referring specifically to lemurs and lorises.

We've presented the traditional system of primate classification in this chapter, even though we acknowledge the need for change, particularly regarding humans and the great apes. Until the new designations are formally adopted and there's more universal usage of the newer terminology, we think it's appropriate to use the standard taxonomy along with discussion of some of the proposed changes.

A Survey of the Living Primates

In this section, we discuss the major primate subgroups. Since it's beyond the scope of this book to cover any species in detail, we present a brief description of each major grouping. Then we take a closer look at the apes.

Prosimians: Lemurs, Lorises and Tarsiers

The most primitive primates are the lemurs and lorises. Remember that by "primitive" we mean that prosimians are more similar to their earlier mammalian ancestors than are the other primates (monkeys, apes, and humans). For example, they retain certain more ancestral characteristics, such as a more pronounced reliance on the sense of smell. Their greater olfactory capabilities (compared to other primates) are reflected in the presence of a moist, fleshy pad, or **rhinarium,** at the end of the nose and in a relatively long snout (Fig. 6-11). Lemurs and lorises also mark territories with scent in a manner not seen in most other primates.

Many other characteristics distinguish lemurs and lorises from the anthropoids (and from tarsiers), including eyes placed more to the side of the face, differences in reproductive physiology, and shorter gestation and maturation periods. Lemurs

rhinarium (rine-air´-ee-um) (*pl.,* rhinaria) The moist, hairless pad at the end of the nose seen in most mammals. The rhinarium enhances an animal's ability to smell.

Lynn Kilgore

Lynn Kilgore

FIGURE 6-11
As you can see, rhinaria come in different shapes and sizes, but they all serve to enhance an animal's sense of smell.

and lorises also have a unique trait called a "dental comb" (Fig. 6-12). The dental comb is formed by forward-projecting lower incisors and canines, and together these modified teeth are used in grooming and feeding. Another characteristic that sets lemurs and lorises apart from anthropoids is the retention of a claw (called a "grooming claw") on the second toe.

Lemurs Lemurs are found only on the island of Madagascar and nearby islands off the east coast of Africa (Fig. 6-13). As the only nonhuman primates on Madagascar, lemurs diversified into numerous and varied ecological niches without competition from monkeys and apes. Thus, the approximately 60 surviving species of lemurs represent an evolutionary pattern that has vanished elsewhere.

Lemurs range in size from the small mouse lemur, with a body length (head and trunk) of only 5 inches, to the indri, with a body length of 2 to 3 feet (Nowak, 1999). While the larger lemurs are diurnal and exploit a wide variety of dietary items, such as leaves, fruits, buds, bark, and shoots, the smaller species (mouse and dwarf lemurs) are nocturnal and insectivorous.

Lemurs display considerable variation regarding numerous other aspects of behavior. Some are mostly arboreal, but others, such as the ring-tailed lemur (Fig. 6-14), are more terrestrial. Some arboreal species are quadrupeds, and others (sifakas and indris) are vertical clingers and leapers (Fig. 6-15). Socially, several species, such as ring-tailed lemurs and sifakas, are gregarious and live in groups of 10 to 25 animals composed of males and females of all ages. Others (the indris) live in family units

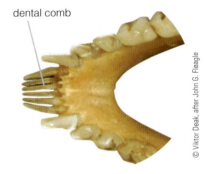

dental comb

© Viktor Deak, after John G. Fleagle

FIGURE 6-12
Prosimian dental comb, formed by forward-projecting incisors and canines.

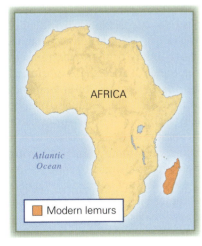

FIGURE 6-13
Geographical distribution of modern lemurs.

AFRICA

Atlantic
Ocean

■ Modern lemurs

Fred Jacobs

FIGURE 6-14
Ring-tailed lemur.

Fred Jacobs

FIGURE 6-15
Sifakas in their native habitat in Madagascar.

FIGURE 6-16
Slow loris.

FIGURE 6-17
Galago, or "bush baby."

composed of a mated pair and their offspring. And several nocturnal forms are mostly solitary.

Lorises Lorises (Fig. 6-16), which resemble lemurs, were able to survive in mainland areas by becoming nocturnal when most other prosimians became extinct. In this way, they were (and are) able to avoid competition with more recently evolved primates, the diurnal monkeys.

There are at least eight loris species, all of which are found in tropical forest and woodland habitats of India, Sri Lanka, Southeast Asia, and Africa. Also included in the same general category are six to nine (Bearder, 1987; Nowak, 1999) galago species (Fig. 6-17), which are widely distributed throughout most of the forested and woodland savanna areas of sub-Saharan Africa.

Locomotion in some, but not all, lorises is a slow climbing form of quadrupedalism. All galagos are highly agile vertical clingers and leapers. Some lorises and galagos are almost entirely insectivorous; others supplement their diet with fruits, leaves, gums, and slugs. Lorises and galagos frequently forage for food alone, and unlike other primates, females leave infants behind in nests until they are older. Feeding ranges overlap, and two or more females occasionally forage together or share the same sleeping nest.

Tarsiers There are five recognized tarsier species (Nowak, 1999; Fig. 6-18), all of which are restricted to island areas in Southeast Asia (Fig. 6-19), where they inhabit a wide range of habitats, from tropical forest to backyard gardens. Tarsiers are nocturnal insectivores that leap from lower branches and shrubs onto prey (which may also include small vertebrates). They appear to form stable pair bonds, and the basic tarsier social unit is a mated pair and their young offspring (MacKinnon and MacKinnon, 1980).

As we have already mentioned, tarsiers present a complex blend of characteristics not seen in other primates. One of the most obvious differences is their enormous eyes, which dominate much of the face and are immobile within their sockets. To compensate for the inability to move the eyes, tarsiers (like owls) are able to rotate their heads 180°.

FIGURE 6-18
Tarsier.

FIGURE 6-19
Geographical distribution of tarsiers.

Anthropoids (Monkeys, Apes, and Humans)

Although there is much variation among anthropoids, they share certain features that, when taken together, distinguish them as a group from prosimians (and most other placental mammals). Here's a partial list of these traits:

1. Generally larger body size
2. Larger brain (in absolute terms and relative to body weight)
3. Reduced reliance on the sense of smell, indicated by absence of a rhinarium and other structures
4. Increased reliance on vision, with forward-facing eyes at the front of the face
5. Greater degree of color vision
6. Back of eye socket formed by a bony plate
7. Blood supply to brain different from that of prosimians
8. Fusion of the two sides of the mandible at the midline to form one bone (in prosimians they are joined by fibrous tissue)
9. Less specialized dentition, as seen in absence of dental comb and some other features
10. Differences in female internal reproductive anatomy
11. Longer gestation and maturation periods
12. Increased parental care
13. More mutual grooming

Approximately 85 percent of all primates are monkeys (about 195 species). Monkeys are divided into two groups separated by geographical area (New World and Old World), as well as by several million years of separate evolutionary history.

New World Monkeys The approximately 70 species of New World monkeys exhibit considerable variation in size, diet, and ecological adaptation (Fig. 6-23 on page 116). They are found throughout most forested areas of southern Mexico and Central and South America (Fig. 6-20). In size, they range from the tiny marmosets and tamarins (about 12 ounces) to the 20-pound howler monkeys (Figs. 6-21 and 6-22). New World monkeys are almost exclusively arboreal, and some never come to the ground. Like Old World monkeys, all except one species (the owl monkey) are diurnal.

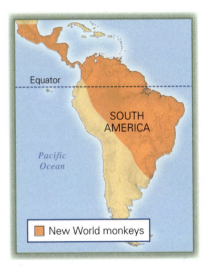

FIGURE 6-20
Geographical distribution of modern New World monkeys.

FIGURE 6-21
A pair of golden lion tamarins.

FIGURE 6-22
Howler monkeys.

FIGURE 6-23
New World monkeys.

Squirrel monkeys

© Kevin Schafer/CORBIS

Female muriqui with infant

Andrew Young

Prince Bernhard's titi monkey (discovered in 2002)

Marc van Roosmalen

White-faced capuchins

© Jay Dickman/CORBIS

Male uakari

R. A. Mittermeier/Conservation International

New World monkeys have traditionally been divided into two families: **Callitrichidae** (marmosets and tamarins) and **Cebidae** (all others). But molecular data along with recently reported fossil evidence indicate that a major regrouping of New World monkeys is in order (Fleagle, 1999).*

Marmosets and tamarins are the smallest of the New World monkeys, and they differ from them in several ways. They're arboreal quadrupeds but instead of nails, they have claws, which they use for climbing. Their diet consists largely of insects, although marmosets eat gums from trees, and tamarins eat fruits. Socially, these small monkeys live in family groups usually composed of a mated pair, or a female and two adult males, and their offspring. Unlike other primates, marmosets and tamarins usually give birth to twins, and they're among the few primate species in which males are extensively involved in infant care.

Cebids range in size from squirrel monkeys (body length 12 inches) to howlers (body length 24 inches). Diet varies, with most relying on a combination of fruits and leaves supplemented, to varying degrees, by insects. Most are quadrupedal; but some, for example, muriquis and spider monkeys (Fig. 6-24) are semibrachiators. Muriquis, howlers, and spider monkeys also have prehensile tails that are used not only in locomotion but also for suspension under branches while feeding. Socially, most cebids are found in groups of both sexes and all age categories. Some (for example, titis) form monogamous pairs and live with their subadult offspring.

Old World Monkeys Except for humans, Old World monkeys are the most widely distributed of all living primates. They are found throughout sub-Saharan Africa and southern Asia, ranging from tropical jungle habitats to semiarid desert and even to seasonally snow-covered areas in northern Japan (Fig. 6-25).

All Old World monkeys are placed in one taxonomic family: **Cercopithecidae**; in turn, this family is divided into two subfamilies: the **cercopithecines** and **colobines**. Most Old World monkeys are quadrupedal and primarily arboreal, but some (baboons, macaques, and langurs) spend much of the day on the ground but return

FIGURE 6-24

Spider monkey. Note the prehensile tail.

Callitrichidae (kal-eh-trick´-eh-dee)

Cebidae (see´-bid-ee)

Cercopithecidae (serk-oh-pith´-eh-sid-ee)

cercopithecines (serk-oh-pith´-eh-seens) The subfamily of Old World monkeys that includes baboons, macaques, and guenons.

colobines (kole´-uh-beans) The subfamily of Old World monkeys that includes the African colobus monkeys and Asian langurs.

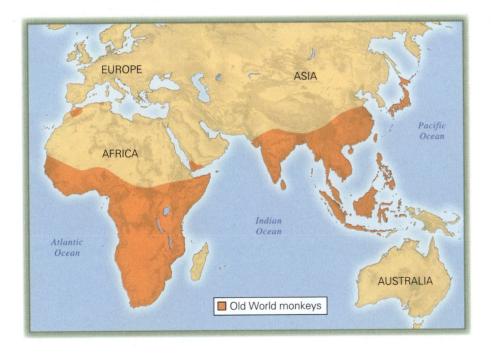

FIGURE 6-25

Geographical distribution of modern Old World monkeys.

---

* One possibility is to include spider monkeys, howler monkeys, and muriquis (woolly spider monkeys) in a third family, Atelidae (see Fig. 6-8). Another is to eliminate the family Callitrichidae altogether and include marmosets and tamarins as a subfamily within the family Cebidae.

FIGURE 6-26
Adult male sykes monkey, one of
several guenon species.

FIGURE 6-27
Savanna baboons.
(a) Male. (b) Female.

(a)

(b)

FIGURE 6-28
Black-and-white colobus monkey.

to the trees in the evening to sleep. They also have areas of hardened skin on the buttocks called **ischial callosities,** which make it possible to sit and sleep for long periods on tree branches.

The cercopithecines are the more generalized of the two groups: They are more omnivorous, and they have cheek pouches for storing food (like hamsters). As a group, the cercopithecines eat almost anything, including fruits, seeds, leaves, grasses, tubers, roots, nuts, insects, birds' eggs, amphibians, small reptiles, and small mammals (the last seen in baboons).

The majority of cercopithecine species, such as the mostly arboreal guenons (Fig. 6-26) and the more terrestrial savanna (Fig. 6-27) and hamadryas baboons, are found in Africa. However, all but one of the several macaque species, which include the well-known rhesus monkey, are distributed across southern Asia and India.

Colobine species have a narrower range of food preferences and mainly eat mature leaves, which is why they're also called "leaf-eating monkeys." The colobines are found mainly in Asia, but both red colobus and black-and-white colobus are exclusively African (Fig. 6-28). Other colobines include several Asian langur species and the proboscis monkey of Borneo.

Locomotion in Old World monkeys includes arboreal quadrupedalism in guenons, macaques, and langurs; terrestrial quadrupedalism in baboons, patas, and macaques; and semibrachiation and acrobatic leaping in colobus monkeys.

Marked differences in body size or shape between the sexes, referred to as **sexual dimorphism,** are typical of some terrestrial species and are particularly pronounced in baboons. In these species, male body weight (up to 80 pounds in baboons) may be twice that of females.

Females of several species, especially baboons and some macaques, have pronounced cyclical changes of the external genitalia. These changes, including swelling and redness, are associated with **estrus,** a hormonally initiated period of sexual receptivity in female nonhuman mammals correlated with ovulation.

Old World monkeys live in a few different kinds of social groups, and there are uncertainties about some species. Colobines tend to live in small groups, with only one or two adult males. Savanna baboons and most macaque species are found in large social units comprising several adults of both sexes and offspring of all ages. Monogamous pairing is uncommon in Old World monkeys, but is seen in a few langurs and possibly one or two guenon species.

FIGURE 6-29
Geographical distribution of modern Asian apes.

Hominoids (Apes and Humans)

The other large grouping of anthropoids, the hominoids, includes apes and humans, and today, apes are found in Asia and Africa. The small-bodied gibbons and siamangs live in Southeast Asia, and the two orangutan subspecies live on the islands of Borneo and Sumatra (Fig. 6-29). In Africa, until the mid- to late twentieth century, gorillas, chimpanzees and bonobos occupied the forested areas of western, central, and eastern Africa, but their habitat is now extremely fragmented, and all are now threatened or highly endangered (see pp. 125–129). Apes and humans differ from monkeys in numerous ways:

1. Generally larger body size, except for gibbons and siamangs
2. Absence of a tail
3. Lumbar area (lower back) shorter and more stable
4. Arms longer than legs (apes only)
5. Differences in position and musculature of the shoulder joint, which is adapted for suspensory behaviors (brachiation and/or feeding)
6. Generally more complex behavior
7. More complex brain and enhanced cognitive abilities
8. Increased period of infant development and dependency

ischial callosities Patches of tough, hard skin on the buttocks of Old World monkeys and chimpanzees.

sexual dimorphism Differences in physical characteristics between males and females of the same species. For example, humans are slightly sexually dimorphic for body size, with males being taller, on average, than females of the same population.

estrus (es´-truss) Period of sexual receptivity in female mammals (except humans), correlated with ovulation. When used as an adjective, the word is spelled "estrous."

Lynn Kilgore

FIGURE 6-30
White-handed gibbon brachiating. Note the long curved fingers, long arms, and heavily muscled shoulders.

Gibbons and Siamangs The eight gibbon species and the closely related siamangs are the smallest of the apes, weighing around 13 and 25 pounds, respectively. Their most distinctive anatomical features are adaptations to feeding while hanging beneath branches and brachiation, at which gibbons and siamangs excel (Fig. 6-30). In fact, gibbons and siamangs are more dedicated to brachiation than any other primate, and this fact is reflected in their extremely long arms, permanently curved fingers, short thumbs, and powerful shoulder muscles. (Their arms are so long that when on the ground, they can't walk quadrupedally, so instead, they walk bipedally with their arms raised to the side.) Gibbons and siamangs mostly eat fruits, although both (especially siamangs) consume a variety of leaves, flowers, and insects.

The basic social unit of gibbons and siamangs is an adult male and female with dependent offspring, and like other species that live in male-female pairs, they aren't sexually dimorphic. Although they've been described as monogamous, in reality, members of pairs sometimes do mate with other individuals. As in marmosets and tamarins, male gibbons and siamangs are very much involved in rearing their young. Both males and females are highly territorial and protect their territories with elaborate whoops and siren-like "songs."

Orangutans Orangutans (*Pongo pygmaeus*) (Fig. 6-31) are represented by two subspecies found today only in heavily forested areas on the Indonesian islands of Borneo and Sumatra (see Fig. 6-29). Due to poaching by humans and continuing habitat loss on both islands, orangutans are severely threatened by extinction in the wild.

Orangutans are very large animals with pronounced sexual dimorphism (males may weigh 200 pounds or more and females less than 100 pounds). In the wild, they lead largely solitary lives, although adult females are usually accompanied by one or two dependent offspring. They're primarily **frugivorous,** but may also eat bark, leaves, insects, and meat (on rare occasions). Orangutans are slow, cautious climbers whose locomotor behavior can best be described as "four-handed," since they tend to use all four limbs for grasping and support. Although they're almost completely arboreal, males in particular also travel quadrupedally on the ground.

Gorillas The largest of all living primates, gorillas (*Gorilla gorilla*) are today confined to forested areas of western and eastern equatorial Africa (Fig. 6-32). There are four generally recognized subspecies, the most numerous of which are the Western lowland gorillas, found in several countries of western central Africa (Fig. 6-33). In 1998, Doran and McNeilage reported an estimated population size of perhaps 110,000.

frugivorous (fru-give´-or-us)
Having a diet composed primarily of fruits.

Noel Rowe

Lynn Kilgore

(a)   (b)

FIGURE 6-31

Orangutans (a) Female. (b) Male.

However, a recently published report (Walsh et al., 2003) suggests that numbers may be far lower.

The Cross River gorilla, a Western lowland gorilla subspecies, was identified in the early 1900s but was thought to be extinct until the 1980s when primatologists became aware of a few small populations restricted to areas along part of the border between Nigeria and Cameroon (Sarmiento and Oates, 2000). Primatologists believe there are only about 250 to 300 of these animals, thus the Cross River gorilla is one of the most endangered of all primates. Currently the International Union for the Conservation of Nature and Natural Resources (IUCN) is developing plans to protect this vulnerable, and little known subspecies Oates et al, 2007).

Eastern lowland gorillas, which haven't really been studied, are found near the eastern border of the Democratic Republic of the Congo (DRC—formerly Zaire). At present, their numbers are unknown and due to warfare in the region researchers fear that many have been killed but it's impossible to know how many.

Mountain gorillas (Fig. 6-34), the most extensively studied of the four subspecies, are restricted to the mountainous areas of central Africa in Rwanda, the DRC, and Uganda. Mountain gorillas have probably never been very numerous, and today

FIGURE 6-32

Geographical distribution of modern African apes.

Lynn Kilgore

Lynn Kilgore

(a)   (b)

FIGURE 6-33

Western lowland gorillas. (a) Male. (b) Female.

(a)   (b)

FIGURE 6-34
Mountain gorillas.
(a) Male. (b) Female.

they are critically endangered and number only about 700. Unfortunately, in September, 2007, rebel forces moved into the gorillas sector of the DRC where at least 300 gorillas live. Since that time, until this writing (November, 2007) it's been impossible to monitor their activities or to protect them.

Gorillas exhibit marked sexual dimorphism, with males weighing up to 400 pounds and females around 150 to 200 pounds. Because of their weight, adult gorillas, especially males, are primarily terrestrial and adopt a quadrupedal knuckle-walking posture on the ground.

Mountain gorillas live in groups consisting of one, or sometimes two, large *silverback* males, a variable number of adult females, and their subadult offspring. The term *silverback* refers to the saddle of white hair across the back of full adult (at least 12 or 13 years of age) male gorillas. Also, a silverback male may tolerate the presence of one or more young adult *blackback* males, probably his sons. Typically, but not always, both females and males leave their **natal group** as young adults. Females join other groups, but males, who appear to be less likely to emigrate, may live alone for a while, or they may join up with other males before eventually forming their own group.

Systematic studies of free-ranging western lowland gorillas weren't begun until the mid-1980s, and not as much is known about them, even though they're the only gorillas you'll see in zoos. The social structure of western lowland gorillas is similar to that of mountain gorillas, but groups are smaller and somewhat less cohesive.

All gorillas are almost exclusively vegetarian. Mountain and western lowland gorillas concentrate primarily on leaves, pith, and stalks, but the latter also eat more fruit. Also, western lowland gorillas, unlike mountain gorillas, which avoid water, frequently wade through swamps while foraging on aquatic plants (Doran and MacNeilage, 1998).

Because of their large body size and enormous strength, gorillas have long been considered ferocious, but in fact they're usually shy and gentle. However, this doesn't mean that gorillas are never aggressive. Among males, competition for females can be extremely violent, and when threatened, males will attack and defend their group from any perceived danger, whether it's another male gorilla or a human hunter. Still, the reputation of gorillas as murderous beasts is nothing more than myth.

Chimpanzees Although chimpanzees are probably the best known of all nonhuman primates (Fig. 6-35), they're often misunderstood because of zoo exhibits, advertising, and television. The true nature of chimpanzees didn't become known until years of fieldwork with wild groups provided a more accurate picture. Today, chimpanzees are found in equatorial Africa, in an area that stretches from the Atlantic Ocean in the

natal group The group in which animals are born and raised. (*Natal* pertains to birth.)

west to Lake Tanganyika in the east. But within this large area, their range is very patchy, and it's becoming even more so with continued forest clearing.

In many ways, chimpanzees are anatomically similar to gorillas, with corresponding limb proportions and upper-body shape. However, the ecological adaptations of chimpanzees and gorillas are different in many ways, and chimpanzees are more arboreal than gorillas. Moreover, while gorillas are typically placid and quiet, chimpanzees are highly excitable, active, and noisy.

Chimpanzees are smaller than orangutans and gorillas, and although they are sexually dimorphic, differences between the sexes aren't as pronounced. While male chimpanzees may weigh over 100 pounds, females can weigh at least 80.

In addition to quadrupedal knuckle walking, chimpanzees (particularly youngsters) may brachiate when they're in trees. Chimpanzees also sometimes walk bipedally for short distances when carrying food or other objects.

Chimpanzees eat a huge variety of foods, including fruits, leaves, insects, nuts, birds' eggs, berries, caterpillars, and small mammals. Moreover, both males and females occasionally take part in group hunting efforts to kill small mammals such as red colobus monkeys, young baboons, bushpigs, and antelope. When hunts are successful, the group (especially members of the hunting party) share the prey.

Chimpanzees live in large, fluid communities ranging in size from 10 to as many as 100 individuals. A group of closely bonded males forms the core of chimpanzee communities, especially in East Africa (Goodall, 1986; Wrangham and Smuts, 1980; Wrangham et al., 1992). But for some West African groups, females appear to be more central to the community (Boesch, 1996; Boesch and Boesch-Ackerman, 2000; Vigilant et al., 2001). Relationships among closely bonded males aren't always peaceful or stable; yet these males cooperatively defend their territory and are highly intolerant of unfamiliar chimpanzees, especially males.

Even though chimpanzees are said to live in communities, it's rare for all members to be together at the same time. Rather, they tend to come and go, so that the individuals they encounter vary from day to day. Adult females usually forage alone or in the company of their offspring, a grouping that might include several individuals, since females with infants sometimes accompany their own mothers and their younger siblings. These associations have been reported at Gombe National Park, Tanzania, where about 40 percent of females remain in the group they were born in (Williams, 1999). But at most other locations, females leave their natal group to join another community. This behavioral pattern may reduce the risk of mating with close relatives, since males apparently never leave the group in which they were born.

Chimpanzee social behavior is complex, and individuals form lifelong attachments with friends and relatives. Indeed, the bond between mothers and infants

(a)   (b)

FIGURE 6-35
Chimpanzees. (a) Male. (b) Female.

Lynn Kilgore

Jill Matsumoto/Jim Anderson

FIGURE 6-36
Female bonobos with young.

can remain strong until one of them dies. This may be a considerable period, because many wild chimpanzees live into their mid-30s and a few into their 40s or even longer.

Bonobos Bonobos (*Pan paniscus*) are found only in an area south of the Zaire River in the DRC (Fig. 6-36). Not officially recognized by European scientists until the 1920s, they remain among the least studied of the great apes. Although ongoing field studies have produced much information (Susman, 1984; Kano, 1992), research has been hampered by more or less continuous civil war. There are no accurate counts of bonobos, but their numbers are believed to be between 10,000 and 20,000 (IUCN, 1996), and they're highly threatened by human hunting, warfare, and habitat loss.

Since bonobos bear a strong resemblance to chimpanzees but are slightly smaller, they've been called "pygmy chimpanzees." However, main anatomical differences between bonobos and chimpanzees are that bonobos have a more linear body build, longer legs relative to arms, a relatively smaller head, a dark face from birth, and tufts of hair at the sides of the face.

Bonobos are more arboreal than chimpanzees, and they're less excitable and aggressive. While aggression isn't unknown, it appears that physical violence both within and between groups is uncommon. Like chimpanzees, bonobos live in geographically based, fluid communities, and they eat many of the same foods, including occasional meat derived from small mammals (Badrian and Malinky, 1984). But bonobo communities aren't centered around a group of closely bonded males. Instead, male-female bonding is more important than in chimpanzees (and most other nonhuman primates), and females aren't peripheral to the group (Badrian and Badrian, 1984). This may be related to bonobo sexuality, which differs from that of other nonhuman primates in that copulation is very frequent and occurs throughout a female's estrous cycle, so sex isn't entirely linked to reproduction. In fact, bonobos are famous for their sexual behavior, engaging in sex frequently and using it to defuse potentially tense situations. Sexual behavior between members of the same sex is also common (Kano, 1992; de Waal and Lanting, 1997).

Humans

Humans are the only living representatives of the habitually bipedal hominids. Our primate heritage is evident in our overall anatomy and genetic makeup and in many aspects of human behavior. With the exception of reduced canine size, human teeth are typical primate (especially ape) teeth. The human dependence on vision and decreased reliance on olfaction, as well as flexible limbs and grasping hands, are rooted in our primate, arboreal past. Humans can even brachiate, as many of us demonstrated during childhood.

In general, humans are omnivorous, although all societies observe certain culturally based dietary restrictions. Even so, as a species with a rather generalized digestive system, we are physiologically adapted to digest an extremely wide assortment of foods. Perhaps to our detriment, we also share with our relatives a fondness for sweets that originates from the importance of high-energy fruits in the diets of many nonhuman primates.

But quite obviously, humans are unique among primates and indeed among all animals. For example, no member of any other species has the ability to write or think about issues such as how they differ from other life-forms. This ability is rooted in the fact that human evolution, during the last 800,000 years or so, has been characterized by dramatic increases in brain size and other neurological changes.

Humans are also completely dependent on culture. Without cultural innovation, it would never have been possible for us to leave the tropics. As it is, humans inhabit every corner of the planet with the exception of Antarctica, and we've even established outposts there. And lest we forget, a fortunate few have even walked on the moon. None of the technologies (indeed, none of the other aspects of culture) that humans have developed over the last several thousand years would have been possible without the highly developed cognitive abilities we alone possess. Nevertheless, the neurological basis for **intelligence** is rooted in our evolutionary past, and it's something we share with other primates. Indeed, research has demonstrated that several nonhuman primate species (most notably chimpanzees, bonobos, and gorillas) display a level of problem solving and insight that most people would have considered impossible 25 years ago (see Chapter 7).

Humans are uniquely predisposed to use spoken language, and for the last 5,000 years or so, we've also used written language. This ability exists because during the course of human evolution, certain neurological and anatomical structures have been modified in ways not seen in any other species. But while nonhuman primates aren't anatomically capable of producing speech, research has shown that to varying degrees, the great apes can communicate by using symbols, which is a foundation for language that humans and the great apes (to a more limited degree) have in common.

Aside from cognitive abilities, the one other trait that sets humans apart from other primates is our unique (among mammals) form of *habitual* bipedal locomotion. This particular trait appeared early in the evolution of our lineage, and over time, we have become more efficient at it because of related changes in the musculoskeletal anatomy of the pelvis, leg, and foot (see Chapter 8). Still, while it's certainly true that human beings are unique intellectually and in some ways anatomically, we are still primates. In fact, fundamentally, humans are somewhat exaggerated African apes.

Endangered Primates

In September 2000, scientists announced that a subspecies of red colobus, named Miss Waldron's red colobus, had officially been declared extinct. This announcement came after a 6-year search for the 20-pound monkey that hadn't been seen for 20 years (Oates et al., 2000). Thus, this species, indigenous to the West African countries of Ghana and the Ivory Coast, has the distinction of being the first nonhuman primate to be declared extinct in the twenty-first century. But it won't be the last. In fact, as of this writing, over half of all nonhuman primate species are now in jeopardy, and some face almost immediate extinction in the wild.

There are three basic reasons for the worldwide depletion of nonhuman primates: habitat destruction, hunting for food, and live capture for export or local trade. Underlying these three causes is one major factor: unprecedented human population growth, which is occurring at a faster rate in developing countries than in the

intelligence Mental capacity; ability to learn, reason, or comprehend and interpret information, facts, relationships, and meanings; the capacity to solve problems, whether through the appplication of previously acquired knowledge or through insight.

developed world. The developing nations of Africa, Asia, and Central and South America are home to over 90 percent of all nonhuman primate species, and these countries, aided in no small part by the United States, China, and the industrialized countries of Europe, are cutting their forests at a rate of about 30 million acres per year. Unbelievably, in the year 2002, deforestation of the Amazon increased by 40 percent over that of 2001. This increase was largely due to land clearing for the cultivation of soybeans. In Brazil, the Atlantic rain forest originally covered some 385,000 square miles. Today, an estimated 7 percent is all that remains of what was once home to countless New World monkeys and thousands of other species.

The motivation behind rain forest destruction is, of course, economic: the short-term gains from clearing forests to create immediately available (but poor) farmland or ranchland; the use of trees for lumber and paper products; and large-scale mining operations (with their necessary roads, digging, and so forth, all of which cause habitat destruction). Furthermore, the demand for tropical hardwoods (such as mahogany, teak, and rosewood) in the United States, Europe, and Japan continues unabated, creating an enormously profitable market for rain forest products.

The Bushmeat Crisis

In many areas, habitat loss has been, and continues to be, the single greatest cause of declining numbers of nonhuman primates. But in the past few years, human hunting has posed an even greater threat (Fig. 6-37). During the 1990s, primatologists and conservationists became aware of a rapidly developing trade in *bushmeat,* meat from wild animals, especially in Africa. The current slaughter, which now accounts for the loss of tens of thousands of nonhuman primates (and other animals) annually, has been compared to the near extinction of the American bison in the nineteenth century.

Wherever primates live, people have always hunted them for food. But in the past, subsistence hunting wasn't a serious threat to nonhuman primate populations, and certainly not to entire species. But now, hunters armed with automatic rifles can, and do, wipe out an entire group of monkeys or gorillas in minutes. In fact, it's now possible to buy bushmeat outside the country of origin. In major cities throughout Europe and the United States, illegal bushmeat is readily available to immigrants

FIGURE 6-37

Red-eared guenons (with red tails) and Preuss' guenons for sale in bushmeat market, Malabo, Equatorial Guinea.

John Oates

Karl Ammann

FIGURE 6-38
These orphaned chimpanzee infants are being bottle-fed at a sanctuary near Pointe Noir, Congo. They will probably never be returned to the wild, and they face a very uncertain future.

who want traditional foods or to nonimmigrants who think it's trendy to eat meat from exotic, and frequently endangered, animals.

It's impossible to know how many animals are killed each year, but the estimates are staggering. The Society for Conservation Biology estimates that about 6,000 kilograms (13,228 pounds) of bushmeat is taken through just seven western cities (New York, London, Toronto, Paris, Montreal, Chicago, and Brussels) every month. No one knows how much of this meat is from primates, but this figure represents only a tiny fraction of all the animals being slaughtered because much smuggled meat isn't detected at ports of entry. Also, the international trade is thought to account for only about 1 percent of the total (Marris, 2006).

Quite clearly, species such as primates, which number only a few hundred or thousand animals, cannot and will not survive this onslaught for more than a few years. In addition, hundreds of infants are orphaned and sold in markets as pets. Although a few of these traumatized orphans make it to sanctuaries, most die within days or weeks of capture (Fig. 6-38).

One major factor in the development of the bushmeat trade has been logging. The construction of logging roads, mainly by French, German, and Belgian lumbar companies, has opened up vast tracts of previously inaccessible forest to hunters. What has emerged is a multimillion dollar trade in bushmeat, a trade in which logging company employees and local government officials participate with hunters, villagers, market vendors, and smugglers who cater to local and overseas markets. In other words, the hunting of wild animals for food, particularly in Africa, has quickly shifted from a subsistence activity to a commercial enterprise of international scope.

Although the slaughter may be best known in Africa, it's by no means limited to that continent. In South America, for example, hunting nonhuman primates for food is common. One report documents that in less than two years, one family of Brazilian rubber tappers killed almost 500 members of various large-bodied species, including spider monkeys, woolly monkeys, and howler monkeys (Peres, 1990). Moreover, live capture and illegal trade in endangered primate species continue unabated in China and Southeast Asia, where nonhuman primates are not only eaten but are also funneled into the exotic pet trade. But just as importantly, primate body parts also figure prominently in traditional medicines, and with increasing human population size, the enormous demand for these products (and products from other, nonprimate species, such as tigers) has placed many species in extreme jeopardy.

Mountain Gorillas at Greater Risk

Mountain gorillas are one of the most endangered nonhuman primate species. All of the approximately 700 mountain gorillas alive today are restricted to a heavily forested area in and around the Virunga mountains (the Virunga Volcanoes Conservation Area) shared by three countries: Uganda, Rwanda, and the DRC. This entire area is a UNESCO (United Nations Educational, Scientific, and Cultural Organization) World Heritage Site. In addition, there is a separate, noncontiguous park in Uganda—the Bwindi Impenetrable Forest, home to about half of all the remaining mountain gorillas. Tourism has been the only real hope of salvation for these magnificent animals, and for this reason, several gorilla groups have been habituated to humans and are heavily protected by park rangers. Nevertheless, poaching, civil war, and land clearing have continued to take a toll on these small populations.

Between January and late July, 2007, nine mountain gorillas were slaughtered in the park. Another is missing and presumed dead. In addition, two infants, orphaned in the attacks, were rescued and taken to a veterinary clinic run by the Dian Fossey Gorilla Fund, where, as of this writing, they are in stable condition (Newport, pers. comm.).

Six of the victims, including the silverback male (Fig. 6-39), were members of one family group of 12. One of the rescued orphans was also from this same group, and after her mother had been killed, she was being carried by her older brother until park rangers were able to capture her. The remnant of this group consists of four immature males and one immature female, and without a silverback, their future is uncertain.

The gorillas weren't shot for meat or because they were raiding crops. They were shot because the existence and protection of mountain gorillas in the park is a hindrance to people who would destroy what little remains of the forests that are home to the gorillas. One of the many reasons for cutting the forests is the manufacture of charcoal, a major source of fuel in rural Rwanda and the DRC.

In 2007, paleoanthropologist Dr. Richard Leakey and a colleague, Dr. Emanuelle de Merode, established WildlifeDirect.org to help support conservationists and especially the rangers who work for little to no pay to protect the mountain gorillas. While administrative costs for WildlifeDirect are mostly provided by the European Union, private contributions go directly to support the rangers and provide them with weapons, boots, and other necessities. (It should be pointed out that in the past few years, more than 120 rangers have been killed while protecting wildlife in the Virungas.) You may want to go to their website (www.wildlifedirect.org), where you can read updates and see photographs and videos posted daily by the rangers. These communications offer fascinating insights into their efforts, conditions in the forest, and updates on gorillas and other species.

FIGURE 6-39

Congolese villagers carrying the body of the silverback gorilla killed in July, 2007. His body was buried with the other members of his group who were also shot.

WildlifeDirect.org

There are several other conservation groups that work to protect mountain gorillas. Also, in 2000, the United Nations Environmental Program established the Great Ape Survival Project (GRASP). GRASP is an alliance of many of the world's major great ape conservation and research organizations. In 2003, GRASP appealed for $25 million to be used in protecting the great apes from extinction. The money (a paltry sum) would be used to enforce laws that regulate hunting and illegal logging. It goes without saying that GRASP and other organizations must succeed if the great apes are to survive in the wild for even 20 more years!

But GRASP and the various conservation organizations face a formidable task just to save mountain gorillas, not to mention the dozens of other primate species at risk. In early September, 2007, rebel forces in the gorilla sector of the DRC attacked a ranger station, where they killed one ranger. Consequently, WildlifeDirect evacuated all rangers from the area, leaving the gorillas unprotected. As of this writing (December, 2007) this situation remains unchanged, although the threat of heavy fighting in the gorilla sector continues to be grave.

As a note of optimism, in November, 2007, the DRC government and the Bonobo Conservation Initiative (in Washington D.C.) created a bonobo reserve consisting of 30,500 square kilometers. This amounts to about 10 percent of the land in the DRC and the government has stated its goal is to set aside an additional five percent for wildlife protection (News in Brief, 2007). This is a huge step forward but it remains to be seen if and how protection is to be enforced.

If you are in your 20s or 30s, you will certainly live to hear of the extinction of some of our marvelous cousins. Many more will undoubtedly slip away unnoticed. Tragically, this will occur, in most cases, before we've even gotten to know them. Each species on earth is the current result of a unique set of evolutionary events that, over millions of years, has produced a finely adapted component of a diverse ecosystem. When it becomes extinct, that adaptation and that part of biodiversity is lost forever. What a tragedy it will be if, through our own mismanagement and greed, we awaken to a world without chimpanzees, mountain gorillas, or the tiny, exquisite lion tamarin. When this day comes, we truly will have lost a part of ourselves, and we will certainly be the poorer for it.

Summary

In this chapter, we introduced you to the primates, the mammalian order that includes prosimians, monkeys, apes, and humans. We discussed how primates, including humans, have retained a number of ancestral characteristics that have permitted them, as a group, to be generalized in terms of diet and locomotor patterns. We also presented a general outline of traits that differentiate primates from other mammals.

We also discussed primate classification and how primatologists are redefining relationships between some lineages. One important change, increasingly favored by primatologists, is placing chimpanzees, gorillas, and orangutans with humans in the family Hominidae. These changes reflect increasing knowledge of the genetic relationships between primate lineages.

You also became acquainted with the major groups of nonhuman primates, especially with regard to their basic social structure, diet, and locomotor patterns. Most primates are diurnal and live in social groups. The only nocturnal primates are lorises, galagos, some lemurs, tarsiers, and owl monkeys. Nocturnal species tend to forage for food alone or with offspring and one or two other animals. Diurnal primates live in a variety of social groupings, including male-female pairs and groups consisting of one male with several females and offspring or those composed of several males and females and offspring.

Finally, we talked about the precarious existence of most nonhuman primates today as they face hunting, capture, and habitat loss. These threats are all imposed by only one primate species, one that arrived fairly late on the evolutionary stage: *Homo sapiens*.

WHY IT MATTERS

Most people don't know much about nonhuman primates, and of those who do, a majority probably don't fully realize how endangered they are. What's worse, even some who do, don't really care because their lives wouldn't substantially change if, say, chimpanzees became extinct in the wild. (Although there could still be captive chimpanzees for a few more decades, this isn't seen as a viable long-term solution.)

The fact is, it *is* important that we know about nonhuman primates, not only for the anthropocentric reason that we can better understand ourselves (although this is true), but also because the living nonhuman primates are the current representatives of a lineage that goes back approximately 60 million years. They can provide us with limitless information as to how evolutionary processes have produced the diversity we see in our own lineage today. From comparative studies, we can identify the genetic causes for certain conditions (such as AIDS) that humans are susceptible to but chimpanzees are able to resist. Although this information may not help us decide what kind of car to buy, or what to have for dinner, it is permitting us to unravel the genetic and behavioral links that connect all primates, including ourselves, in a network of adaptation and evolution. Lastly, the nonhuman primates (and other species, too) are important in their own right, and it's up to us to make sure they survive into the next century. Indeed, this is going to be a truly formidable task.

Critical Thinking Questions

1   How does a classification scheme reflect biological and evolutionary changes in a lineage? Can you give an example of suggested changes as to how primates are classified? What is the basis of these suggestions?

2   How do you think continued advances in genetic research will influence how we look at our species' relationship with nonhuman primates 10 or 15 years from now?

3   What factors are threatening the existence of nonhuman primates in the wild? What can you do to help in the efforts to save nonhuman primates from extinction?

CHAPTER 7

Primate Behavior

Lynn Kilgore

FOCUS QUESTION

How can behavior be a product of evolutionary processes, and what is one example of a behavior that has been influenced by evolution?

▶ **Click!**

Go to the following media resources for interactive activities, more information, and study materials on topics covered in this chapter:

- Anthropology Resource Center
- Student Companion Website for *Essentials of Physical Anthropology,* Seventh Edition
- Online Virtual Laboratories for Physical Anthropology CD-ROM, Fourth Edition

behavior Anything organisms do that involves action in response to internal or external stimuli; the response of an individual, group, or species to its environment. Such responses may or may not be deliberate, and they aren't necessarily the result of conscious decision making.

Introduction

Do you think cats are cruel when they play with mice before they kill them? Or if you've ever fallen off a horse when it leaped aside for no apparent reason, did you think the horse threw you deliberately? If you answered yes to either of these questions, you're not alone. To most people, it does seem cruel for a cat to torment a mouse for no apparent reason. And more than one rider has thought that a horse's eagerness to rid itself of a burden was deliberate mischief (and, admittedly, sometimes it may be). But these views generally demonstrate how little most people really know about nonhuman animal **behavior.**

Because behavior, especially in mammals and birds, has been shaped over evolutionary time by interactions between genetic and environmental factors, it's extremely complex. But most people don't give this much thought, and even those who do don't necessarily accept this basic premise. For example, many social scientists object to the notion of genetic influences on human behavior because of concerns that behaviors will be viewed as fixed and can't be modified by experience (that is, learning). This view could, in turn, be used to support racist and sexist ideologies.

Among the general public, there is also the prevailing notion of a fundamental division between humans and all other animals. In some cultures, this view is fostered by religion; but even when religion isn't a factor, most people see themselves as uniquely set apart from all other species. But at the same time, and in obvious contradiction, they may judge other species from a strictly human perspective and explain certain behaviors in terms of human motivations (for example, cats are cruel to play with mice). Of course, this isn't a valid thing to do for the simple reason that other animals aren't human. Cats sometimes play with mice before they kill them because that's how, as kittens, they learn to hunt. Cruelty doesn't enter into it though, because the cat has no concept of cruelty and no idea of what it's like to be the mouse. Likewise, the horse doesn't deliberately throw you off when it hears leaves rattling in a shrub. It does so because its behavior has been shaped by thousands of generations of horse ancestors who jumped first and asked questions later. It's important to understand that just as cats evolved as predators, horses evolved as prey animals, and their evolutionary history is littered with unfortunate animals that didn't jump at a sound in a shrub. In many cases, those ancestral horses learned, too late, that the sound wasn't caused by a breeze at all. This is a mistake that prey animals don't usually survive, and those that don't leap first leave few descendants.

Of course, this chapter isn't about cats and horses. It's about what we know and hypothesize about the individual and social behaviors of nonhuman primates. But we begin with the familiar examples of cats and horses because we want to point out that many basic behaviors have been shaped by a species' evolutionary history. Also, the same factors that have influenced many behaviors in nonprimate animals also apply to primates. So if we want to discover the underlying principles of behavioral evolution, including that of humans, we first need to identify the interactions between a number of environmental and physiological variables.

The Evolution of Behavior

Scientists study behavior in free-ranging primates from an **ecological** and evolutionary perspective, meaning that they focus on the relationship between behaviors, the natural environment, and various physiological traits of the species in question. This approach is called **behavioral ecology,** and it's based on the underlying assumption that all of the biological components of ecological systems (animals, plants, and even microorganisms) evolved together. Therefore, behaviors are adaptations to environmental circumstances that existed in the past as much as in the present.

Briefly, the cornerstone of this perspective is that *behaviors have evolved through the operation of natural selection.* That is, since certain behaviors are influenced by genes, they're subject to natural selection in the same way physical characteristics are. (Remember that within a specific environmental context, natural selection favors traits that provide a reproductive advantage to the individuals who possess them.) Therefore, behavior constitutes a phenotype, and individuals whose behavioral phenotypes increase reproductive fitness will pass on their genes at a faster rate than others who don't have those favorable behaviors. But this doesn't mean that primatologists think that genes code for specific behaviors, such as a gene for aggression, another for cooperation, and so on. Examining complex behaviors from an evolutionary viewpoint doesn't imply a one gene–one behavior relationship, nor does it suggest that behaviors that are influenced by genes can't be modified through learning.

Much of the behavior of insects and other invertebrates is largely under genetic control. In other words, most behavioral patterns in those species aren't learned; they're innate. But in many vertebrates, especially birds and mammals, the proportion of behavior that's due to learning is substantially increased, and the proportion under genetic control is reduced. This is especially true of primates; and in humans, who are so much a product of culture, most behavior is learned. But at the same time, we know that in mammals and birds, some behaviors are at least partly influenced by certain gene products such as hormones. For example, you're probably aware that increased levels of testosterone increase aggression in many species. You may also know that some forms of depression, schizophrenia, and bipolar disorder are caused by abnormal levels of certain chemicals produced by brain cells.

Behavioral genetics, or the study of how genes influence behavior, is a fairly new field, and we currently don't know the degree to which genes influence behavior in humans or, indeed, other species. But we do know that behavior must be viewed as the product of *complex interactions between genetic and environmental factors.* Among species, there is considerable variability in the limits and potentials for learning and for behavioral **plasticity,** or flexibility. In some, the potentials are extremely broad; in others, they aren't. Ultimately, those limits and potentials are set by genetic factors that natural selection has favored throughout the evolutionary history of every species. That history, in turn, has been shaped by the ecological setting not only of living species, *but also of their ancestors.*

One of the major goals of primatology is to determine how behaviors influence reproductive fitness and how ecological factors have shaped the evolution of these behaviors. While the actual mechanics of behavioral evolution aren't yet fully understood, new technologies are beginning to help scientists answer many questions. For example, genetic analysis has recently been used to establish paternity in a few primate groups, and this has helped support hypotheses about some behaviors (see p. 145). But in general, an evolutionary approach to the study of behavior doesn't provide definitive answers to many research questions. Rather, it provides a valuable framework within which primatologists analyze data to generate and test hypotheses concerning behavioral patterns.

ecological Pertaining to the relationships between organisms and all aspects of their environment (temperature, predators, nonpredators, vegetation, availability of food and water, types of food, disease organisms, parasites, etc.).

behavioral ecology The study of the evolution of behavior, emphasizing the role of ecological factors as agents of natural selection. Behaviors and behavioral patterns have been favored because they increase the reproductive fitness of individuals (i.e., they are adaptive) in specific environmental contexts.

plasticity The capacity to change; in a behavioral context, the ability of animals to modify behaviors in response to differing circumstances.

Because primates are among the most social of animals, social behavior is one of the major topics in primate research. This is a broad subject that includes *all* aspects of behavior that occur in social groupings, even some you may not think of as social behaviors, like feeding or mating. To understand the function of one behavioral element, it's necessary to determine how it's influenced by numerous interrelated factors. As an example, we'll discuss some of the more important variables that influence **social structure.**

Some Factors That Influence Social Structure

Body Size As a general rule, larger animals require fewer calories per unit of weight than smaller animals because they have a smaller ratio of surface area to mass than do smaller animals. Since body heat is lost at the surface, they are better able to retain heat more efficiently, and so they require less energy overall.

FIGURE 7-1

This tiny dwarf lemur has a high BMR and requires an energy-rich diet of insects and other forms of animal protein.

Basal Metabolic Rate (BMR) The BMR concerns **metabolism,** the rate at which the body uses energy to maintain all body functions while in a resting state. It's closely correlated with body size; in general, smaller animals have a higher BMR than larger ones (Fig. 7-1). Consequently, smaller primates, like galagos, tarsiers, marmosets, and tamarins, require an energy-rich diet high in protein (insects), fats (nuts and seeds), and carbohydrates (fruits and seeds). Some larger primates, which tend to have a lower BMR and reduced energy requirements relative to body size, can do well with less energy-rich foods, such as leaves.

Diet Since the nutritional requirements of animals are related to the previous two factors, all three have evolved together. Therefore, when primatologists study the relationships between diet and behavior, they consider the benefits in terms of energy (calories) derived from various food items against the costs (energy expended) of obtaining and digesting them. While small-bodied primates focus on high-energy foods, larger ones don't necessarily need to. For instance, gorillas eat leaves, pith from bamboo stems, and other types of vegetation, and they don't need to use much energy searching for food, since they are frequently surrounded by it (Fig. 7-2).

Distribution of Resources Various types of foods are distributed in different ways. Leaves can be plentiful and dense and will therefore support large groups of animals. Insects, on the other hand, may be widely scattered, and the animals that rely on them usually feed alone or in small groups of two or three.

Fruits, nuts, and berries in dispersed trees and shrubs occur in clumps. These can most efficiently be exploited by smaller groups of animals, so large groups frequently break up into smaller subunits while feeding. Such subunits may consist of one-male, multifemale groups (some baboons) or **matrilines** (macaques). Species that feed on abundantly distributed resources may also live in one-male, multifemale groups, and because food is plentiful, these units are able to join with others to form large, stable communities (for example, howlers and some colobines and some baboons). To the casual observer, these communities can appear to be multimale-multifemale groups.

Some species that rely on foods distributed in small clumps are protective of resources, especially if their feeding area is small enough to be defended. Some live in small groups composed of a mated pair (siamangs) or a female with one or two males (marmosets and tamarins). Naturally, dependent offspring are also included. Lastly, many kinds of food are only seasonally available. These include fruits, nuts, seeds, and berries. Primates that rely on seasonally available foods must exploit a number of different food types and must move about in order to have enough to eat throughout the year. This is another factor that tends to favor smaller feeding groups.

social structure The composition, size, and sex ratio of a group of animals. The social structure of a species is, in part, the result of natural selection in a specific habitat, and it guides individual interactions and social relationships.

metabolism The chemical processes within cells that break down nutrients and release energy for the body to use. (When nutrients are broken down into their component parts, such as amino acids, energy is released and made available for the cell to use.)

matrilines Groups that consists of a female, her daughters, and their offspring. Matrilineal groups are common in macaques.

Predation Primates, depending on their size, are vulnerable to many types of predators, including snakes, birds of prey, leopards, wild dogs, lions, and even other primates. Their responses to predation depend on their body size, social structure, and the type of predator. Typically, where predation pressure is high and body size is small, large communities are advantageous. These may be multimale-multifemale groups or congregations of one-male groups.

Relationships with Other, Nonpredatory Species Many primate species associate with other primate and nonprimate species for various reasons, including predator avoidance. When they share habitats with other species, they exploit somewhat different resources.

Dispersal Another factor that influences social structure and also relationships within groups is dispersal. As is true of most mammals (and indeed, most vertebrates), members of one sex leave the group in which they were born (their *natal group*) about the time they reach puberty. Male dispersal is the most common pattern in primates (ring-tailed lemurs, vervets, and macaques, to name a few). (This is generally true for other animals, too.) Female dispersal is seen in some colobus species, hamadryas baboons, chimpanzees, and mountain gorillas.

Dispersal may have more than one outcome. When females leave, they join another group. Males may do likewise, but in some species (for example, gorillas), they frequently remain solitary for a time, or they may temporarily join an all-male "bachelor" group until they're able to establish a group of their own. But one common theme is that individuals who disperse usually find mates outside their natal group. This commonality has led primatologists to conclude that the most valid explanations for dispersal are probably related to two major factors: reduced competition for mates (particularly between males) and, perhaps even more important, the decreased likelihood of close inbreeding.

Life Histories **Life history traits** are characteristics or developmental stages that typify members of a given species and therefore influence potential reproductive rates. Examples of life history traits include length of gestation, length of time between pregnancies (interbirth interval), period of infant dependency and age at weaning, age at sexual maturity, and life expectancy.

Life history traits have important consequences for many aspects of social life and social structure, and they can also be critical to species survival. Shorter life histories are advantageous to species that live in marginal or unpredictable habitats (Strier, 2003). Since these species mature early and have short interbirth intervals, reproduction can occur at a relatively fast rate. Conversely, species with extended life histories, such as gorillas, are better suited to stable environmental conditions. The extended life spans of the great apes in particular, characterized by later sexual maturation and long interbirth intervals (three to five years), mean that most females will raise only three or four offspring to maturity. This slow reproductive rate is a detriment to species that are threatened with extinction.

Distribution and Types of Sleeping Sites Gorillas are the only nonhuman primates that sleep on the ground. Primate sleeping sites can be in trees or on cliff faces, and their spacing can be related to social structure and predator avoidance.

Activity Patterns Most primates are diurnal, but several small-bodied prosimians and one New World monkey (the owl monkey) are nocturnal. Nocturnal primates tend to forage for food alone or in groups of two or three, and many use concealment to avoid predators.

FIGURE 7-2
This large male mountain gorilla does well on a diet of less-energy-rich leaves and other plant materials.

life history traits Characteristics and developmental stages that influence reproductive rates. Examples include longevity, age at sexual maturity, and length of time between births.

Human Activities Virtually all nonhuman primate populations are now impacted by human hunting and forest clearing (see p. 128). These activities severely disrupt and isolate groups, reduce numbers, and decrease food supplies. Consequently, they can seriously disrupt social groups and change behavior and eventually cause extinction.

Why Be Social?

Group living exposes animals to competition with other group members for resources, so why don't they live alone? After all, competition can lead to injury or even death, and it's costly in terms of energy expenditure. One widely accepted answer to this question is that the costs of competition are offset by the benefits of predator defense provided by associating with others. Groups composed of several adult males and females (multimale-multifemale groups) are advantageous in areas where predation pressure is high, particularly in mixed woodlands and on open savannas. Leopards are the most significant predator of terrestrial primates (Fig. 7-3). Where members of prey species occur in larger groups, the chances of early predator detection (and avoidance) are increased simply because there are more pairs of eyes looking about.

Savanna baboons have long been used as an example of these principles. They're found in semiarid grassland and broken woodland habitats throughout sub-Saharan Africa. To avoid nocturnal predators, savanna baboons sleep in trees, but during the day, they spend much of their time on the ground foraging for food. If a nonhuman predator appears, baboons flee back into the trees, but if they're some distance from safety, adult males (and sometimes females) may join forces to chase the intruder. The effectiveness of male baboons in this regard shouldn't be underestimated, since they've been known to kill domestic dogs and even to attack leopards and lions.

There is probably no single answer to the question of why primates live in groups. More than likely, predator avoidance is a major factor but not the only one. Group living evolved as an adaptive response to a number of ecological variables, and it has served primates well for a very long time.

Primate Social Behavior

Because primates solve their major adaptive problems in a social context, we should expect there to be several behaviors that reinforce the integrity of the group. The better known of these are described in the sections that follow. Remember, all these behaviors have evolved as adaptive responses during more than 50 million years of primate evolution.

FIGURE 7-3

When a baboon strays too far from its troop, as this one has done, it's more likely to fall prey to predators. Leopards are the most serious nonhuman threat to terrestrial primates.

Time Life Pictures/Getty Images

Dominance

Many primate societies are organized into **dominance hierarchies,** which impose a certain degree of order by establishing parameters of individual behavior. Although aggression is frequently a means of increasing one's status, dominance usually serves to reduce the amount of actual physical violence. Not only are lower-ranking animals unlikely to attack or even threaten a higher-ranking one, but dominant animals are usually able to exert control simply by making a threatening gesture.

Individual rank or status can be measured by access to resources, including food items and mating partners. Dominant animals are given priority by others, and they usually don't give way in confrontations.

A number of primatologists think that the primary benefit of dominance is the increased reproductive success of high-ranking animals. This may be true in some cases, but there's good evidence that lower-ranking males also successfully mate. High-ranking females have greater access to food than subordinate females, and since they obtain more energy for the production and care of offspring (Fedigan, 1983), they presumably have higher reproductive success.

Pusey et al. (1997) demonstrated that the offspring of high-ranking female chimpanzees at Gombe Stream National Park, in Tanzania, had significantly higher rates of infant survival. Moreover, their daughters matured faster, which meant they had shorter interbirth intervals and consequently produced more offspring.

An individual's position in the hierarchy isn't permanent and changes throughout life. It's influenced by many factors, including sex, age, level of aggression, amount of time spent in the group, intelligence, perhaps motivation, and sometimes the mother's social position (particularly true of macaques).

In species organized into groups containing a number of females associated with one or several adult males, the males are generally dominant to females. Within such groups, males and females have separate hierarchies, although very high-ranking females can dominate the lowest-ranking males (particularly young males). But there are exceptions to this pattern of male dominance. In many lemur species, females are the dominant sex. Moreover, in species that form bonded pairs (for example, indris and gibbons), males and females are codominant.

All primates *learn* their position in the hierarchy. From birth, an infant is carried by its mother, and it observes how she responds to every member of the group. Just as importantly, it sees how others react to her. Dominance and subordination are indicated by gestures and behaviors, some of which are universal throughout the primate order (including humans), and this gestural repertoire is part of every youngster's learning experience.

Young primates also acquire social rank through play with age peers, and as they spend more time with play groups, their social interactions widen. Competition and rough-and-tumble play allow them to learn the strengths and weaknesses of peers, and they carry this knowledge with them throughout their lives. Thus, through early contact with their mothers and subsequent exposure to peers, young primates learn to negotiate their way through the complex web of social interactions that make up their daily lives.

Communication

Communication is universal among animals and includes scents and unintentional, **autonomic** responses and behaviors that convey meaning. Such attributes as body posture convey information about an animal's emotional state. For example, a purposeful striding gait implies confidence. Moreover, autonomic responses to threatening or novel stimuli, such as raised body hair (most species) or enhanced body odor (gorillas), indicate excitement.

dominance hierarchies Systems of social organization wherein individuals within a group are ranked relative to one another. Higher-ranking animals have greater access to preferred food items and mating partners than lower-ranking individuals. Dominance hierarchies are sometimes called "pecking orders."

communication Any act that conveys information, in the form of a message, to another individual. Frequently, the result of communication is a change in the behavior of the recipient. Communication may not be deliberate but may instead be the result of involuntary processes or a secondary consequence of an intentional action.

autonomic Pertaining to physiological responses not under voluntary control. An example in chimpanzees would be the erection of body hair during excitement. Blushing is a human example. Both convey information regarding emotional states, but neither is deliberate, and communication isn't intended.

Many intentional behaviors also serve as communication. In primates, these include a wide variety of gestures, facial expressions, and vocalizations, some of which we humans share. Among many primates an intense stare indicates a mild threat; and indeed, we humans find prolonged eye contact with strangers very uncomfortable. (For this reason, people should avoid eye contact with captive primates.) Other threat gestures are a quick yawn to expose canine teeth (baboons, macaques; Fig. 7-4); bobbing back and forth in a crouched position (patas monkeys); and branch shaking (many monkey species). High-ranking baboons *mount* the hindquarters of subordinates to express dominance (Fig. 7-5). Mounting may also serve to defuse potentially tense situations by indicating something like, "It's okay, I accept your apology."

Primates also use a variety of behaviors to indicate submission, reassurance, or amicable intentions. Most primates crouch to show submission, and baboons also present or turn their hindquarters toward an animal they want to appease. Reassurance takes the form of touching, patting, hugging, and holding hands (Fig. 7-6). Grooming also serves in a number of situations to indicate submission or reassurance.

A wide variety of facial expressions indicating emotional state is seen in chimpanzees and, especially, in bonobos (Fig. 7-7). These include the well-known play face (also seen in several other primate and nonprimate species), associated with play behavior, and the fear grin (seen in *all* primates) to indicate fear and submission.

Not surprisingly, primates also use a wide assortment of vocalizations for communication. Some, such as the bark of a baboon that has just spotted a leopard, are unintentional startled reactions. Others, such as the chimpanzee food grunt, are heard only in specific contexts, in this case in the presence of food. These vocalizations, whether deliberate or not, inform others of the possible presence of predators or food.

Primates (and other animals) also communicate through **displays,** which are more complicated, frequently elaborate combinations of behaviors. For example,

FIGURE 7-4

An adolescent male savanna baboon threatens the photographer with a characteristic "yawn" that shows the canine teeth. Note also that the eyes are closed briefly to expose light, cream-colored eyelids. This has been called the "eyelid flash."'

FIGURE 7-5

One young male savanna baboon mounts another as an expression of dominance.

FIGURE 7-6

Adolescent savanna baboons holding hands.

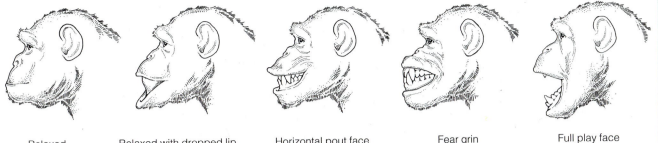

| Relaxed | Relaxed with dropped lip | Horizontal pout face (distress) | Fear grin (fear/excitement) | Full play face |

FIGURE 7-7
Chimpanzee facial expressions.

the exaggerated courtship dances of many male birds, often enhanced by colorful plumage, are displays. Chest slapping and tearing vegetation are common gorilla threat displays.

All nonhuman animals use various body postures, vocalizations, and facial expressions to transmit information. But the array of communicative devices is much richer among nonhuman primates, even though they don't use language the way humans do. Communication is important, because it makes social living possible. Through submissive gestures, aggression is reduced and physical violence is less likely. Likewise, friendly intentions and relationships are reinforced through physical contact and grooming. Indeed, we humans can see ourselves in other primate species most clearly in their use of nonverbal communication, particularly because some of their gestures and facial expressions carry the same meaning as ours do.

Aggressive Interactions

Within primate societies, there is an interplay between aggressive behaviors, which can lead to group disruption, and **affiliative** behaviors, which promote group cohesion. Conflict within a group frequently develops out of competition for resources, including mating partners or food. Instead of actual attacks or fighting, most **intragroup** aggression occurs in the form of various signals and displays, frequently within the context of a dominance hierarchy. Therefore, the majority of tense situations are resolved through various submissive and appeasement behaviors.

However, all conflicts aren't resolved peacefully. Competition between males for mates frequently results in injury and even death. Females also compete with each other, frequently for resources, and especially low-ranking females may starve when food supplies are short (Silk, et al, 2003).

Between groups, aggression is used to protect resources or **territories.** Primate groups are associated with a *home range* where they remain permanently. (Although individuals may leave their home range and join another community, the group itself remains in a particular area.) Within the home range is a portion called the **core area,** which contains the highest concentration of predictable resources, and it's where the group is most frequently found. Although parts of a group's home range may overlap the with home ranges of other groups, core areas of adjacent groups don't overlap. The core area can also be said to be a group's territory, and it's the portion of the home range defended against intrusion.

Not all primates are territorial. In general, territoriality is typical of species whose ranges are small enough to be patrolled and protected (for example, gibbons and vervets). Moreover, in many species, group encounters are frequently nonaggressive.

Male chimpanzees, however, are highly intolerant of unfamiliar chimpanzees, especially other males, and they fiercely defend their territories and resources (Fig. 7-8). Therefore, chimpanzee intergroup interactions are almost always characterized by aggressive displays, chasing, and frequently actual fighting.

displays Sequences of repetitious behaviors that serve to communicate emotional states. Nonhuman primate displays are most frequently associated with reproductive or agonistic behavior, and examples include chest slapping in gorillas or, in male chimpanzees, dragging and waving branches while charging and threatening other animals.

affiliative Pertaining to amicable associations between individuals. Affiliative behaviors, such as grooming, reinforce social bonds and promote group cohesion.

intragroup (*intra,* meaning "within") Within the group, as opposed to between groups (intergroup).

territories Portions of an individual's or group's home range that are actively defended against intrusion, especially by members of the same species.

core area The portion of a home range containing the highest concentration and most reliable supplies of food and water. The core area is defended.

Curt Busse

FIGURE 7-8
Members of a chimpanzee "border patrol" at Gombe survey their territory from a tree.

Beginning in 1974, Jane Goodall and her colleagues witnessed at least five unprovoked and extremely brutal attacks by groups of chimpanzees on other chimpanzees. To explain these attacks, it's necessary to point out that by 1973, the original Gombe chimpanzee community had divided into two distinct groups, one located in the north and the other in the south of what had once been the original group's home range. In effect, the smaller offshoot group had denied the others access to part of their former home range.

By 1977, all seven males and one female of the splinter group were either known or suspected to have been killed. All observed incidents involved several animals, usually adult males, who brutally attacked lone individuals. Although it isn't possible to know exactly what motivated the attackers, it was clear that they intended to incapacitate their victims (Goodall, 1986).

A similar situation was also reported for a chimpanzee group in the Mahale Mountains south of Gombe. Over a 17-year period, all the males of a small community disappeared. Although no attacks were actually observed, there was circumstantial evidence that most of these males met the same fate as the Gombe attack victims (Nishida et al., 1985, 1990).

Even though the precise motivation of chimpanzee intergroup aggression may never be fully explained, it appears that acquiring and protecting resources (including females) are involved (Nishida et al., 1985, 1990; Goodall, 1986; Manson and Wrangham, 1991; Nishida, 1991). Through careful examination of shared aspects of human and chimpanzee social life, we can develop hypotheses regarding how intergroup conflict may have arisen in our own lineage. Early hominids and chimpanzees may have inherited from a common ancestor the predispositions that lead to similar patterns of strife between populations. It's not possible to draw direct comparisons between chimpanzee conflict and modern human warfare owing to later human elaborations of culture, use of symbols (for example, national flags), and language. But it's important to speculate on the fundamental issues that may have led to the development of similar patterns in both species.

Affiliation and Altruism

As you've just seen, even though it can be destructive, a certain amount of aggression helps maintain order within groups and protect resources. Fortunately, to minimize actual violence and to defuse potentially dangerous situations, there are many behaviors that reinforce bonds between individuals and enhance group stability. Common affiliative behaviors include reconciliation, consolation, and simple amicable interactions between friends and relatives. These involve various forms of physical contact; in fact, physical contact is one of the most important factors in primate development, and it's crucial in promoting peaceful relationships in many primate social groups.

Grooming is one of the most important affiliative behaviors in many primate species, so much so that primatologist Alison Jolly (1985) called it the "social cement" of primate societies. Although grooming occurs in other animal species, social grooming is mostly a primate activity, and it plays an important role in day-to-day life (Fig. 7-9). Because grooming involves using the fingers to pick through the fur of another individual (or one's own) to remove insects, dirt, and other materials, it

grooming Picking through fur to remove dirt, parasites, and other materials that may be present. Social grooming is common among primates and reinforces social relationships.

(a)

(b)

(c)

(d)

serves hygienic functions. But it's also an immensely pleasurable activity that members of some species (especially chimpanzees) engage in for long periods of time.

Grooming occurs in a variety of contexts. Mothers groom infants. Males groom sexually receptive females. Subordinate animals groom dominant ones, sometimes to gain favor. Friends groom friends. In general, grooming is comforting. It restores peaceful relationships between animals who have quarreled and provides reassurance during tense situations. In short, grooming reinforces social bonds and consequently helps strengthen and maintain the structure of the group.

Conflict resolution through reconciliation is another important aspect of primate social behavior. Following a conflict, chimpanzee opponents frequently move within minutes to reconcile (de Waal, 1982). Reconciliation takes many forms, including hugging, kissing, and grooming. Even uninvolved individuals may take part, either grooming one or both participants or forming their own grooming parties. In addition, bonobos are unique in their use of sex to promote group cohesion, restore peace after conflicts, and relieve tension within the group (de Waal, 1987, 1989).

Social relationships are crucial to nonhuman primates, and the bonds between individuals can last a lifetime. These relationships serve a variety of functions. Individuals of many species form alliances in which members support each other against outsiders. Alliances, or coalitions, as they are also called, can be used to enhance the status of members. For example, at Gombe, the male chimpanzee Figan achieved alpha status because of support from his brother (Goodall, 1986, p. 424).

FIGURE 7-9
Grooming primates. (a) Patas monkeys; female grooming male. (b) Longtail macaques. (c) Savanna baboons. (d) Chimpanzees.

In fact, chimpanzees so heavily rely on coalitions and are so skillful politically that an entire book, appropriately titled *Chimpanzee Politics* (de Waal, 1982), is devoted to the topic.

Altruism, behavior that benefits another while involving some risk or sacrifice to the performer, is common in many primate species, and altruistic acts sometimes contain elements of what might be interpreted as compassion and cooperation. The most fundamental of altruistic behaviors, the protection of dependent offspring, is ubiquitous among mammals and birds, and in the majority of species, altruistic acts are confined to this context.

Evolutionary explanations of altruism are usually based on one of two premises. The first is that individuals perform acts that benefit others because they share genes with the recipient; thus, by helping a relative, the performer is helping to ensure the survival of the genes they have in common. The second explanation, sometimes called "reciprocal altruism," is that one individual helps another to increase the chances that, at a future date, the recipient might return the favor.

Among primates, however, recipients of altruistic acts may include individuals who aren't offspring and who may not even be closely related to the performer. Stelzner and Strier (1982) witnessed a female baboon chasing a hyena that was in pursuit of a young adult male baboon. This female's unsuccessful rescue attempt was intriguing because not only was she too small to engage the hyena, but she was also unrelated to the victim. Chimpanzees routinely come to the aid of relatives and friends; female langurs join forces to protect infants from infanticidal males; and male baboons protect infants and cooperate to chase predators. In fact, the primate literature abounds with examples of altruistic acts, whereby individuals place themselves at some risk to protect others from attacks by **conspecifics** or predators.

Adoption of orphans is a form of altruism that has been reported for macaques, baboons, and gorillas, and it's common in chimpanzees. When chimpanzee youngsters are orphaned, they are almost always adopted, usually by older siblings who are solicitous and highly protective. Adoption is crucial to the survival of orphans, who would certainly not survive on their own. In fact, it's extremely rare for a chimpanzee orphan less than 3 years of age to survive, even if it's adopted.

There are now hundreds of examples of cooperation and altruism in nonhuman primates, especially chimpanzees. This fact has caused some primatologists to consider the possibility that the common ancestor of humans and chimpanzees had a propensity for cooperation and helping others, at least in certain circumstances (Warneken and Tomasello, 2006).

Empathy, or the ability to identify with the feelings and thoughts of another individual, is required for altruistic behavior, and the degree to which chimpanzees (and other primates) are capable of empathy is debated by primatologists. Some believe there is substantial evidence for it (deWaal, 2007, 1996), but others remain unconvinced (Silk et al., 2005).

Reproduction and Reproductive Behaviors

In most primate species, sexual behavior is tied to the female's reproductive cycle, with females being receptive to males only when they're in estrus. Estrus is characterized by behavioral changes that indicate that a female is receptive. In Old World monkeys and apes that live in multimale groups, estrus is also accompanied by swelling and changes in color of the skin around the genital area. These changes serve as visual cues of a female's readiness to mate (Fig 7-10).

Permanent bonding between males and females isn't common among nonhuman primates. However, male and female savanna baboons sometimes form mating *consortships*. These temporary relationships last while the female is in estrus, and the

altruism Behavior that benefits another individual but at some potential risk or cost to oneself.

conspecifics Members of the same species.

two spend most of their time together, mating frequently. Moreover, lower-ranking male baboons often form "friendships" (Smuts, 1985) with females and occasionally mate with them.

Mating consortships are also sometimes seen in chimpanzees and are common in bonobos. In fact, a male and female bonobo may spend several weeks primarily in each other's company. During this time, they mate often, even when the female isn't in estrus. These relationships of longer duration aren't typical of chimpanzee (*Pan troglodytes*) males and females.

Such a male-female bond may result in increased reproductive success for both sexes. For the male, there is the increased likelihood that he will be the father of any infant the female conceives. At the same time, the female potentially gains protection from predators or other members of her group; and she may also gain some help in caring for offspring she may already have.

Lynn Kilgore

FIGURE 7-10
Estrous swelling of genital tissues in a female chimpanzee.

Female and Male Reproductive Strategies

Reproductive strategies, and especially how they differ between the sexes, have been a primary focus of primate research. The goal of these strategies is to produce and successfully rear to adulthood as many offspring as possible.

Primates are among the most **K-selected** of mammals. By this we mean that individuals produce only a few young, in whom they invest a tremendous amount of parental care. Contrast this pattern with **r-selected** species, where large numbers of offspring are produced but parents invest little or no energy in infant care. Good examples of r-selected species include insects, most fishes, and, among mammals, mice and rabbits.

Considering the degree of care required by young, dependent primate offspring, it's clear that enormous investment by at least one parent is necessary, and in a majority of species, the mother carries most of the burden, certainly before, but also after, birth. Primates are completely helpless at birth. and because they develop slowly, they're exposed to expanded learning opportunities within a *social* environment. This trend has been elaborated most dramatically in great apes and humans, especially the latter. So what we see in ourselves and our close primate relatives (and presumably in our more recent ancestors as well) is a strategy in which at least one parent, usually the mother, makes an extraordinary investment to produce a few "high-quality," slowly maturing offspring.

Finding food and mates, avoiding predators, and caring for and protecting dependent young are difficult challenges for nonhuman primates. Moreover, in most species, males and females use different strategies to meet these challenges.

Female primates spend almost all their adult lives either pregnant, lactating, and/or caring for offspring, and the resulting metabolic demands are enormous. A pregnant or lactating female, although perhaps only half the size of her male counterpart, may require about the same number of calories per day. Even if these demands are met, her physical resources may be drained. For example, analysis of chimpanzee skeletons from Gombe showed significant loss of bone and bone mineral in older females (Sumner et al., 1989).

Given these physiological costs and the fact that her reproductive potential is limited by lengthy intervals between births, a female's best strategy is to maximize the amount of resources available to her and her offspring. Indeed, as we just discussed, females of many primate species (gibbons, marmosets, and macaques, to

reproductive strategies The complex of behavioral patterns that contributes to individual reproductive success. The behaviors need not be deliberate, and they often vary considerably between males and females.

K-selected Pertaining to an adaptive strategy whereby individuals produce relatively few offspring, in whom they invest increased parental care. Although only a few infants are born, chances of survival are increased for each one because of parental investments in time and energy. Examples of K-selected nonprimate species are birds and canids (e.g., wolves, coyotes, and dogs).

r-selected An adaptive strategy that emphasizes relatively large numbers of offspring and reduced parental care (compared to K-selected species). *K-selection* and *r-selection* are relative terms; e.g., mice are r-selected compared to primates but K-selected compared to fish.

name a few) are competitive with other females and aggressively protect resources and territories. In other species, females distance themselves from others to avoid competition. Males, however, face a separate set of challenges. Having little investment in the rearing of offspring and the continuous production of sperm, it's to the male's advantage to secure as many mates and produce as many offspring as possible. One way of doing this is to compete with other males for mating partners.

Sexual Selection

Sexual selection, a phenomenon first described by Charles Darwin, is one outcome of different mating strategies. Sexual selection is a type of selection that operates on only one sex, usually males. The selective agent is male competition for mates and, in some species, mate choice by females. The long-term effect of sexual selection is to increase the frequency of those traits in males that lead to greater success in acquiring mates.

In the animal kingdom, numerous male attributes are the results of sexual selection. For example, female birds of many species are attracted to males with more vividly colored plumage. Selection has thus increased the frequency of alleles that influence brighter coloration in males, and in these species (peacocks are a good example), males are more colorful than females.

Sexual selection in primates is most common in species in which mating is polygynous and there is considerable male competition for females. In these species, sexual selection produces dimorphism with regard to a number of traits, most noticeably body size. As you've seen, males of many primate species are considerably larger than females, and they have larger canine teeth. Conversely, in species that live in pairs (such as gibbons) or where male competition is reduced, sexual dimorphism in canine teeth and body size is either reduced or nonexistent. For this reason, the presence or absence of sexual dimorphism in a species can be a reasonably good indicator of mating structure.

sexual selection A type of natural selection that operates on only one sex within a species. It's the result of competition for mates, and it can lead to sexual dimorphism with regard to one or more traits.

FIGURE 7-11
Hanuman langurs.

Joe MacDonald/Animals Animals

Infanticide as a Reproductive Strategy?

One way males may increase their chances of reproducing is by killing infants fathered by other males. This explanation was first offered in an early study of Hanuman langurs in India (Hrdy, 1977). Hanuman langurs (Fig. 7-11) typically live in groups composed of one adult male, several females, and their offspring. Other males without mates form "bachelor" groups that frequently forage within sight of the one-male associations. These peripheral males occasionally attack and defeat a reproductive male and drive him from his group. Sometimes, following such a takeover, the new male kills some or all of the group's infants (fathered by the previous male).

Such behavior would appear to be counterproductive, especially for a species as a whole. However, individuals act to maximize their *own* reproductive success, no matter what effect their behavior may have on the group or even the species. By killing infants fathered by other animals, male langurs may in fact increase their own chances of fathering offspring, albeit unknowingly. This is because while a female is producing milk and nursing an infant, she doesn't come into estrus and therefore isn't sexually available. But when an infant dies, its mother resumes cycling and becomes sexually receptive. So by killing nursing infants, a new male avoids waiting two to three years for them to be weaned before he can mate with their mothers. This could be advantageous for him, since chances are good that he won't even be in the group for two or three years. He also doesn't expend energy and put himself at risk defending infants who don't carry his genes.

© Peter Henzi

FIGURE 7-12
An immigrant male chacma baboon chases a terrified female and her infant (clinging to her back). Resident males interceded to stop the chase.

Hanuman langurs aren't the only primates that practice infanticide. Infanticide has been observed (or surmised) in many species, such as redtail monkeys, red colobus, blue monkeys, savanna baboons, howlers, orangutans, gorillas, chimpanzees (Struhsaker and Leyland, 1987), and humans. (It should also be noted that infanticide occurs in numerous nonprimate species, including rodents, cats, and horses.) In the majority of reported nonhuman primate examples, infanticide coincides with the transfer of a new male into a group or, as in chimpanzees, an encounter with an unfamiliar female and infant.

Numerous objections to this explanation of infanticide have been raised. Alternative explanations have included competition for resources (Rudran, 1973), aberrant behaviors related to human-induced overcrowding (Curtin and Dohlinow, 1978), and inadvertent killing during aggressive episodes, where it wasn't clear that the infant was actually the target animal (Bartlett et al., 1993). Sussman and colleagues (1995), as well as others, have questioned the actual prevalence of infanticide, arguing that although it does occur, it's not particularly common. These authors have also suggested that if indeed male reproductive fitness is increased through the killing of infants, such increases are negligible. Yet others (Struhsaker and Leyland, 1987; Hrdy et al, 1995) maintain that the incidence and patterning of infanticide by males are not only significant, but consistent with the assumptions established by theories of behavioral evolution.

Henzi and Barrett (2003) report that when chacma baboon males migrate into a new group, they "deliberately single out females with young infants and hunt them down" (Fig. 7-12). The importance of these findings is the conclusion that, at least in chacma baboons, newly arrived males consistently try to kill infants, and their attacks are highly aggressive and purposeful. However, such reports don't prove that infanticide increases a male's reproductive fitness. To do this, primatologists must demonstrate two crucial facts:

1. Infanticidal males *don't* kill their own offspring.
2. Once a male has killed an infant, he subsequently fathers another infant with the victim's mother.

Borries et al. (1999) collected DNA samples from the feces of infanticidal males and their victims in several groups of free-ranging Hanuman langurs specifically to determine if these males killed their own offspring. Their results showed that in all 16 cases where infant and male DNA was available, the males were not related to the infants they either attacked or killed. Moreover, DNA analysis also showed that in four out of five cases where a victim's mother subsequently gave birth, the new infant was fathered by the infanticidal male. Although still more evidence is needed, this DNA evidence strongly suggests that by practicing infanticide, a male may increase his chances of fathering offspring.

polyandry A mating system wherein a female continuously associates with more than one male (usually two or three) with whom she mates. Among nonhuman primates, polyandry is seen only in marmosets and tamarins. It also occurs in a few human societies.

Mothers, Fathers, and Infants

The basic social unit among all primates is the female and her infants (Fig. 7-13). Except in those species in which monogamy or **polyandry** occurs, males usually don't directly participate in the rearing of offspring. The mother-infant bond begins at birth. Although the exact nature of the bonding process isn't fully known, there appear to be predisposing innate factors that strongly attract the female to her infant, so long as she herself has had a sufficiently normal experience with her own mother. This doesn't mean that primate mothers possess innate knowledge of how to care for an infant. In fact, they don't. Monkeys and apes reared in captivity without contact with their own mothers not only don't know how to care for a newborn infant, but may also be afraid of it and attack or even kill it. Thus, learning is critically important in the establishment of a mother's attraction to her infant.

The role of bonding between primate mothers and infants was clearly demonstrated in a famous series of experiments at the University of Wisconsin. Psychologist Harry Harlow (1959) raised infant monkeys with *surrogate* mothers made of wire or a combination of wire and cloth. Other monkeys were raised with no mother at all. In one experiment, infants retained an attachment to their cloth-

FIGURE 7–13
Primate mothers with young.
(a) Mongoose lemur. (b) Chimpanzee.
(c) Patas monkey. (d) Orangutan.
(e) Sykes monkey.

(a)

(b)

(c)

(d)

(e)

covered surrogate mother (Fig. 7-14). But those raised with no mother were incapable of forming lasting affectional ties. These deprived monkeys sat passively in their cages and stared vacantly into space. None of the motherless males ever successfully copulated, and those females who were (somewhat artificially) impregnated either paid little attention to their infants or were aggressive toward them (Harlow and Harlow, 1961). The point is that monkeys reared in isolation were denied opportunities to *learn* the rules of social and maternal behavior. Moreover, and just as essential, they were denied the all-important physical contact so necessary for normal primate psychological and emotional development.

The importance of a normal relationship with the mother is demonstrated by field studies as well. From birth, infant primates are able to cling to their mother's fur, and they're in more or less constant physical contact with her for several months. During this critical period, infants develop a closeness with mothers that doesn't always end with weaning. It may even be maintained throughout life (especially among some Old World monkeys). In fact, mothers and infants may remain close until one or the other dies.

In some species, presumed fathers also participate in infant care (Fig. 7-15). Male siamangs are actively involved, and marmoset and tamarin infants are usually carried on the father's back and transferred to their mother only for nursing.

Primate Cultural Behavior

One important trait that makes primates, and especially chimpanzees and bonobos, attractive as models for behavior in early hominids may be called *cultural behavior*. Although many cultural anthropologists and others prefer to use the term *culture* to refer specifically to human activities, most biological anthropologists consider it appropriate to use the term in reference to nonhuman primates too (McGrew, 1992, 1998; de Waal, 1999; Whiten et al., 1999).

FIGURE 7-14
Infant macaque clinging to cloth mother.

FIGURE 7-15
This male savanna baboon with a youngster on his back is exhibiting infant care, but he may not be the father.

Undeniably, most aspects of culture are uniquely human, and one must be cautious when interpreting nonhuman animal behavior. But again, since humans are products of the same evolutionary forces that have produced other species, they can be expected to show some of the same *behavioral patterns,* particularly of other primates. However, because of increased brain size and learning capacities, humans express many characteristics to a greater degree. We would argue that the *aptitude for culture* as a means of adapting to the natural environment is one such characteristic.

Among other things, cultural behavior is *learned;* it's passed from generation to generation not by genes, but through learning. Whereas humans deliberately teach their young, free-ranging nonhuman primates (with the exception of a few reports) don't appear to do so. But at the same time, like young nonhuman primates, human children also acquire a tremendous amount of knowledge through observation rather than instruction (Fig. 7-16a). Nonhuman primate infants, through observing their mothers and others, learn about food items, appropriate behaviors, and how to use and modify objects to achieve certain ends (Fig. 7-16b). In turn, their own offspring will observe their activities. What emerges is a *cultural tradition* that may eventually come to typify an entire group or even a species.

The earliest reported example of cultural behavior concerned a study group of Japanese macaques on Koshima Island. In 1952, researchers began giving sweet potatoes to the macaques. The following year, a young female named Imo began washing her potatoes in a freshwater stream prior to eating them. Within three years, several monkeys had adopted the practice, but they had switched from using the stream to taking their potatoes to the ocean nearby. Maybe they liked the salt.

The researchers pointed out that dietary habits and food preferences are learned and that potato washing was an example of nonhuman culture. Because the practice arose as an innovative solution to a problem (removing dirt) and gradually spread through the troop until it became a tradition, it was seen as containing elements of human culture.

A study of orangutans in six areas (four Bornean and two Sumatran) identified 19 behaviors that showed sufficient regional variation to be classed as "very likely cultural variants" (van Schaik et al., 2003). Four of these were differences in how nests were used or built. Other behaviors that varied included the use of branches to swat insects and pressing leaves or hands to the mouth to amplify sounds.

Breuer et al (2005) reported seeing two female lowland gorillas in the DRC using branches as tools. In one case, a gorilla used the branch to test the depth of a pool

FIGURE 7–16

(a) This little girl is learning the basic skills of computer use by watching her older sister. (b) A chimpanzee learns the art of termiting through intense observation.

(a)

(b)

of water. Then, as she waded through the pool bipedally she used the branch again, this time as a walking stick.

Chimpanzees exhibit even more elaborate examples of *tool use*. This point is very important, because traditionally, tool use (along with language) was said to set humans apart from other animals. Chimpanzees insert twigs and grass blades into termite mounds in a practice called "termite fishing." When termites grab the twig, the chimpanzee withdraws it and eats them. Chimpanzees modify some of their stems and twigs, in effect making tools from the natural material. For example, a chimpanzee will choose a piece of vine or stem and modify it by removing leaves, then breaking pieces off until it's the appropriate length. Chimpanzees have also been seen making these tools even before the termite mound is in sight.

All this preparation has several implications. First, the chimpanzees are involved in an activity that prepares them for a future (not immediate) task at a somewhat distant location, and this implies planning and forethought. Second, attention to the shape and size of the raw material indicates that chimpanzees have a preconceived idea of what the finished product needs to be in order to be useful. To produce even a simple tool based on a concept is an extremely complex behavior that isn't the exclusive domain of humans. Chimpanzees also crumple and chew handfuls of leaves, which they dip into tree hollows where water accumulates. Then they suck the water from their newly made "leaf sponges." Leaves are also used to wipe substances from fur; twigs as toothpicks; stones as weapons; and objects such as branches and stones may be dragged or rolled to enhance displays.

The recent discovery that chimpanzees also modify and use tools for hunting came as a surprise to primatologists. Preutz and Bertolani (2007) report that savanna chimpanzees in Senegal, West Africa, use sharpened sticks to hunt galagos. Ten different animals (adult males, females, and subadults) repeatedly jabbed sticks into cavities in tree branches and trunks to extract galagos from their sleeping nests. In much the same way that they modify termite sticks, these chimpanzees had stripped off side twigs and leaves. But they'd also chewed the ends to sharpen them, in effect producing a small thrusting spear. Only one galago was actually seen to be retrieved and eaten, and although it wasn't moving or vocalizing, it was unclear if it had actually been killed by the "spear" (Preutz and Bertolani, 2007).

Chimpanzees in several West African study groups use hammerstones along with platform stones to crack nuts and hard-shelled fruits (Boesch et al., 1994; (Fig. 7-17). However, neither the hammerstone nor the platform stone is deliberately manufactured. Like chimpanzees, wild capuchin monkeys use leaves to get water from cavities in trees (Phillips, 1998), and they smash objects against stones (Izawa and Mizuno, 1977). Their use of stones in captivity (both as hammers and anvils) has also been reported (Visalberghi, 1990). But chimpanzees are the only nonhuman primate that consistently and habitually makes and uses tools (McGrew, 1992).

Importantly, chimpanzees show regional variation regarding both the types and methods of tool use. Stone hammers and platforms are used only in West African groups. And at central and eastern African sites, chimpanzees "fish" for termites with stems and sticks, but they don't at some West African locations (McGrew, 1992).

Chimpanzees also show regional dietary preferences (Nishida et al., 1983; McGrew, 1992, 1998). For example, oil palm fruits and nuts are eaten at many locations, including Gombe, but even though these foods are also available in the Mahale Mountains, they aren't eaten by the chimpanzees there. Such regional patterns in tool use and food preferences that

FIGURE 7-17

Chimpanzees in Bossou, Guinea, West Africa, use a pair of stones as hammer and anvil to crack oil-palm nuts.

Tetsuro Matsuzawa

aren't related to availability are reminiscent of the cultural variations seen in humans.

Using sticks, twigs, and stones enhances chimpanzees' ability to exploit resources. They learn these behaviors during infancy and childhood, partly as a result of prolonged contact with the mother. It's also important that exposure to other members of a social group provides additional learning opportunities. These statements can also be appropriately applied to early hominids. While sticks and unmodified stones don't remain to tell tales, our early ancestors surely used these same objects as tools in much the same way chimpanzees do today.

While wild chimpanzees haven't been observed modifying the stones they use, a male bonobo named Kanzi (see also p. 153) learned to strike two stones together to produce sharp-edged flakes. In a study conducted by Sue Savage-Rumbaugh and archaeologist Nicholas Toth, Kanzi was allowed to watch as Toth produced stone flakes, which were then used to open a transparent plastic food container (Savage-Rumbaugh and Lewin, 1994). Although bonobos don't commonly use objects as tools in the wild, Kanzi readily appreciated the usefulness of the flakes in obtaining food. What's more, he was able to master the basic technique of producing flakes without being taught, although at first his progress was slow. Finally, Kanzi realized that if he threw the stone onto a hard floor, it would shatter and he would have an abundance of cutting tools. Although his solution wasn't the one that Savage-Rumbaugh and Toth expected, it was perhaps even more significant because it provided an excellent example of bonobo insight and problem-solving ability. Moreover, Kanzi did eventually learn to produce flakes by striking two stones together, and then he used these flakes to obtain food. These behaviors aren't just examples of tool manufacture and use, albeit in a captive situation; they're also very sophisticated goal-directed activities.

Culture has become the environment in which modern humans live. Quite clearly, the use of sticks in termite fishing and hammerstones to crack nuts is hardly comparable to modern human technology. However, modern human technology had its beginnings in these very types of behaviors. But this doesn't mean that nonhuman primates are "on their way" to becoming human. Remember, evolution isn't goal directed and, even if it were, there's nothing to dictate that modern humans necessarily constitute an evolutionary goal. Such a conclusion is a purely **anthropocentric** view and has no validity in discussions of evolutionary processes.

Language

One of the most significant events in human evolution was the development of language. We've already described several behaviors and autonomic responses that convey information in primates. But although we emphasized the importance of communication to nonhuman primate social life, we also said that nonhuman primates don't use language the way humans do.

The view traditionally held by most linguists and behavioral psychologists has been that nonhuman communication consists of mostly involuntary vocalizations and actions that convey information solely about the emotional state of the animal (anger, fear, and so on). Nonhuman animals haven't been considered capable of communicating about external events, objects, or other animals, either in close proximity or removed in space or time. For example, when a startled baboon barks, other group members know only that it's startled. They don't know why it barked, and they can determine this only by looking around to see what provoked it. In general, then, it's been assumed that in nonhuman animals, including primates, vocalizations, facial expressions, body postures, and so on, don't refer to *specific* external phenomena.

But, for several years, these views have been challenged (Steklis, 1985; King, 1994, 2004). For example, vervet monkeys (Fig. 7-18) use specific vocalizations to refer to particular categories of predators, such as snakes, birds of prey, and leopards (Struhsaker, 1967; Seyfarth, Cheney, and Marler, 1980a, 1980b). When researchers

anthropocentric Viewing nonhuman animals in terms of human motives, and experience and capabilities; emphasizing the importance of humans over everything else.

Lynn Kilgore

FIGURE 7–18
Group of vervets.

made tape recordings of various vervet alarm calls and played them back within hearing distance of free-ranging vervets, they saw different responses to various calls. When the vervets heard leopard-alarm calls, the monkeys climbed trees; eagle-alarm calls caused them to look up; and they responded to snake-alarm calls by looking around at the ground and nearby grass.

These results show that vervets use distinct vocalizations to refer to specific components of the external environment. These calls aren't involuntary, and they don't refer solely to the emotional state (alarm) of the individual, although this information is conveyed. While these findings dispel certain long-held misconceptions about nonhuman communication (at least for some species), they also indicate certain limitations. Vervet communication is restricted to the present; as far as we know, no vervet can communicate about a predator it saw yesterday or one it might see in the future.

Other studies have demonstrated that numerous nonhuman primates, including cottontop tamarins (Cleveland and Snowdon, 1982), Goeldi's monkeys (Masataka, 1983), red colobus (Struhsaker, 1975), and gibbons (Tenaza and Tilson, 1977), produce distinct calls that have specific references. There is also growing evidence that many birds and some nonprimate mammals use specific predator alarm calls (Seyfarth, 1987).

Humans use *language,* a set of written and/or spoken symbols that refer to concepts, other people, objects, and so on. This set of symbols is said to be *arbitrary* because the symbol itself has no inherent relationship with whatever it stands for. For example, the English word *flower,* when written or spoken, neither looks, sounds, smells, nor feels like the thing it represents. Humans can also recombine their linguistic symbols in an infinite number of ways to create new meanings, and we can use language to refer to events, places, objects, and people far removed in both space and time. For these reasons, language is described as a form of communication based on the human ability to think symbolically.

Language, as distinct from other forms of communication, has always been considered a uniquely human achievement, setting humans apart from the rest of the animal kingdom. But work with captive apes has raised some doubts about certain aspects of this notion. Although many people were skeptical about the capacity of nonhuman primates to use language, reports from psychologists, especially those who work with chimpanzees, leave little doubt that apes can learn to interpret visual signs and use them in communication. Other than humans, no mammal can speak. However, the fact that apes can't speak has less to do with lack of intelligence than to differences in the anatomy of the vocal tract and language-related structures in the brain.

Because of unsuccessful attempts by others to teach young chimpanzees to speak, psychologists Beatrice and Allen Gardner designed a study to test language capabilities in chimpanzees by teaching an infant female named Washoe to use ASL (American Sign Language for the deaf). The project began in 1966, and in three years, Washoe acquired at least 132 signs. "She asked for goods and services, and she also asked questions about the world of objects and events around her" (Gardner et al., 1989, p. 6).

Years later, an infant chimpanzee named Loulis was placed in Washoe's care. Psychologist Roger Fouts and colleagues wanted to know if Loulis would acquire signing skills from Washoe and other chimpanzees in the study group. Within just eight days, Loulis began to imitate the signs of others. Moreover, Washoe deliberately *taught* Loulis how to make certain signs. In 1980 Dr. Fouts moved Washoe and Loulis to a facility at Central Washington University where the language studies are ongoing. Washoe, the first signing chimpanzee, died in 2007 at the age of 42.

Dr. Francine Patterson, who taught ASL to Koko, a female lowland gorilla, reports that Koko uses more than 500 signs. Furthermore, Michael, an adult male gorilla who was also involved in the study until his death in 2000, had a considerable sign vocabulary, and the two gorillas regularly communicated with each other using sign language.

In the late 1970s, a 2-year-old male orangutan named Chantek began to use signs after one month of training. Eventually, he acquired approximately 140 signs, which were sometimes used to refer to objects (and people) that weren't present. Chantek also invented signs and recombined them in novel ways, and he appeared to understand that his signs were *representations* of items, actions, and people (Miles, 1990).

Questions have been raised about this type of research. Do the apes really understand the signs they learn, or are they merely imitating their trainers? Do they learn that a symbol is a name for an object or simply that using it will produce that object?

Partly in an effort to address some of these questions and criticisms, psychologist Sue Savage-Rumbaugh taught two chimpanzees named Sherman and Austin to use symbols to categorize *classes* of objects, such as "food" or "tool." This was done in recognition of the fact that in previous studies, apes had been taught symbols for *specific* items. Savage-Rumbaugh recognized that using a symbol as a label is not the same thing as understanding the *representational value* of the symbol. But if the chimpanzees could classify things into groups, it would indicate that they can use symbols referentially.

Sherman and Austin were taught to recognize familiar food items, for which they routinely used symbols, as belonging to a broader category referred to by yet another symbol, "food." Then they were introduced to unfamiliar food items, for which they had no symbols, to see if they would put them in the food category. The fact that they both had perfect or nearly perfect scores further substantiated that they could categorize unfamiliar objects. More importantly, it was clear that they were capable of assigning symbols to indicate an object's membership in a broader grouping. This ability was a strong indication that the chimpanzees understood that the symbols were being used referentially.

However, subsequent work with Lana, who had different language experiences, wasn't as successful. Although Lana was able to sort actual objects into categories, she was unable to assign generic symbols to novel items (Savage-Rumbaugh and Lewin, 1994). Thus, it became apparent that the manner in which chimpanzees are introduced to language influences their ability to understand the representational value of symbols.

Throughout the relatively brief history of ape language studies, a major assumption has been that young chimpanzees must be *taught* to use symbols, in contrast to the ability of human children to learn language through exposure, without being taught. Therefore, it was significant when Savage-Rumbaugh and her colleagues reported that the young bonobo Kanzi, before his toolmaking days, was *spontane-*

Rose A. Sevcik, Language Research Center, Georgia State University; photo by Elizabeth Pugh

FIGURE 7–19

The bonobo Kanzi, as a youngster, using lexigrams to communicate with human observers.

ously acquiring and using symbols when he was just 2½ years old (Savage-Rumbaugh et al., 1986; (Fig. 7-19). His younger half-sister began to use symbols spontaneously when she was only 11 months old. Both animals had been exposed to the use of lexigrams, or illustrated symbols that represent words, when they accompanied their mother to training sessions. But neither had actually been taught and weren't even involved in these sessions.

While the language studies with great apes have shown that they have the ability to use language to a certain degree, and that they have a remarkable degree of cognitive complexity, it nevertheless remains evident that apes don't acquire and use language in the same way humans do. It also appears that not all signing apes understand the referential relationship between symbol and object, person, or action. Nonetheless, there's now abundant evidence that humans aren't the only species capable of some degree of symbolic thought and complex communication.

QUICK REVIEW   **Evolution of Human Language**

Shared cognition abilities of primates, especially apes → Some symbolic capacities

Some symbolic capacities ↓

Neurological reorganization ← Increased communication abilities and development of symbolic thinking

Increased communication abilities and development of symbolic thinking ↓

Anatomical modifications of vocal tract → Full human language: open system, arbitrary use of symbols

The Primate Continuum

It's an unfortunate fact that humans generally view themselves as separate from the rest of the animal kingdom. This perspective is, in no small measure, due to a prevailing lack of knowledge of the behavior and abilities of other species. Moreover, these notions are continuously reinforced through exposure to advertising, movies, and television (Fig. 7-20).

For decades, behavioral psychology taught that animal behavior represents nothing more than a series of conditioned responses to specific stimuli. (This perspective is very convenient for those who wish to use nonhuman animals, for whatever purposes, and remain free of guilt.) Fortunately, this attitude has begun to change in recent years to reflect a growing awareness that humans, although in many ways unquestionably unique, are nevertheless part of a **biological continuum.** Indeed, we are also a part of a behavioral continuum.

Where do humans fit in this biological continuum? Are we at the top? The answer depends on the criteria used. Certainly, we're the most intelligent species if we define intelligence in terms of problem-solving abilities and abstract thought. However, if we look more closely, we recognize that the differences between ourselves and our primate relatives, especially chimpanzees and bonobos, are primarily quantitative and not qualitative.

Although the human brain is absolutely and relatively larger, neurological processes are functionally the same. The necessity of close bonding with at least one parent and the need for physical contact are essentially the same. Developmental stages and dependence on learning are strikingly similar. Indeed, even in the capacity for cruelty and aggression combined with compassion, tenderness, and altruism exhibited by chimpanzees, we see a close parallel to the dichotomy between "evil" and "good" so long recognized in ourselves. The main difference between how chimpanzees and humans express these qualities (and therefore the dichotomy) is one of degree. Humans are much more adept at cruelty and compassion, and we can reflect on our behavior in ways that chimpanzees can't. Like the cat that plays with a mouse, chimpanzees don't seem to understand the suffering they inflict on others. But humans do. Likewise, while an adult chimpanzee may sit next to a dying relative, it doesn't seem to feel the intense grief a human normally does in the same situation.

To arrive at any understanding of what it is to be human, it's important to recognize that many of our behaviors are elaborate extensions of those of our

biological continuum Refers to the fact that organisms are related through common ancestry and that behaviors and traits seen in one species are also seen in others to varying degrees. (When expressions of a phenomeon continuously grade into one another so that there are no discrete categories, they are said to exist on a continuum. Color is such a phenomenon.)

FIGURE 7–20
This unfortunate advertising display is a good example of how humans misunderstand and thus misrepresent our closest relatives.

hominid ancestors and close primate relatives. The fact that so many of us prefer to bask in the warmth of the "sun belt" with literally millions of others reflects our heritage as social animals adapted to life in the tropics. And the sweet tooth that afflicts so many of us is a result of our earlier primate ancestors' predilection for high-energy sugar contained in sweet, ripe fruit. Thus, it's important to recognize our primate heritage as we explore how humans came to be and how we continue to adapt.

Summary

In this chapter, we've presented the major theoretical models for the evolution of behavior in primates, and we've discussed some of the evidence, including some reports that use genetic data to support these models. The subject of the evolution of behavior is extremely complex because it requires research into the interactions of dozens, if not hundreds, of ecological and physiological variables.

The fundamental principle of behavioral evolution is that aspects of behavior (including social behavior) are influenced by genetic factors. And because some behavioral elements are therefore inherited, natural selection can act on them in the same way it acts on physical and anatomical characteristics. We pointed out that in mammals and birds, the proportion of behavior that is due to learning is much greater than it is in insects and most other invertebrates, in which a high proportion of behavior is directly influenced by genes.

Behavioral ecology is the discipline that examines behavior from the perspective of complex ecological relationships and the role of natural selection as it favors behaviors that increase reproductive fitness. This approach generates many models of behavioral evolution that can be applied to all species, including humans. Members of each species inherit a genome that is species-specific, and some part of that genome influences behaviors. But in more complex animals, the genome allows for greater degrees of behavioral flexibility and learning. And in humans, who rely on cultural adaptations for survival, most behavior is learned.

Life history traits or strategies (developmental stages that characterize a species) are important to the reproductive success of individuals. These include length of gestation, number of offspring per birth, interbirth interval, age of sexual maturity, and longevity. Although these characters are strongly influenced by the genome of any species, they are also influenced by environmental and social factors such as nutrition and social status. In turn, nutritional requirements are affected by body size, diet, and basal metabolic rate (BMR).

We discussed numerous examples of cultural behaviors that have been documented for the great apes. These include different types of tool use, which youngsters learn by watching adults. There are also food preferences that vary from one area to another, even though the same types of food are available. These examples represent cultural traditions that may be similar to those that were present among the earliest hominids.

Lastly, we talked about the biological and behavioral continuity within the primate order. Although nonhuman primate cultural behavior and communication are in no way as elaborate as they are in humans, they can be seen as behaviors that are variably expressed throughout the primate order and especially among the great apes and humans.

WHY IT MATTERS

TV shows and popular articles about primate behavior are fun to watch and think about, but can we learn anything useful for our own species by observing primates in their natural settings? Many primatologists argue that it's important to observe other primates simply to learn as much as we can about other species. But there are ways in which knowledge about other primates' lives can be directly useful for humans.

One area that has attracted a great deal of attention is evidence of self-medication by chimpanzees, leading to the suggestion that we may be able to identify beneficial drugs for human diseases by observing chimpanzee dietary behaviors. While studying primate behavior in Tanzania, Harvard primatologist Richard Wrangham noted that chimpanzees occasionally seek out a type of leaf that isn't a normal part of the diet and swallow it whole. Chemical analysis of the leaf revealed that it has high levels of a compound that has antibiotic properties, suggesting that the chimpanzees are using it for intestinal parasite control. Further observations revealed that chimpanzees occasionally use the same plants consumed by people in the area for intestinal parasites, skin infections, and ulcers. Perhaps most significant for human health, some of the plants consumed by chimpanzees contain compounds that are potentially useful for controlling malaria, *Staphylococcus* infections, *E. coli,* and cancer. Perhaps our close relatives will show us as yet unknown medicinal properties of many plant species, but this will require ongoing careful observations of primate behavior.

Critical Thinking Questions

1 Apply some of the topics presented in this chapter to some nonprimate species with which you are familiar. Can you develop some hypotheses to explain the behavior of some domestic species? You might want to speculate on how behavior in domestic animals may differ from that of their wild ancestors. (Chapter 2 might help you here.)

2 Speculate on how the behavioral ecology of nonhuman primates may be helpful in explaining some human behaviors.

3 How might infanticide be seen as a reproductive strategy for males? If this concept were to be applied to human males, do you think some people would object? Why or why not?

CHAPTER 8

Hominid Origins

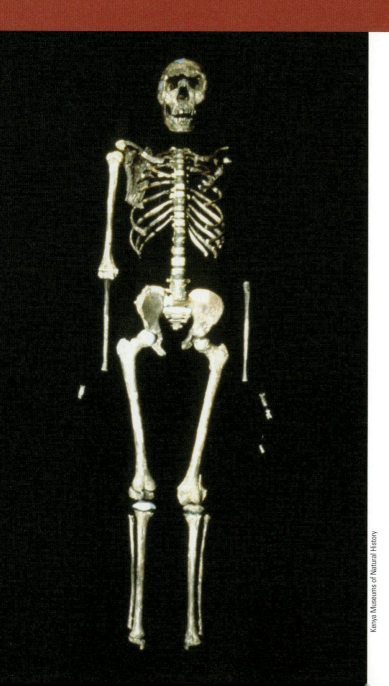

Kenya Museums of Natural History

Who are the oldest members of the human family, and how do these early hominids compare with modern humans?

With modern apes? How do they fit within a biological continuum?

hominids Colloquial term for members of the family Hominidae, which includes all bipedal hominoids back to the divergence from African great apes.

biocultural Pertaining to the concept that biology makes culture possible and that culture influences biology.

Introduction

Our species today dominates our planet as we use our brains and cultural inventions to invade every corner of the earth. Yet, 5 million years ago, our ancestors were little more than bipedal apes, confined to a few regions in Africa. What were these creatures like? When and how did they begin their evolutionary journey?

In the last two chapters, we have seen how and why humans are grouped as primates, both structurally and behaviorally, and how our evolutionary history coincides with that of other primates. However, we are a unique kind of primate, and our ancestors have been adapted to a particular kind of lifestyle for several million years. Some primitive hominoid may have begun this process more than 10 mya, but fossil evidence indicates a much more definite hominid presence sometime after 7 mya. The hominid nature of these remains is revealed by more than the morphological structure of teeth and bones; in many cases, we know that these animals are **hominids** also because of the way they behaved—emphasizing once again the **biocultural** nature of human evolution.

In this chapter, we turn first to the physical evidence of earlier primates and then to the hominid fossils themselves. The earliest fossils identifiable as hominids are all from Africa. They date from as early as 7 million years ago, and after 4 mya, varieties of these early hominids became more plentiful and widely distributed in Africa. It's fascinating to think about all these quite primitive early members of our family living side by side for millions of years, especially when we also try to figure out how these animals managed to co-exist with their different adaptations. Most of these species became extinct. But why? What's more, were some of these apelike animals possibly our direct ancestors?

Hominids, of course, evolved from earlier primates (dating back close to 50 million years ago), and we will briefly review this long and abundant prehominid fossil record to provide a better context for understanding the subsequent evolution of the human lineage. In recent years, paleoanthropologists from several countries have been excavating sites in Africa, and many exciting new finds have been uncovered. However, because many finds have been made so recently, detailed evaluations are still in progress, and conclusions must remain tentative.

One thing is certain, however. The earliest members of the human family were confined to Africa. Only much later did their descendants disperse from the African continent to other areas of the Old World. (This "out of Africa" saga will be the topic of the next chapter.)

Early Primate Evolution

Long before bipedal hominids first evolved in Africa, more primitive primates had diverged from even more distant mammalian ancestors. The roots of the primate order go back to the early stages of the placental mammal radiation as far back as

75–65 mya. Thus, the earliest primates were diverging from early and still primitive placental mammals. We have seen (in Chapter 6) that strictly defining living primates using clear-cut derived features is not an easy task. The further back we go in the fossil record, the more primitive and, in many cases, the more generalized the fossil primates become. Such a situation makes classifying them all the more difficult.

In fact, we only have scarce traces of the earliest primates. Some anthropologists have suggested that recently discovered bits and pieces from North Africa *may* be those of a very small primitive primate. But until more evidence is found, we will just have to wait and see.

Fortunately, a vast number of fossil primates from the Eocene (55–34 mya) have been discovered and now total more than 200 recognized species (see Fig. 5-7, p. 90, for a geological chart). Unlike the available Paleocene forms, those from the Eocene display distinctive primate features. Indeed, primatologist Elwyn Simons (1972, p. 124) called them "the first primates of modern aspect." These animals have been found primarily in sites in North America and Europe (which for most of the Eocene were still connected). It is important to recall that the landmasses that connect continents, as well as the water boundaries that separate them, have obvious impact on the geographical distribution of such terrestrially bound animals as primates (see p. 91).

Some interesting late Eocene forms have also been found in Asia, which was joined to Europe by the end of the Eocene epoch. Looking at the whole array of Eocene primates, it is certain that they were (1) primates, (2) widely distributed, and (3) mostly extinct by the end of the Eocene. What is less certain is how any of them might be related to the living primates. Some of these forms are probably ancestors of the *prosimians*—the lemurs and lorises.* Others are probably related to the tarsier. New evidence of Eocene *anthropoid* origins has recently been discovered at a few sites in North Africa. The earliest of these African fossils go back to 50 mya, but the remains are very fragmentary. More conclusive evidence comes from Egypt and is well dated to 37 mya. At present, it looks likely that the earliest anthropoids first evolved in Africa.

The Oligocene (33–23 mya) has yielded numerous additional fossil remains of several different species of early anthropoids. Most of these forms are *Old World anthropoids,* all discovered at a single locality in Egypt, the Fayum (Fig. 8-1). In addition, there are a few known bits from North and South America that relate only to the ancestry of New World monkeys. By the early Oligocene, continental drift had separated the New World (that is, the Americas) from the Old World (Africa and Eurasia). Some of the earliest Fayum forms, nevertheless, may potentially be close to the ancestry

FIGURE 8–1
(a) Fayum site in Egypt.
(b) Excavations in progress at the Fayum, where dozens of fossil primates have been discovered.

(a)

(b)

© Russell Ciochon

---

* In strict classification terms, especially from a cladistic point of view, lemurs and lorises should be referred to as strepsirhines (see Chapter 6).

TABLE 8.1	Inferred General Paleobiological Aspects of Oligocene Primates			
	Weight Range	**Substratum**	**Location**	**Diet**
Apidium	750–1,600 g (2–3 lb)	Arboreal	Quadruped	Fruit, seeds
Aegyptopithecus	6,700 g (15 lb)	Arboreal	Quadruped	Fruit, some leaves?

Source: After Fleagle, 1999.

of both Old and New World anthropoids. It has been suggested that late in the Eocene or very early in the Oligocene, the first anthropoids (primitive "monkeys") arose in Africa and later reached South America by "rafting" over the water separation on drifting chunks of vegetation. What we call "monkey," then, may have a common Old World origin, but the ancestry of New and Old World varieties remains separate after about 35 mya. The closest evolutionary affinities humans have after this time are with other Old World anthropoids, that is, with Old World monkeys and apes.

The possible roots of anthropoid evolution are illustrated by different forms from the Fayum; one is the genus *Apidium*. Well known at the Fayum, *Apidium* is represented by several dozen jaws or partial dentitions as well as many **postcranial** remains. Because of its primitive dental arrangement, some paleontologists have suggested that *Apidium* may lie near or even before the evolutionary divergence of Old and New World anthropoids. As so much fossil material of teeth and limb bones of *Apidium* has been found, some informed speculation regarding diet and locomotor behavior is possible. It is thought that this small, squirrel-sized primate ate mostly fruits and some seeds and was most likely an arboreal quadruped, adept at leaping and springing (Table 8-1).

The other genus of importance from the Fayum is *Aegyptopithecus*. This genus, also well known, is represented by several well-preserved crania and abundant jaws and teeth. The largest of the Fayum anthropoids, *Aegyptopithecus* is roughly the size of a modern howler monkey (13 to 20 pounds; Fleagle, 1983) and is thought to have been a short-limbed, slow-moving arboreal quadruped (see Table 8-1). *Aegyptopithecus* is important because, better than any other known form, it bridges the gap between the Eocene fossils and the succeeding Miocene hominoids.

postcranial (*post*, meaning "after") In a quadruped, referring to that portion of the body behind the head; in a biped, referring to all parts of the body *beneath* the head (i.e., the neck down).

Nevertheless, *Aegyptopithecus* is a very primitive Old World anthropoid, with a small brain and long snout and not showing any derived features of either Old World monkeys or hominoids. Thus, it may be close to the ancestry of *both* major groups of living Old World anthropoids. Found in geological beds dating to 35–33 mya, *Aegyptopithecus* further suggests that the crucial evolutionary divergence of hominoids from other Old World anthropoids occurred *after* this time (Fig. 8-2).

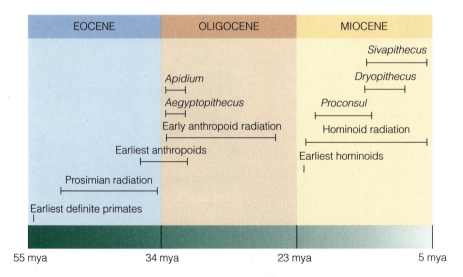

FIGURE 8–2
Major events in early primate evolution.

Miocene Fossil Hominoids

During the approximately 18 million years of the Miocene (23–5 mya), a great deal of evolutionary activity took place. In Africa, Asia, and Europe, a diverse and highly successful group of hominoids emerged (Fig. 8-3). Indeed, there were many more forms of hominoids from the Miocene than are found today (now represented by the highly restricted groups of apes and one species of humans). In fact, the Miocene could be called "the golden age of hominoids." Many thousands of fossils have been found from dozens of sites scattered in East Africa, southern Africa, southwest Asia, into western and southern Europe, and extending into southern Asia and China.

During the Miocene, significant transformations relating to climate and repositioning of landmasses took place. By 23 mya, major continental locations approximated those of today (except that North and South America were separate). Nevertheless, the movements of South America and Australia farther away from Antarctica significantly altered ocean currents. Likewise, the continued movement of the South Asian plate into Asia produced the Himalayan Plateau. Both of these paleogeographical modifications had significant impact on the climate, and the early Miocene was considerably warmer than the preceding Oligocene. Moreover, by 19 mya, the Arabian Plate (which had been separate) "docked" with northeastern Africa. As a result, migrations of animals from Africa directly into southwest Asia (and in the other direction as well) became possible. Among the earliest transcontinental migrants (around 16 mya) were African hominoids who colonized both Europe and Asia at this time.

A problem arises in any attempt to simplify the complex evolutionary situation regarding Miocene hominoids. For example, for many years, paleontologists tended to think of these fossil forms as either "apelike" or "humanlike" and used modern examples as models. But as we have just noted, very few hominoids remain. Therefore, we should not hastily generalize from the living forms to the much more diverse fossil forms; otherwise, we obscure the evolutionary uniqueness of these animals. In addition, we should not expect all fossil forms to be directly or even particularly closely related to living species. Indeed, we should expect the opposite; that is, most lines vanish without descendants.

Over the last three decades, the Miocene hominoid assemblage has been interpreted and reinterpreted. As more fossils are found, the evolutionary picture grows more complicated. The vast array of fossil forms has not yet been completely studied, so conclusions remain tenuous. Given this uncertainty, it is probably best, for the present, to group Miocene hominoids geographically:

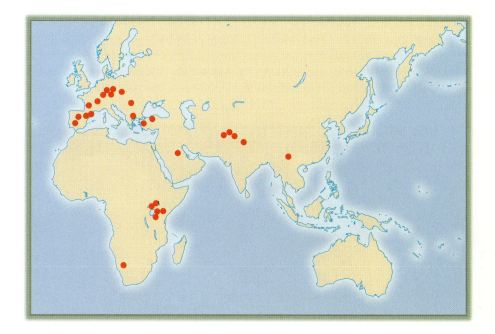

FIGURE 8–3

Miocene hominoid distribution, from fossils thus far discovered.

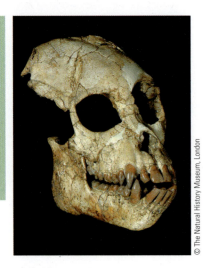

FIGURE 8–4
Proconsul skull, an early Miocene hominoid.

large-bodied hominoids Those hominoids including the great apes (orangutans, chimpanzees, gorillas) and hominids, as well as all ancestral forms back to the time of divergence from small-bodied hominoids (i.e., the gibbon lineage).

FIGURE 8–5
Comparison of a modern chimpanzee (left), *Sivapithecus* (middle), and a modern orangutan (right). Notice that both *Sivapithecus* and the orangutan exhibit a dished face, broad cheekbones, and projecting upper jaw and incisors.

1. *African forms (23–14 mya)* Known especially from western Kenya, these include quite generalized, and in many ways primitive, hominoids. The best-known genus is *Proconsul* (Fig. 8-4). In fact, *Proconsul* is mostly not like an ape, and postcranially it more closely resembles a monkey. It is only some features of the teeth that link these primitive early Miocene forms with hominoids at all.

2. *European forms (16–11 mya)* Known from widely scattered localities in France, Spain, Italy, Greece, Austria, Germany, and Hungary, most of these forms are quite derived. However, this is a varied and not well understood group. The best known of the forms are placed in the genus *Dryopithecus*; the Hungarian and Greek fossils are usually assigned to other genera. The Greek fossils are called *Ouranopithecus,* and remains date to sites 9 to 10 million years of age. Evolutionary relationships are uncertain, but several researchers have suggested a link with the African ape-hominid group.

3. *Asian forms (15–7 mya)* The largest and most varied group from the Miocene fossil hominoid assemblage, geographically dispersed from Turkey through India/Pakistan and east to the highly prolific site Lufeng, in southern China, most of these forms are *highly* derived. The best-known genus is *Sivapithecus* (known from Turkey and Pakistan). The Lufeng material (now totaling more than 1,000 specimens) is usually placed in a separate genus from *Sivapithecus* (and is referred to as *Lufengpithecus*).

Four general points are certain concerning Miocene hominoid fossils: They are widespread geographically; they are numerous; they span a considerable portion of the Miocene, with *known* remains dated between 23 and 6 mya; and at present, they are poorly understood. However, we can reasonably draw the following conclusions:

1. These are hominoids—more closely related to the ape-human lineage than to Old World monkeys.

2. They are mostly **large-bodied hominoids,** that is, more akin to the lineages of orangutans, gorillas, chimpanzees, and humans than to smaller-bodied apes (that is, gibbons).

3. Most of the Miocene forms thus far discovered are so derived that they are probably not ancestral to *any* living form.

4. One lineage that appears well established relates to *Sivapithecus* from Turkey and Pakistan. This form shows some highly derived facial features similar to the modern orangutan, suggesting a fairly close evolutionary link (Fig. 8-5).

5. Evidence of *definite* hominids from the Miocene has not yet been indisputably confirmed. However, exciting new (and not fully studied) finds from Kenya, Ethiopia, and Chad (the latter dating as far back as 7 mya) strongly suggest that hominids diverged sometime in the latter Miocene (see pp. 176–179 for further discussion). As we shall see shortly, the most fundamental feature of the early hominids is the adaptation to bipedal locomotion. In

addition, recently discovered Miocene remains of the first fossils linked closely to gorillas (Suwa et al., 2007) provide further support for a late Miocene divergence (about 10–7 mya) of our closest ape cousins from the hominid line. The only fossil chimpanzee so far discovered is much later in time, and at close to 500,000 years ago (500 kya), is long after the time that hominids split from African apes (McBreaty and Jablonksi, 2005).

Definition of Hominid

The earliest evidence of hominids that has been found dates to the end of the Miocene and mainly includes dental and cranial pieces. But dental features alone don't describe the special features of hominids, and they certainly aren't distinctive of the later stages of human evolution. Modern humans, as well as our most immediate hominid ancestors, are distinguished from the great apes by more obvious features than tooth and jaw dimensions. For example, various scientists have pointed to such distinctive hominid characteristics as bipedal locomotion, large brain size, and tool-making behavior as being significant (at some stage) in defining what makes a hominid a hominid.

It's important to recognize that not all these characteristics developed simultaneously or at the same pace. In fact, over the last several million years of hominid evolution, quite a different pattern has been evident, in which each of the components (dentition, locomotion, brain size, and toolmaking) have developed at quite different rates. This pattern, in which physiological and behavioral systems evolve at different rates, is called **mosaic evolution.** As we first pointed out in Chapter 1 and will emphasize in this and the next chapter, the single most important defining characteristic for the full course of hominid evolution is **bipedal locomotion.** In the earliest stages of hominid emergence, skeletal evidence indicating bipedal locomotion is the only truly reliable indicator that these fossils were indeed hominids. But in later stages of hominid evolution, other features, especially those relating to brain development and behavior, become highly significant (Fig. 8-6).

What's in a Name?

Throughout this book, we refer to members of the human family as hominids (the technical name for the family is Hominidae). This terminology has been widely used for decades, and the inherent evolutionary relationships it reflects are shown in Fig. 8-7a. However, as we mentioned in Chapter 6, there a number of problems with this classification, since it fails to recognize several basic evolutionary relationships among the great apes (most importantly, that chimpanzees and bonobos are more closely related to us and our bipedal predecessors than are other great apes).

As a result of the inadequacies of the traditional classification, a revised one has been proposed (for example, by Wood and Richmond, 2000). In this scheme (Fig. 8-7b), two further levels of classification have been added (subfamily and tribe) to allow finer-tuned and evolutionarily more accurate distinctions. Here, the term *hominid* refers to *all* great apes as well as to the human line ("us"). When referring to the human line ("us") exclusively, the term now used is *hominin,* a distinction made at the taxonomic level of tribe.

This terminology may seem highly confusing; unfortunately, it is—so much so, in fact, that the revised classification has not yet been completely accepted, even by professionals in the field.* Nevertheless, it is important to recognize that

mosaic evolution A pattern of evolution in which the rate of evolution in one functional system varies from that in other systems. For example, in hominid evolution, the dental system, locomotor system, and neurological system (especially the brain) all evolved at markedly different rates.

bipedal locomotion Walking on two feet. Walking habitually on two legs is the single most distinctive feature of the family Hominidae.

---

* The recent annual meetings of the American Association of Physical Anthropologists (2007) give evidence as to how little consensus there is regarding terminology. Three different sessions dealt with fossil evidence of our immediate precursors—and were entitled (for the first time at these meetings) as "Hominin Evolution." A total of 29 of the presentations in these sessions used either "hominid" or "hominin" in their titles, and these were nearly equally split (16 preferred "hominid" and 13 used "hominin").

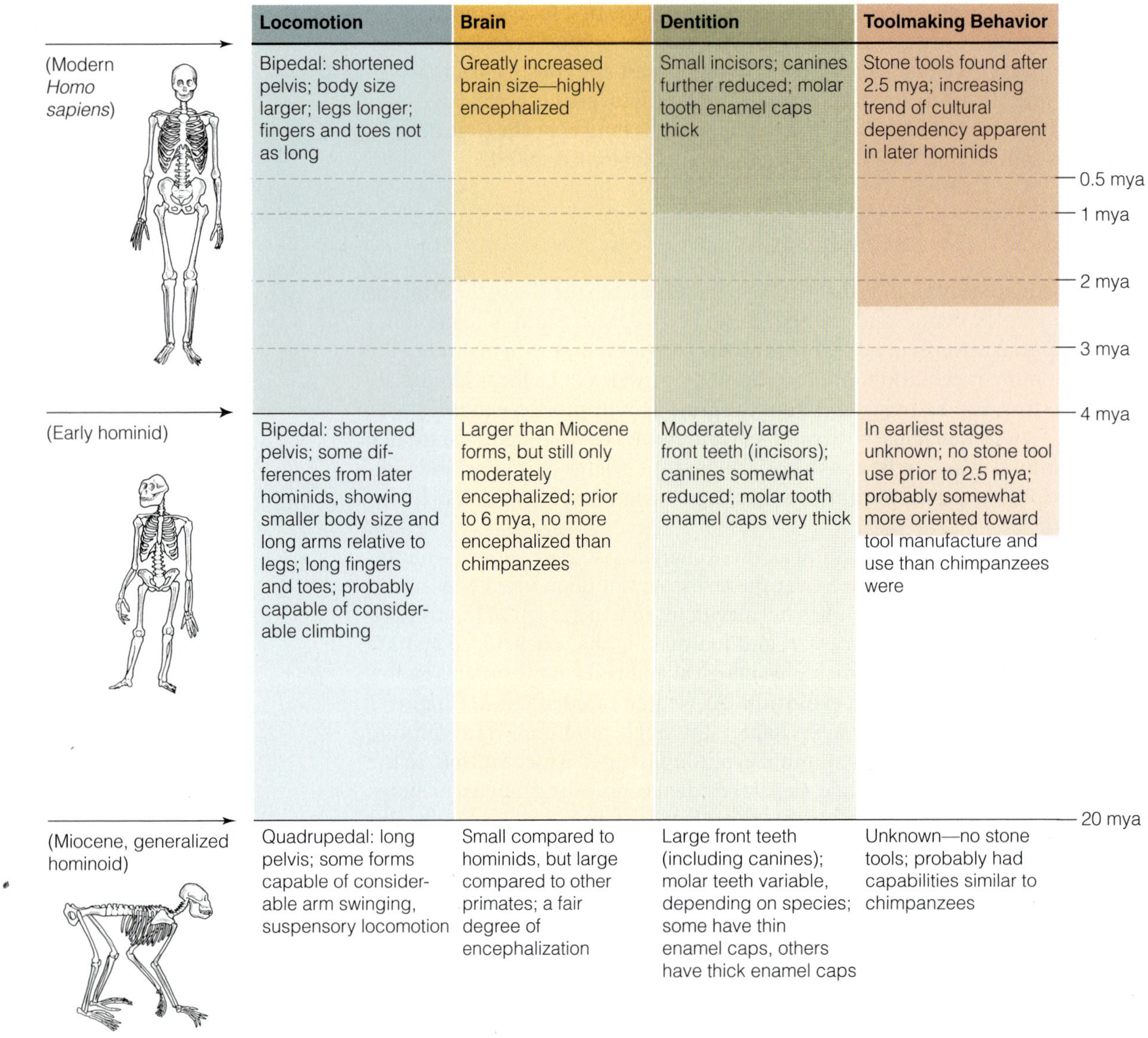

	Locomotion	Brain	Dentition	Toolmaking Behavior
(Modern *Homo sapiens*)	Bipedal: shortened pelvis; body size larger; legs longer; fingers and toes not as long	Greatly increased brain size—highly encephalized	Small incisors; canines further reduced; molar tooth enamel caps thick	Stone tools found after 2.5 mya; increasing trend of cultural dependency apparent in later hominids
(Early hominid)	Bipedal: shortened pelvis; some differences from later hominids, showing smaller body size and long arms relative to legs; long fingers and toes; probably capable of considerable climbing	Larger than Miocene forms, but still only moderately encephalized; prior to 6 mya, no more encephalized than chimpanzees	Moderately large front teeth (incisors); canines somewhat reduced; molar tooth enamel caps very thick	In earliest stages unknown; no stone tool use prior to 2.5 mya; probably somewhat more oriented toward tool manufacture and use than chimpanzees were
(Miocene, generalized hominoid)	Quadrupedal: long pelvis; some forms capable of considerable arm swinging, suspensory locomotion	Small compared to hominids, but large compared to other primates; a fair degree of encephalization	Large front teeth (including canines); molar teeth variable, depending on species; some have thin enamel caps, others have thick enamel caps	Unknown—no stone tools; probably had capabilities similar to chimpanzees

Time scale markers (right side): 0.5 mya, 1 mya, 2 mya, 3 mya, 4 mya, 20 mya

FIGURE 8-6

Mosaic evolution of hominid characteristics: a postulated time line.

the evolutionary relationships depicted (that is, Fig. 8-7b) are more accurate and *are* widely accepted by evolutionary biologists. What to label the various levels remains a decision still in flux. For purposes of clarity in this book, we will continue to use the term *hominid* to refer to the lineage of bipedal hominoids since its divergence from our closest cousins (chimpanzees and bonobos). (If you should see the term *hominin* elsewhere, it is being used synonymously with our usage of *hominid*.)

The Bipedal Adaptation

In our discussion of primate anatomical trends in Chapter 6, we noted a general tendency in all primates for erect body posture and some bipedalism. Of all living primates, however, efficient bipedalism as the primary form of locomotion is seen *only* in hominids. Functionally, the human mode of locomotion is most clearly shown in our striding gait, where weight is alternately placed on a single fully extended hind limb. This specialized form of locomotion has developed to a point where energy levels are used to near peak efficiency. Such is not the case in nonhuman primates, who move bipedally with hips and knees bent and maintain balance in a clumsy and inefficient manner.

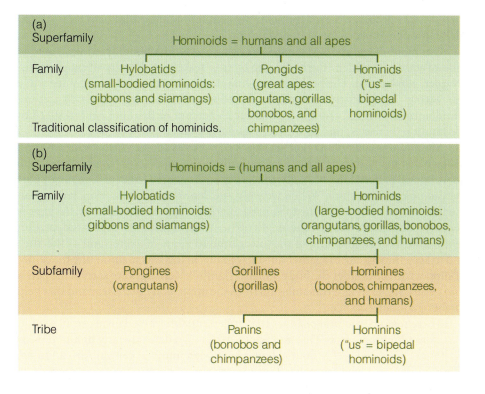

FIGURE 8-7
(a) Traditional classification of hominoids. (b) Revised classification of hominoids. Note that two additional levels of classification are added (subfamily and tribe) to show more precisely and more accurately evolutionary relationships among the apes and humans. In this classification, "hominin" is synonymous with the use of "hominid" in 8-7a.

From a survey of our close primate relatives, it is apparent that while still in the trees, our ancestors were adapted to a fair amount of upper-body erectness. Prosimians, monkeys, and apes all spend considerable time sitting erect while feeding, grooming, or sleeping. Presumably, our early ancestors also displayed similar behavior. What caused these forms to come to the ground and embark on the unique way of life that would eventually lead to humans is still a mystery. Perhaps natural selection favored some Miocene hominoids coming occasionally to the ground to forage for food on the forest floor and forest fringe. In any case, once they were on the ground and away from the immediate safety offered by trees, bipedal locomotion could become a tremendous advantage.

First of all, bipedal locomotion freed the hands for carrying objects and for making and using tools. Such early cultural developments had an even more positive effect on speeding the development of yet more efficient bipedalism—once again emphasizing the dual role of biocultural evolution. In addition, in the bipedal stance, animals have a wider view of the surrounding countryside, and in open terrain, early spotting of predators (particularly the large cats, such as lions, leopards, and saber-tooths) would be of critical importance. We know that modern ground-living primates, such as savanna baboons and vervets, occasionally adopt this posture to "look around" when out in open country. It has also been hypothesized that a bipedal stance would more effectively have aided in cooling early hominids while out in the open. In bipeds, less of the body is exposed directly to the sun than in quadrupeds. Moreover, a greater portion of the body is farther from the ground and thus more removed from heat radiating from the ground surface. It would perhaps have been most adaptive to favor such cooling mechanisms if early hominids had adopted activity patterns exposing them in the open during midday. This last supposition is not really possible to test, but if hominids had ranged more freely at midday, they would have avoided competition from more nocturnal predators and scavengers (such as large cats and hyenas).

Moreover, bipedal walking is an efficient means of covering long distances, and when large game hunting came into play (several million years after the initial adaptation to ground living), further refinements increasing the efficiency of bipedalism may have been favored. Exactly what initiated the process is difficult to say, but all

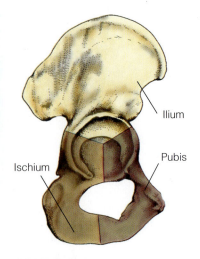

FIGURE 8–8

The human os coxae, composed of three bones (right side shown).

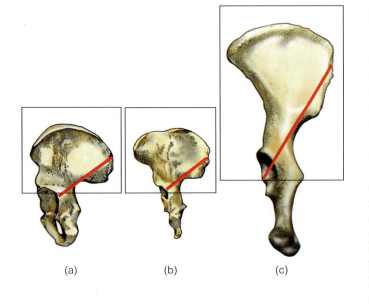

(a) (b) (c)

FIGURE 8–9

Ossa coxae. (a) *Homo sapiens.*
(b) Early hominid (*Australopithecus*) from South Africa. (c) Great ape. Note especially the length and breadth of the iliac blade (boxed) and the line of weight transmission (shown in red).

these factors probably played a role in the adaptation of hominids to their special niche through a special form of locomotion.

Our mode of locomotion is indeed extraordinary, involving, as it does, a unique kind of activity in which "the body, step by step, teeters on the edge of catastrophe" (Napier, 1967, p. 56). The problem is to maintain balance on the "stance" leg while the "swing" leg is off the ground. In fact, during normal walking, both feet are simultaneously on the ground only about 25 percent of the time, and as speed of locomotion increases, this figure becomes even smaller.

Maintaining a stable center of balance in this complex form of locomotion necessitates many drastic structural and functional changes in the basic primate quadrupedal pattern. Functionally, the foot must be altered to act as a stable support instead of a grasping limb. When we walk, our foot is used like a prop, landing on the heel and pushing off on the toes, particularly the big toe. In addition, the leg has become elongated to increase the length of the stride. An efficient bipedal adaptation required further remodeling of the lower limb to allow full extension of the knee and to keep the legs close together during walking, in this way maintaining the center of support directly under the body. Finally, significant changes are seen in the pelvis that permit stable weight transmission from the upper body to the legs and that help further maintain balance.

These major structural changes that are essential for bipedalism are all seen in the earliest hominids from East and South Africa. (To date, no early hominid post-cranial bones have been found in central Africa.) In the pelvis, the ilium (the upper bone of the pelvis, shaped like a blade) is shortened top to bottom, which permits more stable weight support in the erect position by lowering the center of gravity (Figs. 8-8 and 8-9). In addition, the ilium is bent backward and downward, thus altering the position of the muscles that attach along the bone. Most important, these muscles increase in size and act to stabilize the hip. One of these muscles (the *gluteus maximus*) also becomes important as an extensor, pulling the thigh back during running, jumping, and climbing.

Other structural changes shown by even the earliest definitively hominid postcranial evidence further confirm the morphological pattern seen in the pelvis. For example, the vertebral column, known from beautifully preserved specimens from South and East Africa, shows the same forward curvature as in modern hominids, bringing the center of support forward. In addition, the lower limb is elongated and is apparently proportionately about as long as in modern humans. Fossil evidence of a knee fragment from South Africa and pieces from East Africa also shows that full extension of this joint was possible, thus allowing the leg to be completely straightened, as when a field goal kicker follows through.

Fossil evidence of early hominid foot structure has come from two sites in South Africa, and especially important are some recently announced new fossils coming from the same individual as the mostly complete skeleton currently being excavated (see p. 176; Clarke and Tobias, 1995). These foot specimens, consisting of four articulating elements from the ankle and big toe, indicate that the heel and longitudinal arch were both well adapted for a bipedal gait. However, paleoanthropologists Ron Clarke and Phillip Tobias also suggest that the large toe was *divergent* and thus unlike the hominid pattern. If the large toe really did possess this (abducted) anatomical position, it most likely would have aided the foot in grasping. In turn, this grasping ability (as in other primates) would have enabled early hominids to more effectively exploit arboreal habitats. Finally, since anatomical remodeling is always constrained by a set of complex functional compromises, a foot highly capable of grasping and climbing is less capable as a stable platform during bipedal locomotion. Some researchers therefore see early hominids as perhaps not quite as fully committed to bipedal locomotion as are later hominids.

Further evidence for evolutionary changes in the foot comes from two sites in East Africa where numerous fossilized elements have been recovered. As in the remains from South Africa, the East African fossils suggest a well-adapted bipedal gait. The arches are developed, but some differences in the ankle also imply that considerable flexibility was possible (again, probably indicating some continued adaptation to climbing). From this evidence, some researchers have recently concluded that many forms of early hominids probably spent considerable time in the trees. What's more, they may not have been quite as efficient bipedally, as has previously been suggested. Nevertheless, to this point, most researchers think that *all* the early hominids that have been identified from Africa displayed both **habitual** and **obligate bipedalism** (despite the new evidence from South Africa and the earliest traces from central and East Africa, all of which will require further study). For a review of the anatomical features associated with bipedal locomotion, see Figure 8-10.

Biocultural Evolution: The Human Capacity for Culture

One of the most distinctive behavioral features of humans is our extraordinary elaboration of and dependence on **culture.** Certainly other primates, and many other animals, for that matter, modify their environments. As we saw in Chapter 7, chimpanzees especially are now known for such behaviors as using termite sticks, and some even carry rocks to use for crushing nuts. Because of such observations, we're on shaky ground when it comes to drawing sharp lines between early hominid toolmaking behavior and that exhibited by other animals.

Another point to remember is that human culture, at least as it's defined in contemporary contexts, involves much more than toolmaking capacity. For humans, culture integrates an entire adaptive strategy involving cognitive, political, social, and economic components. *Material culture*—or the tools humans use—is but a small portion of this cultural complex.

Still, when we examine the archaeological record of earlier hominids, what's available for study is almost exclusively limited to material culture, especially the residues of stone tool manufacture. This is why it's extremely difficult to learn anything about the earliest stages of hominid cultural development before the regular manufacture of stone tools. As you'll see, this most crucial cultural development has been traced to approximately 2.5 mya (Semaw et al., 1997). Yet because of our contemporary primate models, we can assume that hominids were undoubtedly using other kinds of tools (made of perishable materials) and displaying a whole array of other cultural behaviors long before then. But with no "hard" evidence preserved in the archaeological record, our understanding of the early development of these nonmaterial cultural components remains elusive.

The fundamental basis for human cultural success relates directly to our cognitive abilities. Again, we're not dealing with an absolute distinction, but a relative one. As you've already learned, other primates, as documented in the great apes, have some of the language capabilities exhibited by humans. Even so, modern humans display these abilities in a complexity several orders of magnitude beyond that of any other animal. What's more, only humans are so completely dependent on symbolic communication and its cultural by-products that contemporary *Homo sapiens* could not survive without them.

At this point, you may be wondering when the unique combination of cognitive, social, and material cultural adaptations became prominent in human evolution. In

habitual bipedalism Bipedal locomotion as the form of locomotion shown by hominids most of the time.

obligate bipedalism Bipedalism as the *only* form of hominid terrestrial locomotion. Since major anatomical changes in the spine, pelvis, and lower limb are required for bipedal locomotion, once hominids adapted this mode of locomotion, other forms of locomotion on the ground became impossible.

culture All aspects of human adaptation, including technology, traditions, language, religion, marriage patterns, and social roles. Culture is a set of *learned* behaviors; it is transmitted from one generation to the next through learning and not by biological or genetic means.

answering that question, we must be careful to recognize the manifold nature of culture; we can't expect it to always contain the same elements across species (as when comparing ourselves with nonhuman primates) or through time (when trying to reconstruct ancient hominid behavior). Richard Potts (1993) has critiqued such overly simplistic perspectives and suggests instead a more dynamic approach, one that incorporates many subcomponents (including aspects of behavior, cognition, and social interaction).

We know that the earliest hominids almost certainly didn't regularly manufacture stone tools (at least, none that have been found and identified as such). These earliest members of the hominid lineage, dating back to approximately 7–5 mya, may have carried objects such as naturally sharp stones or stone flakes, parts of carcasses, and pieces of wood around their home ranges. At the very least, we would expect them to have displayed these behaviors to at least the same degree as that exhibited in living chimpanzees.

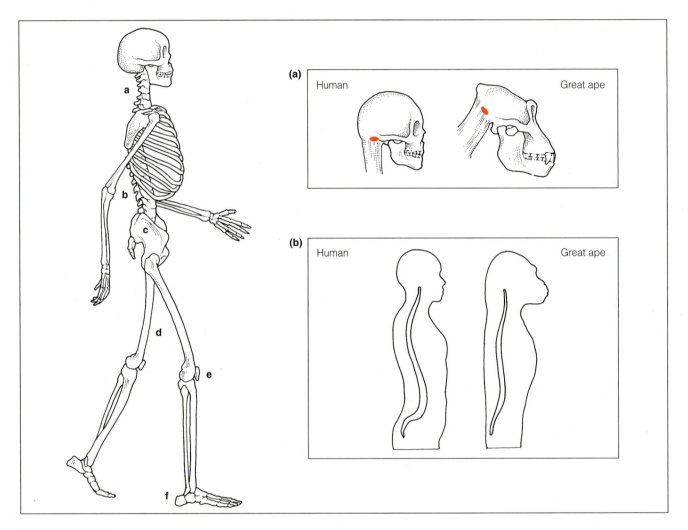

FIGURE 8-10

Major features of hominid bipedalism. During hominid evolution, several major structural features throughout the body have been reorganized (from that seen in other primates) to facilitate efficient bipedal locomotion. These are illustrated here, beginning with the head and progressing to the foot: (a) The *foramen magnum* (shown in red) is repositioned farther underneath the skull, so that the head is more or less balanced on the spine (and thus requires less robust neck muscles to hold the head upright). (b) The spine has two distinctive curves—a backward (thoracic) one and a forward (lumbar) one—that keep the trunk (and weight) centered above the pelvis. (c) The pelvis is shaped more in the form of a basin to support internal organs;

Also, as you'll see later in this chapter, by 6 mya—and perhaps as early as 7 mya—hominids had developed one crucial advantage: They were bipedal and so could more easily carry all kinds of objects from place to place. Ultimately, the efficient exploitation of resources widely distributed in time and space would most likely have led to using "central" spots where key components—especially stone objects—were cached, or collected (Potts, 1991).

What we know for sure is that over a period of several million years, during the formative stages of hominid emergence, many components interacted, but not all of them developed simultaneously. As cognitive abilities developed, more efficient means of communication and learning resulted. Largely because of consequent neurological reorganization, more elaborate tools and social relationships also emerged. These, in turn, selected for greater intelligence, which in turn selected for further neural elaboration. Quite clearly, these mutual dynamic interactions are at the very heart of what we call hominid biocultural evolution.

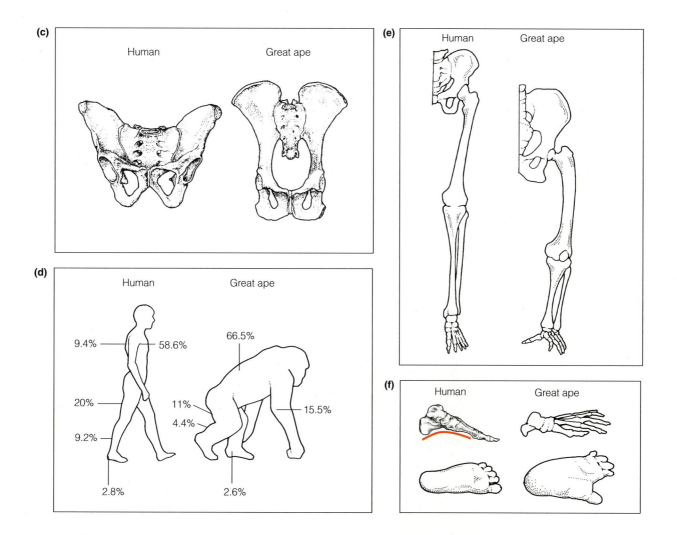

moreover, the ossa coxae (specifically, iliac blades) are shorter and broader, thus stabilizing weight transmission. (d) Lower limbs are elongated, as shown by the proportional lengths of various body segments (e.g., in humans the thigh comprises 20 percent of body height, while in gorillas it comprises only 11 percent). (e) The femur is angled inward, keeping the legs more directly under the body; modified knee anatomy also permits full extension of this joint. (f) The big toe is enlarged and brought in line with the other toes; in addition, a distinctive longitudinal arch forms, helping absorb shock and adding propulsive spring.

Paleoanthropology as a Multidisciplinary Science

multidisciplinary Pertaining to research that involves mutual contributions and cooperation of several different experts from various scientific fields (i.e., disciplines).

sites Locations of discoveries. In paleontology and archaeology, a site may refer to a region where a number of discoveries have been made.

faunal Referring to animal remains; in archaeology, specifically refers to the fossil (or skeletonized) remains of animals.

chronometric (*chronos,* meaning "time," and *metric,* meaning "measure") A dating technique that gives an estimate in actual numbers of years.

artifacts Objects or materials made or modified for use by hominids. The earliest artifacts tend to be tools made of stone or occasionally bone.

To understand human biocultural evolution adequately, we need a broad base of information. The task of recovering and interpreting all the clues left by early hominids is the work of paleoanthropologists. Paleoanthropology is defined as the study of early humans. As such, it is a diverse **multidisciplinary** pursuit seeking to reconstruct every bit of information possible concerning the dating, anatomy, behavior, and ecology of our hominid ancestors. In the last few years, the study of early hominids has marshaled the specialized skills of many diverse scientific disciplines. Included primarily in this growing and exciting adventure are geologists, archaeologists, physical anthropologists, and paleoecologists .

Geologists, usually working with anthropologists (often archaeologists), do the initial survey to locate potential early hominid **sites.** Many sophisticated techniques can contribute to this search, including aerial and satellite photography. Paleontologists may also be involved in this early search, for they can help find geological beds containing **faunal** remains. (Where conditions are favorable for the preservation of such specimens as ancient pigs or baboons, conditions may also be favorable for the preservation of hominid fossils.) In addition, paleontologists can—through comparison with faunal sequences elsewhere—give quick estimates of the approximate age of sites without having to wait for the expensive and time-consuming **chronometric** analyses. In this way, fossil beds of the "right" geological ages (that is, where hominid finds are most likely) can be identified.

Once potential early hominid localities have been identified, much more extensive surveying begins. At this point, the archaeologists take over the search for hominid traces (Fig. 8-11). We do not necessarily have to find the fossilized remains of early hominids (which will always be rare) to know that hominids consistently occupied an ancient land surface. Behavioral clues, or **artifacts,** also inform us directly and unambiguously about early hominid occupation. Modifying rocks according to a consistent plan or simply carrying them over fairly long distances is a behavior exhibited by no other animal but a hominid. Therefore, when we see such behavioral evidence at a site, we know that hominids were once present there.

FIGURE 8-11
Excavations in progress at Olduvai Gorge in Tanzania. This site, more than 1 million years old, was located when a hominid ulna (arm bone) was found eroding out of the side of the gorge.

Robert Jurmain

Dating Methods

One of the essentials of paleoanthropology is placing sites and fossils into a chronological framework. In other words, we want to know how old they are. How, then, do we date sites—or, more precisely, how do we date the geological settings in which sites are found? The question is important, so let us examine some of the dating techniques used by paleontologists, geologists, and paleoanthropologists.

Scientists use two basic types of dating for this purpose: *relative dating* and *chronometric dating* (also known as *absolute dating*). Relative dating methods tell you that something is older or younger than something else, but not by how much. If, for example, a fossil cranium is found at a depth of 50 feet and another cranium at 70 feet at the same site, we usually assume that the cranium at 70 feet is older. We may not know the date (in years) of either one, but we would be able to infer a *relative* sequence. This method of dating is based on **stratigraphy** and is called *stratigraphic dating*. This was one of the first techniques used by scholars working with the vast expanses of geological time. Stratigraphic dating is based on the law of superposition, which states that a lower **stratum** (layer) is older than a higher stratum. Given the fact that much of the earth's crust has been laid down by layer after layer of sedimentary rock, stratigraphic relationships have provided a valuable tool in reconstructing the history of the earth and of life upon it.

Stratigraphic dating does, however, have a number of potential problems. Earth disturbances, such as volcanic activity, river action, and faulting, may shift the strata or materials in them, and the chronology may thus be difficult or impossible to reconstruct. Furthermore, given the widely different rates of accumulation, the elapsed time of any stratum cannot be determined with much accuracy.

Another method of relative dating is *fluorine analysis,* which can be used only to date remains of bone. Bones in the earth are exposed to the seepage of groundwater, which usually contains some fluorine. The longer a bone lies buried, the more fluorine it incorporates during fossilization. Therefore, bones deposited at the same time in the same location should contain the same amount of fluorine.

The use of this technique by Professor Oakley of the British Museum in the early 1950s exposed the famous Piltdown hoax by demonstrating that the human skull was considerably older than the jaw ostensibly found with it (Weiner, 1955). Lying in the same location, the jaw and skull should have absorbed approximately the same quantity of fluorine. But the skull contained significantly more, meaning that if it came from the same site, it had been deposited considerably earlier. The discrepancy of fluorine content led Oakley and others to a much closer examination of the bones, and they found that the jaw was not that of a hominid at all, but one of a juvenile orangutan!

Unfortunately, fluorine is useful only for dating bones from the same location. Because of the differing concentrations in groundwater, accumulation rates will vary from place to place. Also, some groundwater may not contain any fluorine. For these reasons, comparing fossils from different localities using fluorine analysis is not feasible.

Two other relative dating techniques, *biostratigraphy* and *paleomagnetism,* have also proved quite useful in calibrating the ages of early hominid sites. Biostratigraphy is a relative technique based on fairly regular changes seen in the dentition and other anatomical structures in such groups as pigs, rodents, and baboons. Dating of sites is based on the presence of certain fossil species that also occur elsewhere in deposits whose dates have been determined. This technique has proved helpful in cross-correlating the ages of various sites in southern, central, and eastern Africa. A final type of relative dating, paleomagnetism, is based on the shifting nature of the earth's geomagnetic pole. Although now oriented northward, the geomagnetic pole is known to have shifted several times in the past and at times was oriented to the south. By examining magnetically charged particles encased in rock, geologists can determine the orientation of these ancient "compasses." One cannot derive a date in years from this particular technique, but it is used to double-check other techniques.

stratigraphy Study of the sequential layering of deposits.

stratum (*pl.,* strata) Geological layer.

In all these relative dating techniques, the age of geological layers or objects within them is impossible to calibrate. To determine age as precisely as possible, scientists have developed a variety of chronometric techniques, many based on the phenomenon of radioactive decay. The theory is quite simple: Certain radioactive isotopes of elements are unstable, decay, and form an isotopic variant of another element. Since the rate of decay follows a predictable mathematical pattern, the radioactive material serves as an accurate geological clock. By measuring the amount of decay in a particular sample, scientists have devised techniques for dating the immense age of the earth (and of moon rocks) as well as material only a few hundred years old. Several techniques have been employed for a number of years and are now quite well known.

An important chronometric technique used in paleoanthropological research involves potassium-40 (^{40}K), which has a half-life of 1.25 billion years and produces argon-40 (^{40}Ar). That is, half the ^{40}K isotope changes to ^{40}Ar in 1.25 billion years. In another 1.25 billion years, half the remaining ^{40}K would be converted (that is, only one-quarter of the original amount would still be present). Known as the K/Ar, or potassium-argon, method, this procedure has been extensively used in dating materials in the 5–1 mya range, especially in East Africa. Organic material, such as bone, cannot be measured, but the rock matrix in which the fossilized bone is found can be.

Strata that provide the best samples for K/Ar dating are those that have been heated to an extremely high temperature, such as that generated by volcanic activity. Heating drives off previously accumulated argon gas, thus "resetting" the clock to zero. As the material cools and solidifies, ^{40}K continues to break down to ^{40}Ar, but now the gas is physically trapped inside the cooling material. To date the geological material, it is reheated, and the escaping gas is then measured. Potassium-argon dating has been used to date very old events—such as the age of the earth—as well as those less than 2,000 years old.

Another well-known chronometric technique popular with archaeologists involves carbon-14 (^{14}C), with a half-life of 5,730 years. This method has been used to date material as recent as a few hundred years old and can be extended as far back as 75,000 years, although the probability of error rises rapidly after 40,000 years. The physical basis of this technique is also *radiometric;* that is, it is tied to the measurement of radioactive decay of an isotope (^{14}C) into another, more stable form. Radiocarbon dating has proved especially relevant for calibrating the latter stages of human evolution, including the Neandertals and the appearance of modern *Homo sapiens* (see Chapter 11).

Other methods have also proved useful in dating early hominid sites. For example, *fission-track dating* is a chronometric technique that works on the basis of the regular fissioning of uranium atoms. When certain types of crystalline rocks are observed microscopically, the "tracks" left by the fission events can be counted and an approximate age thus calibrated.

Some inorganic artifacts found at hominid sites can be directly dated through the use of **thermoluminescence (TL).** Used especially for dating stone tools that were heated (for example, in a fire), this technique is also used by archaeologists to date clay ceramics found at later sites (which also were subjected to heat). This method, too, relies on the principle of radiometric decay. Many stone tools contain trace amounts of radioactive elements, such as uranium or thorium. When an early human toolmaker placed a stone tool on a fire (a useful method that aided in more precise manufacture), the rapid heating released displaced beta particles trapped within the stone. As the particles escaped, they emitted a dull glow known as thermoluminescence. After that, radioactive decay resumed within the fired stone, again building up electrons at a steady rate. To determine the age of an archaeological sample, the researcher must heat the sample to 500°C and measure its thermoluminescence; from that, the date can be calculated.

Like TL, two other techniques used to date sites from the latter phases of hominid evolution (where neither K/Ar nor radiocarbon dating is possible) are uranium series dating and electron spin resonance (ESR) dating. Uranium series dating relies on radioactive decay of short-lived uranium isotopes, and ESR is similar to TL

thermoluminescence (TL) Technique for dating certain archaeological materials that were heated in the past (such as stone tools) and that release stored energy of radioactive decay as light upon reheating.

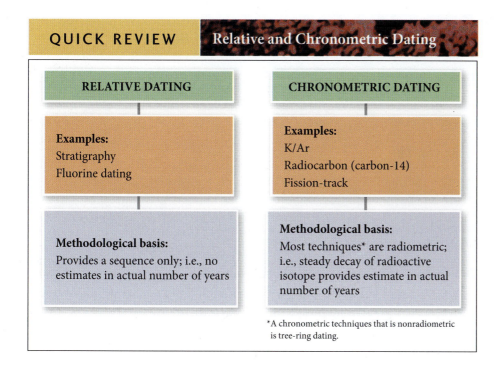

QUICK REVIEW — Relative and Chronometric Dating

RELATIVE DATING	CHRONOMETRIC DATING
Examples: Stratigraphy Fluorine dating	**Examples:** K/Ar Radiocarbon (carbon-14) Fission-track
Methodological basis: Provides a sequence only; i.e., no estimates in actual number of years	**Methodological basis:** Most techniques* are radiometric; i.e., steady decay of radioactive isotope provides estimate in actual number of years

*A chronometric techniques that is nonradiometric is tree-ring dating.

because it's based on measuring trapped electrons. However, while TL is used on heated materials such as clay or stone tools, ESR is used on the dental enamel of animals. All three of these dating methods have been used to provide key dating controls for hominid sites discussed in Chapters 10 and 11.

Many of the techniques just discussed are used together to provide *independent* checks for dating important early hominid sites. Each technique has a degree of error, and only by *cross-correlating* the results can paleoanthropologists feel confident regarding chronological placement of the fossil and archaeological remains they discover. This point is of the utmost importance, for a firm chronology forms the basis for making sound evolutionary interpretations (as discussed later in the chapter).

Finding Early Hominid Fossils

As we discussed earlier, paleoanthropology is a multidisciplinary science, and the finding, surveying, and eventual excavation of hominid sites is a time-consuming and expensive undertaking. What's more, since hominid fossils are never common anywhere and are usually at least partially buried under sediment, finding them also requires no small portion of good luck.

In Africa, most fossil discoveries have come from either East or South Africa. As we'll soon see, a few extremely important discoveries have recently come from central Africa. Nevertheless, more than 99 percent of the early African hominid fossils so far discovered come from the eastern and southern portions of the continent.

In East Africa, early hominid sites are located along the Great Rift Valley. Stretching over more than 2,000 miles, the Rift Valley was formed by geological shifting (actually separation, producing the "rift") between two of the earth's tectonic plates. That is, it's the same geological process as that leading to "continental drift" (discussed in Chapter 5, p. 91). The outcome of these geological upheavals leads to faulting (with earthquakes), volcanoes, and sometimes rapid sedimentation (Fig. 8-12). Paleoanthropologists see all this as a major plus, since it produces a landscape that has many geological exposures revealing at surface level ancient beds that just might contain fossils of all sorts—including hominids. What's more, the chemical makeup of the volcanic sediments makes accurate chronometric dating much more possible.

Paleoanthropological discoveries along the East African branch of the Rift Valley extend from northern Ethiopia, through Kenya, and finally into northern

FIGURE 8-12

View of the main gorge at Olduvai. Note the clear sequence of geological beds. The discontinuity to the right is a major fault line.

Tanzania (Fig. 8-13). Key locales within the Rift Valley where in total more than 2,000 hominid fossils have been found include the extremely productive Middle Awash area of northeastern Ethiopia (containing Aramis, Hadar, and Dikika). In Kenya, crucial discoveries have come from the east and west sides of Lake Turkana and just a bit to the south from the Tugen Hills. Lastly, in northern Tanzania, the remarkably informative paleoanthropological site of Olduvai Gorge has been explored for several decades, and nearby, the Laetoli site has yielded other key fossils as well as extraordinarily well-preserved hominid footprints.

South Africa has also been a very productive area for early hominid discoveries. Over the last 80 years, paleoanthropologists have explored numerous sites, which together have yielded several hundred hominid specimens. The most important South African hominid sites are Taung, Sterkfontein, and Swartkrans.

It's important to recognize that the geological context of all the South African sites is quite different from that in East Africa. The Rift Valley does not extend into southernmost Africa, where, instead, the sediments are composed of layer upon convoluted layer of accumulated limestones. As a result, the geological layers are extremely complex and do not form into such recognizable strata as seen in sites along the East African Rift Valley (see Fig. 8-13). In the South African landscape, caves and fissures form, into which animals fall or perhaps are dragged by predators. Consequently, the hominids accumulate in these caverns and fissures, where they eventually become encased in a rock matrix. Decades ago, the hominids were removed by dynamite. Today, they are retrieved using small hand tools, and only then with extraordinarily painstaking effort (Fig 8-14).

Because the geological setting is so much more difficult in South Africa than in East Africa, the fossils are generally more difficult to locate and usually less well preserved, and chronometric dating is far more difficult. Still, there are some exceptions, as exemplified by an extraordinarily well-preserved skeleton still being excavated at Sterkfontein (see Fig. 8-14).

Early Hominids from Africa

Now that we've reviewed the early primate fossil record as well as the paleoanthropological approaches that allow us to find and date sites, it's time to turn to the fossil record of the earliest hominids themselves.

As you are now well aware, these early hominids come from Africa, and in this chapter we'll cover their comings and goings over a six-million-year period, from 7–1 mya. It's also important to recall from our prior discussion that these hominids

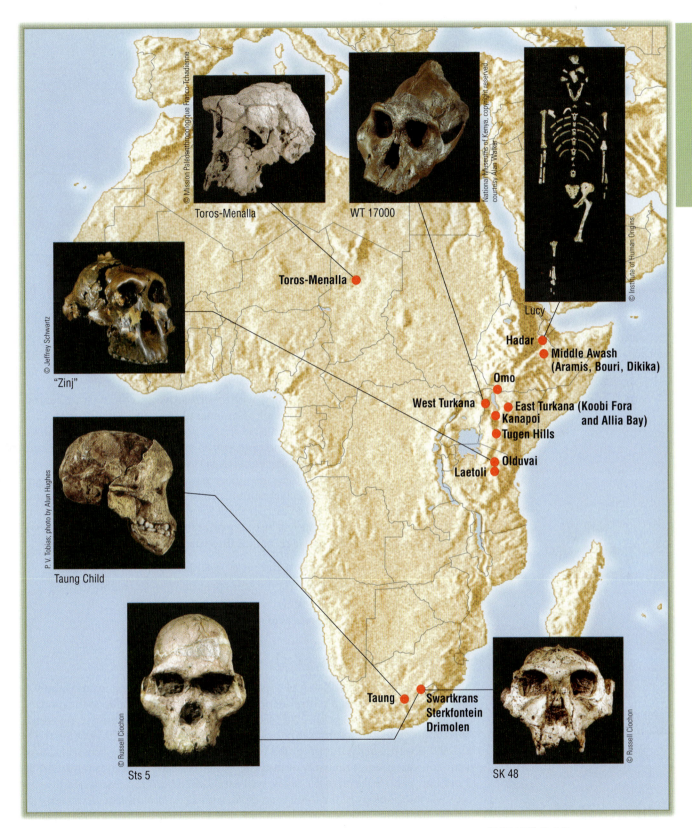

Toros-Menalla

WT 17000

Lucy

"Zinj"

Taung Child

Sts 5

SK 48

Toros-Menalla

Hadar

Middle Awash
(Aramis, Bouri, Dikika)

Omo

West Turkana

East Turkana (Koobi Fora
and Allia Bay)

Kanapoi

Tugen Hills

Olduvai

Laetoli

Taung

Swartkrans
Sterkfontein
Drimolen

FIGURE 8-13

Early hominid finds (pre-*australopith*, *australopith localities*).

John Hodgkiss

FIGURE 8-14

Paleoanthropologist Ronald Clarke carefully excavates a 2-million-year-old skeleton from the lime-stone matrix at Sterkfontein cave. Clearly seen are the cranium (with articulated mandible) and the upper arm bone.

were geographically widely distributed, with fossil discoveries coming from central, East, and South Africa. Paleoanthropologists generally agree that among these early African hominids, there were at least six different genera, which in turn comprised upward of 12 different species. At no time, nor in any other place, were hominids ever as diverse as were these very ancient members of our family.

As you've already guessed, there are quite a few different hominids from many sites, and you'll find that their formal naming can be difficult to pronounce and not easy to remember. So we'll try to discuss these fossil groups in a way that's easy to understand. Our primary focus will be to organize them by time and by major evolutionary trends. In so doing, we recognize three major groups:

- Pre-australopiths— the earliest and most primitive hominids (7–4.4 mya)
- Australopiths—diverse forms, some more primitive, others highly derived (4.2–1 mya)
- Early *Homo*—the first members of our genus (2.4–1.4 mya)

Pre-Australopiths (7.0–4.4 mya)

The oldest and most surprising of these earliest members of the hominid family is a cranium discovered at a central African site called Toros-Menalla in the modern nation of Chad (Brunet et al., 2002; see Fig. 8-14). Provisional dating using faunal correlation (biostratigraphy; see p. 171) suggests a date of nearly 7 mya (Vignaud et al., 2002). Surprisingly, this proposed very early date for this fossil places it at almost 1 million years earlier than *any* of the other proposed early hominids (and close to 3 million years earlier than the oldest well-established hominid discoveries).

The morphology of the fossil is unusual, with a combination of characteristics unlike that found in other early hominids. The braincase is small, estimated at no larger than a modern chimpanzee's (preliminary estimate in the range of 320 to 380 cm³), but it is massively built, with huge browridges in front, a crest on top, and large muscle attachments in the rear (Fig. 8-15). Yet, combined with these apelike features is a smallish vertical face containing front teeth very unlike an ape's. In fact, the lower face, being more tucked in under the brain vault (and not protruding, as in most other early hominids), is more of a *derived* feature more commonly expressed in much later hominids (especially members of genus *Homo*).

© Mission Paléoanthropologique Franco-Tchadienne

FIGURE 8-15

A nearly complete cranium of *Sahelanthropus* from Chad, dating to 7 mya.

In recognition of this unique combination of characteristics, paleoanthropologists have placed the Toros-Menalla remains into a new genus and species of hominid, *Sahelanthropus tchadensis* (Sahel being the region of the southern Sahara in North Africa).

These new finds from Chad have forced an immediate and significant reassessment of early hominid evolution. Two cautionary comments, however, are in order. First, the dating is only approximate, based, as it is, on biostratigraphic correlation with sites in Kenya (1,500 miles to the east). The faunal sequences, nevertheless, seem to be clearly bracketed by two very well-dated sequences in Kenya. Second, and perhaps more serious, is the hominid status of the Chad fossil. Given the facial structure and dentition, it is difficult to see how *Sahelanthropus* could be anything but a hominid. However, some researchers (Wolpoff et al., 2002) have raised questions regarding the evolutionary interpretation of *Sahelanthropus,* suggesting that this fossil may represent an ape rather than a hominid. As we have previously said, the best-defining anatomical characteristics of hominids relate to bipedal locomotion. Unfortunately, no postcranial elements have been recovered from Chad—at least not yet. Consequently, we do not yet know the locomotor behavior of *Sahelanthropus,* and this raises even more fundamental questions: What if further finds show this form not to be bipedal? Should we still consider it a hominid? What, then, are the defining characteristics of our family?

About a million years later than *Sahelanthropus,* two other very early hominids have been found at sites in central Kenya in the Tugen Hills and from the Middle Awash area of northeastern Ethiopia. The earlier of these finds (dated by radiometric methods to about 6 mya) comes from the Tugen Hills and includes mostly dental remains, but also some quite complete lower limb bones, the latter interpreted as clearly indicating bipedal locomotion (Pickford and Senut, 2001; Senut et al., 2001; Galik et al., 2004). Following preliminary analysis of the fossils, the primary researchers have suggested placing these early hominids in a separate genus—*Orrorin*.

The last group of fossil hominids thought to date to the late Miocene (that is, earlier than 5 mya) comes from the Middle Awash in the Afar Triangle of Ethiopia. Radiometric dating places the age of these fossils in the very late Miocene, 5.8–5.2 mya. The fossil remains themselves are very fragmentary. Some of the dental remains resemble some later fossils from the Middle Awash (discussed shortly), and Yohannes Hailie-Selassie, the researcher who first found and described these earlier materials, has provisionally assigned them to the genus *Ardipithecus* (Haile-Selassie et al., 2004; see Quick Review). In addition, some postcranial elements have been preserved, most informatively a toe bone, a phalanx from the middle of the foot (see Appendix A, Fig. A–8). From clues in this bone, Hailie-Selassie concludes that this primate was a well-adapted biped (once again, the best-supporting evidence of hominid status).

From another million years or so later in the geological record in the Middle Awash region, along the banks of the Awash River, a very large and significant assemblage of fossil hominids has been discovered at the Aramis site. Radiometric calibration firmly dates this site at about 4.4 mya.

Fossil remains from Aramis include up to 50 different individuals, and this crucial and quite large fossil assortment includes several dental specimens as well as an upper arm bone (humerus) and some fragmentary cranial remains. Most exciting of all, in 1995, 40 percent of a skeleton was discovered; there are also reports of other partial skeletons from Aramis. However, in all cases, the bones are encased in limestone matrix, thus requiring a long and tedious process to remove the fossils intact from the cement-like material surrounding them. In fact, as of this writing, the Aramis remains (including the skeletons) have not yet been fully described. Nevertheless, details from initial reports are highly suggestive that these remains are, in fact, very early hominids.

First of all, in an Aramis partial cranium, the *foramen magnum* is positioned farther forward in the base of the skull than is the case in quadrupeds (Fig. 8-16). Second, features of the humerus also differ from those seen in quadrupeds, indicating

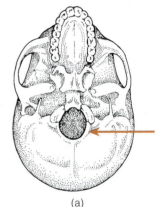

(a)

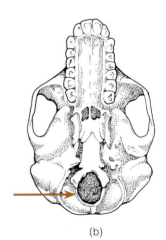

(b)

FIGURE 8-16

Position of the *foramen magnum* in (a) a human and (b) a chimpanzee. Note the more forward position in the human cranium.

TABLE 8.2	Estimated Body Weights and Stature in Plio-Pleistocene Hominids			
	Body Weight		Stature	
	Male	**Female**	**Male**	**Female**
A. afarensis	45 kg (99 lb)	29 kg (64 lb)	151 cm (59 in.)	105 cm (41 in.)
A. africanus	41 kg (90 lb)	30 kg (65 lb)	138 cm (54 in.)	115 cm (45 in.)
South African "robust"	40 kg (88 lb)	32 kg (70 lb)	132 cm (52 in.)	110 cm (43 in.)
East African "robust"	49 kg (108 lb)	34 kg (75 lb)	137 cm (54 in.)	124 cm (49 in.)
H. habilis	52 kg (114 lb)	32 kg (70 lb)	157 cm (62 in.)	125 cm (49 in.)

Source: After McHenry, 1992.

that the Aramis humerus did not function in locomotion to support weight. From these two features, the primary researchers have concluded that the Aramis individuals were *bipedal*. Moreover, initial interpretation of the partial skeleton (while not yet fully cleaned and reported) also suggests obligate bipedalism (Wolpoff, 1999).

Nevertheless, these were clearly quite primitive hominids, displaying an array of characteristics quite distinct from other members of our family. These primitive characteristics include flattening of the cranial base and relatively thin enamel caps on the molar teeth. From measurements of the humerus, body weight for one of the individuals is estimated at 42 kg (93 pounds); if this bone comes from a male individual, this weight estimate is very similar to that hypothesized for other early hominids (Table 8-2).

Thus, current conclusions (which will be either unambiguously confirmed or falsified as the skeleton is fully cleaned and studied) interpret the Aramis remains as among the earliest hominids yet known. These individuals, while very primitive

QUICK REVIEW — Key Pre-Australopith Discoveries

DATES	REGION	HOMINIDS	SITES	EVOLUTIONARY SIGNIFICANCE
4.4 mya	East Africa	*Ardipithecus ramidus*	Aramis	Large collection of fossils, including partial skeletons; bipedal, bur derived
5.2–5.8 mya		*Ardipithecus*	Middle Awash	Fragmentary, but probably bipedal
~6.0 mya		*Orrorin tugenensis*	Tugen Hills	First hominid with postcranial remains
~7.0 mya	Central Africa	*Sahelanthropus tchadensis*	Toros-Menalla	Oldest hominid; well preserved cranium; very small-brained; likely bipedal

hominids, were apparently bipedal, although not necessarily in the same way that later hominids were.

Tim White and colleagues have argued (White et al., 1995) that the fossil hominids from Aramis are so primitive and so different from other early hominids that they should be assigned to a new genus (and, necessarily, a new species as well): *Ardipithecus ramidus*. Most especially, the thin enamel caps on the molars are in dramatic contrast to all other early hominids, who show quite thick enamel.

Another intriguing aspect of all these late Miocene/early Pliocene locales (that is, Tugen Hills, early Middle Awash sites, and Aramis) relates to the ancient environments associated with the suggested earliest of hominids. Rather than the more open grassland savanna habitats so characteristic of most later hominid sites, the environment at all these early locales is more heavily forested. Perhaps we are seeing at Aramis and these other ancient sites the very beginnings of hominid divergence, very soon after the division from the African apes!

Earlier More Primitive Australopiths (4.2–3.0 mya)

The best-known, most widely distributed, and most diverse of the early African hominids are colloquially called **australopiths.** In fact, this diverse and very successful group of hominids is made up of two closely related genera, *Australopithecus* and *Paranthropus*. These hominids have an established time range of over 3 million years, stretching back as early as 4.2 mya and not becoming extinct until apparently close to 1 mya—making them the longest-enduring hominid yet documented. In addition, these hominids have been found in all the major geographical areas of Africa that have, to date, produced early hominid finds, namely South Africa, central Africa (Chad), and East Africa. From all these areas combined, there appears to have been considerable complexity in terms of evolutionary diversity, with numerous species now recognized by most paleoanthropologists.

There are two major subgroups of australopiths, with an earlier group (dated to 4.2-3 mya) composed of at least two different species. These earlier australopiths show several more primitive (ancestral) hominid characteristics than the later australopith group, whose members are more derived, some extremely so. These more derived hominids lived after 2.5 mya and are composed of two different genera, together represented by at least four different species (see Appendix B for a complete listing and more discussion of early hominid fossil finds).

Given the 3-million-year time range as well as quite varied ecological niches, there are numerous intriguing adaptive differences among these varied australopith species. We'll discuss the major adaptations of the various species in a moment. But let's begin by emphasizing those major features that all australopiths share:

1. They are all clearly bipedal (although not necessarily identical to *Homo* in this regard).
2. They all have relatively small brains (at least compared to *Homo*).
3. They all have large teeth, particularly the back teeth, with thick to very thick enamel on the molars.

In short, then, all these australopith species are relatively small-brained, big-toothed bipeds.

The earliest australopiths, dating to 4.2–3.9 mya, come from East Africa from a couple of sites in northern Kenya. Among the fossils finds of these earliest australopiths so far discovered, a few postcranial pieces clearly indicate that locomotion was *bipedal*. There are, however, a few primitive features in the dentition, including a large canine and a **sectorial** lower first premolar (Fig. 8-17).

Since these particular fossils have initially been interpreted as more primitive than all the later members of the genus, paleoanthropologists have provisionally assigned them to a separate species of *Australopithecus*. This important fossil species is now called *Australopithecus anamenisis*, and some researchers suggest that it is a

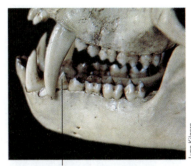
Sectorial lower first premolar

FIGURE 8-17
Left lateral view of the teeth of a male patas monkey. Note how the large upper canine shears against the elongated surface of the *sectorial* lower first premolar.

australopiths A colloquial name referring to a diverse group of Plio-Pleistocene African hominids. They are the most abundant and widely distributed of all early hominids and are also the most completely studied.

sectorial Adapted for cutting or shearing; among primates, refers to the compressed (side-to-side) first lower premolar, which functions as a shearing surface with the upper canine.

Peter Jones

FIGURE 8-18

Hominid footprint from Laetoli, Tanzania. Note the deep impression of the heel and the large toe (arrow) in line (adducted) with the other toes.

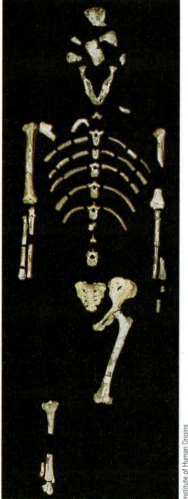

Institute of Human Origins

FIGURE 8-19

"Lucy," a partial hominid skeleton, discovered at Hadar in 1974. This individual is assigned to *Australopithecus afarensis*.

potential ancestor for many later australopiths as well as perhaps early members of the genus *Homo* (White et al., 2006).

Australopithecus afarensis Slightly later and much more complete remains of *Australopithecus* have come from the sites of Hadar (in Ethiopia) and Laetoli (in Tanzania). Much of this material has been known for three decades, and the fossils have been very well studied; indeed, in certain instances, they are quite famous. For example, the Lucy skeleton was discovered at Hadar in 1974, and the Laetoli footprints were first found in 1978. These hominids are classified as members of the species *Australopithecus afarensis*.

Literally thousands of footprints have been found at Laetoli, representing more than 20 different kinds of animals (Pliocene elephants, horses, pigs, giraffes, antelopes, hyenas, and an abundance of hares). Several hominid footprints have also been found, including a trail more than 75 feet long made by at least two—and perhaps three—individuals (Leakey and Hay, 1979; Fig. 8-18). Such discoveries of well-preserved hominid footprints are extremely important in furthering our understanding of human evolution. For the first time, we can make *definite* statements regarding the locomotor pattern and stature of early hominids.

Studies of these impression patterns clearly show that the mode of locomotion of these hominids was bipedal (Day and Wickens, 1980). As we have emphasized, the development of bipedal locomotion is the most important defining characteristic of early hominid evolution. Some researchers, however, have concluded that *A. afarensis* was not bipedal in quite the same way that modern humans are. From detailed comparisons with modern humans, estimates of stride length, cadence, and speed of walking have been ascertained, indicating that the Laetoli hominids moved in a slow-moving ("strolling") fashion with a rather short stride.

One extraordinary discovery at Hadar is the Lucy skeleton (Fig. 8-19), found by Don Johanson eroding out of a hillside. This fossil is scientifically designated as Afar Locality (AL) 288-1, but is usually just called Lucy (after the Beatles song "Lucy in the Sky with Diamonds"). Representing almost 40 percent of a skeleton, this is one of the most complete individuals from anywhere in the world for the entire period before about 100,000 years ago.

Because the Laetoli area was covered periodically by ashfalls from nearby volcanic eruptions, accurate dating is possible and has provided dates of 3.7–3.5 mya. Dating from the Hadar region has not proved as straightforward; however, more complete dating calibration using a variety of techniques has determined a range of 3.9–3 mya for the hominid discoveries from this area.

Several hundred *A. afarensis* specimens, representing a minimum of 60 individuals (and perhaps as many as 100), have been removed from Laetoli and Hadar. At present, these materials represent the largest *well-studied* collection of early hominids and as such are among the most significant of the hominids discussed in this chapter.

Without question, *A. afarensis* is more primitive than any of the other later australopith fossils from South or East Africa (discussed shortly). By "primitive" we mean that *A. afarensis* is less evolved in any particular direction than are later-occurring hominid species. That is, *A. afarensis* shares more primitive features with other early hominoids and with living great apes than do later hominids, who display more derived characteristics.

For example, the teeth of *A. afarensis* are quite primitive. The canines are often large, pointed teeth. Moreover, the lower first premolar is semisectorial (that is, it provides a shearing surface for the upper canine), and the tooth rows are parallel, even converging somewhat toward the back of the mouth (Fig. 8-20).

The cranial portions that are preserved also display several primitive hominoid characteristics, including a crest in the back as well as several primitive features of the cranial base. Cranial capacity estimates for *A. afarensis* show a mixed pattern when compared with later hominids. A provisional estimate for the one partially complete cranium—apparently a large individual—gives a figure of 500 cm³, but another, even more fragmentary cranium is apparently quite a bit smaller and has been estimated at about 375 cm³ (Holloway, 1983). Thus, for some individuals (males?), *A. afarensis* is well within the range of other australopith species (Table 8-3), but others (females?) may have a significantly smaller cranial capacity. However, a detailed depiction of cranial size for *A. afarensis* is not possible at this time; this part of the skeleton is unfortunately too poorly represented. One thing is clear: *A. afarensis* had a small brain, probably averaging for the whole species not much over 420 cm³.

On the other hand, a large assortment of postcranial pieces representing almost all portions of the body of *A. afarenisis* have been found. Initial impressions suggest that relative to lower limbs, the upper limbs are longer than in modern humans (also

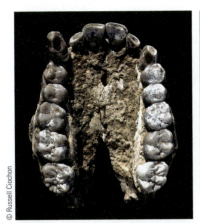

© Russell Ciochon

FIGURE 8-20

Upper jaw of *Australopithecus afarensis* from Hadar, Ethiopia. (Note the parallel tooth rows and large canines.)

TABLE 8.3	Estimated Cranial Capacities in Early Hominids with Comparable Data for Modern Great Apes and Humans	
	Cranial Capacity	
Hominid	**Range (cm³)**	**Average(s) (cm³)**
Early Hominids		
Sahelanthropus		~350
Ardipithecus	Not presently known	Not presently known
Australopithecus afarensis		420
Later australopiths		410–530
Early members of genus *Homo*		631
Contemporary Hominoids		
Human	1150–1750	1330
Chimpanzee	285–500	395
Gorilla	340–752	506
Orangutan	276–540	411
Bonobo		350

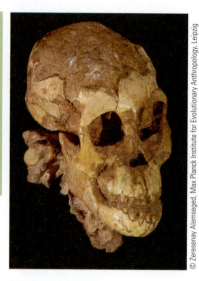

© Zeresenay Alemseged, Max Planck Institute for Evolutionary Anthropology, Leipzig

FIGURE 8-21

Complete skull with attached vertebral column of the infant skeleton from Dikika, Ethiopia, (estimated age, 3.3 mya).

a primitive hominoid condition). (This statement does not mean that the arms of *A. afarensis* were longer than the legs.) In addition, the wrist, hand, and foot bones show several differences from modern humans (Susman et al., 1985). From such excellent postcranial evidence, stature can now be confidently estimated: *A. afarensis* was a short hominid. From her partial skeleton, Lucy is estimated to be only 3 to 4 feet tall (see Fig. 8-19). However, Lucy—as demonstrated by her pelvis—was probably a female, and there is evidence of larger individuals as well. The most economical hypothesis explaining this variation is that *A. afarensis* was quite sexually dimorphic: The larger individuals are male, and the smaller ones, such as Lucy, are female. Estimates of male stature can be approximated from the larger footprints at Laetoli, inferring a height of not quite 5 feet. If we accept this interpretation, *A. afarensis* was a very sexually dimorphic form indeed. In fact, for overall body size, this species may have been as dimorphic as *any* living primate (that is, as much as gorillas, orangutans, or baboons).

An important new find of a mostly complete infant *A. afarensis* skeleton was announced in 2006 (Fig. 8-21). The discovery was made at the Dikika locale in northeastern Ethiopia, very near the Hadar sites mentioned earlier. What's more, the infant comes from the same geological horizon as Hadar, with the same dating (3.3 mya). Although the initial discovery of the fossil was back in 2000, it has taken several years and thousands of hours of preparation to remove portions of the skeleton from the surrounding cemented matrix (full preparation will likely take several more years; Alemseged et al., 2006).

What makes this find of a 3-year-old infant so remarkable is that for the first time in hominid evolution prior to about 100,000 years ago, we have a very well-preserved immature individual. From the infant's extremely well-preserved teeth, scientists hypothesize that she was female. A comprehensive study of her developmental biology has already begun, and many more revelations are surely in store as the Dikika infant is more completely cleaned and studied. For now, and accounting for her immature age, the skeletal pattern appears to be quite similar to adult *A. afarensis*. What's more, the limb proportions, anatomy of the hands and feet, and shape of the scapula (shoulder blade) reveal a similar "mixed" pattern of locomotion. The foot and lower limb indicate that this infant would have been a terrestrial biped; yet, the shoulder and (curved) fingers suggest that she was also capable of climbing about quite ably in the trees.

What makes *A. afarensis* a hominid? The answer is revealed by its manner of locomotion. From the abundant limb bones recovered from Hadar and those beautiful footprints from Laetoli, we know unequivocally that *A. afarensis* walked bipedally when on the ground. (At present, we do not have nearly such good evidence concerning locomotion for *any* of the earlier hominid finds.) Whether Lucy and her contemporaries still spent considerable time in the trees and just how efficiently they walked have become topics of some controversy. Most researchers, however, agree that *A. afarensis* was an efficient habitual biped while on the ground. These hominids were also clearly *obligate* bipeds, which would have hampered their climbing abilities but would not necessarily have precluded arboreal behavior altogether. As one physical anthropologist has surmised: "One could imagine these diminutive early hominids making maximum use of *both* terrestrial and arboreal resources in spite of their commitment to exclusive bipedalism when on the ground. The contention of a mixed arboreal and terrestrial behavioral repertoire would make adaptive sense of the Hadar australopithecine forelimb, hand, and foot morphology without contradicting the evidence of the pelvis" (Wolpoff, 1983, p. 451).

Australopithecus afarensis is a crucial hominid group. Since it comes after the earliest, poorly known group of pre-australopith hominids, but prior to all later australopiths as well as *Homo*, it is an evolutionary bridge, linking together much of what we assume are the major patterns of early hominid evolution. The fact that there are many well-preserved fossils and that they have been so well studied also adds to the paleoanthropological significance of *A. afarensis*. The consensus among most experts over the last several years has been that *A. afarensis* is a potentially strong candidate as the ancestor of *all* later hominids. Some ongoing analysis has recently challenged this hypothesis (Rak et al., 2007), but at least for the moment, this new interpretation has not been widely accepted. Still, it reminds us that science is an intellectual pursuit that constantly reevaluates older views and seeks to provide more systematic explanations about the world around us. When it comes to understanding human evolution, we should always be aware that things might change. So stay tuned.

Later More Derived Australopiths (2.5–1.0 mya)

Following 2.5 mya, hominids became more diverse in Africa. As they adapted to varied niches, australopiths became considerably more derived. In other words, they show physical changes making them quite distinct from their immediate ancestors.

In fact, there were at least three separate lineages of hominids living (in some cases side by side) between 2.5 and 1 mya. One of these is a later form of *Australopithecus;* another is represented by the highly derived three species that belong to the genus *Paranthropus;* and the last consists of early members of the genus *Homo.* Here we'll discuss *Paranthropus* and *Australopithecus. Homo* will be discussed in the next section.

Paranthropus The most derived australopiths are the various members of *Paranthropus.* While all australopiths are big-toothed, *Paranthropus* has the biggest teeth of all, especially as seen in its huge premolars and molars. Along with these massive back teeth, these hominids show a variety of other specializations related to powerful chewing (Fig. 8-23 on page 184). For example, they all have large, deep lower jaws and large attachments for muscles associated with chewing. In fact, these chewing muscles are so prominent that major anatomical alterations evolved in the architecture of their face and skull vault. In particular, the *Paranthropus* face is flatter than that of any other australopith; the broad cheekbones (to which the masseter muscle attaches) flare out; and a ridge develops on top of the skull (this is called a **sagittal crest,** and it's where the temporal muscle attaches).

All these morphological features suggest that *Paranthropus* was adapted for a diet emphasizing rough vegetable foods. However, this does not mean that these very big-toothed hominids did not also eat a variety of other foods, perhaps including some meat. In fact, sophisticated new chemical analyses of *Paranthropus* teeth suggest that their diet may have been quite varied (Sponheimer et al., 2006).

The first member of the *Paranthropus* evolutionary group (clade) comes from a site in northern Kenya on the west side of Lake Turkana. This key find is that of a nearly complete skull, called the "Black Skull" (owing to chemical staining during fossilization), and it dates to approximately 2.5 mya (Fig. 8-22). This skull, with a cranial capacity of only 410 cm^3, is among the smallest for any hominid known, and it has other primitive traits reminiscent of *A. afarensis.* For example, there's a compound crest in the back of the skull, the upper face projects considerably, and the upper dental row converges in back (Kimbel et al., 1988).

But here's what makes the Black Skull so fascinating: Mixed into this array of distinctively primitive traits are a host of derived ones that link it to other members of the robust group (including a broad face, a very large palate, and a large area for the back teeth). This mosaic of features seems to place this individual between earlier *A. afarensis* on the one hand and the later robust *Paranthropus* species on the other. Because of its unique position in hominid evolution, the Black Skull (and the population it represents) has been placed in a new species, *Paranthropus aethiopicus.*

Around 2 mya, different varieties of even more derived members of the *Paranthropus* lineage were on the scene in East Africa. As well documented by finds dated after 2 mya from Olduvai and East Turkana, *Paranthropus* continues to have relatively small cranial

sagittal crest A ridge of bone that runs down the middle of the cranium like a short Mohawk. This serves as the attachment for the large temporal muscles, indicating strong chewing.

FIGURE 8-22

The "black skull," discovered at West Lake Turkana. This specimen is usually assigned to *Paranthropus aethiopicus.* It's called the black skull due to its dark color from the fossilization (mineralization) process.

© Russell Ciochon

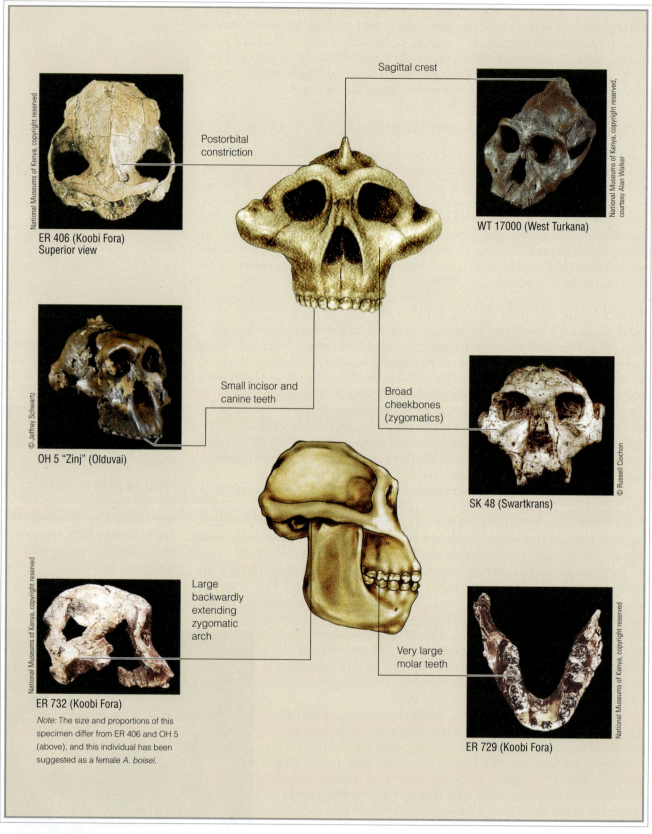

Sagittal crest

Postorbital constriction

ER 406 (Koobi Fora)
Superior view

National Museums of Kenya, copyright reserved

WT 17000 (West Turkana)

National Museums of Kenya, copyright reserved, courtesy Alan Walker

© Jeffrey Schwartz

OH 5 "Zinj" (Olduvai)

Small incisor and canine teeth

Broad cheekbones (zygomatics)

SK 48 (Swartkrans)

© Russell Ciochon

ER 732 (Koobi Fora)

National Museums of Kenya, copyright reserved

Large backwardly extending zygomatic arch

Very large molar teeth

Note: The size and proportions of this specimen differ from ER 406 and OH 5 (above), and this individual has been suggested as a female *A. boisei.*

ER 729 (Koobi Fora)

National Museums of Kenya, copyright reserved

FIGURE 8-23

Morphology and variation of the robust australopiths (*Paranthropus*). (Note both typical features and range of variation as shown in different specimens.)

capacities (ranging from 510 to 530 cm³) and very large, broad faces with massive back teeth and lower jaws. The larger (probably male) individuals also show that characteristic raised ridge (sagittal crest) along the midline of the cranium. Females are not as large or as robust as the males, indicating a fair degree of sexual dimorphism. In any case, the East African *Paranthropus* individuals are all extremely robust in terms of their teeth and jaws—although in overall body size they are much like other australopiths (see Table 8-2). Since these somewhat later East African *Paranthropus** fossils are so robust, they are usually placed in their own separate species, *Paranthropus boisei*.

Paranthropus fossils have also been found at several sites in South Africa. As we discussed earlier (see p. 174), the geological context in South Africa does not allow as precise chronometric dating as is possible in East Africa. Based on less precise dating methods (such as paleomagnetism; see p. 171), *Paranthropus* in South Africa existed about 2–1 mya.

Paranthropus in South Africa is very similar to its close cousin in East Africa, but it's not quite as dentally robust. As a result, paleoanthropologists prefer to regard South African *Paranthropus* as a distinct species—one called *Paranthropus robustus*.

What became of *Paranthropus*? After 1 million years ago these hominids seem to vanish without descendants. Nevertheless, we should be careful not to think of them as "failures." After all, they lasted for 1½ million years, during which time they expanded over a considerable area of sub-Saharan Africa. Moreover, while their extreme dental/chewing adaptations may seem peculiar to us, it was a fascinating "evolutionary experiment" in hominid evolution. And it was an innovation that worked for a long time. Still, these big-toothed cousins of ours did eventually die out. It remains to us, the descendants of another hominid lineage, to find their fossils, study them, and ponder what these creatures were like.

Later *Australopithecus* (*Australopithecus africanus*) From no site dating after 3 mya in East Africa have *Australopithecus* fossils been found. As you know, their close *Paranthropus* kin were doing quite well during this time. Whether *Australopithecus* actually did become extinct in East Africa following 3 mya or whether we just haven't yet found their fossils is impossible to say.

South Africa, however, is another story. A very well-known *Australopithecus* species has been found at four sites in southernmost Africa, in a couple of cases in limestone caves very close to where *Paranthropus* fossils have also been found.

In fact, the very first early hominid discovery from Africa (indeed, from *anywhere*) came from the Taung site and was discovered back in 1924. The story of the discovery of the beautifully preserved child's skull from Taung is a fascinating tale (Fig. 8-24). When first published in 1925 by a young anatomist named Raymond Dart (Fig. 8-25), most experts were unimpressed. They thought Africa to be an unlikely place for the origins of hominids. These skeptics, who had been long focused on European and Asian hominid finds, were initially unprepared to acknowledge Africa's central place in human evolution. Only years later, following many more African discoveries from other sites, did professional opinion shift. With this admittedly slow scientific awareness came the eventual consensus that Taung (which Dart classified as *Australopithecus africanus*) was indeed an ancient member of the hominid family.

Like other australopiths, the "Taung baby" and other *A. africanus* individuals (Fig 8-26) were small-brained, with an adult cranial capacity of about 440 cm³. They were also big-toothed, although not as extremely so as in *Paranthropus*. Moreover, from very well-preserved postcranial remains from Sterkfontein, we know that they also were well-adapted bipeds. The ongoing excavation of the remarkably complete skeleton at Sterkfontein (see Fig. 8-14, p. 176) should tell us about *A. africanus*' locomotion, body size and proportions, and much more.

---

* Note that these later East African *Paranthropus* finds are at least 500,000 years later than the earlier species (*P. aethiopicus*, exemplified by the Black Skull).

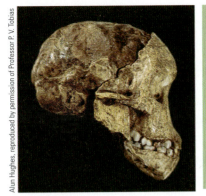
FIGURE 8-24
The Taung child's skull, discovered in 1924. There is a fossilized endocast of the brain in back, with the face and lower jaw in front.

FIGURE 8-25
Raymond Dart, shown working in his laboratory.

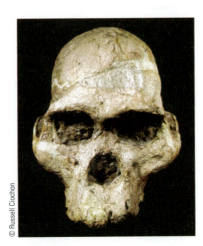
FIGURE 8-26
Australopithecus africanus adult cranium from Sterkfontein.

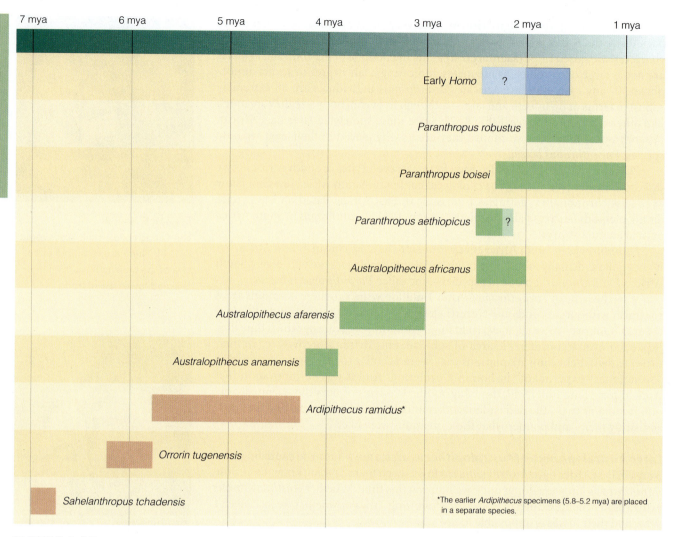

FIGURE 8-27

Time line of early African hominids. Note that most dates are approximations. Question marks indicate those estimates that are most tentative.

The precise dating of *A. africanus*, as with other South African hominids, has been disputed. Over the last several years, it's been assumed that this species existed as far back as 3.3 mya. However, the most recent analysis suggests that *A. africanus* lived approximately between 2.5 and 2.0 mya (Walker et al., 2006). In other words, *A. africanus* overlapped in time considerably with both *Paranthropus* and with early members of the genus *Homo* (Fig. 8-27).

Early *Homo* (2.4–1.4 mya)

In addition to the australopith remains, there's another largely contemporaneous hominid that is quite distinctive. In fact, as best documented by fossil discoveries from Olduvai and East Turkana, these materials have been assigned to the genus *Homo*—and thus are different from all species assigned to either *Australopithecus* or *Paranthropus*.

The earliest appearance of genus *Homo* in East Africa may be as ancient as that of the robust australopiths. (As we have discussed, the Black Skull from West Turkana has been dated to approximately 2.5 mya.) Discoveries in the 1990s from central Kenya and from the Hadar area of Ethiopia suggest that early *Homo* was present in East Africa by 2.4–2.3 mya.

The presence of a **Plio-Pleistocene** hominid with a significantly larger brain than seen in australopiths was first suggested by Louis Leakey in the early 1960s on the basis of fragmentary remains found at Olduvai Gorge. Leakey and his col-

Plio-Pleistocene Pertaining to the Pliocene and first half of the Pleistocene, a time range of 5–1 mya. For this time period, numerous fossil hominids have been found in Africa.

leagues gave a new species designation to these fossil remains, naming them *Homo habilis*. There may, in fact, have been more than one species of *Homo* living in Africa during the Plio-Pleistocene. So, more generally, we'll refer to them all as "early *Homo*." The species *Homo habilis* refers particularly to those early *Homo* fossils from Olduvai.

The *Homo habilis* material at Olduvai dates to about 1.8 mya, but due to the fragmentary nature of the fossil remains, evolutionary interpretations have been difficult. The most immediately obvious feature distinguishing the *H. habilis* material from the australopiths is cranial size. For all the measurable early *Homo* skulls, the estimated average cranial capacity is 631 cm^3, compared to 520 cm^3 for all measurable robust australopiths and 442 cm^3 for the less robust species (McHenry, 1988; see Table 8-3). Early *Homo*, therefore, shows an increase in cranial size of about 20 percent over the larger of the australopiths and an even greater increase over some of the smaller-brained forms. In their initial description of *H. habilis,* Leakey and his associates also pointed to differences from australopiths in cranial shape and in tooth proportions (with early members of genus *Homo* showing larger front teeth relative to back teeth and narrower premolars).

The naming of this fossil material as *Homo habilis* ("handy man") was meaningful from two perspectives. First of all, Leakey argued that members of this group were the early Olduvai toolmakers. Second, and most significantly, by calling this group *Homo*, Leakey was arguing for at least *two separate branches* of hominid evolution in the Plio-Pleistocene. Clearly, only one could be on the main branch eventually leading to *Homo sapiens*. By labeling this new group *Homo* rather than *Australopithecus,* Leakey was guessing that he had found our ancestors.

Because the initial evidence was so fragmentary, most paleoanthropologists were reluctant to accept *H. habilis* as a valid species distinct from *all* australopiths. Later discoveries, especially those from Lake Turkana, of better-preserved fossils have shed further light on early *Homo* in the Plio-Pleistocene.* The most important of this additional material is a nearly complete cranium (Fig. 8-28). With a cranial capacity of 775 cm^3, this individual is well outside the known range for australopiths and actually overlaps the lower boundary for later species of *Homo* (that is, *Homo erectus,* discussed in the next chapter). In addition, the shape of the skull vault is in many respects unlike that of australopiths. However, the face is still quite robust (Walker, 1976), and the fragments of tooth crowns that are preserved indicate that

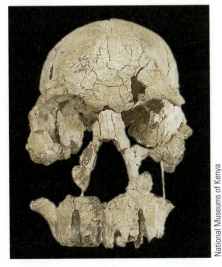
(a)

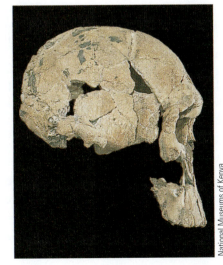
(b)

National Museums of Kenya

FIGURE 8-28

A nearly complete early *Homo* cranium from East Lake Turkana (ER 1470), one of the most important single fossil hominid discoveries from East Africa. (a) Frontal view. (b) Lateral view.

---

* Many of the early *Homo* fossils from East Turkana are classified by many paleoanthropologists into a different species (here called *Homo rudolfensis*) from those found at Olduvai (see Appendix B).

the back teeth in this individual were quite large.* The East Turkana early *Homo* material is generally contemporaneous with the Olduvai remains. The oldest date back to about 1.8 mya, but a newly discovered specimen dates to as recently as 1.44 mya, making it by far the latest surviving early *Homo* fossil yet found (Spoor et al., 2007). In fact, this discovery indicates that a species of early *Homo* coexisted in East Africa for several hundred thousand years with *Homo erectus* (with both species living in the exact same area on the eastern side of Lake Turkana). This new evidence raises numerous fascinating questions regarding how two closely related species existed for so long in the same region.

As in East Africa, early members of the genus *Homo* have also been found in South Africa, apparently living contemporaneously with australopiths. At both Sterkfontein and Swartkrans, fragmentary remains have been recognized as most likely belonging to *Homo* (Fig. 8-29).

On the basis of evidence from Olduvai and East Turkana, we can reasonably postulate that one or more species of early *Homo* were present in East Africa probably by 2.4 mya, developing in parallel with at least two different lines of australopiths. These three hominid lines lived contemporaneously for a minimum of 1 million years, after which both australopith lineages apparently disappeared forever. At the same time, the early *Homo* line was probably evolving into one or more species of later *Homo*.

Interpretations: What Does It All Mean?

By this time, you may think that anthropologists are obsessed with finding small scraps buried in the ground and then assigning them confusing numbers and taxonomic labels impossible to remember. But it's important to realize that the collection of all the basic fossil data is the foundation of human evolutionary research. Without fossils, our speculations would be largely hollow—and most certainly not scientifically testable. Several large, ongoing paleoanthropological projects are now collecting additional data in an attempt to answer some of the more perplexing questions about our evolutionary history.

The numbering of specimens, which may at times seem somewhat confusing, is an effort to keep the designations neutral and to make reference to each individual fossil as clear as possible. The formal naming of finds as *Australopithecus, Paranthropus,* or *Homo habilis* should come much later, since it involves a lengthy series of complex interpretations. Assigning generic and specific names to fossil finds is more than just a convenience; when we attach a particular label, such as *A. africanus,* to a particular fossil, we should be fully aware of the biological implications of such an interpretation.

From the time that fossil sites are first located until the eventual interpretation of hominid evolutionary patterns, several steps take place. Ideally, they should follow a logical order, for if interpretations are made too hastily, they confuse important issues for many years. Here's a reasonable sequence:

1. Selecting and surveying sites
2. Excavating sites and recovering fossil hominids
3. Designating individual finds with specimen numbers for clear reference
4. Cleaning, preparing, studying, and describing fossils
5. Comparing with other fossil material—in a chronological framework if possible
6. Comparing fossil variation with known ranges of variation in closely related groups of living primates and analyzing ancestral and derived characteristics
7. Assigning taxonomic names to fossil material

---

* In fact, some researchers have suggested that all these "early *Homo*" fossils are better classified as *Australopithecus* (Wood and Collard, 1999a).

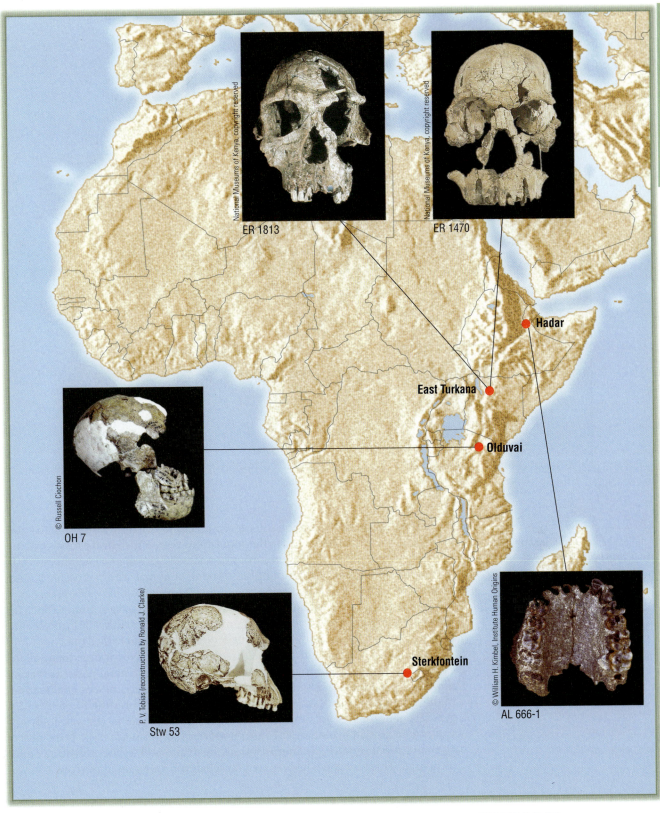

ER 1813

National Museums of Kenya, copyright reserved

ER 1470

National Museums of Kenya, copyright reserved

Hadar

East Turkana

Olduvai

© Russell Ciochon

OH 7

Sterkfontein

P. V. Tobias (reconstruction by Ronald J. Clarke)

Stw 53

© William H. Kimbel, Institute Human Origins

AL 666-1

FIGURE 8-29
Early *Homo* fossil finds.

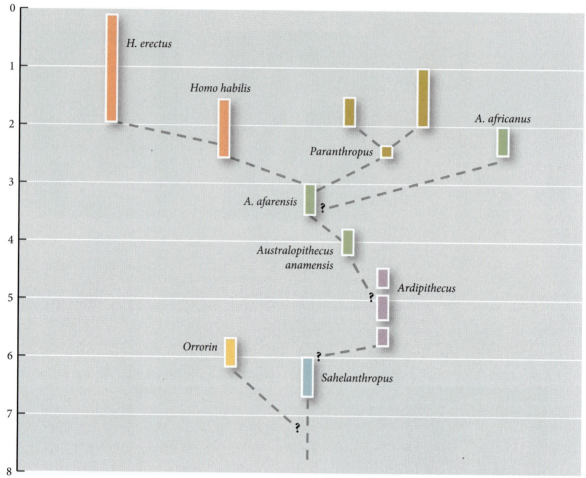

FIGURE 8-30
A tentative early hominid phylogeny. Note the numerous question marks, which indicate continuing uncertainty regarding evolutionary relationships.

But the task of interpretation still isn't complete, for what we really want to know in the long run is what happened to the populations represented by the fossil remains. In looking at the fossil hominid record, we're actually looking for our ancestors. In the process of eventually determining those populations that are our most likely antecedents, we may conclude that some hominids are on evolutionary side branches. If this conclusion is accurate, those hominids necessarily must have become extinct. It's both interesting and relevant to us as hominids to try to find out what influenced some earlier members of our family to continue evolving while others died out.

Although a clear evolutionary picture is not yet possible for organizing all the early hominids discussed in this chapter, there are some general patterns that for now make good sense (Fig 8-30). New finds may of course require serious alterations to this scheme. Science can be exciting but can also be frustrating to many in the general public looking for simple answers to complex questions. For well-informed students of human evolution, it's most important to grasp the basic principles of paleoanthropology and *how* interpretations are made and *why* they sometimes must be revised. This way you'll be prepared for whatever shows up tomorrow.

Seeing the Big Picture: Adaptive Patterns of Early African Hominids

As you are by now aware, there are several different African hominid genera and certainly lots of species. This, in itself, is interesting. Speciation was occurring quite frequently among the various lineages of early hominids—more frequently, in fact, than among later hominids. What explains this pattern?

Evidence has been accumulating at a furious pace in the last decade, but it's still far from complete. What's clear is that we'll never have anything approaching a complete record of early hominid evolution, so significant gaps will remain. After all, we're able to discover hominids only in those special environmental contexts where fossilization was likely. All the other potential habitats they might have exploited are now invisible to us.

Still, patterns are emerging from the fascinating data we do have. First, it appears that early hominid species (pre-australopiths, *Australopithecus*, *Paranthropus*, and early *Homo*) all had restricted ranges. It's therefore likely that each hominid species exploited a relatively small area and could easily have become separated from other populations of its own species. So genetic drift (and to some extent natural selection) could have led to rapid genetic divergence and eventual speciation.

Second, most of these species appear to be at least partially tied to arboreal habitats, although there's disagreement on this point regarding early *Homo* (see Wood and Collard, 1999b; Foley 2002). Also, robust forms (*Paranthropus*) were probably somewhat less arboreal than pre-australopiths or *Australopithecus*. These very big-toothed hominids apparently concentrated at least in part on a diet of coarse, fibrous plant foods, such as roots. Exploiting such resources may have routinely taken these hominids farther away from the trees than their dentally smaller—and perhaps more omnivorous—cousins.

Third, except for some early *Homo* individuals, there's very little in the way of an evolutionary trend of increased body size or of markedly greater encephalization. Beginning with *Sahelanthropus,* brain size was no more than that in chimpanzees—although when controlling for body size, this earliest of all known hominids may have had a proportionately larger brain than any living ape. Close to 6 million years later (that is, the time of the last surviving australopith species), relative brain size increased by no more than 10 to 15 percent. Perhaps tied to this relative stasis in brain capacity, there's no absolute association of any of these hominids with patterned stone tool manufacture.

Although conclusions are becoming increasingly controversial, for the moment, early *Homo* appears to be a partial exception. This group shows both increased encephalization and numerous occurrences of likely association with stone tools (though at many of the sites, australopith fossils were *also* found).

Lastly, all of these early African hominids show an accelerated developmental pattern (similar to that seen in African apes), one quite different from the *delayed* developmental pattern characteristic of *Homo sapiens* (and our immediate precursors). This apelike development is also seen in some early *Homo* individuals (Wood and Collard, 1999a). Rates of development can be accurately reconstructed by examining dental growth markers (Bromage and Dean, 1985), and these data may provide a crucial window into understanding this early stage of hominid evolution.

These African hominid predecessors were rather small, able bipeds, but still closely tied to arboreal and/or climbing niches. They had fairly small brains and, compared to later *Homo,* matured rapidly. It would take a major evolutionary jump to push one of their descendants in a more human direction. For the next chapter in this more human saga, read on.

Summary

Our earliest primate relatives probably diverged from other mammals prior to 65 mya. The first good evidence of prosimian forebears comes much later, from geological beds dating to about 50 mya. The earliest well-dated anthropoid evidence discovered to this point comes from about 37 mya.

Our closest primate ancestors, early hominoids, had a highly successful adaptive radiation during most of the Miocene (23–7 mya), and it was to this time that we can trace the origins of all apes as well as our own hominid lineage.

As a text about human evolution, we naturally concentrate most on the hominid fossil record. The earliest members of our family date as far back as 7 mya. For the next 5 million years, our family stayed geographically restricted to Africa, where it diversified into many different forms. During this 5-million-year span, at least six different hominid genera and upward of 12 species have been identified from the available fossil record. We have organized these fascinating early African hominids into three major groupings:

Pre-australopiths (7–4.4 mya)
Including three genera of very early, and still primitive, hominids (*Sahelanthropus, Orrorin,* and *Ardipithecus*)

Australopiths (4.2–1 mya)
Early, more primitive australopith species (4.2–3 mya), including *Australopithecus anamensis* and *Australopithecus afarensis*

Later, more derived australopith species (2.5–1 mya), including two genera (*Paranthropus* and a later species of *Australopithecus*)

Early *Homo* (2.4–1.4 mya)
The first members of our genus, who around 2 mya likely diverged into more than one species

WHAT'S IMPORTANT — Key Early Hominid Fossil Discoveries from Africa

DATES	HOMINIDS	SITES / REGIONS	THE BIG PICTURE
1.4–1.8 mya	Early *Homo*	Olduvai; E. Turkana (E. Africa)	Bigger-brained; possible ancestor of later *Homo*
2.0–2.5 mya	Later *Australopithecus* (*A. africanus*)	Taung; Sterkfontein (S. Africa)	Quite derived; likely evolutionary dead end
1.0–2.0 mya	Later *Paranthropus*	Several sites (E. and S. Africa)	Highly derived; very likely evolutionary dead end
2.4 mya	*Paranthropus aethiopicus*	W. Turkana (E. Africa)	Earliest robust australopith; likely ancestor of later *Paranthropus*
3.0–3.6 mya	*Australopithecus afarensis*	Laetoli; Hadar (E. Africa)	Many fossils; very well studied; earliest well-documented biped; possible ancestor of all later hominids
4.4 mya	*Ardipithecus ramidus*	Aramis (E. Africa)	Many fossils; not yet well studied; bipedal, but likely quite derived; any likely ancestral relationship to later hominids not yet possible to say
~7.0 mya	*Sahelanthropus*	Toros-Menalla (Central Africa)	The earliest hominid; bipedal?

WHY IT MATTERS

Question: This chapter argues that becoming bipedal contributed to the success of our ancestors and perhaps to our own success as well. But so many people have back problems, and certainly the narrow pelvis of women complicates childbirth. So why hasn't evolution done a better job of making us into well-adapted bipeds?

Answer: First, it's important to remember that the evolutionary process is a series of trade-offs rather than a course to perfection, so it's not surprising that some of the anatomical changes allowing bipedalism seem less than optimal. In fact, the "imperfections" are pretty good evidence against intelligent design. What sort of designer would have a birth canal so narrow and twisted that the baby has to undergo a series of rotations in order to pass its head and shoulders through the canal (see chapter 13)? In fact, complications of birth are the leading cause of death in women throughout the world today, especially in the less industrialized nations.

W. M. Krogman wrote an interesting article in 1951 entitled "The Scars of Human Evolution," in which he discussed the ubiquitous back problems that most of us have as a result of being bipedal. This situation has probably gotten worse since he wrote the article, given that one of the reasons we have problems is all the sitting (often with bad posture) that we do. Anthropologist Robert Anderson, who is also a chiropractor, argues that if we are taught proper walking techniques as children and are more careful of the way we sit, walk, lift, and carry, then we can prevent many of the back problems (especially lower back pain) so often encountered as people enter midlife. In this way, by considering how bipedalism evolved, we may be able to adopt walking and sitting habits that keep our spines more healthy throughout our lives.

Critical Thinking Questions

1. In what ways are the remains of *Sahelanthropus* and *Ardipithecus* primitive? How do we know that these forms are hominids? How sure are we?

2. Assume that you are in the laboratory analyzing the "Lucy" *A. afarensis* skeleton. You also have complete skeletons from a chimpanzee and a modern human. (a) Which parts of the Lucy skeleton are more similar to the chimpanzee? Which are more similar to the human? (b) Which parts of the Lucy skeleton are *most informative?*

3. Discuss the first thing you would do if you found an early hominid fossil and were responsible for its formal description and publication. What would you include in your publication?

4. Discuss two current disputes regarding taxonomic issues concerning early hominids. Try to give support for alternative positions.

5. What is a phylogeny? Construct one for early hominids (7.0–1 mya). Make sure you can describe what conclusions your scheme makes. Also, try to defend it.

CHAPTER 9

The First Dispersal of the Genus *Homo*: *Homo erectus* and Contemporaries

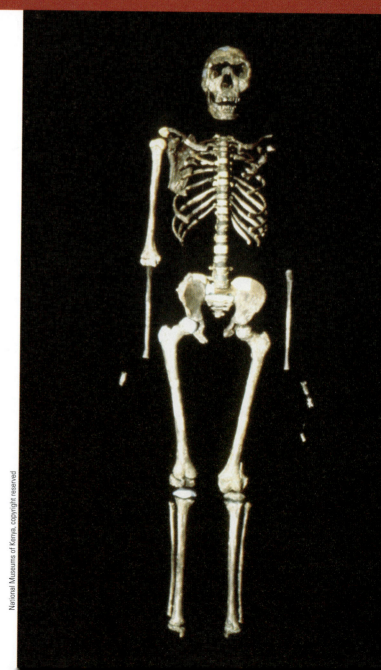

Introduction

Today it's estimated that upward of one million people daily cross national borders. Some individuals travel for business, others for pleasure. Refugees fleeing their homes may feel an urgent need to find safety elsewhere. Regardless, it seems that modern humans have wanderlust—a desire to see distant places. Our most distant hominid ancestors were essentially homebodies, staying in fairly restricted areas, exploiting the local resources, and trying to stay out of harm's way. In this respect, they were much like other primate species.

One thing's for sure: All these early hominids were restricted to Africa. When did the first hominids leave Africa? What were they like, and why might they have left their ancient homeland? Did they differ physically from their australopith and early *Homo* forebearers, and did they have new behavioral and cultural capabilities that helped them successfully exploit new environments?

It would be a romantic misconception to think of these first hominid transcontinental emigrants as "brave pioneers, boldly going where no one had gone before." They weren't deliberately striking out to go someplace in particular. It's not as though they had a map! Still, for what they did, deliberate or not, we owe them a lot.

Sometime, close to 2 million years ago, something decisive occurred in human evolution. As the title of this chapter suggests, for the first time, hominids expanded widely out of Africa into other areas of the Old World. Since all the early hominid fossils have been found *only* in Africa, it seems that hominids were restricted to this continent for perhaps as long as 5 million years. The later, more widely dispersed hominids were quite different both anatomically and behaviorally from their African ancestors. They were much larger, were more committed to a completely terrestrial habitat, used more elaborate stone tools, and perhaps ate meat.

There is some variation among the different geographical groups of these highly successful hominids, and anthropologists still debate how to classify them. Discoveries continue as well. In particular, new finds from Europe are forcing a major reevaluation of exactly which were the first to leave Africa (Fig. 9-1).

Nevertheless, after 2 mya, there's less diversity in these hominids than is apparent in their pre-australopith and australopith predecessors. Consequently, there is universal agreement that the hominids found outside of Africa are all members of genus *Homo*. Thus, taxonomic debates focus solely on how many species are represented. The species for which there is the most evidence is called *Homo erectus*. Furthermore, this is the one group that most paleoanthropologists have recognized for decades and still agree on. Thus, in this chapter we will concentrate our discussion on *Homo erectus*. We'll, however, also discuss alternative interpretations that "split" the fossil sample into more species.

> **Click!**
>
> Go to the following media resources for interactive activities, more information, and study materials on topics covered in this chapter:
>
> - Anthropology Resource Center
> - Student Companion Website for *Essentials of Physical Anthropology,* Seventh Edition
> - Online Virtual Laboratories for Physical Anthropology CD-ROM, Fourth Edition
> - Hominid Fossils CD-ROM: An Interactive Atlas

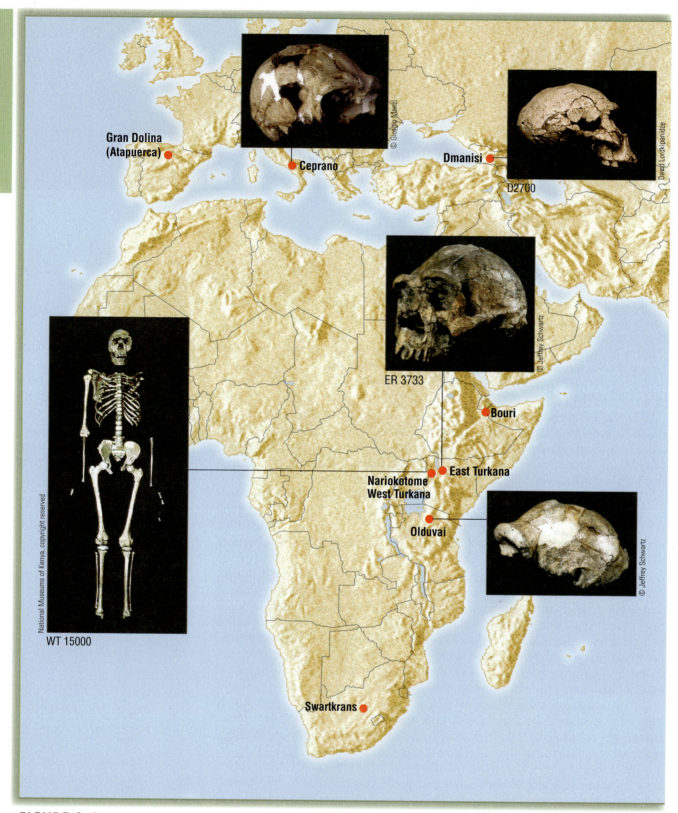

FIGURE 9–1

Major *Homo erectus* sites and localities
of other contemporaneous hominids.

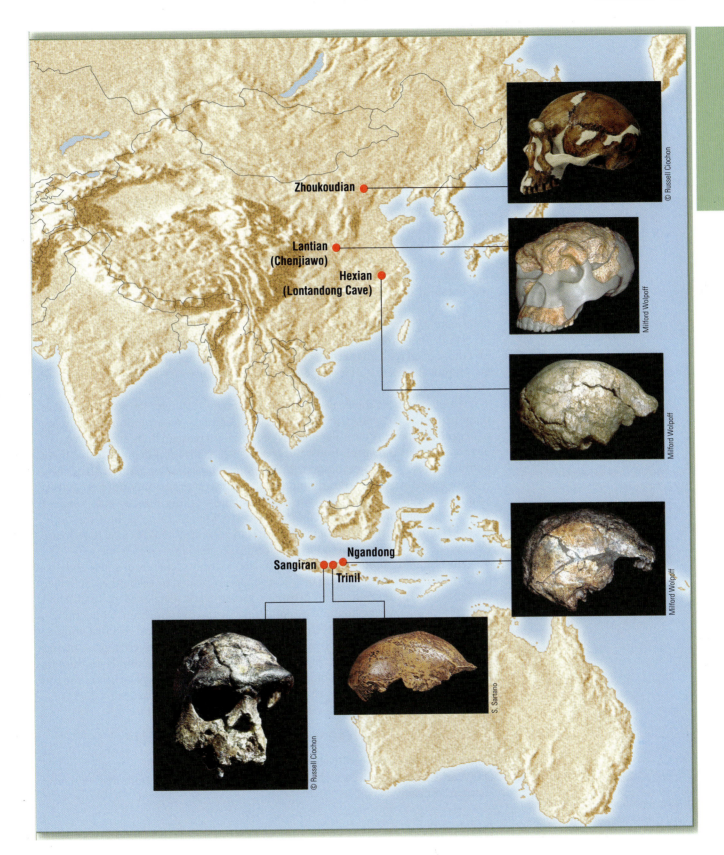

Zhoukoudian

Lantian
(Chenjiawo)

Hexian
(Lontandong Cave)

Ngandong

Sangiran

Trinil

© Russell Ciochon

Milford Wolpoff

Milford Wolpoff

Milford Wolpoff

© Russell Ciochon

S. Sartono

A New Kind of Hominid

The discoveries of fossils now referred to as *Homo erectus* began in the nineteenth century. Later in this chapter, we will discuss in some detail the historical background of these earliest discoveries in Java and the somewhat later discoveries in China. From this work, as well as presumably related finds in Europe and North Africa, a variety of taxonomic names were suggested.

It's important to realize that such taxonomic *splitting* was quite common in the early years of paleoanthropology. More systematic biological thinking came to the fore only after World War II and with the incorporation of the Modern Synthesis into paleontology (see p. 67). Most of the fossils that were given these varied names are now placed in the species *Homo erectus*— or at least they've all been lumped into one genus (*Homo*).

In the last few decades, discoveries from East Africa of firmly dated finds have established the clear presence of *Homo erectus* by 1.8 mya. Some researchers see several anatomical differences between these African representatives of an *erectus*-like hominid and their Asian cousins (hominids that almost everybody refers to as *Homo erectus*). Thus, they place the African fossils into a separate species, one they call *Homo ergaster* (Andrews, 1984; Wood, 1991).

While there are some anatomical differences between the African specimens and those from Asia, they are all clearly *closely* related and quite possibly represent geographical varieties of a single species. We'll thus refer to these hominids as *Homo erectus*.

All analyses have shown that *H. erectus* represents a different **grade** of evolution than their more ancient African predecessors. A grade is an evolutionary grouping of organisms showing a similar adaptive pattern. Increase in body size and robustness, changes in limb proportions, and greater encephalization all indicate that these hominids were more like modern humans in their adaptive pattern than their African ancestors were.* We should point out that a grade only implies general adaptive aspects of a group of animals; it implies nothing directly about shared ancestry (organisms that share common ancestry are said to be in the same *clade*; see p. 82). For example, orangutans and African great apes could be said to be in the same grade, but they are not in the same clade (see p. 111).

The hominids discussed in this chapter are not only members of a new and distinct grade of human evolution; they're also closely related to each other. Whether they all belong to the same clade is debatable. Nevertheless, a major adaptive shift had taken place—one setting hominid evolution in a distinctly more human direction.

We mentioned that there is considerable variation in different regional populations of hominids broadly defined as *Homo erectus*. New discoveries are showing even more dramatic variation, suggesting that some of these hominids may not fit closely at all with this general adaptive pattern (more on this presently). For the moment, however, let's review what *most* of these fossils look like.

The Morphology of *Homo erectus*

Homo erectus populations lived in very different environments over much of the Old World. They all, however, shared several common physical traits that we'll now summarize briefly.

Body Size

As conclusively shown by the discovery of the nearly complete skeleton of "Nariokotome Boy" (from **Nariokotome,** on the west side of Lake Turkana in

grade A grouping of organisms sharing a similar adaptive pattern. Grade isn't necessarily based on closeness of evolutionary relationship, but it does contrast organisms in a useful way (e.g., *Homo erectus* with *Homo sapiens*).

Nariokotome (nar´-ee-oh-koh´-tow-may)

* We did note in Chapter 8 that early *Homo* is a partial exception, being transitional in some respects.

Kenya), we know that *H. erectus* was larger than earlier hominids. From this and other less-complete specimens, anthropologists estimate that some *H. erectus* adults weighed well over 100 pounds, with an average adult height of about 5 feet 6 inches (McHenry, 1992; Ruff and Walker, 1993; Walker and Leakey, 1993). Another point to keep in mind is that *H. erectus* was quite sexually dimorphic—at least as indicated by the East African specimens. For adult males, weight and height in some individuals may have been considerably greater than 100 pounds. In fact, if the Nariokotome Boy had lived to adulthood, he probably would have grown to an adult height of over 6 feet (Walker, 1993).

Increased height and weight in *H. erectus* are also associated with a dramatic increase in robusticity. In fact, a heavily built body was to dominate hominid evolution not just during *H. erectus* times, but through the long transitional era of premodern forms as well. Only with the appearance of anatomically modern *H. sapiens* did a more gracile skeletal structure emerge, and it still characterizes most modern populations.

Brain Size

While *Homo erectus* differs in several respects from both early *Homo* and *Homo sapiens*, the most obvious feature is its cranial size—which is closely related to brain size. Early *Homo* had cranial capacities ranging from as small as 500 cm^3 to as large as 800 cm^3. *H. erectus,* on the other hand, shows considerable brain enlargement, with a cranial capacity of about 700* to 1,250 cm^3 (and a mean of approximately 900 cm^3). However, in making such comparisons, we must bear in mind two key questions: What is the comparative sample, and what were the overall body sizes of the species being compared?

As for the first question, you may recall that many anthropologists are now convinced that more than one species of early *Homo* existed in East Africa around 2 mya. If so, only one of them could have been the ancestor of *H. erectus*. If we choose the smaller-bodied sample of early *Homo* as our presumed ancestral group, then *H. erectus* shows as much as a 40 percent increase in average cranial capacity. But if the comparative sample we use is the larger-bodied group of early *Homo* (for example, skull 1470, from East Turkana), then *H. erectus* shows a 25 percent increase in cranial capacity.

As we've discussed, brain size is closely linked to overall body size. We've focused on the increase in *H. erectus* brain size, but *H. erectus* was also considerably larger overall than earlier members of the genus *Homo*. In fact, when we compare *H. erectus* with the larger-bodied early *Homo* sample, their *relative* brain size is about the same (Walker, 1991). What's more, when we compare the relative brain size of *H. erectus* with that of *H. sapiens,* we see that *H. erectus* was considerably less encephalized than later members of the genus *Homo*.

Cranial Shape

Homo erectus crania display a highly distinctive shape, partly because of increased brain size, but probably more correlated with increased body size. The ramifications of this heavily built cranium are reflected in thick cranial bone, large browridges above the eyes, and a projecting **nuchal torus** at the rear of the skull (Fig. 9-2).

The braincase is long and low, receding from the large browridges with little forehead development. Also, the cranium is wider at the base compared with earlier *and* later species of genus *Homo*. The maximum cranial breadth is below the ear opening, giving the cranium a pentagonal shape (when viewed from behind). In

nuchal torus (nuke´-ul) (*nuchal,* meaning "pertaining to the neck") A projection of bone in the back of the cranium where neck muscles attach; used to hold up the head.

* Even smaller cranial capacities are seen in recently discovered fossils from the Caucasus region of southeastern Europe.

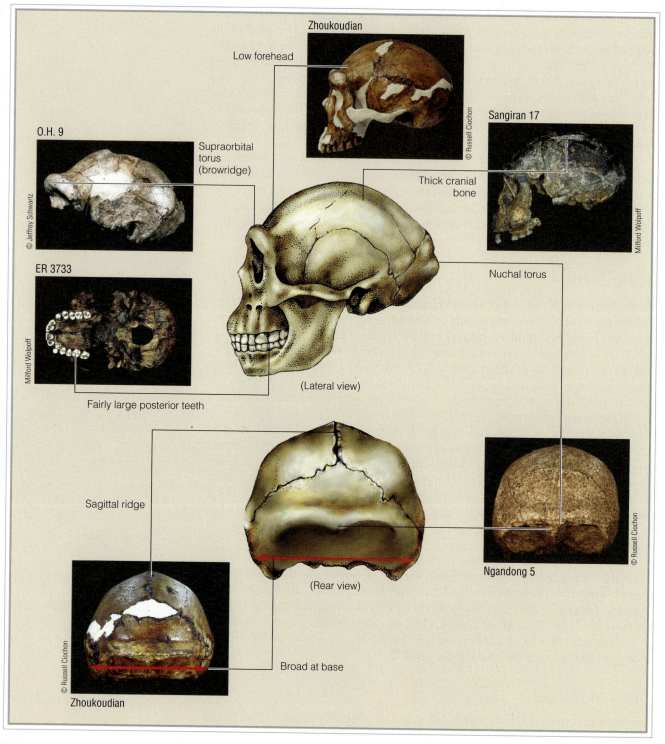

FIGURE 9-2

Morphology and variation in *Homo erectus*.

contrast, the skulls of early *Homo* and *H. sapiens* have more vertical sides, and the maximum width is *above* the ear openings.

Most specimens also have a sagittal ridge (also called a sagittal keel) running along the midline of the skull. Very different from a sagittal crest, the keel is a small ridge that runs front to back along the sagittal suture. The sagittal keel, along with the browridges and the nuchal torus, don't seem to have served an obvious function in the life of *H. erectus*—but most likely reflect bone buttressing in a very robust skull.

The First *Homo erectus:* *Homo erectus* from Africa

Where did *Homo erectus* first appear? The answer seems fairly simple: Most likely, this species initially evolved in Africa, probably in East Africa. Two important pieces of evidence help confirm this hypothesis. First, *all* the earlier hominids prior to the appearance of *H. erectus* come from Africa. What's more, by 1.8 mya, there are well-dated fossils of this species at East Turkana, in Kenya, and not long after at other sites in East Africa.

Still, there's a small wrinkle in this neat view. Around 1.8 mya, in addition to *H. erectus* in East Africa, similar populations were already living far away in both southeastern Asia and in southeastern Europe. Nevertheless, it is very likely that *H. erectus* first arose in East Africa but very quickly migrated to other continents far away from their African homeland. So let's begin at the beginning.

Fossils identified as *H. erectus* have been found at several locales in East Africa. As mentioned, the earliest *H. erectus* fossils come from East Turkana, from the same area where earlier australopith and early *Homo* fossils have been found (see Chapter 8). Indeed, it seems likely that in East Africa around 2–1.8 mya, some form of early *Homo* evolved into *H. erectus*.

The most significant *H. erectus* discovery from East Turkana is a nearly complete skull (Fig. 9-3). Dated at 1.8 mya, this specimen is the oldest *H. erectus* ever found. The cranial capacity is estimated at 848 cm^3, in the lower range for *H. erectus* (700 to 1,250 cm^3), which isn't surprising considering its early date. A second very significant new find from East Turkana is notable because it has the smallest cranium of any *H. erectus* from anywhere in Africa. Dated to around 1.5 mya, the skull has a cranial capacity of only 691 cm^3. As we'll see shortly, there are a couple of crania from southeastern Europe that are even smaller. The small skull from East Turkana also shows more gracile features (such as smaller browridges) than do other East African *H. erectus* individuals. It's been proposed that perhaps this new find is a female and that the variation shown indicates a very high degree of sexual dimorphism in this species (Spoor et al., 2007).

Other important *H. erectus* finds have come from Olduvai Gorge, including a very robust skull discovered there by Louis Leakey back in 1960. The skull is dated at 1.4 mya and has a well-preserved cranial vault with just a small part of the upper face. Estimated at 1,067 cm^3, the cranial capacity of the Olduvai *erectus* skull is the largest of all the African *H. erectus* specimens. The browridge is huge, the largest known for any hominid, but the walls of the braincase are thin. This latter characteristic is seen in most East African *H. erectus* specimens; in this respect, they differ from Asian *H. erectus,* in which cranial bones are thick.

Another remarkable discovery was made in 1984 by Kamoya Kimeu, a member of Richard Leakey's team known widely as an outstanding fossil hunter. Kimeu discovered a small piece of skull on the west side of Lake Turkana at the site known as Nariokotome. The careful excavations that took place there were a resounding success. In fact, the work produced the most complete *H. erectus* skeleton ever found (Fig. 9-4). Known properly as WT 15000, the almost complete skeleton includes facial bones, a pelvis, and most of the limb bones, ribs, and vertebrae. Such well-preserved postcranial elements make for a very unusual and highly useful discovery, because these elements are scarce at other *H. erectus* sites. The Nariokotome skeleton is quite ancient, dated chronometrically to about 1.6 mya. The skeleton is that of a boy about 12 years of age with an estimated height of about 5 feet 3 inches. Had he grown to maturity, it's estimated that his height would have been more than 6 feet—taller than *H. erectus* was previously thought to have been. The postcranial bones look very similar, though not quite identical, to those of modern humans. The cranial capacity of WT 15000 is estimated at 880 cm^3; brain growth was nearly complete, and the boy's adult cranial capacity would have been approximately 909 cm^3 (Begun and Walker, 1993).

FIGURE 9-3

Nearly complete skull of *Homo erectus* from East Lake Turkana, Kenya, dated to approximately 1.8 mya.

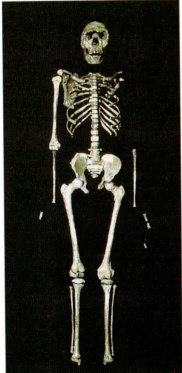

FIGURE 9-4

WT 15000 from Nariokotome, Kenya: the-most complete *H. erectus* specimen yet found.

QUICK REVIEW		Key *Homo erectus* Discoveries from Africa
DATES	SITE	EVOLUTIONARY SIGNIFICANCE
1.4 mya	Olduvai	Large individual, very robust (male?) *H. erectus*
1.6 mya	Nariokotome W. Turkana	Nearly complete skeleton; young male
1.8 mya	E. Turkana	Oldest well-dated *H. erectus*; great amount of variation seen among individuals, possibly due to sexual dimorphism

Two other sites, both from Ethiopia, have yielded *H. erectus* fossils, the most noteworthy coming from the Bouri locale in the Middle Awash region. As you've seen, numerous remains of earlier hominids have come from this area (see Chapter 8 and Appendix B). The recent discovery of a mostly complete cranium from Bouri is important because this individual (dated at approximately 1 mya) is more like Asian *H. erectus* than are most of the earlier East African remains we've discussed (Asfaw et al., 2002). Consequently, the suggestion by several researchers that East African fossils are a different species from (Asian) *H. erectus* isn't supported by the morphology of the Bouri cranium.

Who Were the Earliest African Emigrants?

The fossils from East Africa imply that a new grade of human evolution appeared in Africa not long after 2 mya. Thus, the hominids who migrated to Asia and Europe are generally assumed to be their immediate descendants. This conclusion makes good sense on at least three levels: geography, anatomy, and behavior. As noted, geographically, Africa is where *all* the earlier hominids lived, so *H. erectus* would probably have first appeared there (and East Africa especially would have been a likely locality). Moreover, these were now bigger, brainier hominids capable of traveling longer distances. Finally, they also possessed a more advanced tool kit, which allowed them to exploit a wider range of resources.

Consider the following reasonable hypothesis: *Homo erectus* first evolved in East Africa close to 2 mya and with its new physical/behavioral capacities soon emigrated to other areas of the Old World. This hypothesis helps pull together several aspects of hominid evolution, and much of the fossil evidence after 2 mya supports it. Nevertheless, there are some difficulties, and recently discovered evidence seriously challenges this tidy view.

First, while 1.8 mya is a well-established date for the appearance of *H. erectus* in East Africa, similar hominids also appear at just about the same time in Indonesia and the Caucasus region (see Fig. 9-1). Radiometric dates of sediments on the island of Java have recently placed *H. erectus* there at 1.6 mya. It's possible for us to explain these hominids in Asia at this early date *if* we assume that *H. erectus* evolved in East Africa by 1.8 mya (or slightly earlier) and, in just a few thousand years, expanded rapidly to other regions.

At an even somewhat earlier date, hominids were also present in the Caucasus region of easternmost Europe. Newly discovered fossils from the **Dmanisi** site in the Republic of Georgia (see Fig. 9-1) have been radiometrically dated to 1.75 mya. Not only do the Dmanisi hominids show up early, but they also look different from the usual *H. erectus* we've just briefly described.

Dmanisi (dim´-an-eese´-ee)

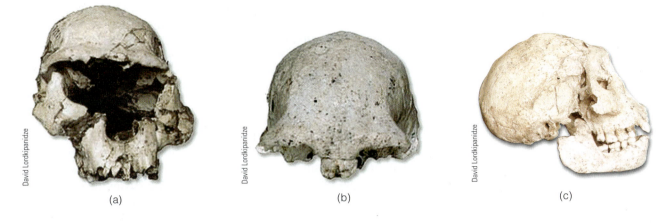

David Lordkipanidze (a)

David Lordkipanidze (b)

David Lordkipanidze (c)

In some respects, the Dmanisi crania are similar to those of *H. erectus* (for example, the long, low braincase, wide base, and sagittal keeling; see especially Fig. 9-5b, and compare with Fig. 9-2). However, other characteristics of the Dmanisi individuals are different from other hominid finds outside of Africa. In particular, the most complete specimen (Fig. 9-5c) has a less-robust and thinner browridge, a projecting lower face, and a relatively large upper canine. At least when viewed from the front, this skull is more reminiscent of the smaller early *Homo* specimens from East Africa than it is of *Homo erectus*. Also, this individual's cranial capacity is very small—estimated at only 600 cm³, well within the range of early *Homo*. In fact, the four Dmanisi crania so far described have relatively small cranial capacities—the other three were estimated at 630 cm³, 650 cm³, and 775 cm³.

Probably the most remarkable discovery yet from Dmanisi is a fourth skull that researchers excavated in 2002 (and published in 2005). This nearly complete cranium is of an older adult male; and surprisingly for such an ancient find, he died with only one tooth remaining in his jaws (Lordkipanidze et al., 2006). Because his jawbones show advanced resorption of bone, it seems that he lived for several years without being able to chew his food (Fig. 9-6). David Lordkipanidze, who leads the excavations at Dmanisi, and his colleagues have suggested that this individual required a fair amount of assistance to survive in an era when the only way to process food was to use your teeth (Lordkipanidze et al., 2005, 2006). However, this contention requires more detailed investigation before it can be confirmed.

Researchers have also recovered some stone tools at Dmanisi. The tools are similar to early ones from Africa, and they're quite different from the seemingly more advanced technology of the **Acheulian** industry broadly associated with African *H. erectus* after 1.4 mya (see p. 211).

The newest evidence from Dmanisi includes several postcranial bones, coming from at least four individuals (Lordkipanidze et al., 2007). This new evidence is especially important because it allows us to make comparisons with what is known of *Homo erectus* from other areas. The Dmanisi fossils have an unusual combination of traits. Firstly, these hominids were not especially tall, with an estimated height ranging from about 4 feet 9 inches to 5 feet 5 inches. Certainly, based on this evidence, they seem much smaller than the full *H. erectus* from East Africa or from Asia. Yet, although very short in stature, they still show body proportions (such as leg length) like that of *H. erectus* (and *H. sapiens*) and quite different from that seen in earlier hominids.

Based on these recent, startling revelations from Dmanisi, we can ask several questions:

1. Was *Homo erectus* the first hominid to leave Africa—or did an earlier form of *Homo* migrate even earlier?

2. Did hominids require a large brain and sophisticated stone tool culture to disperse out of Africa?

3. Was the large, robust body build of *H. erectus* a necessary adaptation for the initial occupation of Eurasia?

FIGURE 9-5

Dmanisi crania discovered in 1999 and 2001 and dated to 1.8–1.7 mya.
(a) Specimen 2282.
(b) Specimen 2280.
(c) Specimen 2700.

David Lordkipanidze

FIGURE 9-6

Most recently discovered cranium from Dmanisi, almost totally lacking in teeth (with both upper and lower jaws showing advanced bone resorption).

Acheulian (ash´-oo-lay-en) Pertaining to a stone tool industry from the Lower and Middle Pleistocene; characterized by a large proportion of bifacial tools (flaked on both sides). Acheulian tool kits are common in Africa, southwest Asia, and western Europe, but they're thought to be less common elsewhere. Also spelled Acheulean.

Of course, since the Dmanisi discoveries are very new, it's important to view any conclusions as highly tentative. But in any case, the recent evidence raises important and exciting possibilities. The Dmanisi findings suggest that the first hominids to leave Africa were quite possibly a very early form of *H. erectus*, possessing smaller brains than later *erectus* and carrying with them a typical African Oldowan stone tool culture. As we mentioned, newly discovered remains of the postcranial skeleton show the Dmanisi individuals were quite small. In fact, they average not much more than five feet in height. Certainly, based on this evidence, they seem much smaller than the full *H. erectus* from East Africa or from Asia.

What we do have so far shows that the Dmanisi hominids were generally very short and small-brained hominids, having none of the adaptations hypothesized to be essential to hominid migration—that is, being tall and having relatively large brains. It's possible we may find that there were *two* migrations out of Africa at this time: one consisting of the small-brained, diminutive Dmanisi hominids and an almost immediate second one that founded the well-recognized *H. erectus* populations of Java and China. All this evidence is so new, however, that it's too soon even to predict what further revisions may be required.

Homo erectus from Indonesia

After the publication of *On the Origin of Species,* debates about evolution were prevalent throughout Europe. While many theorists simply stayed home and debated the merits of natural selection and the likely course of human evolution, one young Dutch anatomist decided to go find evidence of it. Eugene Dubois (1858–1940) enlisted in the Dutch East Indian Army and was shipped to the island of Sumatra, Indonesia, to look for what he called "the missing link."

In October 1891, after moving his search to the neighboring island of Java, Dubois' field crew unearthed a skullcap along the Solo River near the town of Trinil—a fossil that was to become internationally famous (Fig. 9-7). The following year, a human femur was recovered about 15 yards upstream in what Dubois claimed was the same level as the skullcap, and he assumed that the skullcap (with a cranial capacity of slightly over 900 cm³) and the femur belonged to the same individual.

Six sites in eastern Java have yielded all the *H. erectus* fossil remains found to date on that island. The dating of these fossils has been hampered by the complex nature of Javanese geology, but it's been generally accepted that most of the fossils belong to the Early to Middle **Pleistocene** and are between 1.6 and 1 million years old. But as we noted earlier, more precise chronometric dating estimates have suggested that the earliest site may be close to 1.6 million years old, and very late *H. erectus* survivors (from Ngandong) may be as young as 27,000 years old.

The earliest *H. erectus* fossils from Java come from the central part of the island. Beginning with Dubois' famous discovery at Trinil , over 80 different specimens have been located, with many coming from an area called the "Sangiran Dome," located just west of Trinil. Several crania have been found, although only one preserves the face. Cranial capacities range between 813 cm³ and 1,059 cm³.

By far, the most recent group of *H. erectus* fossils from Java come from Ngandong, in an area to the east of the other finds already mentioned. At Ngandong, an excavation along an ancient river terrace produced 11 mostly complete hominid crania. Two specialized dating techniques, discussed in Chapter 8, have determined that animal bones found at the site—and presumably associated with the hominids—are only about 25,000 to 50,000 years old (Swisher et al., 1996). These dates are controversial, but further evidence is now establishing a *very* late survival of *Homo erectus* in Java, long after the species had disappeared elsewhere. So these individuals would be contemporary with *H. sapiens*—which, by this time, had expanded widely throughout the Old World, even into Australia around 40,000 to 60,000 years ago (ya). As we'll see in Chapter 11, even later—and very unusual—

S. Sartano

FIGURE 9-7
The famous Trinil skullcap found by Eugene Dubois in Java.

Pleistocene The epoch of the Cenozoic from 1.8 mya until 10,000 ya. Frequently referred to as the Ice Age, this epoch is associated with continental glaciations in northern latitudes.

hominids have been found elsewhere, apparently evolving while isolated on another Indonesian island.

We can't say much about the *H. erectus* way of life in Java. Very few artifacts have been found, and those have come mainly from river terraces, not from primary sites: "On Java there is still not a single site where artifacts can be associated with *H. erectus*" (Bartstra, 1982, p. 319).

Homo erectus from China

The story of the first discoveries of Chinese *H. erectus* is another saga filled with excitement, hard work, luck, and misfortune. Europeans had known for a long time that "dragon bones," used by the Chinese as medicine and aphrodisiacs, were actually ancient mammal bones. Scientists eventually located one of the sources of these bones near Beijing at a site called **Zhoukoudian.** Serious excavations were begun there in the 1920s, and in 1929, a fossil skull was discovered. The skull turned out to be a juvenile's, and although it was thick, low, and relatively small, there was no doubt that it belonged to an early hominid. The response to this discovery, quite unlike that which greeted Dubois almost 40 years earlier, was enthusiastically favorable.

Zhoukoudian *Homo erectus*

The fossil remains of *H. erectus* discovered in the 1920s and 1930s, as well as some more recent excavations at Zhoukoudian (Fig. 9-8), are by far the largest collection of *H. erectus* material found anywhere. This excellent sample includes 14 skullcaps (Fig. 9-9), other cranial pieces, and more than 100 isolated teeth, but only a scattering of postcranial elements (Jia and Huang, 1990). Various interpretations to account for this unusual pattern of preservation have been offered, ranging from ritualistic treatment or cannibalism by the hominids themselves to the more mundane suggestion that the *H. erectus* remains are simply the leftovers of the meals of giant hyenas.

Zhoukoudian (Zhoh´-koh-dee´-en)

FIGURE 9-8
Zhoukoudian cave.

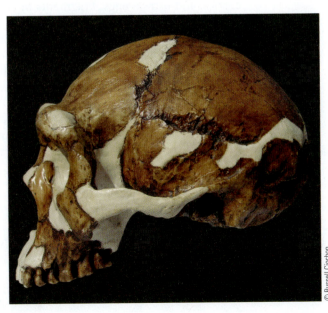

FIGURE 9-9
Composite cranium of Zhoukoudian *Homo erectus,* reconstructed by Ian Tattersall and Gary Sawyer, of the American Museum of Natural History in New York.

QUICK REVIEW		Key *Homo erectus* Discoveries from Asia
DATES	**SITE**	**EVOLUTIONARY SIGNIFICANCE**
50,000–25,000 ya	Ngandong (Java)	Very late survival of *H. erectus* in Java
670,000–410,000 ya	Zhoukoudian (China)	Large sample; most famous *H. erectus* site; shows some *H. erectus* populations well adapted to temperate (cold) environments
1.6 mya	Sangiran	First discovery of *H. erectus* from anywhere; shows dispersal out of Africa by 1.6 mya

At any rate, the hominid remains belong to upward of 40 adults and children and together provide much evidence. Because of meticulous analysis done on the original fossils (before they were lost), the Zhoukoudian fossils have led to a good overall picture of Chinese *H. erectus*. Like the materials from Java, they have typical *H. erectus* features, including a large browridge in front and a nuchal torus behind. Also, the skull has thick bones, a sagittal keel, and a protruding face and, like the Javanese forms, is broadest near the bottom. These specimens have been dated at various times to between 670,000 and 410,000 years old.

Cultural Remains More than 100,000 artifacts have been recovered from this vast site, which was occupied intermittently for many thousands of years. Early on, tools are generally crude and shapeless, but they become more refined over time. Common tools at the site are choppers and chopping tools, but retouched flakes were fashioned into scrapers, points, burins, and awls (Fig. 9-10).

The way of life at Zhoukoudian has traditionally been described as that of hunter-gatherers who killed deer, horses, and other animals and gathered fruits, berries, and ostrich eggs. Fragments of charred ostrich eggshells and abundant deposits of hackberry seeds unearthed in the cave suggest that these hominids supplemented their diet of meat by gathering herbs, wild fruits, tubers, and eggs. Layers of what has long been thought to be ash in the cave (over 18 feet deep at one point) have been interpreted as indicating the use of fire by *H. erectus;* but as we'll see, researchers don't really know whether Beijing hominids could actually make fire.

More recently, several researchers have challenged this picture of Zhoukoudian life. Lewis Binford and colleagues (Binford and Ho, 1985; Binford and Stone, 1986a, 1986b) reject the description of Beijing *H. erectus* as hunters and argue that the evi-

FIGURE 9-10
Chinese tools likely made by *Homo erectus.*

Quartzite chopper

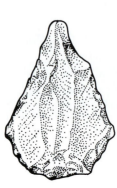

Flint point

Flint awl

Graver, or burin

dence clearly points more accurately to scavenging. Using advanced archaeological techniques of analysis, Noel Boaz and colleagues have even questioned whether the *H. erectus* remains at Zhoukoudian represent evidence of hominid habitation of the cave. By comparing the types of bones, as well as the damage to the bones, with that seen in contemporary carnivore dens, Boaz and Ciochon (2001) have suggested that much of the material in the cave likely accumulated through the activities of a giant extinct hyena. In fact, they hypothesize that most of the *H. erectus* remains, too, are the food refuse of hyena meals.

Boaz and his colleagues do recognize that the tools in the cave, and possibly the cut marks on some of the animal bones, provide evidence of hominid activities at Zhoukoudian. They also recognize that more detailed analysis is required to test their hypotheses and to "determine the nature and scope" of the *H. erectus* presence at Zhoukoudian.

Probably the most intriguing archaeological aspect of the presumed hominid behavior at Zhoukoudian has been the long-held assumption that *H. erectus* deliberately used fire inside the cave. Controlling fire was one of the major cultural breakthroughs of all prehistory. By providing warmth, a means of cooking, an aid to further modify tools, and so forth, controlled fire would have been a giant technological innovation. While some potential early African sites have yielded evidence that to some have suggested hominid control of fire, it's long been concluded that the first *definite* evidence of hominid fire use comes from Zhoukoudian.

Now, more recent evidence has also radically altered this assumption. Much more detailed excavations at Zhoukoudian were carried out in the 1990s. During these excavations, the researchers also carefully collected and analyzed soil samples for distinctive chemical signatures that would show whether fire had occurred in the cave (Weiner et al., 1998). They found that burnt bone was only rarely found in association with tools. And in most cases, the burning appeared to have taken place *after* fossilization—that is, the bones were not cooked. In fact, it turns out that the "ash" layers mentioned earlier aren't actually ash, but naturally accumulated organic sediment. This last conclusion was derived from chemical testing that showed absolutely no sign of wood having been burnt inside the cave. Finally, the "hearths" that have figured so prominently in archaeological reconstructions of presumed fire control at this site are apparently not hearths at all. They are simply round depressions formed in the past by water.

Another provisional interpretation of the cave's geology suggests that the cave wasn't open to the outside like a habitation site, but was accessed only through a vertical shaft. This theory has led archaeologist Alison Brooks to remark, "It wouldn't have been a shelter, it would have been a trap" (quoted in Wuethrich, 1998). These serious doubts about control of fire, coupled with the suggestive evidence of bone accumulation by carnivores, have led anthropologists Noel Boaz and Russell Ciochon to conclude that "Zhoukoudian cave was neither hearth nor home" (Boaz and Ciochon, 2001).

Other Chinese Sites

More work has been done at Zhoukoudian than at any other Chinese site. Even so, there are other paleoanthropological sites worth mentioning. Three of the more important regions outside of Zhoukoudian are Lantian County (including two sites, often simply referred to as Lantian), Yunxian County, and several discoveries in Hexian County (usually referred to as the Hexian finds).

Before the excavation of two sites in Lantian County, Shaanxi Province, in the mid-1960s, Zhoukoudian was widely believed to be the oldest hominid site in China. Dated to 1.15 mya, Lantian is older than Zhoukoudian (Zhu et al., 2003). From the Lantian sites, the cranial remains of two adult *H. erectus* females have been found in association with fire-treated pebbles and flakes as well as ash (Woo, 1966; Fig. 9-11a). One of the specimens, an almost complete mandible containing several teeth, is quite similar to those from Zhoukoudian.

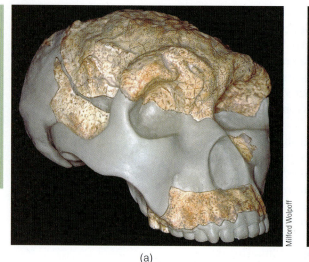

(a)

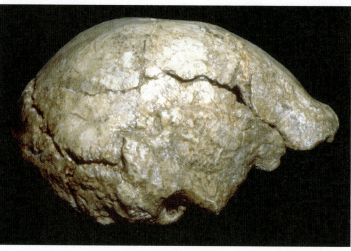

(b)

FIGURE 9-11

(a) Reconstructed cranium of *Homo erectus* from Lantian, China, dated to approximately 1.15 mya. (b) Hexian cranium.

Two badly distorted crania were discovered in Yunxian County, Hubei Province, in 1989 and 1990 (Li and Etler, 1992). A combination of ESR and paleomagnetism dating methods gives us an average dating estimate of 800,000–580,000 ya. If the dates are correct, this would place Yunxian between Lantian and Zhoukoudian in the Chinese sequence. Due to extensive distortion of the crania from ground pressure, it was very difficult to compare these crania with other *H. erectus* fossils; recently, however, French paleoanthropologist Amélie Vialet has restored the crania using sophisticated imaging techniques (Vialet et al., 2005). And from a recent analysis of the fauna and paleoenvironment at Yunxian, the *H. erectus* inhabitants are thought to have had limited hunting capabilities, since they appear to have been limited to the most vulnerable prey, namely, the young and old animals.

In 1980 and 1981, the remains of several individuals, all bearing some resemblance to similar fossils from Zhoukoudian, were recovered from Hexian County, in southern China (Wu and Poirier, 1995) (Fig. 9-11b). A close relationship has been postulated between the *H. erectus* specimens from the Hexian finds and from Zhoukoudian (Wu and Dong, 1985). Indeed, some date the remains to 400,000 ya (Wu et al., 2006), making it contemporaneous with Zhoukoudian; these dates are disputed, and others experts place the age at only 190,000 ya.

The Asian crania from both Java and China share many similar features, which may be explained by *H. erectus* migration from Java to China perhaps around 1 million years ago. African *H. erectus* forms are generally older than most Asian forms, and they're different from them in several ways.

Asian and African *Homo erectus:* A Comparison

The *Homo erectus* remains from East Africa show several differences from the Javanese and Chinese fossils. Some African cranial specimens—particularly the skull from East Turkana (ER 3733), presumably a female, and WT 15000, presumably a male—aren't as strongly buttressed at the browridge and nuchal torus, and their cranial bones aren't as thick. Indeed, some researchers are so impressed by these differences, as well as others in the postcranial skeleton, that they're arguing for a *separate* species status for the African material, to distinguish it from the Asian samples. Bernard Wood, the leading proponent of this view, has suggested that the name *Homo ergaster* be used for the African remains and that *H. erectus* be reserved solely for the Asian material (Wood, 1991). In addition, the very early dates now postulated for the dispersal of *H. erectus* into Asia (Java) would argue for a more than 1-million-year separate history for Asian and African populations.

In any case, this species division has not been fully accepted, and the current consensus (and the one we prefer) is to continue referring to all these hominids as *Homo erectus* (Kramer, 1993; Conroy, 1997; Rightmire, 1998; Asfaw et al., 2002). So, as with some earlier hominids, we'll have to accommodate a considerable degree of intraspecific variation within this species. Wood has concluded, regarding variation within such a broadly defined *H. erectus* species, that "it is a species which manifestly embraces an unusually wide degree of variation in both the cranium and postcranial skeleton" (Wood, 1992, p. 329).

Later *Homo erectus* from Europe

Because of the recent discoveries from Dmanisi (see p. 203), the time frame for the earliest hominid occupation of Europe is being dramatically pushed back. For several decades, researchers assumed that hominids didn't reach Europe until late in the Middle Pleistocene (after 400,000 ya) and were already identifiable as a form very similar to *Homo sapiens*. So they concluded that *H. erectus* (and contemporaries) never got there. But as the new discoveries are evaluated, these assumptions are being discarded, and radical revisions concerning hominid evolution in Europe are becoming necessary.

While not as old as the Dmanisi material, fossils from the Gran Dolina site in northern Spain are extending the antiquity of hominids in western Europe. (Gran Dolina is located in the very productive region called Atapuerca, where later hominid fossils have also been found.) The dating of Gran Dolina, based on specialized techniques discussed in Chapter 8 (see p. 172), is approximately 850,000–780,000 ya (Parés and Pérez-González, 1995; Falguéres et al., 1999). These early Spanish finds are thus *at least* 250,000 years older than any other hominid yet discovered in western Europe. Because all the remains so far identified are fragmentary, assigning these fossils to particular species poses something of a problem; but initial analysis suggests that these fossils aren't *H. erectus*. Spanish paleoanthropologists who have studied the Gran Dolina fossils have decided to place these hominids into another (separate) species, one they call *Homo antecessor* (Bermúdez de Castro et al., 1997; Arsuaga et al., 1999). However, it remains to be seen whether this newly proposed species will prove to be distinct from other species of *Homo* (see p. 213 for further discussion).

Finally, the southern European discovery of a well-preserved cranium from the Ceprano site in central Italy may be the best evidence yet of *H. erectus* in Europe (Ascenzi et al., 1996). Provisional dating of a partial cranium from this important site suggests a date between 800,000 and 900,000 ya (Fig. 9-12). Phillip Rightmire (1998) has concluded that cranial morphology places this specimen quite close to *H. erectus*. Italian researchers have proposed other views. The exact relationship of Ceprano to *H. erectus* remains to be fully determined.

After about 400,000 ya, the European fossil hominid record becomes increasingly abundant. More fossils mean more variation, so it's not surprising that interpretations regarding the proper taxonomic assessment of many of these remains have been debated, in some cases for decades. In recent years, several of these somewhat later "premodern" specimens have been considered either as early representatives of *H. sapiens* or as a separate species, one immediately preceding *H. sapiens*. These enigmatic premodern humans are discussed in Chapter 10. A time line for the *H. erectus* discoveries discussed in this chapter as well as other finds of more uncertain status is shown in Figure 9-13.

FIGURE 9-12

The Ceprano *Homo erectus* cranium from central Italy, provisionally dated to 800,000–900,000 ya. This is the best evidence for *Homo erectus* in Europe.

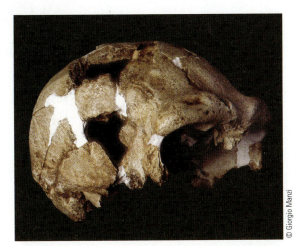

© Giorgio Manzi

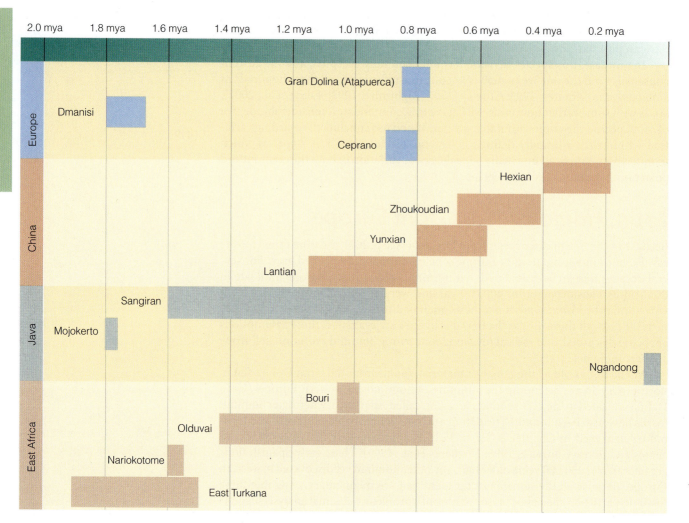

FIGURE 9-13

Time line for *Homo erectus* discoveries and other contemporary hominids.

Note: Most dates are only imprecise estimates. However, the dates from East African sites are chronometrically determined and are thus much more secure. The early dates from Java are also radiometric and are gaining wide acceptance.

QUICK REVIEW		Key *Homo erectus* and Contemporaneous Discoveries from Europe
DATES	SITE	EVOLUTIONARY SIGNIFICANCE
900,000–800,000 ya	Ceprano (Italy)	Well-preserved cranium; best evidence of full *H. erectus* morphology from any site in Europe
850,000–780,000 ya	Gran Dolina (Atapuerca, Spain)	Oldest evidence of hominids in western Europe; likely not *H. erectus*
1.75 mya	Dmanisi (Republic of Georgia)	Oldest well-dated hominids outside of Africa; not like full *H. erectus* morphology, but are small-bodied and small-brained

Technological Trends in *Homo erectus*

During the existence of *H. erectus* in Africa, a new tool kit was developed. The important change in this kit was a core worked on both sides, called a *biface* (known widely as a hand axe or cleaver; Fig. 9-14). The biface had a flatter shape than seen in the rounder earlier Oldowan tools (which in fact probably weren't "tools" at all, but were merely discarded rock blanks from which flakes were removed). Using the biface as a basic part of what's called the Acheulian tool industry, this stone tool technology spread from Africa after 1.4 mya and became the basic *H. erectus* all-purpose lithic tool kit for more than a million years. With the biface as a kind of "Acheulian Swiss army knife," these tools served to cut, scrape, pound, and dig. This most useful tool has been found in Africa, parts of Asia, and later in Europe. Note that Acheulian tool kits also included several types of small tools (Fig. 9-15).

For many years, scientists thought that a cultural "divide" separated the Old World, with Acheulian technology made *only* in Africa, the Middle East, and parts of Europe (elsewhere, the Acheulian was presumed to be absent). But recently reported excavations from more than 20 sites in southern China have forced reevaluation of this hypothesis (Yamei et al., 2000). As we've noted, the most distinctive tools of the Acheulian are bifaces, and they're the very tools thought lacking throughout most of the Pleistocene in eastern Europe and most of Asia. The new archaeological assemblages from southern China are securely dated at about 800,000 ya and contain numerous bifaces, very similar to contemporaneous Acheulian bifaces from Africa (Fig. 9-16). It now appears likely that cultural traditions relating to stone tool technology were largely equivalent over the *full* geographical range of *H. erectus* and its contemporaries.

FIGURE 9-14
Acheulian biface ("hand axe"), a basic tool of the Acheulian tradition.

FIGURE 9-15
Small tools of the Acheulian industry. (a) Side scraper. (b) Point. (c) End scraper. (d) Burin.

FIGURE 9-16
(a) A Middle Pleistocene butchering site at Olorgesailie, Kenya, excavated by Louis and Mary Leakey, who had the catwalk built for observers. (b) A close-up of numerous Acheulian tools, mainly hand axes, found at Olorgesailie in Kenya. Thousands of similar tools were found at this site.

(a)

(b)

While geographical distinctions aren't so obvious, temporal changes in tool technology are evident. Beginning with the Acheulian culture, we find the first evidence that raw materials were being transported more consistently and for longer distances. When Acheulian tool users found a good piece of stone, they often would take it with them as they traveled from one place to another. This behavior suggests foresight: They likely knew that they might need to use a stone tool in the future and that this chunk of rock could later prove useful. This is a major change from the Oldowan, where all stone tools are found very close to their raw material sources.

Evidence of butchering is widespread at *H. erectus* sites, and in the past, such evidence has been cited in arguments for consistent hunting. Researchers formerly interpreted any association of bones and tools as evidence of hunting, but many studies now suggest that cut marks on bones from the *H. erectus* time period often overlay carnivore tooth marks. This means that hominids were gaining access to the carcasses after the carnivores and were therefore scavenging the meat, not hunting the animals. It's also crucial to mention that these hominids were gaining a large amount of their daily calories from gathering wild plants, tubers, and fruits. Like hunter-gatherers of modern times, *H. erectus* individuals were most likely consuming 80 percent of their daily calories from plant materials.

Seeing the Big Picture: Interpretations of *Homo erectus*

Several aspects of the geographical, physical, and behavioral patterns shown by *H. erectus* (broadly defined) seem clear. But new discoveries and more in-depth analyses are helping us to reevaluate our prior ideas. The fascinating fossil hominids discovered at Dmanisi are perhaps the most challenging piece of this puzzle.

Past theories suggest that *Homo erectus* was able to emigrate from Africa owing to more advanced culture and a more modern anatomy as compared to earlier African predecessors. Yet, the Dmanisi cranial remains show that these very early Europeans still had small brains; what's more, *H. erectus* has been found in Java at 1.6 mya, and these hominids were still using Oldowan-style tools.

So it seems that some key parts of earlier hypotheses are not fully accurate. At least some of the earliest emigrants from Africa didn't yet show the entire suite of *H. erectus* physical and behavioral traits. How different the Dmanisi hominids are from the full *H. erectus* pattern remains to be seen, and the discovery of more complete postcranial remains will be most illuminating.

Going a step further, the four crania from Dmanisi are extremely variable; one of them, in fact, does look more like *H. erectus.* It would be tempting to conclude that more than one type of hominid is represented here, but they're all found in the same geological context. The archaeologists who excavated the site conclude that all the fossils are closely associated with each other. The simplest hypothesis is that they all are members of the *same* species. This degree of apparent intraspecific variation is biologically noteworthy, and it's influencing how paleoanthropologists interpret all of these fossil samples.

This growing awareness of the broad limits of intraspecific variation among some hominids brings us to our second consideration: Is *Homo ergaster* in Africa a separate species from *Homo erectus,* as strictly defined in Asia? While this interpretation was popular in the last decade, it now is losing support. The finds from Dmanisi raise fundamental issues of interpretation. Among these four crania from one locality (see Fig. 9-5), we see more variation than between the African and Asian forms, which many researchers have interpreted as different species. Also, the new discovery from Bouri (Ethiopia) of a more *erectus*-looking cranium further weakens the separate-species interpretation of *H. ergaster.*

The separate-species status of the early European fossils from Spain (Gran Dolina) is also not yet clearly established. We still don't have much good fossil evidence from this site; but an early date, prior to 750,000 ya, is well confirmed. Recall also that no other western European hominid fossils are known until at least 150,000 years later, and a seemingly almost contemporaneous find from Italy looks like *H. erectus* (Bischoff et al., 2007). It's quite apparent that later in the Pleistocene, the possible descendants of these hominids are well established both in Africa and in Europe. These later premodern humans are the topic of the next chapter.

When looking back at the evolution of *H. erectus*, we realize how significant this early human's achievements were. It was *H. erectus* who increased in body size with more efficient bipedalism; who embraced culture wholeheartedly as an adaptive strategy; whose brain was reshaped and increased in size to within the range of *H. sapiens;* who became a more efficient scavenger and likely hunter with a greater dependence on meat; and who apparently established more permanent living sites. In short, it was *H. erectus,* committed to a cultural way of life, who transformed hominid evolution to human evolution. As Richard Foley states, "The appearance and expansion of *H. erectus* represented a major change in adaptive strategy that influenced the subsequent process and pattern of human evolution" (1991, p. 425).

Summary

Homo erectus remains are found in geological contexts dating from about 1.8 mya to at least 200,000 ya—and probably much later—and spanning a period of more than 1.5 million years. While the nature and timing of migrations are uncertain, it's likely that *H. erectus* first appeared in East Africa and later migrated to other areas. This widespread and highly successful hominid defines a new and more modern grade of human evolution.

Historically, the first finds were made by Dubois in Java, and later discoveries came from China and Africa. Differences from early *Homo* are notable in *H. erectus'* larger brain, taller stature, robust build, and changes in facial structure and cranial buttressing.

The long period of *H. erectus* existence was marked by a remarkably uniform technology over space and time. Even so, compared to earlier hominids, *H. erectus* and contemporaries introduced more sophisticated tools and probably ate novel and/or differently processed foods. By using these new tools and—at later sites— possibly fire as well, they were also able to move into different environments and successfully adapt to new conditions.

It's generally assumed that certain *H. erectus* populations evolved into later premodern humans, some of which, in turn, evolved into *Homo sapiens.* Evidence supporting such a series of transitions is seen in the Ngandong fossils (and others discussed in Chapter 10), which display both *H. erectus* and *H. sapiens* features. There are still many questions about *H. erectus* behavior—for example, did they hunt, and did they control fire? We also wonder about their relationship to later hominids. Was the mode of evolution gradual or rapid, and which *H. erectus* populations contributed genes? The search for answers continues.

In the What's Important feature on page 214 you'll find a useful summary of the most significant hominid fossils discussed in this chapter.

WHAT'S IMPORTANT   Key Fossil Discoveries of *Homo erectus*

DATES	REGION	SITE	THE BIG PICTURE
25,000 ya–1.6 mya	Asia (Indonesia)	Java (Sangiran and other sites)	Shows *H. erectus* early on (by 1.6 mya) in tropical areas of Southeast Asia; *H. erectus* persisted here for more than 1 million years
400,000–600,000 ya	China	Zhoukoudian	Largest, most famous sample of *H. erectus*; shows adaptation to colder environments; conclusions regarding behavior at this site have been exaggerated and are now questioned
800,000–900,000 ya	Europe (Italy)	Ceprano	Likely best evidence of full-blown *H. erectus* morphology in Europe
1.7–1.8 mya	(Republic of Georgia)	Dmanisi	Very early dispersal to southeastern Europe (by 1.8 mya) of small-bodied, small-brained *H. erectus* population; may represent an earlier dispersal from Africa than one that led to wider occupation of Eurasia
1.6 mya	Africa (Kenya)	Nariokotome	Beautifully preserved nearly complete skeleton; best postcranial evidence of *H. erectus* from anywhere
1.8 mya		East Turkana	Earliest *H. erectus* from Africa; some individuals more robust, others smaller and more gracile; variation suggested to represent sexual dimorphism

WHY IT MATTERS

Question: In this chapter it is argued that increased meat consumption may have been an important behavioral adaptation that led to increased brain and body size in *Homo erectus* and, ultimately, to geographical expansion. Does that mean that modern humans have to eat meat in order to maintain healthy brains and bodies?

Answer: One of the most significant characteristics of humans is that we are a generalized species with flexible adaptations, including diet. But for natural selection to favor increased brain size in the human lineage, as reflected in *Homo erectus*, diet had to change to maintain the energetically expensive brain. In other words, to allow for evolutionary increases in brain size, our ancestors would have had to spend all day gathering and eating the same sorts of plant foods consumed by their ancestors (the australopiths) or they would have had to find foods with greater nutrients per unit of weight. And the food category with the greatest amount of energy and other nutrients per weight is animal protein. Additionally, the pattern of amino acids that humans need for good health matches the pattern found in animal protein, providing more evidence that meat was an important component of ancestral diets. Although animal food sources, including insects, have been consumed by humans for thousands of generations, the types of animal products consumed by most people today are much higher in fat than those consumed in the past. This fat content, as well as the monetary and environmental costs attached to meat, has led many people today to minimize the amount of meat in their diet or to eliminate it entirely. It's probably fine for humans to be entirely vegetarian, as long as combinations of plant foods are used in such a way as to approximate the amino acid content of animal protein. It's particularly important that infants and children obtain appropriate nutrients to maintain healthy brain growth in the first four to five years of life. *Homo erectus* may have been the first of our ancestors to rely on appreciable amounts of animal protein, but as descendants, we are "stuck with" not only a large brain but also the pattern of nutrients required to maintain it.

Critical Thinking Questions

1. Why is the nearly complete skeleton from Nariokotome so important? What kinds of evidence does it provide?

2. Assume that you're in the laboratory and have the Nariokotome skeleton, as well as a skeleton of a modern human. First, given a choice, what age and sex would you choose for the human skeleton, and why? Second, what similarities and differences do the two skeletons show?

3. What fundamental questions of interpretation do the fossil hominids from Dmanisi raise? Does this evidence completely overturn the hypothesis concerning *H. erectus* dispersal from Africa? Explain why or why not.

4. How has the interpretation of *H. erectus* behavior at Zhoukoudian been revised in recent years? What kinds of new evidence from this site have been used in this reevaluation, and what does that tell you about modern archaeological techniques and approaches?

5. You're interpreting the hominid fossils from three sites in East Africa (Nariokotome, Olduvai, and Bouri)—all considered possible members of *H. erectus*. What sorts of evidence would lead you to conclude that there was more than one species? What would convince you that there was just one species? Why do you think some paleoanthropologists (splitters) would tend to see more than one species, while others (lumpers) would generally not? What kind of approach would you take, and why?

CHAPTER 10

Premodern Humans

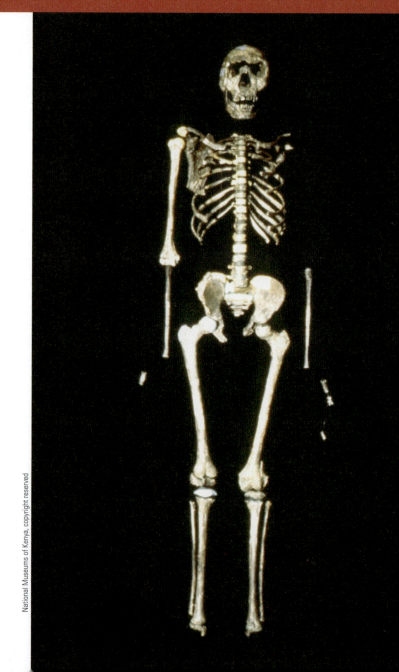

Introduction

What do you think of when you hear the term *Neandertal?* Most people think of imbecilic, bent-over brutes. Yet, Neandertals were quite advanced; they had brains at least as large as ours, and they showed many sophisticated cultural capabilities. What's more, they definitely weren't bent over, but fully erect (as hominids had been for millions of years previously). In fact, Neandertals and their immediate predecessors could easily be called human.

That brings us to possibly the most basic of all questions: What does it mean to be human? The meaning of this term is highly varied, encompassing religious, philosophical, and biological considerations. As you know, physical anthropologists primarily concentrate on the biological aspects of the human organism. All living people today are members of one species, sharing a common anatomical pattern and similar behavioral potentials. We call hominids like us "modern *Homo sapiens,*" and in the next chapter we'll discuss the origin of forms that were essentially identical to living people.

When in our evolutionary past can we say that our predecessors were obviously human? Certainly, the further back we go in time, the less hominids look like modern *Homo sapiens.* This is, of course, exactly what we'd expect in an evolutionary sequence.

We saw in Chapter 9 that *Homo erectus* took crucial steps in the human direction and defined a new *grade* of human evolution. In this chapter, we'll discuss the hominids who continued this journey. Both physically and behaviorally, they're much like modern *Homo sapiens,* though they still show several significant differences. So while most paleoanthropologists are comfortable referring to these hominids as "human," we need to qualify this recognition a bit to set them apart from fully modern people. Thus, in this text, we'll refer to these fascinating immediate predecessors as "premodern humans."

When, Where, and What

Most of the hominids discussed in this chapter lived during the **Middle Pleistocene,** a period beginning 780,000 ya and ending 125,000 ya. In addition, some of the later premodern humans, especially the Neandertals, lived well into the **Late Pleistocene** (125,000–10,000 ya).

The Pleistocene

The Pleistocene has been called the Ice Age because, as had occurred before in geological history, it was marked by periodic continental **glaciations.** During glacial periods, when temperatures dropped dramatically, ice accumulated as a result of

▶ **Click!**

Go to the following media resources for interactive activities, more information, and study materials on topics covered in this chapter:

- Anthropology Resource Center
- Student Companion Website for *Essentials of Physical Anthropology,* Seventh Edition
- Online Virtual Laboratories for Physical Anthropology CD-ROM, Fourth Edition
- Hominid Fossils CD-ROM: An Interactive Atlas

Middle Pleistocene The portion of the Pleistocene epoch beginning 780,000 ya and ending 125,000 ya.

Late Pleistocene The portion of the Pleistocene epoch beginning 125,000 ya and ending approximately 10,000 ya.

glaciations Climatic intervals when continental ice sheets cover much of the northern continents. Glaciations are associated with colder temperatures in northern latitudes and more arid conditions in southern latitudes, most notably in Africa.

more snow falling each year than melting, causing the advance of massive glaciers. As the climate fluctuated, at times it became much warmer. During these **interglacials,** the ice that had built up during the glacial periods melted, and the glaciers retreated back toward the earth's polar regions. The Pleistocene was characterized by numerous advances and retreats of ice, with at least 15 major and 50 minor glacial advances documented in Europe alone (Tattersall et al., 1988).

These glaciations, which enveloped huge swaths of Europe, Asia, and North America as well as Antarctica, were mostly confined to northern latitudes. Hominids living at this time—all still restricted to the Old World—were severely affected as the climate, flora, and animal life shifted during these Pleistocene oscillations. The most dramatic of these effects were in Europe and northern Asia—less so in southern Asia and in Africa. Still, the climate also fluctuated in the south. In Africa, the main effects were related to changing rainfall patterns. During glacial periods, the climate in Africa became more arid, while during interglacials, rainfall increased. The changing availability of food resources certainly affected hominids in Africa; but probably even more importantly, migration routes also swung back and forth. For example, during glacial periods (Fig. 10-1), the Sahara Desert expanded, blocking migration in and out of sub-Saharan Africa (Lahr and Foley, 1998).

In Eurasia, glacial advances also greatly affected migration routes. As the ice sheets expanded, sea levels dropped, more northern regions became uninhabitable, and some key passages between areas became blocked by glaciers. For example, during glacial peaks, much of western Europe would have been cut off from the rest of Eurasia (Fig. 10-2).

During the warmer—and, in the south, wetter—interglacials, the ice sheets shrank, sea levels rose, and certain migration routes reopened (for example, from central into western Europe). Clearly, to understand Middle Pleistocene hominids, it's crucial to view them within their shifting Pleistocene world.

Dispersal of Middle Pleistocene Hominids

Like their *Homo erectus* predecessors, later hominids were widely distributed in the Old World, with discoveries coming from three continents—Africa, Asia, and Europe. For the first time, Europe became more permanently and densely occupied, as Middle Pleistocene hominids have been discovered widely from England, France, Spain, Germany, Italy, Hungary, and Greece. Africa, as well, probably continued as a central area of hominid occupation, and finds have come from North, East, and

interglacials Climatic intervals when continental ice sheets are retreating, eventually becoming much reduced in size. Interglacials in northern latitudes are associated with warmer temperatures, while in southern latitudes the climate becomes wetter.

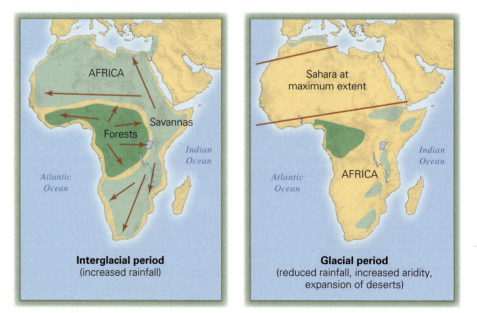

FIGURE 10-1

Changing Pleistocene environments in Africa.

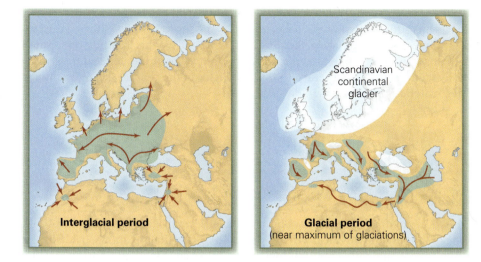

Interglacial period

Scandinavian continental glacier

Glacial period
(near maximum of glaciations)

FIGURE 10-2

Changing Pleistocene environments in Eurasia. Green areas show regions of likely hominid occupation. White areas are major glaciers. Arrows indicate likely migration routes.

South Africa. Finally, Asia has yielded several important finds, most especially from China (see Fig. 10-6 on pp. 222–223). We should point out, though, that these Middle Pleistocene premodern humans didn't vastly extend the geographical range of *Homo erectus,* but largely replaced the earlier hominids in previously exploited habitats. One exception appears to be the more successful occupation of Europe, a region where earlier hominids have only sporadically been found.

Middle Pleistocene Hominids: Terminology

The premodern humans of the Middle Pleistocene (that is, after 780,000 ya) generally succeeded *H. erectus.* Still, in some areas—especially in Asia—there apparently was a long period of coexistence, lasting 300,000 years or longer; you'll recall the very late dates for the Javanese Ngandong *H. erectus* (see p. 204).

The earliest premodern humans exhibit several *H. erectus* characteristics: The face is large, the brows are projected, the forehead is low, and in some cases the cranial vault is still thick. Even so, some of their other features show that they were more derived toward the modern condition than were their *Homo erectus* predecessors. Compared to *H. erectus,* these premodern humans possessed an increased brain size, a more rounded braincase (that is, maximum breadth is higher up on the sides), a more vertical nose, and a less-angled back of the skull (occipital). We should note that the maximum span of time encompassed by Middle Pleistocene premodern humans is at least 500,000 years, so it's no surprise that over time, we can observe certain trends. Later Middle Pleistocene hominids, for example, show even more brain expansion and an even less-angled occipital than do earlier forms.

We know that premodern humans were a diverse group dispersed over three continents. Deciding how to classify them has been in dispute for decades, and anthropologists still have disagreements. However, a growing consensus has recently emerged. Beginning perhaps as early as 850,000 ya and extending to about 200,000 ya, the fossils from Africa and Europe are placed within *Homo heidelbergensis,* named after a fossil found in Germany in 1907. What's more, some Asian specimens possibly represent a regional variant of *H. heidelbergensis.*

Until recently, many researchers regarded these fossils as early, but more primitive, members of *Homo sapiens.* In recognition of this somewhat transitional status, the fossils were called "archaic *Homo sapiens,*" with all later humans also belonging to the species *Homo sapiens.* However, most paleoanthropologists now find this terminology unsatisfactory. For example, Phillip Rightmire concludes that "simply lumping diverse ancient groups with living populations obscures their differences" (1998, p. 226). In our own discussion, we recognize *Homo heidelbergensis* as a transitional species between *Homo erectus* and later hominids (that is, primarily, *Homo sapiens*). Keep in mind, however, that this species was probably an ancestor of both modern humans and Neandertals. It's debatable whether *H. heidelbergensis* actually represents a fully separate species in the *biological* sense, that is, following the biological species concept (see p. 86). Still, it's useful to give this group of premodern humans a separate name to make this important stage of human evolution more easily identifiable. (We'll return to this issue later in the chapter, when we discuss the theoretical implications in more detail.)

Premodern Humans of the Middle Pleistocene

Africa

In Africa, premodern fossils have been found at several sites (Figs. 10-3 and 10-4). One of the best known is Kabwe (Broken Hill). At this site in Zambia, fieldworkers discovered a complete cranium, together with other cranial and postcranial elements belonging to several individuals. In this and other African premodern specimens, we can see a mixture of older and more recent traits. The skull's massive browridge (one of the largest of any hominid), low vault, and prominent occipital torus recall those of *H. erectus*. On the other hand, the occipital region is less angulated, the cranial vault bones are thinner, and the cranial base is essentially modern. Dating estimates of Kabwe and most of the other premodern fossils from Africa have ranged throughout the Middle and Late Pleistocene, but recent estimates have given dates for most of the sites in the range of 600,000–125,000 ya.

A total of eight other crania from South and East Africa also show a combination of retained ancestral with more derived (modern) characteristics, and they're all mentioned in the literature as being similar to Kabwe. The most important of these African finds come from the sites of Florisbad and Elandsfontein in South Africa, Laetoli in Tanzania, and Bodo in Ethiopia (see Fig. 10-6, pp. 222–223).

Bodo is one of the most significant of these other African fossils. A nearly complete cranium, Bodo has been dated to relatively early in the Middle Pleistocene (estimated at 600,000 ya), making it one of the oldest specimens of *Homo heidelbergensis* from the African continent. The Bodo cranium is particularly interesting because it shows a distinctive pattern of cut marks, similar to modifications seen in butchered animal bones. Researchers have thus hypothesized that the Bodo indi-

FIGURE 10-3
The Kabwe (Broken Hill) *Homo heidelbergensis* skull from Zambia. Note the very robust browridges.

FIGURE 10-4
The Bodo cranium, the earliest evidence of *Homo heidelbergensis* in Africa.

QUICK REVIEW	Key Premodern Human (*H. heidelbergensis*) Fossils from Africa	
DATES	SITE	EVOLUTIONARY SIGNIFICANCE
130,000+ ya	Kabwe (Broken Hill) Zambia	Nearly complete skull; mosaic of features (browridge very robust, but brain case expanded)
600,000 ya	Bodo Ethiopia	Earliest example of African *H. heidelbergensis*; likely evidence of butchering

vidual was defleshed by other hominids, but for what purpose is not clear. The defleshing may have been related to cannibalism, though it also may have been for some other purpose, such as ritual. In any case, this is the earliest evidence of deliberate bone processing of hominids *by* hominids (White, 1986).

The general similarities in all these African premodern fossils indicate a close relationship between them, almost certainly representing a single species (most commonly referred to as *H. heidelbergensis*). These African premodern humans also are quite similar to those found in Europe.

Europe

More fossil hominids of Middle Pleistocene age have been found in Europe than in any other region. Maybe it's because more archaeologists have been searching longer in Europe than elsewhere. In any case, during the Middle Pleistocene, Europe was more widely and consistently occupied than it was earlier in human evolution.

The time range of European premodern humans extends the full length of the Middle Pleistocene and beyond. At the earlier end, the Gran Dolina finds from northern Spain (discussed in Chapter 9; see p. 209) are definitely not *Homo erectus*. The Gran Dolina remains may, as proposed by Spanish researchers, be members of a new hominid species. However, Rightmire (1998) has suggested that the Gran Dolina hominids may simply represent the earliest well-dated occurrence of *H. heidelbergensis*, possibly dating as early as 850,000 ya.

More recent and more completely studied *H. heidelbergensis* fossils have been found throughout much of Europe. Examples of these finds come from Steinheim (Germany), Petralona (Greece), Swanscombe (England), Arago (France), and another cave at Atapuerca (Spain). Like their African counterparts, these European premoderns have retained certain *H. erectus* traits, but they're mixed with more derived ones—for example, increased cranial capacity, more rounded occiput, parietal expansion, and reduced tooth size (Fig. 10-5).

The hominids from Atapuerca are especially interesting. These finds come from another cave in the same area as the Gran Dolina discoveries. Dated to between 600,000 and 530,000 ya (Bischoff et al., 2007), a total of at least 28 individuals have been recovered from a site called Sima de los Huesos, literally meaning "pit of bones." In fact, with more than 4,000 fossil fragments recovered, Sima de los Huesos contains more than 80 percent of all Middle Pleistocene hominid remains in the world (Bermudez de Castro et al., 2004). Excavations continue at this remarkable site, where bones have somehow accumulated within a deep chamber inside a cave. From initial descriptions, paleoanthropologists interpret the hominid morphology as showing several indications of an early Neandertal-like pattern, with arching browridges, projecting midface, and other features (Rightmire, 1998).

Milford Wolpoff

FIGURE 10-5

Steinheim cranium, a representative of *H. heidelbergensis* from Germany.

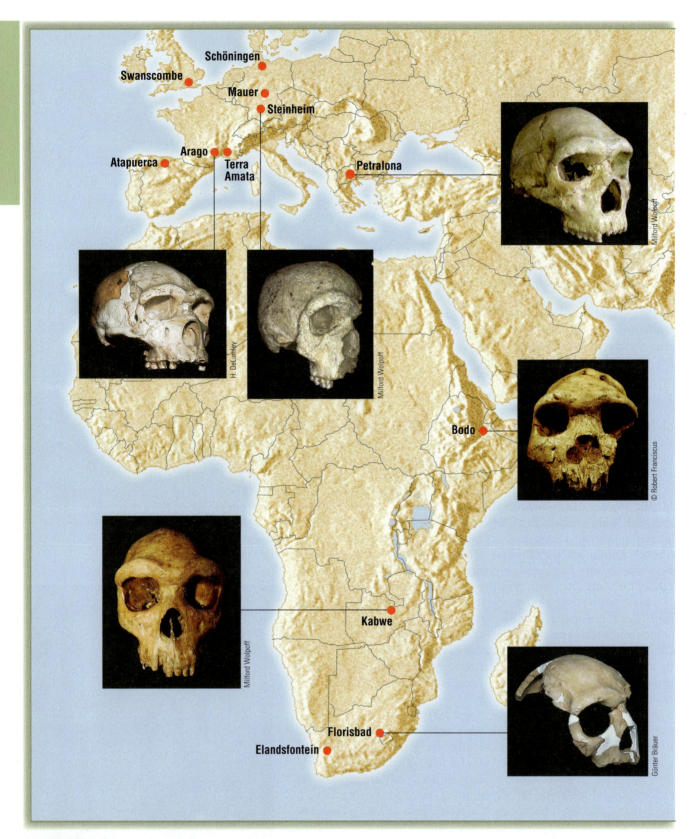

FIGURE 10-6

Fossil discoveries and archaeological localities of Middle Pleistocene premodern hominids.

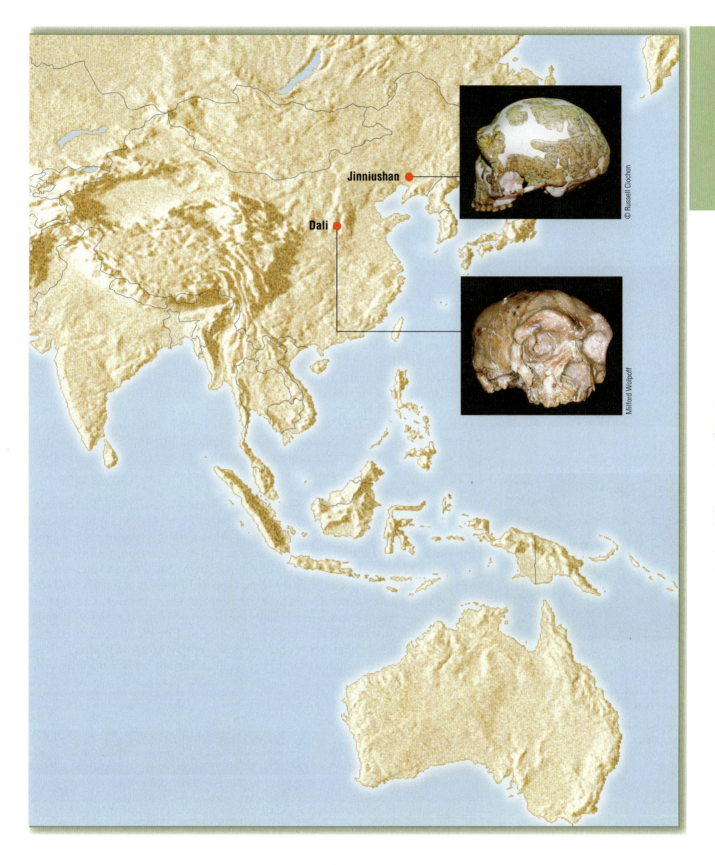

Jinniushan

Dali

QUICK REVIEW	Key Premodern Human (*H. heidelbergensis*) Fossils from Europe	
DATES	**SITE**	**EVOLUTIONARY SIGNIFICANCE**
259,000?–300,000? ya	Swanscombe England	Partial skull, but shows considerable brain expansion
530,000–600,000 ya	Atapuerca (Sima de los Huesos) northern Spain	Large sample; very early evidence of Neandertal ancestry (>500,000 ya); earliest evidence of deliberate disposal anywhere

Asia

Like their contemporaries in Europe and Africa, Asian premodern specimens discovered in China also display both earlier and later characteristics. Chinese paleoanthropologists suggest that the more ancestral traits, such as a sagittal ridge (see p. 200) and flattened nasal bones, are shared with *H. erectus* fossils from Zhoukoudian. They also point out that some of these features can be found in modern *H. sapiens* in China today, indicating substantial genetic continuity. That is, some Chinese researchers have argued that anatomically, modern Chinese didn't evolve from *H. sapiens* in either Europe or Africa; instead, they evolved specifically in China from a separate *H. erectus* lineage. Whether such regional evolution occurred or whether anatomically modern migrants from Africa displaced local populations is the subject of a major ongoing debate in paleoanthropology. This important controversy will be the central focus of the next chapter.

Dali, the most complete skull of the later Middle or early Late Pleistocene fossils in China, displays *H. erectus* and *H. sapiens* traits, with a cranial capacity of 1,120 cm^3 (Fig. 10-7). Like Dali, several other Chinese specimens combine both earlier and later traits. In addition, a partial skeleton from Jinniushan, in northeast China, has been given a provisional date of 200,000 ya (Tiemel et al., 1994). The cranial capacity is fairly large (approximately 1,260 cm^3), and the walls of the braincase are thin. These are both modern features, and they're somewhat unexpected in an individual this ancient—if the dating estimate is indeed correct. Just how to classify these Chinese Middle Pleistocene hominids has been a subject of debate and controversy. Recently, though, a leading paleoanthropologist has concluded that they're regional variants of *H. heidelbergensis* (Rightmire, 2004).

(a)

(b)

FIGURE 10-7

(a) Dali skull and (b) Jinniushan skull, both from China. These two crania are considered by some to be Asian representatives of *Homo heidelbergensis*.

QUICK REVIEW	Key Premodern Human (*H. heidelbergensis*) Fossils from Asia	
DATES	**SITE**	**EVOLUTIONARY SIGNIFICANCE**
180,000–230,000 ya	Dali China	Nearly complete skull; best evidence of *H. heidelbergensis* in Asia
200,000 ya	Jinniushan China	Partial skeleton with cranium showing relatively large brain size; some Chinese scholars suggest it as possible ancestor of early Chinese *H. sapiens*

A Review of Middle Pleistocene Evolution

Premodern human fossils from Africa and Europe resemble each other more than they do the hominids from Asia. The mix of some ancestral characteristics—retained from *Homo erectus* ancestors—with more derived features gives the African and European fossils a distinctive look; thus, Middle Pleistocene hominids from these two continents are usually referred to as *H. heidelbergensis*.

The situation in Asia isn't so tidy. To some researchers, the remains, especially those from Jinniushan, seem more modern than do contemporary fossils from either Europe or Africa. This observation explains why Chinese paleoanthropologists and some American colleagues conclude that the Jinniushan remains are early members of *H. sapiens*. Other researchers (for example, Rightmire, 1998, 2004) suggest that they represent a regional branch of *H. heidelbergensis*.

The Pleistocene world forced many small populations into geographical isolation. Most of these regional populations no doubt died out. Some, however, did evolve, and their descendants are likely a major part of the later hominid fossil record. In Africa, *H. heidelbergensis* is hypothesized to have evolved into modern *H. sapiens*. In Europe, *H. heidelbergensis* evolved into Neandertals. Meanwhile, the Chinese premodern populations may all have met with extinction. Right now, though, there's no consensus on the status or the likely fate of these enigmatic Asian Middle Pleistocene hominids (Fig. 10-8).

Middle Pleistocene Culture

The Acheulian technology of *H. erectus* carried over into the Middle Pleistocene with relatively little change until near the end of the period, when it became slightly more sophisticated. Bone, a very useful tool material, was apparently practically unused during this time. Stone flake tools similar to those of the earlier era persisted, possibly in greater variety. Some of the later premodern humans in Africa and Europe invented a method—the Levallois technique (Fig. 10-9)—for controlling flake size and shape. Requiring several coordinated steps, this was no easy feat, and it suggests increased cognitive abilities in later premodern populations.

Interpreting the distribution of artifacts during the later Middle Pleistocene has generated considerable discussion among archaeologists. As we noted in Chapter 9,

FIGURE 10-8

Time line of Middle Pleistocene hominids. Note that most dates are approximations. Question marks indicate those estimates that are most tentative.

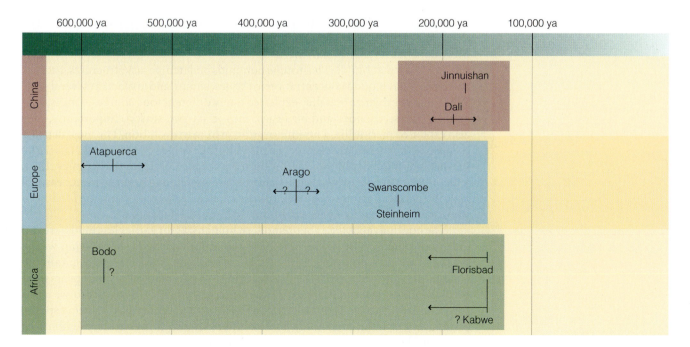

Nodule

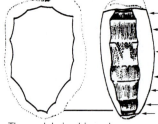

The nodule is chipped on the perimeter.

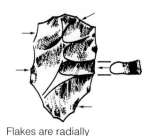

Flakes are radially removed from top surface.

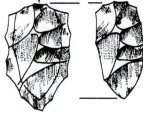

A final blow struck at one end removes a large flake. The flake on the right is the "target design"; that is, it is the goal of the whole process and is the completed tool.

FIGURE 10-9
The Levallois technique.

a general geographical distribution characterizes the Early Pleistocene, with bifaces (mostly hand axes) found quite often at sites in Africa, only rarely at sites in most of Asia, and not at all among the rich assemblage at Zhoukoudian. Also, where hand axes proliferate, the stone tool industry is referred to as Acheulian. At localities without hand axes, various other terms are used—for example, *chopper/chopping tool,* which is a misnomer, since most of the tools are actually flakes.

Acheulian assemblages have been found at many African sites as well as numerous European ones—for example, Swanscombe (England) and Arago (France). Even though there are broad geographical patterns in the distribution of what we call Acheulian, this shouldn't blind us to the considerable intraregional diversity in stone tool industries. Clearly, a variety of European sites do show a typical Acheulian complex, rich in bifacial hand axes and cleavers. However, at other contemporaneous sites in Germany and Hungary, fieldworkers found a variety of small retouched flake tools and flaked pebbles of various sizes, but no hand axes. So it seems that different stone tool industries coexisted in some areas for long periods, and various explanations (Villa, 1983) have been offered to account for this apparent diversity. Some say that different groups of hominids may have produced the tool industries; others suggest that the same group may have produced them when performing different activities at different sites. The type of stone tool manufactured was also affected by the amount and quality of workable rock in the immediate area.

Premodern human populations continued to live both in caves and in open-air sites, but they may have increased their use of caves. Did these hominids control fire? Klein (1999), in interpreting archaeological evidence from France, Germany, and Hungary, suggests that they did. What's more, Chinese archaeologists insist that many Middle Pleistocene sites in China contain evidence of human-controlled fire. Still, not everyone is convinced.

We know that Middle Pleistocene hominids built temporary structures, because researchers have found concentrations of bones, stones, and artifacts at several sites. We also have evidence that they exploited many different food sources—fruits, vegetables, fish, seeds, nuts, and bird eggs, each in its own season. Importantly, they also exploited marine life, a new innovation in human evolution. The most detailed reconstruction of Middle Pleistocene life in Europe comes from Terra Amata, a site in what is now the city of Nice, in southern France (de Lumley and de Lumley, 1973; Villa, 1983). This site provides fascinating evidence relating to short-term, seasonal visits by hominid groups, who built flimsy shelters, gathered plants, ate food from the ocean, and possibly hunted medium- to large-sized mammals.

The hunting capabilities of premodern humans, as for earlier hominids, are still greatly disputed. Most researchers have found little evidence supporting widely practiced advanced hunting. Some more recent finds, however, are beginning to change this view—especially the discovery in 1995 of remarkable wood spears from the Schöningen site in Germany. These large, extremely well-preserved weapons (provisionally dated to about 400,000 ya) were most likely used as throwing spears, presumably to hunt large animals. Also interesting in this context, the bones of numerous horses were recovered at Schöningen.

As documented by the fossil remains as well as artifactual evidence from archae-ological sites, the long period of transitional hominids in Europe continued well into the Late Pleistocene (after 125,000 ya)., But with the appearance and expansion of the Neandertals, the evolution of premodern humans took a unique turn.

Neandertals: Premodern Humans of the Late Pleistocene

Since their discovery more than a century ago, the Neandertals have haunted the minds and foiled the best-laid theories of paleoanthropologists. They fit into the general scheme of human evolution, and yet they're misfits. Classified variously either as *H. sapiens* or as belonging to a separate species, they are like us and yet different. It's not easy to put them in their place. Many anthropologists classify Neandertals within *H. sapiens,* but as a distinctive subspecies, *Homo sapiens neanderthalensis,** with modern *H. sapiens* designated as *Homo sapiens sapiens.* However, not all experts agree with this interpretation. The wide consensus that *Homo heidelbergensis* was a likely ancestor of both Neandertals and modern *Homo sapiens* as well as new archaeological and crucial genetic data have all led to the increasingly common placement of Neandertals into a separate species: *Homo neanderthalensis.*

Neandertal fossil remains have been found at dates approaching 130,000 ya; but in the following discussion of Neandertals, we'll focus on those populations that lived especially during the last major glaciation, which began about 75,000 ya and ended about 10,000 ya (Fig. 10-10). We should also note that the evolutionary roots of Neandertals apparently reach quite far back in western Europe, as evidenced by the 500,000+-year-old remains from Sima de los Huesos, Atapuerca, in northern Spain. The majority of fossils have been found in Europe, where they've been most studied. Our description of Neandertals is based primarily on those specimens, usually called *classic* Neandertals, from western Europe. Not all Neandertals—including others from eastern Europe and western Asia and those from the inter-glacial period just before the last glacial one—exactly fit our description of the classic morphology. They tend to be less robust, possibly because the climate in which they lived was not as cold as in western Europe during the last glaciation.

One striking feature of Neandertals is brain size, which in these hominids actu-ally was larger than that of *H. sapiens* today. The average for contemporary *H. sapi-ens* is between 1,300 and 1,400 cm³, while for Neandertals it was 1,520 cm³. The larger size may be associated with the metabolic efficiency of a larger brain in cold weather. The Inuit (Eskimo), also living in very cold areas, have a larger average brain size than most other modern human populations. We should also point out that the larger brain size in both premodern and contemporary human populations adapted to *cold* climates is partially correlated with larger body size, which has also evolved among these groups (see Chapter 12).

The classic Neandertal cranium is large, long, low, and bulging at the sides. Viewed from the side, the occipital bone is somewhat bun-shaped, but the marked occipital angle typical of many *H. erectus* crania is absent. The forehead rises more vertically than that of *H. erectus,* and the browridges arch over the orbits instead of forming a straight bar (Fig. 10-11).

Compared with anatomically modern humans, the Neandertal face stands out. It projects almost as if it were pulled forward. Postcranially, Neandertals were very

---

* *Thal,* meaning "valley," is the old spelling; but due to rules of taxonomic naming, this spelling is retained in the formal species designation *Homo neanderthalensis* (although the *h* was *never* pronounced). The modern spelling, *tal,* is now used this way in Germany; we follow contemporary usage in the text with the spelling of the colloquial *Neandertal.*

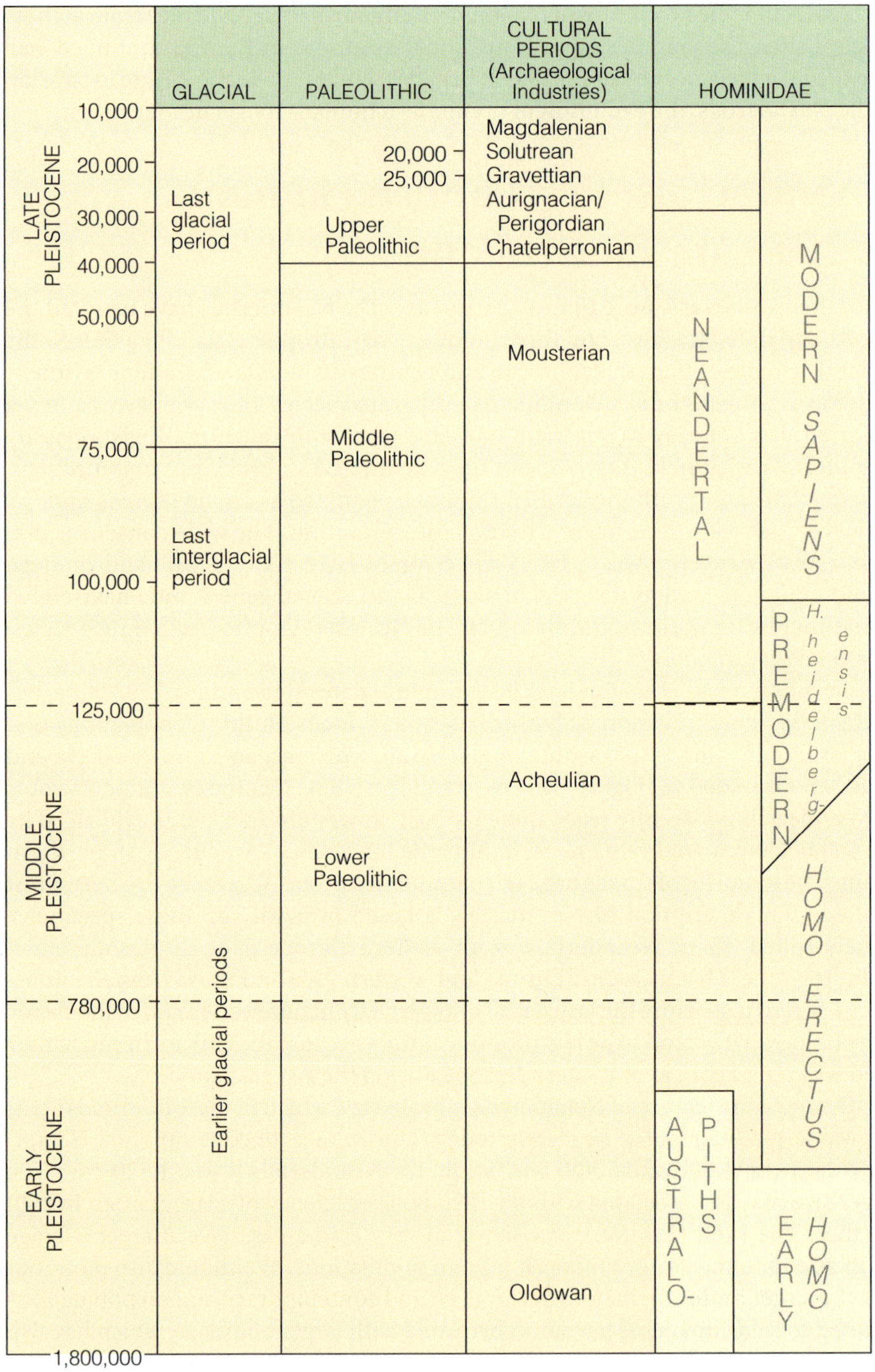

FIGURE 10-10

Correlation of Pleistocene subdivisions with archaeological industries and hominids. Note that the geological divisions are separate and different from the archaeological stages (e.g., Late Pleistocene is *not* synonymous with Upper Paleolithic).

robust, barrel-chested, and powerfully muscled. This robust skeletal structure, in fact, dominates hominid evolution from *H. erectus* through all premodern forms. Still, the Neandertals appear particularly robust, with shorter limbs than seen in most modern *H. sapiens* populations. Both the facial anatomy and the robust postcranial structure of Neandertals have been interpreted by Erik Trinkaus, of Washington University in St. Louis, as adaptations to rigorous living in a cold climate.

For about 100,000 years, Neandertals lived in Europe and western Asia (Fig. 10-12), and their coming and going have raised more questions and controversies than for any other hominid group. As we've noted, Neandertal forebears were transitional forms dating to the later Middle Pleistocene. However, it's not until the Late Pleistocene that Neandertals become fully recognizable.

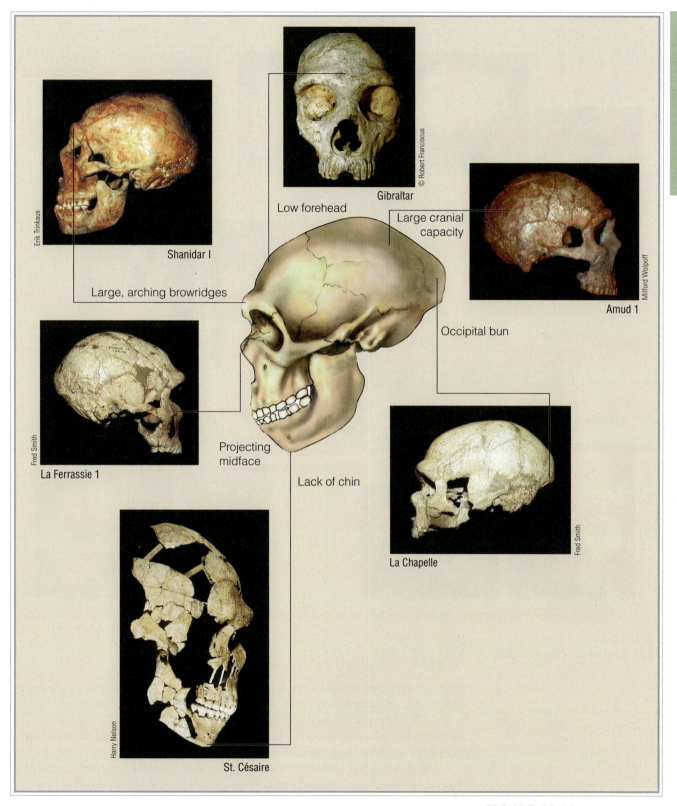

Shanidar I

Gibraltar

Low forehead

Large cranial capacity

Amud 1

Large, arching browridges

Occipital bun

La Ferrassie 1

Projecting midface

Lack of chin

La Chapelle

St. Césaire

FIGURE 10-11

Morphology and variation in Neandertal crania.

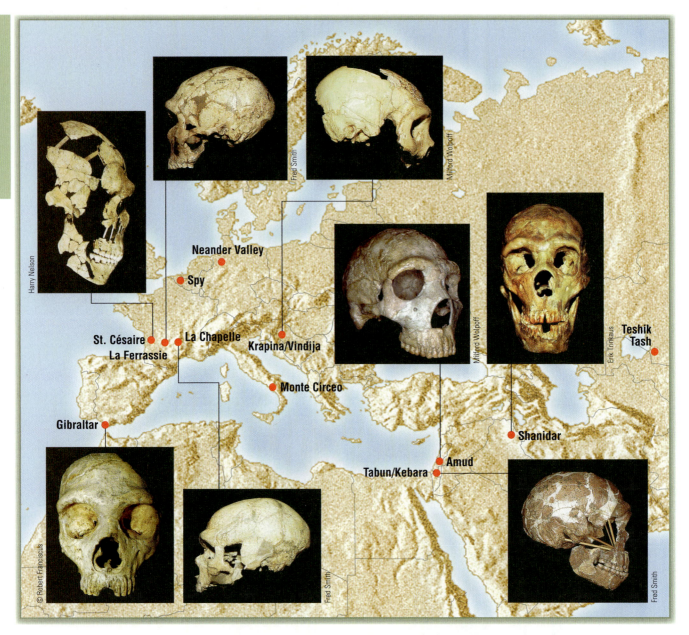

FIGURE 10-12
Fossil discoveries of Neandertals.

Western Europe

One of the most important Neandertal discoveries was made in 1908 at La Chapelle-aux-Saints, in southwestern France. A nearly complete skeleton was found buried in a shallow grave in a **flexed** position. Several fragments of nonhuman long bones had been placed over the head, and over them, a bison leg. Around the body were flint tools and broken animal bones.

The skeleton was turned over for study to a well-known French paleontologist, Marcellin Boule, who depicted the La Chapelle Neandertal as a brutish, bent-kneed, not fully erect biped. Because of this exaggerated interpretation, some scholars, and certainly the general public, concluded that all Neandertals were highly primitive creatures.

Why did Boule draw these conclusions from the La Chapelle skeleton? Today, we think he misjudged the Neandertal posture because this adult male skeleton had osteoarthritis of the spine. Also, and probably more important, Boule and his contemporaries found it difficult to fully accept as a human ancestor an individual who appeared in any way to depart from the modern pattern.

flexed The position of the body in a bent orientation, with arms and legs drawn up to the chest.

The skull of this male, who was possibly at least 40 years of age when he died, is very large, with a cranial capacity of 1,620 cm³. Typical of western European classic forms, the vault is low and long; the browridges are immense, with the typical Neandertal arched shape; the forehead is low and retreating; and the face is long and projecting. The back of the skull is protuberant and bun-shaped (Figs. 10-11 and 10-13).

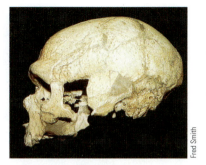

FIGURE 10-13
La Chapelle-aux-Saints. Note the occipital bun, projecting face, and low vault.

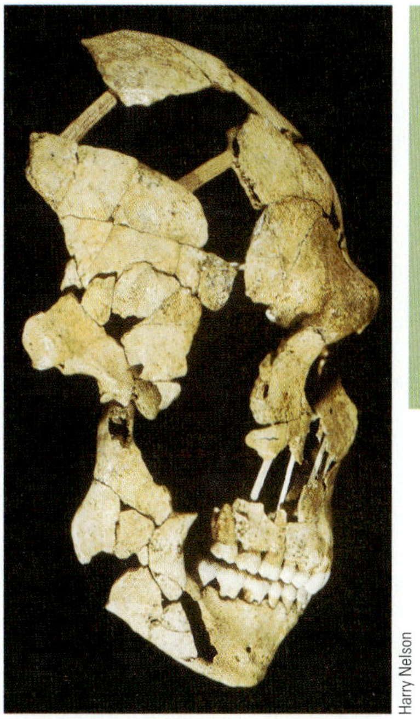

The La Chapelle skeleton isn't a typical Neandertal, but an unusually robust male who "evidently represents an extreme in the Neandertal range of variation" (Brace et al., 1979, p. 117). Unfortunately, this skeleton, which Boule claimed didn't even walk completely erect, was widely accepted as "Mr. Neandertal." But not all Neandertal individuals express the suite of classic Neandertal traits to the degree seen in this one (see Fig. 10-11).

Some of the most recent of the western European Neandertals come from St. Césaire in southwestern France and are dated at about 35,000 ya (Fig. 10-14). The bones were recovered from a bed including discarded chipped blades, hand axes, and other stone tools of an **Upper Paleolithic** tool industry associated with Neandertals. And at another late site in central Europe, radiocarbon dating points to the most recent Neandertal remains at Vindija, in Croatia (discussed shortly), at about 32,000 to 33,000 years old (Smith et al., 1999).

The St. Césaire and Vindija sites are important for several reasons. Anatomically modern humans were living in central and western Europe by about 35,000 ya or a bit earlier. So it's possible that Neandertals and modern *H. sapiens* were living quite close to each other for several thousand years (Fig. 10-15). How did these two groups interact? Evidence from a number of French sites indicates that Neandertals may

FIGURE 10-14
St. Césaire, among the "last" Neandertals.

Upper Paleolithic A cultural period usually associated with modern humans, but also found with some Neandertals, and distinguished by technological innovation in various stone tool industries. Best known from western Europe, similar industries are also known from central and eastern Europe and Africa.

FIGURE 10-15
Time line for Neandertal fossil discoveries.

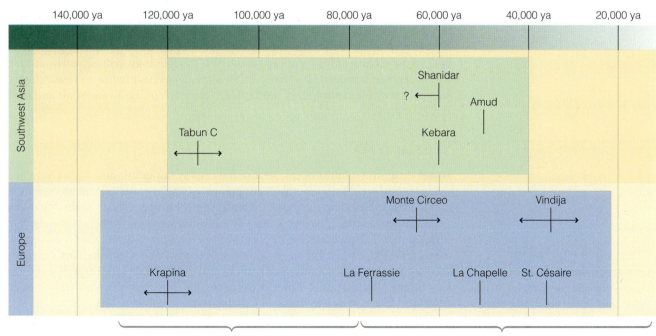

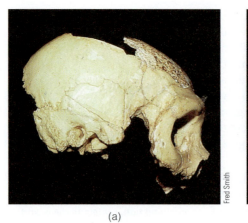
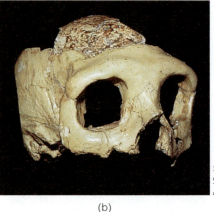

Fred Smith

Fred Smith

(a)   (b)

FIGURE 10-16
Krapina C. (a) Lateral view showing characteristic Neandertal traits. (b) Three-quarters view.

have borrowed technological methods and tools (such as blades) from the anatomically modern populations and thereby modified their own tools, creating a new industry, the **Chatelperronian.**

Central Europe

There are quite a few other European classic Neandertals, including significant finds in central Europe (see Fig. 10-12). At Krapina, Croatia, researchers have recovered an abundance of bones—1,000 fragments representing up to 70 individuals—and 1,000 stone tools or flakes (Trinkaus and Shipman, 1992). Krapina is an old site, possibly the earliest showing the full classic Neandertal morphology, dating back to the beginning of the Late Pleistocene (estimated at 130,000–110,000 ya). And despite the relatively early date, the characteristic Neandertal features of the Krapina specimens, although less robust, are similar to the western European finds (Fig. 10-16). Krapina is also important as an intentional burial site—one of the oldest on record.

About 30 miles from Krapina, Neandertal fossils have also been discovered at Vindija. The site is an excellent source of faunal, cultural, and hominid materials stratified in *sequence* throughout much of the Late Pleistocene. Neandertal fossils consisting of some 35 specimens are dated between about 42,000 and 32,000 ya. (The latter date would be the best verified of the more recent Neandertal discoveries; Higham et al., 2006.) While the overall anatomical pattern is definitely Neandertal, some features of the Vindija individuals, such as smaller browridges and slight chin development, approach the morphology seen in early modern south-central European *H. sapiens*. These similarities have led some researchers to suggest a possible evolutionary link between the late Vindija Neandertals and modern *H. sapiens*.

Western Asia

Israel   In addition to European Neandertals, many important discoveries have been made in southwest Asia. Several specimens from Israel display some modern features and are less robust than the classic Neandertals of Europe, though again, the overall pattern is Neandertal. The best known of these discoveries is from Tabun—short for Mugharet-et-Tabun, meaning "cave of the oven"—at Mt. Carmel, a short drive south from Haifa (Fig. 10-17). Tabun, excavated in the early 1930s, yielded a female skeleton, recently dated by thermoluminescence (TL) at about 120,000–110,000 ya. If this dating is accurate, Neandertals at Tabun were generally contemporary with early modern *H. sapiens* found in nearby caves. (TL dating is discussed on p. 172.)

A more recent Neandertal burial, a male discovered in 1983, comes from Kebara, a neighboring cave of Tabun at Mt. Carmel. A partial skeleton, dated to 60,000 ya,

Chatelperronian   Pertaining to an Upper Paleolithic industry found in France and Spain, containing blade tools and associated with Neandertals.

Harry Nelson

FIGURE 10-17
Excavation of the Tabun Cave, Mt. Carmel, Israel.

contains the most complete Neandertal pelvis so far recovered. Also recovered at Kebara is a hyoid—a small bone located in the throat, and the first ever found from a Neandertal; this bone is especially important because of its usefulness in reconstructing language capabilities.*

Iraq   A most remarkable site is Shanidar cave, in the Zagros Mountains of northeastern Iraq, where fieldworkers found partial skeletons of nine individuals, four of them deliberately buried. Among these individuals is a particularly interesting one called Shanidar 1. This is a skeleton of a male who lived to be approximately 30 to 45 years old, a considerable age for a prehistoric human (Fig. 10-18). His height is estimated at 5 feet 7 inches, and his cranial capacity is 1,600 cm³. Shanidar 1 also exhibits several other fascinating features:

> There had been a crushing blow to the left side of the head, fracturing the eye socket, displacing the left eye, and probably causing blindness on that side. He also sustained a massive blow to the right side of the body that so badly damaged the right arm that it became withered and useless; the bones of the shoulder blade, collar bone, and upper arm are much smaller and thinner than those on the left. The right lower arm and hand are missing, probably not because of poor preservation . . . but because they either atrophied and dropped off or because they were amputated. (Trinkaus and Shipman, 1992, p. 340)

Besides these injuries, the man had further trauma to both legs, and he probably limped. It's hard to imagine how he could have performed day-to-day activities. This is why Erik Trinkaus, who has studied the Shanidar remains, suggests that to survive, Shanidar 1 must have been helped by others: "A one-armed, partially blind, crippled man could have made no pretense of hunting or gathering his own food. That he survived for years after his trauma was a testament to Neandertal compassion and humanity" (Trinkaus and Shipman, 1992, p. 341).

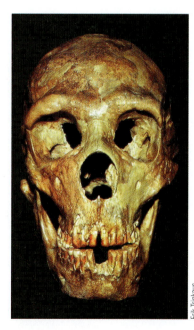

Erik Trinkaus

FIGURE 10-18
Shanidar 1. Does he represent Neandertal compassion for the disabled?

---

* The Kebara hyoid is identical to that of modern humans, suggesting that Neandertals did not differ from modern *H. sapiens sapiens* in this key element.

Key Neandertal Fossil Discoveries

DATES	SITE	EVOLUTIONARY SIGNIFICANCE
30,000 ya — 40,000 ya — 50,000 ya — 60,000 ya — 70,000 ya — 80,000 ya — 90,000 ya — 100,000 ya —	Vindija (Croatia)	Large sample (best evidence of Neandertals in eastern Europe); latest well-dated Neandertal site
	La Chapelle (France)	Most famous Neandertal site; historically provided early, but distorted, interpretation of Neandertals
	Shanidar (Iraq)	Several well-preserved skeletons; good example of Neandertals from southwestern Asia; one individual with multiple injuries
	Tabun (Israel)	Well-preserved and very well-studied fossils showing early evidence of Neandertals in southwestern Asia

Culture of Neandertals

Anthropologists almost always associate Neandertals, who lived in the cultural period known as the Middle Paleolithic, with the **Mousterian** industry—although they don't always associate the Mousterian industry with Neandertals. Early in the last glacial period, Mousterian culture extended across Europe and North Africa into the former Soviet Union, Israel, Iran, and as far east as central Asia and possibly even China. Also, in sub-Saharan Africa, the contemporaneous Middle Stone Age industry is broadly similar to the Mousterian.

Technology

Mousterian Pertaining to the stone tool industry associated with Neandertals and some modern *H. sapiens* groups; also called Middle Paleolithic. This industry is characterized by a larger proportion of flake tools than is found in Acheulian tool kits.

Neandertals improved on previous prepared-core techniques—that is, the Levallois—by inventing a new variation. They trimmed a flint nodule around the edges to form a disk-shaped core. Each time they struck the edge, they produced a flake, and they kept at it until the core became too small and was discarded. In this way, they produced more flakes per core than their predecessors did. They then reworked the flakes into various forms, including scrapers, points, and knives (Fig. 10-19).

Neandertal craftspeople elaborated and diversified traditional methods, and there's some indication that they developed specialized tools for skinning and pre-

FIGURE 10-19

Examples of the Mousterian tool kit, including (from left to right), a Levallois point, a perforator, and a side scraper.

© Randall White

paring meat, hunting, woodworking, and hafting. Even so, in strong contrast to the next cultural period, the Upper Paleolithic, there's almost no evidence that they used bone tools. Still, Neandertals advanced their technology well beyond that of earlier hominids. It's possible that their technological advances helped provide part of the basis for the remarkable changes of the Upper Paleolithic, which we'll discuss in the next chapter.

Subsistence

We know, from the abundant remains of animal bones at their sites, that Neandertals were successful hunters. But while it's clear that Neandertals could hunt large mammals, they may not have been as efficient at this task as were Upper Paleolithic hunters. For example, it wasn't until the beginning of the Upper Paleolithic that the spear-thrower, or atlatl, came into use (see p. 262). Soon after that, the bow and arrow greatly increased efficiency (and safety) in hunting large mammals. Because they had no long-distance weaponry and were mostly limited to thrusting spears, Neandertals may have been more prone to serious injury—a hypothesis supported by paleoanthropologists Thomas Berger and Erik Trinkaus. Berger and Trinkaus (1995) analyzed the pattern of trauma, particularly fractures, in Neandertals and compared it with that seen in contemporary human samples. Interestingly, the pattern in Neandertals, especially the relatively high proportion of head and neck injuries, was most similar to that seen in contemporary rodeo performers. Berger and Trinkaus concluded that "the similarity to the rodeo distribution suggests frequent close encounters with large ungulates unkindly disposed to the humans involved" (Berger and Trinkaus, 1995, p. 841).

We know much more about European Middle Paleolithic culture than any earlier period because it's been studied longer and by more scholars. Recently, however, Africa has been a target not only of physical anthropologists but also of archaeologists, who have added considerably to our knowledge of African Pleistocene hominid history. In many cases, the technology and assumed cultural adaptations in Africa were similar to those in Europe and southwest Asia. We'll see in the next chapter that the African technological achievements also kept pace with, or even preceded, those in western Europe.

Speech and Symbolic Behavior

There are a variety of hypotheses concerning the speech capacities of Neandertals, and many of these views are contradictory. Some researchers argue that Neandertals were incapable of human speech. But the prevailing consensus has been that they *were* capable of articulate speech, maybe even fully competent in the range of sounds produced by modern humans.

However, recent genetic evidence may call for a reassessment of just when fully human language first emerged (Enard et al., 2002). In humans today, mutations in a particular gene (locus) are known to produce serious language impairments. From an evolutionary perspective, what's perhaps most significant concerns the greater variability seen in the alleles at this locus in modern humans as compared to other primates. One explanation for this increased variation is intensified selection acting on human populations, and as we'll see shortly, DNA evidence from Neandertal fossils shows they had already made this transformation.

But even if we conclude that Neandertals *could* speak, it doesn't necessarily mean that their abilities were at the level of modern *Homo sapiens*. Today, paleoanthropologists are quite interested in the apparently sudden expansion of modern *H. sapiens* (discussed in Chapter 11), and they've proposed various explanations for this group's rapid success. Also, as we attempt to explain how and why modern *H. sapiens* expanded its geographical range, we're left with the problem of explaining what happened to the Neandertals. In making these types of interpretations,

TABLE 10.1	Cultural Contrasts* Between Neandertals and Upper Paleolithic Modern Humans
Neandertals	**Upper Paleolithic Modern Humans**
Tool Technology	
Numerous flake tools; few, however, apparently for highly specialized functions; use of bone, antler, or ivory very rare; relatively few tools with more than one or two parts	Many more varieties of stone tools; many apparently for specialized functions; frequent use of bone, antler, and ivory; many more tools comprised of two or more component parts
Hunting Efficiency and Weapons	
No long-distance hunting weapons; close-proximity weapons used (thus, more likelihood of injury)	Use of spear-thrower and bow and arrow; wider range of social contacts, perhaps permitting larger, more organized hunting parties (including game drives)
Stone Material Transport	
Stone materials transported only short distances—just "a few kilometers" (Klein, 1989)	Stone tool raw materials transported over much longer distances, implying wider social networks and perhaps trade
Art	
Artwork uncommon; usually small; probably mostly of a personal nature; some items perhaps misinterpreted as "art"; others may be intrusive from overlying Upper Paleolithic contexts; cave art absent	Artwork much more common, including transportable objects as well as elaborate cave art; well executed, using a variety of materials and techniques; stylistic sophistication
Burial	
Deliberate burial at several sites; graves unelaborated; graves frequently lack artifacts	Burials much more complex, frequently including both tools and remains of animals

*The contrasts are more apparent in some areas (particularly western Europe) than others (eastern Europe, Near East). Elsewhere (Africa, eastern Asia), where there were no Neandertals, the cultural situation is quite different. Even in western Europe, the cultural transformations weren't necessarily abrupt but may have developed more gradually from Mousterian to Upper Paleolithic times. For example, Straus (1995) argues that many of the Upper Paleolithic features weren't consistently manifested until after 20,000 ya.

a growing number of paleoanthropologists suggest that *behavioral* differences are the key.

Researchers believe that Upper Paleolithic *H. sapiens* had some significant behavioral advantages over Neandertals and other premodern humans. Was it some kind of new and expanded ability to symbolize, communicate, organize social activities, elaborate technology, obtain a wider range of food resources, or care for the sick or injured—or was it some other factor? Compared with modern *H. sapiens,* were the Neandertals limited by neurological differences that may have contributed to their demise?

The direct anatomical evidence derived from Neandertal fossils isn't much help in answering these questions. Ralph Holloway (1985) has maintained that Neandertal brains—at least as far as the fossil evidence suggests—aren't significantly different from those of modern *H. sapiens.* What's more, as we've seen, Neandertal vocal tracts (as well as other morphological features), compared with our own, don't appear to have seriously limited them.

Most of the reservations about advanced cognitive abilities in Neandertals are based on archaeological data. Interpretation of Neandertal sites, when compared with succeeding Upper Paleolithic sites—especially those documented in western Europe—have led to several intriguing contrasts, as shown in Table 10-1.

From this type of behavioral and anatomical evidence, Neandertals in recent years have increasingly been viewed as an evolutionary dead end. Right now, we can't say whether their disappearance and ultimate replacement by anatomically modern Upper Paleolithic peoples—with their presumably "superior" culture—was the result of cultural differences alone or whether it was also influenced by biological variation.

Burials

Anthropologists have known for some time that Neandertals deliberately buried their dead. Undeniably, the spectacular discoveries at La Chapelle, Shanidar, and elsewhere were the direct results of ancient burial, which permits preservation that's much more complete. Such deliberate burial treatment goes back at least 90,000 years at Tabun. From a much older site, some form of consistent "disposal" of the dead—not necessarily belowground burial—is evidenced: At Atapuerca, Spain, more than 700 fossilized elements (representing at least 28 different individuals) were found in a cave at the end of a deep vertical shaft. From the nature of the site and the accumulation of hominid remains, Spanish researchers are convinced that the site demonstrates some form of human activity involving deliberate disposal of the dead (Arsuaga et al., 1997).

The recent redating of Atapuerca to more than 500,000 ya suggests that Neandertals—more precisely, their immediate precursors—were, by quite early in the Middle Pleistocene, handling their dead in special ways. Such behavior was previously thought to have emerged only much later, in the Late Pleistocene. As far as current data indicate, this practice is seen in western European contexts well before it appears in Africa or eastern Asia. For example, in the premodern sites at Kabwe and Florisbad (discussed earlier), deliberate disposal of the dead is not documented. Nor is it seen in African early modern sites—for example, the Klasies River Mouth, dated at 120,000–100,000 ya (see p. 250).

Yet, in later contexts (after 35,000 ya), where modern *H. sapiens* remains are found in clear burial contexts, their treatment is considerably more complex than in Neandertal burials. In these later (Upper Paleolithic) sites, grave goods, including bone and stone tools as well as animal bones, are found more consistently and in greater concentrations. Because many Neandertal sites were excavated in the nineteenth or early twentieth century, before more rigorous archaeological methods had been developed, many of these supposed burials are now in question. Still, the evidence seems quite clear that deliberate burial was practiced at several localities. In many cases, the body's *position* was deliberately modified and placed in the grave in a flexed posture (see p. 230).

Finally, as further evidence of Neandertal symbolic behavior, researchers point to the placement of supposed grave goods in burials, including stone tools, animal bones (such as cave bear), and even arrangements of flowers, together with stone slabs on top of the burials. Unfortunately, in many instances, again due to poorly documented excavation, these finds are questionable. Placement of stone tools, for example, is occasionally seen, but it apparently wasn't done consistently. In those 33 Neandertal burials for which we have adequate data, only 14 show definite association of stone tools and/or animal bones with the deceased (Klein, 1989). It's not until the next cultural period, the Upper Paleolithic, that we see a major behavioral shift, as demonstrated in more elaborate burials and development of art.

Genetic Evidence

With the revolutionary advances in molecular biology (discussed in Chapter 3), fascinating new avenues of research have become possible in the study of earlier hominids. It's becoming fairly commonplace to extract, amplify, and sequence ancient DNA from contexts spanning the last 10,000 years or so. For example, researchers have analyzed DNA from the 5,000-year-old "Iceman" found in the Italian Alps.

It's much harder to find usable DNA in even more ancient remains, since the organic components, often including the DNA, have been destroyed during the mineralization process. Still, in the past few years, exciting results have been announced about DNA found in 12 different Neandertal fossils dated between 32,000 and 50,000 ya. These fossils come from sites in France (including La

Chapelle), Germany (from the original Neander Valley locality), Belgium, Italy, Spain, Croatia, and Russia (Krings et al., 1997, 2000; Ovchinnikov et al., 2000; Schmitz et al., 2002; Serre et al., 2004; Green et al., 2006). Newly ascertained ancient DNA evidence strongly suggests that other fossils from central Asia (Uzbekistan and southern Siberia) dated at 38,000–30,000 ya are also Neandertals (Pennisi, 2007).

The technique most often used in studying the Neandertal fossils involves extracting mitochondrial DNA (mtDNA), amplifying it through polymerase chain reaction (PCR; see p. 52), and sequencing nucleotides in parts of the molecule. Results from the Neandertal specimens show that these individuals are genetically more different from contemporary *Homo sapiens* populations than modern human populations are from each other—in fact, about three times as much. Consequently, Krings and colleagues (1997) have hypothesized that the Neandertal lineage separated from that of our modern *H. sapiens* ancestors sometime between 690,000 and 550,000 ya.

Major advances in molecular biology have allowed much more of the Neandertal genetic pattern to be determined with the ability to now sequence big chunks of the *nuclear* DNA (which, as you may recall, contains more than 99 percent of the human genome). In fact, one group of researchers in Germany has already sequenced more than 1 million bases and will likely complete the sequencing for the entire Neandertal genome within the next few years (Green et al. 2006)! Just a couple of years ago this sort of possibility would have seemed like science fiction.

One immediate application of these remarkable new data is further confirmation of the suggested divergence dates derived from mitochondrial DNA. From the studies reported in 2006 and 2007 (Green et al. 2006; Noonan et al., 2006; Pennisi, 2007), the origins of the Neandertals have been traced to approximately 800,000–500,000 ya. Moreover, the early date (>500,000 ya) of the transitional Neandertal fossils at Atapuerca, Spain (Bischoff et al., 2007), further confirms this early divergence date. Lastly, the much more extensive Neandertal nuclear DNA patterns are as distinct from those of modern humans as are the differences seen in mtDNA. Considering the length of time that Neandertals were likely separate from the lineage of modern humans as well as their distinct genetic patterning, it seems reasonable that they should be considered a separate species—or at least a population well on its way to becoming separate (see p. 241).

As more specific areas of the Neandertal nuclear genome are investigated, even more significant information is surely forthcoming, and some of it might prove surprising. For example, one of the first two nuclear loci identified in Neandertals influences skin and hair pigmentation, and the other is thought to be a crucial locus influencing speech and language. The pigmentation locus indicates that at least some Neandertals were redheaded and also were likely light-skinned (Lalueza-Fox et al., 2007). These new data help confirm earlier hypotheses suggesting that Neandertals quite likely had light skin (see Chapter 12 for further discussion).

The second finding relates to the *FOXP2* locus, a genetic region thought to influence speech and language function in modern humans. Interestingly, two distinctive changes in this gene (point mutations) differ in humans from all other living primates, and these exact same genetic modifications have also been identified in Neandertals (Krause et al., 2007). So it appears that this evolutionary change is quite ancient, going back perhaps as far as 500,000 ya. Moreover, it shows that Neandertals did not differ genetically from us in this crucial respect. Did they, then, have full human language? Given that this highly complex behavior is controlled by dozens of genes, we can't really answer this question. For now, the very limited genetic information relating to language doesn't yet show any differences from us. As the two genomes are more closely compared, we should get a much better answer to this intriguing question.

Trends in Human Evolution: Understanding Premodern Humans

As you can see, the Middle Pleistocene hominids are a very diverse group, broadly dispersed through time and space. There is considerable variation among them, and it's not easy to get a clear evolutionary picture. Because we know that regional populations were small and frequently isolated, many of them probably died out and left no descendants. So it's a mistake to see an "ancestor" in every fossil find.

Still, as a group, these Middle Pleistocene premoderns do reveal some general trends. In many ways, for example, it seems that they were *transitional* between the hominid grade that came before them (*H. erectus*) and the one that followed them (modern *H. sapiens*). It's not a stretch to say that all the Middle Pleistocene premoderns derived from *H. erectus* forebears and that some of them, in turn, were probably ancestors of the earliest fully modern humans.

Paleoanthropologists are certainly concerned with such broad generalities as these, but they also want to focus on meaningful anatomical, environmental, and behavioral details as well as underlying processes. So they consider the regional variability displayed by particular fossil samples as significant—but just *how* significant is up for debate. In addition, increasingly sophisticated theoretical approaches are being used to better understand the processes that shaped the evolution of later *Homo,* at both macroevolutionary and microevolutionary levels.

Scientists, like all humans, assign names or labels to phenomena, a point we addressed in discussing classification in Chapter 5. Paleoanthropologists are certainly no exception. Yet, working from a common evolutionary foundation, paleoanthropologists still come to different conclusions about the most appropriate way to interpret the Middle/Late Pleistocene hominids. Consequently, a variety of species names have been proposed in recent years.

Paleoanthropologists who advocate an extreme lumping approach recognize only one species for all the premodern humans discussed in this chapter. These premoderns are classified as *Homo sapiens* and are thus lumped together with modern humans, although they're partly distinguished by such terminology as "archaic *H. sapiens*." As we've noted, this degree of lumping is no longer supported by most researchers. Alternatively, a second, less extreme view postulates modest species diversity and labels the earlier premoderns as *H. heidelbergensis* (Fig. 10-20a).

At the other end of the spectrum, more enthusiastic paleontological splitters have identified at least three species, all distinct from *H. sapiens.* Two of these, *H. heidelbergensis* and *H. neanderthalensis,* were discussed earlier; and a third species, called *Homo helmei,* has recently been proposed (Foley and Lahr, 1997; Lahr and Foley, 1998). It's been suggested that this last group is a possible African ancestor of *both* modern humans and Neandertals, but one that appears fairly late in the Middle Pleistocene (300,000–250,000 ya) and so comes largely after *H. heidelbergensis.* This more complex evolutionary interpretation is shown in Figure 10-20b.

We addressed similar differences of interpretation in Chapters 8 and 9, and we know that disparities like these can be frustrating to students who are new to paleoanthropology. The proliferation of new names is confusing, and it might seem that experts in the field are endlessly arguing about what to call the fossils.

Fortunately, it's not quite that bad. There's actually more agreement than you might think. No one doubts that all these hominids are closely related to each other as well as to modern humans. And everyone agrees that only some of the fossil samples represent populations that left descendants. Where paleoanthropologists disagree is when they start discussing which hominids are the most likely to be closely related to later hominids. The grouping of hominids into evolutionary clusters (clades) and assigning of different names to them is a reflection of differing interpretations—and, more fundamentally, of somewhat differing philosophies.

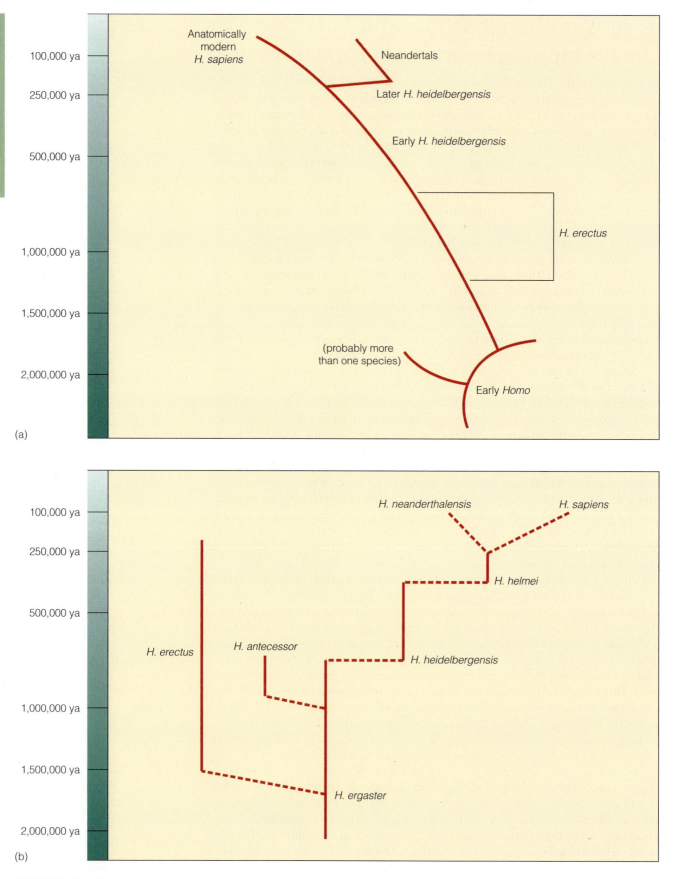

FIGURE 10-20

(a) Phylogeny of genus *Homo*. Only very modest species diversity is implied.

(b) Phylogeny of genus *Homo* showing considerable species diversity (after Foley, 2002).

But we shouldn't emphasize these naming and classification debates too much. Most paleoanthropologists recognize that a great deal of these disagreements result from simple, practical considerations. Even the most enthusiastic splitters acknowledge that the fossil "species" are not true species as defined by the biological species concept (see p. 86). As prominent paleoanthropologist Robert Foley puts it, "It is unlikely they are all biological species. . . . These are probably a mixture of real biological species and evolving lineages of subspecies. In other words, they could potentially have interbred, but owing to allopatry [that is, geographical separation] were unlikely to have had the opportunity" (Foley, 2002, p. 33).

Even so, Foley, along with an increasing number of other professionals, distinguishes these different fossil samples with species names to highlight their distinct position in hominid evolution. That is, these hominid groups are more loosely defined as a type of paleospecies (see p. 89) rather than as fully biological species. Giving distinct hominid samples a separate (species) name makes them more easily identifiable to other researchers and makes various cladistic hypotheses more explicit—and equally important, more directly testable.

The hominids that best illustrate these issues are the Neandertals. Fortunately, they're also the best known, represented by dozens of well-preserved individuals. With all this evidence, researchers can systematically test and evaluate many of the differing hypotheses.

Are Neandertals very closely related to modern *H. sapiens*? Certainly. Are they physically and behaviorally distinct from both ancient and fully modern humans? Yes. Does this mean that Neandertals are a fully separate biological species from modern humans and therefore theoretically incapable of fertilely interbreeding with modern people? Probably not. Finally, then, should Neandertals really be placed in a separate species from *H. sapiens*? For most purposes, it doesn't matter, since the distinction at some point is arbitrary. Speciation is, after all, a *dynamic* process. Fossil groups like the Neandertals represent just one point in this process (see Fig. 5-6, p. 86).

We can view Neandertals as a distinctive side branch of later hominid evolution. Similar to the situation among contemporary baboons—comparing savanna to hamadryas—we could say that Neandertals were an incipient species. Given enough time and enough isolation, they likely would have separated completely from their modern human contemporaries. The new DNA evidence suggests that they were well on their way, very likely approaching full speciation from *Homo sapiens*. But as some fossil and archaeological data are still suggesting, Neandertals perhaps never quite got that far. Their fate, in a sense, was decided for them as more successful competitors expanded into Neandertal habitats. These highly successful hominids were fully modern humans, and in the next chapter we'll focus on their story.

Summary

The Middle Pleistocene (780,000–125,000 ya) was a period of transition in human evolution. Fossil hominids from this period show similarities both with their predecessors (*H. erectus*) and with their successors (*H. sapiens*). They've also been found in many areas of the Old World, in Africa, Asia, and Europe—in the latter case, being the first truly successful occupants of that continent. Because these transitional hominids are more derived and more advanced in the human direction than *H. erectus,* we can refer to them as premodern humans. With this terminology, we also recognize that these hominids display several significant anatomical and behavioral differences from modern humans.

Although there's some dispute about the best way to formally classify the majority of Middle Pleistocene hominids, most paleoanthropologists now prefer to call them *H. heidelbergensis*. Similarities between the African and European Middle Pleistocene hominid samples suggest that they all can be reasonably seen as part of this same species. The contemporaneous Asian fossils, however, don't fit as neatly into this model, and conclusions regarding these premodern humans remain less definite.

Some of the later *H. heidelbergensis* populations in Europe likely evolved into Neandertals. Abundant Neandertal fossil and archaeological evidence has been collected from the Late Pleistocene time span of Neandertal existence, about 130,000–30,000 ya. But unlike their Middle Pleistocene (*H. heidelbergensis*) predecessors, Neandertals are more geographically restricted; they're found only in Europe and southwest Asia. Various lines of evidence—anatomical, archaeological, and genetic—also suggest that they were isolated and distinct from other hominids.

These observations have led to a growing consensus among paleoanthropologists that the Neandertals were largely a side branch of later hominid evolution. Still, there remain significant differences in theoretical approaches regarding how best to deal with the Neandertals; that is, should they be considered as a separate species or as a subspecies of *H. sapiens?* We suggest that the best way to view the Neandertals is within a dynamic process of speciation. Neandertals can thus be interpreted as an incipient species—one in the process of splitting from early *H. sapiens* populations.

In the What's Important feature, you'll find a useful summary of the most significant premodern human fossils discussed in this chapter.

WHAT'S IMPORTANT — Key Fossil Discoveries of Premodern Humans

DATES	REGION	SITE	HOMINID	THE BIG PICTURE
50,000 ya	Western Europe	La Chapelle (France)	Neandertal	Most famous Neandertal discovery; led to false interpretation of primitive, bent-over creature
110,000 ya	Southwestern Asia	Tabun (Israel)	Neandertal	Best evidence of early Neandertal morphology in S. W. Asia
130,000 ya	South Africa	Kabwe (Broken Hill, Zambia)	*H. heidelbergensis*	Transitional-looking fossil; perhaps a close ancestor of early *H. sapiens* in Africa
530,000–600,000 ya	Western Europe	Atapuerca (Sima de los Huesos)	*H. heidelbergensis* (early Neandertal)	Very early evidence of Neandertal ancestry; suggests Neandertals likely are a different species from *H. sapiens*
600,000 ya	East Africa	Bodo (Ethiopia)	*H. heidelbergensis*	Earliest evidence of *H. heidelbergensis* in Africa—and possibly ancestral to later *H. sapiens*

Question: Why should knowing the full genome of Neandertals help us learn something important about ourselves?

Answer: Neandertals are our closest not fully human cousin to ever walk the earth, but they disappeared more than 25,000 years ago. What we have left of them are some very nice fossils, of course. And now we also have begun to sequence their DNA (which is still found in many Neandertal fossils). Moreover, there is a good possibility that we'll soon know the entire Neandertal genomic pattern. Science fiction buffs could easily conjure Jurassic Park—like possibilities of re-creating a living Neandertal (an authentic one and even better than the misunderstood Neandertal seen in insurance ads defending the honor of his group). This is not as crazy as it may sound.

But far more important is what Neandertal DNA can tell us about ourselves. What exactly is it that makes us human, with our full use of language, artistic expression, human emotions, and so forth? Much of what makes the human animal such an unusual hominid is coded in perhaps just a few dozen genes that have been altered by evolution in just the last few hundred thousand years.

By looking at the precise sequences in Neandertal DNA, we have a good chance to see which specific genes have been modified. We can then try to find out how these genes function and begin to explain the biological bases of human intelligence and even perhaps the nature of consciousness.

Critical Thinking Questions

1   Why are the Middle Pleistocene hominids called premodern humans? In what ways are they human?

2   What is the general popular conception of Neandertals? Do you agree with this view? (Cite both anatomical and archaeological evidence to support your conclusion.)

3   Compare the skeleton of a Neandertal with that of a modern human. In which ways are they most alike? In which ways are they most different?

4   What evidence suggests that Neandertals deliberately buried their dead? Do you think the fact that they buried their dead is important? Why? How would you interpret this behavior (remembering that Neandertals were not identical to us)?

5   How are species defined, both for living animals and for extinct ones? Use the Neandertals to illustrate the problems encountered in distinguishing species among extinct hominids. Contrast specifically the interpretation of Neandertals as a distinct species with the interpretation of Neandertals as a subspecies of *H. sapiens*.

CHAPTER 11

The Origin and Dispersal of Modern Humans

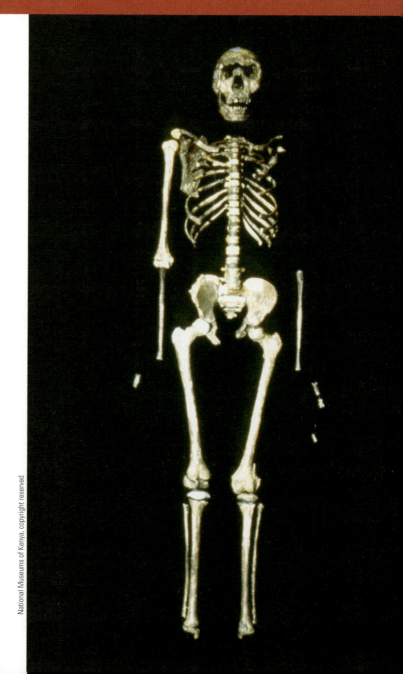

Is it possible to
determine when and
where modern people
first appeared?

FOCUS
QUESTION

Introduction

Today, our species numbers more than 6 billion individuals, scattered all over the globe, but there are no other living hominids but us. The last really close cousin of ours disappeared several thousand years ago. But about 30,000 years ago, modern peoples in Europe may have encountered beings that walked on two legs, hunted large animals, made fire, lived in caves, and fashioned complex tools. These beings were the Neandertals, and imagine what it would have been like to be among a band of modern peoples following game into what is now Croatia and coming across these other *humans,* so like yourself in some ways, so disturbingly odd in others. It's almost certain that such encounters took place, perhaps many times. How strange would it have been to look into the face of a being sharing so much with you, yet being a total stranger both culturally and, to some degree, biologically as well? What would you think seeing a Neandertal for the first time? What do you imagine they would think seeing you?

Sometime, probably close to 200,000 years ago, the first modern *Homo sapiens* evolved in Africa. Within 150,000 years or so, their descendants had spread across most of the Old World, even expanding as far as Australia (and somewhat later to the Americas).

Who were they, and why were these early modern people so successful? What was the fate of the other hominids, such as the Neandertals, who were already long established in areas outside Africa? Did they evolve as well, leaving descendants among some living human populations? Or were they completely swept aside and replaced by African emigrants?

In this chapter, we'll discuss the origin and dispersal of modern *H. sapiens.* All contemporary populations are placed within this species (and the same subspecies as well). Most paleoanthropologists agree that several fossil forms, dating back as far as 100,000 ya, should also be included in the same fully modern group as us. In addition, some recently discovered fossils from Africa also are clearly *H. sapiens,* but they show some (minor) differences from living people and could thus be described as near-modern. Still, we can think of these early African humans as well as their somewhat later relatives as "us."

These first modern humans, who evolved by 195,000 ya, are probably descendants of some of the premodern humans we discussed in Chapter 10. In particular, African populations of *H. heidelbergensis* are the most likely ancestors of the earliest modern *H. sapiens.* The evolutionary events that took place as modern humans made the transition from more ancient premodern forms and then dispersed throughout most of the Old World were relatively rapid, and they raise several basic questions:

1. When (approximately) did modern humans first appear?
2. Where did the transition take place? Did it occur in just one region or in several?

Click!

Go to the following media resources for interactive activities, more information, and study materials on topics covered in this chapter:

- Anthropology Resource Center
- Student Companion Website for *Essentials of Physical Anthropology,* Seventh Edition
- Online Virtual Laboratories for Physical Anthropology CD-ROM, Fourth Edition
- Hominid Fossils CD-ROM: An Interactive Atlas

3. What was the pace of evolutionary change? How quickly did the transition occur?

4. How did the dispersal of modern humans to other areas of the Old World (outside their area of origin) take place?

These questions concerning the origins and early dispersal of modern *Homo sapiens* continue to fuel much controversy among paleoanthropologists. And it's no wonder, for members of early *H. sapiens* are our direct ancestors, which makes them close relatives of all contemporary humans. They were much like us skeletally, genetically, and (most likely) behaviorally, too. In fact, it's the various hypotheses regarding the behaviors and abilities of our most immediate predecessors that have most fired the imaginations of scientists and laypeople alike. In every major respect, these are the first hominids that we can confidently refer to as *fully* human.

In this chapter, we'll also discuss archaeological evidence from the Upper Paleolithic (see p. 231). This evidence will give us a better understanding of the technological and social developments during the period when modern humans arose and quickly came to dominate the planet.

The evolutionary story of *Homo sapiens* is really the biological autobiography of all of us. It's a story that still has many unanswered questions; but several theories can help us organize the diverse information that's now available.

Approaches to Understanding Modern Human Origins

In attempting to organize and explain modern human origins, paleoanthropologists have developed two major theories: the complete replacement model and the regional continuity model. These two views are quite distinct, and in some ways they're completely opposed to each other. What's more, the popular press has further contributed to a wide and incorrect perception of irreconcilable argument on these points by "opposing" scientists. In fact, there's a third theory, which we call the partial replacement model, that's a kind of compromise, incorporating some aspects of the two major theories. Since so much of our contemporary view of modern human origins is influenced by the debates linked to these differing theories, let's start by briefly reviewing each one. Then we'll turn to the fossil evidence itself to see what it can contribute to answering the four questions we've posed.

The Complete Replacement Model: Recent African Evolution

The *complete replacement model* was developed by British paleoanthropologists Christopher Stringer and Peter Andrews (1988). It's based on the origin of modern humans in Africa and later replacement of populations in Europe and Asia (Fig. 11-1). This theory proposes that anatomically modern populations arose in Africa within the last 200,000 years and then migrated from Africa, *completely replacing* populations in Europe and Asia. It's important to note that this model doesn't account for a transition from premodern forms to modern *H. sapiens* anywhere in the world except Africa. A critical deduction of the Stringer and Andrews theory is that anatomically modern humans appeared as the result of a biological speciation event. So in this view, migrating African modern *H. sapiens* could not have interbred with local non-African populations, because the African modern humans were a *biologically* different species. Taxonomically, all of the premodern populations outside Africa would, in this view, be classified as belonging to different species of *Homo*. For example, the Neandertals would be classified as *H. neanderthalensis* (see p. 241 for further discussion). This speciation explanation fits nicely with, and in fact helps explain, *complete* replacement; but Stringer has more recently stated

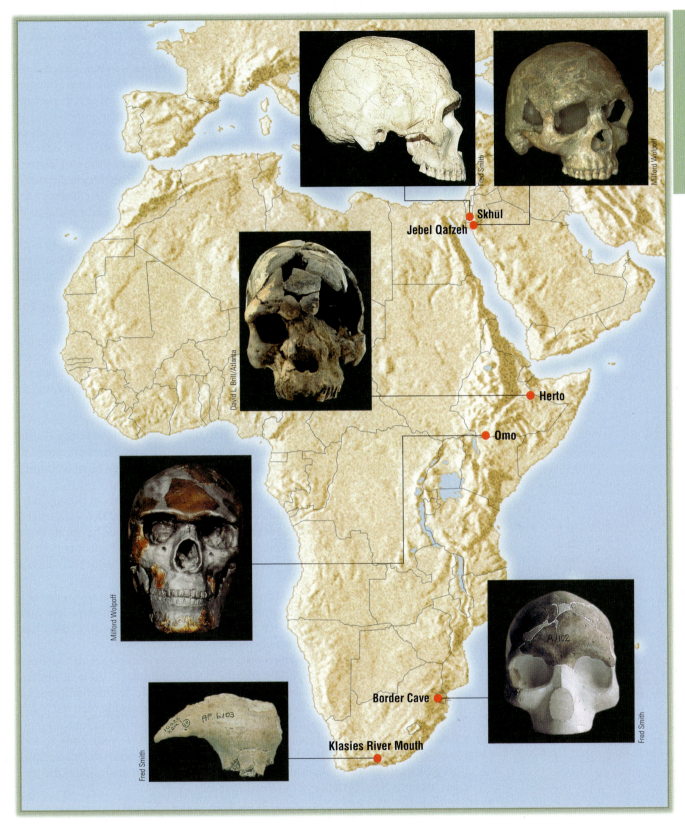

FIGURE 11-1
Modern humans from Africa and the Near East.

that he isn't dogmatic on this issue. He does suggest that even though there may have been potential for interbreeding, apparently very little actually took place.

Interpretations of the latter phases of human evolution have recently been greatly extended by newly available genetic techniques. As we emphasized elsewhere, advances in molecular biology have revolutionized the biological sciences, including physical anthropology, and they've recently been applied to the question of modern human origins. Using numerous contemporary human populations as a data source, geneticists have precisely determined and compared a wide variety of DNA sequences. The theoretical basis of this approach assumes that at least some of the genetic patterning seen today can act as a kind of window on the past. In particular, the genetic patterns observed today between geographically widely dispersed humans are thought to partly reflect migrations occurring in the Late Pleistocene. This hypothesis can be further tested as various types of contemporary population genetic patterning are better documented.

To get a clearer picture of these genetic patterns, geneticists have studied both nuclear and mitochondrial DNA (mtDNA; see p. 39). They consider Y chromosome and mtDNA patterns particularly informative, since neither is significantly recombined during sexual reproduction. As a result, mitochondrial inheritance follows a strictly maternal pattern (inherited through females), while the Y chromosome follows a paternal pattern (transmitted only from father to son).

As these new data have accumulated, consistent relationships are emerging, especially in showing that indigenous African populations have far greater diversity than do populations from elsewhere in the world. The consistency of the results is highly significant, because it strongly supports an African origin for modern humans and some mode of replacement elsewhere.

Certainly, most molecular data come from contemporary species, since DNA is not *usually* preserved in long-dead individuals. Even so, exceptions do occur, and these cases open another genetic window—one that can directly illuminate the past. As discussed in Chapter 10 (see p. 238), Neandertal DNA has been recovered from eight Neandertal fossils.

In addition, nine ancient fully modern *H. sapiens* skeletons from sites in Italy, France, the Czech Republic, and Russia have recently had their mtDNA sequenced (Caramelli et al., 2003, 2006; Kulikov et al., 2004; Serre et al., 2004). The results show mtDNA sequence patterns very similar to the patterns seen in living humans—and thus significantly different from the mtDNA patterns found in the eight Neandertals so far analyzed.

If these results are further confirmed, they provide strong *direct* evidence of a genetic discontinuity between Neandertals and these early fully modern humans. In other words, these data suggest that no—or very little—interbreeding took place between Neandertals and anatomically modern humans.

Still, there's a potentially serious problem with these latest DNA results from the early modern skeletons. The mtDNA sequences are so similar to those of modern humans that they could, in fact, be the result of contamination. That is, the amplified and sequenced DNA could belong to some person who recently handled the fossil. The molecular biologists who did this research took many experimental precautions, following standard practices used by other laboratories. But there's currently no way to rule out such contamination, which would likely have occurred during excavation. Still, the results do fit with an emerging overall agreement on the likely distinctions between Neandertals and modern humans.

Partial Replacement Models

Various alternative perspectives also suggest that modern humans originated in Africa and then, when their population increased, expanded out of Africa into other areas of the Old World. But unlike those who subscribe to the complete replacement hypothesis, supporters of these partial replacement models claim that some interbreeding occurred between emigrating Africans and resident premodern populations elsewhere. So, partial replacement assumes that no speciation event occurred, and all these hominids should be considered members of *H. sapiens*. Günter Bräuer, of the University of Hamburg, suggests that very little interbreeding occurred—a view supported recently by John Relethford (2001) in what he describes as "mostly out of Africa." Fred Smith, of Loyola University, also favors an African origin of modern humans; but his "assimilation" model hypothesizes that in some regions, more interbreeding took place (Smith, 2002).

The Regional Continuity Model: Multiregional Evolution

The regional continuity model is most closely associated with paleoanthropologist Milford Wolpoff, of the University of Michigan, and his associates (Wolpoff et al., 1994, 2001). They suggest that local populations—not all, of course—in Europe, Asia, and Africa continued their indigenous evolutionary development from premodern Middle Pleistocene forms to anatomically modern humans. But if that's true, then we have to ask how so many different local populations around the globe happened to evolve with such similar morphology. In other words, how could anatomically modern humans arise separately in different continents and end up so much alike, both physically and genetically? The multiregional model answers this question by (1) denying that the earliest modern *H. sapiens* populations originated *exclusively* in Africa, challenging the notion of complete replacement; and (2) asserting that significant levels of gene flow (migration) between premodern populations was extremely likely.

Through gene flow and natural selection, according to the multiregional hypothesis, local populations would *not* have evolved totally independently from one another, and such mixing would have "prevented speciation between the regional lineages and thus maintained human beings as a *single,* although obviously *polytypic* [see p. 272], species throughout the Pleistocene" (Smith et al., 1989). Thus, under a multiregional model, there are no taxonomic distinctions between modern and premodern hominids. That is, all hominids following *H. erectus* though modern humans are classified as *H. sapiens*.

Advocates of the multiregional model aren't dogmatic about the degree of regional continuity. They recognize that a likely strong influence of African migrants existed throughout the world and is still detectable today. Agreeing with Smith's assimilation model, this modified multiregionalism suggests that perhaps only minimal gene continuity existed in several regions (for example, western Europe) and that most modern genes are the result of large African migrations and/or more incremental gene flow (Relethford, 2001; Wolpoff et al., 2001).

Seeing the Big Picture

Looking beyond the arguments concerning modern human origins—which the popular media often overstates and overdramatizes—most paleoanthropologists now recognize an emerging consensus view. In fact, new evidence from fossils and especially from molecular comparisons is providing even more clarity. Data from sequenced ancient DNA, various patterns of contemporary human DNA, and the newest fossil finds from Ethiopia all suggest that a "strong" multiregional model is extremely unlikely. Supporters of this more extreme form of multiregionalism claim that modern human populations in Asia and Europe evolved *mostly* from local premodern ancestors—with only minor influence coming from African population expansion. But with the breadth and consistency of the latest research, this strong version of multiregionalism is falsified.

Also, as various investigators integrate these new data, views are beginning to converge even further. Several researchers suggest an out-of-Africa model that leads to virtually complete replacement elsewhere. At the moment, this complete replacement rendition can't be falsified. Still, even devoted advocates of this strong replacement version recognize the potential for at least *some* interbreeding, although they believe it was likely very minor. We can conclude, then, that during the later Pleistocene, one or more major migrations from Africa fueled the world-wide dispersal of modern humans. However, the African migrants might well have interbred with resident populations outside Africa. In a sense, it's all the same, whether we see this process either as very minimal multiregional continuity or as not quite complete replacement.

The Earliest Discoveries of Modern Humans

Africa

In Africa, several early fossil finds have been interpreted as fully anatomically modern forms (see Fig. 11-1). The earliest of these specimens comes from Omo Kibish, in southernmost Ethiopia. Using radiometric techniques, recent redating of a fragmentary skull (Omo 1) demonstrates that, coming from 195,000 ya, this is the earliest modern human yet found in Africa—or, for that matter, anywhere (McDougall et al., 2005). An interesting aspect of fossil finds at this site concerns the variation shown between the two individuals discovered there. Omo 1 (Fig. 11-2) is essentially modern in most respects (note the presence of a chin; Fig. 11-3), but another ostensibly contemporary cranium (Omo 2) is much more robust and less modern in morphology.

Somewhat later African modern human fossils come from the Klasies River Mouth on the south coast and Border Cave, just slightly to the north. Using relatively new techniques, paleoanthropologists have dated both sites to about 120,000–80,000 ya. The original geological context at Border Cave is uncertain, and the fossils may be younger than those at Klasies River Mouth. Although recent reevaluation of the Omo site has provided much more dependable dating, there are still questions remaining about some of the other early African modern fossils. Nevertheless, it now seems very likely that early modern humans appeared in East Africa by shortly after 200,000 ya and had migrated to southern Africa by approximately 100,000 ya. New fossil finds are helping confirm this view.

Herto The announcement in June 2003 of well-preserved *and* well-dated *H. sapiens* fossils from Ethiopia has now gone a long way toward filling gaps in the African fossil record. As a result, these fossils are helping to resolve key issues regarding modern human origins. Tim White, of the University of California, Berkeley, and his colleagues have been working for over a decade in the Middle Awash area of Ethiopia. They've discovered a remarkable array of early fossil hominids (*Ardipithecus* and *Australopithecus anamensis*) as well as somewhat later forms (*H. erectus*). From this same area in the Middle Awash—in the Herto member of the Bouri formation—highly significant new discoveries came to light in 1997. For simplicity, these new hominids are referred to as the Herto remains.

These exciting new Herto fossils include a mostly complete adult cranium and several other fragmentary remains. Well-controlled radiometric dating securely places the remains at between 154,000 and 160,000 ya, making these the best-dated hominid fossils from this time period from anywhere in the world. And note, especially, that

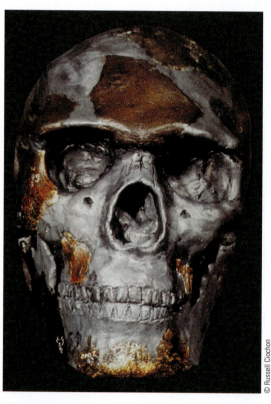

© Russell Ciochon

FIGURE 11-2

Reconstructed skull of Omo I, an early modern human from Ethiopia, dated to 195,000 ya. Note the clear presence of a chin.

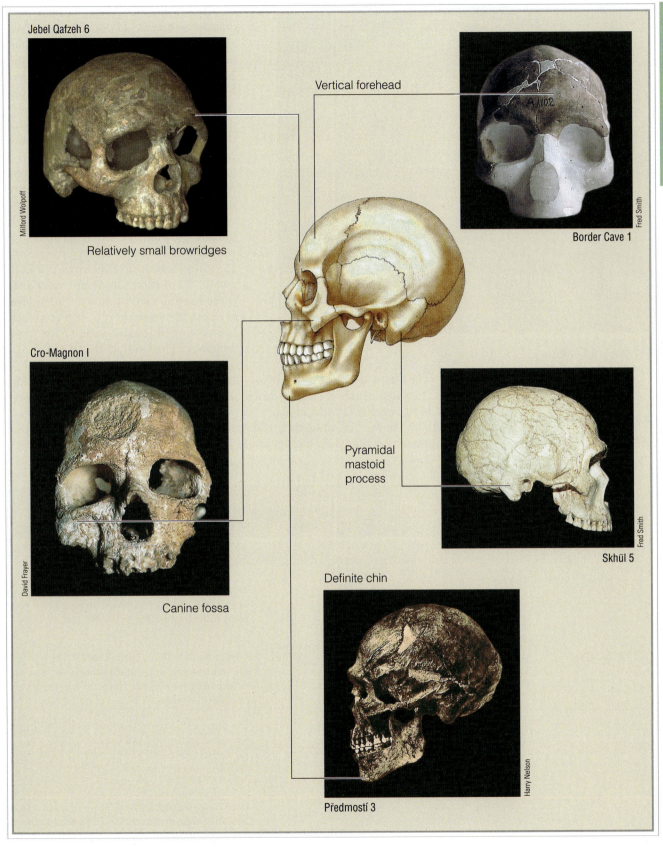

Jebel Qafzeh 6

Relatively small browridges

Milford Wolpoff

Vertical forehead

Border Cave 1

Fred Smith

Cro-Magnon I

David Frayer

Canine fossa

Pyramidal mastoid process

Skhūl 5

Fred Smith

Definite chin

Předmostí 3

Harry Nelson

FIGURE 11-3

Morphology and variation in early specimens of modern *Homo sapiens*.

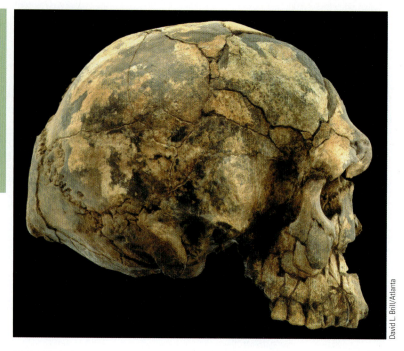

David L. Brill/Atlanta

FIGURE 11-4

Herto cranium from Ethiopia, dated 160,000–154,000 ya. This is the best-preserved early modern *H. sapiens* cranium yet found.

this date is clearly *older* than for any other equally modern *H. sapiens* from anywhere else in the world. Moreover, the preservation and morphology of the remains leave little doubt about their relationship to modern humans. The cranium (Fig. 11-4) is very large, with an extremely long cranial vault. The cranial capacity is 1,450 cm³, well within the range of contemporary *H. sapiens* populations.

White and his team performed comprehensive statistical studies, comparing these fossils with other early *H. sapiens* remains as well as with a large series from modern populations. They concluded that while not identical to modern people, the Herto fossils are near-modern (White et al., 2003). To distinguish these individuals from fully modern humans (*H. sapiens sapiens*), the researchers have placed them in a newly defined subspecies: *Homo sapiens idaltu*. The word *idaltu*, from the Afar language, means "elder."

The Herto fossils are the right age, and they come from the right place. Besides that, they look much like what we might have predicted. These new Herto finds are the most conclusive fossil evidence yet supporting an African origin of modern humans. They're thus compatible with an array of genetic data indicating some form of replacement model for human origins.

QUICK REVIEW	Key Early Modern *Homo sapiens* Discoveries from Africa and the Near East		
DATES	**SITE**	**HOMINID**	**EVOLUTIONARY SIGNIFICANCE**
110,000 ya	Qafzeh (Israel)	*H. sapiens sapiens*	Large sample (at least 20 individuals); definitely modern, but some individuals fairly robust; early date (> 100,000 ya)
115,000 ya	Skhūl	*H. sapiens sapiens*	Minimum of 10 individuals; like Qafzeh modern morphology, but slightly earlier date (and earliest modern humans known outside of Africa)
154,000–160,000 ya	Herto (Ethiopia)	*H. sapiens idaltu*	Very well-preserved cranium; dated > 150,000 ya, the best-preserved early modern human found anywhere
195,000 ya	Omo (Ethiopia)	*H. sapiens*	Dated almost 200,000 ya and the oldest modern human found anywhere; two crania found, one more modern looking than the other

David Frayer

FIGURE 11-5
Mt. Carmel, studded with caves, was home to *H. sapiens sapiens* at Skhūl (and to Neandertals at Tabun and Kebara).

The Near East

In Israel, researchers found early modern *H. sapiens* fossils, including the remains of at least 10 individuals, in the Skhūl Cave at Mt. Carmel (Figs. 11-5 and 11-6a). This is very near the Neandertal site of Tabun, also located at Mt. Carmel. Also from Israel, the Qafzeh Cave has yielded the remains of at least 20 individuals (Fig. 11-6b). Although their overall configuration is definitely modern, some specimens show certain premodern features. Skhūl has been dated to between 100,000 and 130,000 ya (Grün et al., 2005), while Qafzeh has been dated to around 92,000–120,000 ya (Grün and Stringer, 1991). The time line for these fossil discoveries is shown in Figure 11-7.

Such early dates for modern specimens pose some problems for those advocating the influence of local evolution, as proposed by the multiregional model. How early do the premodern *H. sapiens* populations—that is, Neandertals—appear in the Near East? A recent chronometric calibration for the Tabun Cave suggests a date as early as 120,000 ya. This date for Tabun suggests that there's considerable chronological overlap in the occupation of the Near East by Neandertals and modern humans.

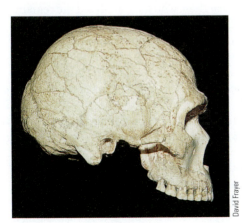

(a)

(b)

David Frayer

Milford Wolpoff

FIGURE 11-6
(a) Skhūl 5. (b) Qafzeh 6. These specimens from Israel are thought to be representatives of early modern *Homo sapiens*. The vault height, forehead, and lack of prognathism are modern traits.

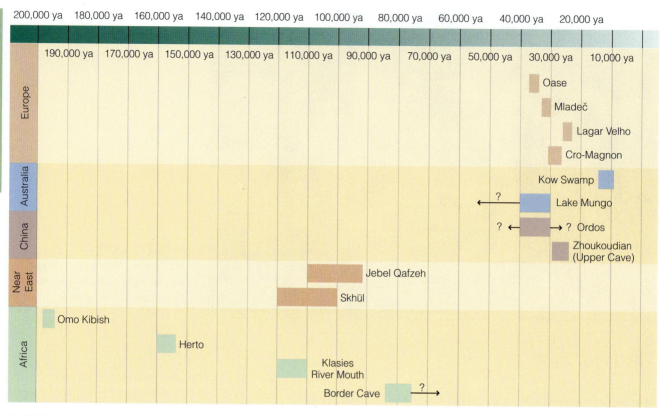

FIGURE 11-7

Time line of modern *Homo sapiens* discoveries. Note that some dates are approximations. Question marks indicate those estimates that are most tentative.

Asia

There are six early anatomically modern human localities in China, the two most significant of which come from the area near the village of Zhoukoudian (Fig. 11-8). The fossils from these Chinese sites are all fully modern, and all are considered to be from the Late Pleistocene with dates likely less than 40,000 ya. Upper Cave at Zhoukoudian, from later strata in the same locale as the famous *H. erectus* finds, has been dated to 27,000 ya.

Just about four miles down the road from the famous Zhoukoudian Cave is another cave called Tianyuan from where an important find came in 2003. Consisting of a fragmentary skull, a few teeth, and several postcranial bones, this fossil is accurately dated by radiocarbon at close to 40,000 ya (Shang et al., 2007). The individual shows mostly modern skeletal features, but also has a few archaic characteristics as well. The Chinese and American team of researchers who have analyzed the remains from Tianyuan suggest they indicate an African origin of modern humans, but also show a good possibility of at least some interbreeding in China with resident archaic populations. More complete analysis and (with some luck) further finds at this new site will help provide a better picture of early modern *H. sapiens* in China. For the moment, this is the best-dated early modern *H. sapiens* from China and one of the two earliest from anywhere in Asia.

The other early find is a partial skull from Niah Cave on the north coast of the Indonesian island of Borneo (see Fig. 11-8). This is actually not a new find, but was, in fact, first excavated 50 years ago. However, until recent more extensive analysis, this find had been relegated to the paleoanthropological back shelf due to uncertainties regarding its archaeological context and dating. Now all this has changed with a better understanding of the geology of the site and new dates strongly supporting an age of more than 35,000 ya and most likely as old as 40,000–45,000 ya, making it perhaps older than Tianyuan (Barker et al., 2007). Like its Chinese counterparts, the

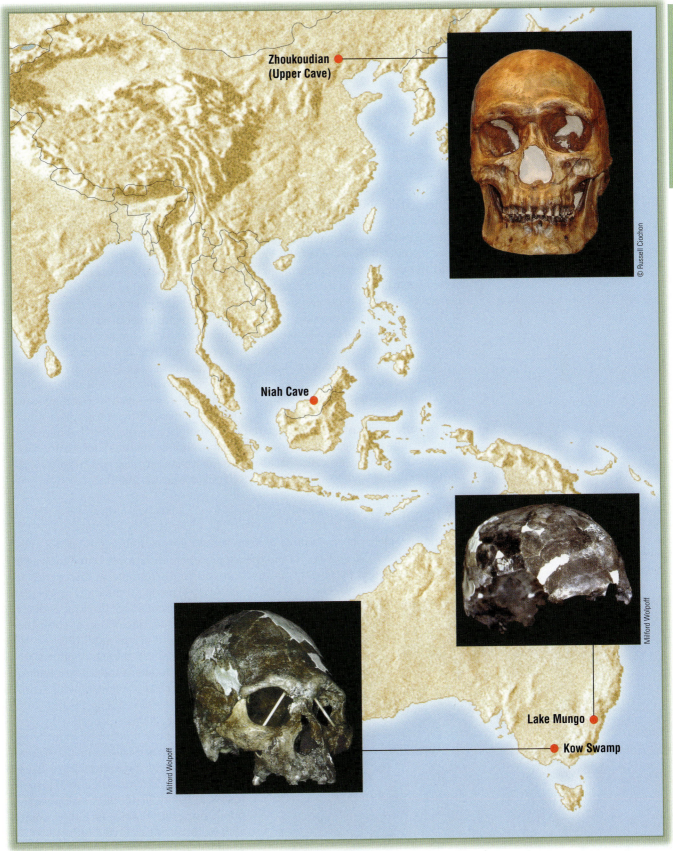

© Russell Ciochon

Zhoukoudian
(Upper Cave)

Niah Cave

Milford Wolpoff

Milford Wolpoff

Lake Mungo

Kow Swamp

FIGURE 11-8
Anatomically modern *Homo
sapiens* from Asia and Australia.

Niah skull is also modern in morphology. It is hypothesized that some population contemporaneous with Niah or somewhat earlier inhabitants of Indonesia were perhaps the first group to colonize Australia.

Australia

During glacial times, the Indonesian islands were joined to the Asian mainland, but Australia was not. It's likely that by 50,000 ya, modern humans inhabited Sahul—the area including New Guinea and Australia. Bamboo rafts may have been the means of crossing the sea between islands, and doing so would have been dangerous and difficult. It's not known just where the future Australians came from, but as noted, Indonesia has been suggested.

Human occupation of Australia appears to have occurred quite early, with some archaeological sites dating to 55,000 ya. There's some controversy about dating of the earliest Australian human remains, which are all modern *H. sapiens*. The earliest finds so far discovered have come from Lake Mungo, in southeastern Australia (see Fig. 11-8). In agreement with archaeological context and radiocarbon dates, the hominids from this site have been dated at approximately 30,000–25,000 ya. Newly determined age estimates, using electron spin resonance (ESR) and uranium-series dating (see p. 173), have dramatically extended the suggested time depth to about 60,000 ya (Thorne et al., 1999). The lack of correlation of these more ancient age estimates with other data, however, has some researchers seriously concerned (Gillespie and Roberts, 2000).

Unlike the more gracile early Australian forms from Lake Mungo are the Kow Swamp people, who are thought to have lived between about 14,000 and 9,000 ya (see Fig. 11-8). These fossils display certain archaic traits—such as receding foreheads, heavy supraorbital tori, and thick bones—that are difficult to explain, since these features contrast with the postcranial anatomy, which matches that of recent native Australians. Regardless of the differing morphology of these later Australians, new genetic evidence indicates that all native Australians are descendants of a *single* migration dating back to about 50,000 ya (Hudjashov et al., 2007).

Central Europe

Central Europe has been a source of many fossil finds, including the earliest anatomically modern *H. sapiens* yet discovered anywhere in Europe. Dated to 35,000 ya, the best dated of these early *H. sapiens* fossils come from recent discoveries at the Oase Cave in Romania (Fig 11-10). Here, cranial remains of three individuals were recovered, including a complete mandible and a partial skull (Fig. 11-9). While quite robust, these individuals are quite similar to later modern specimens, as seen in the clear presence of both a chin and a canine fossa (see Fig. 11-3, p. 251; Trinkaus et al., 2003).

Another early modern human site in central Europe is Mladeč, in the Czech Republic. Several individuals have been excavated here and are dated to approximately 31,000 ya. While there's some variation among the crania, including some with big browridges, Fred Smith (1984) is confident that they're all best classified as modern *H. sapiens* (Fig 11-11). It's clear that by 28,000 ya, modern humans are widely dispersed in central Europe and into western Europe (Trinkaus, 2005).

FIGURE 11-9

Excavators at work within the spectacular cave at Oase, in Romania. The floor is littered with the remains of fossil animals, including the earliest-dated cranial remains of *Homo sapiens* in Europe.

© Mircea Gherase

© Staatliche Museen zu Berlin, Museum für Vor- und Frühgeschichte

Milford Wolpoff

© Erik Trinkaus

David Frayer

Mladeč

Oase

Combe Capelle

Cro-Magnon

FIGURE 11-10
Anatomically modern humans from Europe.

Western Europe

For several reasons, one of them probably serendipity, western Europe and its fossils have received the most attention. Over the last 150 years, many of the scholars interested in this kind of research happened to live in western Europe, and the southern region of France happened to be a fossil treasure trove. Also, early on, discovering and learning about human ancestors caught the curiosity and pride of the local population.

As a result of this scholarly interest, beginning back in the nineteenth century, a great deal of data accumulated, and little reliable comparative information was available from elsewhere in the world. Consequently, theories of human evolution were based almost exclusively on the western European material. It's only been in recent years, with growing evidence from other areas of the world and with the

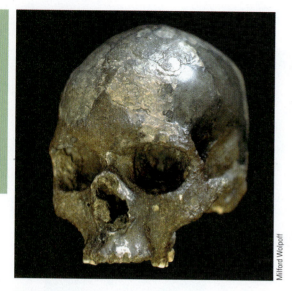

FIGURE 11-11

The Mladeč cranium, from the Czech Republic, is a good example of early modern *Homo sapiens* in central Europe. Along with Oase in Romania, the evidence for early modern *H. sapiens* appears first in central Europe, then later in western Europe.

Cro-Magnon (crow-man´-yon)

Aurignacian Pertaining to an Upper Paleolithic stone tool industry in Europe beginning at about 40,000 ya.

application of new dating techniques, that recent human evolutionary dynamics are being seriously considered from a worldwide perspective.

Western Europe has yielded many anatomically modern human fossils, but by far the best-known sample of western European *H. sapiens* is from the **Cro-Magnon** site. From a rock shelter in southern France, remains of eight individuals were discovered here in 1868.

The Cro-Magnon materials are associated with an **Aurignacian** tool assemblage, an Upper Paleolithic industry. Dated at about 28,000 ya, these individuals represent the earliest of France's anatomically modern humans. The so-called Old Man (Cro-Magnon I) became the original model for what was once termed the Cro-Magnon, or Upper Paleolithic, "race" of Europe (Fig. 11-12). Actually, of course, there's no such valid biological category, and Cro-Magnon I is not typical of Upper Paleolithic western Europeans—and not even all that similar to the other two male skulls found at the site.

Most of the genetic evidence, as well as the newest fossil evidence, from Africa argues against continuous local evolution producing modern groups directly from any Eurasian premodern population (in Europe, these would be Neandertals). Still, for some researchers, the issue isn't completely settled. With all the latest evidence, there's no longer much debate that a *large* genetic contribution from migrating early modern Africans influenced other groups throughout the Old World. What's being debated is just how much admixture might have occurred between these migrating Africans and the resident premodern groups. One group of researchers that has evaluated genetic evidence from living populations (Eswaran et al., 2005) suggests that significant admixture occurred in much of the Old World. What's more, for those paleoanthropologists who also hypothesize that significant admixture (assimilation) occurred in western Europe as well as elsewhere (for example, Trinkaus, 2005), a recently discovered child's skeleton from Portugal provides some of the best evidence of ostensible interbreeding between Neandertals and anatomically modern *H. sapiens*. This important new discovery from the Abrigo do Lagar Velho site (Fig. 11-13) was excavated in late 1998 and is dated to 24,500 ya—that's at least 5,000 years later than the last clearly Neandertal find. Associated with an Upper Paleolithic industry and buried with red ocher and pierced shell is a fairly complete skeleton of a 4-year-old child (Duarte et al., 1999). In studying the remains, Cidália Duarte, Erik Trinkaus, and colleagues found a highly mixed set of anatomical features. Many characteristics, especially of the teeth,

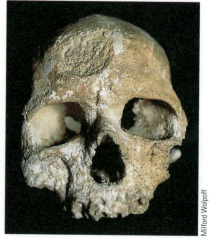

FIGURE 11-12

Cro-Magnon I (France). In this specimen, modern traits are quite clear. (a) Lateral view. (b) Frontal view.

(a)

(b)

	DATES	SITE	HOMINID	EVOLUTIONARY SIGNIFICANCE
QUICK REVIEW		**Key Early Modern *Homo sapiens* from Europe and Asia**		
	24,500 ya	Abrigo do Lagar Velho (Portugal)	*H. sapiens sapiens*	Child's skeleton; some suggestion of possible hybrid between Neandertal and modern human—but it is controversial
	30,000 ya	Cro-Magnon (France)	*H. sapiens sapiens*	Most famous early modern human find in world; earliest evidence of modern humans in France
	40,000 ya	Tianyuan Cave (China)	*H. sapiens sapiens*	Partial skull and a few postcranial bones; oldest modern human find from China
	40,000–45,000 ya	Niah Cave (Borneo, Indonesia)	*H. sapiens sapiens*	Partial skull recently redated more accurately; oldest modern human find from Asia

lower jaw, and pelvis, were like those seen in anatomically modern humans. Yet, several other features—including lack of chin, limb proportions, and muscle insertions—were more similar to Neandertal traits. The authors thus conclude that "the presence of such admixture suggests the hypothesis of variable admixture between early modern humans dispersing into Europe and local Neandertal populations" (Duarte et al., 1999, p. 7608). They suggest that this new evidence strongly supports the partial replacement model while seriously weakening the complete replacement model. Of course, the evidence from one child's skeleton—while intriguing—certainly isn't going to convince everyone.

Something New and Different

As we've seen, by 25,000 years ago, modern humans had dispersed to all major areas of the Old World, and they would soon journey to the New World as well. But at about the same time, remnant populations of earlier hominids still survived in a few remote and isolated corners. We mentioned in Chapter 9 that populations of *Homo erectus* in Java managed to survive on this island long after their cousins had disappeared from other areas, for example, China and East Africa. What's more, even though they persisted well into the Late Pleistocene, physically these Javanese hominids were still very similar to other *H. erectus* individuals (see p. 204).

Even more surprising, it seems that other populations branched off from some of these early inhabitants of Indonesia and either intentionally or accidentally found their way to other, smaller islands to the east. There, under even more extreme isolation pressures, they evolved in an astonishing direction. In late 2004, the world awoke to the startling announcement that an extremely small-bodied, small-brained hominid had been discovered in Liang Bua Cave, on the island of Flores, east of Java (Fig. 11-14). These remains consist of an incomplete skeleton of an adult female (LB1) as well as additional pieces from nine other individuals, which the press have collectively nicknamed "hobbits." The female skeleton is remarkable in several ways (Fig. 11-15), though surprisingly similar to the Dmanisi hominids (from which they may be derived; see p. 203). First, she stood barely 3 feet tall—as short as the smallest

© Portuguese Institute of Archaeology

FIGURE 11-13

The skeleton of the Lagar Velho child thought by some to be a Neandertal–modern human hybrid.

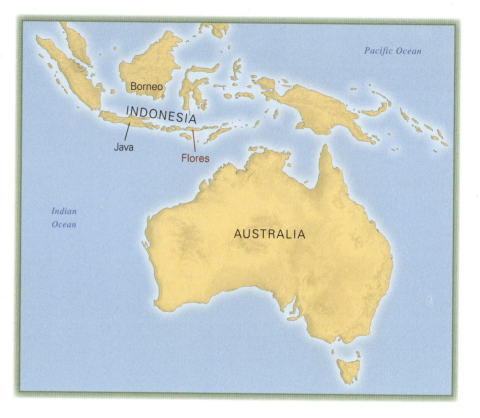

FIGURE 11-14
Location of the Flores site, in Indonesia.

© Peter Brown

FIGURE 11-15
Cranium of adult female *Homo floresiensis* from Flores, Indonesia, dated 18,000 ya.

australopith—and her brain, estimated at a mere 417 cm³ (Falk et al., 2005), was no larger than that of a chimpanzee (Brown et al., 2004). Possibly most startling of all, these extraordinary hominids were still living on Flores just 13,000 ya (Morwood et al., 2004, 2005)!

Where did they come from? As we said, their predecessors were probably *H. erectus* populations like those found on Java. How they got to Flores—some 400 miles away, partly over open ocean—is a mystery. There are several connecting islands, and to get between them, these hominids may have drifted across on rafts; but there's no way to be sure of this.

How did they get to be so physically different from all other known hominids? Here we're a little more certain of the answer. Isolated island populations can quite rapidly diverge from their relatives elsewhere. Among such isolated animals, natural selection frequently favors reduced body size. For example, populations of dwarf elephants are found on islands in the Mediterranean as well as on some channel islands off the coast of southern California. And perhaps most interesting of all, dwarf elephants *also* evolved on Flores; they were found in the same geological beds with the little hominids. The evolutionary mechanism (called "insular dwarfing") thought to explain such extreme body size reduction in both the elephants and the hominids is an adaptation to a reduced amount of resources, leading through selection to smaller size.

Other than short stature, what did the Flores hominids look like? In their cranial shape, thickness of cranial bone, and dentition, they most resemble *H. erectus*, and specifically those from Dmanisi. Still, they have some derived features that also set them apart from all other hominids. For that reason, many researchers have placed them in a separate species, *Homo floresiensis*.

Immediately following the first publication of the Flores remains, considerable controversy arose regarding their interpretation (Jacob et al., 2006; Martin et al., 2006). Some researchers have argued that the small-brained find (LB1) is actually a pathological modern *H. sapiens* afflicted with a severe growth disorder called microcephaly. The researchers who did most of the initial work reject this conclusion and provide some further details to support their original interpretation (for example, Dean Falk's further analysis of microcephalic endocasts, as reported in Bower, 2006).

The conclusion that among this already small-bodied island population the one individual found with a preserved cranium happened to be afflicted with a severe (and rare) growth defect is highly unlikely. Yet, it must also be recognized that long-term, extreme isolation of hominids on Flores leading to a new species showing dramatic body size dwarfing and even more dramatic brain size reduction is also quite unusual.

A third possibility has been suggested by anthropologist Gary Richards, of the University of California, Berkeley. He argues that LB1 (and the other little Flores hominids) are normal *H. sapiens,* but ones that have had a microevolutionary change leading to unusually small body and brain size (Richards, 2006).

So where does this leave us? Because a particular interpretation is unlikely, it is not necessarily incorrect. We do know, for example, that such "insular dwarfing" has occurred in other mammals. For the moment, the most comprehensive analyses indicate that a new hominid species (*H. floresiensis*) did, in fact, evolve on Flores (Nevell et al., 2007; Tocheri et al., 2007). For several researchers, this conclusion still requires more detailed and more convincing evidence. There is some possibility that DNA can be retrieved from the Flores bones and sequenced. Although considered a long shot due to poor bone preservation, analysis of this DNA would certainly help in solving the mystery.

Technology and Art in the Upper Paleolithic

Europe

The cultural period known as the Upper Paleolithic began in western Europe approximately 40,000 years ago (Fig. 11-16). Upper Paleolithic cultures are usually divided into five different industries, based on stone tool technologies: Chatelperronian, Aurignacian, Gravettian, Solutrean, and Magdalenian. Major environmental shifts were also apparent during this period. During the last glacial period, about 30,000 ya, a warming trend lasting several thousand years partially melted the glacial ice. The result was that much of Eurasia was covered by tundra and steppe, a vast area of treeless country dotted with lakes and marshes. In many areas in the north, permafrost prevented the growth of trees but permitted the growth, in the short summers, of flowering plants, mosses, and other kinds of vegetation. This vegetation served as an enormous pasture for herbivorous animals, large and small, and carnivorous animals fed off the herbivores. It was a hunter's paradise, with millions of animals dispersed across expanses of tundra and grassland, from Spain through Europe and into the Russian steppes.

Large herds of reindeer roamed the tundra and steppes, along with mammoths, bison, horses, and a host of smaller animals that served as a bountiful source of food. In addition, humans exploited fish and fowl systematically for the first time, especially along the southern tier of Europe. It was a time of relative abundance, and ultimately Upper Paleolithic people spread out over Europe, living in caves and open-air camps and building large shelters. Far more elaborate burials are also found, most spectacularly at the 24,000-year-old Sungir site near Moscow (Fig. 11-17), where grave goods included a bed of red ocher, thousands of ivory beads, long spears made of straightened mammoth tusks, ivory engravings, and jewelry (Formicola and Buzhilova, 2004). During this period, either western Europe or perhaps portions of Africa achieved the highest population density in human history up to that time.

Humans and other animals in the midlatitudes of Eurasia had to cope with shifts in climatic conditions, some of them quite rapid. For

FIGURE 11-16

Cultural periods of the European Upper Paleolithic and their approximate beginning dates.

GLACIAL	UPPER PALEOLITHIC (beginnings)	CULTURAL PERIODS
W Ü R M	17,000 – 21,000 – 27,000 – 40,000 –	Magdalenian Solutrean Gravettian Aurignacian Chatelperronian
	Middle Paleolithic	Mousterian

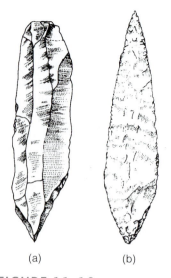

FIGURE 11-18

(a) A burin, a very common Upper Paleolithic tool. (b) A Solutrean blade. This is the best-known work of the Solutrean tradition. Solutrean stonework is considered the most highly developed of any Upper Paleolithic industry.

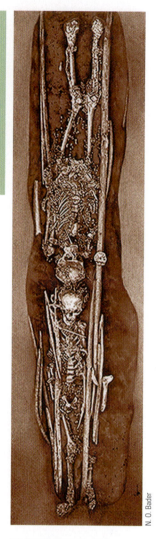

FIGURE 11-17

Skeleton of two teenagers, a male and a female, from Sungir, Russia. Dated 24,000 ya, this is the richest find of any Upper Paleolithic grave.

Magdalenian Pertaining to the final phase of the Upper Paleolithic stone tool industry in Europe.

burins Small, chisel-like tools with a pointed end, thought to have been used to engrave bone, antler, ivory, or wood.

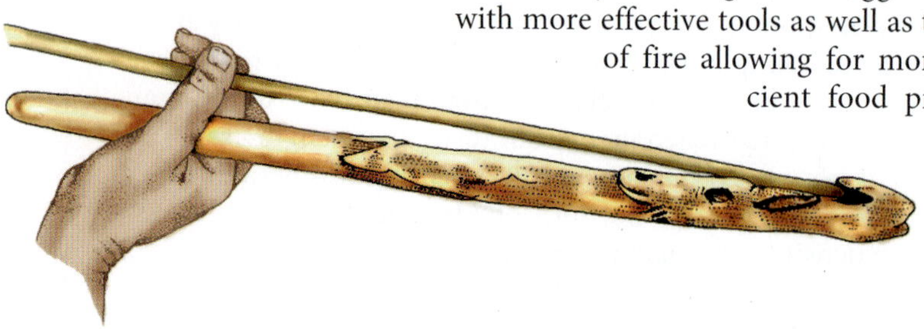

example, at 20,000 ya, another climatic "pulse" caused the weather to become noticeably colder in Europe and Asia as the continental glaciations reached their maximum extent for this entire glacial period, which is called the Würm in Eurasia.

As a variety of organisms attempted to adapt to these changing conditions, *Homo sapiens* had a major advantage: the elaboration of an increasingly sophisticated technology and most likely other components of culture as well. In fact, probably one of the greatest challenges facing numerous Late Pleistocene mammals was the ever more dangerously equipped humans—a trend that has continued to modern times.

The Upper Paleolithic was an age of technological innovation that can be compared to the past few hundred years in our recent history of amazing technological change after centuries of relative inertia. Anatomically modern humans of the Upper Paleolithic not only invented new and specialized tools (Fig. 11-18), but, as we've seen, also experimented with and greatly increased the use of new materials, such as bone, ivory, and antler.

Solutrean tools are good examples of Upper Paleolithic skill and perhaps aesthetic appreciation as well (see Fig. 11-18b). In this lithic (stone) tradition, stoneknapping developed to the finest degree ever known. Using specialized flaking techniques, the artist/technicians made beautiful parallel-flaked lance heads, expertly flaked on both surfaces. The lance points are so delicate that they can be considered works of art that quite possibly never served, nor were they intended to serve, a utilitarian purpose.

The last stage of the Upper Paleolithic, known as the **Magdalenian,** saw even more advances in technology. The spear-thrower, or atlatl, was a wooden or bone hooked rod that acted to extend the hunter's arm, thus enhancing the force and distance of a spear throw (Fig. 11-19). For catching salmon and other fish, the barbed harpoon is a clever example of the craftsperson's skill. There's also evidence that the bow and arrow may have been used for the first time during this period. The introduction of much more efficient manufacturing methods, such as the punch blade technique (Fig. 11-20), provided an abundance of standardized stone blades. These could be fashioned into **burins** (see Fig. 11-18a) for working wood, bone, and antler; borers for drilling holes in skins, bones, and shells; and knives with serrated or notched edges for scraping wooden shafts into a variety of tools.

By producing many more specialized tools, Upper Paleolithic peoples probably had more resources available to them; they may also have had an impact on the biology of these populations. Emphasizing a biocultural interpretation, C. Loring Brace, of the University of Michigan, has suggested that with more effective tools as well as the use of fire allowing for more efficient food process-

FIGURE 11-19

Spear-thrower (atlatl). Note the carving.

(a) A large core is selected and the top portion removed by use of a hammerstone.

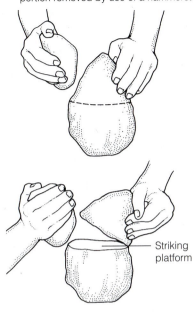

Striking platform

(b) The objective is to create a flat surface called a striking platform.

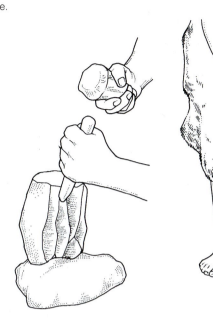

(c) Next, the core is struck by use of a hammer and punch (made of bone or antler) to remove the long narrow flakes (called blades).

(d) Or the blades can be removed by pressure flaking.

(e) The result is the production of highly consistent sharp blades, which can be used, as is, as knives; or they can be further modified (retouched) to make a variety of other tools (such as burins, scrapers, and awls).

FIGURE 11-20
The punch blade technique.

ing, anatomically modern *H. sapiens* wouldn't have required the large teeth and facial skeletons seen in earlier populations.

In addition to their reputation as hunters, western Europeans of the Upper Paleolithic are even better known for their symbolic representation, or what has commonly been called art. Given uncertainties about what actually should be called "art," archaeologist Margaret Conkey, of the University of California, Berkeley, refers to Upper Paleolithic cave paintings, sculptures, engravings, and so forth, as "visual and material imagery" (Conkey, 1987, p. 423). We'll continue using the term *art* to describe many of these prehistoric representations, but you should recognize that we do so mainly as a cultural convention—and perhaps a limiting one.

It's also important to remember that there is an extremely wide geographical distribution of symbolic images, best known from many parts of Europe, but now also well documented from Siberia, North Africa, South Africa, and Australia. Given a 25,000-year time depth of what we call Paleolithic art, and its nearly worldwide distribution, we can indeed observe marked variability in expression.

Besides cave art, there are many examples of small sculptures excavated from sites in western, central, and eastern Europe. Perhaps the most famous of these are the female figurines, popularly known as "Venuses," found at such sites as Brassempouy, France, and Grimaldi, Italy. Some of these figures were realistically carved, and the faces appear to be modeled after actual women. Other figurines may seem grotesque, with sexual characteristics exaggerated, perhaps for fertility or other ritual purposes.

Beyond these quite well-known figurines, there are numerous other examples of what's frequently called portable art, including elaborate engravings on tools and tool handles (Fig. 11-21). Such symbolism can be found in many parts of Europe and was already well established early in the Aurignacian—by 33,000 ya. Innovations in symbolic representations also benefited from, and probably further stimulated, technological advances. New methods of mixing pigments and applying them were important in rendering painted or drawn images. Bone and ivory carving and engraving were made easier with the use of special stone tools (see Fig. 11-18). At

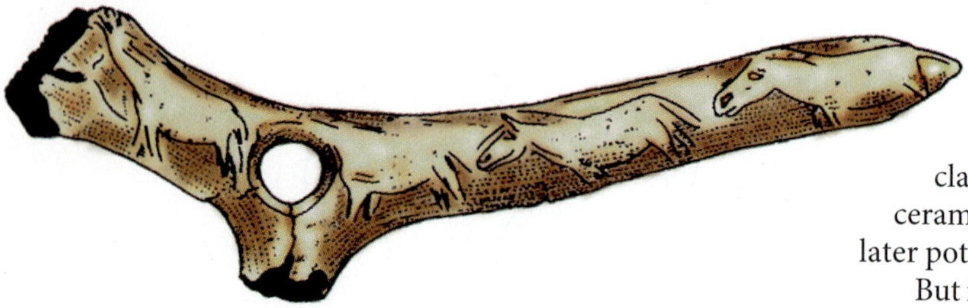

FIGURE 11-21

Magdalenian bone artifact. Note the realistic animal engraving on this object, the precise function of which is unknown.

two sites in the Czech Republic, Dolní Věstonice and Předmostí (both dated at approximately 26,000–27,000 ya), small animal figures were fashioned from fired clay. This is the first documented use of ceramic technology anywhere; in fact, it precedes later pottery invention by more than 15,000 years.

But it wasn't until the final phases of the Upper Paleolithic, particularly during the Magdalenian, that European prehistoric art reached its climax. Cave art is now known from more than 150 separate sites, the vast majority from southwestern France and northern Spain. Apparently, in other areas the rendering of such images did not take place in deep caves. Peoples in central Europe, China, Africa, and elsewhere certainly may have painted or carved representations on rock faces in the open, but these images long since would have eroded. So we're fortunate that the people of at least one of the many sophisticated cultures of the Upper Paleolithic chose to journey below-ground to create their artwork, preserving it not just for their immediate descendants, but for us as well. The most spectacular and most famous of the cave art sites are Lascaux and Grotte Chauvet (in France) and Altamira (in Spain).

In Lascaux Cave, for example, immense wild bulls dominate what's called the Great Hall of Bulls; and horses, deer, and other animals drawn with remarkable skill adorn the walls in black, red, and yellow. Equally impressive, at Altamira the walls and ceiling of an immense cave are filled with superb portrayals of bison in red and black. The "artist" even took advantage of bulges in the walls to create a sense of relief in the paintings. The cave is a treasure of beautiful art whose meaning has never been satisfactorily explained. It could have been religious or magical, a form of visual communication, or simply art for the sake of beauty.

Inside the cave called Grotte Chauvet, preserved unseen for perhaps 30,000 years, are a multitude of images, including dots, stenciled human handprints, and, most dramatically, hundreds of animal representations. Radiocarbon dating has placed the paintings during the Aurignacian, likely more than 35,000 ya, making Grotte Chauvet considerably earlier than the Magdalenian sites of Lascaux and Altamira (Balter, 2006).

Africa

Early accomplishments in rock art, possibly as early as in Europe, are seen in southern Africa (Namibia) at the Apollo 11 rock shelter site, where painted slabs have been identified dating to between 26,000 and 28,000 ya (Freundlich et al., 1980; Vogelsang, 1998). At Blombos Cave, farther to the south, remarkable bone tools, beads, and decorated ocher fragments are all dated to 73,000 ya (Henshilwood et al., 2004; Jacobs et al., 2006). The most recent and highly notable discovery from South Africa comes from another cave located at Pinnacle Point, not far from Blombos. At Pinnacle Point, ocher has been found (perhaps used for personal adornment) as well as clear evidence of systematic exploitation of shellfish and use of very small stone blades (microliths). What is both important and surprising is that the site is dated to approximately 165,000 ya, providing the earliest evidence from anywhere of these behaviors thought by many as characteristic of modern humans (Marean et al., 2007).

In central Africa, there was also considerable use of bone and antler, some of it possibly quite early. Excavations in the Katanda area of the eastern portion of the Democratic Republic of the Congo (Fig. 11-22) have shown remarkable development of bone craftwork. Dating of the site is quite early. Initial results using ESR and TL dating indicate an age as early as 80,000 ya (Feathers and Migliorini, 2001). From these intriguing data, preliminary reports have demonstrated that these technological achievements rival those of the more renowned European Upper Paleolithic (Yellen et al., 1995).

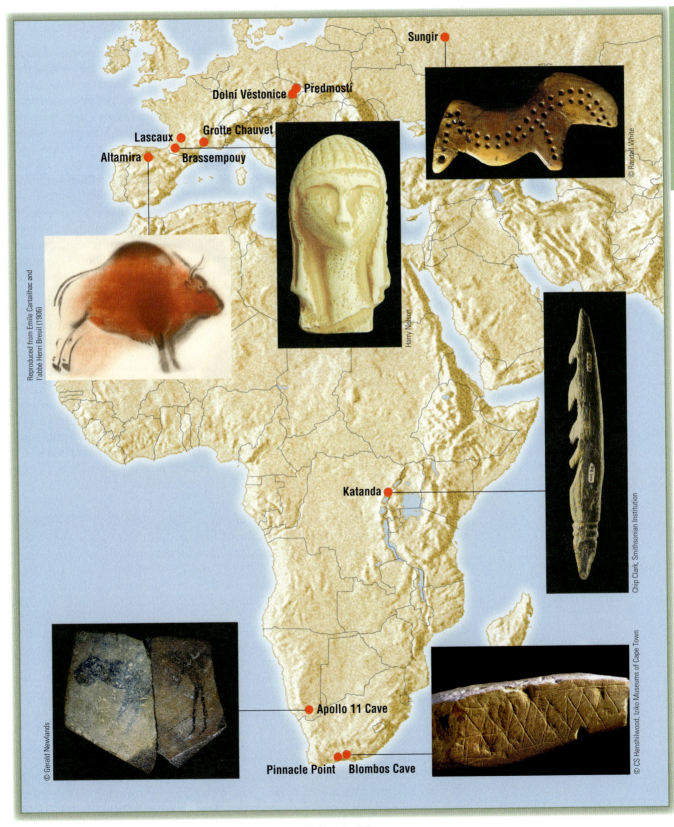

Sungir

Dolní Věstonice   Předmostí

Lascaux   Grotte Chauvet

Altamira   Brassempouy

Reproduced from Emile Cartailhac and l'abbé Henri Breuil (1906)

Harry Nelson

© Randall White

Chip Clark, Smithsonian Institution

Katanda

© Gerald Newlands

Apollo 11 Cave

Pinnacle Point   Blombos Cave

© CS Henshilwood, Iziko Museums of Cape Town

FIGURE 11-22

Symbolic artifacts from the Middle Stone Age of Africa and the Upper Paleolithic in Europe. It is notable that evidence of symbolism is found in Blombos Cave (77,000 ya) and Katanda (80,000 ya), both in Africa, a full 50,000 years *before* any comparable evidence is known from Europe. Moreover, the ochre found at Pinnacle Point is yet another 80,000 years older, dating to more than 160,000 ya.

Summary of Upper Paleolithic Culture

In looking back at the Upper Paleolithic, we can see it as the culmination of 2 million years of cultural development. Change proceeded incredibly slowly for most of the Pleistocene; but as cultural traditions and materials accumulated, and the brain—and, we assume, intelligence—expanded and reorganized, the rate of change quickened.

Cultural evolution continued with the appearance of early premodern humans and moved a bit faster with later premoderns. Neandertals in Eurasia and their contemporaries elsewhere added deliberate burials, technological innovations, and much more.

Building on existing cultures, late Pleistocene populations attained sophisticated cultural and material heights in a seemingly short—by previous standards—burst of exciting activity. In Europe and central Africa particularly, there seem to have been dramatic cultural innovations, among them big game hunting with powerful new weapons, such as harpoons, spear-throwers, and possibly the bow and arrow. Other innovations included body ornaments, needles, "tailored" clothing, and burials with elaborate grave goods—a practice that may indicate some sort of status hierarchy.

This dynamic age was doomed, or so it seems, by the climatic changes of about 10,000 ya. As the temperature slowly rose and the glaciers retreated, animal and plant species were seriously affected, and in turn these changes affected humans. As traditional prey animals were depleted or disappeared altogether, humans had to seek other means of obtaining food.

Grinding hard seeds or roots became important, and as humans grew more familiar with propagating plants, they began to domesticate both plants and animals. Human dependence on domestication became critical, and with it came permanent settlements, new technology, and more complex social organization. This continuing story of human biocultural evolution will be the topic of the remainder of this text.

Summary

For the past two decades, and there's no end in sight, researchers have fiercely debated the date and location of the origin of anatomically modern human beings. One hypothesis (complete replacement) claims that anatomically modern forms first evolved in Africa more than 100,000 ya and then, migrating out of Africa, completely replaced premodern *H. sapiens* in the rest of the world. Another school (regional continuity) takes a completely opposite view and maintains that in various geographical regions of the world, local groups of premodern *H. sapiens* evolved directly to anatomically modern humans. A third hypothesis (partial replacement) takes a somewhat middle position, suggesting an African origin but also accepting some later hybridization outside of Africa.

Recent research coming from several sources is beginning to clarify the origins of modern humans. Molecular evidence, as well as the dramatic new fossil finds from Herto, in Ethiopia, suggests that a multiregional origin of modern humans is unlikely. Sometime, soon after 150,000 ya, complete replacement of all hominids outside Africa may have occurred when migrating Africans displaced the populations in other regions. However, such absolutely *complete* replacement will be very difficult to prove, and it's not really what we'd expect. More than likely, at least some interbreeding probably did take place. Still, it's looking more and more like there wasn't very much intermixing of migrating African populations with other Old World groups.

Archaeological evidence of early modern humans also paints a fascinating picture of our most immediate ancestors. The Upper Paleolithic was an age of extraordinary innovation and achievement in technology and art. Many new and complex tools were introduced, and their production indicates fine skill in working wood, bone, and antler. Cave art in France and Spain displays the masterful ability of Upper

Paleolithic painters, and beautiful sculptures have been found at many European sites. Sophisticated symbolic representations have also been found in Africa and elsewhere. Upper Paleolithic *H. sapiens* displayed amazing development in a relatively short period of time. The culture produced during this period led the way to still newer and more complex cultural techniques and methods.

In the What's Important feature, you'll find a useful summary of the most significant fossil discoveries discussed in this chapter.

WHAT'S IMPORTANT		Key Fossil Discoveries of Early Modern Humans and *Homo floresiensis*		
DATES	REGION	SITE	HOMINID	THE BIG PICTURE
13,000–95,000 ya	Southeast Asia	Flores (Indonesia)	*H. floresiensis*	Late survival of very small-bodied and small-brained hominid on island of Flores; designated as different species (*H. floresiensis*) from modern humans
30,000 ya	Europe	Cro-Magnon (France)	*H. sapiens sapiens*	Famous site historically; good example of early modern humans from France
35,000 ya	Europe	Oase Cave (Romania)	*H. sapiens sapiens*	Earliest well-dated modern human from Europe
110,000 ya	Southwest Asia	Qafzeh (Israel)	*H. sapiens sapiens*	Early site; shows considerable variation
115,000 ya	Southwest Asia	Skhūl (Israel)	*H. sapiens sapiens*	Earliest well-dated modern human outside of Africa; perhaps contemporaneous with neighboring Tabun Neandertal site
154,000–160,000 ya	Africa	Herto (Ethiopia)	*H. sapiens idaltu*	Best-preserved and best-dated early modern human from anywhere; placed in separate subspecies from living *H. sapiens*

WHY IT MATTERS

Question: Are we all originally Africans?

Answer: The answer to this question is easy: Yes, without a doubt. As you know, all the early hominids evolved first in Africa and migrated to other parts of the world only subsequent to several million years of evolutionary history confined solely to Africa. So it is clear that we are all descendants of African ancestors. How recently were all of our ancestors strictly African? Accumulating evidence

(continued on page 268)

is strongly suggesting that we all share an African heritage dating back to no more than 200,000 ya and perhaps as recently as 30,000–40,000 ya.

Most of humanity's genetic patterning arose in the evolutionary crucible of the African continent. These highly successful African hominids then dispersed widely to other areas and did so on several occasions. There were at least two major emigrations out of Africa and perhaps as many as four. The features we see as most distinctive of our species, such as bipedal locomotion, large brain size, and culture, all began in Africa. The most recent evidence provided by fossils, highly detailed genetic data, and archaeological finds further points to our most distinctive fully "human" characteristics also originating in Africa. Artistic expression, body ornamentation, full language, complex social organization, and elaborate tools also perhaps all first developed in the savannas, near the forest edge, or along stream channels in Africa. Only later, as African migrants spread to other areas, do we find these human characteristics outside of Africa.

Our origins are clearly African. Our bodies and brains were shaped as they evolved largely in Africa. All humans share most of their genes with each other, more so than do other primates. This, too, suggests a recent origin of humanity from a restricted ancestral population—one that almost certainly was African. So in every meaningful evolutionary and biocultural aspect, we *are* all Africans. The practical implications are clear as they apply to human social relations. The next time you seriously consider the meaning of race, think about your African roots.

Critical Thinking Questions

1. What anatomical characteristics define *modern* as compared to *premodern* humans? Assume that you're analyzing an incomplete skeleton that may be early modern *H. sapiens*. Which portions of the skeleton would be most informative, and why?

2. Go through the chapter and list all the forms of evidence that you think support the complete replacement model. Now, do the same for the regional continuity model. What evidence do you find most convincing, and why?

3. Why are the fossils recently discovered from Herto so important? How does this evidence influence your conclusions in question 2?

4. What archaeological evidence shows that modern human behavior during the Upper Paleolithic was significantly different from that of earlier hominids? Do you think that early modern *H. sapiens* populations were behaviorally superior to the Neandertals? Be careful to define what you mean by "superior."

5. Why do you think some Upper Paleolithic people painted in caves? Why don't we find such evidence of cave painting from a wider geographical area?

CHAPTER 12

Human Variation and Adaptation

FOCUS QUESTION

How does the contemporary evolutionary-based approach to *understanding human diversity differ from the traditional nineteenth-century approach?*

▶ Click!

Go to the following media resources for interactive activities, more information, and study materials on topics covered in this chapter:

- Anthropology Resource Center
- Student Companion Website for *Essentials of Physical Anthropology,* Seventh Edition
- Online Virtual Laboratories for Physical Anthropology CD-ROM, Fourth Edition
- Basic Genetics for Anthropology CD-ROM 2.0: Principles and Applications

Introduction

At some time or other, you've probably been asked to specify your "race" or "ethnicity" on an application or census form. How did you feel about that? Usually, you can choose from a variety of racial/ethnic categories. Was it easy to pick one? Where would your parents and grandparents fit in?

Notions about human diversity have played a large role in human relations for at least a few thousand years, and they still influence political and social perceptions. While we'd like to believe that informed views have become almost universal, the gruesome tally of genocidal/ethnic cleansing atrocities in recent years tells us that worldwide, we have a long way to go before tolerance becomes the norm.

Most people don't seem to understand the nature of human diversity, and worse yet, many seem quite unwilling to accept what science has to contribute on the subject. Many of the misconceptions, especially those regarding how race is defined and categorized, are rooted in cultural history over the last few centuries. Although many cultures have tried to come to grips with these issues, for better or worse, the most influential of these perspectives were developed in the Western world (that is, Europe and North America). The way many individuals still view themselves and their relationship to other peoples is a legacy of the last four centuries of racial interpretations.

In Chapters 3 and 4, we saw how physical characteristics are influenced by the DNA in our cells. We went on to discuss how individuals inherit genes from parents and how variations in genes (alleles) can produce different expressions of traits. We also focused on how the basic principles of inheritance are related to evolutionary change.

In this chapter, we'll continue to discuss topics that directly relate to genetics, namely biological diversity in humans and how humans adapt physically to environmental challenges. After discussing historical attempts at explaining human phenotypic diversity and racial classification, we'll examine contemporary methods of interpreting diversity. In recent years, several new techniques have emerged that permit direct examination of the DNA molecule, revealing differences between individuals even at the level of single nucleotides. But as discoveries of different levels of diversity emerge, geneticists have also shown that our species is remarkably uniform genetically, particularly when compared with other species.

Historical Views of Human Variation

The first step toward understanding diversity in nature is to organize it into categories that can then be named, discussed, and perhaps studied. Historically, when different groups of people came into contact with one another, they tried to account for the physical differences they saw. Because skin color was so noticeable, it was one of the more frequently explained traits, and most systems of racial classification were based on it.

As early as 1350 B.C., the ancient Egyptians had classified humans based on their skin color: red for Egyptian, yellow for people to the east, white for those to the north, and black for sub-Saharan Africans (Gossett, 1963). In the sixteenth century, after the discovery of the New World, several European countries embarked on a period of intense exploration and colonization in both the New and Old Worlds. One result of this contact was an increased awareness of human diversity.

Throughout the eighteenth and nineteenth centuries, European and American scientists concentrated primarily on describing and classifying the biological variation in humans as well as in nonhuman species. The first scientific attempt to describe the newly discovered variation among human populations was Linnaeus' taxonomic classification (see p. 21), which placed humans into four separate categories (Linnaeus, 1758). Linnaeus assigned behavioral and intellectual qualities to each group, with the least complimentary descriptions going to sub-Saharan, dark-skinned Africans. This ranking was typical of the period and reflected the almost universal European ethnocentric view that Europeans were superior to everyone else.

Johann Friedrich Blumenbach (1752–1840), a German anatomist, classified humans into five races. Although Blumenbach's categories came to be described simply as white, yellow, red, black, and brown, he also used criteria other than skin color. Blumenbach emphasized that categories based on skin color were arbitrary and that many traits, including skin color, weren't discrete phenomena and that their expression often overlapped between groups. He also pointed out that classifying all humans using such a system would omit everyone who didn't neatly fall into a specific category.

Nevertheless, by the mid-nineteenth century, populations were ranked essentially on a scale based on skin color (along with size and shape of the head), with sub-Saharan Africans at the bottom. The Europeans themselves were also ranked, so that northern, light-skinned populations were considered superior to their southern, somewhat darker-skinned neighbors from Italy and Greece.

To many Europeans, the fact that non-Europeans weren't Christian suggested that they were "uncivilized" and implied an even more basic inferiority of character and intellect. This view was rooted in a concept called **biological determinism,** which in part holds that there is an association between physical characteristics and such attributes as intelligence, morals, values, abilities, and even social and economic status. In other words, cultural variations are *inherited* in the same way that biological differences are. It follows, then, that there are inherent behavioral and cognitive differences between groups and that, by nature, some groups are superior to others. Following this logic, it's fairly easy to justify the persecution and even enslavement of other peoples simply because their outward appearance differs from what is familiar.

After 1850, biological determinism was a predominant theme underlying common thinking as well as scientific research in Europe and the United States. Most people, including such notable figures as Thomas Jefferson, Georges Cuvier, Benjamin Franklin, Charles Lyell, Abraham Lincoln, Charles Darwin, and Oliver Wendell Holmes, held deterministic (and what today we'd call racist) views. Commenting on this usually de-emphasized characteristic of more respected historical figures, the late evolutionary biologist Stephen J. Gould (1981, p. 32) remarked that "all American culture heroes embraced racial attitudes that would embarrass public-school mythmakers."

Francis Galton (1822–1911), Charles Darwin's cousin, shared an increasingly common fear among nineteenth-century Europeans that "civilized society" was being weakened by the failure of natural selection to completely eliminate unfit and inferior members (Greene, 1981, p. 107). Galton wrote and lectured on the necessity of "race improvement" and suggested government regulation of marriage and family size, an approach he called **eugenics.** Although eugenics had its share of critics, its popularity flourished throughout the 1930s. Nowhere was it more attractive than

biological determinism The concept that phenomena, including various aspects of behavior (e.g., intelligence, values, morals) are governed by biological (genetic) factors; the inaccurate association of various behavioral attributes with certain biological traits, such as skin color.

eugenics The philosophy of "race improvement" through the forced sterilization of members of some groups and increased reproduction among others; an overly simplified, often racist view that is now discredited.

in Germany, where the viewpoint took a horrifying turn. The false idea of pure races was increasingly extolled as a means of reestablishing a strong and prosperous state, and eugenics was seen as scientific justification for purging Germany of its "unfit." Many of Germany's scientists continued to support the policies of racial purity and eugenics during the Nazi period (Proctor, 1988, p. 143), when these ideologies served as excuses for condemning millions of people to death.

But at the same time, many scientists were turning away from racial typologies and classification in favor of a more evolutionary approach. No doubt for some, this shift in direction was motivated by their growing concerns over the goals of the eugenics movement. Probably more important, however, was the synthesis of genetics and Darwin's theories of natural selection during the 1930s. As discussed in Chapter 4, this breakthrough influenced all the biological sciences, and some physical anthropologists soon began applying evolutionary principles to the study of human variation.

The Concept of Race

All contemporary humans are members of the same **polytypic** species, *Homo sapiens*. A polytypic species is composed of local populations that differ in the expression of one or more traits. Even *within* local populations, there's a great deal of genotypic and phenotypic variation between individuals.

In discussions of human variation, people have traditionally combined various characteristics, such as skin color, face shape, nose shape, hair color, hair form (curly or straight), and eye color. People who have particular combinations of these and other traits have been placed together in categories associated with specific geographical localities. Such categories are called *races*.

We all think we know what we mean by the word *race*, but in reality, the term has had various meanings since the 1500s, when it first appeared in the English language. Race has been used synonymously with *species*, as in "the human race." Since the 1600s, race has also referred to various culturally defined groups, and this meaning is still common. For example, you'll hear people say, "the English race" or "the Japanese race," when they actually mean nationality. Another phrase you've probably heard is "the Jewish race," when the speaker is really talking about an ethnic and religious identity.

So even though *race* is usually a term with biological connotations, it also has enormous social significance. And there's still a widespread perception that certain physical traits (skin color, in particular) are associated with numerous cultural attributes, such as language, occupational preferences, or even morality (however it's defined). As a result, in many cultural contexts, a person's social identity is strongly influenced by the way he or she expresses those physical traits traditionally used to define "racial groups." Characteristics such as skin color are highly visible, and they make it easy to superficially place people into socially defined categories. However, so-called racial traits aren't the only phenotypic expressions that contribute to social identity. Sex and age are also critically important. But aside from these two variables, an individual's biological and/or ethnic background is still inevitably a factor that influences how he or she is initially perceived and judged by others.

References to national origin (for example, African, Asian) as substitutes for racial labels have become more common in recent years, both within and outside anthropology. Within anthropology, the term *ethnicity* was proposed in the early 1950s to avoid the more emotionally charged term *race*. Strictly speaking, ethnicity refers to cultural factors, but the fact that the words *ethnicity* and *race* are used interchangeably reflects the social importance of phenotypic expression and demonstrates once again how phenotype is mistakenly associated with culturally defined variables.

In its most common biological usage, the term *race* refers to geographically patterned phenotypic variation within a species. By the seventeenth century, naturalists were beginning to describe races in plants and nonhuman animals. They had recognized that when populations of a species occupied different regions, they

polytypic Referring to species composed of populations that differ with regard to the expression of one or more traits.

sometimes differed from one another in the expression of one or more traits. But even today, there are no established criteria for assessing races of plants and animals, including humans.

Before World War II, most studies of human variation focused on visible phenotypic variation between large, geographically defined populations, and these studies were largely descriptive. Since World War II, the emphasis has shifted to examining differences in allele frequencies within and between populations, as well as considering the adaptive significance of phenotypic and genotypic variation. This shift in focus occurred partly because of the Modern Synthesis in biology and partly because of further advances in genetics.

In the second half of the twentieth century, the application of evolutionary principles to the study of modern human variation replaced the superficial nineteenth-century view of race *based solely on observed phenotype.* Additionally, the genetic emphasis dispelled previously held misconceptions that races are fixed biological entities that don't change over time and that are composed of individuals who all conform to a particular *type.* Clearly, there are phenotypic differences between humans, and some of these differences roughly correspond to particular geographical locations. But certain questions must be asked. Do readily observable phenotypic variations, like skin color, have adaptive significance? Is genetic drift a factor? What is the degree of underlying genetic variation that influences phenotypic variation? These questions are founded in a completely different perspective from that of 50 years ago and they place considerations of human variation within a contemporary evolutionary framework.

Although, physical anthropology is partly rooted in attempts to explain human diversity, no contemporary anthropologist subscribes to pre-Darwinian and pre–Modern Synthesis concepts of races (human or nonhuman) as fixed biological entities. Also, anthropologists recognize that race isn't a valid concept, especially from a genetic perspective, because the amount of genetic variation accounted for by differences *between* groups is vastly exceeded by the variation that exists *within groups.* Many physical anthropologists also argue that race is an outdated creation of the human mind that attempts to simplify biological complexity by organizing it into categories. Therefore, human races are a product of the human tendency to impose order on complex natural phenomena. In this view, simplistic classification may have been an understandable approach some 150 years ago, but given the current state of genetic and evolutionary science, it's absolutely meaningless today.

Even so, some anthropologists continue to view outwardly expressed phenotypic variations as having the potential to yield information about population adaptation, genetic drift, mutation, and gene flow. Forensic anthropologists, in particular, find the phenotypic criteria associated with race (especially in the skeleton) to have practical applications. Law enforcement agencies frequently call upon them to help identify human skeletal remains. Because unidentified human remains are often those of crime victims, identification must be as accurate as possible. The most important variables in such identification are the individual's sex, age, stature, and ancestry or "racial" and ethnic background. Using metric and nonmetric criteria, forensic anthropologists use various techniques for establishing broad population affinity (that is, a likely relationship) for that individual. Generally, their findings are accurate about 80 percent of the time.

In general, biological anthropologists object to racial taxonomies because traditional classification schemes are *typological,* meaning that categories are distinct and based on stereotypes or ideals that comprise a specific set of traits. So in general, typologies are inherently misleading because any grouping always includes many individuals who don't conform to all aspects of a particular type. In any so-called racial group, there will be people who fall into the normal range of variation for another population based on one or several characteristics. For example, two people of different ancestry might have different skin color, but they could share any number of other traits, including height, head shape, hair color, eye color, or ABO blood

FIGURE 12-1

Some examples of phenotypic variation among Africans.
(a) San (South African)
(b) West African (Bantu)
(c) Ethiopian
(d) Ituri (Central African)
(e) North African (Tunisia)

type. In fact, they could easily share more similarities with each other than they do with many members of their own populations (Fig. 12-1).

The characteristics that have traditionally been used to define races are *polygenic;* that is, they're influenced by several genes and therefore exhibit a continuous range of expression. So it's difficult, if not impossible, to draw distinct boundaries between populations with regard to many traits. This limitation becomes clear if you ask yourself, "At what point is hair color no longer dark brown but medium brown, or no longer light brown but dark blond?" Also, you may want to refer back to Fig. 4-7, p. 66 to see how eye color exhibits continuous gradations from light blue to dark brown.

The scientific controversy over race will fade as we enhance our understanding of the genetic diversity (and also the uniformity) of our species. Given the rapid changes in genome studies, and because very few genes contribute to outward expressions of phenotype, dividing the human species into racial categories isn't a biologically meaningful way to look at human variation. But among the general public, variations on the theme of race will undoubtedly continue to be the most common view of human variation. Keeping all this in mind, it falls to anthropologists and biologists to continue exploring the issue so that, to the best of our abilities, accurate information about human variation is available to anyone who seeks informed explanations of complex phenomena.

Racism

Racism is based on the previously mentioned false belief that along with physical characteristics, humans inherit such factors as intellect and various cultural attributes. Such beliefs also commonly rest on the assumption that one's own group is superior to other groups.

Since we've already alluded to certain aspects of racism, such as the eugenics movement and persecution of people based on racial or ethnic misconceptions, we won't belabor the point here. It's important, though, to point out that racism is hardly a thing of the past, and it's not restricted to Europeans and North Americans of European descent. Racism is a cultural phenomenon, and it's found worldwide.

We end this brief discussion of racism with an excerpt from an article, "The Study of Race," by the late Sherwood Washburn, a well-known physical anthropologist who taught at the University of California, Berkeley. Although written many years ago, the statement is as applicable today as it was then:

> Races are products of the past. They are relics of times and conditions which have long ceased to exist. Racism is equally a relic supported by no phase of modern science. We may not know how to interpret the form of the Mongoloid face, or why Rh is of high incidence in Africa, but we do know the benefits of education and of economic progress. We . . . know that the roots of happiness lie in the biology of the whole species and that the potential of the species can only be realized in a culture, in a social system. It is knowledge and the social system which give life or take it away, and in so doing change the gene frequencies and continue the million-year-old interaction of culture and biology. Human biology finds its realization in a culturally determined way of life, and the infinite variety of genetic combinations can only express themselves efficiently in a free and open society. (Washburn, 1963, p. 531)

Intelligence

As we've shown, belief in the relationship between physical characteristics and specific behavioral attributes is common even today, but there's no scientific evidence to show that personality or any other behavioral trait differs genetically *between* human groups. Most scientists would agree with this last statement, but one question that produces controversy inside scientific circles and among laypeople is whether or not there is a relationship between population affinity and **intelligence**.

Genetic and environmental factors contribute to intelligence, although it's not possible to accurately measure the percentage each contributes. What can be said is that IQ scores and intelligence aren't the same thing. IQ scores can change during a person's lifetime, and average IQ scores of different populations overlap. Such differences in average IQ scores that do exist between groups are difficult to interpret, given the problems inherent in the design of the IQ tests. What's more, complex cognitive abilities, however they're measured, are influenced by multiple loci and are thus polygenic.

Innate factors set limits and define potentials for behavior and cognitive ability in any species. In humans, the limits are broad and the potentials aren't fully known. Individual abilities result from complex interactions between genetic and environmental factors. One product of this interaction is learning, and in turn, the ability to learn is influenced by genetic and other biological components. Undeniably, there are differences among individuals regarding these factors, but it's probably impossible to determine what proportion of the variation in test scores is due to biological factors. Besides, innate differences in abilities reflect individual variation *within* populations, not inherent differences *between* them. Comparing populations based on the results of IQ tests is a misuse of testing procedures. There's no convincing evidence *whatsoever* that populations vary in their cognitive abilities, regardless of what some popular books may suggest. Unfortunately, racist attitudes toward intelligence continue to flourish, despite the lack of evidence of mental inferiority of some populations and mental superiority of others and despite the questionable validity of intelligence tests.

intelligence Mental capacity; ability to learn, reason, or comprehend and interpret information, facts, relationships, and meanings; the capacity to solve problems, whether through the application of previously acquired knowledge or through insight.

Contemporary Interpretations of Human Variation

Since the physical characteristics (such as skin color and hair form) used to define race are *polygenic*, measuring the genetic influence on them hasn't been possible. So physical anthropologists and other biologists who study modern human variation have largely abandoned the traditional perspective of describing superficial phenotypic characteristics in favor of *measuring* actual *genetic* characteristics.

Beginning in the 1950s, studies of modern human variation focused on the various components of blood as well as other aspects of body chemistry. Such traits as the ABO blood types are *phenotypes*, but they are *direct* products of the genotype. (Recall that protein-coding genes direct cells to make proteins, and the antigens on blood cells and many components of blood serum are partly composed of proteins; Fig. 12-2). During the twentieth century, this perspective met with a great deal of success, as eventually dozens of loci were identified and the frequencies of many specific alleles were obtained from numerous human populations. Nevertheless, in all these cases, it was the phenotype that was observed, and information about the underlying genotype remained largely unobtainable. But beginning in the 1990s, with the advent of genomic studies, new techniques were developed. Now that we can directly sequence DNA, we can actually identify entire genes and even larger DNA segments and make comparisons between individuals and populations. A decade ago, only a small portion of the human genome was accessible to physical anthropologists, but now we have the capacity to obtain DNA profiles for virtually every human population on earth. And we can expect that in the next decade, our understanding and knowledge of human biological variation and adaptation will dramatically increase.

polymorphisms Loci with more than one allele. Polymorphisms can be expressed in the phenotype as the result of gene action (as in ABO), or they can exist solely at the DNA level within noncoding regions.

Human Polymorphisms

Traits that differ in expression between populations and individuals are called **polymorphisms,** and they're the main focus of human variation studies. A genetic trait is *polymorphic* if the locus that governs it has two or more alleles. (Refer back to p. 62 for a discussion of the ABO blood group system governed by three alleles at

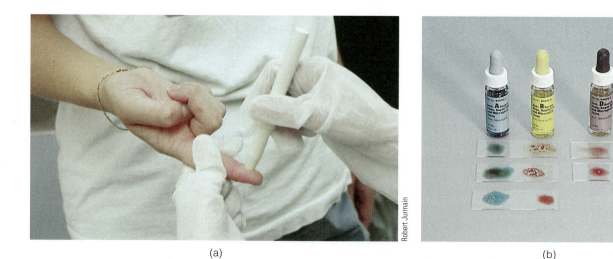

(a)

(b)

Robert Jurmain

Robert Jurmain

FIGURE 12-2

(a) A blood sample is drawn. (b) To determine an individual's blood type, a few drops of blood are treated with specific chemicals. Presence of A and B blood type, as well as Rh, can be detected by using commercially available chemicals. The glass slides below the blue- and yellow-labeled bottles show reactions for the ABO system. The blood on the top slide (at left) is type AB; the middle is type B; and the bottom is type A. The two samples to the right depict Rh-negative blood (top) and Rh-positive blood (bottom).

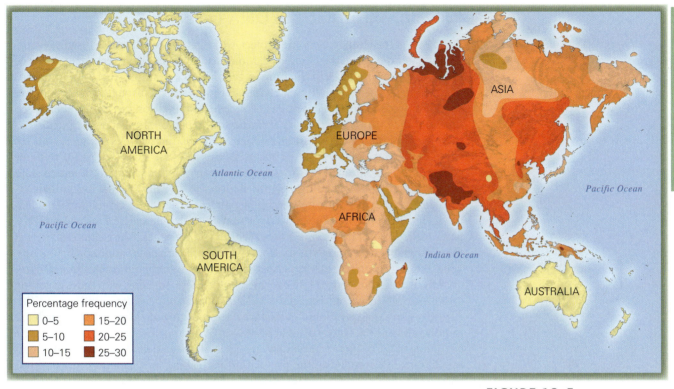

FIGURE 12-3

ABO blood group system. Distribution of the *B* allele in the indigenous populations of the world. (After Mourant et al., 1976.)

one locus.) Since new alleles arise by mutation and their frequency increases or decreases as a result of natural selection, understanding polymorphisms requires evolutionary explanations. Therefore, by studying polymorphisms and comparing allele frequencies between different populations, we can begin to reconstruct the evolutionary events that have caused certain human genetic differences.

By the 1960s, the study of *clinal distributions* of individual polymorphisms had become a popular alternative to the racial approach to human diversity. A **cline** is a gradual change in the frequency of a trait or allele in populations dispersed over geographical space. In humans, the various expressions of many polymorphic traits exhibit a more or less continuous distribution from one region to another, and most of the traits that have been shown to have a clinal distribution are Mendelian. The distribution of the *A* and *B* alleles in the Old World provides a good example of a clinal distribution (Fig. 12-3). Clinal distributions are generally thought to reflect microevolutionary influences of natural selection and/or gene flow. Consequently, clinal distributions are explained in evolutionary terms.

The ABO system is interesting from an anthropological perspective because the frequencies of the *A*, *B*, and *O* alleles vary tremendously among humans. In most groups, *A* and *B* are rarely found in frequencies greater than 50 percent, and usually their frequencies are much lower. Still, most human groups are polymorphic for all three alleles, but there are exceptions. For example, in native South American Indians, frequencies of the *O* allele reach 100 percent. (Actually, you could say that in these groups, the ABO system isn't polymorphic.) Exceptionally high frequencies of *O* are also found in northern Australia, and some islands off the Australian coast show frequencies exceeding 90 percent. In these populations, the high frequencies of the *O* allele are probably due to genetic drift (founder effect), although the influence of natural selection can't be entirely ruled out.

Examining single traits can be informative regarding potential influences of natural selection or gene flow. This approach, however, is limited when we try to sort out population relationships, since the study of single traits, by themselves, can lead to confusing interpretations regarding likely population relationships. A more meaningful approach is to study several traits simultaneously.

cline A gradual change in the frequency of genotypes and phenotypes from one geographical region to another.

Polymorphisms at the DNA Level

As a result of the Human Genome Project, we've gained considerable insight regarding human variation at the DNA level. Molecular biologists have recently discovered many variations in DNA in the human genome. For example, there are hundreds of sites where DNA segments are repeated, in some cases just a few times, in other cases hundreds of times. These areas of nucleotide repetitions are called *microsatellites,* and they vary tremendously from person to person. In fact, every person has their own unique arrangement that defines their distinctive "DNA fingerprint." In Chapter 3, you saw how forensic scientists can now use PCR (see p. 53) to make copies of DNA contained in, for example, a drop of blood, a hair, or a semen stain and then study the "DNA fingerprints" in order to identify specific individuals.

Finally, researchers are now mapping patterns of variation in individual nucleotides. Of course, it's been recognized for some time that changes of individual DNA bases (called "point mutations") occur within coding genes. The sickle-cell allele at the hemoglobin beta locus is the best-known example of a point mutation in humans. What has only been recently appreciated, however, is that point mutations also frequently occur in noncoding DNA segments, and these, together with those in coding regions of DNA, are all referred to as *single nucleotide polymorphisms (SNPs)*. Already, more than a million SNPs have been recognized, 96 percent of which are in noncoding DNA (International SNP Map Working Group, 2001). Thus, at the beginning of the twenty-first century, geneticists have gained access to a vast biological "library," documenting the population patterning and genetic history of our species.

Another area of recent research holds great promise for future advances. Our understanding of polygenic traits has been inadequate because we didn't know the locations of the genes that contribute to them. But now, geneticists can identify specific loci, and soon they'll be able to isolate particular gene variants that contribute to skin color (see p. 64), stature, hypertension, and many other poorly understood human traits. For example, with the publication of the chimpanzee genome and the first opportunity to compare human gene sequences with those seen in our closest relatives, geneticists have identified specific alleles that probably contribute to coronary artery disease and diabetes (The Chimpanzee Sequencing and Analysis Consortium, 2005).

As you can see, the recently developed tools now used by geneticists permit the study of human genetic variation at a level never before conceived. Such research will have a profound influence on our changing views of human diversity in the coming years. Moreover, through the use of these new techniques, the broader history of our species is coming under closer genetic scrutiny.

Human Biocultural Evolution

We've defined culture as the human strategy of adaptation. Humans live in cultural environments that are continually modified by their own activities; thus, evolutionary processes are understandable only within this *cultural* context. You will recall that natural selection pressures operate within specific environmental settings. For humans and many of our hominid ancestors, this means an environment dominated by culture. For example, you learned in Chapter 4 that the altered form of hemoglobin called Hb^S confers resistance to malaria. But the sickle-cell allele hasn't always been an important factor in human populations. Before the development of agriculture, humans rarely, if ever, lived close to mosquito-breeding areas for long periods of time. But with the spread in Africa of **slash-and-burn agriculture,** perhaps in just the last 2,000 years, penetration and clearing of tropical forests occurred. As a result, rain water was left to stand in open, stagnant pools that provided mosquito-breeding areas close to human settlements. DNA analyses have further confirmed such a recent origin and spread of the sickle-cell allele in a population from Senegal,

slash-and-burn agriculture
A traditional land-clearing practice whereby trees and vegetation are cut and burned. In many areas, fields are abandoned after a few years and clearing occurs elsewhere.

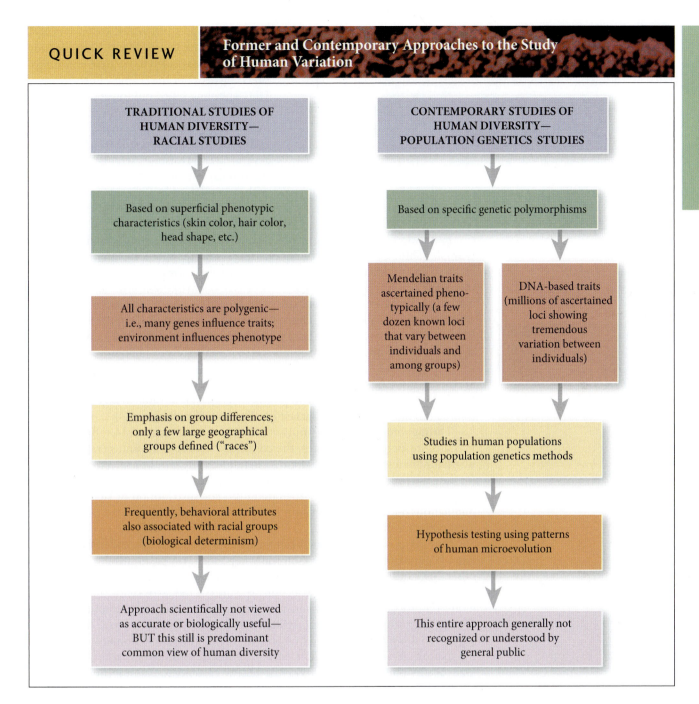

QUICK REVIEW

Former and Contemporary Approaches to the Study of Human Variation

in West Africa. One recent study estimates the origin of the Hb^s mutation in this group at between 1,250 and 2,100 ya (Currat et al., 2002). Thus, it appears that at least in some areas, malaria began to have an impact on human populations only recently. But once it did, it became a powerful selective force.

The increase in the frequency of the sickle-cell allele is a biological adaptation to an environmental change (see p. 72). However, as you learned in Chapter 3, this type of adaptation comes with a huge cost. Heterozygotes (people with sickle-cell trait) have increased resistance to malaria and presumably higher reproductive success, but prior to modern medical treatment, some of their offspring died from the genetic disease sickle-cell anemia; indeed, this situation still persists in much of the developing world. So there is a counterbalance between selective forces with an advantage for carriers *only* in malarial environments. The genetic patterns of recessive traits such as sickle-cell anemia are discussed in Chapter 4.

FIGURE 12-4
Evolutionary interactions affecting the frequency of the sickle-cell allele.

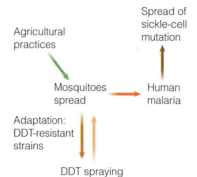

TABLE 12.1	Frequencies of Lactose Intolerance
Population Group	**Percent**
U.S. whites	2–19
Finnish	18
Swiss	12
Swedish	4
U.S. blacks	70–77
Ibos	99
Bantu	90
Fulani	22
Thais	99
Asian Americans	95–100
Native Americans	85

Source: Lerner and Libby, 1976, p. 327.

lactase persistence The ability to continue to produce the enzyme lactase in adults. Most mammals, including humans, lose this ability after they are weaned.

Following World War II, extensive DDT spraying by the World Health Organization began systematically to control mosquito-breeding areas in the tropics. Forty years of DDT spraying killed millions of mosquitoes (and had devastating consequences for some local bird populations); but natural selection, acting on these insect populations, produced several DDT-resistant strains (Fig. 12-4). Accordingly, malaria is again on the rise, with several hundred thousand new cases reported annually in India, Africa, and Central America.

Lactose intolerance, which involves an individual's ability to digest milk, is another example of human biocultural evolution. In all human populations, infants and young children are able to digest milk, an obvious necessity for any young mammal. One ingredient of milk is *lactose,* a sugar that's broken down by the enzyme *lactase.* In most mammals, including many humans, the gene that codes for lactase production "switches off" in adolescence. Once this happens, if a person drinks fresh milk, the lactose ferments in the large intestine, leading to diarrhea and severe gastrointestinal upset. So, as you might expect, adults stop consuming fresh milk products. Among many African and Asian populations (a majority of humankind today), most adults are lactose-intolerant (Table 12-1). But in other populations, including some Africans and Europeans, adults continue to produce lactase and are able to digest fresh milk. This continued production of lactase is called **lactase persistence.**

Throughout most of hominid evolution, milk was unavailable after weaning. Perhaps, in such circumstances, the continued action of an unnecessary enzyme might inhibit digestion of other foods. Therefore, there *may* be a selective advantage for the gene coding for lactase production to switch off. So why can some adults (the majority in some populations) tolerate milk? The distribution of lactose-tolerant populations may provide an answer to this question, and it suggests a powerful cultural influence on this trait.

Europeans, who are generally lactose-tolerant, are partly descended from Middle Eastern populations. Often economically dependent on pastoralism, these groups raised cows and/or goats and probably drank considerable quantities of milk. In such a cultural environment, strong selection pressures would favor lactose tolerance, and modern European descendants of these populations apparently retain this ancient ability. Very interesting genetic evidence from north-central Europe has recently supported this interpretation. DNA analysis of both cattle *and* humans suggest that these species have, to some extent, coevolved and this resulted in cattle that produce high-quality milk and humans with the genetic capacity to digest it (Beja-Pereira et al., 2003). In other words, more than 5,000 years ago, populations of north-central Europe were selectively breeding cattle for higher milk yields. And as these populations were increasing their dependence on fresh milk, they were inadvertently selecting for the gene that produces lactase persistence in themselves.

But perhaps even more informative is the distribution of lactose tolerance in Africa, where the majority of people are lactose-intolerant. But groups such as the Fulani and Tutsi, who have been pastoralists for perhaps thousands of years, have much higher rates of lactose persistence than nonpastoralists. Presumably, like their European counterparts, they've retained the ability to produce lactase because of the continued consumption of fresh milk (Powell et al., 2003).

As we've seen, the geographical distribution of lactase persistence is related to a history of cultural dependence on fresh milk products. There are, however, some populations that rely on dairying but don't have high rates of lactase persistence (Fig. 12-5). It's been suggested that such populations traditionally have consumed their milk in the form of cheese and yogurt, in which the lactose has been broken down by bacterial action (Durham, 1981).

FIGURE 12–5
Natives of Mongolia rely heavily on milk products from goats and sheep, but mostly consume these foods in the form of cheese and yogurt.

The interaction of human cultural environments and changes in lactose tolerance among human populations is another example of biocultural evolution. In the last few thousand years, cultural factors have initiated specific evolutionary changes in human groups. Such cultural factors have probably influenced the course of human evolution for at least 3 million years, and today they are of paramount importance.

Population Genetics

Physical anthropologists use the approach of **population genetics** to interpret microevolutionary patterns of human variation. Population genetics is the area of research that, among other things, examines allele frequencies in populations and attempts to identify the various factors that cause allele frequencies to change in specific groups. As we defined it in Chapter 4, a *population* is a group of interbreeding individuals that share a common **gene pool.** As a rule, a population is the group within which individuals are most likely to find mates.

In theory, this is a straightforward concept. In every generation, the genes (alleles) in a gene pool are mixed by recombination and then reunited with their counterparts (located on paired chromosomes) through mating. What emerges in the next generation is a direct product of the genes going into the pool, which in turn is a product of who is mating with whom.

Factors that determine mate choice are geographical, ecological, and social. If people are isolated on a remote island in the middle of the Pacific, there isn't much chance they'll find a mate outside the immediate vicinity. Such **breeding isolates** are fairly easily defined and are a favorite target of microevolutionary studies. Geography plays a dominant role in producing these isolates by strictly determining the range of available mates. But even within these limits, cultural rules can play a deciding role by prescribing who is most appropriate among those who are potentially available.

Most humans today aren't so clearly defined as members of particular populations as they would be if they belonged to a breeding isolate. Inhabitants of large cities may appear to be members of a single population, but within the city, socioeconomic, ethnic, and religious boundaries crosscut in complex ways to form smaller population segments. In addition to being members of these local population groupings, we are simultaneously members of overlapping gradations of larger populations: the immediate geographical region (a metropolitan area or perhaps a state), a section of the country, a nation, and ultimately, the entire species.

population genetics The study of the frequency of alleles, genotypes, and phenotypes in populations from a microevolutionary perspective.

gene pool The total complement of genes shared by the reproductive members of a population.

breeding isolates Populations that are clearly isolated geographically and/or socially from other breeding groups.

Once specific human populations have been identified, the next step is to ascertain what evolutionary forces, if any, are operating on them. To determine whether evolution is taking place at a given locus, population geneticists measure allele frequencies for specific traits and compare these observed frequencies with a set predicted by a mathematical model called the **Hardy-Weinberg equilibrium** equation. Just how the equation is used is illustrated in Appendix C. The Hardy-Weinberg formula provides a tool to establish whether allele frequencies in a population are indeed changing. In Chapter 4, we discussed several factors that act to change allele frequencies, including:

1. New variation (that is, new alleles produced by mutation)
2. Redistributed variation (that is, *gene flow* or *genetic drift*)
3. Selection of "advantageous" allele combinations that promote reproductive success (that is, *natural selection*)

The Adaptive Significance of Human Variation

Today, biological anthropologists view human variation as the result of the evolutionary factors we have already named: mutation; genetic drift (including founder effect), gene flow; and natural selection (the latter especially seen in adaptations to environmental conditions, both past and present). As we've emphasized, cultural adaptations have also played an important role in the evolution of our species, and although in this discussion we're primarily concerned with biological issues, we must still consider the influence of cultural practices on human adaptive responses.

To survive, all organisms must maintain the normal functions of internal organs, tissues, and cells within the context of an ever-changing environment. Even during the course of a single, seemingly uneventful day, there are numerous fluctuations in temperature, wind, solar radiation, humidity, and so on. Physical activity also places **stress** on physiological mechanisms. The body must accommodate all these changes by compensating in some manner to maintain internal constancy, or **homeostasis,** and all life forms have evolved physiological mechanisms that, within limits, achieve this goal.

Physiological response to environmental change is influenced by genetic factors. We've already defined adaptation as a functional response to environmental conditions in populations and individuals. In a narrower sense, adaptation refers to *long-term* evolutionary (that is, genetic) changes that characterize all individuals within a population or species.

Examples of long-term adaptations in humans include some physiological responses to heat (sweating) or excessive levels of ultraviolet (UV) light (deeply pigmented skin in tropical regions). Such characteristics are the results of evolutionary change in species or populations, and they don't vary as the result of short-term environmental change. For example, the ability to sweat isn't lost in people who spend their entire lives in predominantly cool areas. Likewise, individuals born with dark skin won't become pale, even if they're never exposed to intense sunlight.

Acclimatization is another kind of physiological response to environmental conditions, and it can be short-term, long-term, or even permanent. These responses to environmental factors are partially influenced by genes, but some can also be affected by the duration and severity of the exposure, technological buffers (such as shelter or clothing), and individual behavior, weight, and overall body size.

The simplest type of acclimatization is a temporary and rapid adjustment to an environmental change (Hanna, 1999). Tanning, which can occur in almost everyone, is an example of this kind of acclimatization. Another example (one you've probably experienced but don't know it) is the very rapid increase in hemoglobin production that occurs when people who live at low elevations travel to higher ones.

Hardy-Weinberg equilibrium The mathematical relationship expressing, under ideal conditions, the predicted distribution of alleles in populations; the central theorem of population genetics.

stress In a physiological context, any factor that acts to disrupt homeostasis; more precisely, the body's response to any factor that threatens its ability to maintain homeostasis.

homeostasis A condition of balance, or stability, within a biological system, maintained by the interaction of physiological mechanisms that compensate for changes (both external and internal).

acclimatization Physiological responses to changes in the environment that occur during an individual's lifetime. Such responses may be temporary or permanent, depending on the duration of the environmental change and when in the individual's life it occurs. The *capacity* for acclimatization may typify an entire species or population, and because it's under genetic influence, it's subject to evolutionary factors such as natural selection or genetic drift.

This increase provides the body with more oxygen in an environment where oxygen is less available. In both these examples, the physiological change is temporary. Tans fade once exposure to sunlight is reduced, and hemoglobin production drops to original levels following a return to a lower elevation.

On the other hand, *developmental acclimatization* is irreversible and results from exposure to an environmental challenge during growth and development. Lifelong residents of high altitude exhibit certain expressions of developmental acclimatization.

In the following discussion, we present some examples of how humans respond to environmental challenges. Some of these examples characterize the entire species. Others illustrate adaptations seen in only some populations. And still others illustrate the more short-term process of acclimatization.

Solar Radiation, Vitamin D, and Skin Color

Skin color is a commonly cited example of adaptation through natural selection in humans. In general, prior to European contact, skin color in populations followed a largely predictable geographical distribution, especially in the Old World (Fig. 12-6). Populations with the greatest amount of pigmentation are found in the tropics, while lighter skin color is associated with more northern latitudes, particularly the inhabitants of northwestern Europe.

Skin color is mostly influenced by the pigment *melanin,* a granular substance produced by specialized cells (*melanocytes*) found in the epidermis (Fig. 12-7). All humans have approximately the same number of melanocytes. It's the amount of melanin and the size of the melanin granules that vary. Melanin is important because it acts as a built-in sunscreen by absorbing potentially dangerous UV rays present (although not visible) in sunlight. So melanin protects us from overexposure to UV radiation, which can cause genetic mutations in skin cells. These mutations may lead to skin cancer, which, if left untreated, can eventually spread to other organs and result in death.

As we previously mentioned, exposure to sunlight triggers a protective mechanism in the form of tanning, the result of temporarily increased melanin production

FIGURE 12-6

Geographical distribution of skin color in indigenous human populations. (After Biasutti, 1959.)

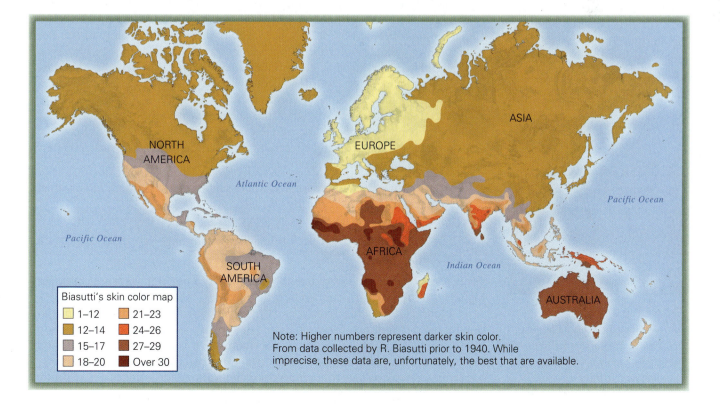

Biasutti's skin color map

1–12	21–23
12–14	24–26
15–17	27–29
18–20	Over 30

Note: Higher numbers represent darker skin color. From data collected by R. Biasutti prior to 1940. While imprecise, these data are, unfortunately, the best that are available.

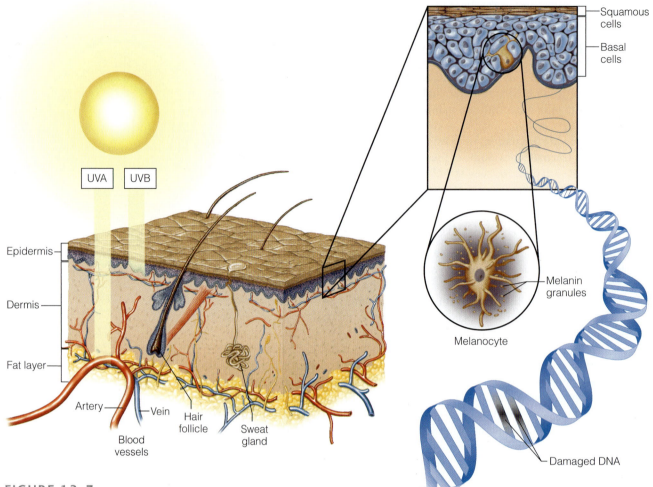

FIGURE 12-7
Ultraviolet rays penetrate the skin and can eventually damage DNA within skin cells. The three major types of cells that can be affected are squamous cells, basal cells, and melanocytes.

FIGURE 12-8
An African albino. This young man has a much greater chance of developing skin cancer than the man standing next to him.

(acclimatization). This response occurs in all humans except albinos, who carry a genetic mutation that prevents their melanocytes from producing melanin (Fig. 12-8). But even people who do produce melanin differ in their ability to tan. For instance, many people of northern European descent have very fair skin, blue eyes, and light hair. Their melanocytes produce small amounts of melanin, but when exposed to sunlight, they have little ability to increase production. And in all populations, women tend not to tan as deeply as men.

Natural selection has favored dark skin in areas nearest the equator, where the sun's rays are most direct and thus where exposure to UV light is most intense. In considering the cancer-causing effects of UV radiation from an *evolutionary* perspective, three points must be kept in mind:

1. Early hominids lived in the tropics, where solar radiation is more intense than in temperate areas to the north and south.
2. Unlike modern city dwellers, early hominids spent their days outdoors.
3. Early hominids didn't wear clothing that would have protected them from the sun.

Given these conditions, UV radiation was probably a powerful agent selecting for high levels of melanin production in early humans.

Jablonski (1992) and Jablonski and Chaplin (2000) offer an additional explanation for the distribution of skin color, one that focuses on the role of UV radiation in the degradation of folate. Folate is a B vitamin that isn't stored in the body and therefore must be replenished through dietary sources. Folate deficiencies in pregnant women are associated with numerous complications, including maternal death;

and in children they can lead to retarded growth and other serious conditions. Folate also plays a crucial role in **neural tube** development very early in embryonic development, and deficiencies can lead to defects, including various expressions of **spina bifida.** The consequences of severe neural tube defects can include pain, infection, paralysis, and even death. It goes without saying that neural tube defects can dramatically reduce the reproductive success of affected individuals.

Some studies have shown that UV radiation rapidly depletes folate serum levels both in laboratory experiments and in fair-skinned individuals. These findings have implications for pregnant women and children and also for the evolution of dark skin in hominids. Jablonski and Chaplin suggest that the earliest hominids may have had light body skin covered with dark hair, as is seen in chimpanzees and gorillas. (Both have darker skin on exposed body parts.) But as loss of body hair in hominids occurred, dark skin evolved rather quickly as a protective response to the damaging effects of UV radiation on folate.

As hominids migrated out of Africa into Europe and Asia, they faced new selective pressures. Not only were they moving away from the tropics, where ultraviolet rays were most direct, but they were also moving into areas where winters were cold and cloudy. Bear in mind, too, that physiological adaptations weren't sufficient to meet the demands of living in colder climates. Therefore, we assume that these populations were wearing animal skins or other types of clothing at least part of the year. Although clothing would have added necessary warmth, it would also have blocked exposure to sunlight. Consequently, the advantages provided by deeply pigmented skin in the tropics were no longer important, and selection for darker skin have been relaxed (Brace and Montagu, 1977).

However, relaxed selection for dark skin probably isn't sufficient to explain the very depigmented skin seen especially in some northern Europeans. Perhaps another factor, the need for adequate amounts of vitamin D, was also critical. The theory concerning the possible role of vitamin D, known as the *vitamin D hypothesis,* offers the following explanation.

Vitamin D is produced in the body partly as a result of the interaction between ultraviolet radiation and a substance similar to cholesterol. It's also available in some foods, including liver, fish oils, egg yolk, butter, and cream. Vitamin D is necessary for normal bone growth and mineralization, and some exposure to ultraviolet radiation is therefore essential. Insufficient amounts of vitamin D during childhood result in *rickets,* a condition that often leads to bowing of the long bones of the legs and deformation of the pelvis (Fig. 12-9). Pelvic deformities are of particular concern for women, because they can lead to a narrowing of the birth canal, which, in the absence of surgical intervention, frequently results in the death of both mother and infant during childbirth.

Rickets may have been a significant selective factor that favored lighter skin in regions with less sunlight. Reduced levels of UV light and the increased use of clothing could have been detrimental to dark-skinned individuals in more northern latitudes. In these people, melanin would have blocked absorption of the already reduced amounts of available ultraviolet radiation required for vitamin D synthesis. Therefore, selection pressures would have shifted over time to favor lighter skin. There is substantial evidence, both historically and in contemporary populations, to support this theory.

During the latter decades of the nineteenth century in the United States, African American inhabitants of northern cities suffered a higher incidence of rickets than whites. (The solution to this problem was fairly simple: the supplementation of milk with vitamin D.) Another example is seen in Britain, where darker-skinned East Indians and Pakistanis show a higher incidence of rickets than people with lighter skin (Molnar, 1983).

Jablonski and Chapin (2000) have also looked at the *potential* for vitamin D synthesis in people with different skin color based on the yearly average UV radiation at various latitudes (Fig. 12-10). Their conclusions support the vitamin D hypothesis to the point of stating that the requirement for vitamin D synthesis in northern latitudes was as important to natural selection as the need for protection from UV radiation in tropical regions.

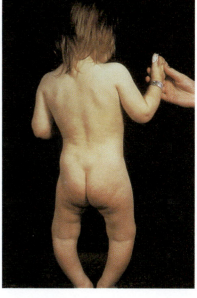

FIGURE 12-9
A child with rickets.

neural tube In early embryonic development, the anatomical structure that develops to form the brain and spinal cord.

spina bifida A condition in which the arch of one or more vertebrae fails to fuse and form a protective barrier around the spinal cord.

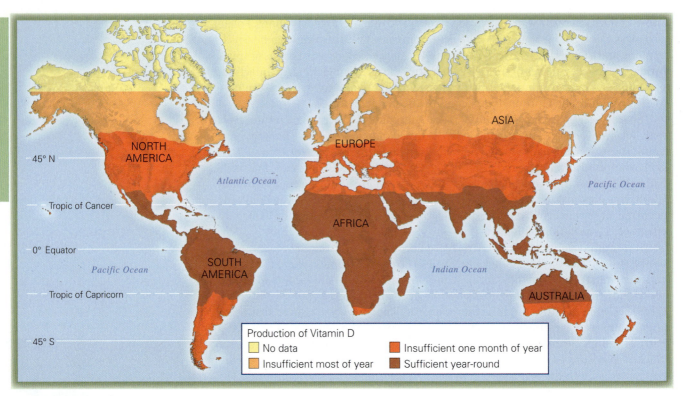

FIGURE 12-10

Populations indigenous to the tropics received enough UV radiation for vitamin D synthesis year-round. In other areas, people have moderately melanized skin and don't receive enough UV light for vitamin D synthesis for one month of the year. In still other areas, even light skin doesn't receive enough UV light for vitamin D synthesis during most of the year. (Adapted from Jablonski and Chaplin, 2000, 2002.)

Except for a person's sex, more social importance has been attached to variation in skin color than to any other single human biological trait. But aside from its probable adaptive significance relative to UV radiation, skin color is no more important physiologically than many other characteristics. However, from an evolutionary perspective, it provides a good example of how the forces of natural selection have produced geographically patterned variation as the consequence of two competing selective forces: the need for protection from overexposure to UV radiation (which can lead to folate depletion and skin cancer) on the one hand, and the necessity for adequate UV exposure to promote vitamin D synthesis on the other.

The Thermal Environment

Mammals and birds have evolved complex mechanisms to maintain a constant internal body temperature. While reptiles rely on exposure to external heat sources to raise body temperature and energy levels, mammals and birds have physiological mechanisms that, within certain limits, increase or reduce the loss of body heat. The optimum internal body temperature for normal cellular functions is species-specific, and for humans it's approximately 98.6°F.

People are found in a wide variety of habitats, with temperatures ranging from over 120°F to less than −60°F. In these extremes, human life wouldn't be possible without cultural innovations. But even accounting for the artificial environments in which we live, such external conditions place the human body under enormous stress.

Response to Heat All available evidence suggests that the earliest hominids evolved in the warm-to-hot savannas of East Africa. The fact that humans cope better with heat than they do with cold is testimony to the long-term adaptations to heat that evolved in our ancestors.

In humans, as well as certain other species, such as horses, sweat glands are distributed throughout the skin. This wide distribution of sweat glands makes it possible to lose heat at the body surface through evaporative cooling, a mechanism that has evolved to the greatest degree in humans. The ability to dissipate heat by sweating is seen in all humans to an almost equal degree, with the average number of sweat glands per individual (approximately 1.6 million) being fairly constant. However, people who aren't generally exposed to hot conditions do experience a period of acclimatization that initially involves significantly increased perspiration rates (Frisancho, 1993). An additional factor that enhances the cooling effects of sweating is increased exposure of the skin because of reduced amounts of body hair. We don't know when in our evolutionary history we began to lose body hair, but it represents a species-wide adaptation.

Although effective, heat reduction through evaporation can be expensive, and indeed dangerous, in terms of water and sodium loss. Up to 3 liters of water can be lost by a human engaged in heavy work in high heat. You can appreciate the importance of this fact if you consider that losing 1 liter of water is approximately equal to losing 1.5 percent of total body weight, and quickly losing 10 percent of body weight can be life threatening. This is why water must be continuously replaced when you exercise on a hot day.

Another mechanism for radiating body heat is **vasodilation,** which occurs when capillaries near the skin's surface widen to permit increased blood flow to the skin. The visible effect of vasodilation is flushing, or increased redness and warming of the skin, particularly of the face. But the physiological effect is to permit heat, carried by the blood from the interior of the body, to be radiated from the skin's surface to the surrounding air. (Some drugs, including alcohol, also produce vasodilation, which accounts for the redder and warmer face some people have after a couple of drinks.)

Body size and proportions are also important in regulating body temperature. Indeed, there seems to be a general relationship between climate and body size and shape in birds and mammals. In general, within a species, body size (weight) increases as distance from the equator increases. In humans, this relationship holds up fairly well, but there are numerous exceptions.

Two rules that pertain to the relationship between body size, body proportions, and climate are *Bergmann's rule* and *Allen's rule*.

1. *Bergmann's rule concerns the relationship of body mass or volume to surface area.* In mammals, body size tends to be greater in populations that live in colder climates. This is because as mass increases, the relative amount of surface area decreases proportionately. Because heat is lost at the surface, it follows that increased mass allows for greater heat retention and reduced heat loss.

2. *Allen's rule concerns shape of the body, especially appendages.* In colder climates, shorter appendages, with increased mass-to-surface ratios, are adaptive because they're more effective at preventing heat loss. Conversely, longer appendages, with increased surface area relative to mass, are more adaptive in warmer climates because they promote heat loss.

According to these rules, the most suitable body shape in hot climates is linear with long arms and legs. In a cold climate, a more suitable body type is stocky with shorter limbs. Several studies have shown that human populations generally conform to these principles. In colder climates, body mass tends, on average, to be greater and characterized by a larger trunk relative to arms and legs (Roberts, 1973). People living in the Arctic tend to be short and stocky, while many sub-Saharan Africans, especially East African pastoralists, are, on average, tall and linear (Fig. 12-11). But there's a great deal of variability regarding human body proportions, and not all populations conform so readily to Bergmann's and Allen's rules.

Response to Cold Human physiological responses to cold combine factors that increase heat production with those that enhance heat retention. Of the two, heat retention is more efficient because it requires less energy. This is an important point because energy is derived from food. Unless resources are abundant, and in winter they frequently aren't, any factor that conserves energy can have adaptive value.

Short-term responses to cold include increased metabolic rate and shivering, both of which generate body heat, at least for a short time. **Vasoconstriction,**

vasodilation Expansion of blood vessels, permitting increased blood flow to the skin. Vasodilation permits warming of the skin and also facilitates radiation of warmth as a means of cooling. Vasodilation is an involuntary response to warm temperatures, various drugs, and even emotional states (blushing).

vasoconstriction Narrowing of blood vessels to reduce blood flow to the skin. Vasoconstriction is an involuntary response to cold and reduces heat loss at the skin's surface.

FIGURE 12-11
(a) This African woman has the linear proportions characteristic of many inhabitants of sub-Saharan Africa. (b) By comparison, the Inuit woman is short and stocky. These two individuals serve as good examples of Bergmann's and Allen's rules.

(a)

(b)

Renee Lynn/Photo Researchers

George Holton/Photo Researchers

another short-term response, restricts heat loss and conserves energy. Humans also have a subcutaneous (beneath the skin) fat layer that provides an insulative layer throughout the body. Behavioral modifications include increased activity, wearing warmer clothing, increased food consumption, and even curling up into a ball.

Increases in metabolic rate (the rate at which cells break up nutrients into their components) release energy in the form of heat. Shivering also generates muscle heat, as does voluntary exercise. But these methods of heat production are expensive because they require an increased intake of nutrients to provide energy. (Perhaps this explains why we tend to have heartier appetites during the winter and frequently eat more fats and carbohydrates, the very sources of energy we require.)

In general, people exposed to chronic cold (meaning much or most of the year) maintain higher metabolic rates than those living in warmer climates. The Inuit (Eskimo) people living in the Arctic maintain metabolic rates between 13 and 45 percent higher than observed in non-Inuit control subjects (Frisancho, 1993). Moreover, the highest metabolic rates are seen in inland Inuit, who are exposed to even greater cold stress than coastal populations. Traditionally, the Inuit had the highest animal protein and fat diet of any human population in the world. Their diet was dictated by the available resource base (fish and mammals but little to no vegetable material), and it served to maintain the high metabolic rates required by exposure to chronic cold.

Vasoconstriction (the opposite of vasodilation) restricts capillary blood flow to the surface of the skin, thus reducing heat loss at the body surface. Because retaining body heat is more economical than creating it, vasoconstriction is very efficient, provided temperatures don't drop below freezing. If temperatures do fall below freezing, continued vasoconstriction can allow the skin's temperature to decline to the point of frostbite or worse.

Long-term responses to cold vary among human groups. For example, in the past, desert-dwelling native Australian populations were exposed to wide temperature fluctuations from day to night. Since they wore no clothing and didn't build shelters, their only protection from temperatures that hovered only a few degrees above freezing was provided by sleeping fires. They also experienced continuous vasoconstriction throughout the night, and this permitted a degree of skin cooling most people would find extremely uncomfortable. But, as there was no threat of frostbite, continued vasoconstriction was an efficient adaptation that helped prevent excessive internal heat loss.

By contrast, the Inuit experience intermittent periods of vasoconstriction and vasodilation. This compromise provides periodic warmth to the skin that helps prevent frostbite in sub-freezing temperatures. At the same time, because vasodilation is intermittent, energy loss is restricted, with more heat retained at the body's core.

These examples illustrate two of the ways that adaptations to cold vary among human populations. Obviously, winter conditions exceed our ability to adapt physiologically in many parts of the world. So if they hadn't developed cultural innovations, our ancestors would have remained in the tropics.

High Altitude

Studies of high-altitude residents have greatly contributed to our understanding of physiological adaptation. As you would expect, altitude studies have focused on inhabited mountainous regions, particularly in the Himalayas, Andes, and Rocky Mountains. Of these three areas, permanent human habitation probably has the longest history in the Himalayas (Moore et al., 1998). Today, perhaps as many as 25 million people live at altitudes above 10,000 feet. In Tibet, permanent settlements exist above 15,000 feet, and in the Andes, they can be found as high as 17,000 feet (Fig. 12-12).

Because the mechanisms that maintain homeostasis in humans evolved at lower altitudes, we're compromised by conditions at higher elevations. At high altitudes, many factors produce stress on the human body. These include **hypoxia** (reduced available oxygen), more intense solar radiation, cold, low humidity, wind (which increases cold stress), a reduced nutritional base, and rough terrain. Of these, hypoxia exerts the greatest amount of stress on human physiological systems, especially the heart, lungs, and brain.

Hypoxia results from reduced barometric pressure. It's not that there's less oxygen in the atmosphere at high altitudes, it's just less concentrated. Therefore, to obtain the same amount of oxygen at 9,000 feet as at sea level, people must make certain physiological alterations that increase the body's ability to transport and efficiently use the oxygen that's available.

At high altitudes, reproduction, in particular, is affected through increased infant mortality rates, miscarriage, low birth weights, and premature birth. An early study (Moore and Regensteiner, 1983) reported that in Colorado, infant deaths are almost twice as common above 8,200 feet (2,500 m) as at lower elevations. One cause of fetal

hypoxia Lack of oxygen. Hypoxia can refer to reduced amounts of available oxygen in the atmosphere (due to lowered barometric pressure) or to insufficient amounts of oxygen in the body.

FIGURE 12-12

(a) A household in northern Tibet, situated at an elevation of over 15,000 feet above sea level. (b) La Paz, Bolivia, at just over 12,000 feet above sea level, is home to more than 1 million people.

(a)

(b)

and maternal death is preeclampsia, a severe elevation of blood pressure in pregnant women after the twentieth gestational week. In another Colorado study, Palmer et al. (1999) reported that among pregnant women living at elevations over 10,000 feet, the prevalence of preeclampsia was 16 percent, compared to 3 percent at around 4,000 feet. In general, the problems related to childbearing are attributed to issues that compromise the vascular supply (and thus oxygen transport) to the fetus.

People born at lower altitudes and high-altitude natives differ somewhat in how they adapt to hypoxia. In people born at low elevations, acclimatization begins to occur within hours of exposure to high altitude. The responses may be short-term modifications, depending on duration of stay. These changes include an increase in respiration rate, heart rate, and production of red blood cells. (Red blood cells contain hemoglobin, the protein responsible for transporting oxygen to organs and tissues.)

Developmental acclimatization occurs in high-altitude natives during growth and development. This type of acclimatization is present only in people who grow up in high-altitude areas, not in those who moved there as adults. Compared with populations at lower elevations, lifelong residents of high altitudes grow somewhat more slowly and mature later. Other differences include greater lung volume and a relatively larger heart. In addition to greater lung capacity, people born at high altitudes are more efficient than migrants at diffusing oxygen from blood to body tissues. Developmental acclimatization to high-altitude hypoxia serves as a good example of physiological plasticity by illustrating how, within the limits set by genetic factors, development can be influenced by environment.

There's evidence that entire *populations* have also genetically adapted to high altitudes. Indigenous peoples of Tibet who have inhabited regions higher than 12,000 feet for around 25,000 years may have made genetic (that is, evolutionary) accommodations to hypoxia. Altitude doesn't appear to affect reproduction in these people to the degree it does in other populations. Infants have birth weights as high as those of lowland Tibetan groups and higher than those of recent (20 to 30 years) Chinese immigrants. This fact may be the result of alterations in maternal blood flow to the uterus during pregnancy (Moore et al., 1991; Moore et al., 2005).

Another line of evidence concerns how the body processes glucose (blood sugar). Glucose is critical because it's the only source of energy used by the brain, and it's also used, although not exclusively, by the heart. Both highland Tibetans and the Quechua (inhabitants of high-altitude regions of the Peruvian Andes) burn glucose in a way that permits more efficient use of oxygen. This implies the presence of genetic mutations in the mitochondrial DNA (mtDNA directs how cells use glucose). It also implies that natural selection has acted to increase the frequency of these advantageous mutations in these groups.

As yet, there's no certain evidence that Tibetans and Quechua have made evolutionary changes to accommodate high-altitude hypoxia (since specific genetic mechanisms that underlie these populations' unique abilities have not been identified). But the data suggest that selection has operated to produce evolutionary change in these two groups. If further study supports these findings, we have an excellent example of evolution in action producing long-term adaptation at the population level.

Infectious Disease

Infection, as opposed to other disease categories, such as degenerative or genetic disease, includes pathological conditions caused by microorganisms (viruses, bacteria, and fungi). Throughout the course of human evolution, infectious disease has exerted enormous selective pressures on populations and consequently has influenced the frequency of certain alleles that affect the immune response. In fact, it would be difficult to overstate the importance of infectious disease as an agent of natural selection in human populations. But as important as infectious disease has been, its role isn't very well documented.

The effects of infectious disease on humans are mediated culturally as well as biologically. Innumerable cultural factors, such as architectural styles, subsistence techniques, exposure to domesticated animals, and even religious practices, all affect how infectious disease develops and persists within and between populations.

Until about 10,000 to 12,000 years ago, all humans lived in small nomadic hunting and gathering groups. These groups rarely remained in one location for long, so they had minimal contact with refuse heaps that house disease **vectors.** But with the domestication of plants and animals, people became more sedentary and began living in small villages. Gradually, villages became towns, and towns, in turn, developed into densely crowded, unsanitary cities.

As long as humans lived in small bands, there was little opportunity for infectious disease to have much impact on large numbers of people. Even if an entire local group or band were wiped out, the effect on the overall population in a given area would have been negligible. Moreover, for a disease to become **endemic** in a population, sufficient numbers of people must be present. Therefore, small bands of hunter-gatherers weren't faced with continuous exposure to endemic disease.

But with the advent of settled living and close proximity to domesticated animals, opportunities for disease greatly increased. As sedentary life permitted larger group size, it became possible for diseases to become permanently established in some populations. Moreover, exposure to domestic animals, such as cattle and fowl, provided an opportune environment for the spread of several **zoonotic** diseases, such as tuberculosis. Humans had no doubt always contracted diseases occasionally from the animals they hunted; but when they began to live with domesticated animals, they were faced with an entire array of new infectious conditions. Also, the crowded, unsanitary conditions that characterized parts of all cities until the late nineteenth century and that persist in much of the world today further added to the disease burden borne by human inhabitants.

AIDS (acquired immunodeficiency syndrome) provides an excellent example of the influence of human infectious disease as a selective agent. In the United States, the first cases of AIDS were reported in 1981. Since that time, perhaps as many as 1.5 million Americans have been infected by HIV (human immunodeficiency virus), the agent that causes AIDS. However, most of the burden of AIDS is borne by developing countries, where 95 percent of all HIV-infected people live. By the end of 2007, an estimated 33.2 million people worldwide were living with HIV infection, and at least 23 million had died.

HIV is transmitted from person to person through the exchange of bodily fluids, usually blood or semen. It's not spread through casual contact with an infected person. Within six months of infection, most infected people test positive for anti-HIV antibodies, meaning that their immune system has recognized the presence of foreign antigens and has responded by producing antibodies. However, serious HIV-related symptoms may not appear for years. HIV is a "slow virus" that may persist in a person's body for several years before the onset of severe illness. This asymptomatic state is called a "latency period," and the average latency period in the United States is more than 11 years.

Like all viruses, HIV must invade certain types of cells and alter the functions of those cells to produce more virus particles in a process that eventually leads to cell destruction. HIV can attack various types of cells, but it especially targets so-called T4 helper cells, which are major components of the immune system. As HIV infection spreads and T4 cells are destroyed, the patient's immune system begins to fail. Consequently, he or she develops symptoms caused by various **pathogens** that are commonly present but usually kept in check by a normal immune response. When an HIV-infected person's T cell count drops to a level indicating that immunity has been suppressed, and when symptoms of "opportunistic" infections appear, the patient is said to have AIDS.

By the early 1990s, scientists were aware of a number of patients who had been HIV positive for 10 to 15 years, but continued to show few if any symptoms. Awareness of these patients led researchers to suspect that some individuals possess

vectors Agents that serve to transmit disease from one carrier to another. Mosquitoes are vectors for malaria, just as fleas are vectors for bubonic plague.

endemic Continuously present in a population.

zoonotic (zoh-oh-no´-tic) Pertaining to a zoonosis (*pl.,* zoonoses), a disease that is transmitted to humans through contact with nonhuman animals.

pathogens Any agents, especially microorganisms such as viruses, bacteria, or fungi, that infect a host and cause disease.

a natural immunity or resistance to HIV infection. This was shown to be true in late 1996 with the publication of two different studies (Dean et al., 1996; Samson et al., 1996) that demonstrated a mechanism for HIV resistance.

These two reports describe a genetic mutation that involves a major "receptor site" on the surface of certain immune cells, including T4 cells. (Receptor sites are protein molecules that enable HIV and other viruses to invade cells.) As a result of the mutation, the receptor site doesn't function properly and HIV can't enter the cell. Current evidence suggests that individuals who are homozygous for a particular (mutant) allele may be completely resistant to many types of HIV infection. In heterozygotes, infection may still occur, but the course of HIV disease is slowed.

For unknown reasons, the mutant allele occurs mainly in people of European descent, among whom its frequency is about 10 percent. Samson and colleagues (1996) reported that in the Japanese and West African groups they studied, the mutation was absent, but Dean and colleagues (1996) reported an allele frequency of about 2 percent among African Americans. They speculated that the presence of the allele in African Americans may be entirely due to genetic admixture (gene flow) with European Americans. They also suggested that this polymorphism exists in Europeans as a result of selective pressures favoring an allele that originally occurred as a rare mutation. But we should point out that the original selective agent was *not* HIV. Instead, it was some other, as yet unidentified pathogen that requires the same receptor site as HIV, and some researchers (Lalani et al., 1999) have suggested that it may have been the virus that causes smallpox. (Lalani et al.,1999, reported that a virus related to the smallpox virus can use the same receptor site as HIV.) While this conclusion hasn't been proved, it offers an exciting avenue of research. It may reveal how a mutation that originally was favored by selection because it provides protection against one type of infection (smallpox) can also increase resistance to another (AIDS).

The best-known epidemic in history was the Black Death (bubonic plague) in the mid-fourteenth century. Bubonic plague is caused by a bacterium and is transmitted from rodents to humans by fleas. In just a few years, this deadly disease had spread (following trade routes and facilitated by rodent-infested ship cargoes) from the Caspian Sea throughout the Mediterranean area to northern Europe. During the initial exposure to this disease, as many as one-third of the inhabitants of Europe died.

A lesser-known but even more devastating example was the influenza **pandemic** that broke out in 1918 at the end of World War I. This was actually one of a series of influenza outbreaks, but it has remained notable for its still unexplained virulence and the fact that it accounted for the death of over 21 million people worldwide.

While we have no clear-cut evidence of a selective role for bubonic plague or influenza, this doesn't mean that one doesn't exist. The tremendous mortality that these diseases (and others) are capable of causing certainly increases the likelihood that they influenced the development of human adaptive responses in ways we haven't yet discovered.

The Continuing Impact of Infectious Disease

It's important to understand that humans and pathogens exert selective pressures on each other, creating a dynamic relationship between disease organisms and their human (and nonhuman) hosts. Just as disease exerts selective pressures on host populations to adapt, microorganisms also evolve and adapt to various pressures exerted on them by their hosts.

Evolutionarily speaking, it's to the advantage of any pathogen not to be so virulent as to kill its host too quickly. If the host dies soon after becoming infected, the viral or bacterial agent may not have time to reproduce and infect other hosts. Thus, selection sometimes acts to produce resistance in host populations and/or to reduce the virulence of disease organisms, to the benefit of both. However, members of

pandemic An extensive outbreak of disease affecting large numbers of individuals over a wide area; potentially a worldwide phenomenon.

populations exposed for the first time to a new disease frequently die in huge numbers. This type of exposure was a major factor in the decimation of indigenous New World populations after contact with Europeans introduced smallpox into Native American groups. This has also been the case with the current worldwide spread of HIV.

Of the known disease-causing organisms, HIV provides the best-documented example of evolution and adaptation in a pathogen. It's also one of several examples of interspecies transfer of infection. HIV is the most mutable and genetically variable virus known. The type of HIV responsible for the AIDS epidemic is HIV-1, which in turn is divided into three major subtypes (Hu et al., 1996; Gao, 1999). Another far less common type is HIV-2, which is present only in populations of West Africa. HIV-2 also exhibits a wide range of genetic diversity, and while some strains cause AIDS, others are far less virulent.

Since the late 1980s, researchers have been comparing the DNA sequences of HIV and a closely related retrovirus called *simian immunodeficiency virus (SIV)*. SIV is found in chimpanzees and several African monkey species. Like HIV, SIV is genetically variable, and each strain appears to be specific to a given species and even subspecies of primate. SIV produces no symptoms in the African monkeys and chimpanzees that are its traditional hosts, but when injected into Asian monkeys, it eventually causes AIDS-like symptoms and death. These findings indicate that the various forms of SIV have shared a long evolutionary history (perhaps several hundred thousand years) with a number of African primate species and that the latter are able to accommodate this virus, which is deadly to their Asian relatives. Moreover, these results substantiate long-held hypotheses that SIV and HIV evolved in Africa.

Comparisons of the DNA sequences of HIV-2 and the form of SIV found in one monkey species (the sooty mangabey) revealed that, genetically, these two viruses are almost identical. These findings led to the generally accepted conclusion that HIV-2 evolved from sooty mangabey SIV. Moreover, sooty mangabeys are hunted for food and also kept as pets in western central Africa, and the transmission of SIV to humans probably occurred through bites and the butchering of monkey carcasses.

A group of medical researchers (Gao et al., 1999) also compared DNA sequences of HIV-1 and the form of SIV found in chimpanzees indigenous to western central Africa. Their results showed that HIV-1 almost certainly evolved from the strain of chimpanzee SIV that infects the central African subspecies *Pan troglodytes troglodytes*.

Unfortunately for both species, chimpanzees are routinely hunted by humans for food in parts of West Africa (see p. 126). Consequently, the most probable explanation for the transmission of SIV from chimpanzees to humans is, as with sooty mangabeys, the hunting and butchering of chimpanzees (Gao et al., 1999; Weiss and Wrangham, 1999; Fig. 12-13). Hence, HIV/AIDS is a zoonotic disease. The DNA evidence further suggests that there were at least three separate human exposures to chimpanzee SIV, and at some point the virus was altered to the form we call HIV. When chimpanzee SIV was first transmitted to humans is unknown. The oldest evidence of human infection is a frozen HIV-positive blood sample taken from a West African patient in 1959. There are also a few documented cases of AIDS

FIGURE 12-13

These people, selling butchered chimpanzees, may not realize that by handling this meat they could be exposing themselves to HIV.

Karl Ammann

infection by the late 1960s and early 1970s. Therefore, although human exposure to SIV/HIV probably occurred many times in the past, the virus didn't become firmly established in humans until the latter half of the twentieth century.

Severe acute respiratory syndrome (SARS) is another contemporary example of zoonotic transmission of disease. Scientists don't know the exact mode of SARS transmission in humans, but many health officials believe that it was initially transmitted to humans through contact with either domesticated animals or wild animals, such as civet cats, sold in Asian markets for food. Indeed, many of the influenza strains that frequently originate in China seem to originate in pigs and fowl that live in very close contact with humans (Clarke, 2003).

In early 2003, an outbreak of SARS in southern China surprised the world health community by quickly spreading through much of Asia, then to North America, South America, and Europe. It was due to air travel that SARS spread so quickly around the world, even though it has a fairly low transmission rate. If it weren't for modern technology, this infection would have been confined to one or perhaps a few villages; and while a small number of people would have died, it would have been a fairly unremarkable event, and it certainly wouldn't have become widely known.

From these SIV/HIV and SARS examples, you can appreciate how, through the adoption of various cultural practices, humans have radically altered patterns of infectious disease. The interaction of cultural and biological factors has influenced microevolutionary change in humans, as in the example of sickle-cell anemia (see p. 72), to accommodate altered relationships with disease organisms.

Until the twentieth century, infectious disease was the number one cause of death in all human populations. Even today, in many developing countries, as much as half of all mortality is due to infectious disease, compared to only about 10 percent in the United States. For example, malaria is a disease of the poor in developing nations. Annually, there are an estimated 1 million deaths due to malaria. That figure computes to one malaria-related death every 30 seconds (Weiss, 2002)! Ninety percent of these deaths occur in sub-Saharan Africa, where 5 percent of children die

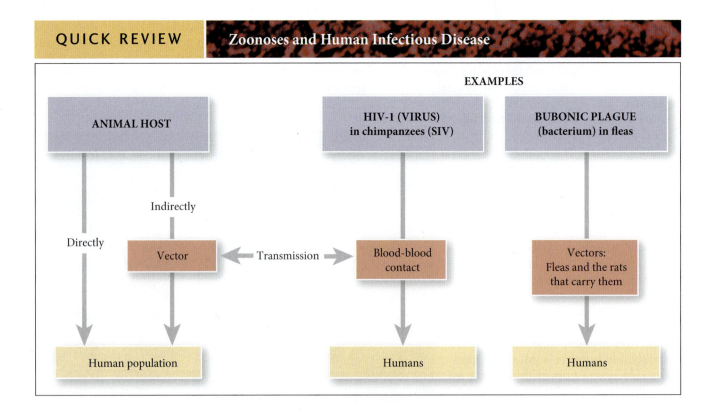

QUICK REVIEW   **Zoonoses and Human Infectious Disease**

of malaria before age 5 (Greenwood and Mutabingwa, 2002; Weiss, 2002). In the United States and other developing nations, with better living conditions and sanitation and especially with the widespread use of antibiotics and pesticides beginning in the late 1940s, infectious disease has given way to heart disease and cancer as the leading causes of death.

Optimistic predictions held that infectious disease would be a thing of the past in developed countries and, with the introduction of antibiotics and better living standards, in developing nations too. But between 1980 and 1992, the number of deaths in the United States in which infectious disease was the underlying cause rose from 41 to 65 per 100,000, an increase of 58 percent (Pinner et al., 1996).

Obviously, AIDS contributed substantially to the increase in mortality due to infectious disease in the United States between 1980 and 1992. By 1992, AIDS was the leading cause of death in men aged 25 to 44 years. As of 1998, mortality due to AIDS had decreased significantly; still, even when subtracting the effect of AIDS in mortality rates, there was a 22 percent increase in mortality rates due to infectious disease between 1980 and 1992 (Pinner et al., 1996).

This increase may partly be due to the overuse of antibiotics. It's estimated that half of all antibiotics prescribed in the United States are used to treat viral conditions such as colds and flu. Because antibiotics are completely ineffective against viruses, such therapy is not only useless, but may also have dangerous long-term consequences. There's considerable concern in the biomedical community over the indiscriminate use of antibiotics since the 1950s. Antibiotics have exerted selective pressures on bacterial species that have, over time, developed antibiotic-resistant strains (an excellent example of natural selection). So, in the past few years we've seen the *reemergence* of many bacterial diseases, including influenza, pneumonia, cholera, and tuberculosis (TB), in forms that are less responsive to treatment.

Tuberculosis is now listed as the world's leading killer of adults by the World Health Organization (Colwell, 1996). In fact, the number of tuberculosis cases has risen 28 percent worldwide since the mid-1980s, with an estimated 10 million people infected in the United States alone. Although not all infected people develop active disease, in the 1990s an estimated 30 million persons worldwide are believed to have died from TB. One very troubling aspect of the increase in tuberculosis infection is that newly developed strains of *Mycobacterium tuberculosis,* the bacterium that causes TB, are resistant to antibiotics and other treatments.

Various treatments for nonbacterial conditions have also become ineffective. One such example is the appearance of chloroquin-resistant malaria, which has rendered chloroquin (the traditional preventive medication) virtually useless in some parts of Africa. And many insect species have also developed resistance to commonly used pesticides.

In addition to threats posed by resistant strains of pathogens, there are other factors that may contribute to the emergence (or reemergence) of infectious disease. Political leaders in some (mostly European) countries and the overwhelming majority of scientists worldwide are becoming increasingly concerned over the potential for global warming to expand the geographical range of numerous tropical disease vectors, such as mosquitoes. And the destruction of natural environments not only contributes to global warming; it also has the potential of causing disease vectors formerly restricted to local areas to spread to new habitats.

Fundamental to all these factors is human population size, which, as it continues to soar, causes more environmental disturbance and, through additional human activity, adds further to global warming. Moreover, in developing countries, where as much as 50 percent of mortality is due to infectious disease, overcrowding and unsanitary conditions increasingly contribute to increased rates of communicable illness. One could scarcely conceive of a better set of circumstances for the appearance and spread of communicable disease, and it remains to be seen if scientific innovation and medical technology are able to meet the challenge.

Summary

In this chapter, we investigated some of the ways in which humans differ from one another, both within and between populations. We first explored how this variation was approached in the past, in terms of racial typologies. We then discussed contemporary approaches that describe simple genetic polymorphisms for which allele frequencies may be calculated, and we emphasized new techniques in which genetic data are obtained from direct analyses of mitochondrial and nuclear DNA. Moreover, we reviewed the theoretical basis of the population genetics approach, the subdiscipline of physical anthropology that seeks to measure genetic diversity among humans. Data on polymorphic traits can be used to understand aspects of human microevolution. For humans, of course, culture also plays a crucial evolutionary role, and the sickle-cell trait and lactase persistence are thus discussed from a biocultural perspective.

The chapter also considered how populations vary with regard to physiological adaptations to a number of environmental conditions, including solar radiation, heat, cold, and high altitude. We also focused on how infectious disease influences evolutionary processes, and we particularly emphasized AIDS/HIV and the dynamic relationship between pathogens and human hosts.

The topic of human variation is very complicated, and the biological and cultural factors that have contributed to that variation and that continue to influence it are manifold. But from an explicitly evolutionary perspective, it is through the investigation of changes in allele frequencies in response to environmental conditions that we will continue to elucidate the diverse adaptive potential that characterizes our species.

WHY IT MATTERS

We've emphasized that most so-called "racial differences" are due to sociocultural and environmental variation and not to major genetic differences between populations. But there are some new medical therapies that target specific populations and they've partly resulted from exploring genetic differences along the lines of geographic ancestry.

One of the goals of the human genome project is to find specific DNA variants associated with disease and to design or recommend treatments that target those genes. Because some of these variants cluster in certain populations, there have been efforts to identify geographical ancestry to predict risks for some chronic and acute diseases. In some cases, this effort has been referred to as "race-based medicine," and the concept has widespread appeal in public health and clinical medicine because of concerns over health disparities, especially in the United States. The result has been the use of the extremely imprecise and biologically inappropriate term *race* to design treatment protocols. In other words, a sociocultural term is being used to make biomedical predictions and treatments. There are several potential problems with this effort.

First, there is a great deal of evidence that clinically observed identification or even self-identification of race or ethnicity is often not congruent with genetic profiles. In fact, it isn't unusual for a person to change his or her perception of self-identified race as life circumstances change (Dressler et al., 2005). Second, if treatment is assigned for a person based on self-reported race rather than on a direct genetic test, serious illnesses may be missed. And finally, using race as a basis for treatment may lead a care provider to miss or minimize the real differences that lead to ill health, including socioeconomic, environmental, nutritional, and cultural settings and backgrounds.

The use of race in determining treatment for genetic diseases and disorders unscientifically simplifies an extremely complex phenomenon and is more likely to result in worse rather than better treatment outcomes. This is especially true in the United States, where virtually all of the statistical variability between blacks and whites in disease risk can be measured by income and sociocultural circumstances (Dressler et al., 2005). To consider the complexities, imagine a drug designed to treat hypertension in African Americans and advertised as such. If a clinician treating an African American for hypertension automatically prescribes that drug and ignores other possible drug candidates, the patient may not benefit at all. On the other hand, if the clinician views that drug as an "African American drug," he or she may not prescribe it for a "white" patient, even though it may be the best choice.

As another example, imagine a clinician who assumes that the sickle-cell allele is found only in people of African descent and therefore misdiagnoses a case of sickle-cell trait in a young white child. Categorizing drugs along racial lines is likely to lead to the same problems that resulted from categorizing people into racial groups. This doesn't mean that the quest for underlying genetic factors involved in disease should be halted; it just means that the search should focus on gene and gene complexes rather than races.

Critical Thinking Questions

1   Imagine you're with some friends talking about variation and how many races there are. One person says that there are three and another thinks that there are five. Would you agree with either one? Why or why not?

2   For the same group of friends in question 1 (none of whom have had a course in biological anthropology), how would you explain how scientific knowledge doesn't support their preconceived notions about human races?

3   In the twentieth century, how did the scientific study of human diversity change from the more traditional approach?

4   Why can we say that variations in human skin color are the result of natural selection in different environments? Why can we say that less-pigmented skin is a result of conflicting selective factors?

5   Do you think that infectious disease has played an important role in human evolution? Do you think it plays a *current* role in human adaptation?

6   How have human cultural practices influenced the patterns of infectious disease seen today? Provide as many examples as you can, including some not discussed in this chapter.

CHAPTER 13

The Anthropological Perspective on the Human Life Course

Bill Hatcher / Getty Images

Frans Lemmen / Getty Images

Given that humans are
part of a biological
continuum, how does
culture make us different
from other species?

FOCUS
QUESTION

Introduction

Throughout this book, we've emphasized the importance of the anthropological perspective for understanding human beings through time and space. As defined in the first chapter, anthropology is the study of humankind. Unlike most other fields that have humans as their focus, the anthropological approach to humankind draws on and integrates research about people from all parts of the earth and from both past and contemporary cultures. An anthropological perspective on the life course will serve as a way of further illustrating the breadth of this approach.

Because this is a physical anthropology text, we've placed primary emphasis on human biological evolution and adaptation. We've learned that our biology is the result of millions of years of evolutionary history: 225 million years of mammalian evolution, 65 million years of primate evolution, 7 million years of hominid evolution, 2–2.5 million years of evolution of the genus *Homo*. But are we just another mammal, just another primate? In most ways, of course we are like other mammals and other primates. But as emphasized throughout the text, modern human beings are the result of *biocultural evolution*. In other words, human biology and behavior today have been shaped by the biological and cultural forces that operated on our ancestors. In fact, it would be fruitless to attempt an understanding of modern human biology and diversity without considering that humans have evolved in the context of culture. It would be like trying to understand the biology of fish without considering that they live in water.

A good place to explore the interaction of biology and culture is the human life course because it's human beings that experience and reflect both biology and sociocultural environments. If we consider how a human develops from an embryo into an adult and examine the forces that operate on that process, then we will have a better perspective of how both biology and culture influence our own lives. Throughout this book, we've focused on the primate order (Chapters 5 and 6), the evolution of the family Hominidae (Chapters 8 through 11), and populations of modern *Homo sapiens* (Chapters 11 and 12). We continue the focus on modern humans in this chapter, but our interest shifts to the life course to understand how past and present evolutionary and cultural forces operate on our own lives.

There is, of course, much variation in the extent to which cultural factors interact with genetically based biological characteristics; these variable interactions influence how characteristics are expressed in individuals. Some genetically based characteristics will be exhibited no matter what the cultural context of growth and development happens to be. If a person inherits two alleles for albinism, for example (see Chapter 4), he or she will be deficient in melanin production and will have lightly colored skin, hair, and eyes. This phenotype will emerge regardless of the cultural environment in which the person lives.

Click!

Go to the following media resources for interactive activities, more information, and study materials on topics covered in this chapter:

- Anthropology Resource Center
- Student Companion Website for *Essentials of Physical Anthropology,* Seventh Edition
- Online Virtual Laboratories for Physical Anthropology CD-ROM, Fourth Edition
- Basic Genetics for Anthropology CD-ROM 2.0: Principles and Applications

Other characteristics, such as intelligence, body shape, and growth will reflect the interaction of environment and genes. We know, for example, that each of us is born with a genetic makeup that influences the maximum stature we can achieve in adulthood. But to reach that maximum stature, we must be properly nourished during our growing years and avoid many childhood diseases and other stresses that inhibit growth. What factors determine whether we are well fed and receive good medical care? In the United States, socioeconomic status is probably the primary determinant of nutrition and health. Thus, socioeconomic status is an example of a cultural factor that affects growth.

Fundamentals of Growth and Development

growth Increase in mass or number of cells.

development Differentiation of cells into different types of tissues and their maturation.

adolescent growth spurt The period during adolescence when well-nourished teens typically increase in stature at greater rates than at other times in the life cycle.

The terms *growth* and *development* are often used interchangeably, but they actually refer to different processes. **Growth** refers to an increase in mass or number of cells, whereas **development** refers to the differentiation of cells into different types of tissues and their subsequent maturation. Some cells are manufactured only once and are usually not replaced if damaged (for example, certain nerve and muscle cells); some cells are continuously dying and being replaced (skin and red blood cells); and some can be regenerated if damaged (cells in the liver, kidneys, and most glands). (See Chapter 3 for discussions of cell division.)

In humans, growth begins at conception and continues until the late teens or early 20s. Typically, well-nourished humans grow fairly rapidly during the first two trimesters (6 months) of fetal development, but growth slows during the third trimester. After birth, growth rates increase and remain fairly rapid for about four years, at which time they decrease again to relatively slow, steady levels that are maintained until puberty. At puberty, there's another very pronounced increase in growth. During this so-called **adolescent growth spurt,** Western teenagers typically grow around 4 inches per year. Subsequent to the adolescent growth spurt, the rate of growth declines again and remains slower until adult stature is achieved by the late teens (Fig. 13-1).

Growth curves for boys and girls are significantly different, with the adolescent growth spurt occurring approximately two years earlier in girls than in boys. At birth, there's slight *sexual dimorphism* in many body measures (for example, height, weight, head circumference, and body fat), but the major divergence in these characteristics doesn't occur until puberty.

FIGURE 13-1

Distance and velocity curves of growth in height for a healthy American girl. (a) The distance curve shows the height attained in a given year. (b) The velocity curve plots the amount gained in a given year.

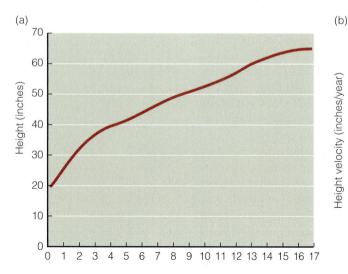

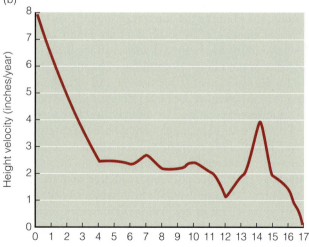

The head is a relatively large part of the body at birth. The continued growth of the brain after birth occurs at a rate far greater than that of any other part of the body, with the exception of the eyeball. At birth, the human brain is about 25 percent of its adult size. By 6 months of age, the brain has doubled in size, reaching 50 percent of adult size. It reaches 75 percent of adult size at age 2½ years, 90 percent by age 5, and 95 percent by age 10. There's only a very small spurt in brain growth at adolescence, making the brain an exception to the growth curves characteristic of most other parts of the body. As we'll see later in this chapter, this pattern of brain growth, including the relatively small amount of growth before birth, is unusual among primates and other mammals. By contrast, the typical picture for most mammalian species is that at least 50 percent of adult brain size has been attained prior to birth. For humans, however, the narrow pelvis necessary for walking bipedally provides limits on the size of the fetal head that can be delivered through it (Rosenberg and Trevathan, 2001). That limitation, in addition to the value of having most brain growth occur in the more stimulating environment outside the womb, has resulted in human infants being born with far less of their total adult brain size than most other mammals.

Nutritional Requirements for Growth

Nutrition has an impact on human growth at every stage of the life cycle. During pregnancy, for example, a woman's diet can have a profound effect on the development of her fetus and the eventual health of the child. Moreover, the effects are transgenerational, because a woman's own supply of eggs is developed while she herself is *in utero* (see Chapter 3). Thus, if a woman is malnourished during pregnancy, the eggs that develop in her female fetus may be damaged in a way that will impact the health of her future grandchildren. Furthermore, a form of fetal programming occurs *in utero* in response to nutritional stress that prepares the individual for lifelong deprivation (Barker, 1998). In the case of food shortage, the size of the liver, muscle tissue, and other organs is reduced to maintain sufficient nutrients for the rapidly developing fetal brain. This often results in a vulnerability to later-life chronic diseases and disorders, especially if the postnatal environment happens to provide excess calories, as often occurs in populations undergoing transitions associated with globalization (Kuzawa, 2005).

Nutrients needed for growth, development, and body maintenance include proteins, carbohydrates, lipids (fats), vitamins, and minerals. The specific amount that we need of each of these nutrients coevolved with the types of foods that were available to human ancestors throughout our evolutionary history. For example, the specific pattern of amino acids required in human nutrition (the **essential amino acids**) reflects an ancestral diet high in animal protein. Unfortunately for modern humans, these coevolved nutritional requirements are often incompatible with the foods that are available and typically consumed today. To understand this mismatch of our nutritional needs and contemporary diets, we need to examine the impact of agriculture on human evolutionary history.

The preagricultural diet, while perhaps high in animal protein, was low in fats, particularly saturated fats. That diet was also high in complex carbohydrates (including fiber), low in salt, and high in calcium. We don't need to be reminded that the contemporary diet that typifies many industrialized societies has the opposite configuration of the one just described. It's high in saturated fats and salt and low in complex carbohydrates, fiber, and calcium (Table 13-1). Although humans are notable for the great flexibility in their diets (Leonard, 2002), there is very good evidence that many of today's diseases in industrialized countries are related to the lack of fit between our diet today and the one with which we evolved (Eaton, Shostak, and Konner, 1988).

Many of our biological and behavioral characteristics evolved because in the past they contributed to adaptation; but today these same characteristics may be

essential amino acids The 9 (of 22) amino acids that must be obtained from the food we eat because they are not synthesized in the body in sufficient amounts.

TABLE 13.1	Preagricultural, Contemporary American, and Recently Recommended Dietary Composition		
	Preagricultural Diet	Contemporary Diet	Recent Recommendations
Total dietary energy (%)			
Protein	33	12	12
Carbohydrate	46	46	58
Fat	21	42	30
Alcohol	~0	(7–10)	—
P:S ratio*	1.41	0.44	1
Cholesterol (mg)	520	300–500	300
Fiber (g)	100–150	19.7	30–60
Sodium (mg)	690	2,300–6,900	1,000–3,300
Calcium (mg)	1,500–2,000	740	800–1,500
Ascorbic acid (mg)	440	90	60

*Polyunsaturated: saturated fat ratio.

Source: Reuse of attached table from p. 84 in *The Paleolithic Prescription,* by S. Boyd Eaton, Marjorie Shostack. Copyright © 1988 by S. Boyd, M.D., Marjorie Shostack, and Melvin Konner, M.D., Ph.D. Reprinted by permission of HarperCollins Publishers, Inc.

maladaptive. An example is our ability to store fat. This capability was an advantage in the past, when food availability often alternated between abundance and scarcity. Those who could store fat during the times of abundance could draw on those stores during times of scarcity and remain healthy, resist disease, and, for women, maintain the ability to reproduce. Today, people with adequate economic resources spend much of their lives with a relative abundance of foods. Considering the number of disorders associated with obesity, the formerly positive ability to store extra fat has now turned into a liability. Our "feast or famine" biology is now incompatible with the constant feast many of us indulge in today.

Perhaps no disorder is as clearly linked with dietary and lifestyle behaviors as the form of diabetes mellitus that typically has its onset in later life, referred to variously as type 2 diabetes or NIDDM (non–insulin dependent diabetes mellitus). A few years ago, type 2 diabetes was something that happened to older people living primarily in the developed world. Sadly, this is no longer true. The World Diabetes Foundation estimates that 80 percent of the new cases of type 2 diabetes that appear between now and 2025 will be in developing nations, and the World Health Organization (WHO) predicts that more than 70 percent of *all* diabetes cases in the world will be in developing nations in 2025. Furthermore, type 2 diabetes is occurring in children as young as 4 (Pavkov et al., 2006), and the mean age of diagnosis in the United States dropped from 52 to 46 between 1988 and 2000 (Koopman et al., 2005). In fact, we would guess that almost everyone reading this book has a friend or family member who has diabetes. What's happened to make this former "disease of old age" and "disease of civilization" reach what some have described as epidemic proportions?

Although there appears to be a genetic link (type 2 diabetes tends to run in families), most fingers point to lifestyle factors. Two lifestyle factors that have been implicated in this epidemic are poor diet and inadequate exercise. Noting that our current diets and activity levels are very different from those of our ancestors,

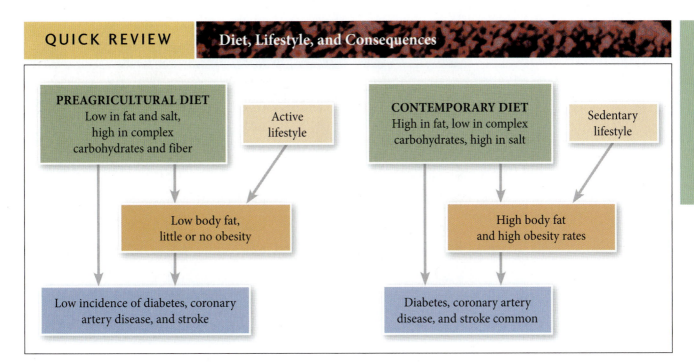

Diet, Lifestyle, and Consequences

PREAGRICULTURAL DIET
Low in fat and salt,
high in complex
carbohydrates and fiber

Active
lifestyle

CONTEMPORARY DIET
High in fat, low in complex
carbohydrates, high in salt

Sedentary
lifestyle

Low body fat,
little or no obesity

High body fat
and high obesity rates

Low incidence of diabetes, coronary
artery disease, and stroke

Diabetes, coronary artery
disease, and stroke common

proponents of evolutionary medicine suggest that diabetes is the price we pay for consuming excessive sugars and other refined carbohydrates while spending our days in front of the TV set or computer monitor. The reason that the incidence of diabetes is increasing in developing nations is that these bad habits are spreading to those nations.

It's clear that both deficiencies and excesses of nutrients can cause health problems and interfere with childhood growth and adult health. Certainly, many people in all parts of the world, both industrialized and developing, suffer from inadequate supplies of food of any quality. We read daily of thousands dying from starvation due to drought, warfare, or political instability. The blame must be placed not only on the narrowed food base that resulted from the emergence of agriculture, but also on the increase in human population that occurred when people began to settle in permanent villages and have more children. Today, the crush of billions of humans almost completely dependent on cereal grains means that millions face undernutrition, malnutrition, and even starvation. Even with these huge populations, however, food scarcity may not be as big a problem as food inequality. In other words, there may be enough food produced for all people on earth, but economic and political forces keep it from reaching those who need it most. (See Chapter 14 for a further discussion of world population growth and related problems.)

Other Factors Influencing Growth and Development

Genetics

Genetic factors set the underlying limitations and potentialities for growth and development, but the life experiences and environments of the organism determine how the body grows within those parameters. How do we assess the relative contributions of genes and the environment in their effects on growth? Much of our information comes from studies of **monozygotic** and **dizygotic twins.** Monozygotic ("identical") twins come from the union of a single sperm and ovum and share

monozygotic twins Twins derived from a single fertilized egg.

dizygotic twins Twins derived from two separate fertilized eggs in the same pregnancy.

TABLE 13.2	Correlation Coefficients for Height Between Monozygotic (MZ) and Dizygotic (DZ) Twin Pairs from Birth to Age 8			
Age	Total *N*	MZ	DZ Same Sex	DZ Different Sex
Birth	629	0.62	0.79	0.67
3 months	764	0.78	0.72	0.65
6 months	819	0.80	0.67	0.62
12 months	827	0.86	0.66	0.58
24 months	687	0.89	0.54	0.61
3 years	699	0.93	0.56	0.60
5 years	606	0.94	0.51	0.68
8 years	444	0.94	0.49	0.65

Source: From Wilson, 1979, after Bogin, 1988. p. 63

100 percent of their genes. Dizygotic ("fraternal") twins come from separate ova and sperm and share only 50 percent of their genes, just as any other siblings from the same parents. If monozygotic twins with identical genes but different growth environments are exactly the same in stature at various ages (that is, show perfect correlation for stature), then we can conclude that genes are the primary, if not the only, determinants of stature. Most studies of twins reveal that under normal circumstances, stature is "highly correlated" for monozygotic twins, leading to the conclusion that stature is under fairly strong genetic control (Table 13-2). Weight, on the other hand, seems to be more strongly influenced by diet, environment, and individual experiences than by genes.

Hormones

One of the primary ways in which genes have an effect on growth and development is through their effects on hormones. Hormones are substances produced in one cell that have an effect on another cell (see p. 42), and examples include estrogen, testosterone, cortisol, and insulin. Most hormones are produced by **endocrine glands,** such as the pituitary, thyroid, and adrenal glands, in addition to the ovaries and testes. Hormones are transported in the bloodstream, and almost all have an effect on growth. The hypothalamus (located at the base of the forebrain) can be considered the relay station, control center, or central clearinghouse for most hormonal action. This control center receives messages from the brain and other glands and sends out messages that stimulate hormonal action. Most of the hormonal messages transmitted from the hypothalamus result in the inhibition or release of other hormones.

Two hormones that are important in growth include growth hormone and insulin. Growth hormone, secreted by the anterior pituitary, promotes growth and has an effect on just about every cell in the body. Tumors and other disorders can result in excessive or insufficient amounts of growth hormone secretion, which in turn can result in gigantism or dwarfism. One group of people who have notably short stature are African Efe pygmies. Recent research suggests that altered levels of growth hormone and its controlling factors interact with nutritional factors and infectious diseases to produce the relatively short adult stature of these people (Shea and Bailey, 1996), providing another example of the interaction of biological and cultural forces.

endocrine glands Glands responsible for secretion of hormones into the bloodstream.

Environmental Factors

As you read in Chapter 12, environmental factors, such as altitude and climate, have effects on growth and development. Perhaps the primary influence of such external factors comes from their effects on nutrition, but there's evidence of independent effects as well. For example, as noted in Chapter 12, infant birth weight is lower at high altitude, and this is so even when such factors as nutrition, smoking, and socio-economic status are taken into consideration. In Colorado, for example, birth weight declines an average of 3.6 ounces per 3,300 feet of elevation gain, even when factors such as gestational age, maternal weight gain, smoking, and prenatal care are considered (Jensen and Moore, 1997). In a Bolivian study, the mean birth weight was 7.8 pounds at low elevations and 7.1 pounds at high elevations (Haas et al., 1980). Most studies of children have found that those at high elevations are shorter and weigh less than those at low elevations.

In general, populations in cold climates tend to be heavier and have longer trunks and shorter extremities than populations in tropical areas. This reflects Bergmann's and Allen's rules, discussed in Chapter 12. Exposure to sunlight also appears to have an effect on growth, most likely through its effects on vitamin D production. Children tend to grow more rapidly in times of high sunlight concentration (that is, in the summer in temperate regions and in the dry season in monsoonal tropical regions). Vitamin D, necessary for skeletal growth, requires sunlight for its synthesis (see pp. 285–286).

Among the most significant environmental factors having an effect on growth and development is infectious disease, such as malaria, influenza, cholera, and tuberculosis (see pp. 290–295). These diseases have their greatest impact during childhood and can delay growth, particularly when coupled with malnutrition. In fact, the effects of infectious disease and malnutrition are said to be *synergistic;* that is, each worsens the effect of the other, so that in combination their effects are potentially more damaging than either is acting alone. Unfortunately, they often occur together because chronic malnutrition lowers resistance to disease organisms that are present in the environment.

The Human Life Cycle

As noted in earlier chapters, primatologists and other physical anthropologists view primate and human growth and development from an evolutionary perspective, with an interest in how natural selection has operated on the life cycle from conception to death, a perspective known as life history theory. Why, for example, do humans have longer periods of infancy and childhood compared with other primates? What accounts for differences seen in the life cycles of such closely related species as humans and chimpanzees? Life history research seeks to answer such questions (see Mace, 2000, for a review).

Life history theory provides ways of predicting the timing of reproduction under favorable circumstances. It begins with the premise that there's only a certain amount of energy available to an organism for growth, maintenance of life, and reproduction. Energy invested in one of these processes isn't available to another. Thus, the entire life course represents a series of trade-offs among various life history traits (see p. 135), such as length of gestation, age at weaning, time spent in growth to adulthood, adult body size, and length of life span. For example, life history theory provides the basis for understanding how fast an organism will grow and to what size, how many offspring can be produced, how long gestation will last, and how long an individual will live. Crucial to understanding life history theory is its link to the evolutionary process: It's the action of natural selection that shapes life history traits, determining which ones will succeed or fail in a given environment. Although it isn't clear if life history theory works in contemporary human populations (Strassman and Gillespie, 2002), it serves as a useful guide for examining the various life cycle phases from evolutionary and ecological perspectives.

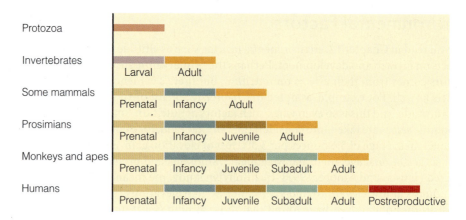

FIGURE 13-2
Life cycle stages for various animal species.

Not all animals have clearly demarcated phases in their lives; moreover, among mammals, humans have more such phases than do other species (Fig. 13-2). Protozoa, among the simplest of animals, have only one phase; many invertebrates have two: larval and adult. Almost all mammals have at least three phases: prenatal, infancy, and adult. Most primates have four phases: prenatal, infancy, juvenile (usually called childhood in humans), and adult. Monkeys, apes, and humans add a phase between the juvenile phase and adulthood that is referred to as the subadult period (adolescence, or teenage, in humans). Finally, for humans there is the addition of a sixth phase in women, the postreproductive years following menopause. One could argue that during the course of primate evolution, more recently evolved forms have longer life spans and more divisions of the life span into phases, or stages.

Most of these life cycle stages are well marked by biological transitions. The prenatal phase begins with conception and ends with birth; infancy is the period of nursing; childhood, or the juvenile phase, is the period from weaning to sexual maturity (puberty in humans); adolescence is the period from puberty to the end of growth; adulthood is marked by the birth of the first child and/or the completion of growth; and menopause is recognized as having occurred one full year after the last menstrual cycle. These biological markers are similar among higher primates, but for humans, there's an added complexity: They occur in cultural contexts that define and characterize them. Puberty, for example, has very different meanings in different cultures. A girl's first menstruation (**menarche**) is often marked with ritual and celebration, and a change in social status typically occurs with this biological transition. Likewise, **menopause** is often associated with a rise in status for women in non-Western societies, whereas it's commonly seen as a negative transition for women in many Western societies. As we shall see, collective and individual attitudes toward these life cycle transitions have an effect on growth, development, and health.

Pregnancy, Birth, and Infancy

The biological aspects of conception and gestation can be discussed in a fairly straightforward way, drawing information from what is known about reproductive biology at the present time: A sperm fertilizes an egg; the resulting zygote travels through a uterine (fallopian) tube to become implanted in the uterine lining; and the embryo develops until it's mature enough to survive outside the womb, at which time birth occurs. But this is clearly not all there is to human pregnancy and birth. Female biology may be similar the world over, but cultural rules and practices are the primary determinants of who will get pregnant, as well as when, where, how, and by whom.

Once a pregnancy has begun, there's much variation in how a woman should behave, what she should eat, where she should and should not go, and how she should interact with other people. Almost every culture known, including our own,

menarche The first menstruation in girls, usually occurring in the early to middle teens.

menopause The end of menstruation in human women, usually occurring at around age 50.

imposes dietary restrictions on pregnant women. Many of these appear to serve an important biological function, particularly that of keeping the woman from ingesting toxins that would be dangerous for the fetus. (Alcohol is a good example of a potential toxin whose consumption in pregnancy is discouraged in the United States.) The food aversions to coffee, alcohol, and other bitter substances that many women experience during pregnancy may be evolved adaptations to protect the embryo from toxins. The nausea of early pregnancy may also function to limit the intake of foods potentially harmful to the embryo at a critical stage of development (Profet, 1988; Williams and Nesse 1991; but see Pike, 2000).

Birth is an event that's celebrated with ritual in almost every culture studied. In fact, the relatively little fanfare associated with childbirth in the United States is unusual by world standards. Because risk of death for both mother and child is so great at birth, it's not surprising that it's surrounded with ritual significance. Perhaps because of the high risk of death, we tend to think that birth is far more difficult for humans than it is for other mammals. But since almost all primate infants have large heads relative to body size, birth is challenging to many primates (Fig. 13-3).

An undeveloped brain seems necessary for birth to occur through a narrow pelvis, but it may also be advantageous for other reasons. For a species as dependent on learning as we are for survival, it may be adaptive for most of our brain growth to take place in the presence of environmental stimuli rather than in the relatively unstimulating environment of the uterus. This may be particularly true for a species dependent on language. The language centers of the brain develop in the first three years of life, when the brain is undergoing its rapid expansion; these three years are considered a critical period for the development of language in the human child.

Infancy is defined as the period during which nursing takes place, typically lasting about four years in humans. When we consider how unusual it is for a mother

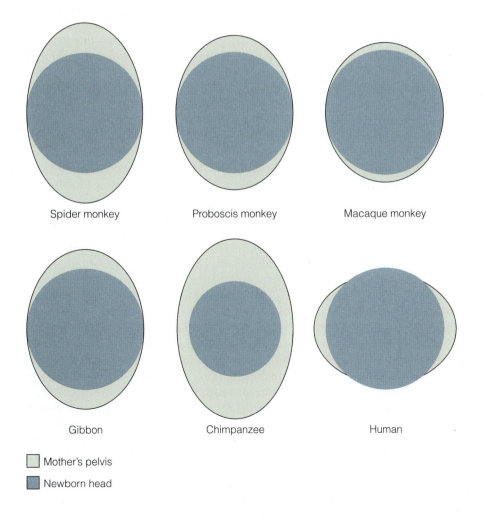

Spider monkey Proboscis monkey Macaque monkey

Gibbon Chimpanzee Human

☐ Mother's pelvis
■ Newborn head

FIGURE 13-3

The relation between the average diameter of the birth canal of adult females and average head length and breadth of newborns of the same species. (After Jolly, 1985.)

to nurse her child for even a year in the United States or Canada, this figure may surprise us. But considering that four or five years of nursing is the norm for the great apes and for women in foraging societies, most anthropologists conclude that four years was the norm for most humans in the evolutionary past (Eaton, Shostak, and Konner, 1988; Dettwyler, 1995). Other lines of evidence confirm this pattern, including the lack of other foods that infants could consume until the origin of agriculture and the domestication of milk-producing animals. In fact, if the mother died during childbirth in preagricultural populations, it's very likely that the child died also, unless there was another woman available who could nurse the child. Jane Goodall has noted that this is also true for chimpanzees: Infants who are orphaned before they are weaned don't usually survive. Even those orphaned after weaning are still emotionally dependent on their mothers and exhibit clinical signs of depression for a few months or years after the mother's death, assuming they survive the trauma (Goodall, 1986).

Human milk, like that of other primates, is extremely low in fats and protein. Such a low nutrient content is typical for species in which mothers are seldom or never separated from their infants and nurse in short, frequent bouts. Not coincidentally, prolonged, frequent nursing suppresses ovulation in marginally nourished women (Konner and Worthman, 1980), especially when coupled with high activity levels and few calorie reserves (Ellison, 2001). Under these circumstances, breast-feeding can help maintain a four-year birth interval, during which infants have no nutritional competition from siblings. Thus, nursing served as a natural (but not foolproof) birth control mechanism in the evolutionary past, as it does in some populations today.

Breast milk also provides important antibodies that contribute to infant survival. Throughout the world, breast-fed infants have far greater survival rates than those who aren't breast-fed or who are weaned too early. The only exception is in societies where scientifically developed milk substitutes are readily available and appropriately used. The importance of adequate nutrients during this period of rapid brain growth can't be overestimated. Thus, it's not surprising that there are many cultural practices designed to ensure successful nursing.

Childhood

Humans have unusually long childhoods, reflecting the importance of learning for our species. Childhood is that time between weaning and puberty when the brain is completing its growth and the acquisition of technical and social skills is taking place. For most other mammals, once weaning has occurred, getting food is left to individual effort. Humans may be unique in the practice of providing food for juveniles (Lancaster and Lancaster, 1983).

In the course of human evolution, it's possible that provisioning children between weaning and puberty may have doubled or even tripled the number of offspring that survived to adulthood (Table 13-3). This long period of extended childcare by older children and adults (especially fathers) probably enhanced the time for learning technological and social skills, also contributing to greater survival and reproductive success. Thus, the costs of extensive parental care were outweighed in human evolutionary history by the benefits of greater reproductive success.

The major causes of childhood death worldwide today are infectious diseases exacerbated by poor nutrition. Pellitier and colleagues (1995) estimate that about 70 percent of deaths of children from birth to age 4 years are due to diarrhea, respiratory infections, malaria, and diseases for which immunizations are available and that as many as 83 percent of these deaths are indirectly attributable to malnutrition, even in a mild to moderate form. It's notable that the leading causes of childhood death in the United States and western Europe aren't typically related to malnutrition and include, for children under 5 years of age, accidents followed by preterm births.

TABLE 13.3	Providing for Juveniles	
	Percent of Those Who Survive	
	Weaning	**Adolescence**
Lion	28	15
Baboon	45	33
Macaque	42	13
Chimpanzee	48	38
Provisioned macaques	82	58
Human Populations		
!Kung*	80	58
Yanomamo†	73	50
Paleoindian‡	86	50

*A hunting and gathering population of southern Africa.
†A horticultural population of South America.
‡A preagricultural people of the Americas.

Source: Adapted from Lancaster and Lancaster, 1983..

Adolescence

A number of biological events mark the transition to adolescence for both males and females. These include increase in body size, change in body shape, and the increased development and enlargement of testes and penes in boys, and breasts in girls. Hormonal changes are the driving forces behind all these physical alterations, especially increased testosterone production in boys and increased estrogen production in girls. As already noted, menarche (the first menstruation) is a clear sign of puberty in girls and is usually the marker of this transition in cultures where the event is ritually celebrated.

A number of factors affect the onset of puberty in humans, including genetics, gestational experience, nutrition, disease, activity levels, and stress. In humans and other primates, females reach sexual maturity before males do. An illustration of the effect of diet and other lifestyle factors on puberty is seen in the trend toward a lower age of menarche that has been noted in human populations in the last hundred years (Fig. 13-4) and the tendency for girls who are very active and thin to mature later than those who are heavier and less active. Socioeconomic factors are also implicated in this trend: In less-developed nations, girls from higher social classes tend to mature earlier than girls from lower social classes. In general, physical development has accelerated in the past several decades along with worldwide improvements in public health and nutrition (Worthman, 1999). Although we have emphasized the gradual decline in the age of maturity observed in the last century, there's a great range of variation within every population. An important lesson from life history theory is that maturation is sensitive to local environmental situations, including diet, health care, and parental care practices.

Adolescence is the time between puberty and the completion of physical growth or the social recognition of adulthood. This social recognition may result from marriage, bearing a child, or a particular accomplishment. In nonhuman primates, the equivalent stage is defined in males as the time from which they are capable of fertilization to the time when physical growth is complete. At this point, they have male-specific features and size and are recognized as adults by other members of

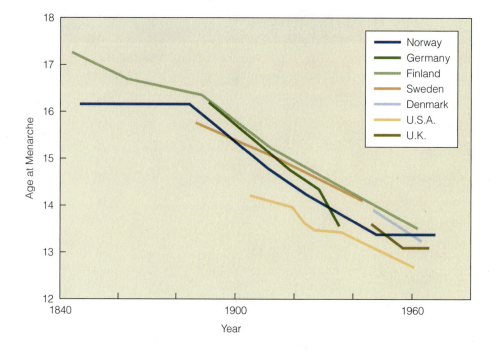

FIGURE 13-4

The secular trend in age at menarche in Europe.

(From Wood, James W., 1994 *Dynamics of Human Reproduction,* New York: Aldine de Gruyter; original redrawn from Eveleth, P.B., and J. M. Tanner, 1976, *Worldwide Variation in Human Growth,* Cambridge: Cambridge University Press.)

the social group. Females begin to engage in sexual behavior, exhibiting signs of sexual receptivity before they are capable of bearing young. These early cycles are usually not ovulatory and define the period of adolescence for them. Adulthood comes with the first pregnancy.

Adulthood

Pregnancy and child care occupy much of a woman's adult life in most cultures, as they likely did throughout hominid evolution. For most women, the years from menarche to menopause are marked by monthly menstruation except when they are pregnant or nursing. A normal menstrual cycle has two phases: the follicular phase, during which the egg is preparing for ovulation, marked by high estrogen production; and the luteal phase, during which the uterus is preparing for implantation, marked by high progesterone production. If the egg is not fertilized, progesterone production drops off and menstruation, the shedding of the uterine lining, occurs. A woman who never becomes pregnant may have as many as 400 cycles between menarche and menopause. Because reliable contraceptives were unavailable in the past, this high number of menstrual cycles is probably a relatively recent phenomenon. It's been suggested, in fact, that highly frequent menstrual cycling may be implicated in several cancers of the female reproductive organs, especially of the breast, uterus, and ovaries (Eaton et al., 1994). During the course of human evolution, females may have had as few as 60 menstrual cycles in their entire lives unless they were sterile or not sexually active.

At the social level, adulthood for women in the majority of world cultures means, in addition to caring for children, participation in economic activities. Adulthood for men typically includes activities related to subsistence, religion, politics, and family. Women may be equally or less involved in these activities, depending on the culture.

For women, menopause, or the end of menstruation, is a sign of entry into a new phase of the life cycle. Estrogen and progesterone production begin to decline toward the end of the reproductive years until ovulation (and thus menstruation) ceases altogether. This occurs at approximately age 50 in all parts of the world. Throughout human evolution, the majority of females (and males) did not survive to age 50; thus, few women lived much past menopause. But today, this event occurs when women have as much as one-third of their active and healthy lives ahead of them. As already noted, such a long postreproductive period isn't found in other primates. Female chimpanzees and monkeys experience decreased fertility in their later years, but most continue to have monthly cycles until their death. Occasional reports of menopause in apes and monkeys have been noted, but it's far from a routine and expected event.

Why do human females have such a long period during which they can no longer reproduce? One theory relates to parenting. Because it takes about 12 to 15 years before a child becomes independent, it's been argued that females are biologically "programmed" to live 12 to 15 years beyond the birth of their last child (Mayer, 1982). This hypothesis assumes that the maximum human life span for preagricultural humans was about 65 years, a figure that corresponds to what is known for contemporary hunter-gatherers and for prehistoric populations.

Another theory that's been gaining attention is known as the "grandmother hypothesis." This proposal argues that natural selection may have favored this long period in women's lives because by ceasing to bear and raise their own children, postmenopausal women would be freed to provide high-quality care for their grandchildren (Fig. 13-5). In other words, an older woman would be more likely to increase her reproductive fitness by enhancing the survival of her older grandchildren (who share one-quarter of her genes) by providing food, shelter, and direct child care than she would by having her own, possibly low-quality infants (Hawkes, O'Connell, and Blurton Jones, 1997; Lahdenperä et al., 2004; but see Peccei, 2001). This is an example of the trade-offs considered by life history theory.

A third theory regarding menopause suggests that it wasn't itself favored by natural selection; rather it's an artifact of the extension of the human life span that's occurred in the last several centuries. To put it another way, the long postreproductive years and associated menopause in women have been "uncovered" by extension of life expectancy because many causes of death are now reduced (Sievert, 2006).

FIGURE 13-5
Hadza woman and grandchild.

Aging

Postreproductive years are physiologically somewhat well defined for women, but "old age" is a very ambiguous concept. In the United States, we tend to associate old age with physical ailments and decreased activity. Thus, a person who's vigorous and active at age 70 might not be regarded as "old," whereas another who's frail and debilitated at age 55 may be considered old.

One reason we're concerned with this definition is that old age is generally regarded negatively and is typically unwelcome in the United States, a culture noted for its emphasis on youth. This attitude is quite different from that of many other societies, where old age brings with it wealth, higher status, and new freedoms, particularly for women. This is because high status is often correlated with knowledge, experience, and wisdom, which are themselves associated with greater age in most societies. Such has been the case throughout most of history, but today, in technologically developed countries, information is changing so rapidly that the old may no longer control the most relevant knowledge.

By and large, people are living longer today than they did in the past because, in part, they aren't dying from infectious disease. Currently, the top five killers in the United States, for example, are heart disease, cancer, stroke, accidents, and chronic obstructive lung disease. Together these account for almost 70 percent of deaths (CDC National Vital Statistics Report, 2000). All these conditions are considered "diseases of civilization" in that most can be accounted for by conditions in the modern environment that weren't present in the past. Examples include cigarette smoke, air and water pollution, alcohol, automobiles, high-fat diets, and environmental carcinogens. It should be noted, however, that the high incidence of these diseases is also a result of people living to older ages because of factors such as improved hygiene, regular medical care, and new medical technologies.

Human Longevity

Relative to most other animals, humans have a long life span (Table 13-4). The maximum life span potential, estimated to be about 120 years, has probably not changed in the last several thousand years, although life expectancy at birth (the average length of life) has increased significantly in the last 100 years, probably owing to the decreased influence of infectious disease, which typically takes its toll on the young (Crews and Harper, 1998).

To some extent, aging is something we do throughout our entire lives. But we usually think of aging as **senescence,** the process of physiological decline in all systems of the body that occurs toward the end of the life course. Actually, throughout adulthood, there's a gradual decline in our cells' ability to synthesize proteins, in immune system function, in muscle mass (with a corresponding increase in fat mass) and strength, and in bone mineral density (Lamberts, van den Beld, and van der Lely, 1997). This decline is associated with an increase in risk for the chronic degenerative diseases that are usually listed as the causes of death in industrialized nations.

Most causes of death that have their effects after the reproductive years won't necessarily be subjected to the forces of natural selection. In evolutionary terms, reproductive success isn't measured by how long we live; rather, as we've emphasized throughout this book, it's measured by how many offspring we produce. So organisms need to survive only long enough to produce offspring and rear them to maturity. Most wild animals die young of infection, starvation, predation, injury, and cold. Obviously, there are exceptions to this statement, especially in larger-bodied animals. Elephants, for example, may live over 50 years; and we know of several chimpanzees at Gombe that have survived into their 40s and even 50s.

TABLE 13.4	Maximum Life Spans for Selected Species	
Organism	**Approximate Maximum Life Span (in years)**
Bristlecone pine	5,000
Tortoise	170
Rockfish	140
Human	120
Blue whale	80
Indian elephant	70
Gorilla	39
Domestic dog	34
Rabbit	13
Rat	5

Source: Stini, 1991.

senescence The process of physiological decline in body function that occurs with aging.

One explanation for why we age and are affected by chronic degenerative diseases like atherosclerosis, cancer, and hypertension is that genes that enhance reproductive success in earlier years (and thus were favored by natural selection) may have detrimental effects in later years. These are referred to as **pleiotropic genes,** meaning that they have multiple effects at different times in the life span or under different conditions (Williams, 1957). For example, genes that enhance the function of the immune system in the early years may also damage tissue so that cancer susceptibility increases in later life (Nesse and Williams, 1994).

Pleiotropy may help us understand evolutionary reasons for aging, but what are the causes of senescence in the individual? Much attention has been focused recently on free radicals, highly reactive molecules that can damage cells. Protection against these by-products of normal metabolism is provided by antioxidants such as vitamins A, C, and E and by a number of enzymes (Kirkwood, 1997). Ultimately, damage to DNA can occur, which in turn contributes to the senescence of cells, the immune system, and other functional systems of the body. Additionally, there is evidence that programmed cell death is also a part of the normal processes of development that can obviously contribute to senescence.

The mitochondrial theory of aging proposes that the free radicals produced by the normal action of the cell's mitochondria (see Chapter 3) as by-products of daily living (for example, eating, breathing, walking) contribute to declining efficiency of energy production and accumulating mutations in mitochondrial DNA (mtDNA). When the mitochondria of an organ fail, there's a greater chance that the organ itself will fail. In this view, as mitochondria lose their ability to function, the body ages as well (Loeb, Wallace, and Martin, 2005; Kujoth et al., 2007).

Another hypothesis for senescence related to ultimate cell death is known as the telomere hypothesis. In this view, the DNA sequence at the end of each chromosome, known as the telomere, is shortened each time a cell divides. Cells that have divided many times throughout the life course have short telomeres, eventually reaching the point at which they can no longer divide and are unable to maintain healthy tissues and organs.

Shortened telomeres have also been implicated in cancer. In laboratory studies, the enzyme telomerase can lengthen telomeres, making the cell "young" again. For this reason, the gene for telomerase has been called the "immortalizing gene." Although this research isn't likely to lead to a lengthening of the life span, it may contribute to better health throughout an individual's lifetime.

Far more important than genes in the aging process, however, are lifestyle factors, such as smoking, physical activity, diet, and medical care. Interestingly, there is evidence that caloric restriction may actually contribute to a longer life span (Kirkwood, 2002). Life expectancy at birth varies considerably from country to country and among socioeconomic classes within a country. Throughout the world, women have higher life expectancies than men. A Japanese girl born in 2004, for example, can expect to live to age 86, a boy to age 79. Girls and boys born in that same year in the United States have life expectancies of 80 and 75, respectively. In contrast to these children in industrialized nations, girls and boys in Mali have life expectancies of only 47 and 44, respectively (data from World Health Organization). Many African nations have seen life expectancy drop below 40 due to deaths from AIDS. For example, before the AIDS epidemic, Botswanans had a life expectancy of almost 65 years; today, life expectancy in Botswana is slightly more than 40 (Fig. 13-6).

A consequence of improved health and life expectancy in conjunction with declining birth rates is an aging population, leading in some parts of the world to a shift toward older median ages and greater numbers of people older than 65 than younger than 20. In demographic terms, these two groups represent dependent categories, and there's increasing concern about the decline in the number of working-aged adults available to support the younger and older segments of a population. In other words, the dependency ratio is increasing, with significant consequences for local and global economies.

pleiotropic genes Genes that have more than one effect; genes that have different effects at different times in the life cycle.

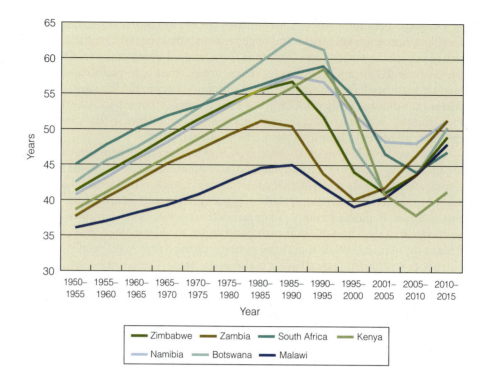

FIGURE 13-6

Changes in life expectancy due to AIDS in seven African nations. (From United Nations, 1998.)

Individuals, Society, and Evolution

Throughout this chapter, we have discussed ways in which evolutionary history, genes, and the environment affect the human life course from infancy until death. Humans are social animals, however, and we now turn our attention to the ways in which natural selection has acted on the behaviors of humans imbedded in social contexts. Examining human social behavior in an evolutionary framework is known as *behavioral ecology,* which we discussed in Chapter 7 in the context of primate behavior. Of course, humans are primates, and many biological anthropologists are interested in the extent to which evolution can explain contemporary human behaviors. Behavioral ecologists suggest that humans, like other animals, behave in ways that increase their fitness, or reproductive success. This includes behaviors affecting mating and parenting success. Finding mates and taking care of offspring require time and energy, and as we know all too well, both of these commodities exist in finite amounts. Thus, reproductive efforts require trade-offs in time, energy, and resources invested in mating and parenting. When we read about these concepts as they pertain to monkeys and apes, most of us probably don't find much to disagree with. But to suggest that evolutionary processes have an impact on human behavior today raises a lot of issues, some of which aren't so easily resolved.

For example, this view argues that natural selection isn't limited to physical and physiological responses, but has had an effect on the way humans think—in other words, on human cognition, perception, and memory. The argument goes something like this: The ability to remember a dangerous event that may have resulted in loss of life would be favorably selected if it prevented a person from being caught in a similar situation. The ability to distinguish a wildebeest (food) from a lion (danger) would be selectively favored. Likewise, economic behaviors involved in the allocation of resources to increase survival and reproductive success would be favored. Other behaviors that have received attention from behavioral ecologists include mate attraction, sexuality, aggression, and violence.

Aggression and violence, particularly on the part of males, have been topics of interest to anthropologists for many decades (for example, Ardrey, 1961; Morris, 1967; Wrangham and Peterson, 1996). For example, contrast the behaviors of our

(a)

(b)

two closest living relatives, chimpanzees and bonobos. Most striking is that chimpanzee society seems to be based on male-male competition and aggression leading occasionally to violence both within and between troops, whereas bonobo society is described as a female-dominated community based on cooperation and peaceful interaction (Fig. 13-7).

To Wrangham and Peterson, these two behavior patterns represent the extremes of human societies and also show potentials for both violence and peace that may be rooted in human evolutionary history. On the other hand, they clearly acknowledge the role of culture and society in fostering aggression and violence in males. Mirroring some of the discussions of terrorism today, chimpanzee communities with abundant resources have far fewer incidents of violence than communities with limited resources; in general, bonobos live in areas of relative resource abundance. But whatever their roots, it appears to many observers that war, genocide, rape, rioting, and terrorism are unwelcome legacies of human evolutionary history. Unfortunately, because of events such as 9/11 in the United States and the war in Iraq, these arguments resonate more profoundly and convincingly than they may have at other times in recent history.   Perhaps the pendulum of thinking about world events will soon swing toward the idea that peaceful cooperation is more fundamental to human behavior.

Are We Still Evolving?

In many ways, culture has enabled us to transcend many of the limitations imposed on us by our biology. But that biology was shaped during millions of years of evolution in environments very different from those in which most of us live today. There is, to a great extent, a lack of fit between our biology and our twenty-first-century cultural environment. Our expectations that scientists can discover a "magic bullet" to enable us to resist any disease that arises have been painfully dashed with death tolls from AIDS reaching catastrophic levels in many parts of the world.

Socioeconomic and political concerns also have powerful effects on our species today. Whether you die of starvation or succumb to disorders associated with overconsumption depends a great deal on where you live, what your socioeconomic status is, and how much control you have over your life, factors not likely to be related to biology. These factors also have an effect on whether or not you are killed in a war or spend most of your life in a safe, comfortable community. Whether or not you are exposed to one of the "new" pathogens, such as HIV, SARS, or tuberculosis, has a lot to do with your lifestyle and other cultural factors, but whether or not

FIGURE 13-7
(a) These chimpanzees exhibit an aggressive reaction when confronted by others. (b) The bonobos show more relaxed expressions.

you die from a particular disease or fail to reproduce because of it still has a lot to do with your biology.

The 4.3 million children dying annually from respiratory infections are primarily those in the developing world, with limited access to adequate medical care, clearly a cultural factor. But in those same areas, lacking that same medical care, are millions of other children who aren't dying from infections. Presumably, among the factors affecting this difference is resistance afforded by genes. By considering this simple example, we can see that human gene frequencies are still changing from one generation to the next in response to selective agents such as disease; thus, our species is still evolving.

Whether we will eventually become a different species or become extinct (remember, extinction is the fate of almost every species that has ever lived on earth) isn't something we can predict. Whether our brains will get larger or our hands will evolve solely to push buttons is the stuff of science fiction, not anthropology. But as long as new pathogens appear or new environments are introduced by technology, there is little doubt that the human species will either continue to evolve or become extinct, just as almost every other species on earth has done.

Culture *has* enabled us to transcend many limits imposed by our biology, and people who never would have been able to do so in the past are today surviving and having children. This in itself means that we are evolving. How many of you would be reading this text if you had been born under the health and economic conditions prevalent 500 years ago?

Summary

This chapter has reviewed the fundamental concepts of growth and development and how those processes occur within the contexts of both biology and culture. Diet has an important effect on growth, and human nutritional requirements themselves result from biocultural evolution. We reviewed the preagricultural human diet with the suggestion that many of our contemporary ills may result from incompatibilities between our evolved nutritional requirements and the foods that are currently consumed. In particular, the preagricultural diet was probably high in complex carbohydrates and fiber and low in fat and sodium. Diets for many contemporary people are low in complex carbohydrates and fiber and high in fat and sodium. This type of diet has been implicated in many current health problems.

The human life cycle can be divided into six phases: prenatal, infancy, juvenile, subadult, adult, and postreproductive. Each is fairly well defined by biological markers. Pregnancy lasts about nine months in humans, and infants are born with only about 25 percent of their adult brain size. This means that human infants are helpless at birth and therefore dependent on at least one parent for a long time. Birth is somewhat more challenging for humans than for other mammals because of the very close correspondence between maternal pelvic size (narrow because of bipedalism) and fetal head size (large, even though the brain is relatively undeveloped). Infancy is the period of nursing, approximately four years for most humans and apes. The unusually long period of childhood in humans is important as the time in which social and technological skills are acquired. Sexual maturation is apparent at puberty, but full adult status isn't achieved until growth has been completed and childbearing capabilities are reached. The last phase of the human life cycle, the postreproductive period, is marked in women by menopause, the cessation of menstruation and ovulation.

The human legacy from evolutionary history includes thought processes and behaviors that reflect natural selection operating on individuals to increase reproductive success, or fitness. Our review of behavioral ecology summarized the ways in which genes, environment, and culture have interacted to produce complex adaptations to equally complex challenges. A critical review of hypotheses for such human behaviors as aggression, violence, nurturance, and reproduction reveals the complexity of this interrelationship.

WHY IT MATTERS

For children who grow up in poverty with limited access to good food, isn't it better that they are small as adults so that they don't require as much food? This argument was presented several years ago as the "small but healthy hypothesis" (Seckler, 1982). It states that small adult stature under circumstances of low resource availability is adaptive in that small adults would need fewer resources and would fare better under chronically stressful conditions. In fact, a great deal of public policy was based on this "small but healthy hypothesis," but the broader anthropological and evolutionary perspectives reveal that small body size also means small organs, less ability to perform work, and lower reproductive success (Martorell, 1989), all of which mean "not healthy" from evolutionary and life span perspectives. And even if a baby whose mother was malnourished during pregnancy is well nourished from birth on (as often happens in adoptions), the child's growth, health, and, for females, future pregnancies appear to be compromised, perhaps even for several generations (Kuzawa, 2005). This awareness has clear implications for public health efforts that attempt to provide adequate nutritional support to pregnant women throughout the world. Furthermore, an emphasis on child immunizations in the context of extreme poverty and malnutrition may be nothing more than prolonging life so that immunized children are able to survive only to die later of malnutrition (Dettwyler, 1994). Children who are well nourished and otherwise healthy are usually able to survive bouts of childhood diseases, even without immunization. Over and over again, we find that the nutritional requirements of our ancestors still have profound effects on us today.

Critical Thinking Questions

1 What is meant by the analogy "Water is to fish as culture is to humans"? Do you think that humans could survive without culture?

2 What are some of the major ways in which human health and life course have changed since the origin of agriculture? Do you think that the transition to agriculture has, in general, been good or bad for human health?

3 Consider the following statement: "In the United States, socioeconomic status is the primary determinant of nutrition and health." Do you agree or disagree with this statement? Why or why not?

4 Do you think that natural selection operates on human behaviors such as parenting and aggression? Provide evidence or examples to support your view.

5 What evidence is there that humans are still evolving?

CHAPTER 14

Lessons from the Past, Lessons for the Future

Craig Mayhew and Robert Simmon, NASA

Near the end of this chapter, you will read the statement that culture is "an adaptive strategy gone awry." Why do we say this? Do you agree with this statement? Why or why not?

Introduction

Virtually every day we read or hear something about global climate change, endangered species, environmental degradation, or one of the many other problems facing humanity (and the planet) today. In this chapter, we briefly discuss some of these challenges that have emerged as a result of our own doing. While many people refuse to believe that humans are responsible for global climate change, the overwhelming consensus among climate scientists is that we are, and this fact really is an "inconvenient truth."

Although anthropology textbooks don't usually dwell on the topics included here, we feel that it's important to consider them, however brief and simplified our treatment must be. We are living during a critical period in the earth's history. Indeed, the future of much of life as we know it will be decided in the next few decades, and these decisions will be irrevocable. Therefore, it's crucial that we, as individuals, cities, and nations, make wise decisions, and to do this we must be well informed. We also think that it's important to consider these problems from an anthropological perspective. This is something not usually done in the media and certainly not by politicians and heads of state. But if we are truly to comprehend the impact that human activities have had on the planet, then such discussions surely must consider our biological and cultural evolution. And we must also emphasize our place in nature and focus on how, since the domestication of plants and animals, we have altered the face of our planet while at the same time shaping the destiny of thousands of species, including our own.

Homo sapiens is one of approximately 1.4 million living species currently known to science. All of these organisms, including bacteria and plants, ultimately are the living results of the same basic evolutionary processes, and all share the same DNA material. But more than any other life-form, humans, through cultural innovation and ever-expanding numbers, have come to dominate the planet.

In our discussion of such topics as evolution and adaptation, we have emphasized the importance of culture in the development of our species. The study of human biological and cultural evolution, coupled with an examination of the results of early human activities, can provide some insights from the past that may help illuminate the future. At the very least, we can provide an anthropological perspective on the serious problems that face us today.

How Successful Are We?

As we've emphasized, humans are animals and, more specifically, primates. Like all life-forms on earth, our very existence is based in the molecule DNA. Since all living things share this same genetic foundation, it's highly probable that all life evolved from a common ancestor and that human beings are part of a continuum

▶ **Click!**

Go to the following media resources for interactive activities, more information, and study materials on topics covered in this chapter:

■ Anthropology Resource Center
■ Student Companion Website for *Essentials of Physical Anthropology,* Seventh Edition
■ Online Virtual Laboratories for Physical Anthropology CD-ROM, Fourth Edition

made up of biologically related species. Yet, we humans tend to regard ourselves as separate from all other species, and as the masters of the planet. In Western cultures, this view has been reinforced by the conventionally held Old Testament assertion that humans shall have *dominion* over all other species. The teachings of Islam and certain other religions and philosophies have similar interpretations. (Actually, the Old Testament's book of Genesis presents two separate versions. The second and lesser-known version conveys a quite different meaning: that humans are to have "stewardship" over other animals.) Also, there's the prevailing view that nature represents an array of resources that exists primarily to be exploited for the betterment of humankind. This view is as widely held today, unfortunately, as ever before.

By most standards, we are a successful species. There are currently around 6.7 billion human beings living on earth. Each one of these 6,700,000,000 individuals is made up of around 20 trillion cells. Nevertheless, we and all other multicellular organisms contribute only a small fraction of all the cells on the planet, the vast majority being bacteria. Thus, if we see life ultimately as a competition among reproducing organisms, bacteria are the winners, hands down.

Bacteria, then, could be viewed as the dominant form of life on earth. However, even when only considering multicellular animals, there are additional lessons in evolutionary humility. As mammals, we are members of a group that includes about 4,000 species. It's also a group that's been on the decline for the last several million years. And as primates, we belong to a group that today consists of only about 250 species, far fewer than there were a few million years ago. By contrast, more than 750,000 insect species have been identified, and there may actually be as many as 30 million (Wilson, 1992)! Number of species (as an indicator of biological diversity) is as good a barometer of evolutionary success as any other, and by this standard, humans can hardly be seen as the most successful of species.

Evolutionary success can also be gauged by species longevity. As we've seen, fossil evidence indicates that humans have been on the scene for between 200,000 and 400,000 years. Such time spans, seen through the perspective of a human lifetime, may seem enormous. But consider this: Our immediate predecessor, *Homo erectus,* existed for over 1.5 million years. In other words, we as a species would need to survive another million years simply to match *Homo erectus.*

Humans and the Impact of Culture

As you have learned, because humans increasingly came to use culture as a means of adapting to the natural environment, biological anthropologists view culture as an adaptive strategy. Stone tools, temporary shelters, animal products (including skin clothing), and the use of fire all permitted earlier populations to leave the tropics and exploit resources in regions previously unavailable to them. Thus, it was culture that enabled humans to become increasingly successful as time passed.

For most of human history, technology remained simple, and the rate of culture change was slow. Indeed, humans enjoyed what could be called a "comfortable" relationship with this adaptive strategy. However, as technologies became more complex, and especially when humans began to adopt an agricultural lifestyle, their relationship with culture became more complicated and, over time, less and less comfortable.

From the archaeological record, it appears that around 15,000 years ago, influenced in part by climate change (not induced by human activity) and the extinction of many large-bodied prey species, some human groups began to settle down, abandoning their nomadic lifestyles. Moreover, by about 10,000 years ago (and probably earlier), some peoples had learned that by keeping domestic animals and growing crops, they had more abundant and reliable food supplies. The domestication of plants and animals is seen as one of the most significant events in human history, one that was eventually to have far-reaching consequences for the entire planet.

Keeping domesticated plants and animals requires a settled way of life, and increased sedentism, combined with more reliable food sources, led to increased population growth. Viewed from the perspective of twenty-first-century humans living in industrialized societies, it might seem that adopting a settled lifestyle would lead to better health and nutrition. Yet, scientists believe that health and nutrition among hunter-gatherers was, in fact, quite good compared to that of humans living in early settlements.

In our discussion of infectious disease in Chapter 12, we considered how contact with nonhuman animals, including domesticated ones, increases our vulnerability to many forms of illness. These illness may be transmitted directly to humans from their animals or indirectly by means of vectors such as fleas. In addition, humans in early settlements increased their exposure to refuse heaps and the flea-infested rodents that found human waste (and grain stores) such an attractive food source. So while living in permanent settlements provides a more reliable resource base, it also comes with the cost of increased exposure to infectious disease. Thus, it can justifiably be said that increased exposure to infectious disease was one of the earliest changes in the harmonious relationship between humans and cultural innovation.

Early agriculturalists, for whom we have only crude population estimates, probably numbered a few million worldwide. At this level, population density was low, but human activity was already beginning to have an impact on the natural environment. In truth, it would be inaccurate to assume that human activities have only recently come to have environmental consequences. In fact, human impact on local environments increased dramatically as soon as people began to live in permanent settlements.

Consequently, many of the earth's features we think of as natural actually came about as the result of human activities. For example, prior to the **Neolithic,** when people began to live in permanent settlements, much of Britain and continental Europe was blanketed with forests and woodlands. The moorlands and, to some extent, the peat bogs that have provided evocative settings for so many English novels are the result of deforestation that began more than 5,000 years ago (Fig. 14-1). In Britain, local woodland clearing by hunter-gatherers began during the late **Mesolithic,** and it accelerated around 5,000 years ago with the adoption of farming. Late Bronze Age peoples (circa 4,000–3,500 years ago) continued the process on an even larger scale, so that by 2,500 years ago, many of England's forests were disappearing (Bell and Walker, 1992). Today, the majority of European woodlands exist as discontinuous patches, the result of processes that continued until fairly recent times but that originated with prehistoric farmers.

Unfortunately, humans began to exploit, and increasingly depend on, nonrenewable resources. Forests can be viewed as renewable resources, provided they are given the opportunity for regrowth. However, in many areas, forest clearing was virtually complete and was inevitably followed by soil erosion, frequent overgrazing, and overcultivation, which led to further soil erosion (Fig. 14-2). Therefore, in those areas, trees became a nonrenewable resource, perhaps the first resource to have this distinction.

Early European explorers and settlers recorded extensive burning of woodlands and forests by indigenous groups of hunter-gatherers in North America and Australia, presumably to clear undergrowth and drive animals from cover. This kind of burning may have been common in many parts of the world prior to the development of agriculture and its

Neolithic The period during which humans began to domesticate plants and animals. The Neolithic is also associated with increased sedentism. Dates for the Neolithic vary from region to region, depending on when domestication occurred.

Mesolithic The period preceding the Neolithic, during which humans increasingly exploited smaller animals (including fish), increased the variety of tools they used, and became somewhat less nomadic.

FIGURE 14-1
The moorland in the foreground is the result of woodland clearing some 2,000 years ago in southwest England.

Lynn Kilgore

© Russ Mittermeier

FIGURE 14-2
Deforestation and erosion in Madagascar.

FIGURE 14-3
Map of deforestation showing the decline in frontier forest over the last 8,000 years. Frontier forests are the remaining natural forest ecosystems. To be considered a frontier forest, an area must contain indigenous treees, be relatively undisturbed by human activity, and be large enough to maintain all of what is believed to be its original biodiversity.

effects weren't inconsequential. But, as people began to live in agricultural communities and later in towns and cities, the impact on forests became devastating. In fact, as shown in Figure 14-3, only about one-fifth of the earth's original forests remain intact today, and much of the clearing occurred centuries and even millennia ago.

There are many reasons for cutting forests, and the earliest of these were to clear the land for cultivation and grazing and to provide firewood and housing material. As small communities grew into towns and cities, wood came to be used for ship-building, fortifications, and even the building of temples and palaces. In short, the human experience over the last 10,000 to 15,000 years wouldn't have been possible without the exploitation of woodlands and forests.

One of the earliest documented examples of humankind's appetite for lumber is the cutting of the famous cedars of Lebanon. Over 3,000 years ago, the eastern

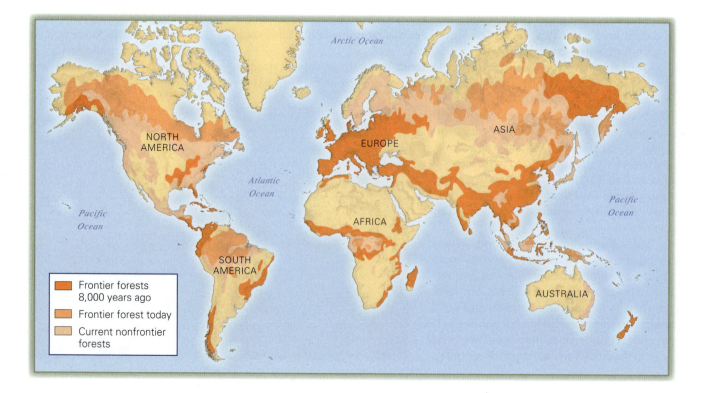

Frontier forests
8,000 years ago

Frontier forest today

Current nonfrontier forests

Mediterranean (modern-day Israel, Jordan, Lebanon, and Syria), southern Turkey, and Mesopotamia (in present-day Iraq) had become major sources of valuable cedar, fir, cypress, and other woods. But by far the most highly prized wood was Lebanese cedar, which was cut and shipped throughout the eastern Mediterranean, where it was used in the construction of buildings and ships (Fig. 14-4). The Old Testament tells us that King Solomon's temple was made of cedar from Lebanon, and numerous other texts, written over several centuries, document the extensive use and desirability of this precious wood. Not surprisingly, the deforestation of the mountains of Lebanon was eventually so complete that the "forest" of today consists of small patches of trees.

Just to prove the old adage "The more things change, the more they stay the same," it's informative to note that classical scholars (most notably Plato and Aristotle) bemoaned the effects of deforestation and other forms of environmental degradation in Greece and other areas of the Mediterranean basin. They warned that the cutting of forests and overuse of land led to soil erosion and agricultural decline, disrupted water supplies, and even caused climate change. Their views, expressed some 2,400 years ago, are verified by combined archaeological and geological data that show sequences of soil accumulation followed by intense human occupation, then soil erosion, and finally abandonment of archaeological sites throughout Greece. Furthermore, this sequence of episodes dates to around 5,000 years ago. But given the relatively small size of human populations, even by the time of the ancient Greeks and Romans, the human impact on ecosystems mostly remained a localized, not global, phenomenon. Nevertheless, these impacts were in some cases significant. The barren landscape of Greece and much of what is now desert in the Middle East and the Sahara Desert in Africa are the legacies of deforestation, overgrazing, and subsequent erosion over the last few thousand years.

Destruction of natural resources in the past has also had severe consequences for people living today. In 1990, a typhoon and subsequent flooding killed over 100,000 people in Bangladesh, and the flooding was at least partly due to previous deforestation in parts of the Himalayas of northern India. There is also evidence that continued erosion and flooding in China are partly the result of deforestation that occurred in the past. Lastly, many scientists have long speculated that the collapse of the Maya civilization of southern Mexico around 1,000 years ago was at least partly due to climate change, overcultivation, and depletion of nutrient-poor tropical soils.

Archaeologists can provide many examples of what humans have done wrong in the past. But just as importantly, they are also able to provide us with positive examples from earlier cultures, innovative techniques that, for all our modern wisdom, we still have yet to match. For example, in the Andean highlands of South America, soil is very poor and subject to erosion. Agricultural peoples living in the region today (in Bolivia and Peru), even with considerable input from modern technology, can barely scrape together a meager existence. Yet, this wasn't always the case. Five hundred years ago, the Inka ancestors of these peoples reaped enormous wealth from this same land and built from it one of the largest, best-organized empires in the world. How did they do it?

By examining Inka agricultural fields, terracing, and irrigation, archaeologist Clark Erickson (1988) was able to reveal the ancient techniques and duplicate many of the same methods. This was no mere academic exercise, however, for the next step was to teach these methods to modern farmers. As a result, crop yields have greatly improved, with less environmental damage, reduced use of fertilizer, and at less expense than before.

Robert Jurmain

FIGURE 14-4
This eighth-century B.C. Assyrian panel depicts the transport of cedar logs from Lebanon to Assyria.

The Loss of Biodiversity

Although the term *biodiversity* is frequently used today, many people don't really understand what it means. Biodiversity is the totality of all living things, from bacteria and fungi to trees and humans. The term refers not only to species, but to individuals and the various genetic combinations they represent, as well as to entire ecosystems. The fact that we are currently losing biodiversity at an unprecedented rate is indisputable. But we don't know the exact rate of loss or what its impact will be.

The geological record indicates that in the past 570 million years, there have been at least 15 mass extinction events, two of which altered all of the earth's ecosystems (Ward, 1994). The first of these occurred some 250 million years ago and resulted from climatic change that followed the joining of all the earth's landmasses into one supercontinent.

The second event happened around 65 million years ago and ended 150 million years of evolutionary processes that, among other things, had produced the dinosaurs. This mass extinction is believed by many researchers to have resulted from climatic changes following the impact of an asteroid.

A third major extinction event, perhaps of the same magnitude, is occurring now, and according to some scientists, it may have begun in the late Pleistocene or early **Holocene** (Ward, 1994). Unlike all other mass extinctions, this one hasn't been caused by continental drift, climate change (so far), or collisions with asteroids. Rather, it's due to the activities of a single species, *Homo sapiens*.

Many scientists, in fact, believe that several large mammalian species were pushed toward extinction by humans, particularly near the end of the Pleistocene, some 10,000 years ago. In North America, at least 57 mammalian species became extinct, including the mammoth, mastodon, giant ground sloth, saber-toothed cat, several large rodents, and numerous grazing animals (Lewin, 1986; Simmons, 1989). There's no dispute that climate change (warming) was a crucial factor in these extinctions, but hunting and other human activities may also have been important. Although we don't know exactly when people first entered North America from Asia, it's certain that they were firmly established by at least 12,000 years ago (and probably much earlier), so they were present when at least some species became extinct.

We have no direct evidence that early American big game hunters contributed to extinctions; but we do have evidence of what can happen to indigenous species when new areas are colonized by humans for the first time. Within just a few centuries of human occupation of New Zealand, the moa, a large flightless bird, was exterminated. Madagascar serves as a similar example. In the last thousand years, after the establishment of permanent human settlements, 14 lemur species and a number of other mammals and birds have become extinct (Jolly, 1985; Napier and Napier, 1985). One of these was a lemur that weighed an estimated 300 pounds (Fleagle, 1999)! Lastly, scientists have debated for years whether the extinction of all large-bodied animals (some 60 species) in Australia during the late Pleistocene was due to human hunting and other activities or to climate change. Recently, Miller and colleagues (1999), using four different techniques, were able to date the rapid extinction of a large flightless bird, *Genyornis newtoni*, to about 50,000 years ago, a date that roughly coincides with the arrival of humans in Australia. This study suggests that the simultaneous extinction of this species in a number of localities occurred during a period of relative climatic stability and therefore is best explained as a consequence of human activities, especially the widespread burning of large areas and subsequent changes in vegetation.

Hunter-gatherers, for whom we have some ethnographic evidence, differed in their views regarding conservation of prey species. Some groups believed that overhunting would anger deities. Others (some Great Basin Indians, for example) killed large numbers only every several years, allowing populations of game species, such as antelope, time to replenish. Still others avoided killing pregnant females or were

Holocene The most recent epoch of the Cenozoic. Following the Pleistocene, it is estimated to have begun 10,000 years ago.

conscientious about using all parts of the body to avoid waste. Nevertheless, there were some groups, such as the Hadza of the Pacific Northwest coast, who appear not to have been especially concerned with conservation.

Moreover, hunting techniques were frequently incompatible with conservation. Prior to domestication of the horse (or its availability in the New World), the only effective way to hunt large herd animals was to organize game drives. In some cases, fire was used to drive stampeding animals into blind canyons or human-made "corrals." Other times, bison were driven over cliffs or into narrow, deep gullies. As you can imagine, this often led to unavoidable waste, as more animals might be killed than could be used, even though it was common practice to store dried meats for future use. Moreover, there might be so many animals that it was impossible to retrieve those at the bottom of the pile.

Since the end of the Pleistocene, human activities have increasingly taken their toll on nonhuman species, but today, species are disappearing at an unprecedented rate. Hunting, which occurs for a number of reasons other than for food, continues to be a factor. Competition with introduced nonnative species, such as pigs, goats, rats, and snakes, has also contributed to the problem. But until recently, the single most important cause of extinction has been habitat reduction. (In some regions though, the importance of habitat loss has now become secondary to the hunting that supplies the bushmeat trade.)

Habitat loss is a direct result of the burgeoning human population and the resulting need for building materials, grazing and agricultural land, and living areas. We are all aware of the risk to such visible species as elephants, pandas, tigers, and mountain gorillas, to name a few. These risks are real, and within your lifetime many of these animals will certainly become extinct, at least in the wild. But the greatest threat to biodiversity is to the countless unknown species that live in the world's rain forests (Fig. 14-5).

It's estimated that over half of all plants and animals on earth live in rain forests. By 1989, these habitats had been reduced to a little less than half their original size—that is, down to about 3 million square miles. The annual net loss between 1980 and 1995 was almost 67,000 square miles. "The loss is equal to the area of a football field every second. Put another way, in 1989 the surviving rain forests occupied an area about that of the continuous forty-eight states of the United States, and they were being reduced by an amount equivalent to the size of Florida every year" (Wilson, 1992, p. 275). By the year 2022, half the world's remaining rain forests will be gone if destruction continues at its present rate. This will result in a loss of between 10 and 22 percent of all rain forest species, or 5 to 10 percent of all plant and animal species on earth (Wilson, 1992).

Lynn Kilgore

FIGURE 14-5
Stumps of recently felled forest trees are still visible in this newly cleared field in Rwanda. The haze is wood smoke from household fires.

Should we care about the loss of biodiversity? If so, why? In fact, it seems that most people don't care, partly because they aren't aware of the problem. Moreover, reasons as to why we should care are usually stated in terms of the benefits (known and unknown) that humans may derive from rain forest species. An example of such a benefit is the chemical taxol (derived from the Pacific yew tree), which may be an effective treatment for ovarian and breast cancer.

It's undeniable that humans stand to benefit from continued research into potentially useful rain forest products. However, anthropocentric reasons aren't the sole justification for preserving the earth's biodiversity. Each species that is lost is the product of millions of years of evolution, and each fills a specific econiche. Quite simply, the destruction of so much of life on earth is within our power. But we must ask ourselves, Is it our right?

The Present Crisis: Our Cultural Heritage?

Overpopulation

If we had to point to one single challenge facing humanity, a problem to which virtually all others are tied, it would have to be human population growth. Human population size has skyrocketed as we've increased our ability to produce food surpluses. As population size increases, more and more land is converted to crops, pasture, and building sites, providing more opportunities for yet more people. Additionally, through the medical advances of the twentieth century, we reduced mortality at both ends of the life cycle. Thus, fewer people die in childhood, and having survived to adulthood, they live longer than ever before. Although these medical advances are unquestionably beneficial to individuals (who hasn't benefited from medical technology?), it's also clear that there are significant detrimental consequences to our species and to the planet.

Population size, if left unchecked, increases exponentially, that is, as a function of some percent, like compound interest in a bank account. Currently, human population increases worldwide at an annual rate of about 1.8 percent. Although this figure may not seem too startling at first, it deserves some examination. It's also useful to discuss doubling time, the amount of time it takes for a population to double in size.

Scientists estimate that around 10,000 years ago, only about 5 million people inhabited the earth (not even half as many as live in Los Angeles County today). By A.D. 1650, there were perhaps 500 million, and by 1800, 1 billion. In other words, between 10,000 years ago and A.D. 1650 (a period of 9,650 years), population size doubled 7½ times. On average, then, the doubling time between 10,000 years ago and 1650 was about 1,287 years. But from 1650 to 1800, population size doubled again, which means that doubling time had been reduced to 150 years (Ehrlich and Ehrlich, 1990). Then, in the 37 years between 1950 and 1987, world population doubled from 2 billion to 4 billion. It's interesting to note that people born in the early 1950s were the first *ever* to see the number of humans on the planet double during their lifetime.

Dates and associated population estimates up to the present are as follows: mid-1800s, 1 billion; 1930s, 2 billion; mid-1960s, 3 billion; mid-1980s, 4 billion; present, 6.7 billion (Fig. 14-6). To state this problem in terms we can appreciate, we add 1 billion people to the world's population approximately every 11 years. That comes out to 90–95 million every year and roughly a quarter of a million every day!

The rate of growth isn't equally distributed among all nations. Although the world's rate of increase has ranged from 1.7 to 2.1 percent since the 1950s (Ehrlich and Ehrlich, 1990), it's the developing countries that share most of the burden (not to be interpreted as blame). During the 1980s, the population of Kenya grew at a

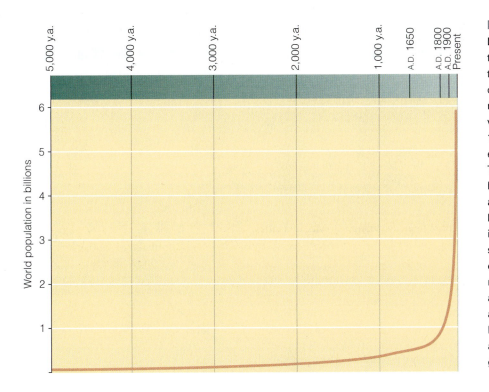

FIGURE 14-6

Line graph depicting exponential growth of human population. Note that for almost all of the last 5,000 years, the number of humans increased very slowly. It was not until 1650 that population size was even half a billion (500 million). The rapid increase to 1 billion by about 1850 is, in-part, attributable to the Industrial Revolution. Population increase occurs as a function of some percent (in some developing countries, the annual rate is over 3 percent). With advances in food production and medical technologies, humans are now undergoing a population explosion, as this graph illustrates.

rate of a little over 4 percent per year, while India added a million per month, and 36,000 babies were born every day in Latin America.

Fortunately, by the end of the twentieth century, rates of human population growth began to decline. The average number of children per female *worldwide* had dropped from 4.3 in 1960 to 2.6 in 2000. Moreover, by 2000, the replacement rate of 2.1 children per female (that is, the number of births, accounting for early infant mortality, required for population size to remain constant) had been achieved in all western European countries, Thailand, and the nonimmigrant population of the United States (Wilson, 2000). It must also be mentioned that for the first time in history, the population of South Africa is now declining, but this fact is due primarily to the high incidence of HIV/AIDS (approximately 30 percent of adults are infected).

The decrease in family size worldwide is attributable to several factors, including the shift to a global economy, the migration of rural populations to urban centers with concomitant shifts in employment from agriculture to manufacturing and service sectors, and, at least in some countries, the increasing empowerment of women that has meant better education, increased opportunities in the workplace, and access to family planning.

The most recent United Nations International Conference on Population and Development set as its goal the development of a plan to contain the world's population to about 7.3 billion by the year 2015 and to prevent future growth. Otherwise, by the year 2050, human numbers could approach 10 billion. The United Nations plan emphasizes women's education, health, and rights throughout the world, but has met with stiff resistance from groups opposed to abortion and contraception. Moreover, many cultures still value large families.

The United Nations goal is admirable and ambitious, but achieving it will be a formidable task. Although the average number of live births per woman has declined, it will still be next to impossible to prevent huge population increases in the next century. Bear in mind that *approximately half of all people currently living in the developing world are less than 15 years old*. These young people haven't reproduced yet, but they will.

You might logically ask if it's possible to make technological changes that would provide food for all these people. This and similar questions are being asked

QUICK REVIEW   **Human Population Growth: Contributing Factors and Consequences**

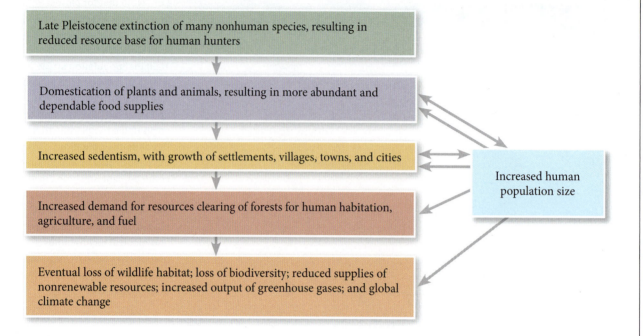

more and more frequently. Certainly, there are methods that would more efficiently use the agricultural lands that are already available, and there are better ways to distribute the food surpluses already produced. But can we continue indefinitely to feed ever-growing numbers of humans? Is there enough land to support an endless demand for housing, crop cultivation, and grazing? Is there enough water? We probably can develop technologies to meet our species' increasing needs for a while. But can we do so and still meet the requirements of thousands of undomesticated species? The answer for the immediate future is: probably not. For the long term, without major changes in human population growth, the answer is: absolutely not.

Global Climate Change

With increases in numbers comes greater consumption of resources. At the same time, activities involved in the production of goods and services produce waste and pollution, all of which leads to further environmental degradation.

Consider for a moment the fact that much of the energy used for human activities is derived from the burning of fossil fuels such as oil and coal. The burning of fossil fuels releases carbon dioxide into the atmosphere, and this, in turn, traps heat. Deforestation, even if the trees aren't burned, also contributes to global warming, since it reduces the number of trees available to absorb carbon dioxide. Moreover, in the tropics, trees are frequently burned as land is cleared, and this releases yet more carbon dioxide. As a sobering note, in Indonesia, an estimated 370,000 to 740,000 acres of forest were burned in 1997 alone. Most of these fires were caused by land-clearing activities in a region already suffering from severe drought. Because these fires also destroyed peat deposits (layers of ancient, decayed vegetation that serve as storehouses of carbon), an estimated 810 million to 2.6 billion metric tons of carbon were released into the atmosphere. (A metric ton is 2,240 pounds.) This amounts to between 13 and 40 percent of the world's annual carbon emissions from the burning of fossil fuels (Page et al., 2002).

The scientific community is now in almost complete agreement that we are seeing the effects of global warming. In 2007, the United Nations Intergovernmental Panel on Climate Change (IPCC)* released a series of reports on global warming. These reports were based on articles published in peer-reviewed scientific publications by over 800 contributing authors from more than 40 different countries (IPCC, 2007). From these reports, the IPCC concluded that climate change is unequivocal and that, during the twentieth century, average global temperatures rose by about 1 degree F. Moreover, there is a more than 95 percent probability that this increase was caused by increased greenhouse gas emissions produced by human activities. (If you want to know more about the IPPC or read more of the IPPC report go to: www.ippc.ch/ippcreports/index/htm).

Unfortunately, in spite of reports by the IPCC and others, the general public and many politicians seem to believe, or want to believe, that the warming we are experiencing is part of a "normal" cycle. At best, this is wishful thinking, as reversing the trend would be monumentally expensive and require individual sacrifice and huge changes in business and industrial practices.

Certainly, there have been dramatic climatic fluctuations throughout earth's history that had nothing to do with human activity. Furthermore, many of these fluctuations were sudden and had devastating consequences. But even if the current warming were part of a natural cycle, scientists are concerned that human-produced greenhouse gases could tip the balance toward a catastrophic global climate change. One source of this concern is the fact that ice core data show that there is significantly more carbon dioxide in the earth's atmosphere than at any time in the last 600,000 years.

Among many scientists, there is uncertainty as to how climate change will be manifested. But, what is certain is this: Since record keeping began in 1860, the 1990s were the hottest decade, followed closely by the 1980s. The year 2002 had the distinction of being the warmest year on record, with 1998 running a close second. The summer of 2003 was the hottest on record in Europe, and for the first time in recorded history, the temperature reached 100°F in London. It's also recognized that the surface temperature of the earth has increased 0.54–1.1°F. The need for concern cannot be overstated. An increase in the mean annual temperature worldwide of even 1–2°F would result in some melting of the polar caps with subsequent flooding of coastal areas. Given these facts, it's disconcerting that the IPCC report predicts that, in a worst case scenario, average annual temperatures could rise by well over 2 degrees F.

In 2007, scientists became alarmed at a sudden, unexpected increase in the loss of Arctic sea ice. Unlike icebergs and glaciers that form on land, sea ice is frozen ocean water. The importance of sea ice to global climate systems can't be overemphasized because it reflects about 80 percent of the sunlight that hits it back into space. By contrast, seawater absorbs approximately 90 percent of the sunlight that hits it. Therefore, as more ice melts, less sunlight is reflected, allowing for increased warming and, in turn, more melting. Because of this, the polar regions are the most sensitive areas on earth to warming, and the loss of sea ice can accelerate climate change.

Since 1979, scientists have been tracking Arctic **sea ice maximum** and **sea ice minimum** data collected from satellites. Satellite images have shown that in September 2007, more sea ice was lost in one season than at any time since 1979, when data collection began. The average minimum area covered by ice between 1979 and 2000 was 2.6 million square miles, but in 2005 that figure was reduced to 2 million square miles (Fig. 14-7). But there was an even more alarming decrease between 2005 and 2007. In just two years, the minimum amount of sea ice was further reduced to less than 1.6 million square miles, an additional loss of 460,000 square miles. Thus, the area of ocean covered by sea ice at its lowest extent in 2007 was 1 million square miles smaller than the average for the period between 1979 and

Sea ice maximum In the Arctic, the greatest amount of sea ice that is present in one year. It occurs in March at the end of the winter season just as the ice quits forming and before it begins to melt.

Sea ice minimum In the Arctic, the least amount of sea ice that is present in one year. Sea ice is at its minimum in September just as the summer melting season ends, but before ice begins to form again.

*The IPCC and former U.S. Vice President Al Gore shared the Nobel Peace Prize in 2007 for their efforts to reduce the threat of climate change.

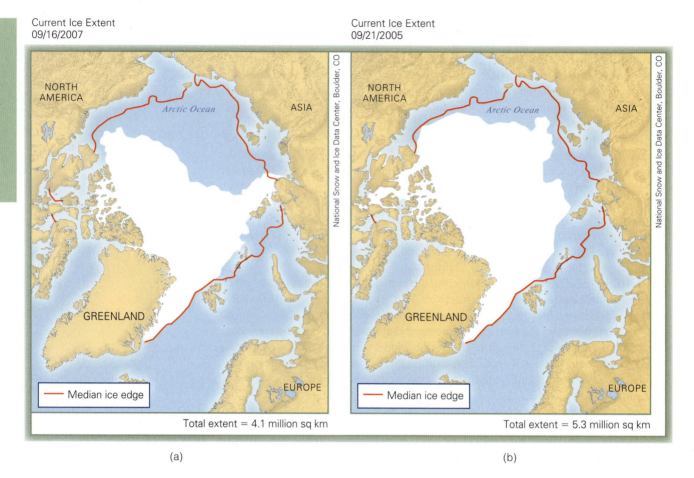

Current Ice Extent
09/16/2007

Current Ice Extent
09/21/2005

(a)

(b)

FIGURE 14-7

In these images derived from satellite data, the area shown in white is the Arctic sea ice minimum (1.59 million square miles) for 2007 (a) compared to the minimum of 2.05 million square miles in 2005 (b). The red line represents the average minimum extent in September for the years 1979 to 2000.

2000. This difference of 1 million square miles represents an area equal in size to Texas and Alaska combined. (National Snow and Ice Data Center, 2007). (You may want to go to the National Snow and Ice Data Center website at http:nsidc.org to view their many satellite image-based graphics and animations.)

By themselves, these statistics may not mean much, but there is rapidly increasing concern among scientists that the polar regions may have reached a "tipping point", a point beyond which the warming process cannot be reversed. In fact, the increase in warming is occurring faster than computer models were predicting just a few years ago. It goes without saying that without sea ice in the summer, polar bears and some seals will become extinct.

Global warming is the result of the interactions of thousands of factors, and the consequences of these interactions aren't possible to predict with accuracy. But the consensus among scientists is that we can anticipate dramatic fluctuations in weather patterns along with alterations in precipitation levels. The results of changing temperatures and rainfall include loss of agricultural lands due to desertification in some regions and flooding in others; increased human hunger; extinction of numerous plant and animal species; and altered patterns of infectious disease. Regarding the latter, health officials are particularly concerned about the spread of mosquito-borne diseases such as malaria, dengue fever, and yellow fever as warmer temperatures increase the geographical range of mosquitoes.

Looking for Solutions

The problems facing our planet reflect an adaptive strategy gone awry. Indeed, it would seem that we no longer enjoy a harmonious relationship with culture. Instead, culture has become the environment in which we live, and every day that environment becomes increasingly hostile. All we need to do is examine the very air we breathe to realize that we have overstepped our limits (Fig. 14-8).

Can the problems we've created be solved? Perhaps, but any objective assessment of the future offers little optimism. Climate change, air pollution, depletion of the ozone layer, and loss of biodiversity are catastrophic problems in a world of 6.7 billion people. How well does the world *now* cope with feeding, housing, and educating its inhabitants? What quality of life do the majority of the world's people enjoy right now? What kind of world have we wrought for the other organisms that share our planet as many are steadily isolated into fragments of what were once large habitats? If these concerns aren't currently overwhelming enough, what kind of world will we see in the year 2050 when the world's population could reach 10 billion?

In recent years, environmental concerns have been more widely discussed. The success of former Vice President Al Gore's documentary film *An Inconvenient Truth* is an indication that the American public is becoming more aware of environmental issues. (Mr. Gore won the Academy Award for Best Documentary for this film in 2007). Some world leaders (particularly in Europe) now at least pay lip service to slowing global warming. All this is well and good, but the real test of any policy will be the willingness of governments to implement policies that certainly will not please everyone.

Industrialized nations must also help developing countries adopt fuel efficient technologies that allow them to raise their standard of living without increasing their output of greenhouse gases. Furthermore, family planning must be adopted to slow population growth. Most cultures are so constructed, however, as to make such a behavioral change very difficult, and sacrifice on the part of the developing world alone wouldn't be adequate to stem the tide. It's entirely too easy for someone from North America to point at the people of Bangladesh and demand that they control their rate of reproduction (it runs two to three times that of the United States). But consider this: The average American uses an estimated 400 times the resources consumed by a resident of Bangladesh (Ehrlich and Ehrlich, 1990)! The United States *alone* produces 25 to 30 percent of all carbon dioxide emissions that end up in earth's atmosphere. In 2007, China caught up with the United States in this regard but over 1.3 billion people live in China compared to 300,000 in the United States. In his book *The Future of Life* (2002), evolutionary biologist E.O. Wilson discusses the issue in terms of "ecological footprints," or the average amount of land and sea required for each person to support his or her lifestyle. This includes all resources consumed for energy, housing, transportation, food, water, and waste disposal. In developing nations the ecological footprint per capita is about 2.5 acres, but in the United States it's 24 acres! Wilson goes on to point out that four additional planet earths would be needed for every person on the planet to reach the current levels of consumption in the United States. Clearly, much of the responsibility for the world's problems rests squarely on the shoulders of the industrialized West.

People living in industrialized nations *must* learn to get along with far fewer resources. To accomplish any meaningful reduction in our wasteful habits, major behavioral changes and personal sacrifice will be required. For example, private automobile transportation (especially with only one passenger), air travel, and large, single-family dwellings are luxuries we enjoy, but they're luxuries the planet can't afford. Who is prepared to make the sacrifices that are required, and where will the leadership come from? The planet already faces serious problems, and there is no time left for indecision. Either we, as members of the dominant species on the planet, find the courage to make dramatic sacrifices, or we are doomed to suffer the consequences of our own folly, and we will.

FIGURE 14-8
Air pollution, increasingly a factor in human respiratory disease, is caused by human activities.

Jerome Wikoff/Visuals Unlimited

Summary

Studies of human evolution have much to contribute to our understanding of how we, as a single species, came to exert such control over the destiny of our planet. It's a truly phenomenal story of how a small, apelike creature walking on two feet across the African savanna challenged nature by learning to make stone tools. From these humble beginnings came large-brained humans who, instead of stone tools, have telecommunications satellites, computers, and nuclear arsenals at their fingertips. The human story is indeed unique and wonderful. Our two feet have carried us not only across the plains of Africa, but onto the polar caps, the ocean floor, and even across the surface of the moon! Surely, if we can accomplish so much in so short a time, we can act responsibly to preserve our home and the wondrous creatures who share it with us.

Critical Thinking Questions

1 How is human culture related to environmental degradation and overpopulation?

2 How are loss of biodiversity, environmental degradation, and human population growth interrelated?

3 Why do we say that culture, as an adaptive strategy, has gone awry? Do you agree with this statement? Why or why not?

Atlas of Primate Skeletal Anatomy

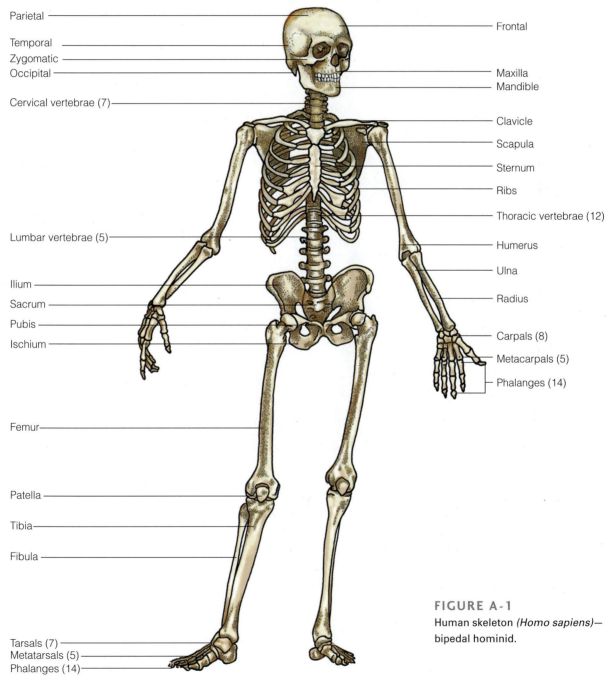

Parietal

Temporal
Zygomatic
Occipital

Cervical vertebrae (7)

Lumbar vertebrae (5)

Ilium
Sacrum
Pubis
Ischium

Femur

Patella

Tibia

Fibula

Tarsals (7)
Metatarsals (5)
Phalanges (14)

Frontal

Maxilla
Mandible

Clavicle

Scapula

Sternum

Ribs

Thoracic vertebrae (12)

Humerus

Ulna

Radius

Carpals (8)

Metacarpals (5)

Phalanges (14)

HUMAN SKELETON

FIGURE A-1
Human skeleton *(Homo sapiens)*—
bipedal hominid.

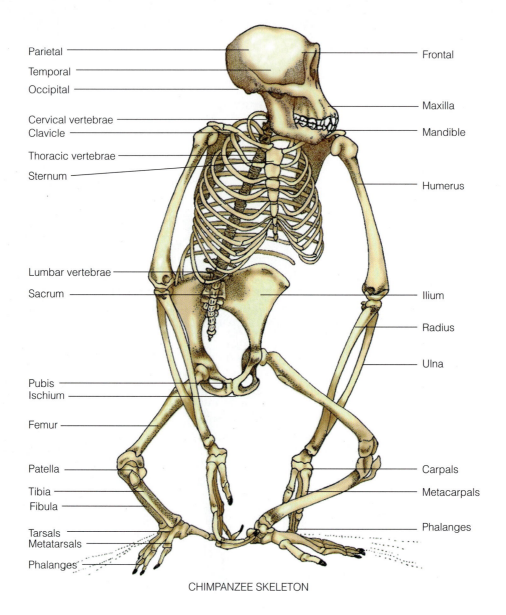

Parietal

Temporal

Occipital

Cervical vertebrae

Clavicle

Thoracic vertebrae

Sternum

Lumbar vertebrae

Sacrum

Pubis

Ischium

Femur

Patella

Tibia

Fibula

Tarsals

Metatarsals

Phalanges

Frontal

Maxilla

Mandible

Humerus

Ilium

Radius

Ulna

Carpals

Metacarpals

Phalanges

CHIMPANZEE SKELETON

FIGURE A-2

Chimpanzee skelton *(Pan troglodytes)*—
knuckle-walking pongid.

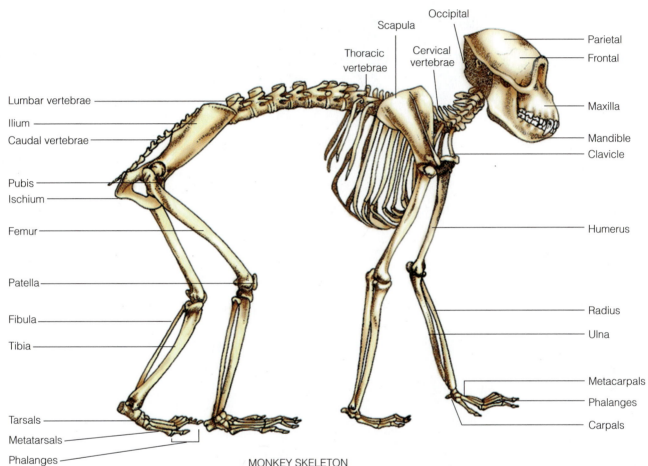

Occipital

Scapula

Parietal

Thoracic
vertebrae

Cervical
vertebrae

Frontal

Lumbar vertebrae

Maxilla

Ilium

Caudal vertebrae

Mandible

Clavicle

Pubis

Ischium

Femur

Humerus

Patella

Radius

Fibula

Ulna

Tibia

Metacarpals

Phalanges

Tarsals

Carpals

Metatarsals

Phalanges

MONKEY SKELETON

FIGURE A-3

Monkey skeleton (rhesus macaque;
Macaca mulatta)—a typical quadrupedal primate.

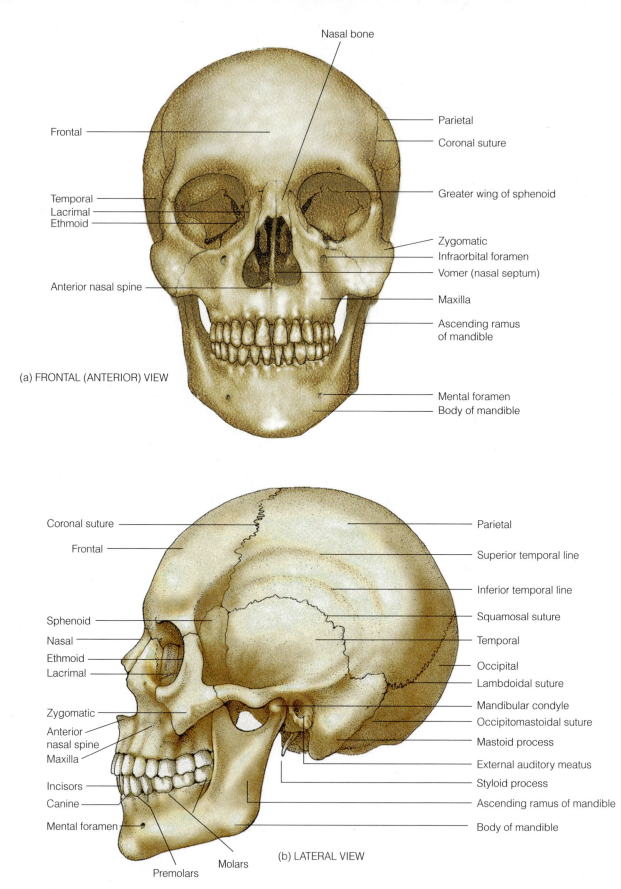

Nasal bone

Frontal

Parietal

Coronal suture

Greater wing of sphenoid

Temporal
Lacrimal
Ethmoid

Zygomatic

Infraorbital foramen

Vomer (nasal septum)

Anterior nasal spine

Maxilla

Ascending ramus
of mandible

(a) FRONTAL (ANTERIOR) VIEW

Mental foramen
Body of mandible

Coronal suture

Parietal

Frontal

Superior temporal line

Inferior temporal line

Sphenoid

Squamosal suture

Nasal

Temporal

Ethmoid

Occipital

Lacrimal

Lambdoidal suture

Zygomatic

Mandibular condyle

Anterior
nasal spine

Occipitomastoidal suture

Mastoid process

Maxilla

External auditory meatus

Incisors

Styloid process

Canine

Ascending ramus of mandible

Mental foramen

Body of mandible

Premolars

Molars

(b) LATERAL VIEW

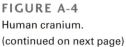

FIGURE A-4

Human cranium.

(continued on next page)

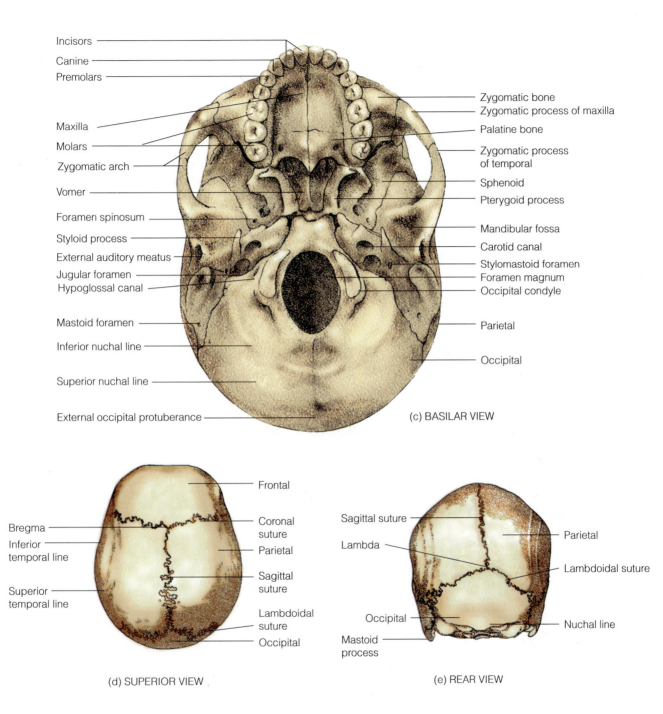

Incisors
Canine
Premolars

Maxilla
Molars
Zygomatic arch

Vomer
Foramen spinosum
Styloid process
External auditory meatus
Jugular foramen
Hypoglossal canal

Mastoid foramen
Inferior nuchal line

Superior nuchal line

External occipital protuberance

Zygomatic bone
Zygomatic process of maxilla
Palatine bone
Zygomatic process of temporal
Sphenoid
Pterygoid process

Mandibular fossa
Carotid canal
Stylomastoid foramen
Foramen magnum
Occipital condyle

Parietal

Occipital

(c) BASILAR VIEW

Frontal
Coronal suture
Parietal
Sagittal suture
Lambdoidal suture
Occipital

Bregma
Inferior temporal line
Superior temporal line

(d) SUPERIOR VIEW

Sagittal suture
Lambda
Occipital
Mastoid process

Parietal
Lambdoidal suture
Nuchal line

(e) REAR VIEW

FIGURE A-4
Human cranium.
(continued)

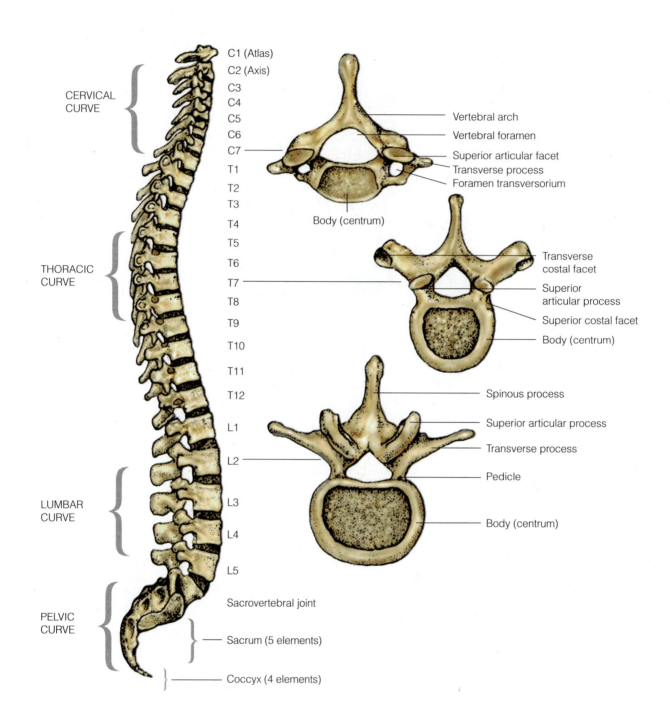

C1 (Atlas)
C2 (Axis)
C3
C4
C5
C6
C7
T1
T2
T3
T4
T5
T6
T7
T8
T9
T10
T11
T12
L1
L2
L3
L4
L5

CERVICAL CURVE

THORACIC CURVE

LUMBAR CURVE

PELVIC CURVE

Vertebral arch
Vertebral foramen
Superior articular facet
Transverse process
Foramen transversorium
Body (centrum)

Transverse costal facet
Superior articular process
Superior costal facet
Body (centrum)

Spinous process
Superior articular process
Transverse process
Pedicle
Body (centrum)

Sacrovertebral joint
Sacrum (5 elements)
Coccyx (4 elements)

FIGURE A-5

Human vertebral column (lateral view) and representative cervical, thoracic, and lumbar vertebrae (superior views).

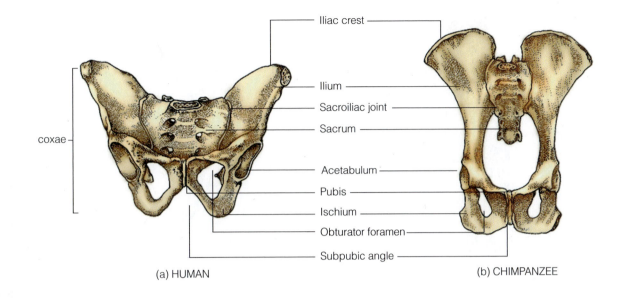

Iliac crest

Ilium
Sacroiliac joint
Sacrum

Acetabulum
Pubis
Ischium
Obturator foramen
Subpubic angle

coxae

(a) HUMAN

(b) CHIMPANZEE

FIGURE A-6
Pelvic girdles.

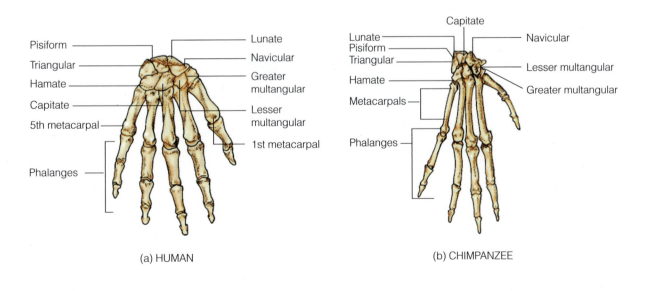

Pisiform
Triangular
Hamate
Capitate
5th metacarpal

Phalanges

Lunate
Navicular
Greater
multangular
Lesser
multangular
1st metacarpal

(a) HUMAN

Capitate

Lunate
Pisiform
Triangular
Hamate

Metacarpals

Phalanges

Navicular

Lesser multangular

Greater multangular

(b) CHIMPANZEE

FIGURE A-7
Hand anatomy.

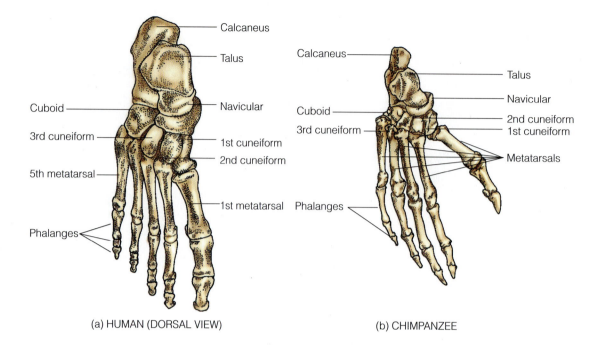

(a) HUMAN (DORSAL VIEW)

Calcaneus

Talus

Navicular

Cuboid

3rd cuneiform

1st cuneiform

2nd cuneiform

5th metatarsal

1st metatarsal

Phalanges

(b) CHIMPANZEE

Calcaneus

Talus

Navicular

2nd cuneiform

1st cuneiform

Cuboid

3rd cuneiform

Metatarsals

Phalanges

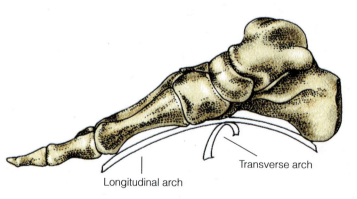

Longitudinal arch

Transverse arch

(c) HUMAN (MEDIAL VIEW)

FIGURE A-8
Foot (pedal) anatomy.

APPENDIX B
Summary of Early Hominid Fossil Finds from Africa

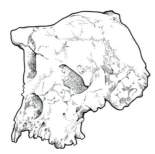

Sahelanthropus
Taxonomic designation:
Sahelanthropus tchadensis
Year of first discovery: 2001
Dating: ~7 mya
Fossil material: Nearly complete cranium, 2 jaw fragments, 3 isolated teeth

Location of finds: Toros-Menalla, Chad, central Africa

Ardipithecus
Taxonomic designation:
Ardipithecus ramidus
Year of first discovery: 1992
Dating: Earlier sites, 5.8–5.6 mya; Aramis, 4.4 mya
Fossil material: Earlier materials: 1 jaw fragment, 4 isolated teeth, postcranial remains (foot phalanx, 2 hand phalanges, 2 humerus fragments, ulna). Later sample (Aramis) represented by many fossils, including up to 50 individuals (many postcranial elements, including at least 1 partial skeleton). Considerable fossil material retrieved from Aramis but not yet published; no reasonably complete cranial remains yet published.

Location of finds: Middle Awash region, including Aramis (as well as earlier localities), Ethiopia, East Africa

Orrorin

Taxonomic designation:
Orrorin tugenensis

Year of first discovery: 2000

Dating: ~6 mya

Fossil material: 2 jaw fragments, 6 isolated teeth, postcranial remains (femoral pieces, partial humerus, hand phalanx). No reasonably complete cranial remains yet discovered.

Location of finds: Lukeino Formation, Tugen Hills, Baringo District, Kenya, East Africa

Australopithecus anamensis

Taxonomic designation:
Australopithecus anamensis

Year of first discovery: 1965 (but not recognized as separate species at that time); more remains found in 1994 and 1995

Dating: 4.2–3.9 mya

Fossil material: Total of 22 specimens, including cranial fragments, jaw fragments, and postcranial pieces (humerus, tibia, radius). No reasonably complete cranial remains yet discovered.

Location of finds: Kanapoi, Allia Bay, Kenya, East Africa

Australopithecus afarensis

Taxonomic designation:
Australopithecus afarensis

Year of first discovery: 1973

Dating: 3.6–3.0 mya

Fossil material: Large sample, with up to 65 individuals represented: 1 partial cranium, numerous cranial pieces and jaws, many teeth, numerous postcranial remains, including partial skeletons. Fossil finds from Laetoli also include dozens of fossilized footprints.

Location of finds: Laetoli (Tanzania), Hadar/Dikika (Ethiopia), also likely found at East Turkana (Kenya) and Omo (Ethiopia), East Africa

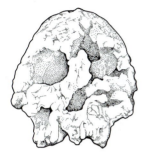

Kenyanthropus

Taxonomic designation:
Kenyanthropus platyops

Year of first discovery: 1999

Dating: 3.5 mya

Fossil material: Partial cranium, temporal fragment, partial maxilla, 2 partial mandibles

Location of finds: Lomekwi, West Lake Turkana, Kenya, East Africa

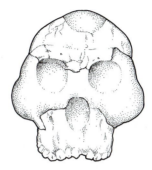

Australopithecus garhi

Taxonomic designation:
Australopithecus garhi

Year of first discovery: 1997

Dating: 2.5 mya

Fossil material: Partial cranium, numerous limb bones

Location of finds: Bouri, Middle Awash, Ethiopia, East Africa

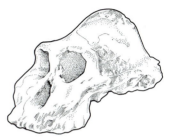

Paranthropus aethiopicus

Taxonomic designation:
Paranthropus *aethiopicus* (also called *Australopithecus aethiopicus*)

Year of first discovery: 1985

Dating: 2.4 mya

Fossil material: Nearly complete cranium

Location of finds: West Lake Turkana, Kenya

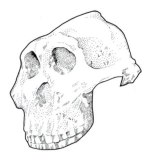

Paranthropus boisei

Taxonomic designation:
Paranthropus *boisei* (also called *Australopithecus* boisei)

Year of first discovery: 1959

Dating: 2.2–1.0 mya

Fossil material: 2 nearly complete crania, several partial crania, many jaw fragments, dozens of teeth. Postcrania less represented, but parts of several long bones recovered.

Location of finds: Olduvai Gorge and Peninj (Tanzania), East Lake Turkana (Koobi Fora), Chesowanja (Kenya), Omo (Ethiopia)

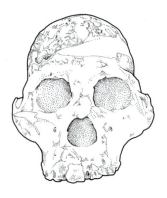
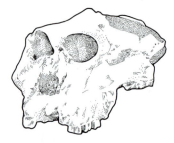

Australopithecus africanus

Taxonomic designation:
Australopithecus africanus

Year of first discovery: 1924

Dating: ~3.0?–2.0 mya

Fossil material: 1 mostly complete cranium, several partial crania, dozens of jaws/partial jaws, hundreds of teeth, 4 partial skeletons representing significant parts of the postcranium

Location of finds: Taung, Sterkfontein, Makapansgat, Gladysvale (all from South Africa)

Paranthropus robustus

Taxonomic designation:
Paranthropus *robustus* (also called *Australopithecus robustusi*)

Year of first discovery: 1938

Dating: ~2–1 mya

Fossil material: 1 complete cranium, several partial crania, many jaw fragments, hundreds of teeth, numerous postcranial elements

Location of finds: Kromdraai, Swartkrans, Drimolen, Cooper's Cave, possibly Gondolin (all from South Africa)

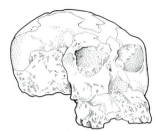

Early *Homo*

Taxonomic designation:
Homo habilis

Year of first discovery:
1959/1960

Dating: 2.4–1.8 mya

Fossil material: 2 partial crania, other cranial pieces, jaw fragments, several limb bones, partial hand, partial foot, partial skeleton

Location of finds: Olduvai Gorge (Tanzania), Lake Baringo (Kenya), Omo (Ethiopia), Sterkfontein (?) (South Africa)

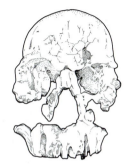

Early *Homo*

Taxonomic designation:
Homo rudolfensis

Year of first discovery: 1972

Dating: 1.8 mya–1.4 mya

Fossil material: 4 partial crania, 1 mostly complete mandible, other jaw pieces, numerous teeth, a few post-cranial elements (none directly associated with crania)

Location of finds: East Lake Turkana (Koobi Fora), Kenya, East Africa

Population Genetics

As noted in Chapter 12, the basic approach in population genetics makes use of a mathematical model called the Hardy-Weinberg equilibrium equation. The Hardy-Weinberg theory of genetic equilibrium postulates a set of conditions in a population where *no* evolution occurs. In other words, none of the forces of evolution are acting, and all genes have an equal chance of recombining in each generation (that is, there is random mating of individuals). More precisely, the hypothetical conditions that such a population would be *assumed* to meet are as follows:

1. The population is infinitely large. This condition eliminates the possibility of random genetic drift or changes in allele frequencies due to chance.
2. There is no mutation. Thus, no new alleles are being added by molecular changes in gametes.
3. There is no gene flow. There is no exchange of genes with other populations that can alter allele frequencies.
4. Natural selection is not operating. Specific alleles confer no advantage over others that might influence reproductive success.
5. Mating is random. There are no factors that influence who mates with whom. Thus, any female is assumed to have an equal chance of mating with any male.

If all these conditions are satisfied, allele frequencies will not change from one generation to the next (that is, no evolution will take place), and a permanent equilibrium will be maintained as long as these conditions prevail. An evolutionary "barometer" is thus provided that may be used as a standard against which actual circumstances are compared. Similar to the way a typical barometer is standardized under known temperature and altitude conditions, the Hardy-Weinberg equilibrium is standardized under known evolutionary conditions.

Note that the idealized conditions that define the Hardy-Weinberg equilibrium are just that: an idealized, *hypothetical* state. In the real world, no actual population would fully meet any of these conditions. But do not be confused by this distinction. By explicitly defining the genetic distribution that would be *expected* if *no* evolutionary change were occurring (that is, in equilibrium), we can compare the *observed* genetic distribution obtained from actual human populations. The evolutionary barometer is thus evaluated through comparison of these observed allele and genotype frequencies with those expected in the predefined equilibrium situation.

If the observed frequencies differ from those of the expected model, then we can say that evolution is taking place at the locus in question. The alternative, of course, is that the observed and expected frequencies do not differ sufficiently to state unambiguously that evolution is occurring at a locus in a population. Indeed, frequently this is the result that is obtained, and in such cases, population geneticists are unable to delineate evolutionary changes at the particular locus under study. Put another way, geneticists are unable to reject what statisticians call the *null hypothesis* (where "null" means nothing, a statistical condition of randomness).

The simplest situation applicable to a microevolutionary study is a genetic trait that follows a simple Mendelian pattern and has only two alleles (*A, a*). As you recall from earlier discussions, there are then only three possible genotypes: *AA, Aa, aa*. Proportions of these genotypes (*AA:Aa:aa*) are a function of the *allele frequencies* themselves (percentage of *A* and percentage of *a*). To provide uniformity for all genetic loci, a standard notation is employed to refer to these frequencies:

Frequency of dominant allele (*A*) = *p*
Frequency of recessive allele (*a*) = *q*

Since in this case there are only two alleles, their combined total frequency must represent all possibilities. In other words, the sum of their separate frequencies must be 1:

$$\underset{\substack{\text{(frequency} \\ \text{of } A \text{ alleles)}}}{p} \quad + \quad \underset{\substack{\text{(frequency} \\ \text{of } a \text{ alleles)}}}{q} \quad = \quad \underset{\substack{\text{(100\% of alleles} \\ \text{at that locus)}}}{1}$$

To ascertain the expected proportions of genotypes, we compute the chances of the alleles combining with one another into all possible combinations. Remember, they all have an equal chance of combining, and no new alleles are being added.

These probabilities are a direct function of the frequency of the two alleles. The chances of all possible combinations occurring randomly can be simply shown as

$$\begin{array}{r} p \;+\; q \\ = \; p \;+\; q \\ \hline pq \;+\; q^2 \\ p^2 \;+\; pq \\ \hline p^2 \;+2pq \;+\; q^2 \end{array}$$

Mathematically, this is known as a binomial expansion and can also be shown as

$$(p + q)(p + q) = p^2 + 2pq + q^2$$

What we have just calculated is simply:

Allele Combination	Genotype Produced	Expected Proportion in Population
Chances of *A* combining with *A*	*AA*	$p \times p = p^2$
Chances of *A* combining with *a*; *a* combining with *A*	*Aa* *aA*	$\left.\begin{array}{l} p \times q \\ p \times q \end{array}\right\} = 2pq$
Chances of *a* combining with *a*	*aa*	$q \times q = q^2$

Thus, p^2 is the frequency of the *AA* genotype, *2pq* is the frequency of the *Aa* genotype, and q^2 is the frequency of the *aa* genotype, where *p* is the frequency of the dominant allele and *q* is the frequency of the recessive allele in a population.

Calculating Allele Frequencies: An Example

How geneticists use the Hardy-Weinberg formula is best demonstrated through an example. Let us assume that a population contains 200 individuals, and we will use the MN blood group locus as the gene to be measured. This gene produces a blood group antigen—similar to ABO—located on red blood cells. Because the *M* and *N* alleles are codominant, we can ascertain everyone's phenotype by taking blood samples and observing reactions with specially prepared antisera. From the phenotypes, we can then directly calculate the *observed* allele frequencies. So let us proceed.

All 200 individuals are tested, and the results are shown in Table C-1. Although the match between observed and expected frequencies is not perfect, it is close enough statistically to satisfy equilibrium conditions. Since our population is not a large one, sampling may easily account for the small observed deviations. Our population is therefore probably in equilibrium (that is, at this locus, it is not evolving). At the minimum, what we can say scientifically is that we cannot reject the *null hypothesis*.

TABLE C-1	Calculating Allele Frequencies in a Hypothetical Population				

Observed Data

Genotype	Number of Individuals	Present	Number of Alleles M	N
MM	80	40%	160	0
MN	80	40%	80	80
NN	40	20%	0	80
Totals	200	100%	240 + 160 = 400	
		Proportion:	.6 + .4 = 1	

*Each individual has two alleles. Thus, a person who is *MM* contributes two *M* alleles to the total gene pool. A person who is *MN* contributes one *M* and one *N*. Two hundred individuals, then, have 400 alleles for the *MN* locus.

Observed Allele Frequencies

$M = .6(p)$

$N = .4(q)$ ($p + q$ should equal 1, and they do)

Expected Frequencies

What are the predicted genotypic proportions if genetic equilibrium (no evolution) applies to our population? We simply apply the Hardy-Weinberg formula: $p^2 + 2pq + q^2$.

$p2$	= (.6)(.6)	=	.36
$2pq$	= 2(.6)(.4) = 2(.24)	=	.48
$q2$	= (.4)(.4)	=	.16
Total			1.00

There are only three possible genotypes (*MM:MN:NN*), so the total of the relative proportions should equal 1; as you can see, they do.

Comparing Frequencies

How do the expected frequencies compare with the observed frequencies in our population?

	Expected Frequency	Expected Number of Individuals	Observed Frequency	Actual Number of Individuals with Each Genotype
MM	.36	72	.40	80
MN	.48	96	.40	80
NN	.16	32	.20	40

APPENDIX D
Sexing and Aging the Skeleton

The field of physical anthropology that is directly concerned with the analysis of skeletal remains is called *osteology*. Using an osteological perspective allows researchers to study skeletons of both human and nonhuman primates to understand the ways in which hominids are similar to, and distinct from, other primates. Moreover, paleoanthropologists also use many of the same techniques to analyze the remains of fossil hominids (which mostly consist of teeth and bones). In more recent contexts, encompassing the last few thousand years, skeletal remains of *Homo sapiens* have been investigated by osteologists to learn about the size, nutritional status, and diseases present in prior human populations.

Two very important questions that osteologists ask when analyzing a skeleton are the sex and age of the individual. Such basic demographic variables as sex and age are crucial in any comprehensive osteological analysis, especially of human remains.

Sexing the Skeleton

During infancy and childhood, male and female skeletons do not differ much. Consequently, osteologists usually cannot determine the sex of a skeleton of someone who died before 13 to 15 years of age. However, during development, *sexual dimorphism* is increasingly manifested in the skeleton, making sex determination feasible in adult remains, provided enough of the skeleton is present. We should mention that molecular techniques are sometimes able to detect the presence of the Y chromosome from bone or dental tissue (thus determining that a skeleton is that of a male). While not used widely, molecularly based sexing is becoming more common in osteological analyses.

The differences between male and female skeletons are most clearly expressed in the pelvis (*pl.,* pelves), and this variation is due to the requirements of childbirth in females. In particular, during hominid evolution, the dual influences of bipedal locomotion and relatively large-brained newborns placed adaptive constraints on pelvic anatomy. As a result, in females the pelvis is generally broader and more splayed out than in males. The most useful criteria for sex determination are listed in Table D-1 and illustrated in Figure D-1. While these criteria, taken together, are good indicators of sex, you should be aware that none, taken in isolation, is accurate in all cases. Moreover, this is not a complete listing of all traits used in sexing skeletons, although it does include those most commonly used.

There are also sex differences in cranial dimensions, most especially relating to facial proportions. However, these differences are not as consistent as those in the pelvis. Therefore, it is important to recognize patterns of cranial variation as they are expressed in different populations. The cranial features most commonly used for sex determination are listed in Table D-2 (see also Fig. D-2). These differences reflect the fact that in males, the skeleton is larger than in females. The bones are denser, and areas of muscle attachment are frequently more robust. However, such differences are not consistently expressed across various populations, and knowledge of relevant population variation is thus important in drawing reasonable determinations of sex.

TABLE D-1	Differences Between the Male and Female Pelvis	
Pelvic Characteristic	**Female**	**Male**
General	Muscle attachments less robust; overall appearance sometimes less massive	Muscle attachments more robust; overall appearance sometimes more massive
Subpubic angle	Wider (more than 90°)	Narrower (less than 90°)
Greater sciatic notch	Wider—more open (more than 68°)	Narrower—more closed (less than 68°)
Ischiopubic ramus (medial view)	Thinner	Thicker
Ventral arc (elevated ridge on ventral surface of pubis	Frequently present	Absent
Sacrum	Wider and straighter	Narrower and more curved

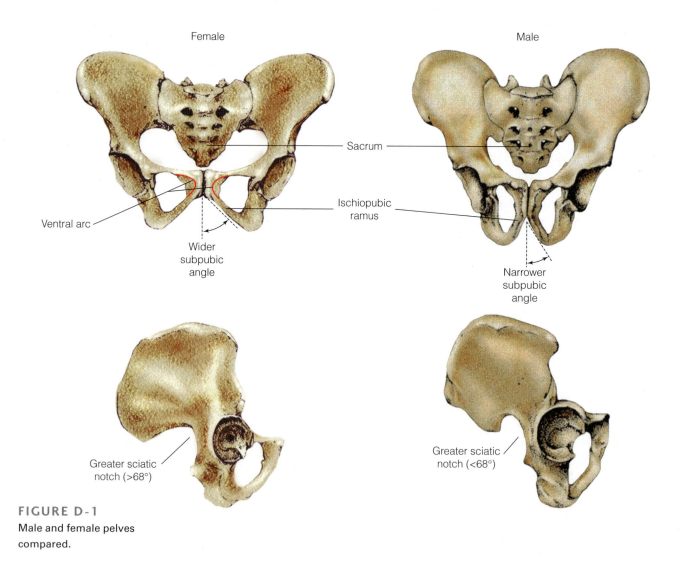

FIGURE D-1
Male and female pelves compared.

TABLE D-2	Differences Between the Male and Female Pelvis	
Cranial Feature	**Female**	**Male**
Points of muscle attachment (e.g., mastoid process)	Less pronounced	Larger, more pronounced
Supraorbital torus (browridge)	Less pronounced or absent	More pronounced
Supraorbital rim (upper margin of eye orbit)	Sharper	More rounded
Palate	More shallow	Deeper

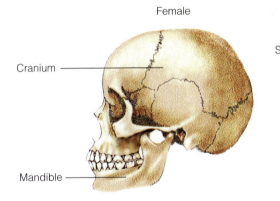

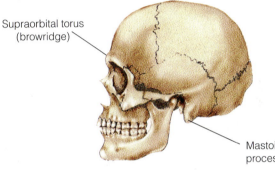

FIGURE D 2
Male and female cranium and mandible.

Determining Age

During growth, the skeleton and dentition undergo developmental changes that occur within known age ranges. Thus, estimating age in individuals who were younger than 20 when they died is based primarily on the presence of deciduous (baby) and permanent teeth, the appearance of ossification centers of bones, and the fusion of the ends of long bones to bone shafts.

Dental Eruption

Age estimation based on dental eruption is useful in individuals up to approximately 15 years of age. The third molar (wisdom tooth) erupts after this time, but the age of eruption of this tooth (if it forms at all) is highly variable. Thus, the third molar is not a very reliable indicator of age except that its presence indicates that the individual was at least a young adult (Fig. D-3).

Bone Growth

The size of long bones, the development of secondary ossification centers (epiphyses), and the degree of fusion of epiphyses to bone shafts are just as important as dental eruption. Postcranial bones are preceded by a cartilage model that is gradually replaced by bone, both in the diaphyses (shafts) and the secondary centers (the ends of the bones, or epiphyses). In children and adolescents, bones continue to grow until the epiphyses fuse to the diaphyses. Because this fusion occurs within different age ranges in different bones, the age of an individual can be estimated by determining which epiphyses have fused and which have

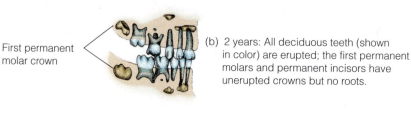

(a) Birth: The crowns for all the deciduous teeth (shown in color) are present; no roots, however, have yet formed.

Gumline

First permanent molar crown

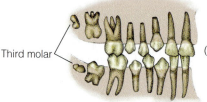

(b) 2 years: All deciduous teeth (shown in color) are erupted; the first permanent molars and permanent incisors have unerupted crowns but no roots.

Third molar

(c) 12 years: All permanent teeth are erupted except the third molar (wisdom tooth).

FIGURE D–3
Dental development.

not (Fig. D-4). The characteristic undulating appearance of the unfused surfaces helps differentiate immature elements from the broken end of a mature bone.

Other Skeletal Changes

Once a person has reached physiological maturity (by the early 20s), determinations of age become more difficult and less precise. Several techniques are used, and these are based on the occurrence of progressive, regular changes in the face of the pubic symphysis (the most common technique), in the sternal ends of the ribs, and in the auricular surface of the ilium (where the ilium articulates with the sacrum). Other indicators are closure of the cranial sutures and cellular changes that are determined by microscopic examination of cross sections of long bones. Degenerative changes, such as arthritis, osteoporosis, and wear of dental enamel, can also aid in the determination of relative age (older versus younger), but they provide imprecise estimates. In fact, it is very difficult to age accurately the skeletons of adults. For example, the presence of severe tooth wear would imply that the individual was not young, but enamel attrition varies between populations and depends on many factors, including diet. Moreover, the appearance of many degenerative changes is influenced by disease, trauma, and the biological makeup of individuals. Thus, at present, osteologists must be content to use broad age ranges when estimating age at death in mature skeletons.

Pubic Symphyseal Face The face of the pubic symphysis in young individuals is characterized by a billowing surface (with ridges and furrows) such as that seen on the surface of an epiphysis (Fig. D-5). The symphyseal face undergoes regular age-related changes from the age of about 18 onward.

The first aging technique based on alterations of the pubic symphysis was developed by T. W. Todd (1920, 1921), utilizing dissection room cadavers. McKern and Stewart (1957) developed a technique by analyzing a sample of American males killed in the Korean War. Both of the samples from which these systems were derived, however, have limitations. The dissection room sample used by Todd contained some individuals of uncertain age, and the Korean War sample was predominantly made up of young white males, with few being older than 35.

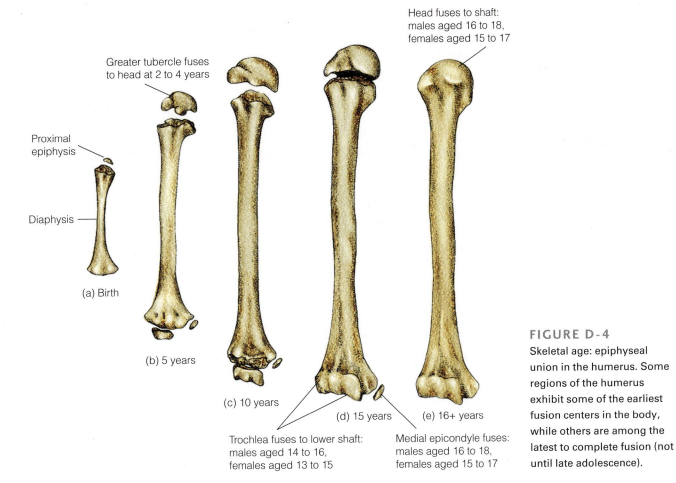

Greater tubercle fuses to head at 2 to 4 years

Head fuses to shaft: males aged 16 to 18, females aged 15 to 17

Proximal epiphysis

Diaphysis

(a) Birth

(b) 5 years

(c) 10 years

(d) 15 years

(e) 16+ years

Trochlea fuses to lower shaft: males aged 14 to 16, females aged 13 to 15

Medial epicondyle fuses: males aged 16 to 18, females aged 15 to 17

FIGURE D-4

Skeletal age: epiphyseal union in the humerus. Some regions of the humerus exhibit some of the earliest fusion centers in the body, while others are among the latest to complete fusion (not until late adolescence).

More recently, a system has been developed by Judy Suchey and colleagues (Katz and Suchey, 1986) based on very well-documented autopsy samples of males and females. These samples have proved more representative of the general population than the earlier samples. Because this technique is derived from data collected from a large sample of people of known age at death, it is currently the most accurate method available for estimating age in adult human skeletal remains.

FIGURE D-5

Skeletal age: remodeling of the pubic symphysis. This area of the pelvis shows systematic changes progressively throughout adult life. Two of these stages are shown in (b) and (c).

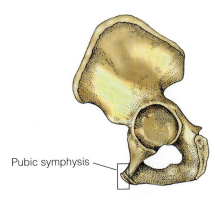

Pubic symphysis

(a) Position of the pubic symphysis.

(b) Age 21. The face of the symphysis shows the typical "billowed" appearance of a young joint; no rim present.

(c) Age mid-50s. The face is mostly flat, with a distinct rim formed around most of the periphery.

Glossary

A

acclimatization Physiological responses to changes in the environment that occur during an individual's lifetime. Such responses may be temporary or permanent, depending on the duration of the environmental change and when in the individual's life it occurs. The *capacity* for acclimatization may typify an entire species or population, and because it's under genetic influence, it's subject to evolutionary factors such as natural selection or genetic drift.

Acheulian (ash´-oo-lay-en) Pertaining to a stone tool industry from the Lower and Middle Pleistocene; characterized by a large proportion of bifacial tools (flaked on both sides). Acheulian tool kits are common in Africa, southwest Asia, and western Europe, but they're thought to be less common elsewhere. Also spelled Acheulean.

adaptation An anatomical, physiological, or behavioral response of organisms or populations to the environment. Adaptations result from evolutionary change (specifically, as a result of natural selection).

adaptive niche The entire way of life of an organism: where it lives, what it eats, how it gets food, how it avoids predators, etc.

adaptive radiation The relatively rapid expansion and diversification of life-forms into new ecological niches.

adolescent growth spurt The period during adolescence when well-nourished teens typically increase in stature at greater rates than at other times in the life cycle.

affiliative Pertaining to amicable associations between individuals. Affiliative behaviors, such as grooming, reinforce social bonds and promote group cohesion.

allele frequency In a population, the percentage of all the alleles at a locus accounted for by one specific allele.

alleles Alternate forms of a gene. Alleles occur at the same locus on partner chromosomes and thus govern the same trait. However, because they are slightly different, their action may result in different expressions of that trait. The term is sometimes used synonymously with *gene*.

altruism Behavior that benefits another individual but at some potential risk or cost to oneself.

amino acids Small molecules that are the components of proteins.

analogies Similarities between organisms based strictly on common function, with no assumed common evolutionary descent.

ancestral (primitive) Referring to characters inherited by a group of organisms from a remote ancestor and thus not diagnostic of groups (lineages) that diverged after the character first appeared.

anthropocentric Viewing nonhuman animals in terms of human motives, and experience and capabilities; emphasizing the importance of humans over everything else.

anthropoids Members of a suborder of Primates, the suborder Anthropoidea (pronounced "ann-throw-poid´-ee-uh"). Traditionally, the suborder includes monkeys, apes, and humans.

anthropology The field of inquiry that studies human culture and evolutionary aspects of human biology; includes cultural anthropology, archaeology, linguistics, and physical, or biological, anthropology.

anthropometry Measurement of human body parts. When osteologists measure skeletal elements, the term *osteometry* is often used.

antigens Large molecules found on the surface of cells. Several different loci govern various antigens on red and white blood cells.

applied anthropology The practical application of anthropological and archaeological theories and techniques. For example, many biological anthropologists work in the public health sector.

arboreal Tree-living; adapted to life in the trees.

artifacts Objects or materials made or modified for use by hominids. The earliest artifacts tend to be tools made of stone or occasionally bone.

Aurignacian Pertaining to an Upper Paleolithic stone tool industry in Europe beginning at about 40,000 ya.

australopiths A colloquial name referring to a diverse group of Plio-Pleistocene African hominids. They are the most abundant and widely distributed of all early hominids and are also the most completely studied.

autonomic Pertaining to physiological responses not under voluntary control. An example in chimpanzees would be the erection of body hair during excitement. Blushing is a human example. Both convey information regarding emotional states, but neither is deliberate, and communication isn't intended.

autosomes All chromosomes except the sex chromosomes.

B

behavior Anything organisms do that involves action in response to internal or external stimuli; the response of an individual, group, or species to its environment. Such responses may or may not be deliberate, and they aren't necessarily the result of conscious decision making (as in one-celled organisms or insects).

behavioral ecology The study of the evolution of behavior, emphasizing the role of ecological factors as agents of natural selection. Behaviors and behavioral patterns have been favored because they increase the reproductive fitness of individuals (i.e., they are adaptive) in specific environmental contexts.

binocular vision Vision characterized by overlapping visual fields provided for by forward-facing eyes. Binocular vision is essential to depth perception.

binomial nomenclature (*binomial,* meaning "two names") In taxonomy, the convention established by Carolus Linnaeus whereby genus and species names are used to refer to species. For example, *Homo sapiens* refers to human beings.

biocultural Pertaining to the concept that biology makes culture possible and that culture influences biology.

biocultural evolution The mutual, interactive evolution of human biology and culture; the concept that biology makes culture possible and that developing culture further influences the direction of biological evolution; a basic concept in understanding the unique components of human evolution.

biological continuum Refers to the fact that organisms are related through common ancestry and that behaviors and traits seen in one species are also seen in others to varying degrees. (When expressions of a phenomenon continuously grade into one another so that there are no discrete categories, they are said to exist on a continuum. Color is such a phenomenon.)

biological determinism The concept that phenomena, including various aspects of behavior (e.g., intelligence, values, morals) are governed by biological (genetic) factors; the inaccurate association of various behavioral attributes with certain biological traits, such as skin color.

biological species concept A depiction of species as groups of individuals capable of fertile interbreeding but reproductively isolated from other such groups.

bipedal locomotion Walking on two feet. Walking habitually on two legs is the single most distinctive feature of the family Hominidae.

bipedally On two feet; walking habitually on two legs.

brachiation A form of locomotion in which the body is suspended beneath the hands and support is alternated from one forelimb to the other; arm swinging.

breeding isolates Populations that are clearly isolated geographically and/or socially from other breeding groups.

burins Small, chisel-like tools with a pointed end, thought to have been used to engrave bone, antler, ivory, or wood.

C

catastrophism The view that the earth's geological landscape is the result of violent cataclysmic events. Cuvier promoted this view, especially in opposition to Lamarck.

centromere The constricted portion of a chromosome. After replication, the two strands of a double-stranded chromosome are joined at the centromere.

cercopithecines (serk-oh-pith'-eh-seens) The subfamily of Old World monkeys that includes baboons, macaques, and guenons.

Chatelperronian Pertaining to an Upper Paleolithic industry found in France and Spain, containing blade tools and associated with Neandertals.

Chordata The phylum of the animal kingdom that includes vertebrates.

Christian fundamentalists Adherents to a movement in American Protestantism that began in the early twentieth century. This group holds that the teachings of the Bible are infallible and are to be taken literally.

chromosomes Discrete structures composed of DNA and protein found only in the nuclei of cells. Chromosomes are visible under magnification only during certain phases of cell division.

chronometric (*chronos,* meaning "time," and *metric,* meaning "measure") A dating technique that gives an estimate in actual numbers of years.

clade A group of organisms sharing a common ancestor. The group includes the common ancestor and all descendants.

classification In biology, the ordering of organisms into categories, such as orders, families, and genera, to show evolutionary relationships.

cladistics An approach to classification that attempts to make rigorous evolutionary interpretations based solely on analysis of certain types of homologous characters (those considered to be derived characters).

cladogram A chart showing evolutionary relationships as determined by cladistic analysis. It's based solely on interpretation of shared derived characters. It contains no time component and does not imply ancestor-descendant relationships.

cline A gradual change in the frequency of genotypes and phenotypes from one geographical region to another.

clones Organisms that are genetically identical to another organism. The term may also be used in referring to genetically identical DNA segments, molecules, and cells.

coding DNA sequences DNA sequences that code for the production of a detectable protein product.

codominance The expression of two alleles in heterozygotes. In this situation, neither allele is dominant or recessive; thus, both influence the phenotype.

codons Triplets of messenger RNA bases that code for specific amino acids during protein synthesis.

colobines (kole´-uh-beans) The subfamily of Old World monkeys that includes the African colobus monkeys and Asian langurs.

communication Any act that conveys information, in the form of a message, to another individual. Frequently, the result of communication is a change in the behavior of the recipient. Communication may not be deliberate but may instead be the result of involuntary processes or a secondary consequence of an intentional action.

complementary In genetics, referring to the fact that DNA bases form base pairs in a precise manner. For example, adenine can bond only to thymine. These two bases are said to be complementary because one requires the other to form a complete DNA base pair.

conspecifics Members of the same species.

continental drift The movement of continents on sliding plates of the earth's surface. As a result, the positions of large landmasses have shifted drastically during the earth's history.

continuum A set of relationships in which all components fall along a single integrated spectrum. All life reflects a single biological continuum.

core area   The portion of a home range containing the highest concentration and most reliable supplies of food and water. The core area is defended.

culture   Behavioral aspects of human adaptation, including technology, traditions, language, religion, marriage patterns, and social roles. Culture is a set of learned behaviors transmitted from one generation to the next through learning and not by biological or genetic mechanisms.

cusps   The elevated portions (bumps) on the chewing surfaces of premolar and molar teeth.

cytoplasm   The portion of the cell contained within the cell membrane, excluding the nucleus. The cytoplasm consists of a semifluid material and contains numerous structures involved with cell function.

D

data   (*sing.,* datum) Facts from which conclusions can be drawn; scientific information.

derived (modified)   Referring to characters that are modified from the ancestral condition and thus are diagnostic of particular evolutionary lineages.

development   Differentiation of cells into different types of tissues and their maturation.

directional change   In a genetic sense, the nonrandom change in allele frequencies caused by natural selection. The change is directional because the frequencies of alleles consistently increase or decrease (they change in one direction), depending on environmental circumstances and the selective pressures involved.

displays   Sequences of repetitious behaviors that serve to communicate emotional states. Nonhuman primate displays are most frequently associated with reproductive or agonistic behavior, and examples include chest slapping in gorillas or, in male chimpanzees, dragging and waving branches while charging and threatening other animals.

diurnal   Active during the day.

dizygotic twins   Twins derived from two separate fertilized eggs in the same pregnancy.

DNA (deoxyribonucleic acid)   The double-stranded molecule that contains the genetic code, a set of instructions for producing bodily structures and functions. DNA is a main component of chromosomes.

dominance hierarchies   Systems of social organization wherein individuals within a group are ranked relative to one another. Higher-ranking animals have greater access to preferred food items and mating partners than lower-ranking individuals. Dominance hierarchies are sometimes called "pecking orders."

dominant   Describing a trait governed by an allele that can be expressed in the presence of another, different allele (i.e., in heterozygotes). Dominant alleles prevent the expression of recessive alleles in heterozygotes. (This is the definition of *complete* dominance.)

E

ecological   Pertaining to the relationships between organisms and all aspects of their environment (temperature, predators, nonpreda-

tors, vegetation, availability of food and water, types of food, disease organisms, parasites, etc.).

ecological niche   The position of a species within its physical and biological environment. A species' ecological niche is defined by such components as diet, terrain, vegetation, type of predators, relationships with other species, and activity patterns, and each niche is unique to a given species. Together, ecological niches make up an ecosystem.

ecological species concept   The concept that a species is a group of organisms exploiting a single niche. This view emphasizes the role of natural selection in separating species from one another.

empirical   Relying on experiment or observation; from the Latin *empiricus,* meaning "experienced."

endemic   Continuously present in a population.

endocrine glands   Glands responsible for secretion of hormones into the bloodstream.

endothermic   (*endo,* meaning "within" or "internal") Able to maintain internal body temperature by producing energy through metabolic processes within cells; characteristic of mammals, birds, and perhaps some dinosaurs.

enzymes   Specialized proteins that initiate and direct chemical reactions in the body.

epochs   Categories of the geological time scale; subdivisions of periods. In the Cenozoic, epochs include the Paleocene, Eocene, Oligocene, Miocene, and Pliocene (from the Tertiary) and the Pleistocene and Holocene (from the Quaternary).

essential amino acids   The 9 (of 22) amino acids that must be obtained from the food we eat because they are not synthesized in the body in sufficient amounts.

estrus   (es´-truss) Period of sexual receptivity in female mammals (except humans), correlated with ovulation. When used as an adjective, the word is spelled "estrous."

ethnocentric   Viewing other cultures from the inherently biased perspective of one's own culture. Ethnocentrism often results in other cultures being seen as inferior to one's own.

ethnographies   Detailed descriptive studies of human societies. In cultural anthropology, an ethnography is traditionally the study of a non-Western society.

eugenics   The philosophy of "race improvement" through the forced sterilization of members of some groups and increased reproduction among others; an overly simplified, often racist view that is now discredited.

evolution   A change in the genetic structure of a population. The term is also frequently used to refer to the appearance of a new species.

evolutionary systematics   A traditional approach to classification (and evolutionary interpretation) in which presumed ancestors and descendants are traced in time by analysis of homologous characters.

F

faunal   Referring to animal remains; in archaeology, specifically refers to the fossil (or skeletonized) remains of animals.

fertility   The ability to conceive and produce healthy offspring.

fitness Pertaining to natural selection, a measure of *relative* reproductive success of individuals. Fitness can be measured by an individual's genetic contribution to the next generation compared to that of other individuals. The terms *genetic fitness, reproductive fitness,* and *differential reproductive success* are also used.

fixity of species The notion that species, once created, can never change; an idea diametrically opposed to theories of biological evolution.

flexed The position of the body in a bent orientation, with arms and legs drawn up to the chest.

forensic anthropology An applied anthropological approach dealing with legal matters. Forensic anthropologists work with coroners, police, and others in identifying and analyzing human remains.

founder effect A type of genetic drift in which allele frequencies are altered in small populations that are taken from, or are remnants of, larger populations.

frugivorous (fru-give´-or-us) Having a diet composed primarily of fruits.

G

gametes Reproductive cells (eggs and sperm in animals), developed from precursor cells in ovaries and testes.

gene A sequence of DNA bases that specifies the order of amino acids in an entire protein, a portion of a protein, or any functional product. A gene may be made up of hundreds or thousands of DNA bases organized into coding and noncoding segments.

gene flow Exchange of genes between populations.

gene pool The total complement of genes shared by the reproductive members of a population.

genetic drift Evolutionary changes—that is, changes in allele frequencies—produced by random factors. Genetic drift is a result of small population size.

genetics The study of gene structure and action, and the patterns of inheritance of traits from parent to offspring. Genetic mechanisms are the foundation for evolutionary change.

genome The entire genetic makeup of an individual or species.

genotype The genetic makeup of an individual. Genotype can refer to an organism's entire genetic makeup or to the alleles at a particular locus.

genus (*pl.,* genera) A group of closely related species.

geological time scale The organization of earth history into eras, periods, and epochs; commonly used by geologists and paleoanthropologists.

glaciations Climatic intervals when continental ice sheets cover much of the northern continents. Glaciations are associated with colder temperatures in northern latitudes and more arid conditions in southern latitudes, most notably in Africa.

grade A grouping of organisms sharing a similar adaptive pattern. Grade isn't necessarily based on closeness of evolutionary relationship, but it does contrast organisms in a useful way (e.g., *Homo erectus* with *Homo sapiens*).

grooming Picking through fur to remove dirt, parasites, and other materials that may be present. Social grooming is common among primates and reinforces social relationships.

growth Increase in mass or number of cells.

H

habitual bipedalism Bipedal locomotion as the form of locomotion shown by hominids most of the time.

Hardy-Weinberg equilibrium The mathematical relationship expressing, under ideal conditions, the predicted distribution of alleles in populations; the central theorem of population genetics.

hemispheres Two halves of the cerebrum that are connected by a dense mass of fibers. (The cerebrum is the large rounded outer portion of the brain.)

hemoglobin A protein molecule found in red blood cells. Hemoglobin binds to oxygen, an ability that allows the blood to carry oxygen throughout the body.

heterodont Having different kinds of teeth; characteristic of mammals, whose teeth consist of incisors, canines, premolars, and molars.

heterozygous Having different alleles at the same locus on members of a chromosome pair.

Holocene The most recent epoch of the Cenozoic. Following the Pleistocene, it is estimated to have begun 10,000 years ago.

homeobox genes (*Hox* genes) An evolutionarily ancient family of regulatory genes that directs the development of the overall body plan and the segmentation of body tissues.

homeostasis A condition of balance, or stability, within a biological system, maintained by the interaction of physiological mechanisms that compensate for changes (both external and internal).

Hominidae The taxonomic family to which humans belong; also includes other, now extinct, bipedal relatives.

hominids Colloquial term for members of the family Hominidae, which includes all bipedal hominoids back to the divergence from African great apes.

homologies Similarities between organisms based on descent from a common ancestor.

hormones Substances (usually proteins) that are produced by specialized cells and travel to other parts of the body, where they influence chemical reactions and regulate various cellular functions.

homoplasy (*homo,* meaning "same," and *plasy,* meaning "growth") The separate evolutionary development of similar characteristics in different groups of organisms.

homozygous Having the same allele at the same locus on both members of a chromosome pair.

Human Genome Project An international effort aimed at sequencing and mapping the entire human genome, completed in 2003.

hybrids Offspring of parents who differ from one another with regard to certain traits or certain aspects of genetic makeup; heterozygotes.

hypotheses (*sing.,* hypothesis) A provisional explanation of a phenomenon. Hypotheses require verification or falsification through testing.

hypoxia   Lack of oxygen. Hypoxia can refer to reduced amounts of available oxygen in the atmosphere (due to lowered barometric pressure) or to insufficient amounts of oxygen in the body.

I

intelligence   Mental capacity; ability to learn, reason, or comprehend and interpret information, facts, relationships, and meanings; the capacity to solve problems, whether through the appplication of previously acquired knowledge or through insight.

interglacials   Climatic intervals when continental ice sheets are retreating, eventually becoming much reduced in size. Interglacials in northern latitudes are associated with warmer temperatures, while in southern latitudes the climate becomes wetter.

interspecific   Between species; refers to variation beyond that seen within the same species to include additional aspects seen between two different species.

intragroup   (*intra*, meaning "within") Within the group, as opposed to between groups (intergroup).

intraspecific   Within species; refers to variation seen within the same species.

ischial callosities   Patches of tough, hard skin on the buttocks of Old World monkeys and chimpanzees.

K

K-selected   Pertaining to an adaptive strategy whereby individuals produce relatively few offspring, in whom they invest increased parental care. Although only a few infants are born, chances of survival are increased for each one because of parental investments in time and energy. Examples of K-selected nonprimate species are birds and canids (e.g., wolves, coyotes, and dogs).

L

lactase persistence   The ability to continue to produce the enzyme lactase in adults. Most mammals, including humans, lose this ability after they are weaned.

large-bodied hominoids   Those hominoids including the great apes (orangutans, chimpanzees, gorillas) and hominids, as well as all ancestral forms back to the time of divergence from small-bodied hominoids (i.e., the gibbon lineage).

Late Pleistocene   The portion of the Pleistocene epoch beginning 125,000 ya and ending approximately 10,000 ya.

life history traits   Characteristics and developmental stages that influence reproductive rates. Examples include longevity, age at sexual maturity, and length of time between births.

locus   (*pl.*, loci) (lo´-kus, lo-sigh´) The position on a chromosome where a given gene occurs. The term is sometimes used interchangeably with *gene,* but this usage is technically incorrect.

M

macaques   (muh-kaks´) A group of Old World monkeys comprising several species, including rhesus monkeys. Most macaque species live in India, other parts of Asia, and nearby islands.

macroevolution   Large-scale changes that occur in populations only after many generations, such as the appearance of a new species (speciation).

Magdalenian   Pertaining to the final phase of the Upper Paleolithic stone tool industry in Europe.

matrilines   Groups that consists of a female, her daughters, and their offspring. Matrilineal groups are common in macaques.

meiosis   Cell division in specialized cells in ovaries and testes. Meiosis involves two divisions and results in four daughter cells, each containing only half the original number of chromosomes. These cells can develop into gametes.

menarche   The first menstruation in girls, usually occurring in the early to middle teens.

Mendelian traits   Characteristics that are influenced by alleles at only one genetic locus. Examples include many blood types, such as ABO. Many genetic disorders, including sickle-cell anemia and Tay-Sachs disease, are also Mendelian traits.

menopause   The end of menstruation in human women, usually occurring at around age 50.

Mesolithic   The period preceding the Neolithic, during which humans increasingly exploited smaller animals (including fish), increased the variety of tools they used, and became somewhat less nomadic.

messenger RNA (mRNA)   A form of RNA that's assembled on a sequence of DNA bases. It carries the DNA code to the ribosome during protein synthesis.

metabolism   The chemical processes within cells that break down nutrients and release energy for the body to use. When nutrients are broken down into their component parts, such as amino acids, energy is released and made available for use by the cell.

microevolution   Small genetic changes that occur within a species. A human example is the variation seen in the different ABO blood types.

Middle Pleistocene   The portion of the Pleistocene epoch beginning 780,000 ya and ending 125,000 ya.

midline   An anatomical term referring to a hypothetical line that divides the body into right and left halves.

mitochondria   (*sing.,* mitochondrion) Structures contained within the cytoplasm of eukaryotic cells that convert energy, derived from nutrients, to a form that's used by the cell.

mitochondrial DNA (mtDNA)   DNA found in the mitochondria. mtDNA is inherited only from the mother.

mitosis   Simple cell division; the process by which somatic cells divide to produce two identical daughter cells.

molecules   Structures made up of two or more atoms. Molecules can combine with other molecules to form more complex structures.

monozygotic twins   Twins derived from a single fertilized egg.

morphology   The form (shape, size) of anatomical structures; can also refer to the entire organism.

mosaic evolution   A pattern of evolution in which the rate of evolution in one functional system varies from that in other systems. For example, in hominid evolution, the dental system, locomotor system, and neurological system (especially the brain) all evolved at markedly different rates.

Mousterian   Pertaining to the stone tool industry associated with Neandertals and some modern *H. sapiens* groups; also called Middle Paleolithic. This industry is characterized by a larger proportion of flake tools than is found in Acheulian tool kits.

multidisciplinary   Pertaining to research that involves mutual contributions and cooperation of several different experts from various scientific fields (i.e., disciplines).

mutation   A change in DNA. The term can refer to changes in DNA bases as well as to changes in chromosome number or structure.

N

natal group   The group in which animals are born and raised. (*Natal* pertains to birth.)

natural selection   The most critical mechanism of evolutionary change, first articulated by Charles Darwin; refers to genetic change or changes in the frequencies of certain traits in populations due to differential reproductive success between individuals.

neocortex   The more recently evolved portions of the brain's cortex that are involved with higher mental functions and composed of areas that integrate incoming information from different sensory modalities.

Neolithic   The period during which humans began to domesticate plants and animals. The Neolithic is also associated with increased sedentism. Dates for the Neolithic vary from region to region, depending on when domestication occurred.

neural tube   In early embryonic development, the anatomical structure that develops to form the brain and spinal cord.

nocturnal   Active during the night.

noncoding DNA sequences   sequences that do not code for identifiable proteins but in many cases influence the actions of coding sequences.

nuchal torus   (nuke´-ul) (*nuchal,* meaning "pertaining to the neck") A projection of bone in the back of the cranium where neck muscles attach; used to hold up the head.

nucleic acids   Organic acids made up of nucleotides. DNA and RNA are nucleic acids.

nucleus   A structure (organelle) found in all eukaryotic cells. The nucleus contains chromosomes (nuclear DNA).

nucleotides   Basic units of the DNA molecule, composed of a sugar, a phosphate, and one of four DNA bases.

O

obligate bipedalism   Bipedalism as the *only* form of hominid terrestrial locomotion. Since major anatomical changes in the spine, pelvis, and lower limb are required for bipedal locomotion, once hominids adapted this mode of locomotion, other forms of locomotion on the ground became impossible.

omnnivorous   Having a diet consisting of many kinds of foods, such as plant materials (seeds, fruits, leaves), meat, and insects.

organelles   Structures contained within cells. There are many kinds of organelles, and each type has a different function.

osteology   The study of skeletal material. Human osteology focuses on the interpretation of skeletal remains from archaeological

sites, skeletal anatomy, bone physiology, and growth and development. Some of the same techniques are used in paleoanthropology to study early hominids.

P

paleoanthropology   The interdisciplinary approach to the study of earlier hominids, their chronology, physical structure, archaeological remains, habitats, etc.

paleopathology   The branch of osteology that studies the evidence of disease and injury in human skeletal (or, occasionally, mummified) remains from archaeological sites.

paleospecies   Species defined from fossil evidence, often covering a long time span.

pandemic   An extensive outbreak of disease affecting large numbers of individuals over a wide area; potentially a worldwide phenomenon.

pathogens   Any agents, especially microorganisms such as viruses, bacteria, or fungi, that infect a host and cause disease.

phenotypes   The observable or detectable physical characteristics of an organism; the detectable expressions of genotypes.

phylogenetic species concept   Splitting many populations into separate species based on an identifiable parental pattern of ancestry.

phylogenetic tree   A chart showing evolutionary relationships as determined by evolutionary systematics. It contains a time component and implies ancestor-descendant relationships.

placental   A type (subclass) of mammal. During the Cenozoic, placentals became the most widespread and numerous mammals and today are represented by upward of 20 orders, including the primates.

plasticity   The capacity to change; in a behavioral context, the ability of animals to modify behaviors in response to differing circumstances.

pleiotropic genes   Genes that have more than one effect; genes that have different effects at different times in the life cycle.

Pleistocene   The epoch of the Cenozoic from 1.8 mya until 10,000 ya. Frequently referred to as the Ice Age, this epoch is associated with continental glaciations in northern latitudes.

Plio-Pleistocene   Pertaining to the Pliocene and first half of the Pleistocene, a time range of 5–1 mya. For this time period, numerous fossil hominids have been found in Africa.

polyandry   A mating system wherein a female continuously associates with more than one male (usually two or three) with whom she mates. Among nonhuman primates, polyandry is seen only in marmosets and tamarins. It also occurs in a few human societies.

polygenic   Referring to traits that are influenced by genes at two or more loci. Examples of such traits are stature, skin color, and eye color. Many polygenic traits are also influenced by environmental factors.

polymerase chain reaction (PCR)   A method of producing thousands of copies of a DNA segment using the enzyme DNA polymerase.

polymorphisms   Loci with more than one allele. Polymorphisms can be expressed in the phenotype as the result of gene action (as in

ABO), or they can exist solely at the DNA level within noncoding regions.

polytypic   Referring to species composed of populations that differ with regard to the expression of one or more traits.

population   Within a species, a community of individuals where mates are usually found.

population genetics   The study of the frequency of alleles, genotypes, and phenotypes in populations from a microevolutionary perspective.

postcranial   (*post*, meaning "after") In a quadruped, referring to that portion of the body behind the head; in a biped, referring to all parts of the body *beneath* the head (i.e., the neck down).

predisposition   The capacity or inclination to do something. An organism's capacity for behavioral or anatomical modification is related to the presence of preexisting traits.

prehensility   Grasping, as by the hands and feet of primates.

primates   Members of the order of mammals Primates (pronounced "pry-may´-tees"), which includes prosimians, monkeys, apes, and humans.

primatologists   Scientists who study the evolution, anatomy, and behavior of nonhuman primates. Those who study behavior in non-captive animals are usually trained as physical anthropologists.

primatology   The study of the biology and behavior of nonhuman primates (prosimians, monkeys, and apes).

principle of independent assortment   The distribution of one pair of alleles into gametes does not influence the distribution of another pair. The genes controlling different traits are inherited independently of one another.

principle of segregation   Genes (alleles) occur in pairs (because chromosomes occur in pairs). During gamete production, the members of each gene pair separate, so that each gamete contains one member of each pair. During fertilization, the full number of chromosomes is restored, and members of gene or allele pairs are reunited.

prosimians   Members of a suborder of Primates, the suborder Prosimii (pronounced "pro-sim´-ee-eye"). Traditionally, the suborder includes lemurs, lorises, and tarsiers.

protein synthesis   The assembly of chains of amino acids into functional protein molecules. The process is directed by DNA.

proteins   Three-dimensional molecules that serve a wide variety of functions through their ability to bind to other molecules.

punctuated equilibrium   The concept that evolutionary change proceeds through long periods of stasis punctuated by rapid periods of change.

Q

quadrupedal   Using all four limbs to support the body during locomotion; the basic mammalian (and primate) form of locomotion.

quantitatively   Pertaining to measurements of quantity and including such properties as size, number, and capacity. When data are quantified, they're expressed numerically and can be tested statistically.

R

r-selected   An adaptive strategy that emphasizes relatively large numbers of offspring and reduced parental care (compared to K-selected species). *K-selection* and *r-selection* are relative terms; e.g., mice are r-selected compared to primates but K-selected compared to fish.

random assortment   The chance distribution of chromosomes to daughter cells during meiosis; along with recombination, a source of variation resulting from meiosis.

recessive   Describing a trait that isn't expressed in heterozygotes; also refers to the allele that governs the trait. For a recessive allele to be expressed, there must be two copies of it (i.e., the individual must be homozygous).

recognition species concept   A depiction of species in which the key aspect is the ability of individuals to identify members of their own species for purposes of mating (and to avoid mating with members of other species). In theory, this type of selective mating is a component of a species concept emphasizing mating and is therefore compatible with the biological species concept.

recombinant DNA technology   A process in which genes from the cell of one species are transferred to somatic cells or gametes of another species.

recombination   Sometimes called crossing over; the exchange of genetic material between partner chromosomes during meiosis.

regulatory genes   Genes that code for the production of proteins that can bind to DNA and modify the action of genes. Many are active only during certain stages of development.

relativistic   Pertaining to relativism; viewing entities as they relate to something else. Cultural relativism is the view that cultures have merits within their own historical and environmental contexts and that they shouldn't be judged through comparison with one's own culture.

replicate   To duplicate. The DNA molecule is able to make copies of itself.

reproductive strategies   The complex of behavioral patterns that contributes to individual reproductive success. The behaviors need not be deliberate, and they often vary considerably between males and females.

reproductive success   The number of offspring an individual produces and rears to reproductive age; an individual's genetic contribution to the next generation.

reproductively isolated   Pertaining to groups of organisms that, mainly because of genetic differences, are prevented from mating and producing offspring with members of other groups.

rhinarium   (rine-air´-ee-um) (*pl.*, rhinaria) The moist, hairless pad at the end of the nose seen in most mammals. The rhinarium enhances an animal's ability to smell.

ribonucleic acid (RNA)   A single-stranded molecule similar in structure to DNA. Three forms of RNA are essential to protein synthesis: messenger RNA (mRNA), transfer RNA (tRNA), and ribosomal RNA (rRNA).

ribosomes   Structures composed of a form of RNA called ribosomal RNA (rRNA) and protein. Ribosomes are found in the cell's cytoplasm and are essential to the manufacture of proteins.

S

sagittal crest A ridge of bone that runs down the middle of the cranium like a short Mohawk. This serves as the attachment for the large temporal muscles, indicating strong chewing.

savanna (also spelled savannah) A large flat grassland with scattered trees and shrubs. Savannas are found in many regions of the world with dry and warm to hot climates.

science A body of knowledge gained through observation and experimentation; from the Latin *scientia*, meaning "knowledge."

scientific method An approach to research whereby a question is asked, a hypothesis (or provisional explanation) is stated, and that hypothesis is tested by collecting and analyzing data.

scientific testing The precise repetition of an experiment or expansion of observed data to provide verification; the procedure by which hypotheses and theories are verified, modified, or discarded.

sea ice maximum In the Arctic, the greatest amount of sea ice that is present in one year. It occurs in March at the end of the winter season just as the ice quits forming and before it begins to melt.

sea ice minimum In the Arctic, the least amount of sea ice that is present in one year. Sea ice is at its minimum in September just as the summer melting season ends, but before ice begins to form again.

sectorial Adapted for cutting or shearing; among primates, refers to the compressed (side-to-side) first lower premolar, which functions as a shearing surface with the upper canine.

selective pressures Forces in the environment that influence reproductive success in individuals.

senescence The process of physiological decline in body function that occurs with aging.

sensory modalities Different forms of sensation (e.g., touch, pain, pressure, heat, cold, vision, taste, hearing, and smell).

sex chromosomes In mammals, the X and Y chromosomes.

sexual dimorphism Differences in physical characteristics between males and females of the same species. For example, humans are slightly sexually dimorphic for body size, with males being taller, on average, than females of the same population.

sexual selection A type of natural selection that operates on only one sex within a species. It's the result of competition for mates, and it can lead to sexual dimorphism with regard to one or more traits.

shared derived Relating to specific character traits shared in common between two life-forms and considered the most useful for making evolutionary interpretations.

sickle-cell anemia A severe inherited hemoglobin disorder in which red blood cells collapse when deprived of oxygen. It results from inheriting two copies of a mutant allele. This mutation is caused by a single base substitution in the DNA.

sites Locations of discoveries. In paleontology and archaeology, a site may refer to a region where a number of discoveries have been made.

slash-and-burn agriculture A traditional land-clearing practice whereby trees and vegetation are cut and burned. In many areas, fields are abandoned after a few years and clearing occurs elsewhere.

social structure The composition, size, and sex ratio of a group of animals. The social structure of a species is, in part, the result of natural selection in a specific habitat, and it guides individual interactions and social relationships.

somatic cells All the cells in the body except gametes (eggs and sperm).

specialized Evolved for a particular function; usually refers to a specific trait (e.g., incisor teeth), but may also refer to the entire way of life of an organism.

speciation The process by which a new species evolves from an earlier species. Speciation is the most basic process in macroevolution.

species A group of organisms that can interbreed to produce fertile offspring. Members of one species are reproductively isolated from members of all other species (that is, they can't mate with them to produce fertile offspring).

spina bifida A condition in which the arch of one or more vertebrae fails to fuse and form a protective barrier around the spinal cord.

stereoscopic vision The condition whereby visual images are, to varying degrees, superimposed on one another. This provides for depth perception, or the perception of the external environment in three dimensions. Stereoscopic vision is partly a function of structures in the brain.

stratigraphy Study of the sequential layering of deposits.

stratum (*pl.*, strata) Geological layer.

stress In a physiological context, any factor that acts to disrupt homeostasis; more precisely, the body's response to any factor that threatens its ability to maintain homeostasis.

T

taxonomy The branch of science concerned with the rules of classifying organisms on the basis of evolutionary relationships.

territories Portions of an individual's or group's home range that are actively defended against intrusion, especially by members of the same species.

theory A broad statement of scientific relationships or underlying principles that has been substantially verified through the testing of hypotheses.

thermoluminescence (TL) Technique for dating certain archaeological materials that were heated in the past (such as stone tools) and that release stored energy of radioactive decay as light upon reheating.

theropods Small- to medium-sized ground-living dinosaurs, dated to approximately 150 mya and thought to be related to birds.

transfer RNA (tRNA) The type of RNA that binds to amino acids and transports them to the ribosome during protein synthesis.

transmutation The change of one species to another. The term *evolution* did not assume its current meaning until the late nineteenth century.

U

uniformitarianism The theory that the earth's features are the result of long-term processes that continue to operate in the present as they did in the past. Elaborated on by Lyell, this theory opposed catastrophism and contributed strongly to the concept of immense geological time.

Upper Paleolithic   A cultural period usually associated with modern humans, but also found with some Neandertals, and distinguished by technological innovation in various stone tool industries. Best known from western Europe, similar industries are also known from central and eastern Europe and Africa.

V

variation (genetic)   Inherited differences among individuals; the basis of all evolutionary change.

vasoconstriction   Narrowing of blood vessels to reduce blood flow to the skin. Vasoconstriction is an involuntary response to cold and reduces heat loss at the skin's surface.

vasodilation   Expansion of blood vessels, permitting increased blood flow to the skin. Vasodilation permits warming of the skin and also facilitates radiation of warmth as a means of cooling. Vasodilation is an involuntary response to warm temperatures, various drugs, and even emotional states (blushing).

vectors   Agents that serve to transmit disease from one carrier to another. Mosquitoes are vectors for malaria, just as fleas are vectors for bubonic plague.

vertebrates   Animals with segmented, bony spinal columns; includes fishes, amphibians, reptiles, birds, and mammals.

W

worldview   General cultural orientation or perspective shared by members of a society.

Z

zoonotic   (zoh-oh-no´-tic) Pertaining to a zoonosis (*pl.*, zoonoses), a disease that is transmitted to humans through contact with nonhuman animals.

zygote   A cell formed by the union of an egg cell and a sperm cell. It contains the full complement of chromosomes (in humans, 46) and has the potential to develop into an entire organism.

Bibliography

Alemseged, Z., F. Spoor, W. H. Kimbel et al.
2006 "A Juvenile Early Hominin Skeleton from Dikika, Ethiopia." *Nature*, 443:296–301.

Ardrey, R.
1961 *African Genesis* New York: Macmillan.

Arsuaga, Juan-Luis, Carlos Lorenzo, Ana Gracia, et al.
1999 "The Human Cranial Remains from Gran Dolina Lower Pleistocene Site (Sierra de Atapuerca, Spain)." *Journal of Human Evolution*, 37:431–457.

Arsuaga, J. L., I. Martinez, A. Gracia, et al.
1997 "Sima de los Huesos (Sierra de Atapuerca, Spain): The Site." *Journal of Human Evolution*, 33:109–127.

Ascenzi, A., I. Bidditu, P. F. Cassoli, et al.
1996 "A Calvarium of Late *Homo erectus* from Ceprano, Italy." *Journal of Human Evolution*, 31:409–423.

Asfaw, B., W. H. Gilbert, Y. Beyene, et al.
2002 "Remains of *Homo erectus* from Bouri, Middle Awash, Ethiopia." *Nature*, 416:317–320.

Badrian, A. and N. Badrian
1984 "Social Organization of *Pan paniscus* in the Lomako Forest, Zaire." In: *The Pygmy Chimpanzee*, Randall L. Susman (ed.), New York, NY: Plenum Press, pp. 325–346.

Badrian, N., and R. K. Malenky
1984 "Feeding Ecology of *Pan paniscus* in the Lomako Forest, Zaire." In: *The Pygmy Chimpanzee,* Randall L. Susman (ed.), New York, NY: Plenum Press, pp. 275–299.

Balter, Michael
2006 "Radiocarbon Dating's Final Frontier." News Focus, *Science*, 313:1560–1563.

Barker, Graeme, Huw Barton, Michael Bird, et al.
2007 "The Human Revolution in Lowland Tropical Southeast Asia: the Antiquity and Behavior of Anatomically Modern Humans at Niah Cave (Sarawak, Borneo)." *Journal of Human Evolution*, 52:243–261.

Bartlett, Thad Q., Robert W. Sussman, and James M. Cheverud
1993 "Infant Killing in Primates: A Review of Observed Cases with Specific References to the Sexual Selection Hypothesis." *American Anthropologist*, 95:958–990.

Bearder, Simon K.
1987 "Lorises, Bushbabies & Tarsiers: Diverse Societies in Solitary Foragers." In: *Primate Societies*, Smuts, B. B., D. L. Cheney, and R. M. Seyfath (eds.), pp. 11–24.

Begun, D. and A.Walker
1993 "The Endocast." In: *The Nariokotome* Homo erectus *Skeleton*. A. Walker and R. E. Leakey (eds.), Cambridge, MA: Harvard University Press, pp. 326–358.

Beja-Pereira, A., G. Luikart, P. R. England, et al.
2003 "Gene-culture Coevolution Between Cattle Milk Protein Genes and Human Lactase Genes." *Nature Genetics,* 35:311–313.

Bell, Martin and Michael J. C. Walker
1992 *Late Quaternary Environmental Change.* New York: John Wiley and Sons.

Berger, Thomas and Erik Trinkaus
1995 "Patterns of Trauma Among the Neandertals." *Journal of Archaeological Science*, 22:841–852.

Bermudez de Castro, J. M., J. Arsuaga, E. Carbonell, et al.
1997 "A Hominid from the Lower Pleistocene of Atapuerca, Spain. Possible Ancestor to Neandertals and Modern Humans." *Science*, 276:1392–1395.

Bermudez de Castro, J. M., M. Martinon-Torres, E. Carbonell, et al.
2004 "The Atapuerca Sites and their Contribution to the Knowledge of Human Evolution in Europe." *Evolutionary Anthropology*, 13:25–41.

Binford, Lewis R. and Chuan Kun Ho
1985 "Taphonomy at a Distance: Zhoukoudian, 'The Cave Home of Beijing Man'?" *Current Anthropology*, 26:413–442.

Binford, Lewis R. and Nancy M. Stone
1986a "The Chinese Paleolithic: An Outsider's View." *AnthroQuest*, 1986:14–20.

———
1986b "Zhoukoudian: A Closer Look." *Current Anthropology*, 27(5):453–475.

Bininda-Emonds, R.P. Olaf, Marcel Cordillo, et al.
2007 "The Delayed Rise of Present-Day Mammals." *Nature*, 446:507–512

Bischoff, J. L., R. W. Williams, R. J. Rosebauer, et al.
2007 "High-Resolution U-series Dates from the Sima de los Huesos Hominids Yields 600+V/-66 kyrs: Implications for the Evolution of the Early Neanderthal Lineage." *Journal of Archaeological Science*, 34:763–770.

Boaz, N. T. and R. L. Ciochon
2001 "The Scavenging of *Homo erectus pekinensis*." *Natural History*, 110:46–51.

Boesch, C.
1996 "Social Grouping Tai Chimpanzees." In: *Great Ape Societies*. W. C. McGrew, L. Marchant, and T. Nishida (eds), Cambridge, UK: Cambridge University Press. pp. 101–113.

Boesch, C. and H. Boesch-Achermann
2000 *The Chimpanzees of the Tai Forest*. Oxford, UK: Oxford University Press.

Boesch, C. and H. Boesch
1989   "Hunting Behavior of Wild Chimpanzees in the Tai National Park." *American Journal of Physical Anthropology*, 78:547–573.

Boesch, C. P. Marchesi, N. Marchesi, et al.
1994   "Is Nut Cracking in Wild Chimpanzees a Cultural Behaviour?" *Journal of Human Evolution*, 26:325–338.

Bogin, Barry
1988   *Patterns of Human Growth*. Cambridge: Cambridge University Press.

Borries, C., K. Launhardt, C. Epplen, et al.
1999   "DNA Analyses Support the Hypothesis that Infanticide is Adaptive in Langur Monkeys." *Proceedings of the Royal Society of London*, 266:901–904.

Bower, Bruce
2006   "Evolution's Mystery Woman." *Science News*, 170:330–332.

Brace, C. L. and Ashley Montagu
1977   *Human Evolution* (2nd Ed.). New York, NY: Macmillan.

Brace, C. Loring, H. Nelson, and N. Korn
1979   *Atlas of Human Evolution* (2nd Ed.). New York, NY: Holt, Rinehart & Winston.

Breuer, T., M. Ndoundou-Hockemba, and V. Fishlock.
2005   "First Observations of Tool Use in Wild Gorillas." *PloS Biology*. 3(11):e380 doi:10.1371/journal.pbio.0030380

Bromage, Timothy G. and Christopher Dean
1985   "Re-evaluation of the Age at Death of Immature Fossil Hominids." *Nature*, 317:525–527.

Brown, P., T. Sutiikna, M. K. Morwood, et al.
2004   "A New Small-Bodied Hominin from the Late Pleistocene of Flores, Indonesia." *Nature*, 431:1055–1061.

Brown, T. M. and K. D. Rose
1987   "Patterns of Dental Evolution in Early Eocene Anaptomorphine Primates Comomyidael from the Bighorn Basin, Wyoming." *Journal of Paleontology*, 61:1–62.

Brunet, M., F. Guy, D. Pilbeam, et al.
2002   "A New Hominid from the Upper Miocene of Chad, Central Africa." *Nature*, 418:145–151.

Caramelli, D., C. Lalueza-Fox, S. Condemi, et al.
2006   "A Highly Divergent mtDNA Sequence in a Neandertal Individual from Italy." *Current Biology*, 16:R630–R632.

Caramelli, David, Carlos Lalueza-Fox, Cristiano Vernesi, et al.
2003   "Evidence for Genetic Discontinuity Between Neandertals and 24,000-year-old Anatomically Modern Humans." *Proceedings of the National Academy of Sciences, USA*, 100:6593–6597.

Cartmill, Matt
1972   "Arboreal Adaptations and the Origin of the Order Primates." In: *The Functional and Evolutionary Biology of Primates*, R. H. Tuttle (ed.), Chicago, IL: Aldine-Atherton, pp. 97–122.

———
1992   "New Views on Primate Origins." *Evolutionary Anthropology*, 1:105–111.

Chen, F-C., and Li, W-H.
2001   "Genomic Divergences Between Humans and Other Hominoids and the Effective Population Size of the Common Ancestor of Humans and Chimpanzees." *American Journal of Human Genetics*, 68:444–456.

Chen, F. C., E. J. Vallender, H. Wang, C. S. Tzeng, and W. H. Li
2001   "Genomic Divergence between Human and Chimpanzee Estimated from Large-scale Alignments of Genomic Sequences." *Journal of Heredity*, 92:481–489.

Cheng, Z., M. Ventura, X. She, P. Khaitovich, T. Graves, et al.
2005   "A Genome-wide Comparison of recent Chimpanzee and Human Segmental Duplications." *Nature*, 437:88–93.

The Chimpanzee Sequencing and Analysis Consortium.
2005   "Initial Sequence of the Chimpanzee Genome and Comparison with the Human Genome." *Nature*, 437:69–87.

Chisholm, J. S.
1993   "Death, Hope, and Sex: Life-history theory and the development of reproductive strategies." *Current Anthropology*, 34 (1), 1–24.

Ciochon, Russell L. and Robert S. Corruccini (eds.)
1983   *New Interpretations of Ape and Human Ancestry*. New York: Plenum Press.

Clarke, Ronald J. and Phillip V. Tobias
1995   "Sterkfontein Member 2 Foot Bones of the Oldest South African Hominid." *Science*, 269:521–524.

Cleveland, J. and C. T. Snowdon
1982   "The Complex Vocal Repertoire of the Adult Cotton-top Tamarin *(Saguinus oedipus oedipus)*." *Zeitschrift Tierpsychologie*, 58:231–270.

Colwell, Rita R.
1996   "Global Climate and Infectious Disease: The Cholera Paradigm." *Science*, 274:2025–2031.

Conkey, M.
1987   "New Approaches in the Search for Meaning? A Review of the Research in 'Paleolithic Art.'" *Journal of Field Archaeology*, 14:413–430.

Conroy, Glenn C.
1990   *Primate Evolution*. New York, NY: W. W. Norton.

———
1997   *Reconstructing Human Origins*: A Modern Synthesis. New York, NY: Norton.

Crews, D. E. and G. J. Harper
1998   "Ageing as Part of the Developmental Process." In: *The Cambridge Encyclopedia of Human Growth and Development*, S. J. Ulijaszek et al. (eds.) Cambridge, UK: Cambridge University Press, pp. 425–427.

Cummings, Michael
2000   *Human Heredity. Principles and Issues (5th Ed.)*. St. Paul, MN: Wadsworth/West Publishing Co.

Currat, M., G. Trabuchet, D. Rees, et al.
2002   "Molecular Analysis of the Beta-Globin Gene Cluster in the Niokholo Mandenka Population Reveals a Recent Origin of the Beta S Senegal Mutation." *American Journal of Human Genetics*, 70:207–223.

Curtin, R. and P. Dolhinow
1978   "Primate Social Behavior in a Changing World." *American Scientist*, 66:468–475.

Daeschler, Edward B., Neil H. Shubin, and Farish A. Jenkins, Jr.
2006   "A Darwinian Tetrapod-Like Fish and the Evolution of the Tetrapod Body Plan." *Nature*, 440:757–763.

Dart, Raymond
1959   *Adventures with the Missing Link*. New York, NY: Harper & Brothers.

Darwin, Charles
1859   *On the Origin of Species.* A Facsimile of the First Edition, Cambridge, MA: Harvard University Press (1964).

1871   *The Descent of Man and Selection in Relation to Sex.* Princeton, NJ: Princeton University Press (1981).

Day, M. H. and E. H. Wickens
1980   "Laetoli Pliocene Hominid Footprints and Bipedalism." *Nature,* 286:385–387.

Dean, M., M. Carring, C. Winkler, et al.
1996   "Genetic Restriction of HIV-1 Infection and Progression to AIDS by a Deletion Allele of the CKR5 Structural Gene." *Science,* 273:1856–1862.

de Lumley, Henry and M. de Lumley
1973   "Pre-Neanderthal Human Remains from Arago Cave in Southeastern France." *Yearbook of Physical Anthropology,* 16:162–168.

Demuth, J. P., T. D. Bie, J. E. Stajich, N. Cristianini, and M. W. Hahn
2006   "The Evolution of Mammalian Gene Families." *PloS ONE* 1(1):e85. doi:10.1371/journal.pone.0000085.

Dene, H. T., M. Goodman, and W. Prychodko
1976   "Immunodiffusion Evidence on the Phylogeny of the Primates." *In: Molecular Anthropology,* M. Goodman, R. E. Tashian, and J. H. Tashian (eds.), New York: Plenum Press, pp. 171–195.

Desmond, Adrian and James Moore
1991   *Darwin.* New York, NY: Warner Books.

Dettwyler, K. A.
1995   "A Time to Wean: The Hominid Blueprint for the Natural Age of Weaning in Modern Human Populations." In: P. Stuart-Macadam & K. A. Dettwyler (Eds.), *Breastfeeding: Biocultural Perspectives..* New York, NY: Aldine de Gruyter, pp. 39–73.

de Waal, Frans
1982   Chimpanzee Politics. London, UK: Jonathan Cape.

1987   "Tension Regulation and Nonreproductive Functions of Sex in Captive Bonobos *(Pan paniscus)*." *National Geographic Research,* 3:318–335.

1989   *Peacemaking among Primates.* Cambridge, MA: Harvard University Press.

1996   *Good Natured: The Origins of Right and Wrong in Humans and Other Animals.* Cambridge, MA.: Harvard University Press.

1999   "Cultural Primatology Comes of Age." *Nature,* 399:635–636.

2007   "With a Little Help from a Friend." *PloS Biology,* 5(7):1406–1408.

de Waal, F. and F. Lanting.
1997   *Bonobo: The Forgotten Ape.* Berkeley, CA: University of California Press.

Dominy, N. J. and P. W. Lucas
2001   "Ecological Importance of Trichromatic Vision to Primates." *Nature,* 410:363–366.

Doran, D. M. and A. McNeilage
1998   "Gorilla Ecology and Behavior." *Evolutionary Anthropology,* 6:120–131.

Dressler WW, K.S. Oths, and C.G. Gravlee
2005   "Race and Ethnicity in Public Health Research: Models to Explain Health Disparities. *Annual Review of Anthropology,* 34: 231–252.

Duarte, C., J. Mauricio, P. B. Pettitt, et al.
1999   "The Early Upper Paleolithic Human Skeleton from the Abrigo do Lagar Velho (Portugal) and Modern Human Emergence in Iberia." *Proceedings of the National Academy of Sciences, USA,* 96:7604–7609.

Durham, William
1981   Paper presented to the Annual Meeting of the American Anthropological Association, Washington, D.C., Dec. 1980. Reported in *Science,* 211:40.

Eaton, S. Boyd, M. Shostak, and M. Konner
1988   *The Paleolithic Prescription.* New York, NY: Harper and Row.

Ehrlich, Paul R. and Anne H. Ehrlich
1990   *The Population Explosion.* New York, NY: Simon & Schuster.

Ellison, P. T
2001   *On Fertile Ground: A Natural History of Human Reproduction.* Cambridge, MA: Harvard University Press

Erickson, Clark
1998   "Applied Archaeology and Rural Development: Archaeology's Potential Contribution to the Future." *In:* M. Whiteford and S. Whiteford (eds.), *Crossing Currents: Continuity and Change in Latin America.* Upper Saddle, NJ: Prentice-Hall, pp. 34–45.

Enard, W., M. Przeworski, S. E. Fisher, et al.,
2002   "Molecular Evolution of FOXP2, a Gene Involved in Speech and Language." *Nature,* 418:869–872.

Eswaran, V., H. Harpending, and A. R. Rogers
2005   "Genomics Refutes an Exclusively African Origin of Humans." *Journal of Human Evolution,* 49:1–18.

Ewald, P. W.
1994   *Evolution of Infectious Disease.* New York, NY: Oxford University Press.

1999   "Evolutionary Control of HIV and Other Sexually Transmitted Viruses." In: *Evolutionary Medicine,* W. R. Trevathan, E. O. Smith, and J. J. McKenna, (eds.), New York, NY: Oxford University Press.

Falguères, Christophe, Jean-Jacques Bahain, Yugi Yokoyama, et al.
1999   "Earliest Humans in Europe: The Age of TD6 Gran Dolina, Atapuerca, Spain." *Journal of Human Evolution,* 37:345–352.

Falk, D., C. Hildebolt, K. Smith, et al.
2005   "The Brain of LB1, *Homo floresiensis.*" *Science,* 308:242–245.

Feathers, James K. and Elena Migliorini
2001   Luminescence Dating at Katanda – A Reassessment. *Quaternary Science Reviews,* 20:961–966.

Fedigan, L. M.
1983   "Dominance and Reproductive Success in Primates." *Yearbook of Physical Anthropology,* 26:91–129.

Fischman, Josh
2005   "Family Ties." *National Geographic,* 207(April):16–27.

Fleagle, John

1983 "Locomotor Adaptations of Oligocene and Miocene Hominoids and their Phyletic Implications." *In*: R. L. Ciochon and R. S. Corruccini (eds.), q.v., pp. 301–324.

_____

1988/ *Primate Adaptation and Evolution.* New York, NY:
1999 Academic Press. (2nd Ed.), 1999.

Foley, R. A.

1991 "How Many Species of Hominid Should There Be?" *Journal of Human Evolution*, 30: 413–427.

_____

2002 "Adaptive Radiations and Dispersals in Hominin Evolutionary Ecology." *Evolutionary Anthropology*, 11(Supplement 1):32–37.

Foley, R.A. and M.M. Lahr

1997 "Mode 3 Technologies and the Evolution of Modern Humans." *Cambridge Archaeological Journal*: 7:3–36.

Formicola, Vincenzo and Alexandra P. Buzhilova

2004 "Double Child Burial from Sunghir (Russia): Pathology and Inferences for Upper Paleolithic Funerary Practices." *American Journal of Physical Anthropology*, 124:189–198.

Freundlich, J. C., H. Schwabedissen and E. Wendt

1980 "Köln Radiocarbon Measurements II." *Radiocarbon*, 22:68–81.

Frisancho, A. Roberto

1993 *Human Adaptation and Accommodation.* Ann Arbor, MI: University of Michigan Press.

Galik, K., B. Senut, M. Pickford, et al.

2004 "External and Internal Morphology of the Bar, 1002'00 *Orrorin tugenensis* Femur." *Science*, 305:1450–1453.

Gao, Feng, Elizabeth Bailes, David L. Robertson, et al.

1999 "Origin of HIV-1 in the Chimpanzee *Pan troglodytes troglodytes*." *Nature*, 397:436–441.

Gardner, R. Allen, B. T. Gardner, and T. T. van Cantfort (eds.)

1989 *Teaching Sign Language to Chimpanzees.* Albany, NY: State University of New York Press.

Giles, J. and J. Knight

2003 "Dolly's Death Leaves Researchers Woolly on Clone Ageing Issue." *Nature*, 421:776.

Gillespie, B. and R. G. Roberts

2000 "On the Reliability of Age Estimate for Human Remains at Lake Mungo." *Journal of Human Evolution*, 38:727–732.

Gingerich, Phillip D.

1985 "Species in the Fossil Record: Concepts, Trends, and Transitions." *Paleobiology*, 11:27–41.

Goodall, Jane

1986 *The Chimpanzees of Gombe.* Cambridge, NY: Harvard University Press.

Goodman, M., C. A. Porter, J. Czelusniak, et al.

1998 "Toward a Phylogenetic Classification of Primates Based on DNA Evidence Complemented by Fossil Evidence." *Molecular Phylogenetics and Evolution*, 9:585–598.

Gossett, T. F.

1963 *Race, the History of an Idea in America.* Dallas, TX: Southern Methodist University Press.

Gould, Stephen

1981 *The Mismeasures of Man.* New York, NY: W. W. Norton.

_____

1987 *Time's Arrow, Time's Cycle.* Cambridge, NY: Harvard University Press.

Gould, Stephen Jay and Niles Eldredge

1977 "Punctuated Equilibria: The Tempo and Mode of Evolution Reconsidered." *Paleobiology*, 3:115–151.

Grant, P. R.

1982 "Variation in the Size and Shape of Darwin's Finch Eggs." *Auk*, 99:5–23.

_____

1986 *Ecology and Evolution of Darwin's Finches.* Princeton, NJ: Princeton University Press.

Green, R. E., J. Krause, E. Ptak, A. W. Briggs, et al.

2006 "Analysis of One Million Base Pairs of Neanderthal DNA." *Nature*, 444:330–336.

Greene, John C.

1981 *Science, Ideology, and World View.* Berkeley, CA: University of California Press.

Greenwood, B. and T. Mutabingwa

2002 "Malaria in 2000." *Nature*, 415:670–672.

Gross, Liza

2006 "Scientific Illiteracy and the Partisan Takeover of Biology." PLoS Biol., 4:e167.

Groves, C. P.

2001a *Primate Taxonomy.* Washington, DC: Smithsonian Institution Press.

_____

2001b "Why Taxonomic Stability Is a Bad Idea, or Why Are There So Few Species of Primates (or Are There?)." *Evolutionary Anthropology*, 10:191–197.

Grün, R. and C. B. Stringer

1991 "ESR Dating and the Evolution of Modern Humans." *Archaeometry*, 33:153–199.

Grün, R., C. B. Stringer, F. McDermott, et al.

2005 "U-series and ESR Analysis of Bones and Teeth Relating to the Human Burials from Skhūl." *Journal of Human Evolution*, 49:316–334.

Haas, J. D., E. A. Frongillo, Jr., C. D. Stepick, et al.

1980 "Altitude, Ethnic and Sex Difference in Birth Weight and Length in Bolivia." *Human Biology*, 52:459–477.

Haile-Selassie, Y., G. Suwa, and T. D. White

2004 "Late Miocene Teeth from Middle Awash, Ethiopia, and Early Hominid Dental Evolution." *Science*, 303:1503–1505.

Hanna, J. M.

1999 "Climate, Altitude, and Blood Pressure." *Human Biology*, 71:553–582.

Harlow, H. F.

1959 "Love in Infant Monkeys." *Scientific American*, 200:68–74.

Harlow, H. F. and M. K. Harlow

1961 "A Study of Animal Affection." *Natural History*, 70:48–55.

Hawkes, K., J. F. O'Connell, and N. G. Blurton Jones

1997 "Hadza Women's Time Allocation, Offspring Provisioning, and the Evolution of Long Postmenopausal Life Spans." *Current Anthropology*, 38:551–577.

Henshilwood, C. S., F. d'Errico, M. Vanhaeren, et al.

2004 "Middle Stone Age Shell Beads from South Africa." *Science*, 304:404.

Henzi, P. and L. Barrett

2003 "Evolutionary Ecology, Sexual Conflict, and Behavioral Differentiation Among Baboon Populations." *Evolutionary Anthropology*, 12:217–230.

Higham, Tom, Christopher Bronk Ramsey, Ivor Karavanic, et al.
2006 "Revised Direct Radiocarbon Dating of the Vindija G₁ Upper Paleolithic Neandertals." *Proceedings of the National Academy of Sciences*, 103:553–557.

Holloway, Ralph L.
1983 "Cerebral Brain Endocast Pattern of *Australopithecus afarensis* Hominid." Nature, 303:420–422.

———
1985 "The Poor Brain of *Homo sapiens neanderthalensis*." In: *Ancestors, The Hard Evidence*, E. Delson (ed.). New York, NY: Alan R. Liss, pp. 319–324.

Howell, F. C.
1999 "Paleo-demes, Species, Clades, and Extinctions in the Pleistocene Hominin Record." *Journal of Anthropological Research*, 55:191–243.

Hrdy, Sarah Blaffer
1977 *The Langurs of Abu*. Cambridge, MA: Harvard University Press.

Hrdy, Sarah Blaffer, Charles Janson, and Carel van Schaik
1995 "Infanticide: Let's Not Throw Out the Baby with the Bath Water." *Evolutionary Anthropology*, 3:151–154.

Hu, Dale J., Timothy J. Dondero, Mark A. Rayfield, et al.
1996 "The Emerging Genetic Diversity of HIV. The Importance of Global Surveillance for Diagnostics, Research, and Prevention." *Journal of the American Medical Association*, 275:210–216.

Hudjashou Georgi, Toomas Kivisid, Peter A. Underhill et al.,
2007 "Revealing the Prehistoric Settlement of Australia by Y Chromosome and mtDNA Analysis." *Proceedings of the National Academy of Sciences*, 104:8726–8730.

The International SNP Map Working Group
2001 "A Map of Human Genome Sequence Variation Containing 1.42 Million Single Nucleotide Polymorphisms." *Nature*, 409:928–933.

Izawa, K. and A. Mizuno
1977 "Palm-Fruit Cracking Behaviour of Wild Black-Capped Capuchin (*Cebus apella*)." *Primates*, 18:773–793.

IUCN (International Union for Conservation of Nature and Natural Resources)
1996/ Red List of Threatened Species. www.iucnredlist.org
2004

Jablonski, N. G.
1992 "Sun, Skin Colour, and Spina Bifida: An Exploration of the Relationship between Ultraviolet Light and Neural Tube Defects." *Proceedings of the Australian Society of Human Biology*, 5:455–462.

Jablonski, N. G. and G. Chaplin
2000 "The Evolution of Skin Coloration." *Journal of Human Evolution*, 39:57–106.

———
2002 "Skin Deep". *Scientific American*, 287:74–81.

Jacob, T., E. Indriati, R. P. Soejono, et al.
2006 "Pygmoid Australomelanesian *Homo sapiens* Skeletal Remains from Liang Bua, Flores: Population Affinities and Pathological Abnormalities." *Proceedings of the National Academy of Sciences*, 103:13421–13426.

Jacobs, Z. G.A.T. Duller, A.G. Wintle, and C.S. Heshilwood
2006 "Extending the Chronology of Deposits at Blombos Cave, South Africa, Back to 140 ka Using Optical Dating of Single and Multiple Grains of Quartz." *Journal of Human Evolution*, 51:255–273.

Jensen, G. M. and L. G. Moore
1997 "The Effect of High Altitude and Other Risk Factors on Birthweight: Independent or Interactive Effects?" *American Journal of Public Health*, 87(6):1003–1007.

Jia, L. and W. Huang
1990 *The Story of Peking Man*. New York, NY: Oxford University Press.

Jolly, Alison
1985 *The Evolution of Primate Behavior* (2nd Ed.). New York, NY: Macmillan.

Kano, T.
1992 *The Last Ape. Pygmy Chimpanzee Behavior and Ecology*. Stanford, CA: Stanford University Press.

Katz, D. and Suchey, J.M.
1986 Age Determination of the Male Os Pubis. *American Journal of Physical Anthropology* 69:427–435.

Keynes, Randal
2002 *Darwin, His Daughter and Human Evolution*. New York, NY: Riverhead Books.

Kimbel, W. H., T. D. White, and D. C. Johanson
1988 "Implications of KNM-WT-17000 for the Evolution of 'Robust' *Australopithecus*." In: *Evolutionary History of the "Robust" Australopithecines* (Foundations of Human Behavior), F. E. Grine (ed.), Somerset, NJ: Aldine Transaction, pp. 259–268.

King, B. J.
1994 *The Information Continuum*. Santa Fe, NM: School of American Research.

———
2004 *Dynamic Dance: Nonvocal Communication in the African Great Apes*. Cambridge, MA: Harvard University Press.

Kirkwood, T. B. L.
1997 "The Origins of Human Ageing." *Philosophical Transactions of the Royal Society of London B.*, 352:1765–1772.

———
2002 "Evolution of Ageing." *Mechanisms of Ageing and Development*, 123:737–745.

Klein, Richard G.
1989/ *The Human Career. Human Biological and Cultural*
1999 *Origins* (2nd Ed.). Chicago, IL: University of Chicago Press.

Konner, Melvin and Carol Worthman
1980 "Nursing Frequency, Gonadal Function, and Birth Spacing among !Kung Hunter-Gatherers." *Science*, 207:788–791.

Koopman, R. J., A. G. Mainous, V. A. Diaz, et al.
2005 "Changes in Age at Diagnosis of Type 2 Diabetes Mellitus in the United States, 1988 to 2000." *Annals of Family Medicine*, 3:60–69.

Kramer, Andrew
1993 "Human Taxonomic Diversity in the Pleistocene: Does *Homo erectus* Represent Multiple Hominid Species?" *American Journal of Physical Anthropology*, 91:161–171.

Krause, Johannes, Carlos Lalueza-Fox, Ludavic Orlando, et al.
2007 "The Derived FOXP2 Variant of Modern Humans Was Shared with Neandertals." *Current Biology*, 17:1908–1912.

Krings, Matthias, Anne Stone, Ralf W. Schmitz, et al.
1997   "Neandertal DNA Sequences and the Origin of Modern Humans." *Cell*, 90:19–30.

Kujoth, G. C., P. C. Bradshaw, S. Haroon, and T. A. Prolla.
2007   "The Role of Mitochondrial DNA Mutations in Mammalian Aging. *PLoS Genetics*, 3:e24.

Kulikov, Eugene E., Audrey B. Poltaraus, and Irina A. Lebedeva
2004   "DNA Analysis of Sunghir Remains: Problems and Perspectives." Poster Presentation, European Paleopathology Association Meetings, Durham, U.K, August 2004.

Lack, David
1966   *Population Studies of Birds*. Oxford: Clarendon.

Lahdenperä, M., V. Lummaa, S. Helle, M. Tremblay and A. F. Russell
2004   "Fitness Benefits of Prolonged Post-Reproductive Lifespan in Women. *Nature*, 428:178–181.

Lahr, Marta Mirazon and Robert Foley
1998   "Towards a Theory of Human Origins: Geography, Demography, and Diversity in Recent Human Evolution." *Yearbook of Physical Anthropology*, 41:137–176.

Lalani, A. S., J. Masters, W. Zeng, et al.
1999   "Use of Chemokine Receptors by Poxviruses." *Science*, 286:1968–71.

Lalueza-Fox, Carles, Hogler Römpler, David Caramelli, et al.
2007   A Melanocortin Receptor Allele Suggests Varying Pigmentation Among Neanderthals." *Science Express*, Oct 25, 2007.

Lamberts, S. W. J., A. W. van den Beld, and A. J. van der Lely
1997   "The Endocrinology of Aging." *Science*, 278:419–424.

Lamason, R.L., M-A.P.K. Mohideen, J.R. Mest et al.
2005   "SLC24A5, a Putative Cation Exchanger, Affects Pigmentation in Zebrafish and Humans." *Science*, 310:1782–1786.

Lancaster, J. B. and C. S. Lancaster
1983   "Prenatal Investment: The Hominid Adaptation." *In:* Ortner, D. J. (ed.), *How Humans Adapt: A Biocultural Odyssey*. Washington DC: Smithsonian Institution Press.

Leakey, M. D. and R. L. Hay
1979   "Pliocene Footprints in Laetolil Beds at Laetoli, Northern Tanzania." *Nature*, 278:317–323.

Lerner, I. M. and W. J. Libby
1976   *Heredity, Evolution, and Society*. San Francisco, CA: W. H. Freeman and Company.

Lewin, Roger
1986   "Damage to Tropical Forests, or Why Were There So Many Kinds of Animals?" *Science*, 234:149–150.

Lewontin, R. C.
1972   "The Apportionment of Human Diversity." In: *Evolutionary Biology* (Vol. 6), T. Dobzhansky, et al. (eds.), New York, NY: Plenum, pp. 381–398.

Li, T. and D. A. Etler
1992   "New Middle Pleistocene Hominid Crania from Yunxian in China." *Nature*, 357:404–407.

Loeb, L. A., D. C. Wallace and G. M. Martin.
2005   "The Mitochondrial Theory of Aging and its Relationship to Reactive Oxygen Species Damage and Somatic mtDNA Mutations." *Proceedings of the National Academy of Sciences (PNAS)*, 102:18769–18770.

Lordkipanidze, David, Abesalom Vekua, Reid Ferring, et al.
2005   "The Earliest Toothless Hominin Skull." *Nature*, 434:717–718.

Lordkipandize, David, Tea Jashashuil, Abesalom Vekua, et al.
2007   "Postcranial Evidence from Early *Homo* from Dmanisi, Georgia." *Nature*, 449:305–310.

Lordkipandize D., A. Vekua, R. Ferring, P. Rightmire, et al.
2006   "A Fourth Hominid Skull from Dmanisi, Georgia." *The Anatomical Record: Part A,* 288:1146–1157.

Mace, R.
2000   "Evolutionary Ecology of Human Life History: A Review." *Animal Behaviour* 59:1–10.

MacKinnon, J. and K. MacKinnon
1980   "The Behavior of Wild Spectral Tarsiers." *International Journal of Primatology*, 1:361–379.

Manson, J. H. and R. Wrangham
1991   "Intergroup Aggression in Chimpanzees and Humans." *Current Anthropology,* 32:369–390.

Marean, Curtis W., Miryam Bar-Matthews, Jocelyn Bernatchez, et al.
2007   "Early Human Use of Marine Resources and Pigment in South Africa During the Middle Pleistocene." *Nature*, 449:905–908.

Marris, Emma
2006   "Bushmeat Surveyed in Western Cities. Illegally Hunted Animals Turn Up in Markets from New York to London." *News@Nature.com*. doi:10.1038/news060626-10

Martin, Robert D., Ann M. Maclaranon, James C. Phillips, and William B. Dobyns
2006   "Flores Hominid: New Species or Microcephalic Dwarf?" *The Anatomical Record: Part A,* 288:1123–1145.

Masataka, N.
1983   "Categorical Responses to Natural and Synthesized Alarm calls in Goeldi's Monkeys *(Callimico goeldi)*." *Primates*. 24:40–51.

Mayer, Peter
1982   "Evolutionary Advantages of Menopause." *Human Ecology*, 10:477–494.

Mayr, Ernst
1970   *Population, Species, and Evolution*. Cambridge, MA: Harvard University Press.

McBrearty, Sally and Nina G. Jablonski
2005   "First Fossil Chimpanzee." *Nature*, 437:105–108.

McDougall, I.; F. H. Brown, J. G. Fleagle
2005   "Stratigraphic Placement and Age of Modern Humans from Kibish, Ethiopia." *Nature*, 433: 733–736.

McGrew, W. C.
1992   *Chimpanzee Material Culture. Implications for Human Evolution*. Cambridge: Cambridge University Press.

———
1998   "Culture in Nonhuman Primates?" *Annual Review of Anthropology*, 27:301–328.

McHenry, Henry
1988   "New Estimates of Body Weight in Early Hominids and Their Significance to Encephalization and Megadontia in 'Robust' Australopithecines." In: *Evolutionary History of the "Robust" Australopithecines* (Foundations of Human Behavior), F. E. Grine (ed.), Somerset, NJ: Aldine Transaction, pp. 133–148.

1992 "Body Size and Proportions in Early Hominids." *American Journal of Physical Anthropology*, 87:407–431.

McKern, T. W., and Stewart T. D.
1957 *Skeletal Age Changes in Young American Males*. Natick, MA: Quartermaster Research and Development Command, Technical Report EP-45.

McKusick, V. A. (with S. E. Antonarakis, et al.)
1998 *Mendelian Inheritance in Man*. (12th Ed.). Baltimore, MD: Johns Hopkins University Press.

Mervis, J.
2006 "Judge Jones Defines Science—And Why Intelligent Design Isn't." *Science*, 311:34.

Miles, H. Lyn Whire
1990 "The Cognitive Foundations for Reference in a Signing Orangutan." In: *Language and Intelligence in Monkeys and Apes: Comparative Developmental Perspectives*, S. T. Parker and K. R. Gibson (eds.), New York, NY: Cambridge University Press, pp. 511–539.

Miller, G. H., J. W. Magee, B. J. Johnson, et al.
1999 "Pleistocene extinction of *Genyornis newtoni*: Human Impact on Australian Megafauna." *Science*, 283:205–208.

Molnar, Stephen
1983 *Human Variation. Races, Types, and Ethnic Groups* (2nd Ed.). Englewood Cliffs, NJ: Prentice-Hall.

Moore, L. G. and J. G. Regensteiner
1983 "Adaptation to High Altitude." *Annual Reviews of Anthropology*, 12:285–304.

Moore, L. G., et al.
1994 "Genetic Adaptation to High Altitude." *In: Sports and Exercise Medicine*, Stephen C. Wood and Robert C. Roach (eds.), New York, NY: Marcel Dekker, Inc., pp. 225–262.

Moore, L. G., S. Niermeyer, and S. Zamudio
1998 "Human Adaptation to High Altitude: Regional and Life-Cycle Perspectives." *American Journal of Physical Anthropology, Suppl*. 27:25–64.

Moore, L.G., M. Shriver, L. Bemis, and E. Vargas
2006 "An Evolutionary Model for Identifying Genetic Adaptation to High Altitude." *Advances in Experimental Medicine and Biology*, 588:101–118.

Moore, L. G., S. Zamudio, J. Zhuang, et al.
2001 "Oxygen Transport in Tibetan Women During Pregnancy at 3,658 M." *American Journal of Physical Anthropology*, 114:42–53.

Morris, D.
1967 *The Naked Ape*. New York: Dell.

Morwood, M. J., P. Brown, T. Jatmiko, et al.
2005 "Further Evidence for Small-Bodied Hominins from the Late Pleistocene of Flores, Indonesia." *Nature*, 437:1012–1017.

Morwood, M. J., R. P. Suejono, R. G. Roberts, et al.
2004 "Archaeology and Age of a New Hominin from Flores in Eastern Indonesia." *Nature*, 431:1087–1091.

Mourant, A.E., A.C. Kopec, and K. Domaniewska-Sobczak.
1976. *The Distribution of the Human Blood Groups and Other Polymorphisms*, 2d ed. London, England: Oxford University Press.

Muchmore, E. A., S. Diaz , and A. Varki
1998 "A Structural Difference Between the Cell Surfaces of Humans and the Great Apes. *American Journal of Physical Anthropology*, 107:187–98.

Murphy, W. J., E. Elzirik, W. E. Johnson, et al.
2001 "Molecular Phylogenetics and the Origins of Placental Mammals." *Nature*, 409:614–618.

Napier, John
1967 "The Antiquity of Human Walking." *Scientific American*, 216:56–66.

Napier, J. R. and P. H. Napier
1967 *A Handbook of Living Primates*. New York, NY: Academic Press.

1985 *The Natural History of the Primates*. London: British Museum of Natural History.

National Snow and Ice Data Center.
2007 http://nsdic.org/

Nesse, R. M. and G. C. Williams
1994 *Why We Get Sick. The New Science of Darwinian Medicine*. New York, NY: Vintage Books.

Nevell, L., A Gordon, and B. Wood
2007 "*Homo floresiensis* and *Homo sapiens* Size-Adjusted Cranial Shape Variations." *American Journal of Physical Anthropology, Supplement*, 14:177–178 (Abstract).

Newport, S.
2007 WildlifeDirect.org. Personal communication.

News in Brief
2007 "Congolese Government Creates Bonobo Reserve." *Nature*. 450:470 doi:10.1038/450470f

Ni, Xijun, Yuanqing Wang, Yaoming Hu, and Chuankui Li
2004 "A Euprimate Skull from the Early Eocene of China." *Nature*, 427:65–68.

Nishida, T.
1991 "Comments.: In: "Intergroup Aggression in Chimpanzees and Humans," J. H. Manson and R. Wrangham, *Current Anthropology*, 32:369–390, pp. 381–382.

Nishida, T., M. Hiraiwa-Hasegawa, T. Hasegawa, and Y. Takahata
1985 "Group Extinction and Female Transfer in Wild Chimpanzees in the Mahale National Park, Tanzania." *Zeitschrift Tierpsychologie*, 67:284–301.

Nishida, T., H. Takasaki, and Y. Takahata
1990 "Demography and Reproductive Profiles." In: *The Chimpanzees of the Mahale Mountains*, T. Nishida (ed.), Tokyo: University of Tokyo Press, pp. 63–97.

Nishida, T., R. W. Wrangham, J. Goodall, and S. Uehara
1983 "Local Differences in Plant-feeding Habits of Chimpanzees between the Mahale Mountains and Gombe National Park, Tanzania." *Journal of Human Evolution*, 12:467–480.

Noonan, James P., G. Coop, S. Kudaravalli, D. Smith, et al.
2006 "Sequencing and Analysis of Neanderthal Genomic DNA." *Science*, 314:1113–1118.

Nowak, Ronald M.
1999 *Walker's Primates of the World*. Baltimore, MD: Johns Hopkins University Press.

Oates, John F., Michael Abedi-Lartey, W. Scott McGraw, et al.
2000 "Extinction of a West African Red Colobus Monkey." *Conservation Biology*, 14:1526–1532.

Oates, J. F., R. A. Bergl, J. Sunderland-Groves, and A. Dunn
2007 "*Gorilla gorilla* ssp. *Diehli*. In: IUCN 2007. *2007 IUCN Red List of Threatened Species*.

Ovchinnikov, Igor V., Anders Gotherstrom, Galina P. Romanova, et al.
2000   "Molecular Analysis of Neanderthal DNA from the Northern Caucasus." *Nature*, 404:490–493.

Padian, Kevin and Luis M. Chiappe
1998   "The Origin of Birds and Their Flight." *Scientific American*, 278:38–47.

Page, S. E., F. Siegert, J. O. Rieley, H-D. V. Boehm, A Jaya, and S. Limin
2002   "The Amount of Carbon Released from Peat and Forest Fires in Indonesia During 1997." *Nature*, 420:61–65.

Pagel, M., C. Venditti, and A. Meade
2006   "Large Punctuational Contribution of Speciation to Evolutionary Divergence at the Molecular Level." *Science*, 314:119–121.

Palmer, S. K., L. G. Moore, D. Young, et al.
1999   "Altered Blood Pressure Course During Normal Pregnancy and Increased Preeclampsia at High Altitude (3100 meters) in Colorado." *American Journal of Obstetrics and Gynecology*, 189:1161–1168.

Parés, Josef M. and Alfredo Pérez-González
1995   "Paleomagnetic Age for Hominid Fossils at Atapuerca Archaeological Site, Spain." *Science*, 269:830–832.

Peccei, Jocelyn Scott
2001   "Menopause: Adaptation or Epiphenomenon?" *Evolutionary Anthropology*, 10:43–57.

Pelletier, D. L., E. A. Frongillo, D. G. Schroeder, and J. P. Habicht
1995   "The Effects of Malnutrition on Child Mortality in Developing Countries." *Bulletin of the World Health Organization*, 73:443–448.

Pennisi, Elizabeth
2007   "No Sex Please, We're Neandertals." *Science*, 316:967

Peres, C. A.
1990   "Effects of Hunting on Western Amazonian Primate Communities." *Biological Conservation* 54:47–59.

Phillips, K. A.
1998   "Tool Use in Wild Capuchin Monkeys." *American Journal of Primatology*, 46:259–261.

Pickford, Martin and Brigitte Senut
2001   "The Geological and Faunal Context of Late Miocene Hominid Remains from Lukeino, Kenya." *Comptes Rendus de l'Académie des Sciences, Ser. 11A, Earth and Planetary Science*, 332:145–152.

Pike, I. L.
2000   "The Nutritional Consequences of Pregnancy Sickness: A Critique of a Hypothesis." *Human Nature*, 11 (3), 207–232.

Pinner, R. W., S. M. Teutsch, L. Simonson, et al.
1996   "Trends in Infectious Diseases Mortality in the United States." *Journal of the American Medical Association*, 275:189–193.

Potts, Richard
1984   "Home Bases and Early Hominids." *American Scientist*, 72:338–347.

_____
1991   "Why the Oldowan? Plio-Pleistocene Toolmaking and the Transport of Resources." *Journal of Anthropological Research*, 47:153–176.

_____
1993   "Archeological Interpretations of Early Hominid Behavior and Ecology." In: *The Origin and Evolution of Humans and Humanness*, D. T. Rasmussen (ed.), Boston, MA: Jones and Bartlett, pp. 49–74.

Powell, K. B.
2003   "The Evolution of Lactase Persistence in African Populations." *American Journal of Physical Anthropology*, Supplement 36:170 (Abstract).

Pruetz, J.D., and P. Bertolani
2007   "Savanna Chimpanzees, *Pan troglodytes verus*, Hunt with Tools." *Current Biology*, 17:412–417

Proctor, Robert
1988   "From Anthropologie to Rassenkunde." In: *Bones, Bodies, Behavior. History of Anthropology* (Vol. 5), W. Stocking, Jr. (ed.), Madison, WI: University of Wisconsin Press, pp. 138–179.

Profet, M.
1988   "The Evolution of Pregnancy Sickness as a Protection to the Embryo Against Pleistocene Teratogens." *Evolutionary Theory*, 8:177–190.

Pusey, A., J. Williams, and J. Goodall
1997   "The Influence of Dominance Rank on the Reproductive Success of Female Chimpanzees." *Science*, 277:828–831.

Rak, Yoel, Avishag Ginzburg, and Eli Geffen
2007   "Gorilla-Like Anatomy on *Australopithecus afarensis* Mandibles Suggests *Au. afarensis* link to Robust Australopiths." *Proceedings of the National Academy of Sciences*, 104:6568–6572.

Relethford, John H.
2001   *Genetics and the Search for Modern Human Origins.*" New York, NY: Wiley-Liss.

The Rhesus Macaque Genome Sequencing and Analysis Consortium.
2007   "Evolutionary and Biomedical Insights from the Rhesus Macaque Genome." *Science*. 316:222–234.

Richards, Gary D.
2006   "Genetic, Physiologic, and Ecogeographic Factors Contributing to Variation in *Homo sapiens: Homo floresiensis* Reconsidered." *Journal of Evolutionary Biology*, 19:1744–1767.

Riddle, Robert D. and Clifford J. Tabin
1999   "How Limbs Develop." *Scientific American*, 280:74–79.

Ridley, Mark
1993   *Evolution.* Boston, MA: Blackwell Scientific Publications.

Rightmire, G. P.
1998   "Human Evolution in the Middle Pleistocene: The Role of *Homo heidelbergensis*." *Evolutionary Anthropology*, 6:218–227.

_____
2004   "Affinities of the Middle Pleistocene Cranium from Dali and Jinniushan." *American Journal of Physical Anthropology, Supplement* 38:167 (Abstract).

Rose, M. D.
1991   "Species Recognition in Eocene Primates." *American Journal of Physical Anthropology*, Supplement, 12:153 (Abstract).

Rosenberg, K. and W. Trevathan
2001   "The Evolution of Human Birth." *Scientific American*, 285:72–77.

Rudran, R.

1973 "Adult Male Replacement in One-Male Troops of Purple-Faced Langurs (*Presbytis senex senex*) and its Effect on Population Structure." *Folia Primatologica,* 19:166–192.

Ruff, C. B. and Alan Walker

1993 "The Body Size and Shape of KNM-WT 15000." In: *The Nariokotome* Homo erectus *Skeleton,* A. Walker and R. E. Leakey (eds.), Cambridge, MA: Harvard University Press, pp. 234–265.

Samson, M., F. Libert, B. J. Doranz, et al.

1996 "Resistance to HIV-1 Infection in Caucasian Individuals Bearing Mutant Alleles of the CCR-5 Chemokine Receptor Gene." *Nature* 382:722–725.

Sarmiento, E. E. and J. F. Oates

2000 "The Cross River Gorilla: A Distinct Subspecies *Gorilla gorilla diehli* Matschie 1904." *American Museum Novitates* 3304:1–55.

Savage-Rumbaugh, S. and R. Lewin

1994 *Kanzi: The Ape at the Brink of the Human Mind.* New York, NY: John Wiley and Sons.

Savage-Rumbaugh, S., K. McDonald, R. A. Sevic, W. D. Hopkins, and E. Rupert

1986 "Spontaneous Symbol Acquisition and Communicative Use by Pygmy Chimpanzees *(Pan paniscus)*." *Journal of Experimental Psychology: General,* 115:211–235.

Schmitz, Ralf W., David Serre, Georges Bonani, et al.

2002 "The Neandertal Type Site Revisited: Interdisciplinary Investigations of Skeletal Remains from the Neander Valley, Germany." *Proceedings of the National Academy of Sciences,* 99:13342–13347.

Scriver, C. R.

2001 *The Metabolic and Molecular Bases of Inherited Disease.* New York, NY: McGraw Hill.

Semaw, S., P. Renne, W. K. Harris, et al.

1997 "2.5-million-Year-Old Stone Tools from Gona, Ethiopia." *Nature,* 385:333–336.

Senut, Brigitte, Martin Pickford, Dominique Grommercy, et al.

2001 "First Hominid from the Miocene (Lukeino Formation, Kenya)." *Comptes Rendus de l'Académie des Sciences, Ser. 11A, Earth and Planetary Science,* 332:137–144.

Serre, David, André Langaney, Marie Chech, et al.

2004 "No Evidence of Neandertal mtDNA Contribution to Early Modern Humans." *PloS Biology,* 2:313–317.

Seyfarth, Robert M.

1987 "Vocal Communication and Its Relation to Language." In: *Primate Societies,* B. Smuts, D. L. Cheney, R. M. Seyfarth, et al. (eds.), Chicago, IL: University of Chicago Press, pp. 440–451.

Seyfarth, Robert M., Dorothy L. Cheney, and Peter Marler

1980a "Monkey Responses to Three Different Alarm Calls." *Science,* 210:801–803.

———

1980b "Vervet Monkey Alarm Calls." *Animal Behavior,* 28:1070–1094.

Shang, Hong, Haowen Tong, Shuangguan Zhang, et al.

2007 "An Early Modern Human from Tianyuan Cave, Zhoukoudian, China." *Proceedings of the National Academy of Sciences,* 104:6573–6578.

Shea, Brian T. and Robert C. Baily

1996 "Allometry and Adaptation of Body Proportions and Stature in African Pygmies." *American Journal of Physical Anthropology,* 100:311–340

Shubin, Neil H., Edward B. Daeschler, and Farish A. Jenkins, Jr.

2006 "The Pectoral Fin of *Tiktaalik roseae* and the Origin of the Tetrapod Limb." Nature, 440:764–771.

Shubin, Neil, Cliff Tabin, and Sean Carroll

1997 "Fossil Genes, and the Evolution of Animal Limbs." *Nature,* 388:639–648.

Sievert, Lynette Leidy

2006 *Menopause: A Biocultural Perspective.* New Brunswick, NJ: Rutgers University Press.

Silk, J. B., S. C. Alberts, and J. Altmann

2003 "Social Bonds of Female Baboons Enhance Infant Survival." *Science,* 302:1231–1234.

Silk, J. B., S. F. Brosman, J. Vonk, et al.

2005 Chimpanzees are Indifferent to the Welfare of Unrelated Group Members. *Nature,* 437:1357–1359.

Simmons, J. G.

1989 *Changing the Face of the Earth.* Oxford: Basil Blackwell Ltd.

Simons, E. L.

1972 *Primate Evolution.* New York: Macmillan.

Smith, F. H.

1984 "Fossil Hominids from the Upper Pleistocene of Central Europe and the Origin of Modern Europeans." In: *The Origins of Modern Humans,* F. H. Smith and F. Spencer (eds.), New York, NY: Alan R. Liss, pp. 187–209.

———

2002 "Migrations, Radiations and Continuity: Patterns in the Evolution of Late Pleistocene Humans. In: *The Primate Fossil Record.* W. Hartwig (ed.), Cambridge: Cambridge University Press, pp. 437–456.

Smith, F. H., A. B. Falsetti, and S. M. Donnelly

1989 "Modern Human Origins." *Yearbook of Physical Anthropology,* 32:35–68.

Smith, F. H., E. Trinkaus, P. B. Pettitt, et al.

1999 "Direct Radiocarbon Dates for Vindija G1 and Velika Pécina Late Pleistocene Hominid Remains." *Proceedings of the National Academy of Sciences,* 96:12281–12286.

Smuts, Barbara

1985 *Sex and Friendship in Baboons.* Hawthorne, NY: Aldine de Gruyter.

Snyder, M. and M. Gerstein

2003 "Genomics. Defining Genes in the Genomics Era." *Science,* 300:258–260.

Sponheimer, M., B. H. Passey, D. J. de Ruiter, et al.

2006 "Isotopic Evidence for Dietary Variability in the Early Hominin *Paranthropus robustus*." *Science,* 314:980–982.

Spoor, F., M.G. Leakey, P.N. Gathago, et al.

2007 "Implications of New Early *Homo* Fossils from Ileret, East of Lake Turkana, Kenya." *Nature,* 448:688–691.

Steklis, H. D.

1985 "Primate Communication, Comparative Neurology, and the Origin of Language Reexamined." *Journal of Human Evolution,* 14:157–173.

Stelzner, J. and K. Strier

1981 "Hyena Predation on an Adult Male Baboon." *Mammalia,* 45:106–107.

Strassman, B. I. and B. Gillespie

2002 "Life-history Theory, Fertility, and Reproductive Success in Humans." *Proceedings of the Royal Society of London B,* 269:553–562.

Strier, Karen B.

2003 *Primate Behavioral Ecology* (2nd Ed.). Boston, MA: Allyn and Bacon.

Stringer, C. B. and P. Andrews

1988 "Genetic and Fossil Evidence for the Origin of Modern Humans." *Science,* 239:1263–1268.

Struhsaker, T. T.

1967 "Auditory Communication among Vervet Monkeys (*Cercopithecus aethiops*)." In: *Social Communication Among Primates,* S. A. Altmann (ed.), Chicago, IL: University of Chicago Press.

———

1975 *The Red Colobus Monkey.* Chicago, IL: University of Chicago Press.

Struhsaker, T. T. and L. Leland

1979 "Socioecology of Five Sympatric Monkey Species in the Kibale Forest, Uganda." In: *Advances in the Study of Behavior, Vol. 9.* J.S. Rosenblatt, R.A. Hinde, C. Beer, and M.C. Busnel (eds.), New York, NY: Academic Press, pp. 159–229.

———

1987 "Colobines: Infanticide by Adult Males." In: *Primate Societies,* B. Smuts, D. L. Cheney, R. M. Seyfarth, et al. (eds.), Chicago, IL: University of Chicago Press, pp. 83–97.

Sua, Gen, Reikp T. Kono, Shigehiro Katoh, et al.

2007 "A New Species of Great Ape from the Late Miocene Epoch of Ethiopia." *Nature,* 448:921–924.

Sumner, D. R., M. E. Morbeck, and J. Lobick

1989 "Age-Related Bone Loss in Female Gombe Chimpanzees." *American Journal of Physical Anthropology,* 72:259.

Susman, Randall L. (ed.)

1984 *The Pygmy Chimpanzee: Evolutionary Biology and Behavior.* New York, NY: Plenum.

Susman, Randall L., Jack T. Stern, and William L. Jungers

1985 "Locomotor Adaptations in the Hadar Hominids." In: *Ancestors: The Hard Evidence,* E. Delson (ed.), New York, NY: Alan R. Liss, pp. 184–192.

Sussman, Robert W.

1991 "Primate Origins and the Evolution of Angiosperms." *American Journal of Primatology,* 23:209–223.

Sussman, R. W., J. M. Cheverud, and T.Q. Bartlett

1995 "Infant Killing as an Evolutionary Strategy: Reality or Myth?" *Evolutionary Anthropology,* 3:149–151.

Suwa, G., R. T. Kono, S. Katch, B. Asfaw, and Y. Beyene

2007 "A New Species of Great Ape from the Late Miocene Epoch in Ethiopia." *Nature,* 448:921–924.

Swisher, C. C., W. J. Rink, S. C. Anton, et al.

1996 "Latest *Homo erectus* of Java: Potential Contemporaneity with Homo sapiens in Southwest Java." *Science,* 274:1870–1874.

Szalay, F. S. and E. Delson

1979 *Evolutionary History of the Primates.* New York, NY: Academic Press.

Tattersall, I., E. Delson, and J. Van Couvering

1988 *Encyclopedia of Human Evolution and Prehistory.* New York, NY: Garland Publishing.

Tenaza, R. and R. Tilson

1977 "Evolution of Long-Distance Alarm Calls in Kloss' Gibbon." *Nature,* 268:233–235.

Teresi, Dick

2002 *Lost Discoveries. The Ancient Roots of Modern Science—from the Babylonians to the Maya.* New York, NY: Simon and Schuster.

Thieme, H.

1997 "Lower Palaeolithic Hunting Spears from Germany." *Nature,* 385:807–810.

Thorne, A., R. Grün, G. Mortimer, et al.

1999 "Australia's Oldest Human Remains: Age of the Lake Mungo 3 Skeleton." *Journal of Human Evolution,* 36:591–612.

Tiemel, C., Y. Quan, and W. En

1994 "Antiquity of *Homo sapiens* in China." *Nature,* 368:55–56.

Tocheri, Matthew W., Caley M. Orr, Susan G. Larson, et al.

2007 "The Primitive Wrist of *Homo floresiensis* and Its Implications fro Hominin Evolution." *Science,* 1743–1745.

Todd, T. W.

1920 "Age Changes in the Pubic Bone. I. The Male White Pubis." *American Journal of Physical Anthropology* 3:285–339.

———

1921 "Age Changes in the Ppubic bone. III. The Pubis of the White Female. *American Journal of Physical Anthropology* 4: 26–39.

Trinkaus, E.

2005 "Early Modern Humans." *Annual Reviews of Anthropology,* 34:207–230.

Trinkaus, E., S. Milota, R. Rodrigo, et al.

2003 "Early Modern Human Cranial Remains from Pestera cu Oase, Romania." *Journal of Human Evolution,* 45:245–253.

Trinkaus, E. and P. Shipman

1992 *The Neandertals.* New York, NY: Alfred A. Knopf.

van Schaik, C. P., M. Ancrenaz, G. Bogen, et al.

2003 "Orangutan Cultures and the Evolution of Material Culture." *Science,* 299:102–105.

Varki, A.

2000 "A Chimpanzee Genome Project Is a Biomedical Imperative." *Genome Research,* 8:1065–1070.

Vialet, A., L. Tianyuan, D. Grimaud-Herve, et al.

2005 "Proposition de Reconstitution du Deuxième Crâne d'*Homo erectus* de Yunxian (Chine)." *Comptes rendus. Palévol,* 4:265–274.

Vigilant, L., M. Hofreiter, H. Siedel, and C. Boesch

2001 Paternity and Relatedness in Wild Chimpanzee Communities. *Proceedings of the National Academy of Sciences,* 98:12890–12895.

Vignaud, P., P. Duringer, H. MacKaye, et al.

2002 "Geology and Palaeontology of the Upper Miocene Toros-Menalla Hominid Locality, Chad." *Nature,* 418:152–155.

Villa, Paola

1983 *Terra Amata and the Middle Pleistocene Archaeological Record of Southern France.* University of California

Publications in Anthropology, Vol. 13. Berkeley, CA: University of California Press.

Visalberghi, E.
1990   "Tool Use in Cebus." *Folia Primatologica*, 54:146–154.

Vogelsang, R.
1998   *The Middle Stone Age Fundstellen in Süd-west Namibia*. Köln: Heinrich Barth Institut.

Walker, A.
1976   "Remains Attributable to *Australopithecus* from East Rudolf." In: *Earliest Man and Environments in the Lake Rudolf Basin*, Y. Coppens (ed.), Chicago, IL: University of Chicago Press, pp. 484–489.

_____
1991   "The Origin of the Genus *Homo*." In: *Evolution of Life*, S. Osawa and T. Honjo (eds.), Tokyo: Springer-Verlag, pp. 379–389.

_____
1993   "The Origin of the Genus *Homo*." In: *The Origin and Evolution of Humans and Humanness*, D. T. Rasmussen (ed.), Boston, MA: Jones and Bartlett, pp. 29–47.

Walker, Alan and R. E. Leakey
1993   *The Nariokotome* Homo erectus *Skeleton*. Cambridge, MA: Harvard University Press.

Walker, J., R.A. Cliff, and A.G. Latham
2006   "U-Pb Isoptoic Age of the Stw 573 Hominid from Sterkfontein, South Africa." *Science*, 314:1592–1594.

Walsh, P. D., K. A. Abernathy, M. Bermejo, et al.
2003   "Catastrophic Ape Decline in Western Equatorial Africa." *Nature*, 422:611–614.

Ward, Peter
1994   *The End of Evolution*. New York, NY: Bantam.

Warneken, F. and M. Tomasello
2006   "Altruistic Helping in Human Infants and Young Chimpanzees." *Science*, 311:1301–1303.

Washburn, S. L.
1963   "The Study of Race." *American Anthropologist*, 65:521–531.

Waterston, R. H., K. Lindblad-Toh, E. Birney, et al. (Mouse Genome Sequencing Consortium)
2002   "Initial Sequencing and Comparative Analysis of the Mouse Genome." *Nature*, 421:520–562.

Watson, J. B. and F. H. C. Crick
1953a   "Genetical Implications of the Structure of the Deoxyribonucleic Acid." *Nature*, 171:964–967.

_____
1953b   "A Structure for Deoxyribonucleic Acid." *Nature*, 171:737–738.

Weiner, J. S.
1955   *The Piltdown Forgery*. London: Oxford University Press.

Weiner, Steve, Qinqi Xu, Paul Goldberg, et al.
1998   "Evidence for the Use of Fire at Zhoukoudian, China." *Science*, 281:251–253.

Weiss, Kenneth
2003   "Come to Me My Melancholic Baby!" *Evolutionary Anthropology*, 12:3–6.

Weiss, Robin A. and Richard W. Wrangham
1999   "From Pan to Pandemic." *Nature*, 397:385–386.

Weiss, U.
2002   "Nature Insight: Malaria." *Nature*, 415:669.

White, T. D.
1986   "Cut Marks on the Bodo Cranium: A Case of Prehistoric Defleshing." *American Journal of Physical Anthropology*, 69:503–509.

White, T. D., B. Asfaw, D. DeGusta, et al.
2003   "Pleistocene *Homo sapiens* from Middle Awash Ethiopia." *Nature*, 423:742–747.

_____
1995   "Corrigendum (White, et al., 1994)". *Nature*, 375:88.

White, T. D., Giday WoldeGabriel, B. Asfaw, et al.
2006   "Asa Issie, Aramis and the Origin of *Australopithecus*." *Nature*, 440:883–889.

Whiten, A., J. Goodall, W. C. McGrew, et al.
1999   "Cultures in Chimpanzees." *Nature*, 399:682–685.

Wildman, Derek E., Monica Uddin, Guozhen Liu, et al.
2003   "Implications of Natural Selection in Shaping 99.4% Nonsynonymous DNA Identity Between Humans and Chimpanzees: Enlarging Genus *Homo*." *Proceedings of the National Academy of Sciences*, 100:7181–7188.

Williams, G. C.
1957   "Pleiotopy, Natural Selection, and the Evolution of Senescence." *Evolution,* 11:398–411.

Williams, George C. and Randolph M. Nesse
1991   "The Dawn of Darwinian Medicine." *The Quarterly Review of Biology*, 66:1–22.

Williams, J. M.
1999   *Female Strategies and the Reasons for Territoriality in Chimpanzees. Lessons from Three Decades of Research at Gombe*. Unpublished Ph.D. Thesis. University of Minnesota.

Wilmut, I., A. E. Schnieke, J. McWhir, et al.
1997   "Viable Offspring Derived from Fetal and Adult Mammalian Cells." *Nature*, 385:810–813.

Wilson, E. O.
1992   *The Diversity of Life*. Cambridge, MA: The Belknap Press of Harvard University Press.

Wolpoff, Milford H.
1983   "*Ramapithecus* and Human Origins. An Anthropologist's Perspective of Changing Intepretations." In: *New Interpretations of Ape and Human Ancestry*, Russell L. Ciochon and Robert S. Corruccini (eds.), New York, NY: Plenum Press, pp. 651–676.

_____
1999   *Paleoanthropology*. 2nd ed. New York, NY: McGraw-Hill.

Wolpoff, M., A. G. Thorne, F. H. Smith, et al.
1994   "Multiregional Evolutions: A World-Wide Source for Modern Human Populations." In: *Origins of Anatomically Modern Humans*, M. H. Nitecki and D. V. Nitecki (eds.), New York, NY: Plenum Press, pp. 175–199.

Wolpoff, M. H., J. Hawks, D. Frayer, and K. Hunley
2001   "Modern Human Ancestry at the Peripheries: A Test of the Replacement Theory." *Science*, 291:293–297.

Wolpoff, Milford H., Brigitte Senut, Martin Pickford, and John Hawks
2002   "Paleoanthropology (Communication Arising): *Sahelanthropus* or '*Sahelpithecus*'"? *Nature*, 419:581–582.

Woo, J.
1966   "The Skull of Lantian Man." *Current Anthropololgy*, 5:83–86.

Wood, Bernard
1991   *Koobi Fora Research Project IV: Hominid Cranial Remains from Koobi Fora*. Oxford: Clarendon Press.

_____
1992   "Origin and Evolution of the Genus Homo." *Nature*, 355:783–790.

Wood, Bernard and Mark Collard
1999a   "The Human Genus." *Science*, 284:65–71.

_____
1999b   "The Changing Face of Genus *Homo*." *Evolutionary Anthropology*, 8:195–207.

Wood, B. and B. G. Richmond
2000   "Human Evolution: Taxonomy and Paleobiology." *Journal of Anatomy*, 197:19–60.

Worthman, C. M.
1999   "Evolutionary Perspectives on the Onset of Puberty." In: *Evolutionary Medicine*. W. R. Trevathan, E. O. Smith, and J. J. McKenna (eds.), New York, NY: Oxford University Press.

Wrangham, R. W. and B. B. Smuts
1980   "Sex Differences in the Behavioural Ecology of Chimpanzees in Gombe National Park, Tanzania." *J. Reprod. Fert., Supplement*, 28:13–31.

Wrangham, R., A. Clark, and G. Isabiryre-Basita
1992   "Female Social Relationships and Social Organization of Kibale Forest Chimps." In: *Topics in Primatology*, vol. 1, Human Origins, T. Nishida, W. McGrew, P. Marler, et al. (eds), Tokyo: Tokyo University Press, pp. 81–98.

Wrangham, R. and D. Peterson
1996   *Demonic Males: Apes and the Origins of Human Violence*. New York, NY: Houghton Mifflin.

Wu, Rukang and Xingren Dong
1985   "*Homo erectus* in China." In: *Palaeoanthropology and Palaeolithic Archaeology in the People's Republic of China*, R. Wu and J. W. Olsen (eds.), New York, NY: Academic Press, pp. 79–89.

Wu, X. and F. E. Poirier
1995   *Human Evolution in China*. Oxford: Oxford University Press.

Wu, X., L. A. Schepartz, D. Falk, and L. Wu
2006   "Endocranial Cast of Hexian *Homo erectus* from South China." *American Journal of Physical Anthropology*, 130:445–454.

Wuehrich, B.
1998   "Geological Analysis Damps Ancient Chinese Fires." *Science*, 28:165–166.

Yamei, H., R. Potts, Y. Baoyin, et al.
2000   "Mid-Pleistocene Acheulean-like Stone Technology of the Bose Basin, South China." *Science*, 287:1622–1626.

Yellen, J. E., A. S. Brooks, E. Cornelissen, et al.
1995   "A Middle Stone Age Worked Bone Industry from Katanda, Upper Semliki Valley, Zaire." *Science*, 268:553–556.

Young, David.
1992   *The Discovery of Evolution*. Cambridge: Natural History Museum Publications, Cambridge University Press.

Zhu, R. X., Z. S. An, R. Potts, et al.
2003   "Magnetostratigraphic Dating of Early Humans in China." *Earth Science Reviews*, 61:341–359.

Credits

1, Chapter opener, © (top) Russell Ciochon; (bottom left) Craig King; (bottom right) David Haring; **2,** Fig. 1-1, Peter Jones; **3,** Fig. 1-2, © Bettmann/Corbis; **5,** Fig. 1-3a–c, Lynn Kilgore; Fig. 1-3d, Justin Horocks/iStockphoto; **8,** Fig. 1-4, © Kenneth Garrett/NGS Image Collection; Fig. 1-5, Lynn Kilgore; **9,** Fig. 1-6, Judith Regensteiner; Fig. 1-7, Kathleen Galvin; **10,** Fig. 1-8, Robert Jurmain; Fig. 1-9, Bonnie Pedersen/Arlene Kruse; **11,** Fig. 1-10a and b, Lynn Kilgore; Fig. 1-11a, Lorna Pierce/Judy Suchey; Fig. 1-11b, D. France; **12,** Fig. 1-12, Linda Levitch; **17,** Chapter opener, © Russell Ciochon; **20,** Fig. 2-1, J. van (Johannes) Loon; **22,** Fig. 2-2, American Museum of Natural History; **23,** Fig. 2-4, Mathieu-Ignace van Brée; **24,** With permission from the Master of Haileybury; Fig. 2-6, © National Portrait Gallery, London; **25,** The Natural History Museum, London; Fig. 2-8, © Bettmann/Corbis; **27,** Fig. 2-11, Wolf: John Giustina/Getty Images; Dogs surrounding wolf: Lynn Kilgore and Lin Marshall; **28,** Fig. 2-12, © National Portrait Gallery, London; **29,** Fig. 2-13a, Michael Tweedie/Photo Researchers; Fig. 2-13b, Breck P. Kent/Animals Animals; **37,** Chapter opener, © Russell Ciochon; **39,** Fig. 3-1, Dr. Michael S. Donnenberg; **40,** Fig. 3-3, A. Barrington Brown/Photo Researchers, Inc.; **47,** Fig. 3-10, Biophoto Associates/Science Source/Photo Researchers; **53,** Fig. 3–15, Cellmark Diagnostics, Abingdon, UK; **56,** Chapter opener, © Russell Ciochon; **57,** Fig. 4-1, Raychel Ciemma and Precision Graphics; **65,** Fig. 4-6, Ray Carson, University of Florida News and Public Affairs; **66,** Fig. 4-7a–f; Lynn Kilgore; Fig. 4-7g, Robert Jurmain; **71,** Fig. 4-9, Lynn Kilgore; **72,** Fig. 4-10a and b, © Dr. Stanley Flegler/Visuals Unlimited; **77,** Chapter opener, © Russell Ciochon; **94,** Fig. 5-12, J. C. Stevenson/Animals Animals; **98,** Chapter opener, Lynn Kilgore; **101,** Fig. 6-1a–e, Lynn Kilgore; **103,** Fig. 6-3 a and b, Lynn Kilgore; Fig. 6-4, Lynn Kilgore; **105,** Fig. 6-5, © Russell Ciochon; **106,** Fig. 6-6, (Howler species), Raymond Mendez/Animals Animals; (Spider and woolly monkeys), Robert L. Lubeck/Animals Animals; (Prince Bernhard's titi), Marc van Roosmalen; (Marmosets and tamarins), © Zoological Society of San Diego, photo by Ron Garrison; (Muriqui), Andrew Young; (White-faced capuchins), © Jay Dickman/Corbis; (Squirrel monkeys), © Kevin Schafer/Corbis; (Uakari), R. A. Mittermeier/Conservation International; **107,** Fig. 6-6 (Baboon species), Bonnie Pedersen/Arlene Kruse; (Macaque

species), Jean De Rousseau; (Gibbons and siamangs), Lynn Kilgore; (Tarsier species), David Haring, Duke University Primate Zoo; (Orangutans), © Tom McHugh/Photo Researchers, Inc.; (Colobus species) Robert Jurmain; (Galagos), Bonnie Pedersen/Arlene Kruse; (Chimpanzees and bonobos), Arlene Kruse/Bonnie Pedersen; (Mountain and lowland gorillas), Lynn Kilgore; (Cercopithecus species), Robert Jurmain; (Loris species), San Francisco Zoo; (Langur species), Joe MacDonald/Animals Animals; (Lemurs), Fred Jacobs; **108,** Fig. 6-7a–d, Redrawn from original art by Stephen D. Nash in John G. Fleagle, Primate Adaptation and Evolution, 2nd ed., 1999. Reprinted by permission of publisher and Stephen Nash; **109,** Fig. 6-8, Lynn Kilgore; **113,** Fig. 6-11a and b, Lynn Kilgore; Fig. 6-12, © Viktor Deak, after John G. Fleagle; Fig. 6-14, Fred Jacobs; Fig. 6-15, Fred Jacobs; **114,** Fig. 6-16, San Francisco Zoo; Fig. 6-17, Bonnie Pedersen/Arlene Kruse; Fig. 6-18, David Haring, Duke University Primate Zoo; **115,** Fig. 6-12, Ron Garrison, © Zoological Society of San Diego; Fig. 6-22, Raymond Mendez/Animals Animals; **116,** Fig. 6-23, (Muriqui), Andrew Young; (Squirrel monkeys), © Kevin Schafer/Corbis; (Prince Bernhard's titi), Marc van Roosmalen; (Uakari), R. A. Mittermeier/Conservation International; (White-faced capuchins), © Jay Dickman/Corbis; **117,** Fig. 6-24, Robert L. Lubeck/Animals Animals; **118,** Fig. 6-26, Robert Jurmain; Fig. 6-27a and b, Bonnie Pedersen/Arlene Kruse; Fig. 6-28, Lynn Kilgore; **120,** Fig. 6-30, Lynn Kilgore; **121,** Fig. 6-31a, Noel Rowe; Fig. 6-31b, Lynn Kilgore; **121,** Fig. 6-33a and b, Lynn Kilgore; **122,** Fig. 6-34a and b, Lynn Kilgore; **123,** Fig. 6-35a, Lynn Kilgore; Fig. 6-35b, Jill Matsumoto/Jim Anderson; **124,** Fig. 6-36, Ellen Ingmanson; **126,** Fig. 6-37, John Oates; **127,** Fig. 6-38, Karl Ammann; **128,** Fig. 6-39, WildlifeDirect.org; **131,** Chapter opener, Lynn Kilgore; **134,** Fig. 7-1, © Russ Mittermeir; **135,** Fig. 7-2, Lynn Kilgore; **136,** Fig. 7-3, Time Life Pictures/Getty Images; **138,** Fig. 7-4, Lynn Kilgore; Fig. 7-5, Lynn Kilgore; Fig. 7-6, Lynn Kilgore; **140,** Fig. 7-8, Curt Busse; **141,** Fig. 7-9a, Robert Jurmain; Fig. 7-9b, Meredith Small; Fig. 7-9c and d, Arlene Kruse/Bonnie Pedersen; **143,** Fig. 7-10, Lynn Kilgore; **144,** Fig. 7-11, Joe MacDonald/Animals Animals; **145,** Fig. 7-12, © Peter Henzi; **146,** Fig. 7-13a, Courtesy, David Haring, Duke University Primate Center; Fig. 7-13b, Arlene Kruse/Bonnie Pedersen; Fig. 7-11c, Robert Jurmain; Fig. 7-11d, © Tom McHugh/Photo Researchers, Inc.; Fig. 7-11e, Robert Jurmain; **147,** Fig. 7-14, Harlow Primate Laboratory, University of Wisconsin; Fig. 7-15, Lynn Kilgore; **148,** Fig. 7-16a, Lynn Kilgore; Fig. 7-16b, Manoj Shah/The Image Bank; **149,** Fig. 7-17, Tetsuro Matsuzawa; **151,** Fig. 7-18, Lynn Kilgore; **153,** Fig. 7-19, Rose A. Sevcik, Language Research Center, Georgia State University; photo by Elizabeth Pugh; **154,** Fig. 7-20, Lynn Kilgore; **157,** Chapter opener, Kenya Museums of Natural History; **159,** Fig. 8-1, © Russell Ciochon; **162,**

Index

Page numbers in *italics* indicate figures or illustrations. Page numbers in **bold** indicate definitions.

Genetic disorders, *62*, 63
Genetic drift, 70–71, *70–71*, 74, *75*, 86
Genetic processes, 4, 5, 7, 38
    acquired characteristics, inheritance of, 22, *23*
    autosomes and, 48
    behavior patterns and, 133
    blending process of inheritance and, 32
    cell division and, 46–52, *47–49*, *51–52*
    cloning and, 50, 53
    comparative genomics, 54
    culture and, 4
    definition of, 9
    genes and, 44–46, *45*
    genome and, 32
    growth/development, 303–304, *304*
    Hardy-Weinberg equilibrium equation and, 282
    human variation and, 8, 9
    Mendelian genetic principles, 57–61, *58–61*
    molecular anthropology and, 9, *10*
    new frontiers in, 52–54
    physical anthropology and, 9
    predisposition for culture and, 4–5
    sex chromosomes and, 48
    trait inheritance, 9
    See also Biological systems; DNA (deoxyribonucleic acid); Evolution; Evolutionary theory; Heredity; Human variation/adaptation; Inheritance; Molecular anthropology; Natural selection; RNA (ribonucleic acid)
Genome, 32, 53–54
Genotype, 60, 61, *61*, *63*, 66, 87
Genus, 21, 89
Geographic isolation, 29, 86–87, 225
Geologic time scale, 24, 90–92, *90*, *92*
Gibbons, 108, 119, *119*, 120, *120*
Gibraltar site, *230*
Glaciations, 217–218, *218–219*, 231, 262
Global community, 14–15
Global warming, 5, 319, 328–330, *330*
Gombe National Park, *10*, 123, 137, 140, 141, 149
Goodall, Jane, 140, 308
Gore, Al, 329, 331
Gorilla gorilla, 120
Gorillas, 4, 120–122, *121–122*
    chromosomes in, 46, *47*
    classification of, 111, *112*
    Eastern lowland gorillas, 121
    endangered status of, 128–129
    habitats of, 105
    infanticide and, 145
    knuckle walking, 109
    Mountain gorillas, 121–122, *122*, 128–129, *128*

    natal groups and, 122
    silverback males, 122
    sleep site selection, 135
    tool use, 148–149
    Western lowland gorillas, 120–121, *121*, 122
    See also Hominoids; Primates
Gould, Stephen J., 271
Government policy:
    creationism/intelligent design and, 34, 35
    endangered species and, 10, 128, 129
    environmental legislation and, 7
    See also Development pressures
Grade of evolution, 198
Gradualism, 95–96
Gran Dolina *Homo erectus*, 209, 210, *210*, 213, 221
Grand Designer role, 19–20
Great Ape Survival Project (GRASP), 129
Great Hall of Bulls, 264
Great Rift Valley, 173–174, *175*
Grooming behaviors, 140–142, *141*
Grooming claw, 113
Grotte Chauvet cave art, 264, *265*
Growth/development, 9, 10
    adolescent growth spurts, 300
    environmental factors and, 305
    fundamentals of, 300–301, *300*
    genetic factors in, 303–304, *304*
    hormones and, 304
    nutritional requirements, 301–303, *302*
    See also Human life cycle

H

Habitat loss, 324–326, *325*
Habitual bipedalism, 124, 125, 167, 182
Hadar region, 180–181, 182, *189*, 192
Haplorhines, 111
Hardy-Weinberg equilibrium equation, 282
Harlow, Harry, 146
Hemoglobin, 42, *43*
Henzi, P., 145
Heredity, 57
    additive effect in polygenic systems, 64
    allele frequency, evolution and, 68, 69, 74
    alleles and, 60, *60*, 61–64
    antigens and, 62–63, *63*
    blending theory and, 57, 58
    carriers, recessive alleles and, 63
    continuous variation and, 64–66, *65–66*
    dominant/recessive traits and, 59–64, *60–61*, *62–63*
    evolutionary processes and, 28–29, 30–31, 67–68, 74, *75*
    evolution, current definition of, 68
    gene flow and, 69, *75*
    gene pools and, 71
    genetic disorders and, *62*, 63

    genetic drift, founder effect and, 70–71, *70–71*
    genetic vs. environmental factors and, 66–67
    genotypes and, 60, 61, *61*, *63*
    heterozygous individuals and, 60
    homoxygous individuals and, 60
    hybrids and, 58
    independent assortment principle, 61
    locus on a chromosome, 60, *60*
    Mendelian genetic principles, 57–61, *58–61*
    Mendelian traits in humans, 61–63, *62–63*, 65, 66, 67
    mitochondrial inheritance and, 67
    modern evolutionary theory and, 67–68
    mutation and, 44, 45, 67–68, 69
    phenotypes and, 60, 61, *61*, 63, *63*, 66–67
    polydactyly and, 57
    polygenic inheritance, 64–66, *65–66*
    populations and, 68
    random assortment and, 61
    segregation principle, 58–59, *59*
    variation and, 69–71, 72–73, *72–73*, *75*
    See also Evolutionary theory; Genetic processes; Macroevolution; Natural selection
Herto site, *247*, 250, 252, *252*, 267
Heterodont dentition, 93
Heterozygous individuals, 60, 63, 73, 279
Hexian *Homo erectus*, *197*, 208, *208*, 210
High-altitudes, 289–290, *289*, 305
HIV/AIDS, 5, 16, 35–36, 291–292, 293–295, *293*, 313, *314*, 315, 327
HMS *Beagle*, 25–26
Hobbits, 259–261
Holloway, Ralph, 236
Holocene epoch, 324
Homeobox/hox genes, 45–46, *46*, 81
Homeostasis, 282, 289
Homeothermic body temperature, 93
Hominidae family, 2, 3, 111, 112
    See also Hominid fossil discoveries; Hominids
Hominid fossil discoveries, 158, 173–174, 192
    adaptive patterns, early African hominids and, 190–191
    Australopithecus afarensis, 180–183, *180–182*
    Australopithecus africanus, 185–186, *185*
    bipedal gait and, 177, 178, 179, 182
    black skull, 183, *183*, 186
    cranial capacities, 181, *181*
    Dikika infant skeleton, 182, *182*)
    early hominid finds, 174–176, *175*, 192
    early *Homo* finds, 186–188, *187*, *189*
    foramen magnum and, 177–178, *177*

omnivorous diet, 101, 105
prehensile tails and, 109, 117
prehensility and, 100, *101*, 104
prosimians, 99, 112–114, *113–114*
rhinarium and, 112, *113*
social grouping of, 103, 119
specialized characteristics and, 100, *101*
stereoscopic vision in, 102
visual predation hypothesis and, 104
See also Evolutionary theory;
    Hominids; Mammalian evolution;
    Primate behavior
Primatology, 9–10, *10*, 100
Primitive traits, 82
Proconsul, 162, *162*
Property inheritance, 4
Prosimians, 3, 99, 108, 111, 112–113
    dental comb and, 113, *113*
    hominid evolution and, 159–160, *160*
    lemurs, 108, 111, *111*, 113–114, *113*
    lorises, 111, *111*, 114, *114*
    rhinarium and, 112, *113*
    tarsiers, 111, 114, *114*
    See also Primate behavior; Primates
Protein synthesis, 39, 42–44, *43–44*
Proteins, 39, 42–43
PTC tasting, *62*
Punch blade technique, 262, *263*
Punctuated equilibrium, 96
Punnett squares, 60, *61*
Pusey, A., 137
Pygmies, 304

Q

Qafzeh Cave site, 252, 253, *253*, 267
Quadrupedal gait, 108, *108*, 164
Quantitative data, 13

R

r-selected species, 143
Racial variation, 65, 271
    biological determinism and, 271
    ethnicity and, 272, 273
    eugenics and, 271–272
    phenotypic variation and, 272–273,
        274, *274*
    polygenic characteristics and, 274
    polytypic species and, 272
    race, concept of, 272–274
    racism and, 274–275
    skin color scale, 271
    See also Human variation/adaptation
Racism, 8, 274–275
Radioactive isotopes, 172
Rain forest habitat, 325, 326
Random assortment, 61
Ray, John, 21
Recessive traits, 59–60, *60–62*
    blood types and, 62–63, *63*

carriers and, 63
codominance and, 63
genetic disorders and, *62*, 63
misconceptions about, 63–64
See also Heredity
Reciprocal altruism, 142
Recognition species concept, 87
Recombinant DNA technology, 53
Recombination process, 50, 71, *75*
Reconciliation behaviors, 141–142
Reform Movement (Britain), 25
Refugees, 6
Regional continuity model, 249
Regulatory genes, 45–46
Relative dating, 171–172, 173
Relativistic viewpoint, 14–15
Relethford, John, 249
Religion, 4, 6, 7, 33
    evolutionary theory and, 18, 19–20, 25,
        33–34
    planetary systems and, 21
Replacement models. *See* Complete
    replacement model; Partial
    replacement models; Regional
    continuity model
Replication of DNA, 41, *42*
Reproduction:
    consortships, 142–143
    differential net reproductive success, 32
    estrus, 119, 142, *143*
    high altitudes and, 289–290
    human pregnancy/birth/infancy,
        306–308, *307*
    hybrids and, 87, 89
    life history theory and, 305
    meiosis and, 50
    postreproductive years/human aging,
        311–312
    primate species and, 142–145
    reproductively isolated organisms, 21,
        29, 87
    reproductive strategies, 143–144
    reproductive success/fitness, 29, 31, 32,
        133
    selective breeding and, 87
    sexual reproduction, 27–28
    sexual selection and, 144
    See also Evolutionary theory; Genetic
        processes; Natural selection
Reproductive strategies, 143–144
Reptiles:
    brain structure, 92, *93*
    homeothermic body temperature, 93
    teeth in, 93, *93*
The Rhesus Macaque Genome Sequencing
    and Analysis Consortium, 54
Rhinarium, 112, *113*
Ribonucleic acid. *See* RNA
Ribosomes, 39, 40
Richards, Gary, 261

Rickets, 285, *285*
Rift Valley fossils, 173–174, *176*
Rightmire, Phillip, 219, 221
Rituals, 6
RNA (ribonucleic acid), 39
    codons and, 44
    messenger RNA, 39, 44, *44*
    protein synthesis and, 44, *44*
    ribosomal RNA, 39, 40
    transcription of, 44, *44*
    transfer RNA, 39, 44
    See also Biological systems; DNA
        (deoxyribonucleic acid); Genetic
        processes

S

Sagittal crest, 183, *183–184*, 185, 224
Sahelanthropus tchadensis, 177, 178, *181,
    190*, 191, 192
Samson, M., 292
Sangiran *Homo erectus, 197, 200*, 206, *210,*
    214
SARS, 315
Savage-Rumbaugh, Sue, 150, 152
Savanna, 2, 3
Schöningen site, *222*, 226
Science, 12
Scientific method, 12–14
    absolutes and, 13
    data collection, 13
    development of, 20–21
    falsification of hypotheses and, 13
    hypotheses and, 12, 13
    hypothesis testing and, 13, 18
    quantitative data and, 13
    scientific testing of hypotheses and, 13
Scientific revolution, 20–21, *20*
Scientific testing of hypotheses, 13
Sea ice maximum/minimum, 329–330, *330*
Sectorial lower premolar, 179, *179*
Segregation principle of inheritance,
    58–59, *59*, 74
Selective breeding, 87
Selective pressures, 100
Senescence, 312
Senses:
    neocortex, 103
    olfaction in primates, 102
    sensory modalities, information from,
        103
Sensory modalities, 103
Sex chromosomes, 48, 52
Sexual dimorphism, 88, 119, 122, 144, 201,
    300
Sexual reproduction, 27
    See also Reproduction
Sexual selection, 144
Shanidar site, *230–231*, 233, *233*, 234, 237
Shared derived traits, 84
Siamangs, 120

Sickle-cell anemia, 62 (table), 72, 73, *73*, 74, 278–279, *280*
Sima de los Huesos site, 221, 224, 227, 242
Simian immunodeficiency virus (SIV), 293, 294
Simons, Elwyn, 159
Single nucleotide polymorphisms (SNPs), 278
Sivapithecus, 162
Skeletal remains:
    faunal remains, 170
    forensic anthropology and, 11, *11*
    hyoid bone, 233
    Laetoli site, 3
    osteology, 10
    paleopathology and, 10, 11, *11*
    postcranial remains, 160
    See also Fossils; Hominid fossil
        discoveries
Skhūl site, *247, 251,* 252, 253, *253,* 267
Skin color, 64–65, 271, 272, 283–286, *283–286*
Slash-and-burn agriculture, 278
Sleeping site selection, 135
Smallpox, 292
Smith, Fred, 249, 256
Social organization, 4
    extinct societies, 6
    female-dominated community, 325, *325*
    influential factors in, 134–136
    intragroup aggression and, 139
    medical anthropology and, 6
    natal groups, 122
    primates and, 103, 119, 122, 123, 124, 134, 136
    See also Anthropology; Primate
        behavior
Society for Conservation Biology, 127
Sociocultural environments, 299
Solar radiation, 283–286, *283–286,* 305
Somatic cells, 40, 46, 47, 48
South Africa. *See* Africa; Hominid fossil
    discoveries
Spear-thrower, 262, *262*
Specialized characteristics, 95, 100, *101*
Speciation, 4, 18, 22, 29, 86, *86,* 87, 96, 246, 249
Species, 3
    adaptive zones and, 89
    alterations in, 22
    biological species concept, 86
    catastrophism doctrine and, 23
    concept of, 21
    definition of, 86–89
    ecological niches and, 87, 89
    ecological species concept, 87
    endangered species, 10
    evolution and, 4, 86–87
    extinct species, 3, 9, 11, 22–23
    fixity of, 19–20

fossil records, interpretation of, 88–89
geographic isolation and, 86
interspecies/intraspecies variations, 88
mutability of, 26–28
natural historians and, 8
paleospecies, 89
phylogenetic species concept, 87
recognition species concept, 87
relativistic viewpoint and, 15
reproduction, criterion of, 21
selective pressures and, 29, 87
sexual dimorphism, 88
speciation, 4, 18, 22, 29, 86, *86,* 87, 96
transmutation and, 25
See also Classification; Macroevolution
Speech:
    Neandertals and, 235–236, 238
    See also Language
Spina bifida, 285
Spy site, *230*
Standard deviation, 65–66
Staphylococcus bacteria, 35
Statistics, 65–66
St. Césaire site, *230–231,* 231
Steinheim site, 221, *221–222,* 225
Stelzner, J., 142
Stereoscopic vision, 102
Sterkfontein, 174, *175, 176, 185,* 188, *189,* 192
Stratigraphy, 171, 173
Stratum, 171
Strepsirhines, 111, 112
Stress, 282
    See also Environmental factors; Trauma
Strier, K., 142
Stringer, Christopher, 246
Subsistence strategies, 6
Sungir site, 261, *262, 265*
Sussman, R. W., 104, 145
Swanscombe site, 221, *222,* 224, *225,* 226
Swartkrans site:
    hominid fossils, 174, *175, 184,* 188
    Homo erectus fossils, *196*
Symbolic behavior, 235–236
Symbolic representation, 263–264, *265*
Symbols, 6, 140, 151
Synergistic effects, 305
Syphilis, 10

T

Taboos, 6
Tabun site, 134, *230–231,* 232, 233, 237, 242, 253, *253*
Tanzania:
    Olduvai Gorge, *170*
    skeletal remains, 3
    See also Gombe National Park;
        Hominid fossil discoveries; Laetoli
        site
Tarsiers, 111, 114, *114*

Taung, 174, *175,* 185, *185,* 192
Taxonomy, 21, 80, 89
    See also Classification
Tay-Sachs disease, *62,* 71
Technology, 4, 5, *5,* 6
    archaeology and, 7
    design, anthropometric techniques
        and, 8
    DNA fingerprinting, 53, *53*
    dominance/recessiveness and, 64
    molecular anthropology and, 9
    recombinant DNA technology, 53
    See also Tools
Teeth, 5
    Australopithecus afarensis, 181, *181*
    cusps, 105
    dental combs, 113, *113*
    dental formulae, 105
    Dikika infant skeleton and, 182
    early *Homo,* 187–188
    heterodont dentition, 93
    homodont dentition, 93
    hypodontia, upper lateral incisors and, *62*
    midline of the jaw, 105
    morphology of teeth, 105
    Paranthropus, 183, *184*
    permanent dentition, absence of, *62*
    primates and, 101, 105, *105,* 108
    reptile vs. mammalian teeth, 93, *93*
    sectorial lower premolar, 179, *179*
Terra Amata, *222*
Territory protection, 139
Teshik Tash site, *230*
Thalassemia, *62,* 71
Theory, 12, 18
    See also Evolutionary theory
Thermal environment, 286–289, *288,* 305
Thermoluminescence (TL), 172, 173, 232, 264
Tianyuan Cave site, 254, 259
Time. *See* Dating methods; Geologic time
    scale
Tobias, Phillip, 166
Tools:
    Acheulian industry, 203, 211, *211,* 225, 226
    Aurignacian industry, 258
    burins, 262, *262*
    Chatelperronian industry, 232
    chopper/chopping tools, 226
    cultural environment and, 4, *5*
    hominids and, 3, 167, 168
    Homo erectus tool use, 211–212, *211*
    Levallois technique, 255, *256*
    Madgalenian industry, 262
    Mousterian industry, 234
    Neandertals and, 234–235, *234*
    premodern humans and, 225–226, *226*
    primate tool use, 148–150, *148–149*

World Political Map

ARCTIC CIRCLE

GREENLAND
(KALAALLIT NUNAAT)
(Den.)

ICELAND

UNITED
KINGDOM

IRELAND
(EIRE)

ALASKA
(U.S.)

CANADA

UNITED STATES

*Atlantic
Ocean*

PORTUGAL

SPAIN

AZORE IS.
(Port.)

CANARY IS.
(Sp.)

MOROCCO

TROPIC OF CANCER

MEXICO

BAHAMAS

CUBA

JAMAICA

BELIZE

HONDURAS

GUATEMALA

EL SALVADOR

NICARAGUA

COSTA RICA

PANAMA

HAITI

DOMINICAN REP.

PUERTO
RICO (U.S.)

NETHERLANDS
ANTILLES (Neth.)

ANTIGUA & BARBUDA

GUADELOUPE (Fr.)

DOMINICA

MARTINIQUE (Fr.)

BARBADOS

GRENADA

TRINIDAD & TOBAGO

CAPE VERDE IS.

MAURITANIA

MA

SENEGAL

GAMBIA

GUINEA BISSAU

SIERRA LEONE

LIBERIA

GUINEA

IVORY
COAST

GHANA

EQUATORIAL

HAWAII
(U.S.)

*Pacific
Ocean*

VENEZUELA

GUYANA

SURINAME

FRENCH GUIANA
(Fr.)

COLOMBIA

EQUATOR

ECUADOR

GALAPAGOS IS.
(Ecuador)

BRAZIL

PERU

WESTERN
SAMOA

AMERICAN
SAMOA (U.S.)

SOCIETY IS.
(Fr.)

FRENCH
POLYNESIA
(Fr.)

TAHITI (Fr.)

BOLIVIA

TONGA

PARAGUAY

TROPIC OF CAPRICORN

PITCAIRN IS.
(U.K.)

EASTER ISLAND
(Chile)

CHILE

*Atlantic
Ocean*

URUGUAY

ARGENTINA

0   500   1000   1500 miles

0   1000   2000 kms

Equatorial Scale

FALKLAND IS.
(U.K.)

ANTARCTIC CIRCLE

180°   160°W   140°W   120°W   100°W   80°W   60°W   40°W   20°W   0°

80°N   60°N   40°N   20°N   0°   20°S   40°S   60°S   80°S